SUBJECT & STRATEGY

A WRITER'S READER

FIFTEENTH EDITION

SUBJECT & STRATEGY

A WRITER'S READER

PAUL ESCHHOLZ

University of Vermont

ALFRED ROSA

University of Vermont

 bedford/st.martin's
Macmillan Learning
Boston | New York

For Bedford/St. Martin's

Vice President, Editorial, Macmillan Learning Humanities: Edwin Hill
Executive Program Director for English: Leasa Burton
Senior Program Manager for Readers and Literature: John E. Sullivan III
Executive Marketing Manager: Joy Fisher Williams
Director of Content Development: Jane Knetzger
Developmental Editor: Leah Rang
Editorial Assistant: Cari Goldfine
Content Project Manager: Pamela Lawson
Senior Workflow Project Manager: Lisa McDowell
Production Supervisor: Robert Cherry
Media Project Manager: Allison Hart
Manager of Publishing Services: Andrea Cava
Editorial Services: Lumina Datamatics, Inc.
Composition: Lumina Datamatics, Inc.
Permissions Editor: Angela Boehler
Photo Researcher: Richard Fox, Lumina Datamatics, Inc.
Text Permissions Manager: Kalina Ingham
Text Permissions Researcher: Elaine Kosta, Lumina Datamatics, Inc.
Design Director, Content Management: Diana Blume
Text Design: Lumina Datamatics, Inc.
Cover Design: William Boardman
Cover Image: Emilija Manevska/Getty Images
Printing and Binding: LSC Communications

Manufactured in the United States of America.

1   2   3   4   5   6   23   22   21   20   19   18

For information, write: Bedford/St. Martin's, 75 Arlington Street, Boston, MA 02116

ISBN 978-1-319-13195-1 (Student Edition)
ISBN 978-1-319-15744-9 (Instructor's Edition)

Acknowledgments
Text acknowledgments and copyrights appear at the back of the book on pages 603–605, which constitute an extension of the copyright page. Art acknowledgments and copyrights appear on the same page as the art selections they cover.

At the time of publication all Internet URLs published in this text were found to accurately link to their intended website. If you do find a broken link, please forward the information to cari.goldfine@macmillan.com so that it can be corrected for the next printing.

Preface for Students

❝ It is easy to see good thinking in good writing. ❞

—JIM TASSÉ, student

We have always believed that learning to write is an indispensable skill set for an educated person and that writing courses are perhaps the most valuable ones that you will take during your college career. Why? Well, writing has worked for us, and our students have told us how valuable their writing skills have been, often several semesters after finishing a course with us. One alum, after being in the work world for a number of years, told us, "There have been no skills of more importance to me professionally than my abilities to read critically and write clearly." In the opening to this preface, Jim Tassé, one of our former students, tells us in his own words how important writing is for critical thinking, and the quotes from Katie Angeles, Katherine Kachnowski, and Keith Eldred (whose essays all appear in this book) show how good reading and writing has impacted their school work and lives, too. Our students soon discover that writing is not only helpful in communicating their thoughts to others but often more useful in clarifying their own thinking in the first place. You have probably noticed this yourself in both high school and college classes.

We have long considered writing to be one of the best ways to learn. By analyzing the issues we all face, the earth itself, its people, and their ideas, we deconstruct what we experience and then reassemble in writing all that we have gathered, creating an essay reflecting our unique perspective. Writing about a subject brings us to a level of understanding that we would find very difficult to achieve by simply reading or hearing about it. When, in our writing, we consider all that we learn from our reading, not just the facts and ideas but the ways that authors have seen the world, we also bring into focus the importance of reading in the writing process. Reading and writing are inseparable parts of the same process. As has often been said, writing is the making of reading; in fact, you are the first reader of what you write. Engaging

v

> ❝ Reading is always helpful because you gain a lot of information and ideas that you wouldn't have available any other way. ❞
>
> —KATIE ANGELES, student

in both processes will deepen your education and bring you satisfaction in later life and in your career. Soon you will be reading with the eye of a writer and writing with your readers in mind, which is, after all, the point of *Subject & Strategy*.

During the summer of 2017 we were fortunate enough to sit in on a roundtable discussion with college students from all over the country who were interning with our publisher, Bedford/St. Martin's. The focus of the roundtable was students' experiences with writing classes. While some of the students found the courses difficult and didn't always understand why they were engaging in certain sentence- or paragraph-level classroom exercises in their courses, most recognized the value of learning how to organize, revise, and polish a piece of writing. Learning to write can be a lonely activity, and the consensus of students was that they would have found it helpful to talk to other writers along the way. Our main takeaway from this roundtable discussion was that it's not only important for students using our book to see student-level work, but it is also important for them to hear what these students were thinking and feeling while they were working on their essays.

We suspect you might feel this way, too. Throughout the book you will find many examples of student writing, from the paragraph level to whole essays. In fact, you'll find one student essay for each chapter from Chapters 2–14. Each of the essays is on a topic of the student's own choosing and is, we believe, comparable in length and quality to what most instructors expect from students in writing courses today. Notes in the margins explain the writer's choices and show you where the strategy discussed in the chapter is in play, giving you models for writing these types of essays. The essays, written by students like you in their college writing courses, can help you establish realistic goals and standards for your writing, as well as suggest ways of identifying and solving the sorts of problems a particular assignment may present.

> ❝ I think you're always learning when you're writing. Every paper I write, I do think I become a better writer, at least a little bit. I also find that writing about a subject helps me to understand the subject better. ❞
>
> —KATHERINE KACHNOWSKI, student

However, to meet this real need of hearing from writers about their writing, in this new edition of *Subject & Strategy* we are happy to include a new feature after each student essay in Chapters 4–14: "Student Reflection."

We interviewed the student writers, asking them to think about the experience of taking a paper through multiple drafts. They share how they chose their topic and generated ideas, how they determined suitable writing strategies to meet their purposes, how many drafts they wrote and what kinds of revisions they made, how peer responses proved beneficial, and how they solved any problems that arose during the writing process. On occasion, the student writers expressed their anxieties about writing, what came easily and what was frustrating, and how they coped with the difficulties of expressing themselves clearly. The quotes in this preface are also from students reflecting on the value of reading and writing.

> ❝I think I write so much that I have forgotten I'm doing it. Writing has made it easier to find my way, period.❞
> —KEITH ELDRED, student

To highlight the usefulness of the student writing in this edition, we have made it easy to find with a colorful design, as in the image on this page. These blue boxes have three important elements:

1. The model student essay, annotated to point out the writing strategies the writer uses

2. The student reflection, in which we interviewed students about their process writing the essay

3. "Your Response," an opportunity to consider how you might learn from the student writer's strategy or process as you develop your own essay

---

Student Reflection
Andrew Kauser

Q. Your narration is chronological. Did you consider other patterns of organization?

A. I didn't think much about patterns other than chronological. For the most part, I felt I had no choice but to write it that way. I did have difficulty in beginning the narrative because I wasn't sure whether I wanted to write it in the past or the present tense. I made many attempts at different beginnings, from describing waking up on the morning of my flight to describing how I spent my summer flying. Once I found a beginning that I liked, it was relatively easy to write the rest of the essay because I just wrote about the events in the order that they happened. The beginning solved my tense problem as well.

These student writing boxes appear at the end of each rhetorical chapter introduction, after the instruction on each writing strategy but before the professional writing selections. After all, the writing you do in your college class is a bridge to the professional writing you will produce in your future careers.

We've put more student voices into this edition because your experiences with reading and writing—and what you have to say about them—are important to us and to other student writers like you. Learning about the topics that interest you when you read and the struggles you face when you write helps us make *Subject & Strategy* a better book to guide you as you develop your writing skills. We would enjoy hearing more from you and reading the exciting essays you'll write in your course this year.

Preface for Instructors

Subject & Strategy is a reader for college writers. The seventy-one selections in this edition were chosen to entertain students and to contribute to their self-awareness and understanding of the world around them. Above all, however, we've brought together readings and thought-provoking apparatus to help students become better writers.

As its title suggests, *Subject & Strategy* places equal emphasis on the content and form of good writing. While all readers pay attention to content, far fewer notice the strategies—narration, description, illustration, process analysis, comparison and contrast, division and classification, definition, cause and effect analysis, and argumentation—that writers, artists, filmmakers, journalists, and storytellers use to organize their work and to make their subjects understandable and effective for a given audience. Because these strategies are such an essential element of the writer's craft, we have designed *Subject & Strategy* to help students understand what they are and how they work. Each selection skillfully models the use of the strategies, while questions, writing prompts, visuals, and other pedagogy further support students in writing well-constructed essays of their own.

As in the fourteen previous editions of *Subject & Strategy*, we have relied heavily on writing teachers throughout the country to help us develop the improvements to this edition. For this fifteenth edition, we also depended on students who are in the midst of their college careers, actively writing and facing the challenges of writing assignments. Thanks to a discussion we had with college students with diverse majors who were interning with Bedford/St. Martin's, as well as surveys asking students to review the fourteenth edition and proposed new readings, we were able to learn firsthand about students' experiences in writing classes. We learned from these students that it's important for student writers using our book to not only see student work, but also to hear what these students were thinking and feeling while they were working on their essays.

The many examples of student writing you can assign from *Subject & Strategy*, from the paragraph level to whole essays, are, we believe, comparable in length and quality to what most of you expect from students in your writing courses today. The student essays can help you establish realistic goals and standards for their writing, as well as suggest ways of identifying and solving the sorts of problems a particular assignment may present. You can use the new feature after each student essay—"Student Reflection"—to emphasize for students the need to consider one's own writing process for each assignment. By recognizing what worked and what didn't, students can improve their next writing experience. Including these interviews with the student writers in *Subject & Strategy* also, we believe, allows students to identify with the writers' journeys as peers. It is a nice supplement to the "Writers on Writing" chapter and another way to emphasize that all writers face challenges, all writers revise, and all writers are constantly improving and adapting to new contexts, assignments, and audiences.

ENDURING FEATURES OF *SUBJECT & STRATEGY*

We continue to include the key features—developed and refined over fourteen previous editions—that have made *Subject & Strategy* a classic introductory text.

Timely, Teachable, and Diverse Readings

Seventy-one selections—fifty-eight professional selections and thirteen student essays—offer a broad spectrum of subjects, styles, and cultural points of view. The work of well-known writers—including Maya Angelou, Stephen King, and Bharati Mukherjee—as well as emerging voices—including Issa Rae, Shaun King, Jennifer Ackerman, James Rebanks, and Derald Wing Sue—demonstrates for students the versatility and strengths of the different rhetorical strategies when writing about classic and contemporary issues.

Thorough Coverage of the Reading and Writing Processes

Chapter 1, "Reading," discusses effective reading habits and illustrates attentive, analytical reading of essays and visuals using Cherokee Paul McDonald's "A View from the Bridge," Thomas L. Friedman's "My Favorite Teacher," a photograph of a street scene, and a graphic about energy savings when using recycled materials.

Chapter 2, "Writing," offers writing advice and provides a case study of a student paper in progress, which illustrates one student's writing process and shows what can be accomplished with careful, thoughtful revision.

Chapter 3, "Writers on Writing," showcases inspiration, insight, and advice on writing well from professional writers Russell Baker, Anne Lamott, Linda S. Flower, and Stephen King, and from student writer Ricardo Rodríguez-Padilla.

Detailed Introductions to Each Rhetorical Strategy

The introduction to each rhetorical chapter opens with an example of the strategy at work in everyday life and then examines its use in written texts. Annotated excerpts from professional readings provide example-driven instruction that discusses the various purposes for which writers use the strategy and offers advice on how to use it in various college disciplines. This discussion is followed by detailed, practical advice on how to write an essay using the strategy, including guidelines on selecting topics, developing thesis statements, considering audiences, gathering evidence, and using other rhetorical strategies in support of the dominant strategy.

Unique Cross-Disciplinary Connections

Each rhetorical chapter introduction includes a "Using the Strategy Across the Disciplines" section that shows students how rhetorical strategies are used and combined outside the composition classroom—whether in the humanities, the natural sciences, or the social sciences. The examples move students from a main idea to a research question and then show what dominant strategy and supporting strategies could be used to best answer that question.

Annotated Student Essays

An annotated student essay appears in each rhetorical chapter, offering students realistic models for successfully incorporating a particular strategy into their own writing. Following each student essay are the student writer's reflection on the writing process and a prompt for student readers, encouraging students to analyze and evaluate the overall effectiveness of the rhetorical strategies employed in the example and to consider how they might apply the writer's technique to their own writing.

Extensive Rhetorical Apparatus for Professional Essays

Numerous questions and prompts for thought, discussion, in-class activities, and writing accompany each professional essay:

- **Preparing to Read** prompts ask students to write about their own knowledge and experiences with the subject of each selection before they read.

- **Thinking Critically about the Text** prompts ask students to analyze, elaborate on, or take issue with a key aspect of each selection.

- **Questions on Subject** focus students' attention on the content of each selection as well as on the author's purpose. These questions help students check their comprehension and provide a basis for classroom discussion.

- **Questions on Strategy** direct students to the various rhetorical strategies and writing techniques the writer has used. These questions encourage students to put themselves in the writer's place and to consider how they might employ the strategies in their own writing. In addition, questions in this section ask students to identify and analyze places where the author has used one or more rhetorical strategies to enhance or develop the essay's dominant strategy.

- **Strategy in Action** activities accompanying each essay—usually requiring no more than ten to fifteen minutes of class time and designed for students to complete individually, in small groups, or as a class—allow students to apply their understanding of the strategies at work in a given selection.

- **Writing Suggestions** focus on the particular rhetorical strategy under discussion and explore the subject of the essay or a related topic. Select questions include **Writing with Sources** and **Writing in the Workplace** headings to offer practice in these skills.

Advice for Writing Researched Essays

Chapter 14, "Writing with Sources," helps students master this essential academic skill by offering sound, detailed advice on avoiding plagiarism and effectively integrating sources through quotation, summary, and paraphrase. The chapter also features four essays (one student, three professional) that integrate outside sources. Questions and prompts direct students' attention to how they can use sources persuasively in their own writing.

Chapter 15, "A Brief Guide to Researching and Documenting Essays," provides an overview of the research process, with a focus on finding, evaluating, and analyzing sources; taking notes; and documenting sources. MLA citation models following the 2016 *MLA Handbook* are provided for the most widely used types of sources, along with a sample documented student essay.

Editing Advice

Chapter 16, "Editing for Grammar, Punctuation, and Sentence Style," provides a concise guide to twelve of the most common writing challenges, from sentence run-ons and fragments to wordiness and lack of sentence variety.

Thematic Contents

Immediately after the main table of contents, a second table of contents groups the reading selections into general thematic categories to provide students further opportunities for topics and discussion. Additional prompts for thematic writing assignments, based on the content of individual selections, can be found in the appendix.

Glossary of Rhetorical Terms

The glossary at the end of *Subject & Strategy* provides concise definitions of terms boldfaced in the text and called out in the questions that follow each reading selection.

NEW TO THIS EDITION OF *SUBJECT & STRATEGY*

Substantially updated for its fifteenth edition, *Subject & Strategy* combines the currency of a brand-new text with the effectiveness of a thoroughly class-tested one. Guided by comments and advice from instructors and students across the country who have used previous editions, we have made a number of meaningful changes to the text.

New Readings, Compelling Perspectives

Twenty-two readings—about 30 percent of this edition's selections—are new, including

- **Pop culture critic Linda Holmes** on the overwhelming choices we face as cultural consumers in "The Sad, Beautiful Fact That We're All Going to Miss Almost Everything"
- **Civil rights activist Shaun King** on how writing can give power to the undeserving in "No, I Won't Be Writing about Black-on-Black Crime"
- **Supermodel Paulina Porizkova** on how different countries treat women in "America Made Me a Feminist"

A Fresh Take on Argument

To reflect the multiplicity of possible perspectives on any complex topic and to encourage students to consider arguments in a multifaceted, nuanced way, we offer a new argument cluster: **"The Changing Nature of Work: What Is the Value of a Career—Now and in the Future?"** This group of readings explores how our approaches to jobs and careers are shifting. Student Caitlin McCormick, cultural anthropologist Ilana Gershon, and economist Noah Smith explore how class power structures, changing business practices, and robots affect the future of work.

Increased Focus on Student Voice

To bring more attention to student writing, and to show student readers how their peers address writing challenges, each rhetorical strategy chapter introduction now culminates in a three-part student feature:

- **An annotated student essay** models how the student implemented the writing strategy;
- **A reflection** shares the process each student went through in writing the essay;
- **A response question** prompts student readers to consider how they can implement the model student's techniques into their own writing.

The Preface for Students also showcases quotations about reading and writing from real student writers who appear in this book.

Challenging My Fears
Andrew Kauser

Context set — writer driving to airport on chilly autumn morning for first solo flight	Cedars Airport, just off the western tip of Montreal, is about a half-hour drive from my house. Today's drive is boring as usual except for the chill which runs up the back of my legs because of the cold breeze entering through the rusted floorboards. I peer through the dew-covered windshield to see the leaves changing color. Winter is on its way.

Your Response

What did you learn from Andrew's essay and reflection? What challenges do you expect to face as you write your own narrative essay? Based on Andrew's experiences and the practical advice discussed earlier in this chapter (pages 82–87), how will you overcome those challenges?

A New, Colorful Design

A fresh look improves navigation between headings and reading selections, makes annotations on selections easier to follow, and highlights important sections, such as the new student feature that bridges the writing instruction and reading selections in each chapter.

New Visualizing the Strategy Activities

Half of the chapter opening images are new, spanning genres from infographics and flowcharts to cartoons and photographs. These images are accompanied by a Visualizing the Strategy activity that builds visual literacy by asking students to identify and analyze the chapter's rhetorical strategy in an image. Additional images in reading selections and prompts about visuals in the apparatus offer more opportunities for students to engage with the strategies in other media.

WE'RE ALL IN. AS ALWAYS.

Bedford/St. Martin's is as passionately committed to the discipline of English as ever, working hard to provide support and services that make it easier for you to teach your course your way.

Find **community support** at the Bedford/St. Martin's English Community (community.macmillan.com), where you can follow our *Bits* blog for new teaching ideas, download titles from our professional resource series, and review projects in the pipeline.

Choose **curriculum solutions** that offer flexible custom options, combining our carefully developed print and digital resources, acclaimed works from Macmillan's trade imprints, and your own course or program materials to provide the exact resources your students need. Our approach to customization makes it possible to create a project uniquely suited for your students, and based on your enrollment size, return money to your department and raise your institutional profile with a high-impact author visit through the Macmillan Author Program ("MAP").

Rely on **outstanding service** from your Bedford/St. Martin's sales representative and editorial team. Contact us or visit macmillanlearning.com to learn more about any of the following options.

Choose from Alternative Formats of *Subject & Strategy*

Bedford/St. Martin's offers a range of formats. Choose what works best for you and your students:

- *Paperback* To order the paperback edition, use ISBN 978-1-319-13195-1.
- *Popular e-book formats* For details of our e-book partners, visit **macmillanlearning.com/ebooks**.

Select Value Packages

Add value to your text by packaging any Bedford/St. Martin's resource, such as *LaunchPad Solo for Readers and Writers*, with *Subject & Strategy* at a significant discount. Contact your sales representative for more information.

LaunchPad Solo for Readers and Writers allows students to work on what they need help with the most. At home or in class, students learn at their own pace, with instruction tailored to each student's unique needs. *LaunchPad Solo for Readers and Writers* features:

- **Prebuilt units that support a learning arc**. Each easy-to-assign unit comprises a pre-test check, multimedia instruction and assessment, and a post-test that assesses what students have learned about critical reading, writing process, using sources, grammar, style, and mechanics. Dedicated units also offer help for multilingual writers.

- **Diagnostics that help establish a baseline for instruction**. Assign diagnostics to identify areas of strength and areas for improvement and to help students plan a course of study. Use visual reports to track performance by topic, class, and student as well as improvement over time.

- **A video introduction to many topics**. Introductions offer an overview of the unit's topic, and many include a brief, accessible video to illustrate the concepts at hand.

- **Twenty-five reading selections with comprehension quizzes**. Assign a range of classic and contemporary essays, each of which includes a label indicating Lexile level to help you scaffold instruction in critical reading.

- **Adaptive quizzing for targeted learning**. Most units include Learning-Curve, game-like adaptive quizzing that focuses on the areas in which each student needs the most help.

- **Additional reading comprehension quizzes**. *Subject & Strategy* includes multiple-choice quizzes, which help you quickly gauge your students' understanding of the assigned reading. These are available in *LaunchPad Solo for Readers and Writers*.

Order ISBN 978-1-31922-436-3 to package *LaunchPad Solo for Readers and Writers* with *Subject & Strategy* at a significant discount. Students who rent or buy a used book can purchase access, and instructors may request free access, at **macmillanlearning.com/readwrite**.

Instructor Resources

You have a lot to do in your course. We want to make it easy for you to find the support you need—and to get it quickly.

Instructor's Manual for Subject & Strategy is available as a PDF that can be downloaded from macmillanlearning.com. Visit the instructor resources tab for *Subject & Strategy*. The instructor's manual includes sample syllabi, additional writing suggestions, and responses to each question and prompt in the book.

COUNCIL OF WRITING PROGRAM ADMINISTRATORS (WPA) OUTCOMES STATEMENT FOR FIRST-YEAR COMPOSITION

The following chart provides detailed information on how *Subject & Strategy* helps students build proficiency and achieve the learning outcomes that writing programs across the country use to assess their students' work: rhetorical knowledge; critical thinking, reading, and writing; writing processes; and knowledge of conventions.

WPA Outcomes	Relevant Features of *Subject & Strategy*, 15th Edition
RHETORICAL KNOWLEDGE	
Learn and use key rhetorical concepts through analyzing and composing a variety of texts	• **The organization of *Subject & Strategy* supports students' understanding of rhetorical strategy.** Chapters 4–12 explore in detail the different writing strategies most often required of college students. Comprehensive and practical chapter introductions explain how the strategies suit authors' purposes. Chapter 13, Combining Strategies, highlights how professional writers use multiple strategies to convey their messages. • **In Chapter 1, students learn how to read rhetorically**, using annotation as an effective skill to analyze and evaluate texts according to their rhetorical purpose (pp. 3–12).
	• **Chapter 2 shows students how to identify their purpose and audience** (pp. 26–41) through an understanding of the assignment or research question. • **Boxes provide additional support for analyzing and composing texts:** see "Questions for Analyzing and Evaluating" (p. 12) and "Questions about Audience" (p. 29). • **Questions on Subject** following each reading focus on the author's purpose. • **Questions on Strategy** focus on the dominant and supporting strategies used to achieve that purpose. • **Writing Suggestions** following each reading prompt students to write using the rhetorical element or strategy focused on in that chapter. • ***Ethos, logos,* and *pathos* are introduced in relation to the rhetorical situation** (pp. 378–380) in Chapter 12, Argumentation.

WPA Outcomes	Relevant Features of *Subject & Strategy*, 15th Edition
RHETORICAL KNOWLEDGE *(continued)*	

Gain experience reading and composing in several genres to understand how genre conventions shape and are shaped by readers' and writers' practices and purposes	• **The seventy-one readings in the book span a variety of topics, disciplines, and genres.** Chapters 4–13 are organized by rhetorical pattern, with four professional and one student reading selection per chapter to give students experience and practice (Chapter 12 has more professional selections).
	
	• **Each reading selection features a robust apparatus** that gives students practice analyzing and writing for a variety of purposes and in a range of styles. In addition to Questions on Subject, Questions on Strategy, and Writing Suggestions,
	
	   • **Strategy in Action activities** provide opportunities for applied learning with exercises that enable students to work (often in groups) on rhetorical elements, techniques, or patterns.
	
	   • **Writing in the Workplace** prompts also connect rhetorical strategies to real-world genres such as business plans.
	
	   • **Using the Strategy Across the Disciplines** sections in each rhetorical chapter introduction show how to apply strategies in a range of disciplines with different purposes.

Develop facility in responding to a variety of situations and contexts calling for purposeful shifts in voice, tone, level of formality, design, medium, and/or structure	• **Chapter introductions** explain how each rhetorical element and strategy is used to achieve an author's purpose. • **"Writing for an Academic Audience"** (p. 29) in Chapter 2 explains how to choose the correct tone for writing in college classes. • The **"Formal versus Informal Writing" box** (pp. 29–30) offers a helpful reference for understanding the differences in voice, tone, and sentence structure. • **"Step 3: Organize and Write Your First Draft"** (pp. 33–37) in Chapter 2 introduces students to the importance of structure. Most essays and instruction highlight the writer's chosen organization.
Understand and use a variety of technologies to address a range of audiences	• **A Visualizing the Strategy activity** accompanies chapter opening images, which vary from photographs to flowcharts and infographics. Students may re-create these visuals to express strategy in different media using different software and technologies to present their work.

WPA Outcomes	Relevant Features of *Subject & Strategy*, 15th Edition
RHETORICAL KNOWLEDGE *(continued)*	
Match the capacities of different environments (e.g., print and electronic) to varying rhetorical situations	• Research coverage in Chapters 14 and 15 gives instructions specific to research and project planning, from taking notes to finding and evaluating sources, in both print and online spaces.
CRITICAL THINKING, READING, AND COMPOSING	
Use composing and reading for inquiry, learning, critical thinking, and communicating in various rhetorical contexts	• **Chapter 1, Reading, gives students tools to read critically and learn to read as a writer** so they can understand the rhetorical context and the writer's choices in order to apply those tools to their own writing. • **Chapter 2, Writing, presents writing as inquiry**, as a tool for gathering ideas and exploring topics. • **"Choosing Strategies Across the Disciplines"** (pp. 35–36) in Chapter 2 shows students how to take a topic or main idea in another course and models how to turn the topic into a question, answered by a dominant and supporting writing strategy. Specific examples appear in Chapters 4–12. • **Students are encouraged to write to learn** through small-stakes writing activities or full essays appropriate to the rhetorical strategy of the chapter. Question sets for each reading selection include Preparing to Read, Thinking Critically about the Text, Questions on Subject, Questions on Strategy, and Writing Suggestions.
Read a diverse range of texts, attending especially to relation-ships between asser-tion and evidence, to patterns of organization, to the interplay between verbal and nonverbal elements, and to how these features function for different audiences and situations	• **A lively collection of 58 classic and contemporary essays from professional writers and 13 essays from student writers provide outstanding models for students.** Each selection has been carefully chosen to engage students and to clearly illustrate the rhetorical strategy at work in the chapter. • **Annotated professional writing excerpts show the rhetorical choices** each writer makes to achieve his or her purpose. • **The Thematic Contents list** (pp. xliii–xlviii) offers flexibility, grouping readings by topic so students can use the selection in the book to collect and analyze information on their subject of choice. Themes include gender, the immigrant experience, the natural world, and technology, among others. Thematic writing suggestions are included in the appendix.

WPA Outcomes	Relevant Features of *Subject & Strategy*, 15th Edition
CRITICAL THINKING, READING, AND COMPOSING *(continued)*	
	• **Chapter 13, Combining Strategies**, explains more varied organizational writing strategies, showing how to combine patterns for effective writing. • **At least one reading per chapter features a question with an image** to encourage students to analyze the relationship between visual and verbal elements (e.g., Jeannette Walls, Mitch Albom, Shaun King). • **Chapter 12, Argumentation**, explains making and supporting claims. • **Chapter 14, Writing with Sources**, provides thorough coverage on integrating sources responsibly.
Locate and evaluate (for credibility, sufficiency, accuracy, timeliness, bias, and so on) primary and secondary research materials, including journal articles and essays, books, scholarly and professionally established and maintained databases or archives, and informal electronic networks and internet sources	***Subject & Strategy* offers practical instruction on working with sources** to guide students in one of their biggest writing challenges: incorporating supporting evidence from other writers into their essays. • Chapter 2, Writing, offers students clear advice for how to "Gather Ideas and Formulate a Thesis" (pp. 30–33). • Chapter 14, Writing with Sources, and Chapter 15, A Brief Guide to Researching and Documenting Essays, review the steps and skills involved in research and synthesis, with dedicated sections on "Finding and Using Sources" in print and online (p. 540), "Evaluating Your Sources" (p. 544), and "Analyzing Your Sources" (p. 546). The chapter includes a model MLA-style research paper and model for citation. • Helpful charts in Chapter 15 make useful reference tools; see, e.g., "Refining Keyword Searches on the Web" (p. 543), "Strategies for Evaluating Print and Online Sources" (pp. 544–45), and "Checklist for a Working Bibliography of Sources" (pp. 547–48).
Use strategies — such as interpretation, synthesis, response, critique, and design/redesign — to compose texts that integrate the writer's ideas with those from appropriate sources	• **Students are asked to interpret, respond, and critique** each reading and identify the writer's choices, engaging in academic conversation through the questions and prompts that accompany each selection. • **Chapter 14, Writing with Sources**, models strategies for taking effective notes from sources; using signal phrases to integrate quotations, summaries, and paraphrases smoothly; synthesizing sources; and avoiding plagiarism. • See also the previous section, "Locate and evaluate...."

WPA Outcomes	Relevant Features of *Subject & Strategy*, 15th Edition
PROCESSES	

Develop a writing project through multiple drafts	• **Chapter 2, Writing, leads students through a series of numbered steps to move from assignment to final draft:**
	  • Step 1: Understand Your Assignment
	  • Step 2: Gather Ideas and Formulate a Thesis
	  • Step 3: Organize and Write Your First Draft
	  • Step 4: Revise Your Essay
	  • Step 5: Edit and Proofread Your Essay
	• **"A Student Essay in Progress"** (pp. 42–49) in Chapter 2 follows student Keith Eldred from assignment through brainstorming, draft, and revision to final essay.
	• **Helpful boxes serve as reference tools during the writing process** to guide students in successfully choosing and employing a strategy: e.g., "Direction Words" (p. 26), "Determining What Strategies to Use with a Specific Assignment" (p. 35), and "Tips for Revising Your Draft" (p. 37).
	• **Chapter 16, Editing for Grammar, Punctuation, and Sentence Style**, provides sound advice, examples, and solutions for the editing problems that trouble students most.

Develop flexible strategies for reading, drafting, reviewing, collaborating, revising, rewriting, rereading, and editing	• **Students' reflection interviews show how they developed writing strategies** to overcome challenges and compose successful essays. "Your Response" prompts ask student readers to consider the writer's choices and how they might apply the writer's strategies to their own work. • **Inquiry-based reference boxes** guide students to making reading, writing, and revision choices. See, e.g., "Questions for Analyzing and Evaluating" (p. 12), "Will Your Thesis Hold Up to Scrutiny?" (p. 33), and "Questions for Revising the Larger Elements of Your Essay" (p. 39).
Use composing processes and tools as a means to discover and reconsider ideas	• **Chapter 2 includes sections to help students brainstorm and prewrite** with notes, clustering, and outlining; see "Finding a Subject Area and Focusing on a Topic" (pp. 27–30) and "Gather Ideas and Formulate a Thesis" (pp. 30–33). • **The reading apparatus guides students to use writing to discover new ideas and writing topics:** Preparing to Read, Thinking Critically about the Text, Questions on Subject, Questions on Strategy, and Writing Suggestions.

WPA Outcomes	Relevant Features of *Subject & Strategy*, 15th Edition
PROCESSES *(continued)*	
Experience the collaborative and social aspects of writing processes	• **Group discussion and writing** can easily begin with Visualizing the Strategy, Preparing to Read, and Thinking Critically about the Text prompts, which immediately precede and follow each reading selection. • **Students can share their writing and ideas** with their classmates and learn from each other with Strategy in Action activities.
Learn to give and to act on productive feedback to works in progress	*Subject & Strategy* **encourages peer review as part of the writing and revision process:** • In Chapter 2, "Taking Advantage of Peer Critiques" (p. 38) emphasizes for students the importance of peer feedback. • "A Brief Guide to Peer Critiquing" box (p. 38) can be used as a reference tool for peer review. • Each rhetorical chapter's "Questions for Revising and Editing" boxes (e.g., p. 86) can also be used as a tool for peer revision of a particular writing strategy.
Adapt composing processes for a variety of technologies and modalities	• The book assumes that most students compose in digital spaces, and instructions in a number of Writing Suggestions and other prompts reflect and encourage this use of the digital space. • **Strategies for collecting and managing data in digital formats** for the purpose of research assume that students are working mostly online and with technology; see Chapters 14 and 15.
Reflect on the development of composing practices and how those practices influence their work	• **Preparing to Read** prompts before each reading ask students to discover and apply their prior knowledge to the reading selection. • **Student Reflection** interviews following each student essay demonstrate student writers' reflective processes. • **"Your Response"** prompts following these interviews encourage students to consider how they might learn from other student writers' processes and make similar choices in their own writing.

WPA Outcomes	Relevant Features of *Subject & Strategy*, 15th Edition
KNOWLEDGE OF CONVENTIONS *(continued)*	
Develop knowledge of linguistic structures, including grammar, punctuation, and spelling, through practice in composing and revising	**Chapter 16, Editing for Grammar, Punctuation, and Sentence Style**, covers common grammar and mechanics errors and presents clear examples of corrections to help students write with minimal errors. Coverage includes run-ons and comma splices, sentence fragments, subject-verb agreement, pronoun-antecedent agreement, verb tense shifts, misplaced and dangling modifiers, faulty parallelism, weak nouns and verbs, and academic diction and tone.
Understand why genre conventions for structure, paragraphing, tone, and mechanics vary	• Chapter introductions for each rhetorical strategy in Chapters 4–13 explain how each strategy serves a writer's purpose. • Questions on Strategy highlight authors' specific choices, such as short paragraphs or strategic use of fragments, and ask students to consider why the author made a certain choice.
Gain experience negotiating variations in genre conventions	**Strategy in Action activities and Writing Suggestions** following each reading selection encourage students to apply the rhetorical strategies to real-world genres and situations and use them in their writing.
Learn common formats and/or design features for different kinds of texts	• Visualizing the Strategy prompts encourage students to focus on design elements in visual texts. • Though *Subject & Strategy* offers no specific coverage of formatting documents in MLA style, citations follow MLA style formatting, unless otherwise noted.
Explore the concepts of intellectual property (such as fair use and copyright) that motivate documentation conventions	• **Chapter 14, Writing with Sources**, explains why outside sources are rhetorically useful and help writers articulate positions in the conversation and extend their own ideas, and how doing so requires thoughtful documentation when integrating using quotation, paraphrase, or summary. • **"Avoiding Plagiarism," (pp. 507–11) and the "Preventing Plagiarism" reference box (p. 510)** further define and explore these concepts.
Practice applying citation conventions systematically in their own work	**Chapter 15, A Brief Guide to Researching and Documenting Essays**, offers detailed guidance on taking notes to avoid plagiarism and provides model citations in MLA style.

ACKNOWLEDGMENTS

We are gratified by the reception and use of the fourteen previous editions of *Subject & Strategy*. Composition teachers in hundreds of community colleges, liberal arts colleges, and universities have used the book. Many teachers responded to our detailed review questionnaire, thus helping tremendously in conceptualizing the improvements to this edition. We thank Jacqueline Beamen, Camden County College; Janet M. Black, Colorado Christian University; Birdena Brookins, Rowan College at Gloucester County; Katawna Caldwell-Warren, Eastfield College; Heather Chacon, Greensboro College; Phillip Chamberlin, Hillsborough Community College; Mark A. Graves, Morehead State University; Jennifer Jared, University of La Verne; Denise Lagos, Union County College; Elaine Lux-Koman, Nyack College; Felicia M. Maisey, Gwynedd Mercy University; Rebecca R. Mullane, Moraine Park Technical College; Corrine Peschka, The University of Texas at El Paso; Maria Rankin-Brown, Pacific Union College; Lynn Reid, Fairleigh Dickinson University; Eileen Figure Sandlin, Northwood University; Judy H. Schmidt, Harrisburg Area Community College; Nancy A. Shaffer, The University of Texas at El Paso; Arna A. Shines, Tougaloo College; and Megan Trexler, Delaware County Community College.

We also wish to thank the exceptional students whose input in round-table discussions and surveys influenced the direction of this new edition: Laura Agosto, Baruch College; Kayshawna Brown, Cristo Rey New York High School; Tiana Burnett, Fairleigh Dickinson University; Annie Campbell, Wheaton College; Annabelle Chan, Baruch College; Bethany Christian, Mercy College; Nathanael Christian, State University of New York at New Paltz; George Cunningham, University at Buffalo; Sarah Fornshell, Columbia University; Aislyn Fredsall, Northeastern University; Mila Gauvin, Harvard College; Belinda Huang, Emerson College; Gabi Jackson, Fairleigh Dickinson University; Katherine Kachnowski, The Ohio State University; Anne-Clarisse Magtaan, University of Texas at Austin; Andrew Matthews; Grand Valley State University; Sara McLaughlin, Fordham University; Matthew Mercado, Texas A&M at College Station; Daniel Monteagudo, Rochester Institute of Technology; Meg Moran, University of Scranton; Nick Rizzuti, Hofstra University; Isabella Salerni, Tulane University; Danielle Straub, Hunter College; Claire Strickland, New York University; Alexandra Torres, University at Buffalo; Sarah Vogel, Fairleigh Dickinson University; Haley Wade, Barnard College; and Kayla Williamson, Spring Arbor University.

Thanks go also to the Bedford/St. Martin's team: Leah Rang, our thoughtful, creative, and untiring editor; John Sullivan, Senior Program

Manager for Readers and Literature; Leasa Burton, Executive Program Director for English; and Edwin Hill, Vice President, Editorial, Macmillan Learning Humanities. We would also like to acknowledge Pamela Lawson, Joy Fisher Williams, Aubrea Bailis, and Cari Goldfine. Special thanks go to Sarah Federman for her assistance with developing the Instructor's Manual. We are also happy to recognize those students whose work appears in *Subject & Strategy* for their willingness to contribute their time and effort in writing and rewriting their essays: Katie Angeles, Barbara Bowman, Kevin Cunningham, Keith Eldred, LeeLee Goodson, Jake Jamieson, Katherine Kachnowski, Andrew Kauser, Paula Kersch, Bill Peterson, Howard Solomon Jr., Jim Tassé, Mundy Wilson-Piper. We are grateful to all of our writing students at the University of Vermont for their enthusiasm for writing and for their invaluable responses to materials included in this book. And we also thank our families for sharing in our commitment to quality teaching and textbook writing.

Finally, we thank each other. Since 1971 we have collaborated on many textbooks on language and writing, all of which have gone into multiple editions. With this fifteenth edition of *Subject & Strategy*, we enter more than forty-five years of working together. Ours must be one of the longest-running and most mutually satisfying writing partnerships in college textbook publishing. The journey has been invigorating and challenging as we have come to understand the complexities and joys of good writing and have sought new ways to help students become better writers.

PAUL ESCHHOLZ

ALFRED ROSA

Contents

2 Writing 25

5 Description   113

6 Illustration 153

8 Comparison and Contrast 225

Sojourner Truth, *Ain't I a Woman?*   395
"Nobody ever helps me into carriages, or over mud-puddles, or gives me any best place!"

Abraham Lincoln, *Second Inaugural Address*   398
"Both parties deprecated war, but one of them would make war rather than let the nation survive, and the other would accept war rather than let it perish, and the war came."

Nancy Armour, *Participation Awards Do Disservice*   402
"If we're honest with ourselves, the trophies, ribbons and medals we hand out so willingly are more about us than the children getting them."

William Galston, *Telling Americans to Vote, or Else*   406
"A democracy can't be strong if its citizenship is weak."

Roger Cohen, *The Organic Fable*   411
"The takeaway from the study could be summed up in two words: Organic, schmorganic."

Nikki Giovanni, *Campus Racism 101*   415
"There are discomforts attached to attending predominantly white colleges, though no more so than living in a racist world."

Siobhan Crowley, *On the Subject of Trigger Warnings*   422
"I would hate for students to miss an opportunity to work through their trauma in my classroom, where I can mediate discussions to ensure that comments are not hurtful."

Roger McNamee, *I Invested Early in Google and Facebook. Now They Terrify Me.*   426
"The big internet companies know more about you than you know about yourself, which gives them huge power to influence you, to persuade you to do things that serve their economic interests."

14 Writing with Sources 497

16 Editing for Grammar, Punctuation, and Sentence Style 561

Thematic Contents

THE NATURAL WORLD

PEER PRESSURE

WRITERS ON WRITING

SUBJECT & STRATEGY

A WRITER'S READER

Images-USA / Alamy

CHAPTER 1

Reading

SUBJECT & STRATEGY PLACES EQUAL EMPHASIS ON CONTENT AND FORM — that is, on the *subject* of an essay and on the *strategies* an author uses to write it. All readers pay attention to content. Far fewer, however, notice form — the strategies authors use to organize their writing and the means they use to make it clear, logical, and effective.

When you learn to read actively and analytically, you come to appreciate the craftsmanship involved in writing — a writer's choice of an appropriate organizational strategy or strategies and his or her use of descriptive details, representative and persuasive examples, sentence variety, and clear, appropriate, vivid diction.

VISUALIZING READING

Founded in 2009, Little Free Library is a nonprofit organization that helps people build little, unconventional libraries. As of November 2016, there were over fifty thousand registered Little Free Libraries in the United States and seventy other countries. What does the photograph indicate about how a Little Free Library operates? What do the little library and its surroundings tell you about the neighborhood — or about the community's attitudes toward reading? Does the little library look like it's being used? How do you know? Finally, what do you think a library like this does for a community and its people?

DEVELOPING AN EFFECTIVE READING PROCESS

Active, analytical reading requires, first of all, that you commit time and effort to it. Second, it requires that you try to take a positive interest in what you are reading, even if the subject matter is not immediately appealing. To help you get the most out of your reading, this chapter provides guidelines for an effective reading process.

Step 1: Prepare Yourself to Read the Selection

Instead of diving right into any given selection in *Subject & Strategy*, you need first to establish a context for what you will be reading. What's the essay about? What do you know about the author's background and reputation? Where was the essay first published? Who was the intended audience? And, finally, how much do you already know about the subject of the selection?

The materials that precede each selection in this book—the title, headnote, and Preparing to Read prompt—are intended to help you establish this context. From the *title* you often discover the writer's position on an issue or attitude toward the topic. The title can also give clues about the writer's intended audience and reasons for composing the piece.

Each *headnote* contains four essential elements:

1. A *photo* of the author lets you put a face to a name.
2. The *biographical information* provides details about the writer's life and work, as well as his or her reputation and authority to write on the subject.
3. The *publication information* for the selection tells you when the essay was published and where it first appeared. This information can also give you insight into the intended audience.
4. The *content and rhetorical highlights* of the selection preview the subject and point out key aspects of the writing strategies used by the author.

Finally, the Preparing to Read *journal prompt* encourages you to reflect and record your thoughts and opinions on the topic of the essay before you begin reading.

Carefully review the following context-building materials that accompany Cherokee Paul McDonald's "A View from the Bridge" to see how they can help you establish a context for the reading. The essay itself appears with annotations on pages 8–10.

Title

A View from the Bridge

Author

CHEROKEE PAUL MCDONALD

Headnote

A fiction writer and journalist, Cherokee Paul McDonald was raised and schooled in Fort Lauderdale, Florida. In 1970, he returned home from a tour of duty in Vietnam and joined the Fort Lauderdale Police Department, where he remained until 1980, when he resigned with

Courtesy of Simon Dearden

Biographical information

the rank of sergeant. During this time, McDonald received a degree in criminal science from Broward Community College. He left the police department to become a writer and worked a number of odd jobs before publishing his first book, *The Patch*, in 1986. McDonald has said that almost all of his writing comes from his police work, and his common themes of justice, balance, and fairness reflect his life as part of the "thin blue line" (the police department). In 1991, he published *Blue Truth*, a memoir. His first novel, *Summer's Reason*, was released in 1994, and *Into the Green: A Reconnaissance by Fire*, a memoir of his three years as an artillery forward observer in Vietnam, appeared in 2001.

Publication information

"A View from the Bridge" was originally published in *Sunshine*, a monthly magazine filled with uplifting short articles and stories, in 1990. The essay shows McDonald's usual expert handling of fish and fishermen, both in and out of water, and reminds us that things are not

Content and rhetorical highlights

always as they seem. Notice his selective use of details to describe the young fisherman and the fish he has hooked on his line.

Preparing to Read

Journal prompt

The great American philosopher and naturalist Henry David Thoreau has written: "The question is not what you look at, but what you see." We've all had the experience of becoming numb to sights or experiences that once struck us with wonderment; but sometimes, with luck, something happens to renew our appreciation. Think of an example from your own experience. What are some ways we can retain or recover our appreciation of the remarkable things we have come to take for granted?

From reading these preliminary materials, what expectations do you have for "A View from the Bridge"? While McDonald's *title* does not give any specific indication of his topic, it does suggest that he will be writing about the view from a particular bridge and that what he sees is worth sharing with his readers. The *biographical note* reveals that McDonald, a Vietnam veteran and former police officer, is a fiction writer and journalist. The titles of his books suggest that much of his writing comes from his military and police work, where he developed important observational skills and sensitivity to people and the environment. From the *publication information* for the selection, you learn that the essay first appeared in 1990 in *Sunshine*, a monthly magazine with short, uplifting human-interest articles for a general readership. The *content and rhetorical highlights* advise you to look at how McDonald's knowledge about fish and fishing and his use of descriptive details help him paint a verbal picture of the young fisherman and the battle he has with the fish on his line. Finally, the *journal prompt* asks for your thoughts on why we become numb to experiences that once awed us. What, for you, is the difference between to "look at" and to "see," and how can we preserve our appreciation for the awesome things that we sometimes take for granted? After reading McDonald's essay, you can compare your reflections on "seeing" with what McDonald learned from his own experience with the boy who fished by the bridge.

Step 2: Read the Selection

Always read the selection at least twice, no matter how long it is. The first reading lets you get acquainted with the essay and get an overall sense of what the writer is saying and why. As you read, you may find yourself modifying the sense of the writer's message and purpose that you derived from the title, headnote, and your response to the writing prompt. Circle words you do not recognize so that you can look them up in a dictionary. Put a question mark alongside any passages that are not immediately clear. However, you will probably want to delay most of your annotating until a second reading so that your first reading can be fast, enabling you to concentrate on the larger issues of message and purpose.

Step 3: Reread the Selection

Your second reading should be quite different from your first. You will know what the essay is about, where it is going, and how it gets there; now you can relate the individual parts of the essay more accurately to the whole. Use your second reading to test your first impressions, developing and deepening your sense of how (and how well) the essay is written. Pay special attention to the author's purpose and means of achieving it. You can look for strategies of organization in the "Organizational Strategies" box in Chapter 2 (page 33) and style and adapt them to your own work.

Step 4: Annotate the Selection

When you annotate a selection, you should do more than simply underline what you think are important points. It is easy to underline so much that the notations become meaningless, and it's common to forget why you underlined passages in the first place. Instead, as you read, write down your thoughts in the margins or on a separate piece of paper. Mark the selection's main point when you find it stated directly. Look for the strategy or strategies the author uses to explore and support that point and jot down this information. If you disagree with a statement or conclusion, object in the margin: "No!" If you feel skeptical, write "Why?" or "Explain." If you are impressed by an argument or turn of phrase, write "Good point!" Place vertical lines or a star in the margin to indicate especially important points.

Remember that there are no hard-and-fast rules for annotating elements. Choose a method of annotation that will make sense to you when you go back to recollect your thoughts and responses to the essay. Jot down whatever marginal notes come naturally to you. Most readers combine brief written responses with underlining, circling, highlighting, stars, or question marks.

What to Annotate in a Text

Here are some examples of what you may want to mark in a selection as you read:

- Memorable statements or important points
- Key terms or concepts
- Central issues or themes
- Examples that support a major point
- Unfamiliar words
- Questions you have about a point or passage
- Your responses to a specific point or passage

Above all, don't let annotating become burdensome. A word or phrase is usually as good as a sentence. One helpful way to focus your annotations is to ask yourself questions such as those in the "Questions for Analyzing and Evaluating" box (page 12) while reading the selection a second time. As you read "A View from the Bridge," observe what Julie Dwire, one of our students, chose to annotate.

▷ An Example: Student Annotations for Cherokee Paul McDonald's "A View from the Bridge"

Sets the scene

I was coming up on the little bridge in the Rio Vista neighborhood of Fort Lauderdale, deepening my stride and my breathing to negotiate the slight incline without altering my pace. And then, as I neared the crest, I saw the kid.   1

Nice description

He was a lumpy little guy with baggy shorts, a faded T-shirt and heavy sweat socks falling down over old sneakers.   2

Partially covering his shaggy blond hair was one of those blue baseball caps with gold braid on the bill and a sailfish patch sewn onto the peak. Covering his eyes and part of his face was a pair of those stupid-looking '50s-style wrap-around sunglasses.   3

Why "fumbling"?

He was fumbling with a beat-up rod and reel, and he had a little bait bucket by his feet. I puffed on by, glancing down into the empty bucket as I passed.   4

"Hey, mister! Would you help me, please?"   5

The shrill voice penetrated my jogger's concentration, and I was determined to ignore it. But for some reason, I stopped.   6

Jogger sounds irritated

With my hands on my hips and the sweat dripping from my nose I asked, "What do you want, kid?"   7

"Would you please help me find my shrimp? It's my last one and I've been getting bites and I know I can catch a fish if I can just find that shrimp. He jumped outta my hand as I was getting him from the bucket."   8

Shrimp is clearly visible, so why does kid ask for help?

Exasperated, I walked slowly back to the kid, and pointed.   9

"There's the damn shrimp by your left foot. You stopped me for *that*?"   10

As I said it, the kid reached down and trapped the shrimp.   11

Kid's polite

"Thanks a lot, mister," he said.   12

I watched as the kid dropped the baited hook down into the canal. Then I turned to start back down the bridge.   13

That's when the kid let out a "Hey! Hey!" and the prettiest 14
tarpon I'd ever seen came almost six feet out of the water, twist-
ing and turning as he fell through the air.

Dialogue enhances drama

"I got one!" the kid yelled as the fish hit the water with a 15
loud splash and took off down the canal.

I watched the line being burned off the reel at an alarming 16
rate. The kid's left hand held the crank while the extended fingers felt for the drag setting.

Jogger gets involved once kid hooks fish

"No, kid!" I shouted. "Leave the drag alone . . . just keep that 17
damn rod tip up!"

Then I glanced at the reel and saw there were just a few 18
loops of line left on the spool.

"Why don't you get yourself some decent equipment?" I 19
said, but before the kid could answer I saw the line go slack.

"Ohhh, I lost him," the kid said. I saw the flash of silver as 20
the fish turned.

Starts coaching kid

"Crank, kid, crank! You didn't lose him. He's coming back 21
toward you. Bring in the slack!"

The kid cranked like mad, and a beautiful grin spread across 22
his face.

"He's heading in for the pilings," I said. "Keep him out of 23
those pilings!"

The kid played it perfectly. When the fish made its play for 24
the pilings, he kept just enough pressure on to force the fish out.
When the water exploded and the silver missile hurled into the
air, the kid kept the rod tip up and the line tight.

Impressive fish

As the fish came to the surface and began a slow circle in 25
the middle of the canal, I said, "Whooee, is that a nice fish or
what?"

The kid didn't say anything, so I said, "Okay, move to the 26
edge of the bridge and I'll climb down to the seawall and pull
him out."

When I reached the seawall I pulled in the leader, leaving 27
the fish lying on its side in the water.

"How's that?" I said. 28

"Hey, mister, tell me what it looks like." 29

Kid makes strange request

"Look down here and check him out," I said, "He's 30
beautiful."

But then I looked up into those stupid-looking sunglasses 31
and it hit me. The kid was blind.

Wow!

"Could you tell me what he looks like, mister?" he said 32
again.

"Well, he's just under three, uh, he's about as long as one of 33
your arms," I said. "I'd guess he goes about 15, 20 pounds. He's
mostly silver, but the silver is somehow made up of *all* the colors, if you know what I mean." I stopped. "Do you know what
I mean by colors?"

The kid nodded. 34

"Okay. He has all these big scales, like armor all over his 35
body. They're silver too, and when he moves they sparkle. He
has a strong body and a large powerful tail. He has big round
eyes, bigger than a quarter, and a lower jaw that sticks out past
the upper one and is very tough. His belly is almost white and
his back is a gunmetal gray. When he jumped he came out
of the water about six feet, and his scales caught the sun and
flashed it all over the place."

By now the fish had righted itself, and I could see 36
the bright-red gills as the gill plates opened and closed. I
explained this to the kid, and then said, more to myself, "He's
a beauty."

"Can you get him off the hook?" the kid asked. "I don't want 37
to kill him."

I watched as the tarpon began to slowly swim away, tired 38
but still alive.

By the time I got back up to the top of the bridge the kid 39
had his line secured and his bait bucket in one hand.

He grinned and said, "Just in time. My mom drops me off 40
here, and she'll be back to pick me up any minute."

He used the back of one hand to wipe his nose. 41

"Thanks for helping me catch that tarpon," he said, "and for 42
helping me to see it."

I looked at him, shook my head, and said, "No, my friend, 43
thank you for letting *me* see that fish."

I took off, but before I got far the kid yelled again. 44

"Hey, mister!" 45

I stopped. 46

"Someday I'm gonna catch a sailfish and a blue marlin and 47
a giant tuna and *all* those big sportfish!"

As I looked into those sunglasses I knew he probably would. 48
I wished I could be there when it happened.

Student Reflection
Julie Dwire on Annotating a Reading

Q. How do you know what things you annotate?

A. Now that's a good question, because I haven't always been as comfortable with marking up an essay as I was when I read and annotated "A View from the Bridge" about seven weeks into the semester. The first time my instructor asked me to annotate a reading back in September I really wasn't sure what I was doing. I tried to make notes while I was reading the piece the first time. How was I supposed to know what was important and what wasn't when I didn't even know where the essay was going? I ended up underlining way too much, and most of what I did underline or comment upon was related to content. I remember being a little self-conscious about what I was writing in the margins, too. Once I realized that marginal notes were for my eyes—to help me better remember and understand an essay and to see how it was written—I relaxed and started to develop a sense of what to look for and what to question.

From my first reading of the McDonald essay, I learned the narrator was telling a story about an encounter he'd had with a young fisherman who he discovers is blind. With a basic understanding of the storyline in mind, during my second reading I set about making annotations that focused on the two central characters, key points in the development of the story, and the writer's method or technique in "showing" his story. As I reflect on my annotations now, I see that I was interested in those descriptive details that gave me insight into the jogger and the fisherman; in key points of the interaction between these characters; and in how the writer used dialogue to develop his story, how he was able to keep the kid's blindness a mystery for so long, and how he left me with a clear understanding of why he had written this piece.

Step 5: Analyze and Evaluate the Selection

As you continue to study the selection, analyze it for a deeper understanding and appreciation of the author's craft and try to evaluate its overall effectiveness as a piece of writing. The "Questions for Analyzing and Evaluating" box that follows on page 12 gives you some questions you may find helpful as you start the process.

Questions for Analyzing and Evaluating

1. What is the writer's topic?
2. What is the writer's main point or thesis?
3. What is the writer's purpose in writing?
4. What strategy or strategies does the writer use? *Where* and *how* does the writer use them?
5. Do the writer's strategies suit his or her subject and purpose? Why or why not?
6. How effective is the essay? Does the writer make his or her points clear and persuade the reader to accept them?

Each essay in *Subject & Strategy* is followed by study questions similar to these but specific to the essay. Some of the questions help you analyze the content, while others help you analyze the writer's use of the rhetorical strategies. As you read the essay a second time, look for details related to these questions and then answer the questions as fully as you can.

THE READING PROCESS IN ACTION: THOMAS L. FRIEDMAN'S "MY FAVORITE TEACHER"

To give you practice using the five-step reading process that we have just explored, we present an essay by Thomas L. Friedman, including the headnote material and the Preparing to Read prompt. Before you read Friedman's essay, think about the title, the biographical and rhetorical information in the headnote, and the journal prompt. Make some notes of your expectations about the essay and write out a response to the prompt. Next, continue following the five-step process outlined in this chapter. As you read the essay for the first time, try not to stop; take it all in as if in one breath. The second time through, pause to annotate the text. Finally, using the questions listed in the "Questions for Analyzing and Evaluating" box in the previous section, analyze and evaluate the essay.

My Favorite Teacher

THOMAS L. FRIEDMAN

New York Times foreign affairs columnist Thomas L. Friedman was born in Minneapolis, Minnesota, in 1953. He graduated from Brandeis University in 1975 and received a Marshall Scholarship to pursue modern Middle East studies at St. Anthony's College, Oxford University, where he earned a master's degree. He has worked for the *New York Times* since 1981 — first in Lebanon, then in Israel, and since 1989 in Washington, D.C. He was awarded the Pulitzer Prize in 1983 and 1988 for his reporting and again in 2002 for his com-

Nancy Ostertag/Getty Images for AFI

mentary. Friedman's 1989 best seller *From Beirut to Jerusalem* received the National Book Award for nonfiction. His most recent books are *The World Is Flat: A Brief History of the Twenty-First Century* (2005), *Hot, Flat, and Crowded: Why We Need a Green Revolution — And How It Can Renew America* (2008), and *That Used to Be Us: How America Fell Behind in the World It Invented and How We Can Come Back* (2011), with Michael Mandelbaum. From 2013 to 2014, Friedman contributed to the climate change documentary series "Years of Living Dangerously." His most recent book is *Thank You for Being Late: An Optimist's Guide to Thriving in the Age of Accelerations* (2016).

In the following essay, which first appeared in the *New York Times* on January 9, 2001, Friedman pays tribute to his tenth-grade journalism teacher. As you read Friedman's profile of Hattie M. Steinberg, note the descriptive detail he selects to create the dominant impression of "a woman of clarity in an age of uncertainty."

Preparing to Read

If you had to name your three favorite teachers of all time, who would they be? Why do you consider each one a favorite? Which one, if any, are you likely to remember twenty-five years from now? Why?

Last Sunday's *New York Times Magazine* published its annual review of 1 people who died last year who left a particular mark on the world. I am sure all readers have their own such list. I certainly do. Indeed, someone who made the most important difference in my life died last year — my high school journalism teacher, Hattie M. Steinberg.

I grew up in a small suburb of Minneapolis, and Hattie was the leg- 2 endary journalism teacher at St. Louis Park High School, Room 313. I took her intro to journalism course in 10th grade, back in 1969, and have never needed, or taken, another course in journalism since. She was that good.

Hattie was a woman who believed that the secret for success in life was 3 getting the fundamentals right. And boy, she pounded the fundamentals of journalism into her students — not simply how to write a lead or accurately transcribe a quote, but, more important, how to comport yourself in a professional way and to always do quality work. To this day, when I forget to wear a tie on assignment, I think of Hattie scolding me. I once interviewed an ad exec for our high school paper who used a four-letter word. We debated whether to run it. Hattie ruled yes. That ad man almost lost his job when it appeared. She wanted to teach us about consequences.

Hattie was the toughest teacher I ever had. After you took her journalism course in 10th grade, you tried out for the paper, *The Echo*, which she supervised. Competition was fierce. In 11th grade, I didn't quite come up to her writing standards, so she made me business manager, selling ads to the local pizza parlors. That year, though, she let me write one story. It was about an Israeli general who had been a hero in the Six-Day War, who was giving a lecture at the University of Minnesota. I covered his lecture and interviewed him briefly. His name was Ariel Sharon. First story I ever got published. 4

> 66 **The Internet can make you smarter, but it can't make you smart.** 99

Those of us on the paper, and the yearbook that she also supervised, lived in Hattie's classroom. We hung out there before and after school. Now, you have to understand, Hattie was a single woman, nearing sixty at the time, and this was the 1960s. She was the polar opposite of "cool," but we hung around her classroom like it was a malt shop and she was Wolfman Jack. None of us could have articulated it then, but it was because we enjoyed being harangued by her, disciplined by her, and taught by her. She was a woman of clarity in an age of uncertainty. 5

We remained friends for thirty years, and she followed, bragged about, and critiqued every twist in my career. After she died, her friends sent me a pile of my stories that she had saved over the years. Indeed, her students were her family—only closer. Judy Harrington, one of Hattie's former students, remarked about other friends who were on Hattie's newspapers and yearbooks: "We all graduated forty-one years ago; and yet nearly each day in our lives something comes up—some mental image, some admonition that makes us think of Hattie." 6

Judy also told the story of one of Hattie's last birthday parties, when one man said he had to leave early to take his daughter somewhere. "Sit down," said Hattie. "You're not leaving yet. She can just be a little late." 7

That was my teacher! I sit up straight just thinkin' about her. 8

Among the fundamentals Hattie introduced me to was the *New York Times*. Every morning it was delivered to Room 313. I had never seen it before then. Real journalists, she taught us, start their day by reading the *Times* and columnists like Anthony Lewis and James Reston. 9

I have been thinking about Hattie a lot this year, not just because she died on July 31, but because the lessons she imparted seem so relevant now. We've just gone through this huge dot-com-Internet-globalization bubble—during 10 which a lot of smart people got carried away and forgot the fundamentals of how you build a profitable company, a lasting portfolio, a nation state, or a thriving student. It turns out that the real secret of success in the information age is what it always was: fundamentals—reading, writing, and arithmetic; church, synagogue, and mosque; the rule of law and good governance.

The Internet can make you smarter, but it can't make you smart. It can extend   11
your reach, but it will never tell you what to say at a P.T.A. meeting. These fundamentals cannot be downloaded. You can only upload them, the old-fashioned way, one by one, in places like Room 313 at St. Louis Park High. I only regret that I didn't write this column when the woman who taught me all that was still alive.

Once you have read and reread Friedman's essay, write your own answers to the six basic questions in the "Questions for Analyzing and Evaluating" box (page 12). Then compare your answers with the following answers written by Gary Ortiz, one of our writing students.

1. **What is the writer's *topic*?**

   Friedman's topic is his high school journalism teacher, Hattie M. Steinberg; more broadly, his topic is the "secret for success in life," as taught to him by Steinberg.

2. **What is the writer's *main point* or *thesis*?**

   Friedman writes about Steinberg because she was "someone who made the most important difference in my life" (paragraph 1). His main point seems to be that "Hattie was a woman who believed that the secret for success in life was getting the fundamentals right" (3). Friedman learned this from Hattie and applied it to his own life. He firmly believes that "the real secret of success in the information age is what it always was: fundamentals" (10).

3. **What is the writer's *purpose* in writing?**

   Friedman's purpose is to memorialize Steinberg and to explain the importance of the fundamentals that she taught him more than forty years ago. He wants his readers to realize that there are no shortcuts or quick fixes on the road to success. Without the fundamentals, success often eludes people.

4. **What *strategy* or *strategies* does the writer use? *Where* and *how* does the writer use them?**

   Overall, Friedman uses the strategy of illustration, fleshing out his profile of Steinberg with specific examples of the fundamentals she instilled in her students (paragraphs 3 and 9). Friedman uses description as well to develop his profile of Steinberg. We learn that she was Friedman's "toughest teacher" (4), that she was "a single woman, nearing sixty at the time," that she was "the polar opposite of 'cool,'" and that she was "a woman of clarity in an age of uncertainty" (5). Finally, Friedman's brief narratives about an advertising executive, Ariel Sharon, Steinberg's classroom hangout, and one of the teacher's last birthday parties give readers insight into her personality by showing us what she was like instead of simply telling us.

5. **Do the writer's *strategies* suit his *subject* and *purpose*? Why or why not?**

Friedman uses exemplification as a strategy to show why Steinberg had such a great impact on his life. Friedman knew that he was not telling Steinberg's story, or writing narration, as much as he was showing what a great teacher she was. Using examples of how Steinberg affected his life and molded his journalistic skills allows Friedman to introduce his teacher as well as to demonstrate her importance.

In developing his portrait of Steinberg in this way, Friedman relies on the fundamentals of good journalism. When taken collectively, his examples create a poignant picture of this teacher. Steinberg would likely have been proud to see her former student demonstrating his journalistic skills in paying tribute to her.

6. **How effective is the essay? Does the writer make his points clear and persuade the reader to accept them?**

Friedman's essay serves his purpose extremely well. He helps his readers visualize Steinberg and understand what she gave to each of her journalism students. In his concluding two paragraphs, Friedman shows us that Steinberg's message is as relevant today as it was more than forty years ago, in St. Louis Park High School, Room 313.

Student Reflection
Gary Ortiz on Answering Study Questions

Q. What is the value of writing out answers to the study questions?
A. The study questions help me to really understand what an essay's about and how it was written. At first I thought that these questions were a waste of time, and my answers usually showed it—brief and superficial. If my instructor had asked me, "What's your purpose?" after I wrote a draft of my first essay, I probably would have responded, "To do the assignment." But the more we talked in class about the questions for each reading, the more I began to see how my answers, especially to the writing strategy questions, could help my own writing. I read the Friedman essay several times, making notes the second time through. As I wrote my answers, I realized that Friedman's essay is a good essay because he knew his subject and why he was writing about her—and his descriptive details show that so clearly. I eventually discovered that doing the study questions helped me annotate better, which also gave me confidence to say more in class.

READING PHOTOGRAPHS AND VISUAL TEXTS

Subject & Strategy has a visual dimension to complement the many verbal texts. Each chapter offers you at least two images to analyze or interpret. Adding this visual medium to the mix of written essays and text-based analytical activities and assignments gives you an opportunity to see not only another approach to themes and strategies but also how a different medium portrays these themes and strategies.

There's nothing unnatural or wrong about looking at a photograph and naming its subject or giving it a label. For example, summarizing the content of the following photograph is easy enough. We'd simply say, *"Here's a photograph of a man sitting in front of a store."*

Mark Henley/Panos Pictures

The problem comes when we mistake *looking* for *seeing*. If we think we are seeing and truly perceiving but are only looking, we miss a lot. Our visual sense can become uncritical and nonchalant, perhaps even dismissive of what's going on in a photograph.

To reap the larger rewards, we need to move in more closely on an image. If we take a closer look, we will see all kinds of important details that we perhaps missed the first time around—just like when we take a closer look at a piece of writing. We see elements in harmony as well as conflict. We see comparisons and contrasts. We see storytelling. We see process and change. We see highlights and shadows, foreground and background, light and dark, and a myriad of shades in between. There is movement—even in still photographs. There is tension and energy, peace and harmony, and line and texture. We see all this because we are seeing and not merely looking.

When one of our writing classes examined the photograph of the man, they generated the following list of observations:

- A man sits on a ledge that is low to the ground. He is possibly traveling because he has two bags, one of which is so heavy that a wheeled cart is useful. Behind him is a store-window display with mannequins posed in various positions.

- A casual observer might think the scene is in a mall, but closer observation reveals that the ledge is alongside an outdoor sidewalk. The glass of the store window reflects the activity of a busy urban street. We see the side of a bus reflected there. The man holds a cigarette in his right hand, evidence that he is outside.

- The light square tiles of the sidewalk contrast with the round-edged, glossy dark ledge.

- The man is not particularly meticulous about his appearance and seems unbothered by the street potentially dirtying his clothes. His white shirt is unbuttoned and rumpled. His loose-fitting camouflage jacket and baseball cap suggest that he prioritizes comfort over style. The shadow on his cap indicates flexible, broken-in fabric. He may wear the hat often.

- The man stares blankly ahead, uninterested in the goings-on outside the photograph. If he tried to observe the area in front of him, the cart's handle would obscure his view. His posture is rounded, and his arms rest on his knees. He seems tired. Perhaps it's late in the day or, if he has been traveling, it's been a complicated journey.

- In contrast to the man's appearance and manner, the front-window display is formal and fashionable. We see decorative plant fronds in an ornate holder. Luxurious, fringed blankets and jacquard pillows rest on the right side of a squared, modern white bench. The headless, seated mannequin is styled with great care, dressed in skinny high heels, a short dress, and a three-buttoned jacket with a fur collar. The sharp angles of the mannequin's elbows strike a self-assured, confident pose.

- It's clear that the store carries upscale women's clothes and home furnishings. The clean, litter-free street suggests that the store may be in a well-kept area, perhaps catering to upscale shoppers.
- The fact that both the mannequin and the man wear light, open jackets suggests a temperate, cool time of year. If we were to zoom in on the window's text placard, we would see Chinese characters, suggesting that this scene is in a Chinese city.
- The most striking thing about the photograph is the juxtaposition of the weary, casually dressed man with the formal and upscale mannequin in the store window. The man seems content to sit and smoke his cigarette, showing little interest in his surroundings.

Based on these detailed observations, our students identified a number of themes at work in the photo: class and lifestyle differences, cultural contradictions, and the clash between concepts like work and leisure. Additionally, they saw that several rhetorical strategies are at work: comparison and contrast predominantly but also description and illustration.

Just as written texts have an author with a purpose, strategy, and style, visual texts also have creators: photographers, illustrators, graphic designers, and so on. Sometimes the author may be a business or an organization, as in the case of an advertisement or a public service announcement. To become a strong reader of visual texts, you can start with the same questions for analyzing and evaluating that you use for essays:

Questions for Analyzing and Evaluating Visuals

1. What is the creator's topic?
2. What is the creator's main point or thesis?
3. What is the creator's purpose in photographing/illustrating/designing?
4. What strategy or strategies does the creator use? *Where* and *how* does the creator use them?
5. Do the creator's strategies suit his or her subject and purpose? Why or why not?
6. How effective is the visual text? Does the creator make his or her viewpoint clear and persuade the reader or viewer to accept that viewpoint?

Photographs are not the only visual texts that we encounter in our daily lives. Both in print and on the Internet, governments, organizations, and individuals present us with visual information in graphs, diagrams, flow-charts, and ads.

Consider the following Recycling Saves Energy poster published by the North Carolina Department of Environmental Quality to promote public awareness of pressing environmental issues. In recent years, we've all heard a great deal about the need to recycle more, to conserve energy, and to reduce global warming. Often, however, we are not shown or told about how these three environmental issues might be interrelated.

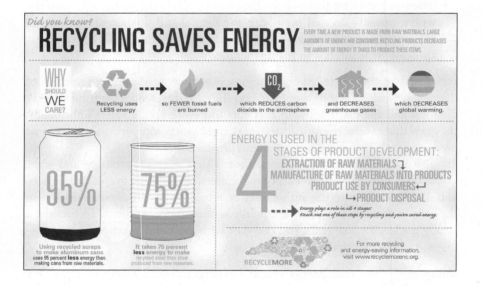

First, think about how recycling and energy are related and about what your everyday recycling habits might contribute to conservation. Then take the time to carefully analyze the graphic and write down observations about what you see. Here is what our students observed:

- The poster is divided into two halves. The top half answers two basic questions: "Did you know recycling saves energy?" and "Why should we care?" The bottom half provides two specific ways of looking at how recycling saves energy.

- The first question on the top half is answered with a simple two-sentence statement. The answer—"Recycling Saves Energy"—is also the argument of the poster, represented in large type using all capital letters, which makes it appear like a title.

- The second question on the top half is answered using a visual causal chain, using common symbols to show how recycling ultimately decreases global warming. The simple symbols are also similar to emoji, making the poster seem current and familiar.

- The two cans depicted on the bottom left show percentages to compare how much energy is saved when using recycled aluminum and steel instead of raw materials to manufacture the cans. The cans' differing sizes and how much they are "filled" reinforce the statistics, and the recognizable shapes of soda and food cans serve as a reminder to recycle everyday items.

- The four-stage process of product development using raw materials is described in a flowchart on the bottom right. When recycling replaces any one of these steps, energy is saved.

- The image of the state of North Carolina (which created or commissioned the graphic) is filled with recycle symbols, implying the entire state can and should be involved in recycling. It also provides a pathway to more information on the Web site.

Similar close analysis of the other visuals in this book will enhance your understanding of how themes and strategies work in these visual texts. Practice in visual analysis will, in turn, add to your understanding of the reading selections. In reading, too, we need to train ourselves to pay close attention to catch all nuances and to be attuned to what is *not* expressed as well as to what is. By sharpening our observational skills, we penetrate to another level of meaning—a level not apparent to a casual reader. Finally, strengthening your ability to see and read deeply will also strengthen your ability to write. We need to see first, clearly and in detail, before we attempt, as writers, to find the appropriate words to help others see.

THE READING-WRITING CONNECTION

Reading and writing are two sides of the same coin. Active reading is one of the best ways to learn to write and to improve writing skills. By reading we can see how others have communicated their experiences, ideas, thoughts, and feelings in their writing. We can study how they have effectively used the various elements of the essay—thesis, organizational strategies, beginnings and endings, paragraphs, transitions, effective sentences, word choice, tone, and figurative language—to say what they wanted to say.

By studying the style, technique, and rhetorical strategies of other writers — by reading, in effect, *as* writers — we learn how to write more effectively ourselves.

▶ Reading as a Writer

What does it mean to read as a writer? Most of us have not been taught to read with a writer's eye, to ask why we like one piece of writing and not another. Likewise, most of us do not ask ourselves why one piece of writing is more believable or convincing than another. When you learn to read with a writer's eye, you begin to answer these important questions and, in the process, come to appreciate what is involved in selecting a subject.

At one level, reading stimulates your imagination by providing you with ideas on what to write about. After reading Thomas L. Friedman's "My Favorite Teacher," David P. Bardeen's "Not Close Enough for Comfort," or Jeannette Walls's "A Woman on the Street," you might decide to write about a turning point in your life. Or, after reading Maya Angelou's "Sister Flowers" or Robert Ramírez's "The Barrio," you might be inspired to write about a person or place of similar personal significance to you.

Reading also provides you with information, ideas, and perspectives that can serve as jumping-off points for your own essays. For example, after reading Paulina Porizkova's "America Made Me a Feminist," you might want to elaborate on what she has written, agreeing with her examples or generating better ones, or qualify or take issue with her argument. Similarly, if you wanted to write an essay in which you take a stand on an issue, you would find the essays on various controversies in Chapter 12, "Argumentation," an invaluable resource.

Reading actively and analytically will also help you recognize effective writing and learn to emulate it. When you see, for example, how Nikki Giovanni uses a strong thesis statement in "Campus Racism 101" to control the parts of her essay about the value of black students attending predominantly white colleges, you can better appreciate the importance of having a clear thesis statement in your writing. When you see the way Nancy Armour uses transitions in "Participation Awards Do Disservice" to link key phrases and important ideas so that readers can recognize how the parts of her essay are meant to flow together, you have a better idea of how to achieve such coherence in your writing. And when you see how Suzanne Britt uses a point-by-point organizational pattern in "Neat People vs. Sloppy People" to show the differences between neat and sloppy people, you see a powerful way in which you can organize an essay using the strategy of comparison and contrast.

Perhaps the most important reason to master the skill of reading like a writer is that, for everything you write, you will be your own first reader. How well you scrutinize your own drafts will affect how well you revise them, and revising well is crucial to writing well.

Alison J. Bechdel/*The New Yorker*, © Conde Nast

CHAPTER 2

Writing

NOTHING IS MORE IMPORTANT TO YOUR SUCCESS IN SCHOOL AND IN THE workplace than learning to write well. You've heard it so often you've probably become numb to the advice. Let's ask the big question, however: Why is writing well so important? The simple answer is that no activity develops your ability to think and communicate better than writing does. Writing allows you to expand your thoughts and to "see" and reflect critically on what you think. In that sense, writing also involves its twin sister, reading. Small wonder, then, that employers in all fields are constantly looking for people who can read and write well. Simply put, employers want to hire and retain the best minds they can to further their business objectives, and the ability to read and write well is a strong indication of a good mind.

Moreover, in today's technology-driven economy, there is virtually no field of work that doesn't require clear, accurate, and direct expression in writing, whether it be writing cover letters and résumés, internal e-mails, self-appraisals, laboratory reports, contract bids, proposals, loan or grant applications, sales reports, market analyses, or any other document. Perhaps more than any other factor, your ability to organize your thoughts and clearly present them will affect your overall success on the job and in life.

College is a practical training ground for learning to write. In college, with the help of instructors, you will write essays, analyses, term papers, reports, reviews of research, critiques, and summaries. Take advantage of the opportunity college provides to develop your skills as a writer: What you learn now will be fundamental not only to your education but also to your later success.

VISUALIZING WRITING

This single graphic panel is Alison Bechdel's depiction of her creative process, a mix of brainstorming, research, planning, writing, drawing, breaks, distractions, and successes. As she would surely attest, writing well takes *time*. Consider the image. What tone does it strike, and how does Bechdel establish that tone visually? Would you say her writing process is effective? Do you identify with her process? How would you illustrate the process differently?

DEVELOPING AN EFFECTIVE WRITING PROCESS

Writers cannot rely on inspiration alone to produce effective writing. Good writers follow a writing *process*: They analyze their assignment, gather ideas, draft, revise, edit, and proofread. But the writing process is rarely as simple and straightforward as this. Often it moves back and forth among different stages. Moreover, writing is personal—no two people go about it the same way. Still, it is possible to describe basic guidelines for developing a writing process, and these will allow you to devise your own reliable method for undertaking a writing task.

Step 1: Understand Your Assignment

A great deal of the writing you do in college will be in response to very specific assignments. Your American history professor may ask you to write a paper in which you explain the causes of the Spanish-American War, or your environmental studies professor may ask you to evaluate both pro and con arguments for hybrid city buses. It is important, therefore, that you understand exactly what your instructor is asking you to do. The best way to understand assignments such as these (or exam questions) is to identify *subject* words (words that indicate the content of the assignment) and *direction* words (words that indicate your purpose or the writing strategy you should use). In the first example, the subject words are *Spanish-American War* and the direction word is *explain*. In the second example, the subject words are *hybrid city buses* and the direction word is *evaluate*.

Most direction words are familiar to us, but we are not always sure how they differ from one another or exactly what they are asking us to do. The following list of direction words, along with explanations of what they call for, will help you analyze paper and exam assignments.

Direction Words

- *Analyze*: take apart and examine closely
- *Argue*: make a case for a particular position
- *Categorize*: place into meaningful groups
- *Compare*: look for differences; stress similarities
- *Contrast*: look for similarities; stress differences
- *Critique*: point out positive and negative features
- *Define*: provide the meaning for a term or concept
- *Evaluate*: judge according to some standard
- *Explain*: make plain or comprehensible
- *Illustrate*: show through examples
- *Interpret*: explain the meaning of something
- *List*: catalog or enumerate steps in a process

- *Outline*: provide abbreviated structure for key elements
- *Prove*: demonstrate truth through logic, fact, or example
- *Review*: summarize key points
- *Synthesize*: bring together or make connections among elements
- *Trace*: delineate a sequence of events

Finding a Subject Area and Focusing on a Topic.   Although you will often be given specific assignments in your writing course, you may sometimes have the freedom to choose your subject matter and topic. In this case, begin by determining a broad subject that you like to think about and might enjoy writing about—a general subject like the Internet, popular culture, or foreign travel. Something you've recently read—one of the essays in *Subject & Strategy*, for example—may help bring particular subjects to mind. You might consider a subject related to your career ambitions—perhaps business, law, medicine, architecture, or computer programming. Another option is to list some subjects you enjoy discussing with friends: food, sports, television programs, or politics. Select several likely subjects and explore their potential. Your goal is to arrive at a narrowed topic.

Suppose, for example, you select as possible subject areas "farming" and "advertising." You could develop each according to the following chart:

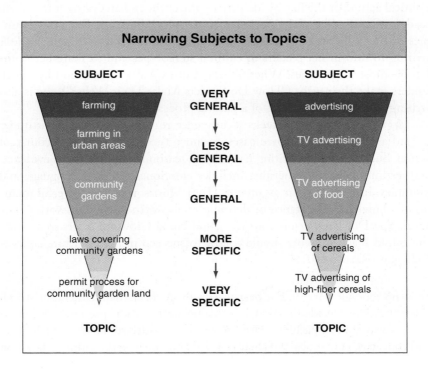

Narrowing Subjects to Topics

SUBJECT		SUBJECT
farming	**VERY GENERAL**	advertising
farming in urban areas	**LESS GENERAL**	TV advertising
community gardens	**GENERAL**	TV advertising of food
laws covering community gardens	**MORE SPECIFIC**	TV advertising of cereals
permit process for community garden land	**VERY SPECIFIC**	TV advertising of high-fiber cereals
TOPIC		**TOPIC**

Determining Your Purpose.   All effective writing springs from a clear purpose. Most good writing seeks specifically to accomplish any one of the following purposes:

- To express thoughts and feelings about life experiences
- To inform readers by explaining something about the world around them, sometimes by analyzing, evaluating, or critiquing someone's actions, words, writing, or creations
- To persuade readers to adopt some belief or take some action

In *expressive writing*, you put your thoughts and feelings before all other concerns. When Cherokee Paul McDonald reacts to watching a young boy fishing ("A View from the Bridge"), when David P. Bardeen narrates the story of his difficulty in coming out to his twin brother ("Not Close Enough for Comfort"), and when Jeannette Walls describes seeing her homeless mother ("A Woman on the Street"), each one is writing from experience. In each case, the writer has clarified an important life experience and has conveyed what he or she learned from it.

Informative writing focuses on telling the reader something about the outside world. In informative writing, you report, explain, analyze, define, classify, compare, describe a process, or examine causes and effects. Many writers of the think-pieces popular today respond to a cultural phenomenon, political action, or the like by identifying the event and analyzing it to inform readers of a trend or of their opinion on a topic. When Issa Rae gives examples of times she was expected to act a certain way ("The Struggle"), she is writing to inform her readers of cultural stereotypes and to share her opinion on those stereotypes. When Alicia Ault explains the method by which spiders make their webs ("How Do Spiders Make Their Webs?"), she is also writing to inform her readers of a natural process.

Argumentative writing seeks to influence readers' thinking and attitudes toward a subject and, in some cases, to move them to a particular course of action. Such persuasive writing uses logical reasoning, authoritative evidence, and testimony, and it sometimes includes emotionally charged language and examples. In writing their arguments, Toni Morrison uses a powerful memory to show the importance of defining one's worth outside of work ("The Work You Do, The Person You Are"), and Nikki Giovanni offers some rules she thinks black students should follow to succeed in mainly white colleges ("Campus Racism 101").

Knowing Your Audience.   The best writers always keep their audience in mind. Once they have decided on a topic and a purpose, writers present their material in a way that empathizes with their readers, addresses readers' difficulties and concerns, and appeals to their rational and emotional faculties. Based on knowledge of their audience, writers make conscious decisions on content, sentence structure, and word choice.

When you write, your audience might be an individual (your instructor), a group (the students in your class), a specialized group (art history majors), or a general readership (readers of your student newspaper). To help identify your audience, ask yourself the questions posed in the following box.

Questions about Audience

- Who are my readers? Are they a specialized or a general group?
- What do I know about my audience's age, gender, education, religious affiliation, economic status, and political views?
- What does my audience know about my subject? Are they experts or novices?
- What does my audience need to know about my topic to understand my discussion of it?
- Will my audience be interested, open-minded, resistant, or hostile to what I have to say?
- Do I need to explain any specialized language so that my audience can understand my subject? Is there any language that I should avoid?
- What do I want my audience to do as a result of reading my essay?

Writing for an Academic Audience.   Academic writing most often uses the conventions of formal standard English, or the language of educated professionals. Rather than being heavy or stuffy, good academic writing is lively and engaging and holds the reader's attention by presenting interesting ideas supported with facts, statistics, and detailed information. Informal writing, usually freer and simpler in form, is typically used in notes, journal entries, e-mail, text messages, instant messaging, and the like.

In order not to lessen the importance of your ideas and your credibility, be sure that informal writing does not carry over into your academic writing, unless allowed by the assignment. Always keeping your audience and purpose in mind will help you achieve an appropriate style.

Formal versus Informal Writing

Formal Writing	Informal Writing
Uses standard English, the language of public discourse typical of newspapers, magazines, books, and speeches	Uses nonstandard English, slang, colloquial expressions (*anyways, dude, freaked out*), and shorthand (*OMG, IMHO*)
Uses mostly third person	Uses first and second person most often

(continued on next page)

Avoids most abbreviations (*professor, brothers, miles per gallon, Internet, digital video recorder*)	Uses abbreviations and acronyms (*prof., bros., mpg, Net, DVR*)
Uses an impersonal tone (*The speaker took questions from the audience at the end of her lecture.*)	Uses an informal tone (*It was great the way she answered questions at the end of her talk.*)
Uses longer, more complex sentences	Uses shorter, simpler sentences
Adheres to the rules and conventions of proper grammar	Takes a casual approach to the rules and conventions of proper grammar

Step 2: Gather Ideas and Formulate a Thesis

Ideas and information, facts and details lie at the heart of good prose. Ideas grow out of information; information supports ideas. Before you begin to draft, gather as many ideas as possible and as much information as you can about your topic in order to inform and stimulate your readers intellectually.

Brainstorming.   A good way to generate ideas and information about a topic is to *brainstorm*: Simply list everything you know about the topic, freely associating one idea with another. At this point, order is not important. Write quickly, but if you get stalled, reread what you have written to jog your mind in new directions. Keep your list handy so that you can add to it over the course of several days.

Here, for example, is student Anita Mangat's brainstorming list on why Martin Luther King Jr.'s "I Have a Dream" speech is enduring. (If you're not familiar with the speech, you can find video recordings online.)

WHY "I HAVE A DREAM" IS MEMORABLE

- Delivered on steps of Lincoln Memorial during civil rights demonstration in Washington, D.C.; crowd of more than 200,000 people
- Repetition of "I have a dream"
- Allusions to the Bible, spirituals
- "Bad check" metaphor and other memorable figures of speech
- Echoes other great American writings — Declaration of Independence and Gettysburg Address
- Refers to various parts of the country and embraces all races and religions
- Sermon format
- Displays energy and passion

Clustering.   Clustering allows you to generate material and to sort it into meaningful groupings. Put your topic, or a key word or phrase about your topic, in the center of a sheet of paper and draw a circle around it. Draw four or five (or more) lines radiating out from this circle and jot down main ideas about your topic; draw circles around them as well. Repeat the process by drawing lines from the secondary circles and adding examples, details, and any questions you have.

Here is student Jael Jose's cluster on television news programs:

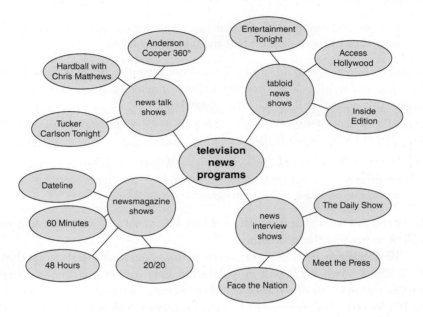

Researching.   You may want to supplement what you know about your topic with research. This does not necessarily mean formal library work or even online research. Firsthand observations and interviews with people knowledgeable about your topic are also forms of research. Whatever your form of research, take careful notes so you can accurately paraphrase an author or quote an interviewee. (For more on conducting research and documenting sources, see Chapter 15).

Rehearsing Ideas.   Consider rehearsing what you are going to write by taking ten or fifteen minutes to talk your way through your paper with a roommate, friend, or family member. Rehearsing in this way may suit your personality and the way you think. Moreover, rehearsing may help you generate new ideas or find gaps in your research.

Formulating a Thesis.   The thesis of an essay is its main idea, the major point the writer is trying to make.

A thesis should be:

- The most important point you make about your topic
- More general than the ideas and facts used to support it
- Focused enough to be covered in the space allotted for the essay

The thesis is often expressed in one or two sentences called a *thesis statement*. Here is an example of a thesis statement about television news programs:

> The so-called serious news programs are becoming too much like tabloid news shows in both their content and their presentation.

A thesis statement should not be a question but rather an assertion. If you find yourself writing a question for a thesis statement, answer the question first—this answer will be your thesis statement.

An effective strategy for developing a thesis statement is to begin by writing, "What I want to say is that . . ."

> *What I want to say is that* unless language barriers between patients and health care providers are bridged, many patients' lives in our most culturally diverse cities will be endangered.

Later you can delete the formulaic opening *What I want to say is that*, and you will be left with a thesis statement.

To determine whether your thesis is too general or too specific, think hard about how easy it will be to present data—that is, facts, statistics, names, examples or illustrations, and opinions of authorities—to support it. If you stray too far in either direction, your task will become much more difficult. A thesis statement that is too general will leave you overwhelmed by the number of issues you must address. For example, the statement "Malls have ruined the fabric of American life" would lead to the question "How?" To answer it, you would probably have to include information about traffic patterns, urban decay, environmental damage, economic studies, and so on. To cover all of this in the time and space you have for a typical college paper would mean taking shortcuts, and your paper would be ineffective. On the other hand, too specific a thesis statement will leave you with too little information to present. "The Big City Mall should not have been built because it reduced retail sales at existing Big City stores by 21.4 percent" does not leave you with any opportunity to develop an argument.

The thesis statement is usually presented near the beginning of the essay. One common practice in shorter college papers is to position the thesis statement as the final sentence of the first paragraph.

> ## Will Your Thesis Hold Up to Scrutiny?
>
> Once you have a possible thesis statement in mind for an essay, answer the following questions:
>
> - Does my thesis statement take a clear position on an issue? If so, what is that position?
> - Is my thesis the most important point I make about my topic?
> - Is my thesis neither too general nor too specific? Will I be able to argue it in the time and space allotted?

Step 3: Organize and Write Your First Draft

There is nothing mysterious or difficult about the nine organizational strategies discussed in this book. In fact, you're familiar with most of them already. Whenever you tell a story, for example, you use the strategy *narration*. When you need to make a decision, you *compare and contrast* the things you must choose between. When you want to describe how to make a pizza, you use the *process analysis* strategy to figure out how to explain it. What might make these strategies seem unfamiliar, especially in writing, is that most people use them more or less intuitively. Sophisticated thinking and writing, however, do not come from simply using these strategies but rather from using them consciously and purposefully.

> ## Organizational* Strategies
>
> | | |
> |---|---|
> | **Narration** | Telling a story or giving an account of an event |
> | **Description** | Presenting a picture in words |
> | **Illustration** | Using examples to explain a point or an idea |
> | **Process analysis** | Explaining how something is done or happens |
> | **Comparison and contrast** | Demonstrating likenesses and differences |
> | **Division and classification** | Breaking down a subject into its parts and placing them in appropriate categories |
> | **Definition** | Explaining what something is |
> | **Cause and effect analysis** | Explaining the causes of an event or the effects of an action |
> | **Argumentation** | Using reason and logic to persuade |
>
> *Also known as *rhetorical* or *writing* strategies.

Writing strategies are not like blueprints or 3D printers that determine in advance exactly how the final product will be shaped. Rather, these strategies are flexible and versatile, with only a few fundamental rules or directions to define their shape—like the rules for basketball, chess, or other strategic games. Such directions leave plenty of room for imagination and variety. In addition, because these strategies are fundamental ways of thinking, they will help you in all stages of the writing process—from prewriting and the first draft through revising and editing your composition.

Determining a Strategy for Developing Your Essay.   Good essays often employ components of more than one strategy. In determining which strategies to use, the language of the writing assignment is very important. If a description is called for, if you need to examine causes and effects, or, as is often the case, if you are asked to argue for a position on an important issue, the language of the assignment will include key direction words and phrases that will indicate the primary strategy or strategies you should use in developing your essay.

Determining What Strategies to Use with a Specific Assignment

Key Direction Words and Phrases	Suggested Writing Strategy
Give an account of; tell the story of; relate the events of	*Narration*
Describe; present a picture; discuss the details of	*Description*
Show; demonstrate; enumerate; discuss; give examples of	*Illustration*
Explain how something is done; explain how something works; explain what happens; analyze the steps	*Process analysis*
Compare; contrast; explain differences; explain similarities; evaluate	*Comparison and contrast*
Divide and classify; explain what the components are; analyze the parts of	*Division and classification*
Explain; define a person, place, or thing; give the meaning of	*Definition*
Explain causes; explain effects; give the reasons for; explain the consequences of	*Cause and effect analysis*
Argue for or against; make a case for or against; state your views on; persuade; convince; justify	*Argumentation*

Often in academic writing your instructor may not give you a specific assignment; instead, he or she may ask only that you write a paper of a specific length. In such cases, you are left to determine for yourself what strategy or strategies might best accomplish your purpose. If you are not given a specific assignment and are uncertain as to what strategy or strategies you should use in developing your essay, you might try the following four-step method:

Determining What Strategies to Use with an Open Assignment

1. State the main idea of your essay in a single phrase or sentence.
2. Restate the main idea as a question — in effect, the question your essay will answer.
3. Look closely at both the main idea and the question for key words or concepts that go with a particular strategy, just as you would when working with an assignment that specifies a topic.
4. Consider other strategies that would support your primary strategy.

Choosing Strategies Across the Disciplines.   The following examples show how a student writing in different disciplines might decide what strategies to use. In each of the nine rhetorical chapters in *Subject & Strategy*, we include lists similar to the one presented below, but with each demonstrating the use of that strategy in different disciplines:

American Literature

1. MAIN IDEA: John Updike relies on religion as a major theme in his fiction.
2. QUESTION: In what instances does John Updike use religion as a major theme?
3. STRATEGY: Illustration. The phrase *in what instances* suggests that it is necessary to show examples of where Updike uses the theme of religion to further his narrative purposes.
4. SUPPORTING STRATEGY: Definition. What is meant by *religion* needs to be clear.

Biology

1. MAIN IDEA: Mitosis is the process by which cells divide.
2. QUESTION: How does the process of mitosis work?
3. STRATEGY: Process analysis. The words *how*, *process*, and *work* suggest a process analysis essay.
4. SUPPORTING STRATEGY: Illustration. A good process analysis includes examples of each step in the process.

Political Science

1. **MAIN IDEA:** The threat of terrorism has changed the way people think about air travel.
2. **QUESTION:** What effects does terrorism have on air travel?
3. **STRATEGY:** Cause and effect. The phrase *what effects* asks for a list of the effects.
4. **SUPPORTING STRATEGY:** Narration. A powerful anecdote from a traveler would help readers empathize with the effects.

These are just a few examples of how to decide on a writing strategy and supporting strategies. In every case, your reading can guide you in recognizing the best plan to follow. In Chapter 13, you will learn more about combining strategies.

Writing Your First Draft.   First drafts are exploratory and sometimes unpredictable. While writing your first draft, you may find yourself getting away from your original plan. What started as a definition essay may develop into a process analysis or an effort at argumentation. For example, a definition of *manners* could become an instructive process analysis on how to be a good host, or it could turn into an argument that respect is based on the ways people treat one another. A definition of *democracy* could evolve into a process analysis of how democracy works in the United States or into an argument for democratic forms of government.

If your draft is leaning toward a different strategy from the one you first envisioned, don't force yourself to revert to your original plan. Allow your inspiration to take you where it will. When you finish your draft, you can see whether the new strategy works better than the old one or whether it would be best to go back to your initial strategy. Use your first draft to explore your ideas; you will always have a chance to revise later.

It may also happen that, while writing your first draft, you run into a difficulty that prevents you from moving forward. For example, suppose you want to tell about something that happened to you, but you aren't certain whether you should be using the pronoun *I* so frequently. If you turn to the essays in Chapter 4 to see how authors of narrative essays handle this concern, you will find that it may not be a problem at all. For an account of a personal experience, it's perfectly acceptable to write *I* as often as you need to. Or suppose that after writing several pages describing someone you think is quite a character, you find that your draft seems flat and doesn't express how lively and funny the person really is. If you read the introduction to Chapter 5, you will learn that descriptions need lots of factual, concrete detail; the chapter selections give further proof of this. You suddenly realize that just such detail is what's missing from your draft.

If you do run into difficulties writing your first draft, don't worry or get upset. Even experienced writers run into problems at the beginning. Just try to keep going. Think about your topic and consider your details and what you want to say. You might even want to go back and look over your original brainstorming work for additional inspiration.

Step 4: Revise Your Essay

Once you have completed your first draft, set it aside awhile and do something else. When you are refreshed and again ready to give it your full attention, you are ready to revise.

Revision is a vital part of the writing process. It is not to be confused with editing or "cleaning up" a draft but should be regarded as a set of activities wherein a rough draft may be transformed into a polished essay that powerfully expresses your ideas. In fact, many writers believe that all writing is essentially *re*writing. When you revise, you give yourself a chance to re-see how well you have captured your subject, to see what has worked and what still needs to be done.

In revising, you might need to reorganize your paragraphs or the sentences within some paragraphs, generate more information because you have too few examples, revise your thesis statement so that it better fits your argument, or find better transitions to bind your sentences and thoughts together. Many writers find revision not an arduous task but a very satisfying process because they are able to bring their work into sharper focus and give themselves a better chance of connecting with their audience. Best of all, when you revise, you are not staring at a blank page but rearranging the building blocks you have already created.

Tips for Revising Your Draft

- Make revisions on a hard copy of your paper. Triple-space your draft so that you can make changes more easily.

- If you are revising on a computer, try tracking your changes or using the comment balloon features to make notes and see how much you have changed. Save your drafts as different file names so you can compare drafts to see how much you have revised.

- On a computer or by hand, highlight the main ideas in your paragraphs to be sure you have clear points. You might highlight your transitions in a second color to be sure your ideas are organized logically.

- Read your paper aloud, listening for parts that do not make sense.

- Have a fellow student or writing center tutor read your essay and critique it.

The following sections offer proven techniques for initiating and carrying out one or more revisions of your developing essays.

Taking Advantage of Peer Critiques.   Peer critiquing is one of the best ways to encourage revision and improve your drafts. Peer critiquing requires an audience, one or more people who are reading or listening to you read what you have written. By asking some simple but important questions, your listeners can verify that what you intended to say is what they heard. If there are some discrepancies, it's usually because you have not expressed yourself as well as you thought you have, and you need to revise. Often there are problems with the purpose for writing and the articulation of a thesis, with lesser problems concerning organization, evidence, and other paragraphs and sentences.

When you critique work with other students—yours or theirs—it is important to maximize the effectiveness and efficiency of the exercise. The tips outlined in the "A Brief Guide to Peer Critiquing" box will help you get the most out of peer critiques.

A Brief Guide to Peer Critiquing

When critiquing someone else's work:

- Read the essay carefully. Read it to yourself first and, if possible, have the writer read it to you at the beginning of the session. Some flaws only become obvious when read aloud.

- Ask the writer to state his or her purpose for writing and to identify the thesis statement within the essay itself.

- Be positive but be honest. Never denigrate the paper's content or the writer's effort, but do your best to identify how the writer can improve the essay through revision.

- Try to address the most important issues first. Think about the thesis and the organization of the essay before moving on to more specific topics like word choice.

- Identify what works well and point to clear examples in the writer's work.

- Do not be dismissive, do not dictate changes, and do not attempt to fix everything. Ask questions that encourage the writer to reconsider parts of the essay that you find confusing or ineffective.

When someone critiques your work:

- Give your reviewer a copy of your essay before your meeting, if possible.

- Listen carefully to your reviewer and try not to argue each issue. Record comments and evaluate them later.

- Do not get defensive or explain what you wanted to say if the reviewer misunderstands what you meant. Try to understand the reviewer's point of view and learn what you need to revise to clear up the misunderstanding.
- Consider every suggestion, but use only the ones that make sense to you in your revision.
- Be sure to thank your reviewer for his or her effort on your behalf.

Revising the Larger Elements of Your Essay.   During revision, you should focus first on the larger issues of thesis, purpose, content, organization, and paragraph structure to make sure your writing says what you want it to say. One way to begin is to make an informal outline of your first draft—not as you planned it but as it actually came out. What does your outline tell you about the strategy you used? Does this strategy suit your purpose? Perhaps you meant to compare your two grandmothers, but you have not clearly shown their similarities and differences. Consequently, your draft is not one unified comparison and contrast essay but two descriptive essays spliced together.

Even if you are satisfied with the overall strategy of your draft, an outline can still help you make improvements. Perhaps your classification essay on types of college students is confusing because you create overlapping categories: international students, computer science majors, and athletes (an international student could, of course, be a computer science major, an athlete, or both). You may uncover a flaw in your organization, such as a lack of logic in an argument or faulty parallelism in a comparison and contrast. Now is the time to discover these problems and to fix them.

The following list of questions addresses the larger elements of your essay: thesis, purpose, organization, paragraphs, and evidence. Use it as a guide when reviewing your work as well as when reviewing the work of others during peer critique sessions.

Questions for Revising the Larger Elements of Your Essay

- Have I focused my *topic*?
- Does my *thesis statement* clearly identify my topic and make an assertion about it?
- Is the *writing strategy* I have chosen the best one for my purpose?
- Are my *paragraphs* adequately developed, and does each one support my thesis?
- Have I accomplished my *purpose*?

Writing Beginnings and Endings. Beginnings and endings are very important to the effectiveness of an essay, but writing them can be daunting.
Inexperienced writers often feel they must write their essays sequentially,
but it is usually better to write both the beginning and the ending after you
have completed most or all of the rest of an essay. Once you see how your
essay develops, you will know better how to capture the reader's attention and
introduce the rest of the essay. As you work through the revision process, ask
yourself the questions in the following box.

Questions for Revising Beginnings and Endings

- Does my introduction grab the reader's attention?
- Is my introduction confusing in any way? How well does it relate to the rest of
  the essay?
- If I state my thesis in the introduction, how effectively have I presented it?
- Does my essay come to a logical conclusion, or does it seem to just stop?
- Does the conclusion relate well to the rest of the essay? Am I careful not to
  introduce topics or issues that I did not address in the essay?
- Does my conclusion underscore important aspects of the essay, or is it merely
  a mechanical rehashing of what I wrote earlier?

Revising the Smaller Elements of Your Essay. Once you have addressed the
larger elements of your essay, you should turn your attention to the finer
elements of sentence structure, word choice, and usage. The "Questions for
Revising Sentences" box focuses on these concerns.

If, after serious efforts at revision, you still find yourself dissatisfied with
specific elements of your draft, look at some of the essays in *Subject & Strategy*

Questions for Revising Sentences

- Do my sentences convey my thoughts clearly, and do they emphasize the
  most important parts of my thinking?
- Are all my sentences complete sentences?
- Are my sentences stylistically varied? Do I alter their pattern and rhythm for
  emphasis? Do I use some short sentences for dramatic effect?
- Are all my sentences written in the active voice?
- Do I use strong action verbs and concrete nouns?
- Is my diction fresh and forceful? Do I avoid wordiness?
- Have I achieved an appropriate degree of formality in my writing?
- Have I committed any errors in usage?

to see how other writers have dealt with similar situations. For example, if you don't like the way the essay starts, find some beginnings you think are particularly effective. What characterizes those beginnings? If your paragraphs don't seem to flow into one another, examine how various writers use transitions. If you have lapsed into informal language, take a look at how other writers express themselves. If an example seems unconvincing, examine the way other writers include details, anecdotes, facts, and statistics to strengthen their illustrations.

Remember that the readings in this text are a resource for you as you write, as are the strategy chapter introductions, which outline the basic features of each strategy. In addition, the readings in Chapter 3, "Writers on Writing," will provide you with inspiration and advice to help you through the writing process.

Step 5: Edit and Proofread Your Essay

During the *editing* stage, you check your writing for errors in grammar, punctuation, capitalization, spelling, and manuscript format. Chapter 16 of this book provides help for common problems with grammar, punctuation, and sentence style. A dictionary and a grammar handbook may be necessary for less common or more specific editing questions.

After editing, proofread your work carefully before turning it in. Though you may have used your computer's spell-checker, you might find that you have typed *their* instead of *there* or *form* instead of *from*. (A computer program often won't know the difference, as long as you've spelled *some* word correctly.)

Questions to Ask during Editing and Proofreading

- Do I have any sentence fragments, comma splices, or run-on sentences?
- Have I used commas properly in all instances?
- Do my verbs agree in number with their antecedents?
- Do my pronouns clearly and correctly refer to their antecedents?
- Do any dangling or misplaced modifiers make my meaning unclear?
- Do I use parallel grammatical structures correctly in my sentences?
- Have I used specific nouns and strong verbs wherever possible?
- Have I made any unnecessary shifts in person, tense, or number?
- Have I eliminated unnecessary words?
- Are my sentences appropriately varied and interesting?
- Have I checked for misspellings, mistakes in capitalization, commonly confused words like *its* and *it's*, and typos?
- Have I followed the prescribed guidelines for formatting my manuscript?

A STUDENT ESSAY IN PROGRESS

When he was a first-year student at the University of Vermont, Keith Eldred enrolled in Written Expression, an introductory writing course. As he worked on his essay, we interviewed Keith to learn what he was doing and how he felt about the writing process as he moved toward the completion of his essay.

Near the middle of the semester, Keith's assignment was to write a three-to five-page definition essay. After reading the introduction to Chapter 10 in *Subject & Strategy* and the essays his instructor assigned from that chapter, Keith was ready to get to work.

Step 1: Keith's Assignment

Q. What did you think about the assignment you were given?
A. I was intrigued by the assignment to write an essay using definition as a strategy. I knew from the start that I didn't want to write what I thought would be some dry essay clarifying an established definition by unraveling or expanding it. I just thought that making my own definition would show that I was being insightful, maybe creative. I guess I wanted writing the essay to be fun.

Step 2: Keith's Ideas

Q. Where do you get your ideas?
A. I had learned about the concept of the Hindu mantra in the religion course I was taking at the time, and I thought I'd explore the concept, narrowing my focus to the topic of mantras as they operate in the secular world. To get started I decided to brainstorm for ideas. My brainstorming provided me with several examples of what I decided to call *secular mantras*, a dictionary definition of the word *mantra*, and the idea that a good starting point for my rough draft might be the story of "The Little Engine That Could."

KEITH'S NOTES

Mantra: "a mystical formula of invocation or incantation" (*Webster's*)

Counting to ten when angry

"Little Engine That Could" (possible beginning)

"Let's Go Bulls" — action because crowd wants players to say it to themselves

Swearing (not always a mantra)

Tennis star — "Get serious!"

"Come on, come on" (at traffic light)

"Geronimo" "Ouch!"

Hindu mythology

Step 3: Keith's First Draft

Q. Did you just write about the items on your list as they appeared?
A. After studying my list of ideas, I organized them in a scratch outline, then wrote my first draft based on the outline and what I learned from *Subject & Strategy* about using definition.

KEITH'S OUTLINE

1. Begin with story of "Little Engine That Could"

2. Talk about the magic of secular mantras

3. Dictionary definition and Hindu connections

4. Examples of individuals using mantras

5. Crowd chants as mantras — Bulls

6. Conclusion — talk about how you can't get through the day without using mantras

Secular Mantras: Magic Words
Keith Eldred

Do you remember "The Little Engine That Could"? If you recall, it's the story about the tiny locomotive that hauled the train over the mountain when the big, rugged locomotives wouldn't. Do you remember how the Little Engine strained and heaved and chugged "I think I can—I think I can—I think I can" until she reached the top of the mountain? That's a perfect example of a secular mantra in action.

A secular mantra (pronounced "man-truh") is any word or group of words that helps a person use his or her energy. The key word here is "helps"—repeating a secular mantra doesn't *create* energy; it just makes it easier to channel a given amount. The Little Engine, for instance, obviously had the strength to pull the train up the mountain; apparently, she could have done it without saying a word. But we all know she wouldn't have been able to, any more than any one of us would be able to skydive the first time without yelling "Geronimo" or not exclaim "Ouch" if we touched a hot stove. Some words and phrases simply have a certain magic that makes a job easier or that makes us feel better when we repeat them. These are secular mantras.

2

It is because of their magical quality that these expressions are called "secular mantras" in the first place. A mantra (Sanskrit for "sacred counsel") is "a mystical formula of invocation or incantation" used in Hinduism (*Webster's*). According to Hindu mythology, Manu, lawgiver and progenitor of humankind, created the first language by teaching people the thought-forms of objects and substances. "VAM," for example, is the thought-form of what we call "water." Mantras, groups of these ancient words, can summon any object or deity if they are miraculously revealed to a seer and properly repeated silently or vocally. Hindus use divine mantras to communicate with gods, acquire superhuman powers, cure diseases, and for many other purposes. Hence, everyday words that people concentrate on to help themselves accomplish tasks or cope with stress act as secular mantras.

3

All sorts of people use all sorts of secular mantras for all sorts of reasons. A father counts to 10 before saying anything when his son brings the car home dented. A tennis player faults and chides himself, "Get serious!" A frustrated mother pacing with her wailing baby mutters, "You'll have your own kids someday." A college student writhing before an exam instructs himself not to panic. A freshly grounded child glares at his mother's back and repeatedly promises never to speak to her again. Secular mantras are everywhere.

4

Usually, we use secular mantras to make ourselves walk faster or keep silent or do some other act. But we can also use them to influence the actions of other persons. Say, for instance, the Chicago Bulls are behind in the final minutes of a game. Ten thousand fans who want them to win scream, "Let's go, Bulls!" The Bulls are roused and win by 20 points. Chalk up the victory to the fans' secular mantra, which transferred their energy to the players on the court.

5

If you're not convinced of the power of secular mantras, try to complete a day without using any. Don't mutter anything to force yourself out of bed. Don't utter a sound when the water in the shower is cold. Don't grumble when the traffic lights are long. Don't speak to the computer when it's slow to boot up. And don't be surprised if you have an unusually long, painful, frustrating day.

6

Step 4: Keith's Revised Essay

Q. How did you know what to do when it came time to revise your first draft?

A. I read the first draft of my paper to two of my fellow students, who jotted down questions for me as I read. I was surprised by both their interest in my topic and how thought-provoking their questions were. They had questions about secular mantras in particular, and I immediately realized that I needed to do more work in that area. My definition wasn't as clear as I originally thought. With the answers I gave them, which they wrote down, they were able to provide me a list of really helpful ideas and suggestions for revising my first draft.

KEITH'S PEER REVIEW

- Do a better job of defining *secular mantra* — expand it and be more specific — maybe tell what secular mantras are not.

- Get more examples, especially from everyday experience and TV.

- Don't eliminate background information about mantras.

- Thought Chicago Bulls example didn't work — keep or delete?

- Keep "The Little Engine That Could" example at the beginning of the draft.

- Write new conclusion — present conclusion doesn't follow from what you have written.

Q. What did you do in subsequent drafts of your paper?

A. In other drafts, I worked on each of the areas my classmates had suggested. While revising I found it helpful to reread portions of the selections in Chapter 10 to see how those writers had solved problems. My reading led me to new insights about how to strengthen my essay. As I revised further, I found that I needed to make other unanticipated changes, too. I revised my definitions of *mantra* and *secular mantras* to include the meanings for the related *terms*.

Revised historical definition of mantra

Mantra means "sacred counsel" in Sanskrit and refers to a "mystical formula of invocation or incantation" used in Hinduism (*Webster's*). According to Hindu mythology, the god Manu created the first language by teaching humans the thought-form of every object and substance. "VAM," for example, was what he told them to call the stuff we call "water." But people altered or forgot most of Manu's thought-forms. Followers of Hinduism believe mantras, groups of these ancient words revealed anew by gods to seers, can summon specific objects or deities if they are properly repeated, silently or vocally. Hindus repeat mantras to gain superhuman powers, cure diseases, and for many other purposes. Sideshow fakirs chant "AUM" ("I agree" or "I accept") to become immune to pain when lying on beds of nails.

Expanded definition of secular mantra

Our "mantras" are "secular" because, unlike Hindus, we do not attribute them to gods. Instead, we borrow them from tradition or invent them to fit a situation, as the Little Engine did. They work not by divine power but because they help us, in a way, to govern transmissions along our central nervous systems.

Added explanation of how secular mantras work

Secular mantras give our brains a sort of dual signal-boosting and signal-damping capacity. The act of repeating them pushes messages, or impulses, with extra force along our nerves or interferes with incoming messages we would rather ignore. We can then perform actions more easily or cope with stress that might keep us from functioning the way we want to. We may even accomplish both tasks at once. A skydiver might yell "Geronimo," for example, both to amplify the signals telling his legs to jump and to drown out the ones warning him he's dizzy or scared.

Q. What revisions did you make to better align your conclusion with all that you had written to that point?
A. I rewrote the conclusion, adding more examples of secular mantras, this time drawing largely from television advertising. Finally, I made my conclusion more of a natural outgrowth of my thesis and purpose, and it turned out to fit my essay much better.

Sentence of examples moved from paragraph 4

You probably have favorite secular mantras already. Think about it. How many of us haven't uttered the following at least once: "Just do it"; "I'm lovin' it"; "Got milk?"; "Can you hear me now?"; or "Have it your way"? How about the phrases you mumble to yourself from your warm bed on chilly mornings? And those words you chant to ease your impatience when the traffic lights are endless? And the reminders you mutter so

Final sentence, which links to thesis and purpose, added

that you'll remember to buy bread at the store? If you're like most people, you'll agree that your life is much less painful and frustrating because of those magic words and phrases.

Step 5: Keith's Edited Essay

Q. What did you think about your work when you finished your essay?
A. I had worked hard revising my essay and I was excited about how well it had turned out. I also knew that I was not quite finished yet because I needed to edit. My instructor had told me to avoid the use of first and second person and to correct sentences starting with conjunctions like *and* or *but*. I also had to correct smaller errors in word choice, spelling, etc. I had put aside fixing those errors until I was sure my essay had all of the bigger elements in place.

KEITH'S EDITING

~~Do you~~ remember "The Little Engine That Could"? ~~If you recall, it's~~ That's the story about the tiny locomotive that hauled the train over the mountain when the big, rugged locomotives wouldn't. ~~Do you~~ remember how the Little Engine strained and heaved and chugged, "I think I can—I think I can—I think I can" until she reached the top of the mountain? That's a perfect example of a secular mantra in action.

Q. So, as the deadline arrived, how did you feel about the work you had done in writing "Secular Mantras"?
A. Well, it was a lot of work, to be sure. I was somewhat surprised, however, that after I came up with an original idea, I had such a sense of accomplishment in the end. The essay got better as I worked on it, and that was a good feeling. The peer review helped me to improve my essay a lot. It was amazing how much reading aloud helped, too. I could hear the clunky parts before anyone even mentioned them.

Keith's Final Draft

Secular Mantras
Keith Eldred

"The Little Engine That Could" is a story about a tiny locomotive that hauls a train over a mountain when the big, rugged locomotives refuse: The Little Engine strains and heaves and chugs, repeating "I think I can—I think I can—I think I can" until she reaches the top of the mountain. This refrain—"I think I can—I think I can"—is a perfect example of a secular mantra in action.

1

A secular mantra (pronounced "man-truh") is any word or group of words that focuses energy when consciously repeated. Most readers of this essay have already used a secular mantra today without realizing it. Some additional explanation is necessary, however, in order to understand what distinguishes a secular mantra from any other kind of phrase.

To be a secular mantra, a phrase must help the speaker focus and use energy. Thus, "I wish I were at home" is not a secular mantra if it's simply a passing thought. The same sentence becomes a secular mantra if, walking home on a cold day, a person repeats the sentence each time she takes a step, willing her feet to move in a steady, accelerated rhythm and take her quickly someplace warm. By the same token, every curse word a person mutters in order to bear down on a job is a secular mantra, while every curse word that same person unthinkingly repeats is simple profanity.

It is important to understand, however, that secular mantras only help people use energy: They don't create it. The Little Engine, for instance, obviously had enough power to pull the train up the mountainside—she could have done it without a peep. Still, puffing "I think I can" clearly made her job easier, just as, say, chanting "left-right-left" makes marching in step easier for soldiers. Any such word or phrase that, purposefully uttered, helps a person perform something difficult qualifies as a secular mantra.

Why, though, use the term *secular mantra* to describe these phrases, rather than something else? *Mantra* means "sacred counsel" in Sanskrit and refers to a "mystical formula of invocation or incantation" used in Hinduism (*Webster's*). According to Hindu mythology, the god Manu created the first language by teaching humans the thought-form of every object and substance. *VAM*, for example, was what Manu taught humans to call "water." People unfortunately forgot or altered most of Manu's thought-forms, however. Followers of Hinduism believe that mantras, groups of these ancient words revealed anew by gods to seers, can summon specific objects or deities if they are properly repeated, silently or aloud. Hindus repeat mantras to gain superhuman powers, cure diseases, and for many other purposes. Sideshow fakirs chant *AUM* ("I agree" or "I accept") to become immune to pain when lying on a bed of nails.

The mantras that are the topic of this paper are called *secular* because Western culture does not claim that they are divine in origin; instead, they derive from tradition or are invented to fit a situation, as in the case of the Little Engine. In addition, most Westerners assume that they work not by divine power but through the mind-body connection, by helping govern transmissions along the central nervous system.

The Western, scientific explanation for the power of secular mantras runs something like this: Secular mantras give people's brains a sort of dual signal-boosting and signal-damping capacity. The act of repeating them pushes messages, or impulses, with extra force along the nerves or blocks incoming messages that would interfere with the task at hand. People repeating mantras are thus enabled to perform actions more easily or cope with stress that might keep them from functioning optimally. Mantras may even convey both benefits at once: A skydiver might yell "Geronimo!," for example, both to amplify the signals telling his legs to jump and to drown out the signals warning him he's dizzy or afraid.

Anyone can use words in this way to help accomplish a task. A father might count to ten to keep from bellowing when Junior returns the family car with a huge dent. A tennis player who tends to fault may shout "Get serious!" as he serves, to concentrate harder on controlling the ball. An exhausted new mother with her wailing baby can make her chore less painful by muttering, "Someday you'll do chores for me." Chanting "Grease cartridge" always cools this writer's temper because doing so once headed off a major confrontation with a friend while working on a cantankerous old Buick.

Most readers of this essay probably have favorite secular mantras already. Most people—at least those exposed in any way to contemporary popular culture—have at one point uttered one of the following: "Just do it"; "No worries"; "It's all good"; "I'm king of the world!!"; "We are the champions!"; or something similar. Many people have ritual phrases they mutter to get themselves to leave their warm beds on chilly mornings; others blurt out habitual phrases to help them get over impatience when traffic lights don't change or to help them endure a courtesy call to a neighbor they've never really liked. Most people, if they really think about it, will admit that the seeming magic of secular mantras has made their lives much less painful, less frustrating, and perhaps even a little more fun.

While it's not perfect, "Secular Mantras" is a fine essay of definition. Keith provides a clear explanation of the concept, offers numerous examples to illustrate it, and suggests how mantras work and how we use them. Keith's notes, rough draft, samples of revised and edited paragraphs, and final draft demonstrate how such effective writing is accomplished. By reading analytically—both his own writing and that of experienced writers—Keith came to understand the requirements of the strategy of definition. An honest and thorough appraisal of his rough draft led to thoughtful revisions, resulting in a strong and effective piece of writing.

CHAPTER 3

Writers on Writing

LIKE ANY OTHER CRAFT, WRITING INVOLVES LEARNING BASIC SKILLS AS well as more sophisticated techniques that can be refined and then shared among fellow writers. Some of the most important lessons a writer encounters may come from the experiences of other writers: suggestions, advice, cautions, corrections, encouragement. This chapter contains essays in which writers discuss their habits, difficulties, and judgments while they express both the joy and the hard work of writing. These writers deal with the full range of the writing process — from freeing the imagination in journal entries to correcting punctuation errors for the final draft. The advice they offer is pertinent and sound.

Often readers want to know what a particular writer looks like — simple curiosity. Sometimes readers think they can see some connection between a writer's appearance and what he or she has written. Of course, such speculation is not reliable. Still, author photos do add to our knowledge of a writer's biography and help us understand that there is a person behind the words and ideas we see on the page, which is why, when possible, we have included a photograph of the author for each essay in *Subject & Strategy*.

VISUALIZING WRITERS ON WRITING

Sometimes we have the opportunity to see a writer at work, as with this photo of Maya Angelou. While we cannot be certain what the circumstances were when the photo was taken, we can make some informed guesses. Rather than sitting at a desk cluttered with papers or perhaps a typewriter (or a computer), Angelou has found a place more like each of us may have found at some time. What visual cues suggest where she is or what she may be writing? What does the photograph suggest about the subject of her writing — how personal or objectified her subject is or what her attitude toward it might be? What other visual details do you see in the photo, and how do they support your interpretation of the photo, of the writer, or of the writing process?

Learning to Write Dumb Things Again

RICARDO RODRÍGUEZ-PADILLA

Ricardo Rodríguez-Padilla was born in San Juan, Puerto Rico, in 1993 and graduated from Columbia University, where he won the David Estabrook Romine Prize for his research and writing as an undergraduate. Having worked for several years in economics consulting, he is currently a doctoral student in economics at Harvard University. In this essay, which appeared in the 2011–2012 issue of Columbia's *Morningside Review*, Rodríguez-Padilla recalls his childhood passion for writing and his reengagement with writing in the more complex contexts of academic coursework, intellectual discovery, and approaching adulthood.

Ricardo Rodríguez-Padilla

Preparing to Read

Did you write stories or poems as a child? Did you find it pleasurable or rewarding? Or did you prefer a different means of expression, such as drawing, making music, or doing some other creative activity? How valuable were those activities or creations to you then, and how valuable are they to you now?

> "I am myself the substance of my book, and there is no reason why you should waste your leisure on so frivolous and unrewarding a subject."
> —Michel de Montaigne

You are violently introduced to the world one day when you least expect it. You aren't really ready to leave the warmth, safety, and comfort of your mother's womb—and let's face it, the world is probably not ready for you either. Yet, after some long, arduous hours of intense labor, there you are—small and fat and hopefully the most adorable thing anyone has ever seen. Throughout those first few glorious years, you lead a sheltered life: your mom coddles you and puts you to sleep, your father puts to use those diaper skills he's learned with your older sister and, for some reason, people seem to want to stay up all night whenever you are simply singing your baby-tunes. You pipe down for just a second, and the moment you start singing your heart out, in comes your mom or dad again, sleep-deprived and insistent on rocking you to sleep. It doesn't work—all you want to do is sing, and sing you shall.

Eventually though, you realize those baby-tunes you have been singing all night are actually horrid, loud, annoying *crying*. As you grow, you realize how inadequate all your previous attempts at self-expression have been, and unless you rebel against society and insist on crying, or you've been endowed with the gift of a great voice, a great hand, or any other requisite for talent in the visual and plastic arts, one of your last resorts for self-expression is becoming a writer.

Honestly, you have not really been looking forward to it. At first the ink seems impersonal, the letters on the page distant vestiges of what first originated as a thought in a living, real, human brain. Yet slowly, as you get used to the cadences and the syntax and the grammar and the words — those *words*, those *words*! There are so many words that it's probably the nearest you've ever come to actually experiencing infinity! You realize that the words are as alive as that thought inside your head and that the alphabet is not the stale, inadequate means of expression you initially thought it to be.

> " You realize that the words are as alive as that thought inside your head and that the alphabet is not the stale, inadequate means of expression you initially thought it to be. "

And so you let fly. You begin writing a story about some bears living in the mountains and how they eat fish and sleep and find friendship and love in the beauty of nature. "That's deep," your teacher says. She gives you a gold star. You proudly bring the story back to Mom. She gives you a hug for it. Dad congratulates you and hangs it on the fridge. You go to sleep thinking you've made your parents proud — and you truly, truly have.

And so, surprised that you might actually have a talent in something you like, you keep on writing. Your writing gets longer, more complex, and so do the criticisms of your teachers. You grow up writing dumb novels about two brothers who go camping and get lost yet ultimately find their way home. You write about a boggart living in a castle in Denmark and, your sister — God bless her — with love and dedication prints them out from her new desktop computer and manually pastes the pages together to make an actual book. Yet, slowly, people stop caring. Teachers no longer give you gold stars and the principal no longer marvels at how much you love to write.

Eventually, the "teachers" becomes "professors" — a more serious and formal denotation you don't quite understand. They expect you to write more serious and formal pieces than you did before. And so, lost in all the work and friends and hormones and new-found loves, you let your writing slip. It becomes one of those things you used to love. Your parents still keep those novels you used to write as a child, despite your suggestion that they burn them. Luckily, your dad insists on keeping them and hides them, safe from your zeal to destroy anything embarrassing from the past.

As the years go on, you write less to impress your parents and your teachers, and more to get an A on that essay or that test. Maybe you even occasionally attempt to write novels, works that begin with sentences like "The silverware's ready, Mrs. Fairfax," that will astound the world by their simplicity and depth and will be spoken about for centuries to come. Yet for some reason you never get beyond the second page. You have lost it. You give up. You look at those novels you wrote as a child and wonder how you did it. You smile at their green paper spines, those illustrations your father made for the covers and fake reviews your sister wrote critiquing your work and calling each one "Your best novel yet." You wish that trend would continue; you wish that every new work you'd write would be that best novel yet. That it would capture human experience and hold it eternal and beautiful between the covers of *your* book. That some child would pick it up one day and find the mystery of humanity revealed. Yet, you can't write. It seems to be all gone, and you begin to wonder.

Maybe you've forgotten that those "dumb" novels were the most import- 8 ant thing to you. You wrote from the heart back then, about the things you cared about. You didn't care to be the next Kate Chopin or Oscar Wilde. You didn't worry that you might not write the most beautiful, elaborate sentences that would capture a moment and hold a scene in its grasp. You didn't concern yourself with trying to be the next Hemingway by drafting short, simple sentences that nevertheless said so much. You simply wrote, and it was beautiful. It was beautiful because your parents thought it was and because, captured within those cardboard covers, in size 20 Comic Sans, it was the essence of your childhood and what you most loved.

When you finally reach college, you are already disillusioned with your 9 writing and accept the fact that you'll never be the next Virginia Woolf. You've resigned yourself to writing that paper analyzing St. Augustine's rise to transcendence through interiority, how it mirrors Diotima's ladder in Plato's *Symposium,* and how the physical world is but a medium through which to reach eternal truth. And then you reach U. Writing, thinking you've gotten to yet another class that will teach you vague notions of being a writer. You will learn how to cite MLA properly and get on with writing serious essays.

But then, because you are writing so often and working with your own 10 ideas, you realize that you can write about the things you like again. That you can take Oscar Wilde and leaf through *The Importance of Being Earnest* and find new things you'd never seen before. That you can draw connections in unexpected places, delve into an essay through an interesting exhibit, and—most unexpectedly—discover that the exhibit could even be yourself. You can be the subject of your own writing.

And so you write about the thrill you got when someone you were inter- 11 ested in actually liked your post on Facebook, but how your friends were unable to understand your emotions, and how you wondered what that says about the effect the Internet is having on human relationships. You write about affirmative action and how you got into college. By writing about yourself, you discover that once more there's something new and beautiful inside you. That you have interesting things to say. That you can join a conversation between Oscar Wilde and a doctor of theology about the nature of identity. And you learn that, ultimately, you're more complex than you thought. You learn what Oscar Wilde meant when he said, "Only the shallow know themselves," and you strive to dive deeper and deeper into the recesses of your complexity to discover more of yourself (1244). At the same time, Virginia Woolf tells you that the meaning of life was "little daily miracles, illuminations, matches struck unexpectedly in the dark" (161). You wonder how you'll make sense of it all.

So you write more to make sense of it all for yourself. And you realize   12
you are also still writing, not just for yourself, but for your parents. And your sister. You always write for them. You realize in a year of being far away from them, living in a 120-square-foot dorm in New York City, that you've always written thinking of them as the audience. That's why you send them essays and papers that have already been corrected, pretending you need their feedback or their help, even when you can't help feeling that you're wasting their time on feedback that won't really matter, at least not to the grade. Yet, you're relieved to hear when they call you back and marvel at how beautifully you write.

So maybe, just maybe, when it seems like it's lost, it'll all come back if   13
you write about yourself and for yourself—and for the people who matter to you most. Because everything you do—you realize—is always for those three people, those three who accepted you and loved you when you were least ready to come into the world, and when they were probably not even sure they were ready for you either. You write for them. For illustrating your covers and for binding the pages together and for reading your dumb books when they had so much more work to do. Finally, you remember Virginia Woolf defining those "little daily miracles, illuminations, matches struck unexpectedly in the dark," those transient moments that encapsulate the purpose of your existence and give meaning to your life (161). She had said, simply: "here was one" (161). And you realize: Your family. Here was one. Your writing. Here was one. Yourself. Here was one.

Works Cited

Montaigne, Michel de. *Essays*. Penguin Books, 1958, p. 23.

Wilde, Oscar. "Phrases and Philosophies for the Use of the Young." *Collins Complete Works of Oscar Wilde*, edited by Owen D. Edwards et al. Collins, 2003, pp. 1244–45.

Woolf, Virginia. *To the Lighthouse*. Harcourt, 1955.

Thinking Critically about the Text

The writer prefaces his essay with an epigraph (or opening quotation) from Michel de Montaigne (1533–1592). Montaigne was a philosopher and writer during the French Renaissance who, perhaps more than any other figure, popularized the personal essay as a serious literary and intellectual form. Why do you think Rodríguez-Padilla chose this epigraph? Does his essay support Montaigne's point about personal writing? Does the quotation shed any light on the act of writing about "dumb" things?

Discussing the Craft of Writing

1. While this appears to be an autobiographical essay, Rodríguez-Padilla uses the second person (*you*) instead of the first person (*I*). Why do you think he chose to write from this perspective? What does this **point of view** imply about the writer's **audience** — and about his **purpose** in writing the essay?

2. The title of the essay refers to "dumb things." What are they, specifically? Does the writer really believe that they are "dumb"? Why would it be important to learn how to write about them again?

3. What different motives and **purposes** for writing does Rodríguez-Padilla discuss here? Do they shed light on his motives for writing this particular essay?

4. Rodríguez-Padilla celebrates the purity, honesty, and directness of his own — and perhaps all — childhood writing: "You wrote from the heart back then, about the things you cared about. You didn't care to be the next Kate Chopin or Oscar Wilde" (paragraph 8). Yet, this essay begins with a quotation from Montaigne and includes several literary references. Do you see that as a **paradox**? Is writing "from the heart" compatible with writing in a sophisticated or intellectually demanding way? Why, or why not?

5. As Rodríguez-Padilla discusses the formal writing he does for his coursework, he claims, "You can be the subject of your own writing" (paragraph 10). Do you agree with him? When you reflect on your own academic work (say, essays about literary texts in English classes), is your individual **voice** present in that writing? Should it be? Explain.

6. On the surface, this is a deeply personal essay about one writer's experiences. What insights or "takeaways" does it provide that you can apply to your own writing or identity as a writer?

Discovering the Power of My Words

RUSSELL BAKER

Yvonne Hemsey/Getty Images

Russell Baker has had a long and distinguished career as a newspaper reporter and columnist. He was born in Morrisonville, Virginia, in 1925 and graduated from Johns Hopkins University. In 1947, he secured his first newspaper job, as a reporter for the *Baltimore Sun*, then moved to the *New York Times* in 1954, where he wrote the "Observer" column from 1962 to 1998. His incisive wit, by turns melancholic and sharp-edged, is well represented in such quips as these: "Children rarely want to know who their parents were before they were parents, and when age finally stirs their curiosity, there is no parent left to tell them" and "Is fuel efficiency really what we need most desperately? I say that what we really need is a car that can be shot when it breaks down."

Baker's columns have been collected in numerous books over the years. In 1979, he was awarded the Pulitzer Prize, journalism's highest award, as well as the George Polk Award for Commentary. Baker's memoir, *Growing Up* (1983), also received a Pulitzer. His autobiographical follow-up, *The Good Times*, was published in 1989. His other works include *Russell Baker's Book of American Humor* (1993); *Inventing the Truth: The Art and Craft of Memoir*, with William Zinsser and Jill Ker Conway (revised 1998); and *Looking Back* (2002), a collection of Baker's essays for the *New York Review of Books*. From 1993 to 2004 he hosted the distinguished PBS series *Exxon Mobil Masterpiece Theatre*.

The following selection is from *Growing Up*. As you read Baker's account of how he discovered the power of his own words, note particularly the joy he felt hearing his writing read aloud.

Preparing to Read

What has been your experience with writing teachers in school? Have any of them helped you become a better writer? What kind of writer do you consider yourself now — excellent, above average, good, below average? Why?

The notion of becoming a writer had flickered off and on in my head . . . but it wasn't until my third year in high school that the possibility took hold. Until then I'd been bored by everything associated with English courses. I found English grammar dull and baffling. I hated the assignments to turn out "compositions," and went at them like heavy labor, turning out leaden, lackluster paragraphs that were agonies for teachers to read and for me to write. The classics thrust on me to read seemed as deadening as chloroform.

When our class was assigned to Mr. Fleagle for third-year English I anticipated another grim year in that dreariest of subjects. Mr. Fleagle was notorious among City students for dullness and inability to inspire. He was said to be stuffy, dull, and hopelessly out of date. To me he looked to be sixty or seventy and prim to a fault. He wore primly severe eyeglasses, his wavy hair was primly cut and primly combed. He wore prim vested suits with neckties blocked primly against the collar buttons of his primly starched white shirts. He had a primly pointed jaw, a primly straight nose, and a prim manner of speaking that was so correct, so gentlemanly, that he seemed a comic antique.

I anticipated a listless, unfruitful year with Mr. Fleagle and for a long time was not disappointed. We read *Macbeth*. Mr. Fleagle loved *Macbeth* and wanted us to love it, too, but he lacked the gift of infecting others with his own passion. He tried to convey the murderous ferocity of Lady Macbeth one day by reading aloud the passage that concludes

> . . . I have given suck, and know
> How tender 'tis to love the babe that milks me.
> I would, while it was smiling in my face,
> Have plucked my nipple from his boneless gums . . .

The idea of prim Mr. Fleagle plucking his nipple from boneless gums was too much for the class. We burst into gasps of irrepressible snickering. Mr. Fleagle stopped.

"There is nothing funny, boys, about giving suck to a babe. It is the — the very essence of motherhood, don't you see."

He constantly sprinkled his sentences with "don't you see." It wasn't a question but an exclamation of mild surprise at our ignorance. "Your pronoun needs an antecedent, don't you see," he would say, very primly. "The purpose of the Porter's scene, boys, is to provide comic relief from the horror, don't you see."

Late in the year we tackled the informal essay. "The essay, don't you see, is the . . ." My mind went numb. Of all forms of writing, none seemed so boring as the essay. Naturally we would have to write informal essays. Mr. Fleagle distributed a homework sheet offering us a choice of topics. None was quite so simpleminded as "What I Did on My Summer Vacation," but most seemed to be almost as dull. I took the list home and dawdled until the night before the essay was due. Sprawled on the sofa, I finally faced up to the grim task, took the list out of my notebook, and scanned it. The topic on which my eye stopped was "The Art of Eating Spaghetti."

This title produced an extraordinary sequence of mental images. Surging up from the depths of memory came a vivid recollection of a night in Belleville when all of us were seated around the supper table — Uncle Allen, my mother, Uncle Charlie, Doris, Uncle Hal—and Aunt Pat served spaghetti for supper. Spaghetti was an exotic treat in those days. Neither Doris nor I had ever eaten spaghetti, and none of the adults had enough experience to be good at it. All the good humor of Uncle Allen's house reawoke in my mind as I recalled the laughing arguments we had that night about the socially respectable method for moving spaghetti from plate to mouth.

Suddenly I wanted to write about that, about the warmth and good feeling 8 of it, but I wanted to put it down simply for my own joy, not for Mr. Fleagle. It was a moment I wanted to recapture and hold for myself. I wanted to relive the pleasure of an evening at New Street. To write it as I wanted, however, would violate all the rules of formal composition I'd learned in school, and Mr. Fleagle would surely give it a failing grade. Never mind. I would write something else for Mr. Fleagle after I had written this thing for myself.

When I finished it the night was half gone and there was no time left 9 to compose a proper, respectable essay for Mr. Fleagle. There was no choice next morning but to turn in my private reminiscence of Belleville. Two days passed before Mr. Fleagle returned the graded papers, and he returned everyone's but mine. I was bracing myself for a command to report to Mr. Fleagle immediately after school for discipline when I saw him lift my paper from his desk and rap for the class's attention.

> ❝ **And he started to read. My words! He was reading *my words* out loud to the entire class. What's more, the entire class was listening.** ❞

"Now, boys," he said, "I want to read 10 you an essay. This is titled 'The Art of Eating Spaghetti.'"

And he started to read. My words! 11 He was reading *my words* out loud to the entire class. What's more, the entire class was listening. Listening attentively. Then somebody laughed, then the entire class was laughing, and not in contempt and ridicule, but with open-hearted enjoyment. Even Mr. Fleagle stopped two or three times to repress a small prim smile.

I did my best to avoid showing pleasure, but what I was feeling was pure 12 ecstasy at this startling demonstration that my words had the power to make people laugh. In the eleventh grade, at the eleventh hour as it were, I had discovered a calling. It was the happiest moment of my entire school career. When Mr. Fleagle finished he put the final seal on my happiness by saying, "Now that, boys, is an essay, don't you see. It's—don't you see—it's of the very essence of the essay, don't you see. Congratulations, Mr. Baker."

For the first time, light shone on a possibility. It wasn't a very heartening 13 possibility, to be sure. Writing couldn't lead to a job after high school, and it was hardly honest work, but Mr. Fleagle had opened a door for me. After that I ranked Mr. Fleagle among the finest teachers in the school.

Thinking Critically about the Text

In his opening paragraph, Baker states, "I hated the assignments to turn out 'compositions,' and went at them like heavy labor, turning out leaden, lackluster paragraphs that were agonies for teachers to read and for me to write." Have you ever had any assignments like these? How are such assignments different from Mr. Fleagle's assignment to write an informal essay about "The Art of Eating Spaghetti"? How do you think Baker would respond to the following cartoon about writing assignments?

"*When writing your essays, I encourage you to think for yourselves while you express what I'd most agree with.*"

Matthew Henry Hall, www.matthewhenryhall.com

Discussing the Craft of Writing

1. How does Baker describe his teacher, Mr. Fleagle, in the second paragraph? What **dominant impression** does Baker create of this man?

2. Mr. Fleagle's homework assignment offered Baker and his classmates "a choice of topics." Is it important to have a "choice" of what you write about? Explain.

3. Once Baker's eye hits the topic of "The Art of Eating Spaghetti" on Mr. Fleagle's list, what happens? What triggers Baker's urge to write about the night his Aunt Pat served spaghetti for supper?

4. Why is Baker reluctant to submit his finished essay?

5. In paragraph 11, Baker states, "And he started to read. My words! He was reading *my words* out loud to the entire class. What's more, the entire class was listening. Listening attentively." Why was this episode so memorable to Baker? What surprised him most about it?

6. What insights into the nature of writing does Baker's narrative offer? Explain.

Shitty First Drafts

ANNE LAMOTT

Born in San Francisco in 1954, Anne Lamott graduated from Goucher College in Baltimore and is
the author of seven novels, including *Rosie* (1983),
All New People (1989), *Blue Shoes* (2002), and
Imperfect Birds (2010). She has also been a food
reviewer for *California* magazine, a book reviewer
for *Mademoiselle*, and a columnist for *Salon.* Her
nonfiction books include *Operating Instructions:
A Journal of My Son's First Year* (1993), in which
she describes life as a single parent; *Traveling
Mercies: Some Thoughts on Faith* (1999), in
which she charts her journey toward faith in

AP Photo/Nati Harnik

God; *Plan B: Further Thoughts on Faith* (2005); *Some Assembly Required: A Journal
of My Son's First Son* (2012); *Help, Thanks, Wow: The Three Essential Prayers*
(2012); *Small Victories: Spotting Improvable Moments of Grace* (2014); and *Halle-
lujah Anyway: Rediscovering Mercy* (2017). Lamott has taught at the University of
California–Davis, as well as at writing conferences around the country. Reflecting
on the importance of writing and reading, Lamott has written, "Writing and reading
decrease our sense of isolation. They deepen and widen and expand our sense of
life: They feed the soul."

 In the following selection, taken from Lamott's popular book about writing, *Bird
by Bird: Some Instructions on Writing and Life* (1994), she argues for the need to let
go and write those "shitty first drafts" that lead to clarity and sometimes brilliance in
subsequent drafts.

Preparing to Read

Many professional writers view first drafts as something they have to do before they
can begin the real work of writing — revision. How do you view the writing of your first
drafts? What patterns, if any, do you see in your writing behavior when working on
them? Is the work liberating or restricting? Pleasant or unpleasant?

N ow, practically even better news than that of short assignments is 1
the idea of shitty first drafts. All good writers write them. This is
how they end up with good second drafts and terrific third drafts.
People tend to look at successful writers, writers who are getting their books
published and maybe even doing well financially, and think that they sit
down at their desks every morning feeling like a million dollars, feeling
great about who they are and how much talent they have and what a great
story they have to tell; that they take in a few deep breaths, push back their
sleeves, roll their necks a few times to get all the cricks out, and dive in,

typing fully formed passages as fast as a court reporter. But this is just the fantasy of the uninitiated. I know some very great writers, writers you love who write beautifully and have made a great deal of money, and not *one* of them sits down routinely feeling wildly enthusiastic and confident. Not one of them writes elegant first drafts. All right, one of them does, but we do not like her very much. We do not think that she has a rich inner life or that God likes her or can even stand her. (Although when I mentioned this to my priest friend Tom, he said you can safely assume you've created God in your own image when it turns out that God hates all the same people you do.)

> " All good writers write them. This is how they end up with good second drafts and terrific third drafts. "

Very few writers really know what they are doing until they've done it. Nor do they go about their business feeling dewy and thrilled. They do not type a few stiff warm-up sentences and then find themselves bounding along like huskies across the snow. One writer I know tells me that he sits down every morning and says to himself nicely, "It's not like you don't have a choice, because you do—you can either type or kill yourself." We all often feel like we are pulling teeth, even those writers whose prose ends up being the most natural and fluid. The right words and sentences just do not come pouring out like ticker tape most of the time. Now, Muriel Spark is said to have felt that she was taking dictation from God every morning—sitting there, one supposes, plugged into a Dictaphone, typing away, humming. But this is a very hostile and aggressive position. One might hope for bad things to rain down on a person like this.

For me and most of the other writers I know, writing is not rapturous. In fact, the only way I can get anything written at all is to write really, really shitty first drafts.

The first draft is the child's draft, where you let it all pour out and then let it romp all over the place, knowing that no one is going to see it and that you can shape it later. You just let this childlike part of you channel whatever voices and visions come through and onto the page. If one of the characters wants to say, "Well, so what, Mr. Poopy Pants?," you let her. No one is going to see it. If the kid wants to get into really sentimental, weepy, emotional territory, you let him. Just get it all down on paper, because there may be something great in those six crazy pages that you would never have gotten to by more rational, grown-up means. There may be something in the very last line of the very last paragraph on page six that you just love, that is so beautiful or wild that you now know what you're supposed to be writing about, more or less, or in what direction you might go—but there was no way to get to this without first getting through the first five and a half pages.

I used to write food reviews for *California* magazine before it folded. (My writing food reviews had nothing to do with the magazine folding, although every single review did cause a couple of canceled subscriptions. Some readers took umbrage at my comparing mounds of vegetable puree with various ex-presidents' brains.) These reviews always took two days to write. First I'd go to a restaurant several times with a few opinionated, articulate friends in tow. I'd sit there writing down everything anyone said that was at all interesting or funny. Then on the following Monday I'd sit down at my desk with my notes, and try to write the review. Even after I'd been doing this for years, panic would set in. I'd try to write a lead, but instead I'd write a couple of dreadful sentences, xx them out, try again, xx everything out, and then feel despair and worry settle on my chest like an X-ray apron. It's over, I'd think, calmly. I'm not going to be able to get the magic to work this time. I'm ruined. I'm through. I'm toast. Maybe, I'd think, I can get my old job back as a clerk-typist. But probably not. I'd get up and study my teeth in the mirror for a while. Then I'd stop, remember to breathe, make a few phone calls, hit the kitchen and chow down. Eventually I'd go back and sit down at my desk, and sigh for the next ten minutes. Finally I would pick up my one-inch picture frame, stare into it as if for the answer, and every time the answer would come: All I had to do was to write a really shitty first draft of, say, the opening paragraph. And no one was going to see it.

So I'd start writing without reining myself in. It was almost just typing, just making my fingers move. And the writing would be *terrible*. I'd write a lead paragraph that was a whole page, even though the entire review could only be three pages long, and then I'd start writing up descriptions of the food, one dish at a time, bird by bird, and the critics would be sitting on my shoulders, commenting like cartoon characters. They'd be pretending to snore, or rolling their eyes at my overwrought descriptions, no matter how hard I tried to tone those descriptions down, no matter how conscious I was of what a friend said to me gently in my early days of restaurant reviewing. "Annie," she said, "it is just a piece of *chicken*. It is just a bit of *cake*."

But because by then I had been writing for so long, I would eventually let myself trust the process—sort of, more or less. I'd write a first draft that was maybe twice as long as it should be, with a self-indulgent and boring beginning, stupefying descriptions of the meal, lots of quotes from my black-humored friends that made them sound more like the Manson girls than food lovers, and no ending to speak of. The whole thing would be so long and incoherent and hideous that for the rest of the day I'd obsess about getting creamed by a car before I could write a decent second draft. I'd worry that people would read what I'd written and believe that the accident had really been a suicide, that I had panicked because my talent was waning and my mind was shot.

The next day, though, I'd sit down, go through it all with a colored pen, take out everything I possibly could, find a new lead somewhere on the

6

7

8

second page, figure out a kicky place to end it, and then write a second draft. It always turned out fine, sometimes even funny and weird and helpful. I'd go over it one more time and mail it in.

Then, a month later, when it was time for another review, the whole process would start again, complete with the fears that people would find my first draft before I could rewrite it.

Almost all good writing begins with terrible first efforts. You need to start somewhere. Start by getting something—anything—down on paper. A friend of mine says that the first draft is the down draft—you just get it down. The second draft is the up draft—you fix it up. You try to say what you have to say more accurately. And the third draft is the dental draft, where you check every tooth, to see if it's loose or cramped or decayed, or even, God help us, healthy.

What I've learned to do when I sit down to work on a shitty first draft is to quiet the voices in my head. First there's the vinegar-lipped Reader Lady, who says primly, "Well, *that's* not very interesting, is it?" And there's the emaciated German male who writes these Orwellian memos detailing your thought crimes. And there are your parents, agonizing over your lack of loyalty and discretion; and there's William Burroughs, dozing off or shooting up because he finds you as bold and articulate as a houseplant; and so on. And there are also the dogs: let's not forget the dogs, the dogs in their pen who will surely hurtle and snarl their way out if you ever *stop* writing, because writing is, for some of us, the latch that keeps the door of the pen closed, keeps those crazy ravenous dogs contained.

Quieting these voices is at least half the battle I fight daily. But this is better than it used to be. It used to be 87 percent. Left to its own devices, my mind spends much of its time having conversations with people who aren't there. I walk along defending myself to people, or exchanging repartee with them, or rationalizing my behavior, or seducing them with gossip, or pretending I'm on their TV talk show or whatever. I speed or run an aging yellow light or don't come to a full stop, and one nanosecond later am explaining to imaginary cops exactly why I had to do what I did, or insisting that I did not in fact do it.

I happened to mention this to a hypnotist I saw many years ago, and he looked at me very nicely. At first I thought he was feeling around on the floor for the silent alarm button, but then he gave me the following exercise, which I still use to this day.

Close your eyes and get quiet for a minute, until the chatter starts up. Then isolate one of the voices and imagine the person speaking as a mouse. Pick it up by the tail and drop it into a mason jar. Then isolate another voice, pick it up by the tail, drop it in the jar. And so on. Drop in any high-maintenance parental units, drop in any contractors, lawyers, colleagues, children, anyone who is whining in your head. Then put the lid on, and watch all these mouse people clawing at the glass, jabbering away, trying to make you feel like shit because you won't do what they want—won't give them more money, won't be more successful, won't see them more often. Then imagine that there is a volume-control button on the bottle. Turn it all the way up for a minute, and listen to the stream of angry, neglected, guilt-mongering voices. Then turn it all the way down and watch the frantic mice lunge at the glass, trying to get to you. Leave it down, and get back to your shitty first draft.

A writer friend of mine suggests opening the jar and shooting them 15 all in the head. But I think he's a little angry, and I'm sure nothing like this would ever occur to you.

Thinking Critically about the Text

What do you think of Lamott's use of the word *shitty* in her title and in the essay itself? Is it in keeping with her **tone**? Are you offended by the word? Explain. What would be lost or gained if she used a different word?

Discussing the Craft of Writing

1. Lamott says that the perception most people have of how writers work is different from the reality. She refers to this in paragraph 1 as the "fantasy of the uninitiated." What does she mean?

2. In paragraph 7, Lamott refers to a time when, through experience, she "eventually let [herself] trust the process — sort of, more or less." She is referring to the writing process, of course, but why "more or less"? Do you think her wariness is personal, or is she speaking for all writers? Explain.

3. From what Lamott has to say, is writing a first draft more about content or psychology? Do you agree when it comes to your own first drafts? Explain.

4. What is Lamott's **thesis**?

5. Lamott adds humor to her argument for "shitty first drafts." Give some examples. Does her humor add to or detract from the points she makes? Explain.

6. In paragraph 5, Lamott narrates her experiences in writing a food review, during which she refers to an almost ritualistic set of behaviors. What is her **purpose** in telling her readers this story about her difficulties? Is this information helpful? Explain.

Writing for an Audience

LINDA S. FLOWER

Linda S. Flower was born in 1944. She received her bachelor's degree from Simpson College and her doctorate from Rutgers University. She is currently a professor of English at Carnegie Mellon University, where she directed the Business Communication program for a number of years and is currently the director of the Center for the Study of Writing and Literacy. She has been a leading researcher on the composing process, and the results of her investi-

Courtesy of Linda Flower

gations shaped and informed her influential writing text *Problem-Solving Strategies for Writing in College and Community* (1997). Her other work includes *Talking Across Difference* (2004) and *Community Literacy and the Rhetoric of Public Engagement* (2008).

In this selection, which is taken from *Problem-Solving Strategies*, Flower's focus is on audience — the people for whom we write. She believes that writers must establish a "common ground" between themselves and their readers that lessens their differences in knowledge, attitudes, and needs. Although we can never be certain who might read what we write, it is nevertheless important for us to have a target audience in mind. Many of the decisions that we make as writers are influenced by those real or imagined readers.

Preparing to Read

Imagine for a moment that you just received a speeding ticket for going sixty-five miles per hour in a thirty-mile-per-hour zone. How would you describe the episode to your best friend? To your parents? To the judge in court? Sketch out the three versions. What differences, if any, do you find in the three versions? Explain.

T he goal of the writer is to create a momentary common ground   1
between the reader and the writer. You want the reader to share your
knowledge and your attitude toward that knowledge. Even if the
reader eventually disagrees, you want him or her to be able for the moment
to *see things as you see them*. A good piece of writing closes the gap between
you and the reader.

ANALYZE YOUR AUDIENCE

The first step in closing that gap is to gauge the distance between the two of   2
you. Imagine, for example, that you are a student writing your parents, who
have always lived in New York City, about a wilderness survival expedition
you want to go on over spring break. Sometimes obvious differences such as

age or background will be important, but the critical differences for writers usually fall into three areas: the reader's *knowledge* about the topic; his or her *attitude* toward it; and his or her personal or professional *needs*. Because these differences often exist, good writers do more than simply express their meaning; they pinpoint the critical differences between themselves and their reader and design their writing to reduce those differences. Let us look at these areas in more detail.

Knowledge

This is usually the easiest difference to handle. What does your reader need 3 to know? What are the main ideas you hope to teach? Does your reader have enough background knowledge to really understand you? If not, what would he or she have to learn?

Attitudes

When we say a person has knowledge, we usually refer to his conscious 4 awareness of explicit facts and clearly defined concepts. This kind of knowledge can be easily written down or told to someone else. However, much of what we "know" is not held in this formal, explicit way. Instead it is held as an

> **A good piece of writing closes the gap between you and the reader.**

attitude or image — as a loose cluster of associations. For instance, my image of lakes includes associations many people would have, including fishing, water skiing, stalled outboards, and lots of kids catching night crawlers with flashlights. However, the most salient or powerful parts of my image, which strongly color my whole attitude toward lakes, are thoughts of cloudy skies, long rainy days, and feeling generally cold and damp. By contrast, one of my best friends has a very different cluster of associations: to him a lake means sun, swimming, sailing, and happily sitting on the end of a dock. Needless to say, our differing images cause us to react quite differently to a proposal that we visit a lake. Likewise, one reason people often find it difficult to discuss religion and politics is that terms such as "capitalism" conjure up radically different images.

As you can see, a reader's image of a subject is often the source of atti- 5 tudes and feelings that are unexpected and, at times, impervious to mere facts. A simple statement that seems quite persuasive to you, such as "Lake Wampago would be a great place to locate the new music camp," could have little impact on your reader if he or she simply doesn't visualize a lake as a "great place." In fact, many people accept uncritically any statement that fits in with their own attitudes—and reject, just as uncritically, anything that does not.

Whether your purpose is to persuade or simply to present your perspective, it helps to know the image and attitudes that your reader already holds. The more these differ from your own, the more you will have to do to make him or her *see* what you mean. 6

Needs

When writers discover a large gap between their own knowledge and attitudes and those of the reader, they usually try to change the reader in some way. Needs, however, are different. When you analyze a reader's needs, it is so that you, the writer, can adapt to him. If you ask a friend majoring in biology how to keep your fish tank from clouding, you don't want to hear a textbook recitation on the life processes of algae. You expect a friend to adapt his or her knowledge and tell you exactly how to solve your problem. 7

The ability to adapt your knowledge to the needs of the reader is often crucial to your success as a writer. This is especially true in writing done on a job. For example, as producer of a public affairs program for a television station, 80 percent of your time may be taken up planning the details of new shows, contacting guests, and scheduling the taping sessions. But when you write a program proposal to the station director, your job is to show how the program will fit into the cost guidelines, the FCC requirements for relevance, and the overall programming plan for the station. When you write that report, your role in the organization changes from producer to proposal writer. Why? Because your reader needs that information in order to make a decision. He may be *interested* in your scheduling problems and the specific content of the shows, but he *reads* your report because of his own needs as station director of the organization. He has to act. 8

In college, where the reader is also a teacher, the reader's needs are a little less concrete but just as important. Most papers are assigned as a way to teach something. So the real purpose of a paper may be for you to make connections between two historical periods, to discover for yourself the principle behind a laboratory experiment, or to develop and support your own interpretation of a novel. A good college paper doesn't just rehash the facts; it demonstrates what your reader, as a teacher, needs to know—that you are learning the thinking skills his or her course is trying to teach. 9

Effective writers are not simply expressing what they know, like a student madly filling up an examination bluebook. Instead they are *using* their knowledge: reorganizing, maybe even rethinking their ideas to meet the demands of an assignment or the needs of their reader. 10

Thinking Critically about the Text

What does Flower believe constitutes a "good college paper" (paragraph 9)? Do you agree? Why, or why not?

Discussing the Craft of Writing

1. How, according to Flower, does a competent writer close the gap between himself or herself and the reader? How does a writer determine what a reader's "personal or professional *needs*" (paragraph 2) are?

2. What, for Flower, is the difference between knowledge and attitude? Why is it important for writers to understand this difference?

3. In paragraph 4, Flower discusses the fact that many words have both positive and negative associations. How do you think words come to have associations (**connotations/denotations**)? Consider, for example, such words as *home*, *anger*, *royalty*, *welfare*, *politician*, and *strawberry shortcake*.

4. Flower wrote this selection for college students. How well did she assess your needs as a member of this audience? Does Flower's use of language and examples show a sensitivity to her audience? Provide specific examples to support your view.

5. When using technical language in a paper on a subject you are familiar with, why is it important for you to know your audience? Explain. How could your classmates, friends, or parents help you?

Reading to Write

STEPHEN KING

Born in 1947, Stephen King is a 1970 graduate of the University of Maine. He worked as a janitor in a knitting mill, a laundry worker, and a high school English teacher before he struck it big with his writing. Today, many people consider King's name synonymous with the macabre; he is, beyond dispute, the most successful writer of horror fiction today. He has written dozens of novels and hundreds of short stories, novellas, and screenplays, among other works. His books have sold well over 350 million copies worldwide, and many of his novels have been made into popular

BERTRAND LANGLOIS/AFP/ Getty Images

motion pictures, including *Stand by Me*, *Misery*, *The Green Mile*, and *It*. His fiction, starting with *Carrie* in 1974, includes *Salem's Lot* (1975), *The Shining* (1977), *The Dead Zone* (1979), *Christine* (1983), *Pet Sematary* (1983), *The Girl Who Loved Tom Gordon* (1999), *Everything's Eventual: Five Dark Tales* (2002), *11/22/63: A Novel* (2012), *The Bazaar of Bad Dreams* (2015), and (with his son Owen King), *The Outsider* (2017). Other works include *Danse Macabre* (1980), a nonfiction look at horror in the media, and *On Writing: A Memoir of the Craft* (2000).

In the following selection taken from *On Writing*, King discusses the importance of reading in learning to write. Reading, in his words, "offers you a constantly growing knowledge of what has been done and what hasn't, what is trite and what is fresh, what works and what just lies there dying (or dead) on the page."

Preparing to Read

In your opinion, are reading and writing connected in some way? If the two activities are related, what is the nature of that relationship? Do you have to be a reader to be a good writer, or is writing an activity that can be learned quite apart from reading?

f you want to be a writer, you must do two things above all others: Read a 1
lot and write a lot. There's no way around these two things that I'm aware of, no shortcut.

I'm a slow reader, but I usually get through seventy or eighty books a year, 2
mostly fiction. I don't read in order to study the craft; I read because I like to read. It's what I do at night, kicked back in my blue chair. Similarly, I don't read fiction to study the art of fiction, but simply because I like stories. Yet there is a learning process going on. Every book you pick up has its own lesson or lessons, and quite often the bad books have more to teach than the good ones.

When I was in the eighth grade, I happened upon a paperback novel 3
by Murray Leinster, a science fiction pulp writer who did most of his work

during the forties and fifties, when magazines like *Amazing Stories* paid a penny a word. I had read other books by Mr. Leinster, enough to know that the quality of his writing was uneven. This particular tale, which was about mining in the asteroid belt, was one of his less successful efforts. Only that's too kind. It was terrible, actually, a story populated by paper-thin characters and driven by outlandish plot developments. Worst of all (or so it seemed to me at the time), Leinster had fallen in love with the word *zestful*. Characters watched the approach of ore-bearing asteroids with *zestful smiles*. Characters sat down to supper aboard their mining ship with *zestful anticipation*. Near the end of the book, the hero swept the large-breasted, blonde heroine into a *zestful embrace*. For me, it was the literary equivalent of a smallpox vaccination: I have never, so far as I know, used the word *zestful* in a novel or a story. God willing, I never will.

> " If you want to be a writer, you must do two things above all others: Read a lot and write a lot. "

Asteroid Miners (which wasn't the title, but that's close enough) was an   4
important book in my life as a reader. Almost everyone can remember losing his or her virginity, and most writers can remember the first book he/she put down thinking: *I can do better than this, Hell, I* am *doing better than this!* What could be more encouraging to the struggling writer than to realize his/her work is unquestionably better than that of someone who actually got paid for his/her stuff?

One learns most clearly what not to do by reading bad prose—one   5
novel like *Asteroid Miners* (or *Valley of the Dolls*, *Flowers in the Attic*, and *The Bridges of Madison County*, to name just a few) is worth a semester at a good writing school, even with the superstar guest lecturers thrown in.

Good writing, on the other hand, teaches the learning writer about style,   6
graceful narration, plot development, the creation of believable characters, and truth-telling. A novel like *The Grapes of Wrath* may fill a new writer with feelings of despair and good old-fashioned jealousy—"I'll never be able to write anything that good, not if I live to be a thousand"—but such feelings can also serve as a spur, goading the writer to work harder and aim higher. Being swept away by a combination of great story and great writing—of being flattened, in fact—is part of every writer's necessary formation. You cannot hope to sweep someone else away by the force of your writing until it has been done to you.

So we read to experience the mediocre and the outright rotten; such   7
experience helps us to recognize those things when they begin to creep into our own work, and to steer clear of them. We also read in order to measure

ourselves against the good and the great, to get a sense of all that can be done. And we read in order to experience different styles.

You may find yourself adopting a style you find particularly exciting, and there's nothing wrong with that. When I read Ray Bradbury as a kid, I wrote like Ray Bradbury—everything green and wondrous and seen through a lens smeared with the grease of nostalgia. When I read James M. Cain, everything I wrote came out clipped and stripped and hard-boiled. When I read Lovecraft, my prose became luxurious and Byzantine. I wrote stories in my teenage years where all these styles merged, creating a kind of hilarious stew. This sort of stylistic blending is a necessary part of developing one's own style, but it doesn't occur in a vacuum. You have to read widely, constantly refining (and redefining) your own work as you do so. It's hard for me to believe that people who read very little (or not at all in some cases) should presume to write and expect people to like what they have written, but I know it's true. If I had a nickel for every person who ever told me he/she wanted to become a writer but "didn't have time to read," I could buy myself a pretty good steak dinner. Can I be blunt on this subject? If you don't have time to read, you don't have the time (or the tools) to write. Simple as that.

Reading is the creative center of a writer's life. I take a book with me everywhere I go, and find there are all sorts of opportunities to dip in. The trick is to teach yourself to read in small sips as well as in long swallows. Waiting rooms were made for books—of course! But so are theater lobbies before the show, long and boring checkout lines, and everyone's favorite, the john. You can even read while you're driving, thanks to the audiobook revolution. Of the books I read each year, anywhere from six to a dozen are on tape. As for all the wonderful radio you will be missing, come on—how many times can you listen to Deep Purple sing "Highway Star"?

Reading at meals is considered rude in polite society, but if you expect to succeed as a writer, rudeness should be the second-to-least of your concerns. The least of all should be polite society and what it expects. If you intend to write as truthfully as you can, your days as a member of polite society are numbered, anyway.

Where else can you read? There's always the treadmill, or whatever you use down at the local health club to get aerobic. I try to spend an hour doing that every day, and I think I'd go mad without a good novel to keep me company. Most exercise facilities (at home as well as outside it) are now equipped with TVs, but TV—while working out or anywhere else—really is about the last thing an aspiring writer needs. If you feel you must have the news analyst blowhards on CNN while you exercise, or the stock market blowhards on MSNBC, or the sports blowhards on ESPN, it's time for you to question how serious you really are about becoming a writer. You must be prepared to do some serious turning inward toward the life of the imagination, and that means, I'm afraid, that Geraldo, Keith Olbermann, and Jay Leno must go. Reading takes time, and the glass teat takes too much of it.

Once weaned from the ephemeral craving for TV, most people will find they enjoy the time they spend reading. I'd like to suggest that turning off that endlessly quacking box is apt to improve the quality of your life as well as the quality of your writing. And how much of a sacrifice are we talking about here? How many *Frasier* and *ER* reruns does it take to make one American life complete? How many Richard Simmons infomercials? How many whiteboy/fatboy Beltway insiders on CNN? Oh man, don't get me started. Jerry-Springer-Dr.-Dre-Judge-Judy-Jerry-Falwell-Donny-and-Marie, I rest my case.

When my son Owen was seven or so, he fell in love with Bruce Springsteen's E Street Band, particularly with Clarence Clemons, the band's burly sax player. Owen decided he wanted to learn to play like Clarence. My wife and I were amused and delighted by this ambition. We were also hopeful, as any parent would be, that our kid would turn out to be talented, perhaps even some sort of prodigy. We got Owen a tenor saxophone for Christmas and lessons with Gordon Bowie, one of the local music men. Then we crossed our fingers and hoped for the best.

Seven months later I suggested to my wife that it was time to discontinue the sax lessons, if Owen concurred. Owen did, and with palpable relief—he hadn't wanted to say it himself, especially not after asking for the sax in the first place, but seven months had been long enough for him to realize that, while he might love Clarence Clemons's big sound, the saxophone was simply not for him—God had not given him that particular talent.

I knew, not because Owen stopped practicing, but because he was practicing only during the periods Mr. Bowie had set for him: half an hour after school four days a week, plus an hour on the weekends. Owen mastered the scales and the notes—nothing wrong with his memory, his lungs, or his eye-hand coordination—but we never heard him taking off, surprising himself with something new, blissing himself out. And as soon as his practice time was over, it was back into the case with the horn, and there it stayed until the next lesson or practice time. What this suggested to me was that when it came to the sax and my son, there was never going to be any real playtime; it was all going to be rehearsal. That's no good. If there's no joy in it, it's just no good. It's best to go on to some other area, where the deposits of talent may be richer and the fun quotient higher.

Talent renders the whole idea of rehearsal meaningless; when you find something at which you are talented, you do it (whatever *it* is) until your fingers bleed or your eyes are ready to fall out of your head. Even when no one is listening (or reading, or watching), every outing is a bravura performance, because you as the creator are happy. Perhaps even ecstatic. That goes for reading and writing as well as for playing a musical instrument, hitting a baseball, or running the four-forty. The sort of strenuous reading and writing program I advocate—four to six hours a day, every day—will not seem strenuous if you really enjoy doing these things and have an aptitude for them; in fact, you may be following such a program already. If you feel you need permission to do all the reading and writing your little heart desires, however, consider it hereby granted by yours truly.

The real importance of reading is that it creates an ease and intimacy 17 with the process of writing; one comes to the country of the writer with one's papers and identification pretty much in order. Constant reading will pull you into a place (a mind-set, if you like the phrase) where you can write eagerly and without self-consciousness. It also offers you a constantly growing knowledge of what has been done and what hasn't, what is trite and what is fresh, what works and what just lies there dying (or dead) on the page. The more you read, the less apt you are to make a fool of yourself with your pen or word processor.

Thinking Critically about the Text

What does King mean when he writes that reading a bad novel is "worth a semester at a good writing school, even with the superstar guest lecturers thrown in" (paragraph 5)? Do you take his observation seriously? In your own words, what can one learn about writing by reading a bad novel? What can one learn by reading a good novel?

Discussing the Craft of Writing

1. In paragraph 3, King berates the author Murray Leinster for his repeated use of the word *zestful*. He says he himself has, as far as he knows, never used the word. Why do you suppose he doesn't like the word? Have you ever used it in your own writing? Explain. (Glossary: **Diction**)

2. In paragraph 7, King says that "we read in order to experience different styles." What **examples** does he use to support this statement? If you have learned from someone else's style, what exactly was it that you learned?

3. Authors, especially those as famous as King, are very much sought after as guests on television shows, at writing conferences, and at celebrity and charity events. Why does King believe that it is incompatible for one to be both a member of polite society and an author? Do you agree with him? Why or why not?

4. King does not like TV. What does he find wrong with it, especially for writers?

5. Admittedly, not everyone who wants to write well also aspires to be a great novelist. What value, if any, does King's advice about reading and writing have for you as a college student? Explain.

6. How do you react to the following cartoon? What is a Klout score? Do you find the cartoon humorous? Why or why not? Do you think Stephen King would find it humorous?

"I'm sorry, Paige, but grades are based on the quality of the writing, not on your Klout score."

Matthew Diffee The New Yorker Collection/The Cartoon Bank

LIFE IN THE WOODS

I WENT TO THE WOODS BECAUSE I WISHED TO LIVE DELIBERATELY.

I BROUGHT ALONG A FEW THINGS IN CASE I GOT BORED.

THERE I EXPERIENCED THE PROFOUND JOY OF SOLITUDE...

AND MADE SURE EVERYONE ELSE KNEW ABOUT IT.

#majestic

I MARCHED TO THE RHYTHMS OF NATURE, THE SOUNDS OF THE FOREST...

AND THE BEAT OF MY KILLER WILDERNESS PLAYLIST.

THE WOODS WERE FILLED WITH MANY WONDROUS CREATURES.

I TURNED THEM INTO MEMES.

CONDESCENDING OWL IS WISER THAN YOU

DEVIL SQUIRREL WANTS YOUR SOUL

CONFUSED GOOSE FLIES NORTH FOR WINTER

ALONE IN THE DARKNESS, I FOUND TRUE ILLUMINATION...

BY THE LIGHT OF MY EVER-GLOWING SCREENS.

Grant Snider, Incidental Comics

CHAPTER 4

Narration

WHAT IS NARRATION?

Whenever you recount an event or tell a story or an anecdote to illustrate an idea, you are using narration. In its broadest sense, narration is any account of an event, or a series of events, presented in a logical sequence. The tremendous popularity in our culture of narrative forms like action movies, television dramas, celebrity gossip, graphic novels, and even the Facebook status update attests to the fact that nearly everyone loves a good story. Given a decent character and a good beginning, we all want to find out what happens next.

VISUALIZING NARRATION

Take a minute to read Grant Snider's graphic narrative "Life in the Woods." Notice that Snider constructs his narrative with a series of pictures and accompanying text that provide snapshots of the narrator's experience in the woods. What aspects of the story are conveyed by the visual elements? What is left to the written elements? What do you think is the narrator's purpose in going to the woods? In your opinion, how satisfying was the narrator's experience? Which visual elements led you to your conclusion? What do you think is Snider's point in creating this graphic narrative?

UNDERSTANDING NARRATION AS A WRITING STRATEGY

The most basic and most important purpose of narration is to *share* a meaningful experience with readers, perhaps one that offers new insight about the writer or others. Another important purpose of narration is to *report* and *instruct*—to give the facts, to tell what happened. Journalists and historians, in reporting events of the near and more distant past, provide us with information that we can use to form opinions about a current issue or to better understand the world around us. A biographer gives us another person's life as a document of an individual's past but also, perhaps, as a portrait of more general human potential. And naturalists recount the drama of encounters between predators and prey in the wild to remind us of the power of nature. We expect writers to make these narratives as objective as possible and to distinguish between facts and opinions.

A narrative may present a straightforward message or moral, or it may make a more subtle point about us and the world we live in. Consider, for example, the following narrative by E. J. Kahn Jr. about the invention of Coca-Cola as both a medicine and a soft drink, from his book *The Big Drink: The Story of Coca-Cola.*

Establishes context for narrative Uses third-person point of view Organizes narrative chronologically, using time markers Focuses on the discovery that led to Coca-Cola's popularity as a soft drink	In 1886—a year in which, as contemporary Coca-Cola officials like to point out, Conan Doyle unveiled Sherlock Holmes and France unveiled the Statue of Liberty—[John Styth] Pemberton unveiled a syrup that he called Coca-Cola. He had taken out the wine and added a pinch of caffeine, and, when the end product tasted awful, had thrown in some extract of cola (or kola) nut and a few other oils, blending the mixture in a three-legged iron pot in his back yard and swishing it around with an oar. He distributed it to soda fountains in used beer bottles, and [his bookkeeper Frank M.] Robinson, with his flowing bookkeeper's script, presently devised a label on which "Coca-Cola" was written in the fashion that is still employed. Pemberton looked upon his concoction less as a refreshment than as a headache cure, especially for people whose throbbing temples could be traced to overindulgence. On a morning late in 1886, one such victim of the night before dragged himself into an Atlanta drugstore and asked for a dollop of Coca-Cola. Druggists customarily stirred a teaspoonful of syrup into a glass of water, but in this instance the factotum on duty was too lazy to walk to the fresh-water tap, a couple of feet off. Instead, he mixed the syrup with some charged water, which was closer at hand. The suffering customer perked up almost at once, and word quickly spread that the best Coca-Cola was a fizzy one.

A good narrative essay, like the preceding paragraph, has four essential features:

1. *Context*: The writer makes clear when the action happened, where it happened, and to whom.
2. *Point of view*: The writer establishes and maintains a consistent relationship to the action, either as a participant or as a reporter looking on.
3. *Selection of detail*: The writer carefully chooses what to include, focusing on actions and details that are most important to the story while playing down or even eliminating others.

4. *Organization*: The writer arranges the events of the narrative in an appropriate sequence, often a strict chronology with a clear beginning, middle, and end.

As you read the selections in this chapter, watch for these features and for how each writer uses them to tell his or her story. Think about how each writer's choices affect the way you react to the selections.

Narration is often used in combination with one or more of the other rhetorical strategies. In an essay that is written primarily to explain a process — reading a book, for example — a writer might find it useful to tell a brief story or anecdote of an instance when the process worked especially well (Mortimer Adler, "How to Mark a Book"). In the same way, a writer attempting to define the term *poverty* might tell several stories to illustrate clearly the many facets of poverty (Jo Goodwin Parker, "What Is Poverty?"). Finally, a writer could use narrative examples to persuade — for example, to argue against handing out participation awards (Nancy Armour, "Participation Awards Do Disserve") or to demonstrate the resilience of family members in the hospitality industry to argue for the importance of service workers (Caitlin McCormick, "The Gingham Apron").

USING NARRATION ACROSS THE DISCIPLINES

When writing essays in the academic disciplines, you will have many opportunities to use the strategy of narration to both organize and strengthen the presentation of your ideas. To determine whether narration is the right strategy for you in a particular paper, use the guidelines described in Chapter 2, "Determining a Strategy for Developing Your Essay" (pages 34–35). Consider the following examples, which show how these guidelines work for typical college papers:

American History

1. **MAIN IDEA:** Although Abraham Lincoln was not the chief speaker at Gettysburg on November 19, 1863, the few remarks he made that day shaped the thinking of our nation as perhaps few other speeches have.

2. **QUESTION:** What happened at Gettysburg on November 19, 1863, that made Abraham Lincoln's speech so memorable and influential?

3. **STRATEGY:** Narration. The thrust of the main idea as well as the direction words *what happened* say "tell me the story," and what better way to tell what happened than to narrate the day's events?

4. SUPPORTING STRATEGY: Cause and effect analysis. The story and how it is narrated can be used to explain the impact of this speech on our nation's thinking.

Anthropology

1. MAIN IDEA: Food-gathering and religious activities account for a large portion of the daily lives of native peoples in rural Thailand.
2. QUESTION: What happens during a typical day or week in rural Thailand?
3. STRATEGY: Narration. The direction words in both the statement of the main idea (*account* and *daily*) and the question (*what happens*) call out for a narration of what happens during any given day.
4. SUPPORTING STRATEGY: Illustration. The paper might benefit from specific examples of the various chores related to food gathering as well as examples of typical religious activities.

Life Science

1. MAIN IDEA: British bacteriologist Sir Alexander Fleming discovered penicillin quite by accident in 1928, and that discovery changed the world.
2. QUESTION: How did Fleming happen to discover penicillin, and why was this discovery so important?
3. STRATEGY: Narration. The direction words *how* and *did happen* call for the story of Fleming's accidental discovery of penicillin.
4. SUPPORTING STRATEGIES: Argument and cause and effect analysis. The claims that Fleming's discovery was *important* and *changed the world* suggest that the story needs to be both compelling and persuasive and should also explain its world-changing effects.

PRACTICAL ADVICE FOR WRITING AN ESSAY OF NARRATION

As you plan, write, and revise your narrative essay, be mindful of the writing process guidelines described in Chapter 2. Also, pay particular attention to the basic requirements and essential ingredients for this writing strategy.

▶ Planning Your Essay of Narration

Planning is an essential part of writing a good narrative essay. You can save yourself a great deal of inconvenience by taking the time to think about the key components of your essay before you actually begin to write.

Select a Topic That Has Meaning for You. In your writing course, you may have the freedom to choose the story you want to narrate, or your instructor may give you a list of topics from which to choose. Instead of jumping at the first topic that looks good, however, brainstorm a list of events that have had an impact on your life and that you could write about. Such a list might include your first blind date, making a team, the death of a loved one, a trip to the Grand Canyon, the breakup of a relationship, or getting into college.

As you narrow your options, look for an event or an incident that is particularly memorable. Memorable experiences are memorable for a reason; they offer us important insights into our lives. Such experiences are worth narrating because people want to read about them.

Determine Your Point and Purpose.   Before you begin writing, ask yourself why the experience you have chosen is meaningful. What did you learn from it? How are you different as a result of the experience? What has changed? Your narrative point (the meaning of your narrative) and purpose in writing will influence which events and details you include and which you leave out. Suppose you choose to write about how you learned to ride a bicycle. If you mean mainly to entertain, you will probably include unusual incidents unique to your experience. If your purpose is mainly to report or inform, it will make more sense to concentrate on the kinds of details that are common to most people's experience. The most successful narrative essays, however, do more than entertain or inform. While narratives do not ordinarily have a formal thesis statement, readers will more than likely expect your story to make a statement or to arrive at some meaningful conclusion — implied or explicit — about your experience.

Establish a Context.   Early in your essay, perhaps in the opening paragraphs, establish the context, or setting, of your story — the world within which the action took place:

> *When it happened* — morning; 11:37 on the dot; 1997; winter
> *Where it happened* — in the street; at Chipotle; in Pocatello, Idaho
> *To whom it happened* — to me; to my father; to the intern; to Teri

Without a clear context, your readers can easily get confused or even completely lost. And remember, readers respond well to specific contextual information because such details make them feel as if they are present, ready to witness the narrative.

Choose the Most Appropriate Point of View.   Consider what point of view to take in your narrative. Did you take part in the action? If so, it will seem most natural for you to use the first-person (*I, we*) point of view. On the other hand, if you weren't there at all and must rely on other sources for your information, you will probably choose the third-person (*he*, *she*, *it*, *they*) point of view, as did the author writing about the invention of Coca-Cola earlier in this chapter. However, if you were a witness to part or all of what happened but not a participant, then you will need to choose between the more immediate and subjective quality of the first person and the more distanced, objective effect of the third person. Whichever you choose, you should maintain the same point of view throughout your narrative.

Gather Details That "Show, Don't Tell."   When writing your essay, you will need enough detail about the action, the people involved, and the context to let your readers understand what is going on. Start collecting details by asking yourself the traditional reporter's questions:

- *Who* was involved?
- *What* happened?
- *Where* did it happen?
- *When* did it happen?
- *Why* did it happen?
- *How* did it happen?

Generate as many details as you can because you never know which ones will ensure that your essay *shows* and doesn't *tell* too much.

As you write, you will want to select and emphasize details that support your point, serve your purpose, and show the reader what is happening. You should not, however, get so carried away with details that your readers become confused or bored by excess information: In good storytelling, deciding what to leave out can be as important as deciding what to include.

▶ Organizing Your Essay of Narration

Identify the Sequence of Events in Your Narrative.   Storytellers tend to follow an old rule: Begin at the beginning, and go on till you come to the end; then stop. Chronological organization is natural in narration because it is a retelling of the original order of events; it is also easiest for the writer to manage and the reader to understand.

Some narratives, however, are organized using a technique called *flashback*: The writer may begin midway through the story, or even at the end, with an important or exciting event, and then use flashbacks to fill in what happened earlier, leading up to that event. Some authors begin in the present and then use flashbacks to shift to the past to tell the story. Whatever organizational pattern you choose, words and phrases like "for a month," "afterward," and "three days earlier" will help you and your reader keep the sequence of events straight.

▶ Writing Your Essay of Narration

Keep Your Verb Tense Consistent.   Most narratives are presented in the past tense, and this is logical: They recount events that have already happened, even if very recently. But writers sometimes use the present tense to create an effect of immediacy, as if the events were happening as you read about them. The important thing is to be consistent. If you are recounting an event that has already occurred, use the past tense throughout. For an event in the present, use the present tense consistently. If you find yourself jumping from a present event to a past event, as in the case of a flashback, you will need to switch verb tenses to signal the change in time.

Use Narrative Time for Emphasis.   The number of words or pages you devote to an event does not usually correspond to the number of minutes or hours the event took to happen. You may require several pages to recount an important or complex quarter of an hour but then pass over several hours or days in a sentence or two. Length has less to do with chronological time than with the amount of detail you include, and that's a function of the amount of emphasis you want to give to a particular incident.

Use Transitional Words to Clarify Narrative Sequence.   Transitional words like *after, next, then, earlier, immediately,* and *finally* are useful, as they help your readers smoothly connect and understand the sequence of events that make up your narrative. Likewise, specific time markers like "on April 20," "two weeks earlier," and "in 2004" can indicate time shifts and can signal to readers how much time has elapsed between events.

   Inexperienced writers sometimes overuse transitional words; this makes their writing style wordy and tiresome. Use these conventional transitions when you really need them, but when you don't—when your readers can follow your story without them—leave them out.

Use Dialogue to Bring Your Narrative to Life.   Having people in a narrative speak is a very effective way of showing rather than telling or summarizing what happened. Snippets of actual dialogue make a story come alive and feel immediate to the reader.

   Consider this passage from an early draft of a student narrative:

> I hated having to call a garage, but I knew I couldn't do the work myself and I knew they'd rip me off. Besides, I had to get the car off the street before the police had it towed. I felt trapped without any choices.

Now compare this early draft with the following revised draft, in which the situation is revealed through dialogue.

> "University Gulf, Glen speaking. What can I do for ya?"
>
> "Yeah, my car broke down. I think it's the timing belt, and I was wondering if you could give me an estimate."
>
> "What kind of car is it?" asked Glen.
>
> "A Nissan Sentra."
>
> "What year?"
>
> "2008," I said, emphasizing the 8.
>
> "Oh, those are a bitch to work on. Can ya hold on for a second?"
>
> I knew what was coming before Glen came back on the line.

With dialogue, readers can hear the direct exchange between the car owner and the mechanic. You can use dialogue in your own writing to deliver a sense of immediacy to the reader.

▶ Revising and Editing Your Essay of Narration

When writing a narrative essay, it is often critical to find fellow students or friends to read your draft. They will catch any missing details or inconsistencies in the narrative that you, being familiar or too close to material, might have missed. We include guidelines for peer review in the "A Brief Guide to Peer Critiquing" box in Chapter 2 (pages 38–39).

You will also want to ask yourself the following questions and revisit Chapter 16, "Editing for Grammar, Punctuation, and Sentence Style" before you turn in a final draft.

Questions for Revising and Editing: Narration

1. Is my narrative well focused, or do I try to cover too great a period of time?

2. What is my reason for telling this story? Is that reason clearly stated or implied for readers?

3. Have I established a clear context for my readers? Is it clear when the action happened, where it happened, and to whom?

4. Have I used the most effective point of view to tell my story? How would my story be different had I used a different one?

5. Have I selected details that help readers understand what is going on, or have I included unnecessary details that get in the way of what I'm trying to say? Do I give enough examples of the important events in my narrative?

6. Is the chronology of events clear? Have I taken advantage of opportunities to add emphasis, drama, or suspense with flashbacks or other complications of the chronological organization?

7. Have I used transitional expressions or time markers to help readers follow the sequence of events?

8. Have I used dialogue to reveal a situation, or have I told about or summarized the situation too much?

9. Have I avoided run-on sentences and comma splices? Have I used sentence fragments only deliberately to convey mood or tone?

10. Have I avoided other errors in grammar, punctuation, and mechanics? Is my sentence style as clear, smooth, and persuasive as possible?

11. Is the meaning of my narrative clear, or have I left my readers thinking, "So what?"

STUDENT ESSAY USING NARRATION AS A WRITING STRATEGY

Andrew Kauser was born in Montreal, Canada. As a child, he often went on weekend-long flying trips with his father, who is a pilot; these experiences instilled in him a passion for flying and a desire to get his own pilot's license one day. In the following essay, Kauser writes how he felt as he took that most important step in becoming a licensed pilot, the first solo flight.

Challenging My Fears
Andrew Kauser

Context set — writer driving to airport on chilly autumn morning for first solo flight

Cedars Airport, just off the western tip of Montreal, is about a half-hour drive from my house. Today's drive is boring as usual except for the chill which runs up the back of my legs because of the cold breeze entering through the rusted floorboards. I peer through the dew-covered windshield to see the leaves changing color. Winter is on its way. [1]

Writer tells story in present tense and uses first-person point of view

Events are presented in chronological order

Finally, I arrive at the airport; while my instructor waits, I do my aircraft check. I curse as I touch the steely cold parts of the aircraft. Even though the discomfort is great, I do my check slowly. Hurrying could make me miss a potential problem. It is better to find a problem on the ground instead of in the air. The check takes about fifteen minutes, and by this time my fingertips are white. Everything appears to be in order so now it is time to start up. [2]

My instructor and I climb into the cockpit of the 3
airplane and strap ourselves in. The plane has been
out all night, and it is just as cold inside as it is outside.
My back shivers as I sit in the seat, and the controls are
painfully cold to touch. The plane starts without a hint
of trouble, and in one continuous motion I taxi onto the
runway. At full throttle we begin to increase our speed
down the runway. In a matter of seconds we leave the
ground. The winds are calm and the visibility is endless. It's a beautiful day to fly.

The object of today's lesson is to practice taking off 4
and landing. The first "touch and go" is so smooth that I
surprise both myself and my instructor. Unfortunately,
my next two attempts are more like "smash and goes."
I land once more; this time it is not as jarring as my last
two, and my instructor gives me the O.K. to do a circuit
alone. We taxi to the hanger, and he gets out.

Confined in the small cockpit with my seatbelt 5
strapped around me as tightly as it will go, I look out the
window and watch my human security blanket walking
back toward the hangars. The calm feeling with which
I began the day quickly disappears. I feel like a soldier
being sent to the front lines. I begin to feel smothered by
the enclosed cockpit. My stomach tightens around the
breakfast I ate and squeezes out my last breath. I gulp for
air, and my breathing becomes irregular. My mind still
functions, though, and I begin to taxi toward the runway.

It is a long taxi, and I have ample time to think 6
about what I am about to do. I remember the time
when my father had to land on a football field when his
engine quit. My eyes scan the instruments quickly in
hope of finding something comforting in all the dials.
My hands are still feeling quite cool. I reach out and
pull the lever for cabin heat. A rush of warm air satu-
rated with the smell of the engine fills the cockpit. This
allows me some comfort as my mind begins to wander.
The radio crackles and breaks my train of thought. A
student pilot in the air with his instructor announces
that he is on final approach for landing. While still taxi-
ing, I look through the Plexiglas windscreen to watch
him land. The plane hits hard and bounces right back
into the air. It comes down again, and as though on
springs, leaps back into the air. Once again it comes
down and this time stays.

*Central idea
introduced:
solo flight*

*Figurative
language
describes
writer's feelings*

*Key word "taxi"
repeated to make
a transition*

*Selection of detail
reveals writer's
state of mind*

At the parking area off the runway, I close the throttle and bring the plane to a stop. I check the instruments and request clearance for take-off from the tower. While I wait, I try to calm down.

7

Now hold your breath and count to ten. Look, the chances of dying in a car accident are twenty times greater, I think to myself. Somehow that isn't very comforting. The radio crackles, and I exhale quickly. Permission is granted.

8

Dramatic short sentence announces the start of the solo

I taxi onto the runway and come to a stop. I mentally list my options, but they are very few. One is to get up the courage to challenge my fears; the other, to turn the plane around and shamefully go back to the hangar. Well, the choices are limited, but the ultimate decision seems fairly obvious. I reach out and push the throttle into the full open position. The engine roars to life. The decision to go has been made. The plane screams down the runway, and at fifty-five knots I pull back on the controls. In one clean movement, the plane and I leave the ground.

9

Writer makes connection to title

The noise of the engine is the only thing I can hear as the air pressure begins to clog my ears. My mind still racing, I check my instruments. The winds are still calm, and the plane cuts through the air without a hint of trouble. Warm gas-laden air streams through the vents as the sun streaks into the cockpit through the passenger window, and I begin to feel quite hot. At seven hundred feet above the ground, I turn left, check for any traffic, and continue climbing. At twelve hundred feet, I turn left onto the downward portion of the circuit which is parallel to the runway.

10

This is a longer stretch, and I take a moment to gaze down at the ground below. The view is simply amazing. The trees are all rich bright colors, and I can see for miles. Then it hits me. *I'm* flying alone. It's great, almost tranquil, no instructor yelling things into my ear, just the machine and myself. A relaxed feeling comes over me, and I start to enjoy the flight. I check my instruments again and start to descend as I turn left.

11

Choice of details shows the writer's growing calm once airborne

Turning on the final approach, I announce my intentions on the radio. The nice feeling of calm leaves me just as quickly as it came. What is there to worry about, Andrew? All you have to do is land the airplane, preferably on the runway. My heart starts to pound

12

quickly, almost to the beat of the motor. Where is my instructor? Why am I alone?

Writer addresses himself directly as he once again challenges his fears

Lower the nose, Andrew. Don't lose speed. Give it some more power, maintain your glidepath. That's it. Bank a little to the left. Now you're doing it, just a little further. My ears begin to pop as the pressure on them decreases, and the motor gets quieter as I start to decrease power. The plane passes over the threshold of the runway. I begin to raise the nose. The wheels utter a squeal as they touch down, but the impact quickly sends the plane back into the air. The wheels hit again; this time they stay down, and I roll to a stop.

Short sentences enhance tension and drama of landing

Writer comments on the meaning of his first solo flight

Back at the hangar, I climb out of the plane and shudder as the cool air hits me again. A smile comes across my face, and it persists. I told myself that I would just be cool about it and not try to show any emotion, but it isn't going to work. I can't stop smiling as my instructor congratulates me. I smile because I know that I was successful in challenging and over-coming my fears.

13

14

Student Reflection
Andrew Kauser

Q. Your narration is chronological. Did you consider other patterns of organization?

A. I didn't think much about patterns other than chronological. For the most part, I felt I had no choice but to write it that way. I did have difficulty in beginning the narrative because I wasn't sure whether I wanted to write it in the past or the present tense. I made many attempts at different beginnings, from describing waking up on the morning of my flight to describing how I spent my summer flying. Once I found a beginning that I liked, it was relatively easy to write the rest of the essay because I just wrote about the events in the order that they happened. The beginning solved my tense problem as well.

Q. Why did you feel your narration was worth telling? What was your purpose?

A. The experience I had with flying was fresh in my mind, and at the time it seemed to be the most interesting thing that had happened to me recently. The purpose of the narrative was to share my experience of flying with the class. When I used to fly with my dad, I was afraid of flying because I didn't know how to operate the plane. In a way, it was a challenge to myself to find out how to fly. I guess I just wanted to tell the readers that you don't get anywhere by just sitting around being afraid.

Q. You don't use any dialogue, or do you?
A. In paragraph 12 of the narration I do use dialogue—dialogue without quotation marks, however. It is a kind of interior monologue in which I hear my instructor talking to me. I tried other ways of writing the paragraph, but it really didn't come off as well. This passage was very easy for me to write because it was exactly what I was thinking when I was up there.

Q. In writing the essay, what gave you the most trouble? How did you go about solving the problem(s)?
A. I ran into two problems. The first problem, as I said, was in starting the essay. I knew what I wanted to write about and pretty much what I wanted to say, but I couldn't find a proper beginning for the narrative. I made many attempts at an introduction, but none of them really worked. Finally, I cut a lot of material out that I didn't need and made my beginning much shorter. The second problem I had was trying to make the audience grasp what I was talking about. The first time I read my essay to the class, their reaction was that I didn't use enough detail and so they really didn't feel as though they were there with me. I consequently included many more details when I read the essay, and they were able to understand the experience better.

Q. How important was it for you to set a context for the essay?
A. Context is very important in anything that you write, but especially a narrative. The experience I recount in my essay took place in a specific time and place. It wouldn't have been the same narrative if it had taken place in some other city or country. Basically, the narrative is specific to that situation, and it wouldn't be credible to me in another situation.

Your Response

What did you learn from Andrew's essay and reflection? What challenges do you expect to face as you write your own narrative essay? Based on Andrew's experiences and the practical advice discussed earlier in this chapter (pages 82–87), how will you overcome those challenges?

The Terror

JUNOT DÍAZ

Junot Díaz's writing focuses on Dominican culture and history and on the immigrant experience. Born in 1968 in the Dominican Republic, Díaz moved to New Jersey with his family at age six. He graduated from Rutgers University, working as a dishwasher and gas station attendant and delivering pool tables to help pay his way through school. After college, he served as an editorial assistant at Rutgers University Press and then went on to earn his MFA from Cornell University in 2005. Currently, he is a professor of writing at Massachusetts Institute of Technology and fiction editor at the *Boston Review*.

Photo by D Dipasupil/FilmMagic/ Getty Images

Díaz's books include the short story collection *Drown* (1995), the Pulitzer Prize–winning *The Brief Wondrous Life of Oscar Wao* (2007), and *This Is How You Lose Her* (2012). Some of his many awards include a MacArthur "Genius" Fellowship, the National Book Critics Circle Award, and the PEN/O. Henry Award. All of his books have been national best sellers. Díaz is also a cofounder of Voices of Our Nation workshop, an organization whose goal "is to develop emerging writers of color through programs and workshops taught by established writers of color."

This essay appeared in the July 2015 *The New York Times Magazine*, in an issue focused on the theme of mental health. As you read, pay close attention to the way Díaz uses language to convey his emotions and to reflect on his experience.

Preparing to Read

What books were powerful to you when you were in middle school, and why? How did they, or any one book in particular, influence your actions and behavior?

I got jumped at a pretty bad time in my life. Not that there's ever a *good* time. 1

What I mean is that I was already deep in the vulnerability matrix. I 2 had just entered seventh grade, was at peak adolescent craziness and, to make matters worse, was dealing with a new middle school whose dreary white middle-class bigotry was cutting the heart out of me. I wasn't two periods into my first day before a classmate called me a "sand nigger," as if it were no big deal. Someone else asked me if my family ate dogs every day or only once in a while. By my third month, that school had me feeling like the poorest, ugliest immigrant freak in the universe.

My home life was equally trying. My father abandoned the family 3 the year before, plunging our household into poverty. No sooner than that happened, my brother, who was one year older and my best friend and protector, was found to have leukemia, the kind that in those days had a real nasty habit of killing you. One day he was sprawled on our front stoop in London Terrace holding court, and the next he was up in Newark, 40 pounds lighter and barely able to piss under his own power, looking as if he were one bad cold away from the grave.

I didn't know what to do with myself. I tried to be agreeable, to make friends, but that didn't work so hot; mostly I just slouched in my seat, hating my clothes and my glasses and my face. Sometimes I wrote my brother letters. Made it sound as though I were having a great time at school — a ball. 4

> **Eventually the bruises and the rage faded, but not the fear. The fear remained. An awful withering dread that coiled around my bowels — that followed me into my dreams.**

And then came the beat-down. Not at school, as I would have expected, but on the other side of the neighborhood. At the hands and feet of these three brothers I dimly knew. The youngest was my age, and on the day in question we had a spat over something — I can't remember what. I do remember pushing him down hard onto the sidewalk and laughing about it, and the kid running off in tears, swearing he was going to kill me. Then the scene in my head jumps, and the next thing I know, the kid comes back with his two older brothers, and I'm getting my face punched in. The older brothers held me down and let the younger brother punch me all he wanted. I cried out for my brother, but he was in Beth Israel Hospital, saving no one. I remember one of the older ones saying, "Hit him in the *teeth*." 5

As these things go, it wasn't too bad. I didn't actually lose any teeth or break any limbs or misplace an eye. Afterward, I even managed to limp home. My mother was at the hospital, so no one noticed that I had gotten stomped. Even took my blackened eye to classes the next day, but because my assailants attended another school, I didn't have to tell the truth. I said, "It happened in karate." 6

My first real beat-down, and I was furious and ashamed, but above all else I was afraid. Afraid of my assailants. Afraid they would corner me again. Afraid of a second beat-down. Afraid and afraid and afraid. Eventually the bruises and the rage faded, but not the fear. The fear remained. An awful withering dread that coiled around my bowels — that followed me into my dreams. ("Hit him in the *teeth*.") I guess I should have told someone, but I was too humiliated. And besides, my No. 1 confidant, my brother, wasn't available. 7

So I locked up the whole miserable affair deep inside. I thought that would help, but avoidance only seemed to give it more strength. 8

Without even thinking about it, I started doing everything I could to duck the brothers. I shunned their part of the neighborhood. I started looking around buildings to make sure the coast was clear. I stayed in the apartment a lot more, reading three, four books a week. And whenever I saw the brothers, together or individually—in a car, on a bike, on foot—the fear would spike through me so powerfully that I felt as though I was going to lose my mind. In *Dune*, a novel I adored in those days, Frank Herbert observed that "Fear is the mind-killer," and let me tell you, my man knows of what he speaks. When the brothers appeared, I couldn't think for nothing. I would drop whatever I was doing and *get away*, and it was only later, after I calmed down, that I would realize what I had done. 9

The brothers didn't pursue me. They would jeer at me and occasionally throw rocks, but even if they weren't chasing me in the flesh, they sure were chasing me in spirit. After these encounters, I would be a mess for days: depressed, irritable, hypervigilant, ashamed. I hated these brothers from the bottom of my heart, but even more than them, I hated myself for my cowardice. 10

Before that attack, I had felt fear plenty of times—which poor immigrant kid hasn't?—but after my beating, *I became afraid*. And at any age, that is a dismal place to be. 11

Given all the other crap I was facing, my adolescence was never going to win any awards. But sometimes I like to think that if that beat-down didn't happen, I might have had an easier time of it. Maybe a whole bunch of other awfulness would not have happened. But who can really know? In the end, the fear become another burden I had to shoulder—like having a sick brother or brown skin in a white school. 12

Took me until I was a sophomore in high school—yes, that long—before I finally found it in me to start facing my terror. By then, my older brother was in remission and wearing a wig to hide his baldness. Maybe his improbable survival was what gave me courage, or maybe it was all the Robert Cormier I was reading—his young heroes were always asking themselves, "Do I dare disturb the universe?" before ultimately deciding that yes, they did dare. Whatever it was, one day I found myself fleeing from a sighting of the brothers, and suddenly I was brought up short by an appalling vision: me running away forever. 13

I forced myself to stop. I forced myself to turn toward them, and it felt as if the whole world was turning with me. I couldn't make myself walk toward them, I could barely even look at them, so I settled for standing still. As the brothers approached, the ground started tilting out from under me. One of them scowled. 14

And then, without a word, they walked past. 15

Thinking Critically about the Text

Were you ever bullied, either emotionally or physically? Remember the circumstances and how you felt. Did you alter any of your routines to try to avoid whoever was bothering you, and were you successful? Did you have a protector you could rely on (as Díaz described his brother to be before he got sick)? How and when did the bullying stop?

Questions on Subject

1. Why do Díaz's classmates call him names and ask him if his family eats dogs?

2. Why do you think Díaz wrote to his brother making "it sound as though I were having a great time" (paragraph 4)? Why would he lie?

3. In paragraph 11, Díaz writes that he "had felt fear plenty of times" but that "after my beating, *I became afraid*." What is the difference between feeling fear and being afraid? Provide examples from your own life to support your answer.

4. Díaz quotes the writer Robert Cormier's heroes, who ask themselves, "Do I dare disturb the universe?" (paragraph 13). Does Díaz think he disturbed the universe in the course of this story, and if so, how?

Questions on Strategy

1. Díaz's essay opens dramatically: "I got jumped at a pretty bad time in my life." But instead of narrating the details of his beating immediately, he provides three paragraphs of background, or context, first. Why do you think he delays telling readers about the actual beating? How would the essay be different if he had described the beating in the first paragraph?

2. Díaz shares just a few details to make us understand how sick his brother is. What details does he use, and why are they powerful?

3. In paragraph 5, Díaz switches from past to present tense for one sentence: "Then the scene in my head jumps, and the next thing I know, the kid comes back with his two older brothers, and I'm getting my face punched in." What is the effect of this shift in tense?

4. What time markers does Díaz use to help him organize, or **sequence**, his narrative? Locate and list as many as you can. How do they help the reader understand Díaz's story, both in the past and in the present?

Narration in Action

Write your birth date at the top of a piece of paper and the date you're doing this activity at the bottom. In between, fill in any significant dates you can think of. There are no rules about what to record, as long as each event has some importance to you. Some possible entries might be:

- the first day of preschool or kindergarten
- accomplishing something important (such as reading a book, learning to swim, teaching someone something, winning an award or a race)

- the birth of a younger sibling or a niece or nephew
- moving to a new home or new school
- learning to drive

Once your list is finished, add details about each event. As you do so, you'll notice that you're already comfortable with some of the key elements of narrative: context, organization, and details.

Writing Suggestions

1. Think of a time you were deeply frightened of something or someone. If you have moved past that fear, try to explain how you did so. What inspiration or combination of circumstances helped you find the courage to stop being afraid? If you are still afraid, what strategies do you use to cope? What do you think might help you find the courage to move past your fear? Using Díaz's narrative as a model, write an essay about an event related to this fear. Be sure to establish a context for this event, select meaningful details, and consider how you want to organize those details.

2. **Writing in the Workplace.** Imagine that you will be attending a national conference, representing the office where you work. For one of the opening small-group sessions, you have been asked to prepare a three- to five-minute narrative in which you tell a revealing story about yourself as a way of introducing yourself to the group. What do you think others would be interested in knowing about you? Does the story you choose relate to your imagined career in any way? You may find it helpful to review the list of significant events you created for the Narration in Action activity for this reading.

Not Close Enough for Comfort

DAVID P. BARDEEN

David P. Bardeen was born in 1974 in New Haven, Connecticut, and grew up in Seattle, Washington. He graduated cum laude from Harvard University in 1996 and then worked for J. P. Morgan & Co. as an investment banking analyst. In 2002, he received his JD from the New York University School of Law, where he was the managing editor of the school's *Law Review*. After graduation, he

Courtesy of David Bardeen

joined the law firm Cleary, Gottlieb, Steen & Hamilton, where his practice focused on international business transactions involving clients in Latin America. Currently, he is corporate counsel with Ziff Brothers Investments. A freelance writer on a variety of topics, he is also active with Immigration Equality, a national organization fighting for the equality for lesbian, gay, bisexual, transgender, and HIV-positive immigrants.

In the following article, which appeared in the *New York Times Magazine* on February 29, 2004, Bardeen tells the story of a lunch meeting at which he reveals a secret to his twin brother, a secret that had derailed their relationship for almost fifteen years.

Preparing to Read

Recall a time when a parent, sibling, friend, teacher, or some other person close to you kept a secret from you. How did the secret affect your relationship? How did you feel once the secret was revealed? How has the relationship fared since?

had wanted to tell Will I was gay since I was twelve. As twins, we shared   1
everything back then: clothes, gadgets, thoughts, secrets. Everything except this. So when we met for lunch more than a year ago, I thought that finally coming out to him would close the distance that had grown between us. When we were kids, we created our own language, whispering to each other as our bewildered parents looked on. Now, at twenty-eight, we had never been further apart.

I asked him about his recent trip. He asked me about work. Short ques-   2
tions. One-word answers. Then an awkward pause.

Will was one of the last to know. Partly it was his fault. He is hard to   3
pin down for brunch or a drink, and this was not the sort of conversation I wanted to have over the phone. I had actually been trying to tell him for more than a month, but he kept canceling at the last minute—a friend was in town, he'd met a girl.

But part of me was relieved. This was the talk I had feared the most. Coming out is, in an unforgiving sense, an admission of fraud. Fraud against yourself primarily, but also fraud against your family and friends. So, once I resolved to tell my secret, I confessed to my most recent "victims" first. I told my friends from law school—those I had met just a few years earlier and deceived the least—then I worked back through college to the handful of high-school friends I still keep in touch with.

Keeping my sexuality from my parents had always seemed permissible, so our sit-down chat did not stress me out as much as it might have. We all mislead our parents. "I'm too sick for school today." "No, I wasn't drinking." "Yes, Mom, I'm fine. Don't worry about me." That deception is understood and, in some sense, expected. But twins expect complete transparency, however romantic the notion.

> **I had wanted to tell Will I was gay since I was twelve. As twins, we shared everything back then: clothes, gadgets, thoughts, secrets. Everything except this.**

Although our lives unfolded along parallel tracks—we went to college together, both moved to New York and had many of the same friends—Will and I quietly drifted apart. When he moved abroad for a year, we lost touch almost entirely. Our mother and father didn't think this was strange, because like many parents of twins, they wanted us to follow divergent paths. But friends were baffled when we began to rely on third parties for updates on each other's lives. "How's Will?" someone would ask. "You tell me," I would respond. One mutual friend, sick of playing the intermediary, once sent me an e-mail message with a carbon copy to Will. "Dave, meet Will, your twin," it said. "Will, let me introduce you to Dave."

Now, here we were, at lunch, just the two of us. "There's something I've been meaning to tell you," I said. "I'm gay." I looked at him closely, at the edges of his mouth, the wrinkles around his eyes, for some hint of what he was thinking.

"O.K.," he said evenly.

"I've been meaning to tell you for a while," I said.

"Uh-huh." He asked me a few questions but seemed slightly uneasy, as if he wasn't sure he wanted to hear the answers. Do Mom and Dad know? Are you seeing anyone? How long have you known you were gay? I hesitated.

I've known since I was young, and to some degree, I thought Will had always known. How else to explain my adolescent melancholy, my withdrawal, the silence when the subject changed to girls, sex, and who was hot. As a teenager I watched, as if from a distance, as my demeanor went from outspoken to sullen. I had assumed, in the self-centered way kids often do, that everyone noticed this change—and that my brother had guessed the reason. To be fair, he asked me once in our twenties, after I had ended yet another brief relationship with a woman. "Of course I'm not gay," I told him, as if the notion were absurd.

"How long have you known?" he asked again. 12

"About fifteen years," I said. Will looked away. 13

Food arrived. We ate and talked about other things. Mom, Dad, the 14 mayor, and the weather. We asked for the check and agreed to get together again soon. No big questions, no heart to heart. Just disclosure, explanation, follow-up, conclusion. But what could I expect? I had shut him out for so long that I suppose ultimately he gave up. Telling my brother I was gay hadn't made us close, as I had naively hoped it would; instead it underscored just how much we had strayed apart.

As we left the restaurant, I felt the urge to apologize, not for being gay, of 15 course, but for the years I'd kept him in the dark, for his being among the last to know. He hailed a cab. It stopped. He stepped inside, the door still open.

"I'm sorry," I said. 16

He smiled. "No, I think it's great." 17

A nice gesture. Supportive. But I think he misunderstood. 18

A year later, we are still only creeping toward the intimacy everyone 19 expects us to have. Although we live three blocks away from each other, I can't say we see each other every week or even every two weeks. But with any luck, next year, I'll be the one updating our mutual friends on Will's life.

Thinking Critically about the Text

How do you think Will felt when David announced that he was gay? Do you think Will had any clue about David's sexual orientation? What in Will's response to David's announcement led you to this conclusion? Why do you think it was so difficult for them to recapture the "intimacy everyone expects [them] to have" (paragraph 19) in the year following David's coming out to Will?

Questions on Subject

1. Why do you suppose Bardeen chose to keep his sexual orientation a secret from his brother? Why was this particular "coming out" so difficult? Was Bardeen realistic in thinking that "Will had always known" (paragraph 11) that he was gay?

2. What does Bardeen mean when he says, "But twins expect complete transparency, however romantic the notion" (paragraph 5)?

3. Why does Bardeen feel the need to apologize to his brother as they part? Do you think his brother understood the meaning of the apology? Why, or why not?

4. What do you think Bardeen had hoped would happen after he confided his secret to his brother? Was this hope unrealistic?

Questions on Strategy

1. Bardeen narrates his coming out using the first-person pronoun *I*. Why is the first-person **point of view** particularly appropriate for telling a story such as this one? Explain.

2. How has Bardeen **organized** his narrative? In paragraphs 3 through 6, Bardeen uses flashbacks to give readers a context for his relationship with his twin. What would have been lost or gained had he begun his essay with paragraphs 3 through 6?

3. During the lunch-meeting part of the narrative (paragraphs 7-17), Bardeen uses **dialogue**. What does he gain by doing this? Why do you suppose he uses dialogue sparingly elsewhere?

4. Bardeen uses a number of short sentences and deliberate sentence fragments. What effect do these have on you? Why do you suppose he uses some sentence fragments instead of complete sentences? Identify some particularly strong examples from the text to support your answer.

Narration in Action

Good narrative depends on a sense of continuity or flow, a logical ordering of events and ideas. The following sentences, which make up the first paragraph of E. B. White's essay "Once More to the Lake," have been rearranged. Place the sentences in what seems to be a coherent sequence based on such language signals as transitions, repeated words, pronouns, and temporal references. Be prepared to explain your reason for the placement of each sentence.

1. I have since become a salt-water man, but sometimes in summer there are days when the restlessness of the tides and the fearful cold of the sea water and the incessant wind that blows across the afternoon and into the evening make me wish for the placidity of a lake in the woods.

2. We all got ringworm from some kittens and had to rub Pond's Extract on our arms and legs night and morning, and my father rolled over in a canoe with all his clothes on; but outside of that the vacation was a success and from then on none of us ever thought there was any place in the world like that lake in Maine.

3. A few weeks ago this feeling got so strong I bought myself a couple of bass hooks and a spinner and returned to the lake where we used to go, for a week's fishing and to revisit old haunts.

4. One summer, along about 1904, my father rented a camp on a lake in Maine and took us all there for the month of August.

5. We returned summer after summer — always on August 1st for one month.

Writing Suggestions

1. Using your Preparing to Read response for this selection, write an essay about a secret you once had and how it affected relationships with those close to you. What exactly was your secret? Why did you decide to keep this information secret? How did you feel while you kept your secret? What happened when you revealed your secret? What insights into secrets do you have as a result of this experience?

2. The following photograph was taken at a gay pride festival in 2012. How do you "read" this photograph? (For a discussion of how to analyze photographs, see "Reading Photographs and Visual Texts" in Chapter 1, pages 17–21). How do you interpret the message on her T-shirt? How do her expression and her surroundings impact your reading of this photo? Using Bardeen's essay, this photograph, and your own observations and experiences, write an essay about the mixed feelings and emotions as well as the potential misunderstandings attendant on coming out.

© Ed Simons/Alamy Stock Photo

The Work You Do,
The Person You Are

TONI MORRISON

Matthew Horwood / Getty Images

A Nobel Prize–winning novelist, editor, and professor, Toni Morrison was born in Lorain, Ohio, in 1931. She earned a bachelor's degree from Howard University and received a master's in English from Cornell University. In the mid-1960s, she began a career as a fiction editor at Random House, where she worked with prominent authors such as Chinua Achebe and Toni Cade Bambara. She published her own first book of fiction, *The Bluest Eye*, in 1970. In the years that followed, Morrison produced a string of celebrated novels, including *Sula* (1973), *Song of Solomon* (1977), and — perhaps most famously — *Beloved* (1987). Her work often explores the intersections of race, female identity, and history, among other themes. In the early 1980s, she left her publishing career to write and teach at the State University of New York, Rutgers University, and Princeton University, where she held the Robert F. Goheen Chair in the Humanities. In addition to the Nobel Prize, Morrison has received the Pulitzer Prize, the American Book Award, and the Presidential Medal of Freedom.

In this short narrative, first published as part of a 2017 *New Yorker* magazine series on the subject of work, Morrison recalls her childhood experience cleaning the house of a relatively affluent woman. In reflecting on the pleasures and pressures of this job, she comes to an insightful conclusion about her relationship with work.

Preparing to Read

Have you ever had a paying job? Do you have one now? To what degree do you define yourself and your identity by the work you do or plan to do in your intended career? If you have not worked, how much do you think your identity is defined by your role as a student?

All I had to do for the two dollars was clean Her house for a few hours   1
after school. It was a beautiful house, too, with a plastic-covered sofa and chairs, wall-to-wall blue-and-white carpeting, a white enamel stove, a washing machine and a dryer—things that were common in Her neighborhood, absent in mine. In the middle of the war, She had butter, sugar, steaks, and seam-up-the-back stockings.

I knew how to scrub floors on my knees and how to wash clothes in our   2
zinc tub, but I had never seen a Hoover vacuum cleaner or an iron that wasn't heated by fire.

Part of my pride in working for Her was earning money I could squander: 3
on movies, candy, paddleballs, jacks, ice-cream cones. But a larger part of my

pride was based on the fact that I gave half my wages to my mother, which meant that some of my earnings were used for real things—an insurance-policy payment or what was owed to the milkman or the iceman. The pleasure of being necessary to my parents was profound. I was not like the children in folktales: burdensome mouths to feed, nuisances to be corrected, problems so severe that they were abandoned to the forest. I had a status that doing routine chores in my house did not provide—and it earned me a slow smile, an approving nod from an adult. Confirmations that I was adultlike, not childlike.

In those days, the forties, children were not just loved or liked; they were needed. They could earn money; they could care for children younger than themselves; they could work the farm, take care of the herd, run errands, and much more. I suspect that children aren't needed in that way now. They are loved, doted on, protected, and helped. Fine, and yet . . .

Little by little, I got better at cleaning Her house—good enough to be given more to do, much more. I was ordered to carry bookcases upstairs and, once, to move a piano from one side of a room to the other. I fell carrying the bookcases. And after pushing the piano my arms and legs hurt so badly. I wanted to refuse, or at least to complain, but I was afraid She would fire me, and I would lose the freedom the dollar gave me, as well as the standing I had at home—although both were slowly being eroded. She began to offer me her clothes, for a price. Impressed by these worn things, which looked simply gorgeous to a little girl who had only two dresses to wear to school, I bought a few. Until my mother asked me if I really wanted to work for castoffs. So I learned to say "No, thank you" to a faded sweater offered for a quarter of a week's pay.

> " Go to work. Get your money. And come on home. "

Still, I had trouble summoning the courage to discuss or object to the increasing demands She made. And I knew that if I told my mother how unhappy I was she would tell me to quit. Then one day, alone in the kitchen with my father, I let drop a few whines about the job. I gave him details, examples of what troubled me, yet although he listened intently, I saw no sympathy in his eyes. No "Oh, you poor little thing." Perhaps he understood that what I wanted was a solution to the job, not an escape from it. In any case, he put down his cup of coffee and said, "Listen. You don't live there. You live here. With your people. Go to work. Get your money. And come on home."

That was what he said. This was what I heard:

1. Whatever the work is, do it well—not for the boss but for yourself.
2. You make the job; it doesn't make you.
3. Your real life is with us, your family.
4. You are not the work you do; you are the person you are.

I have worked for all sorts of people since then, geniuses and morons,   8
quick-witted and dull, bighearted and narrow. I've had many kinds of jobs,
but since that conversation with my father I have never considered the level
of labor to be the measure of myself, and I have never placed the security of
a job above the value of home.

Thinking Critically about the Text

In this essay, Morrison relates a deeply personal story. What larger, perhaps even
universal, meaning does her narrative have for others?

Questions on Subject

1. What was the most profound pleasure that Morrison took in earning money?

2. Morrison suspects that children are viewed and treated differently now than they
were in the 1940s. How would you summarize the difference, as she sees it?

3. What did Morrison's employer begin to offer her as part of her payment? What
was Morrison's response, and why do you think she responded that way?

4. Morrison became unhappy with certain aspects of the job, but she did not
want to tell her mother about her concerns. Why? What does her response
say about the impact parents can have on their children's careers?

Questions on Strategy

1. Often, narratives begin with background and context to orient the reader.
Does Morrison provide such context in the opening of "The Work You Do, The
Person You Are"? Do you find her approach confusing? Clear? Should she
supply more background information? Explain your answer.

2. Where in the essay does Morrison use transitional words or phrases to clarify
the sequence of events? Point to specific examples.

3. Morrison quotes her father's words directly. But then she conveys them to the
reader by "what [she] heard." Why do you think she does this? And why does
she choose to present her points as a numbered list?

4. Morrison refers to her employer by using only the capitalized pronouns "She"
and "Her." Why do you think she made that choice?

Narration in Action

Narration should do more than merely recount events in a sequence. Indeed, effective narrative writing usually presents, explores, and resolves conflict(s): problems,
tensions, questions. With this in mind, look again at Morrison's brief personal narrative. In a class discussion, or within small groups, identify all the conflicts presented in the essay. Then, explain how the writer resolves them in the narrative.
Finally, discuss how the resolution of the essay's conflict (or conflicts) leads to the
writer's thesis or key insights.

Writing Suggestions

1. In the conclusion of her essay, Morrison writes, "I have never considered the level of labor to be the measure of myself, and I have never placed the security of a job above the value of home." How do you respond to her key insight? Refer back to your answers to the questions in Preparing to Read. How do you see the connection between your current job, your role as a student, or your imagined career (on one hand) and your identity (on the other)? Do you measure yourself by your achievements, either as a student now or in terms of the professional life you imagine for yourself in the future? Write a narrative about yourself that addresses the issues about work and home that Morrison discusses in her essay.

2. Morrison's narrative is personal and specific. Yet, she reflects on — and interprets — her experience through writing in a way that makes her auto-biographical story significant for readers. Keeping Morrison's essay in mind, write a narrative about an experience in your own life that shaped or changed your point of view about a topic, problem, or question. What was the conflict? What was your reaction? What are the key details and events related to the experience? You may want to incorporate a numbered list of insights, as Morrison does. As best as you can, try to avoid reducing your experience to a pat lesson, moral, or cliché.

A Shepherd's Life

JAMES REBANKS

Ian Rutherford/REX/Shutterstock.com

Shepherd, farmer, and best-selling author James Rebanks was born in 1975 and grew up in a sheepherding family in the Lake District of northern England. He left school at fifteen to travel and work on his family's farm. Later, Rebanks completed his formal education at Oxford University, but he returned to focus on cultivating sheep. "There's a false hierarchy," he told the British newspaper *The Daily Mail* in 2015. "People think book stuff is hard and that you only work on a farm if you've got no brains. But it's the reverse. It takes way more brains to breed Herdwick sheep. There are layers and layers of things you need to know. It takes generations to build a great flock." As both a consultant at his own company and an expert adviser to the United Nations Educational, Scientific and Cultural Organization (UNESCO), Rebanks also works on sustainable tourism and the preservation of cultural heritage in the Lake District.

While he has been writing since the late 1990s, Rebanks became an Internet celebrity when his Twitter feed (@herdyshepherd1) became a surprise sensation in 2012. He wrote about this phenomenon in a 2013 article for the *Atlantic* magazine, "Why This Shepherd Loves Twitter." In 2015, he published the memoir *The Shepherd's Life: A Tale of the Lake District*, from which the selection below is excerpted.

Preparing to Read

Rebanks writes about what it means to remain in the place — and within the traditions — where he was born and grew up. How do you view your own hometown? Do you see it as a place where people (in Rebanks's words) are "doing something" with their lives? Do you feel compelled to move away? Or do you identify with Rebanks's desire to stay?

I realized we were different, really different, on a rainy morning in 1987. I was in an assembly at the 1960s shoddy built concrete comprehensive school in our local town. I was thirteen or so years old. Sitting surrounded by a mass of other academic non-achievers listening to an old battle-weary teacher lecturing us how we should aim to be more than just farmworkers, joiners, brickies, electricians, and hairdressers. We were basically sorted aged twelve between those deemed intelligent (who were sent to a "grammar school") and those of us that weren't (who stayed at the "comprehensive"). Her words flowed past us without registering, a sermon she'd delivered many times before. It was a waste of time and she knew it. We were firmly set, like our fathers and grandfathers, mothers and grandmothers before us, on being what we were, and had always been. Plenty of us were bright enough, but we had no intention of displaying it in school. It would have been dangerous.

There was a chasm between that headmistress and us. The kids who gave a damn had departed the year before, leaving the losers to fester away the next three years in a place no one wanted to be. The result was something akin to a guerrilla war between largely disillusioned teachers and some of the most bored and aggressive kids imaginable. We played a game as a class where the object was to smash school equipment of the greatest value in one lesson and pass it off as an accident. 2

I was good at that kind of thing. 3

The floor was littered with broken microscopes, biological specimens, crippled stools, and torn books. A long-dead frog pickled in formaldehyde lay sprawled on the floor, doing the breaststroke. The gas taps were burning like an oil rig and a window was cracked. The teacher stared at us with tears streaming down her face, destroyed, as a lab technician tried to restore order. One math lesson was improved for me by a fistfight between a pupil and the teacher before the lad ran for it down the stairs and across the muddy playing fields, only to be knocked down by the teacher. We cheered as if it were a great tackle in a game of rugby. From time to time someone would try (incompetently) to burn the school down. One day some kid climbed up the drainpipe at the edge of the playground, like Spider-Man minus the outfit, and then he sat on the roof of the gym, his legs dangling over the edge. He just sat there grinning inanely, thirty-five feet above the tarmac. The news went round the school like the wind, kids running to see the kid that had "gone crazy." We stood below, curiously, until some joker shouted "jump" and everyone laughed. I stood back a few steps just in case. The teachers went crazy, running to and fro, calling the fire service and police. No one was quite sure if he'd gone up there to jump off. Eventually they talked him off the roof. No one ever really knew why he did it, but we didn't see him in school much after that. 4

On another occasion, I argued with our dumbfounded headmaster that school was really a prison and "an infringement of my human rights." He looked at me strangely, and said, "But what would you do at home?" Like this was an impossible question to answer. "I'd work on the farm," I answered, equally amazed that he couldn't see how simple this was. He shrugged his shoulders hopelessly, told me to stop being ridiculous and go away. When people got into serious trouble, he sent them home. So I thought about putting a brick through his window, but didn't dare. 5

So in that assembly in 1987 I was daydreaming through the windows into the rain, wondering what the men on our farm were doing, and what I should have been doing, when I realized the assembly was about the valleys of the Lake 6

District, where my grandfather and father farmed. I switched on. After a few minutes of listening, I realized this bloody teacher woman thought we were too stupid and unimaginative to "do anything with our lives." She was taunting us to rise above ourselves. We were too dumb to want to leave this area with its dirty dead-end jobs and its narrow-minded provincial ways. There was nothing here for us—we should open our eyes and see it. In her eyes to want to leave school early and go and work with sheep was to be more or less an idiot.

> ❝ The idea that we, our fathers, and mothers might be proud, hardworking, and intelligent people doing something worthwhile or even admirable was beyond her. ❞

The idea that we, our fathers, and mothers might be proud, hardworking, and intelligent people doing something worthwhile or even admirable was beyond her. For a woman who saw success as being demonstrated through education, ambition, adventure, and conspicuous professional achievement we must have seemed a poor sample. No one ever mentioned "university" in this school. No one wanted to go anyway. People who went away ceased to belong; they changed and could never really come back. We knew that in our bones. Schooling was a way out, but we didn't want it, and we'd made our choice. Later I would understand that modern people the world over are obsessed with the importance of "going somewhere" and "doing something" with your life. The implication is an idea I have come to hate, that staying local and doing physical work doesn't count for much. 7

I listened, getting more and more aggravated, as she claimed to love our land. But she talked about it, and thought of it, in terms that were completely alien to my family and me. She loved a wild landscape, full of mountains, lakes, leisure, and adventure, lightly peopled with folk who I had never met. The Lake District in her monologue was the playground for an itinerant band of climbers, poets, walkers, and daydreamers . . . people who, unlike our parents or us, had "really done something." She would utter the name Wordsworth in reverential tones and look in vain for us to respond with interest. 8

I'd never heard of him. 9

I don't think anyone in that hall, who wasn't a teacher, had. 10

Thinking Critically about the Text

Rebanks narrates a childhood experience that left him "more and more aggravated" (paragraph 8). In his telling, Rebanks's teachers and headmaster had a perception of him — and of life in general — that he disagreed with profoundly. Can you recall an experience like this in your own life, when teachers or other authority figures had a different point of view that made you frustrated and angry? How did you respond?

Questions on Subject

1. Rebanks writes that "[p]lenty of us were bright enough [to escape manual labor], but we had no intention of displaying it in school. It would have been dangerous" (paragraph 1). What do you think he means? Why would it have been "dangerous" to display intelligence?

2. What **dominant impression** of his school does Rebanks create in the fourth paragraph? How does he construct that impression?

3. In paragraph 6, Rebanks realizes that the assembly and the teacher's lecture are actually "about" something. What realization does he have? What idea is the teacher communicating? How does Rebanks respond?

4. According to Rebanks, "modern people" are obsessed with "going somewhere" or "doing something" with their lives. This point of view implies an idea that Rebanks has grown to hate. What is the idea? Why does he hate it?

Questions on Strategy

1. Rebanks is supposedly narrating the events of a "rainy morning in 1987" (paragraph 1). Where in the essay does he **transition** between his main narrative and other observations? How do these shifts affect the reader's sense of narrative time?

2. The third paragraph is one sentence long. Why do you think Rebanks chose to **emphasize** the paragraph in this way? What effect does it have?

3. In paragraph 8, Rebanks recounts his teacher's **description** of the Lake District. What do her details reveal about her ideals? Why does her characterization bother Rebanks?

4. Rebanks writes that the teacher giving the lecture "would utter the name Wordsworth in reverential tones and look in vain for us to respond with interest" (paragraph 8). Who is William Wordsworth? Why would the teacher refer to him in this context? What effect does including Wordsworth's name and its **connotations** have on the reader? What does Rebanks's response reveal?

Narration in Action

Consider the following prompt as the conclusion of a story: "The student stood up from her chair. She stared at the other students and then stared at the instructor. Without saying a word, she walked to the door and left the classroom." What happened that led to this situation? Working in small groups, come up with a brief narrative chain of events that explains the student's actions. When you are finished, compare your narrative with the narratives of other groups. How do they differ? How are they similar? What narrative explanations are the most convincing, and why?

Writing Suggestions

1. In this narration, Rebanks recalls an event from his childhood that angered and frustrated him. At the same time, the experience helped clarify his thinking and shape his point of view about work, life, and his community. What experiences in your own life have formed your identity or influenced your perspective? Choose a single, memorable event to focus your account. Then, write a narrative that begins with the basic template of Rebanks's opening sentence: "I realized _____ on a _____ in _____." Remember that important milestones (graduation, your first breakup, a memorable trip) can also be less obvious events that nevertheless led to an important realization.

2. Narration must do more than merely recount events in a sequence. Effective narrative writing usually presents, explores, and resolves conflict(s): problems, tensions, questions. In "The Shepherd's Life," Rebanks narrates and highlights the conflict with the teachers and authorities at his school, sometimes providing details of explicit conflict and argument. At the same time, good narration must suggest some resolution or self-knowledge from these confrontations, as Rebanks's writing does here. Think of a conflict in your own life with others, or even with yourself. Then, write a narrative account of the conflict that tries to resolve it or that at least suggests some insight from narrating and reflecting on the conflict.

Library of Congress, Prints & Photographs Division, FSA/OWI Collection, LC-USF34-013407-C

CHAPTER 5

Description

WHAT IS DESCRIPTION?

DESCRIBING SOMETHING WITH WORDS IS OFTEN COMPARED TO PAINTING a verbal picture. Both verbal description (like a magazine article profiling a celebrity) and visual description (like a photograph, painting, or drawing accompanying the article) seek to transform fleeting perceptions into lasting images—through words by authors and pixels, paints, or pencils used by artists. Both verbal and visual descriptions enable us to imaginatively experience the subject using some or all of our five senses. Both kinds of description convey information about a subject, telling us something we didn't know before. Both can convey a dominant impression of the subject. And, finally, both verbal and visual descriptions can be classed as objective or subjective, depending on how much they reveal the perspective of the person doing the describing.

VISUALIZING DESCRIPTION

This famous photograph — one of a series of portraits of Ella Watson, a custodial worker in a federal government building, taken by Gordon Parks in August 1942 — is a good example of description conveyed through strictly visual cues. In this portrait, Ella Watson poses with a broom and a mop, the tools she uses as a custodian, in front of a prominent backdrop of the American flag. How do you interpret the meaning of the composition that Parks, an African American, has set before his viewers? Is it one of harmony, conflict, dedication, loyalty, irony, or something else? What do the combined details of the visual convey about the United States?

UNDERSTANDING DESCRIPTION AS A WRITING STRATEGY

Writers often use the strategy of description to *inform* — to provide readers with specific data. You may need to describe the results of a chemical reaction for a lab report, the style of a Renaissance painting for an art history term paper, the physical capabilities and limitations of a stroke patient for a case study, or the acting of Charlize Theron in a movie you want your friends to see. Such descriptions will sometimes be scientifically objective, sometimes intensely impressionistic. The approach you use will depend on the subject itself, the information you want to communicate about it, and the format in which the description appears.

Another important use of description is to create a mood or atmosphere or even to convey your own views — to develop a dominant impression. Consider, for example, the following description by Bernd Heinrich from his book *One Man's Owl* (1987). In this selection, Heinrich describes trekking through the woods in search of owls. First, try to see, hear, smell, and feel the scene he describes: Form the jigsaw puzzle of words and details into a complete experience. Once you've accomplished this, define the dominant impression Heinrich creates.

<table>
<tr><td>Sets the scene with description of landscape</td><td>By mid-March in Vermont, the snow from the winter storms has already become crusty as the first midday thaws refreeze during the cold nights. A solid white cap compacts the snow, and you can walk on it without breaking through to your waist. The maple sap is starting to run on warm days, and one's blood quickens.</td></tr>
<tr><td>Describes sights and sounds of birds in early spring</td><td>Spring is just around the corner, and the birds act as if they know. The hairy and downy woodpeckers drum on dry branches and on the loose flakes of maple bark, and purple finches sing merrily from spruces. This year the reedy voices of the pine siskins can be heard everywhere on the ridge where the hemlocks grow, as can the chickadees' two-note, plaintive song. Down in the bog, the first red-winged blackbirds have just returned, and they can be heard yodeling from the tops of dry cattails. Flocks of rusty blackbirds fly over in long skeins, heading north.</td></tr>
<tr><td>Reveals his position and relies on auditory details as night approaches</td><td>From where I stand at the edge of the woods overlooking Shelburne Bog, I feel a slight breeze and hear a moaning gust sweeping through the forest behind me. It is getting dark. There are eery creaking and scraping noises. Inside the pine forest it is becoming black, pitch black. The songbirds are silent. Only the sound of the wind can be heard above the distant honks of Canada geese flying below the now starry skies. Suddenly I hear a booming hollow "hoo-hoo-*hoo*-hoo — ." The</td></tr>
</table>

> deep resonating hoot can send a chill down any spine, as indeed it has
> done to peoples of many cultures. But I know what the sound is, and
> it gives me great pleasure.

Heinrich could have described the scene with far fewer words, but that description would likely not have conveyed his dominant impression—one of the comfort with his natural surroundings. Heinrich reads the landscape with subtle insight; he knows all the different birds and understands their springtime habits. The reader can imagine the smile on Heinrich's face when he hears the call of the owl.

▎ Types of Description

There are essentially two types of description: objective and subjective. *Objective description* is as factual as possible, emphasizing the actual qualities of the subject being described while subordinating the writer's personal responses. For example, a witness to a mugging would try to give authorities a precise, objective description of the assailant, unaffected by emotional responses, so that a positive identification could be made. In the excerpt from his book, Bernd Heinrich objectively describes what he sees: "The hairy and downy woodpeckers drum on dry branches and on the loose flakes of maple bark, and purple finches sing merrily from the spruces."

Subjective or *impressionistic description*, on the other hand, conveys the writer's personal opinion or impression of the object, often in language rich in modifiers and figures of speech. A food critic describing a memorable meal would write about it impressionistically, using colorful or highly subjective language. (In fact, relatively few words in English can describe the subtleties of smell and taste in neutral terms.) In "A Woman on the Street," Jeannette Walls uses objective and subjective description techniques to capture a picture of her mother and what she sees as her dilemma.

Notice that with objective description, it is usually the person, place, or thing being described that stands out, whereas with subjective description, the response of the person doing the describing is the most prominent feature. Most topics, however, lend themselves to both objective and subjective description, depending on the writer's purpose. You could write, for example, one of the following:

Objective: I have *exactly four weeks* to finish a history term paper.

Subjective: I have *all the time in the world* to finish my history term paper.

Subjective: I have *an outrageously short amount of time* to finish my history term paper.

Each type of description can be accurate and useful in its own way.

Although descriptive writing can stand alone, and often does, it is also used with other types of writing. In a narrative, descriptions provide the context for the story—and make the characters, settings, and events come alive. Description may also help to define an unusual object or animal, such as a giraffe, or to clarify the steps of a process, such as diagnosing an illness. Wherever it is used, good description creates vivid and specific pictures that clarify, create a mood, and build a dominant impression.

USING DESCRIPTION ACROSS THE DISCIPLINES

When writing essays in the academic disciplines, you will have many opportunities to use the strategy of description to both organize and strengthen the presentation of your ideas. To determine whether description is the right strategy for you in a particular essay, review the guidelines in Chapter 2, "Determining a Strategy for Developing Your Essay" (pages 34–35). Consider the following examples:

History

1. **MAIN IDEA:** Roman medicine, while primitive in some ways, was in general very advanced.
2. **QUESTION:** What primitive beliefs and advanced thinking characterize Roman medicine?
3. **STRATEGY:** Description. The direction word *characterize* signals the need to describe Roman medical practices and beliefs.
4. **SUPPORTING STRATEGY:** Comparison and contrast might be used to set off Roman practices and beliefs from those in later periods of history.

Chemistry

1. **MAIN IDEA:** The chemical ingredients in acid rain are harmful to humans and the environment.
2. **QUESTION:** What are the components of acid rain?
3. **STRATEGY:** Description. The direction word *components* suggests the need for a description of acid rain, including sulfuric acid, carbon monoxide, carbon dioxide, chlorofluorocarbons, and nitric acid.
4. **SUPPORTING STRATEGIES:** Cause and effect might be used to show the harm caused by acid rain. Process analysis might be used to explain how acid rain develops.

Psychology

1. **MAIN IDEA:** Law enforcement officers who are under abnormal stress manifest certain symptoms.
2. **QUESTION:** What comprises the symptoms?

3. **STRATEGY:** Description. The direction word *comprises* suggests the need for a picture or description of the *symptoms*.

4. **SUPPORTING STRATEGIES:** Comparison and contrast might be used to differentiate those officers suffering from stress. Process analysis might be used to explain how to carry out an examination to identify the symptoms of stress. Argumentation might be used to indicate the need for programs to test for excessive stress on the job.

PRACTICAL ADVICE FOR WRITING AN ESSAY OF DESCRIPTION

As you plan, write, and revise your essay of description, be mindful of the writing process guidelines described in Chapter 2. Pay particular attention to the basic requirements and essential ingredients of this writing strategy.

▶ Planning Your Essay of Description

Planning is an essential part of writing a good description essay. You can save yourself a great deal of work by taking the time to think about key building blocks of your essay before you actually begin to write.

Determine Your Purpose.   Begin by determining your purpose: Are you trying to inform, express your emotions, persuade, or entertain? While it is not necessary, or even desirable, to state your purpose explicitly, you must have a purpose that your readers recognize. If your readers do not see a purpose in your writing, they may be tempted to respond by asking, "So what?" Making your reason for writing clear in the first place will help you avoid this pitfall.

Use Description in the Service of an Idea.   Your readers will want to know why you chose to describe what you did. You should always write description with a thesis in mind, an idea you want to convey. For example, you might describe a canoe trip as one of both serenity and exhilarating danger to symbolize the contrasting aspects of nature. In his essay "A View from the Bridge" (see pages 8–10), Cherokee Paul McDonald uses description in the service of an idea, and that idea is description itself: McDonald needs to describe a fish so that a blind boy can "see" it. In the process of describing, the author comes to an epiphany: The act of describing the fish brings him closer to the essence of it. He realizes then that he has received from the boy more than he has given.

Show, Don't Tell: Use Specific Nouns and Action Verbs.   Inexperienced writers often believe that adjectives and adverbs are the basis for effective descriptions. They're right in one sense, but not wholly so. Although strong adjectives and adverbs are crucial, description also depends on well-chosen, specific nouns

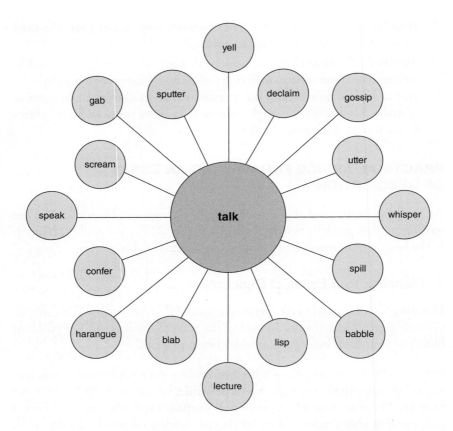

and verbs. *Vehicle* is not nearly as descriptive as something more specific—*Jeep*, *snowmobile*, or *Honda Civic*. Similarly, the verb *talk* does far less to describe the *way* something is said than do many possible substitutes (see the preceding diagram). The more specific and strong you make your nouns and verbs, the more lively and interesting your descriptions will be.

When you have difficulty thinking of specific action nouns and verbs to use, reach for a thesaurus—but only if you are sure you can discern the best word for your purpose. Most word-processing programs have a thesaurus utility, and there are many reasonable versions online as well. A thesaurus will help you keep your descriptions from getting repetitive and will be invaluable when you need to find a specific word with just the right meaning.

▶ Organizing Your Essay of Description

Create a Dominant Impression.   After generating as many details as possible describing your subject, reread them and select those that will be most helpful in developing a dominant impression. Suppose that you wish to depict the hospital emergency room as a place of great tension. You will naturally choose details to reinforce that sense of tension: the worried looks on the faces of a couple sitting in the corner, the quick movements of the medical staff as they tend to a patient on a wheeled stretcher, the urgent whisperings of two interns out in the hallway, the incessant paging of Dr. Thomas. If the dominant impression you want to create is of the emergency room's sterility, however, you will choose different details: the smell of disinfectant, the spotless white uniforms of the staff members, the stainless steel tables and chairs, the gleaming instruments the nurse hands to the physician.

Organize Your Details to Create a Vivid Picture.   Once you have decided which details to include and which to leave out, you need to arrange your details in an order that serves your purpose and is easy for the reader to follow.

In describing some subjects, one pattern that might make sense is to imagine what the reader would experience first. A description of an emergency room, for example, could begin at the entrance, move through the waiting area, pass the registration desk, and proceed into the treatment cubicles. A description of a restaurant kitchen might conjure up the smells and sounds that escape through the swinging doors even before moving on to the first glimpse inside the kitchen. Other patterns of organization include moving from general to specific, from smallest to largest, from least to most important, or from the usual to the unusual. The last details you present will probably stay in the reader's mind the longest, and the first details will also have special force.

Before you begin your first draft, you may find it useful to sketch an outline of your description. Here's a sample outline for Bernd Heinrich's description of his trek through the late winter landscape in search of owls (pages 114–15):

Description of Shelburne Bog

Dominant impression: Comfort with the natural surroundings

Paragraph 1: Snow-crusted landscape in mid-March

Paragraph 2: Activity and sounds of the birds (e.g., woodpeckers, finches, chickadees, and red-winged blackbirds) described from the edge of the woods

Paragraph 3: Activity and sounds inside the pine forest behind the speaker, culminating with the familiar call of the owl

Such an outline can remind you of the dominant impression you want to create and can suggest which specific details may be most useful to you.

▶ Revising and Editing Your Essay of Description

As the author, you are familiar with the scenes, people, or items you are describing. It might be helpful to find a fellow classmate to read your draft to ensure that he or she can vividly "see" whatever you are describing. The

"Brief Guide to Peer Critiquing" box in Chapter 2 (pages 38–39) will help to guide your classmate's review, just as the tips on common writing problems in Chapter 16 will help you in your own self-review.

Questions for Revising and Editing: Description

1. Do I have a clear purpose for my description? Have I answered the "so what" question?

2. Is the subject of my description interesting and relevant to my audience?

3. What senses have I chosen to use to describe it? For example, what does it look like, sound like, or smell like? Does it have a texture or taste that is important to mention?

4. Which details must I include in my essay? Which are irrelevant or distracting to my purpose and should be discarded?

5. Have I achieved the dominant impression I wish to leave with my audience?

6. Does the organization I have chosen for my essay make it easy for the reader to follow my description?

7. How carefully have I chosen my descriptive words? Are my nouns and verbs strong and specific?

8. Have I used figurative language, if appropriate, to further strengthen my description?

9. Does my paper contain any errors in grammar, punctuation, or mechanics? Is my sentence style as clear, smooth, and persuasive as possible?

STUDENT ESSAY USING DESCRIPTION AS A WRITING STRATEGY

Jim Tassé wrote the following essay while he was a student majoring in English and religion. As his essay "Trailcheck" reveals, Tassé is an enthusiastic skier. His experience working on ski patrol during winter breaks provided him with the subject for a striking description.

Trailcheck
Jim Tassé

Context — early morning in January and preparations for trailcheck

At a quarter to eight in the morning, the sharp cold of the midwinter night still hangs in the air of Smuggler's Notch. At the base of Madonna Mountain, we stamp our feet and turn up our collars while waiting for Dan to get the chairlift running. Trailcheck always begins with this cold, sleepy wait—but it can continue in many

1

Description of
trailcheck begins
with explanation of
what it is

different ways. The ski patrol has to make this first run
every morning to assess the trail conditions before the
mountain opens—and you never know what to expect
on top of the Mad Dog, Madonna Mountain. Sometimes
we take our first run down the sweet, light powder that
fell the night before; sometimes we have to ski the rock-
hard boilerplate ice that formed when yesterday's mush
froze. But there's always the cold—the dank, bleary cold
of 8 a.m. in January.

Use of present
tense gives
immediacy to the
description

I adjust my first-aid belt and heft my backpack up a   2
little higher, cinching it tight. I shiver, and pull my hat
down a bit lower. I am sleepy, cold, and impatient. Dan's
finally got the lift running, and the first two patrollers,
Chuck and Ken, get on. Three more chairs get filled,
and then there's me. Looks like I'm riding up alone. The
chairlift jars me a little more awake as it hits the back
of my boots. I sit down and am scooped into the air.

Description of
total experience
is enhanced by
appealing to
reader's senses —
especially touch,
hearing, and sight

It's a cold ride up, and I snuggle my chin deep into   3
my parka. The bumps of the chair going over the lift-
tower rollers help keep me awake. Trees piled high and
heavy with snow move silently past. Every so often, in
sudden randomness, a branch lets go a slide and the
air fills with snow dust as the avalanche crashes from
branch to branch, finally landing with a soft thud on
the ground. Snow dances in the air with kaleidoscopic
colors, shining in the early daylight.

Well-selected
details contribute
to description of
wintry mountain
and magic of
the day

I imagine what it would have been like on the   4
mountain on a similar day three hundred years ago.
A day like this would have been just as beautiful, or
maybe even more so—the silent mountain, all trees
and cold and sunshine, with no men and no lifts. I
think of the days when the fog rolls out of the notch,
and the wind blows cold and damp, and the trees
are close and dark in the mist, and I try to imagine
how terrifyingly wild the mountain would have been
centuries ago, before the white man came and installed
the chairlift that takes me to the top so easily. I think
how difficult it would have been to climb through the
thick untamed forest that bristles out of the mountain's
flanks, and I am glad I don't have to walk up Madonna
this sleepy-eyed morning.

I watch the woods pass, looking for the trails of   5
small animals scrolled around the trees. Skiing should
be nice with all the new snow. Arriving at the top,

I throw up the safety bar, tip my skis up, make contact, stand, and ski clear of the lift. The view from the mountaintop is incredible. I can see over the slopes of Stowe, where another patrol is running trailcheck just as we are. Across the state, Mt. Washington hangs above the horizon like a mirage. Back toward Burlington, I can see the frozen lake sprawling like a white desert.

I toss my backpack full of lunch and books to Marty, who's going into the patrol shack to get the stove fired up. I stretch my legs a little as we share small talk, waiting for the mountain captain to say we can go down. I tighten my boots. Finally, Ken's radio crackles out the word, and I pull down my goggles and pole forward.

Wake up! The first run of the day. Trailcheck. Today the run is heaven—eight inches of light dry powder. My turns are relaxed giant slaloms that leave neat S's in the snow behind me. No need to worry about ice or rocks—the snow covers everything with an airy cushion that we float on, fly on, our skis barely on the ground. We split up at the first intersection, and I bear to the left, down the Glades. My skis gently hiss as they break the powder, splitting the snow like a boat on calm water. I blast through deep drifts of snow, sending gouts and geysers of snow up around me. The air sparkles with snow, breaking the light into flecks of color.

What a day! Some mornings I ride up in fifteen-below-zero cold, only to ski down icy hardpack on which no new snow has fallen for days. There are rocks and other hazards to be noted and later marked with bamboo poles so skiers don't hit them. Fallen branches must be cleared from the trail. On days like that, when the snow is lousy and I have to worry about rocks gouging the bottoms of the skis, trailcheck is work—cold, necessary work done too early in the morning. But when the run is like today, the suffering is worthwhile.

I yelp with pleasure as I launch myself off a knoll and gently land in the soft whiteness, blasting down a chute of untracked powder that empties out into a flatter run. I can hear the other patroller whooping and yelling with me in the distance. Turns are effortless; a tiny shift of weight and the skis respond like wings. I come over the next pitch, moving fast, and my skis hit an unseen patch of ice; my tails slide, too late to get the edge in, and POOF! I tumble into the snow in an

Opening sentence and then two fragments signal the end of the ride and the beginning of the trailcheck

Strong action verbs bring the description alive

Contrast enhances description of the trailcheck

Dominant impression of ecstatic play

explosion of snow dust. For a second I lie panting. Then I wallow in ecstasy, scooping the handfuls of powder over myself, the sweet light snow tingling in the air. After a moment I hop up and continue down, sluicing the S-turns on the whipped-cream powder.

Reaching the patrol room, I click off my skis and stamp the snow from myself. No longer do I feel the night's cold breath in the air—just the sting of the melting snow on my face. Ken looks at me as I drip and glisten over my trail report, and asks: "Good run, Jim?"

10

Concluding comment sums up the writer's experience in one word

I grin at him and say, "Beau-ti-ful!"

11

Student Reflection
Jim Tassé

Q. Do you enjoy writing?
A. Yes, I've always been interested in writing, though it's something I always feel I'm not doing well enough. What I like most is turning phrases, putting things into my own words. And I use writing to get a handle on what I know. Sometimes it's papers for my professors, sometimes it's just ramblings in my journal—I'll have a couple of beers and start jotting something down.

Q. What do you least enjoy about writing? What is hardest for you?
A. Clarity, I guess. Like I said, I'm hardly ever satisfied with anything I've written, and I always think I could make it better by doing another draft. And the more drafts you do, the more challenging it gets, because the work you do seems to be finer and finer. You're looking for rough spots to polish, and as a piece gets better and you find more and more good about it, the rough spots become hidden even more. So each draft becomes more of a challenge, but I'm always eager to get at it.

Q. Show me a rough spot and what you did about it.
A. Okay. Here's the first draft of paragraph 3, about riding up the chairlift.

The ride up gives one a chance to do some serious thinking. You're barely awake, and your first question is usually, "What the hell am I doing here?" But when you see the sun racing between tree branches piled high with snow, and bathing Mt. Mansfield in early morning coral light—you let that question slide. There is great beauty to a mountain in the morning in the winter, and the patrol is always the first to see it. Inevitably I wonder what the mountain would've been like had it remained as it was a hundred years ago: silent, cold, all trees and animals—a lonely, dangerous place for a man to be. But we've changed this mountain. . . .

And it goes on. If you look at the final version, you'll see that I made a lot of changes. Now the subject doesn't shift around from *one* to *you* to *I* to *we*. And instead of saying that the mountain is beautiful, I tried to show how beautiful it was.

Q. Anything else?
A. Paragraph 7 is new. My instructor suggested it; he said it wasn't clear what trailcheck is for, and by telling about the hazards we sometimes have to deal with I could make that day's run seem even more perfect. I didn't have to add this but it seemed worth trying, and I liked the result. I like to get feedback from a reader. It helps me to have things like this pointed out.

Q. We've talked about how you finish a writing project. How do you get started?
A. That depends. Sometimes I'll make an observation and comment on it. Or I'll think of an experience I'd like to write about. I like description; I can just put myself into a situation, appreciate it, and try to get my readers to see it as I do.

Q. How do you prepare? Do you take notes, or make an outline?
A. I guess I'm unorthodox, the way I work. When I start on a piece of writing, I start to put it together in my mind, get an idea of its shape, even start finding words. Sometimes if it isn't shaping up, I'll drop it for a while and come back to it, and sometimes something will click and I'll see what I have to do. Then I'll start on a draft. I've never been a person to use outlines or anything like that, or very rarely.

Q. Then it's the first rough draft, not notes or an outline, that's your raw material?
A. That's right.

Your Response

What did you learn from Jim's essay and reflection? What challenges do you expect to face as you write your own descriptive essay? Based on Jim's experiences and the practical advice discussed earlier in this chapter (pages 117–20), how will you overcome those challenges?

A Woman on the Street

JEANNETTE WALLS

Jeannette Walls was born in 1960 in Phoenix, Arizona, and later moved with her family to San Francisco, California, to Battle Mountain, Nevada, and to Welch, West Virginia. At age seventeen, she entered Barnard College in New York City, and she graduated with honors in 1984. After college, she interned and then became a reporter for the *Phoenix*, a small newspaper in Brooklyn, New

Photo by Andrew Testa/REX/ Shutterstock.com

York. Walls is best known for her gossip reporting on "The Scoop" on MSNBC (1998–2007) and for *The Glass Castle* (2005), a memoir of her childhood years growing up in a nomadic, and at times homeless, family. *The Glass Castle* remained on the *New York Times* best-seller list for more than 200 weeks; sold over 2.5 million copies; was translated into twenty-two languages; and was adapted into a 2017 film starring Brie Larson, Woody Harrelson, and Naomi Watts. Walls has written three other books: *Dish: The Inside Story on the World of Gossip* (2000), *Half-Broke Horses: A True-Life Novel* (2009), and *The Silver Star* (2013).

In "A Woman on the Street," the first chapter of *The Glass Castle*, Walls describes a chance sighting of her mother scavenging in a Dumpster in New York City and a subsequent meeting to try to help "improve" her mother's homeless life.

Preparing to Read

Do you ever wonder about the homeless, their lives before becoming homeless, or their beliefs and values? Does the way we think about the homeless depend mostly on how we describe them, or are there real aspects of their lives that support our impressions? If you know someone who is homeless, what qualities does that person possess that others might not know?

I was sitting in a taxi, wondering if I had overdressed for the evening, when I looked out the window and saw Mom rooting through a Dumpster. It was just after dark. A blustery March wind whipped the steam coming out of the manholes, and people hurried along the sidewalks with their collars turned up. I was stuck in traffic two blocks from the party where I was heading. 1

Mom stood fifteen feet away. She had tied rags around her shoulders to keep out the spring chill and was picking through the trash while her dog, a black-and-white terrier mix, played at her feet. Mom's gestures were all familiar—the way she tilted her head and thrust out her lower lip when studying items of potential value that she'd hoisted out of the Dumpster, 2 the way her eyes widened with childish glee when she found something she liked. Her long hair was streaked with gray, tangled and matted, and her eyes had sunk deep into their sockets, but still she reminded me of the mom she'd been when I was a kid, swan-diving off cliffs and painting in the desert and reading Shakespeare aloud. Her cheekbones were still high and strong, but the skin was parched and ruddy from all those winters and summers exposed to the elements. To the people walking by, she probably looked like any of the thousands of homeless people in New York City.

It had been months since I laid eyes on Mom, and when she looked up,   3
I was overcome with panic that she'd see me and call out my name, and that someone on the way to the same party would spot us together and Mom would introduce herself and my secret would be out.

I slid down in the seat and asked the driver to turn around and take me   4
home to Park Avenue.

The taxi pulled up in front of my building, the doorman held the door for   5
me, and the elevator man took me up to my floor. My husband was working late, as he did most nights, and the apartment was silent except for the click of my heels on the polished wood floor. I was still rattled from seeing Mom, the unexpectedness of coming across her, the sight of her rooting happily through the Dumpster. I put some Vivaldi on, hoping the music would settle me down.

I looked around the room. There were the turn-of-the-century bronze-   6
and-silver vases and the old books with worn leather spines that I'd collected at flea markets. There were the Georgian maps I'd had framed, the Persian rugs, and the overstuffed leather armchair I liked to sink into at the end of the day. I'd tried to make a home for myself here, tried to turn the apartment into the sort of place where the person I wanted to be would live. But I could never enjoy the room without worrying about Mom and Dad huddled on a sidewalk grate somewhere. I fretted about them, but I was embarrassed by them, too, and ashamed of myself for wearing pearls and living on Park Avenue while my parents were busy keeping warm and finding something to eat.

> ❝ I fretted about them, but I was embarrassed by them, too, and ashamed of myself for wearing pearls and living on Park Avenue while my parents were busy keeping warm and finding something to eat. ❞

What could I do? I'd tried to help them countless times, but Dad would   7
insist they didn't need anything, and Mom would ask for something silly, like a perfume atomizer or a membership in a health club. They said that they were living the way they wanted to.

After ducking down in the taxi so Mom wouldn't see me, I hated 8
myself—hated my antiques, my clothes, and my apartment. I had to do
something, so I called a friend of Mom's and left a message. It was our system of staying in touch. It always took Mom a few days to get back to me,
but when I heard from her, she sounded, as always, cheerful and casual, as
though we'd had lunch the day before. I told her I wanted to see her and
suggested she drop by the apartment, but she wanted to go to a restaurant.
She loved eating out, so we agreed to meet for lunch at her favorite Chinese
restaurant.

Mom was sitting at a booth, studying the menu, when I arrived. She'd 9
made an effort to fix herself up. She wore a bulky gray sweater with only a
few light stains, and black leather men's shoes. She'd washed her face, but her
neck and temples were still dark with grime.

She waved enthusiastically when she saw me. "It's my baby girl!" she 10
called out. I kissed her cheek. Mom had dumped all the plastic packets of
soy sauce and duck sauce and hot-and-spicy mustard from the table into her
purse. Now she emptied a wooden bowl of dried noodles into it as well. "A
little snack for later on," she explained.

We ordered. Mom chose the Seafood Delight. "You know how I love my 11
seafood," she said.

She started talking about Picasso. She'd seen a retrospective of his work 12
and decided he was hugely overrated. All the cubist stuff was gimmicky, as
far as she was concerned. He hadn't really done anything worthwhile after
his Rose Period.

"I'm worried about you," I said. "Tell me what I can do to help." 13

Her smile faded. "What makes you think I need your help?" 14

"I'm not rich," I said. "But I have some money. Tell me what it is you 15
need."

She thought for a moment. "I could use an electrolysis treatment." 16

"Be serious." 17

"I am serious. If a woman looks good, she feels good." 18

"Come on, Mom." I felt my shoulders tightening up, the way they invari- 19
ably did during these conversations. "I'm talking about something that could
help you change your life, make it better."

"You want to help me change my life?" Mom asked. "I'm fine. You're the 20
one who needs help. Your values are all confused."

"Mom, I saw you picking through trash in the East Village a few days 21
ago."

"Well, people in this country are too wasteful. It's my way of recycling." 22
She took a bite of her Seafood Delight. "Why didn't you say hello?"

"I was too ashamed, Mom. I hid." 23

Mom pointed her chopsticks at me. "You see?" she said. "Right there. 24
That's exactly what I'm saying. You're way too easily embarrassed. Your
father and I are who we are. Accept it."

"And what am I supposed to tell people about my parents?" 25

"Just tell the truth," Mom said. "That's simple enough." 26

Thinking Critically about the Text

"A Woman on the Street" is a description of Walls's mother, but you soon realize
that the essay is equally about Walls as a daughter. Explain how Walls is able to
"turn the tables" on herself.

Questions on Subject

1. Do you think Walls's mother is happy? Why, or why not?

2. Is Walls's mother against material possessions? How do you know?

3. Why do you suppose Walls's mother refuses to go to her daughter's apartment?

4. In the end, what point is her mother trying to make Walls understand? What
   does she mean when she says to her daughter, "I'm fine. You're the one that
   needs help. Your values are all confused" (paragraph 20)? Are Walls's values
   confused? Explain.

Questions on Strategy

1. How does Walls describe her mother? What details does she reveal about her?

2. How does Walls describe herself? What details does she reveal about herself?

3. Why do you think Walls makes paragraph 4 a single sentence?

4. Walls uses certain words and phrases to quickly draw distinctions between
   the life her mother is leading and the life she herself is leading. Point out a half
   dozen of those terms and phrases and explain how they work as a kind of
   descriptive shorthand.

Description in Action

Think about your topic — the person, place, thought, or concept that lies at the
center of your descriptive essay. Make a list of all the details that you could gather
about it using your five senses, as well as those that simply come to mind when
you consider your topic. Determine a dominant impression that you would like to
create, and then choose from your list the details that will best help you form it.
Your instructor may have you and your classmates go over your lists together and
discuss how effectively your choices build dominant impressions.

Writing Suggestions

1. In paragraph 6, Walls says of her own apartment, "I tried to make a home for myself here, tried to turn the apartment into the sort of place where the person I wanted to be would live." Write an essay in which you consider the idea that homelessness might be as much a state of mind as a physical reality. In other words, does one have to be without a home to be homeless? Can one be homeless living in a wonderful house with all its creature comforts? What makes a person have a sense of belonging, and a sense of warmth, comfort, safety, and satisfaction? Describe that life.

2. Some people believe that our nation is increasingly becoming a place where the middle class is disappearing and the rich and the poor are becoming both more prevalent and more distant from one another. Study the following photograph. What details express or contradict this belief in our changing social class structure? Write an essay in which you explore the complications of such an economic and lifestyle change. For example, is the idea that the middle class is disappearing accurate in your view? What about the idea that there are more rich and poor people? Can you support your position with facts? How does your description and analysis of the photograph support or argue against a changing social demographic?

Eco Images/Getty Images

The Barrio

ROBERT RAMÍREZ

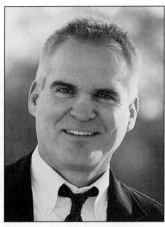

Robert Ramírez was born in 1949 and was raised in Edinburg, Texas, near the Mexican border. He graduated from the University of Texas–Pan American and then worked in several communications-related jobs before joining KGBT-TV in Harlingen, Texas, where he was an anchor. He then moved to finance and worked for a time in banking and as a development officer responsible for alumni fund-raising for his alma mater.

Courtesy of Robert Ramírez

Ramírez's knowledge of the barrio allows him to paint an affectionate portrait of barrio life that nevertheless has a hard edge. His barrio is colorful but not romantic, and his description raises important societal issues as it describes the vibrant community. "The Barrio" was originally published in *Pain and Promise: The Chicano Today* (1972), edited by Edward Simmen.

Preparing to Read

Describe the neighborhood in which you grew up or the most memorable neighborhood you have encountered. Did you like it? Why, or why not? How strong was the sense of community between neighbors? How did it contrast with other neighborhoods nearby?

The train, its metal wheels squealing as they spin along the silvery   1
tracks, rolls slower now. Through the gaps between the cars blinks a
streetlamp, and this pulsing light on a barrio street-corner beats slower,
like a weary heartbeat, until the train shudders to a halt, the light goes out, and
the barrio is deep asleep.

Throughout Aztlán (the Nahuatl term meaning "land to the north"), trains   2
grumble along the edges of a sleeping people. From Lower California, through
the blistering Southwest, down the Rio Grande to the muddy Gulf, the darkness and mystery of dreams engulf communities fenced off by railroads, canals,
and expressways. Paradoxical communities, isolated from the rest of the town
by concrete columned monuments of progress, yet stranded in the past. They
are surrounded by change. It eludes their reach, in their own backyards, and
the people, unable and unwilling to see the future, or even touch the present,
perpetuate the past.

Leaning from the expressway or jolting across the tracks, one enters   3
a different physical world permeated by a different attitude. The physical
dimensions are impressive. It is a large section of town which extends for

fifteen blocks north and south along the tracks, and then advances eastward, thinning into nothingness beyond the city limits. Within the invisible (yet sensible) walls of the barrio are many, many people living in too few houses. The homes, however, are much more numerous than on the outside.

Members of the barrio describe the entire area as their home. It is a home, but it is more than this. The barrio is a refuge from the harshness and the coldness of the Anglo world. It is a forced refuge. The leprous people are isolated from the rest of the community and contained in their section of town. The stoical pariahs of the barrio accept their fate, and from the angry seeds of rejection grow the flowers of closeness between outcasts, not the thorns of bitterness and the mad desire to flee. There is no want to escape, for the feeling of the barrio is known only to its inhabitants, and the material needs of life can also be found here. 4

> ❝ The barrio is a refuge from the harshness and the coldness of the Anglo world. ❞

The *tortillería* fires up its machinery three times a day, producing steaming, round, flat slices of barrio bread. In the winter, the warmth of the tortilla factory is a wool *sarape* in the chilly morning hours, but in the summer, it unbearably toasts every noontime customer. 5

The *panadería* sends its sweet messenger aroma down the dimly lit street, announcing the arrival of fresh, hot sugary *pan dulce*. 6

The small corner grocery serves the meal-to-meal needs of customers, and the owner, a part of the neighborhood, willingly gives credit to people unable to pay cash for foodstuffs. 7

The barbershop is a living room with hydraulic chairs, radio, and television, where old friends meet and speak of life as their salted hair falls aimlessly about them. 8

The pool hall is a junior level country club where 'chucos, strangers in their own land, get together to shoot pool and rap, while veterans, unaware of the cracking, popping balls on the green felt, complacently play dominoes beneath rudely hung *Playboy* foldouts. 9

The *cantina* is the night spot of the barrio. It is the country club and the den where the rites of puberty are enacted. Here the young become men. It is in the taverns that the young dude shows his *machismo* through the quantity of beer he can hold, the stories of *rucas* he has had, and his willingness and ability to defend his image against hardened and scarred old lions. 10

No, there is no frantic wish to flee. It would be absurd to leave the familiar and nervously step into the strange and cold Anglo community when the needs of the Chicano can be met in the barrio. 11

The barrio is closeness. From the family living unit, familial relationships stretch out to immediate neighbors, down the block, around the corner, 12 and to all parts of the barrio. The feeling of family, a rare and treasurable sentiment, pervades and accounts for the inability of the people to leave. The barrio is this attitude manifested on the countenances of the people, on the faces of their homes, and in the gaiety of their gardens.

The color-splashed homes arrest your eyes, arouse your curiosity, and 13 make you wonder what life scenes are being played out in them. The flimsy, brightly colored, wood-frame houses ignore no neon-brilliant color. Houses trimmed in orange, chartreuse, lime-green, yellow, and mixtures of these and other hues beckon the beholder to reflect on the peculiarity of each home. Passing through this land is refreshing like Brubeck, not narcotizing like revolting rows of similar houses, which neither offend nor please.

In the evenings, the porches and front yards are occupied with men 14 calmly talking over the noise of children playing baseball in the unpaved extension of the living room, while the women cook supper or gossip with female neighbors as they water their *jardines*. The gardens mutely echo the expressive verses of the colorful houses. The denseness of multicolored plants and trees gives the house the appearance of an oasis or a tropical island hideaway, sheltered from the rest of the world.

Fences are common in the barrio, but they are fences and not the walls of 15 the Anglo community. On the western side of town, the high wooden fences between houses are thick, impenetrable walls, built to keep the neighbors at bay. In the barrio, the fences may be rusty, wire contraptions or thick green shrubs. In either case you can see through them and feel no sense of intrusion when you cross them.

Many lower-income families of the barrio manage to maintain a com- 16 fortable standard of living through the communal action of family members who contribute their wages to the head of the family. Economic need creates interdependence and closeness. Small barefooted boys sell papers on cool, dark Sunday mornings, deny themselves pleasantries, and give their earnings to *mamá*. The older the child, the greater the responsibility to help the head of the household provide for the rest of the family.

There are those, too, who for a number of reasons have not achieved a 17 relative sense of financial security. Perhaps it results from too many children too soon, but it is the homes of these people and their situation that numbs rather than charms. Their houses, aged and bent, oozing children, are fissures in the horn of plenty. Their wooden homes may have brick-pattern asbestos tile on the outer walls, but the tile is not convincing.

Unable to pay city taxes or incapable of influencing the city to live up 18 to its duty to serve all the citizens, the poorer barrio families remain trapped in the nineteenth century and survive as best they can. The backyards have well-worn paths to the outhouses, which sit near the alley. Running water is considered a luxury in some parts of the barrio. Decent drainage is usually unknown, and when it rains, the water stands for days, an incubator of health hazards and an avoidable nuisance. Streets, costly to pave, remain rough, rocky trails. Tires do not last long, and the constant rattling and shaking grind away a car's life and spread dust through screen windows.

The houses and their *jardines*, the jollity of the people in an adverse world, 19 the brightly feathered alarm clock pecking away at supper and cautiously eyeing the children playing nearby, produce a mystifying sensation at finding the noble savage alive in the twentieth century. It is easy to look at the positive qualities of life in the barrio, and look at them with a distantly envious feeling. One wishes to experience the feelings of the barrio and not the hardships. Remembering the illness, the hunger, the feeling of time running out on you, the walls, both real and imagined, reflecting on living in the past, one finds his envy becoming more elusive, until it has vanished altogether.

Back now beyond the tracks, the train creaks and groans, the cars jostle 20 each other down the track, and as the light begins its pulsing, the barrio, with all its meanings, greets a new dawn with yawns and restless stretchings.

Thinking Critically about the Text

Does Ramírez's essay leave you with a positive or negative image of the barrio? Is it a place you would like to live in, visit, or avoid? Explain your answer.

Questions on Subject

1. Based on Ramírez's essay, what is the barrio? Why do you think that Ramírez uses the image of the train to introduce and close his essay about the barrio?

2. Why do you think Ramírez refers to the barrios of the Southwest as "paradoxical communities" (paragraph 2)?

3. In paragraph 4, Ramírez states that residents consider the barrio something more than a home. What does he mean? In what ways is it more than just a place where they live?

4. Why are the color schemes of the houses in the barrio striking? How do they **contrast** with houses in other areas of town?

Questions on Strategy

1. Explain Ramírez's use of the imagery of walls and fences to describe a sense of cultural isolation. What might this imagery symbolize?

2. Ramírez uses several **metaphors** throughout his essay. Identify them and discuss how they contribute to the essay.

3. Ramírez **begins** his essay with a relatively positive picture of the barrio but ends on a more disheartening note. Why has he organized his essay this way? What might the effect have been if he had reversed the images?

4. Ramírez goes into detail about the many groups living in the barrio. How does his subtle use of **division** and **classification** add to his description? In what ways do the groups he identifies contribute to the unity of life in the barrio?

Description in Action

Using action verbs can make a major difference in the quality of your writing. Review a draft of a descriptive essay that you have written and look for at least three weak verbs — verbs that do not add very much descriptive punch — and make a list of at least three alternatives you could use in place of each one. Be sure that the meaning of each of your alternative action verbs supports your meaning and fits the context in which you use it.

Writing Suggestions

1. Ramírez frames his essay with the image of a train rumbling past the sleeping residents. Using Ramírez's essay as a model, write a descriptive essay about the place where you currently live and use a metaphorical image to frame your essay. What image is both a part of where you live and an effective **metaphor** for it?

2. Write a **comparison and contrast** essay in which you compare where you live now with another residence. Where are you more comfortable? What about your current surroundings do you like? What do you dislike? How does it compare with your hometown, your first apartment, or another place you have lived? If and when you move on, where do you hope to go?

Sister Flowers

MAYA ANGELOU

Best-selling author and poet Maya Angelou (1928–2014) was an educator, historian, actress, playwright, civil rights activist, producer, and director. She is best known as the author of *I Know Why the Caged Bird Sings* (1970), the first book in a series that constitutes her autobiography, and for "On the Pulse of the Morning," a characteristically optimistic poem on the need for personal and national renewal that she read at President Clinton's inauguration in 1993. Starting with her beginnings in St. Louis in 1928, Angelou's autobiography presents a joyful triumph over hardships

© Syracuse Newspapers/Frank Ordonez/The Image Works

that test her courage and threaten her spirit. It includes the titles *All God's Children Need Traveling Shoes* (1986), *Wouldn't Take Anything for My Journey Now* (1993), and *Heart of a Woman* (1997). The sixth book in the series, *A Song Flung Up to Heaven*, was published in 2002. Angelou reflects on her often difficult relationship with her mother in *Mom & Me & Mom* (2013). Several volumes of her poetry were collected in *Complete Collected Poems of Maya Angelou* in 1994.

In the following excerpt from *I Know Why the Caged Bird Sings*, Angelou describes a family friend who had a major impact on her early life. As you read, notice the way Angelou describes Sister Flowers's physical presence, her stately manners, and the guidance she offered Angelou as a youngster.

Preparing to Read

Think about a major crisis you have had to face. Was there someone who came to your aid, offering solid advice and comforting support? How would you describe that person? What physical and personality traits characterize that person?

For nearly a year [after I was raped], I sopped around the house, the Store, the school, and the church, like an old biscuit, dirty and inedible. Then I met, or rather got to know, the lady who threw me my first life line.

Mrs. Bertha Flowers was the aristocrat of Black Stamps. She had the grace of control to appear warm in the coldest weather, and on the Arkansas summer days it seemed she had a private breeze which swirled around, cooling her. She was thin without the taut look of wiry people, and her printed voile dresses and flowered hats were as right for her as denim overalls for a farmer. She was our side's answer to the richest white woman in town.

Her skin was a rich black that would have peeled like a plum if snagged, but then no one would have thought of getting close enough to Mrs. Flowers to ruffle her dress, let alone snag her skin. She didn't encourage familiarity. She wore gloves too.

I don't think I ever saw Mrs. Flowers laugh, but she smiled often. A slow   4
widening of her thin black lips to show even, small white teeth, then the slow effortless closing. When she chose to smile on me, I always wanted to thank her. The action was so graceful and inclusively benign.

She was one of the few gentlewomen I have ever known, and has re-   5
mained throughout my life the measure of what a human being can be.

Momma had a strange relationship with her. Most often when she   6
passed on the road in front of the Store, she spoke to Momma in that soft yet carrying voice, "Good day, Mrs. Henderson." Momma responded with "How you, Sister Flowers?"

Mrs. Flowers didn't belong to our church, nor was she Momma's famil-   7
iar. Why on earth did she insist on calling her Sister Flowers? Shame made me want to hide my face. Mrs. Flowers deserved better than to be called Sister. Then, Momma left out the verb. Why not ask, "How *are* you, *Mrs. Flowers?*" With the unbalanced passion of the young, I hated her for show-ing her ignorance to Mrs. Flowers. It didn't occur to me for many years that they were as alike as sisters, separated only by formal education.

Although I was upset, neither of the women was in the least shaken by   8
what I thought an unceremonious greeting. Mrs. Flowers would continue her easy gait up the hill to her little bungalow, and Momma kept on shelling peas or doing whatever had brought her to the front porch.

Occasionally, though, Mrs. Flowers would drift off the road and down   9
to the Store and Momma would say to me, "Sister, you go on and play." As she left I would hear the beginning of an intimate conversation. Momma persistently using the wrong verb, or none at all.

"Brother and Sister Wilcox is sho'ly the meanest—""Is," Momma? "Is"?   10
Oh, please, not "is," Momma, for two or more. But they talked, and from the side of the building where I waited for the ground to open up and swal-low me, I heard the soft-voiced Mrs. Flowers and the textured voice of my grandmother merging and melting. They were interrupted from time to time by giggles that must have come from Mrs. Flowers (Momma never giggled in her life). Then she was gone.

She appealed to me because she was like people I had never met person-   11
ally. Like women in English novels who walked the moors (whatever they were) with their loyal dogs racing at a respectful distance. Like the women who sat in front of roaring fireplaces, drinking tea incessantly from silver trays full of scones and crumpets. Women who walked over the "heath" and read morocco-bound books and had two last names divided by a hyphen. It would be safe to say that she made me proud to be Negro, just by being herself.

She acted just as refined as whitefolks in the movies and books and she   12
was more beautiful, for none of them could have come near that warm color
without looking gray by comparison.

> ❝ **She acted just as refined as whitefolks in the movies and books and she was more beautiful, for none of them could have come near that warm color without looking gray by comparison.** ❞

It was fortunate that I never saw her   13
in the company of powhitefolks. For since
they tend to think of their whiteness as
an evenizer, I'm certain that I would have
had to hear her spoken to commonly
as Bertha, and my image of her would
have been shattered like the unmendable
Humpty-Dumpty.

One summer afternoon, sweet-milk   14
fresh in my memory, she stopped at the
Store to buy provisions. Another Negro
woman of her health and age would have
been expected to carry the paper sacks
home in one hand, but Momma said, "Sister Flowers, I'll send Bailey up to
your house with these things."

She smiled that slow dragging smile, "Thank you, Mrs. Henderson.   15
I'd prefer Marguerite, though." My name was beautiful when she said it.
"I've been meaning to talk to her, anyway." They gave each other age-group
looks.

Momma said, "Well, that's all right then. Sister, go and change your   16
dress. You going to Sister Flowers's."

The chifforobe was a maze. What on earth did one put on to go to Mrs.   17
Flowers's house? I knew I shouldn't put on a Sunday dress. It might be sacri-
legious. Certainly not a house dress, since I was already wearing a fresh one.
I chose a school dress, naturally. It was formal without suggesting that going
to Mrs. Flowers's house was equivalent to attending church.

I trusted myself back into the Store.   18

"Now, don't you look nice." I had chosen the right thing, for once. . . .   19

There was a little path beside the rocky road, and Mrs. Flowers walked   20
in front swinging her arms and picking her way over the stones.

She said, without turning her head, to me, "I hear you're doing very good   21
school work, Marguerite, but that it's all written. The teachers report that
they have trouble getting you to talk in class." We passed the triangular farm
on our left and the path widened to allow us to walk together. I hung back in
the separate unasked and unanswerable questions.

"Come and walk along with me, Marguerite." I couldn't have refused   22
even if I wanted to. She pronounced my name so nicely. Or more correctly,
she spoke each word with such clarity that I was certain a foreigner who
didn't understand English could have understood her.

"Now no one is going to make you talk—possibly no one can. But bear   23
in mind, language is man's way of communicating with his fellow man and it
is language alone which separates him from the lower animals." That was a
totally new idea to me, and I would need time to think about it.

"Your grandmother says you read a lot. Every chance you get. That's good,   24
but not good enough. Words mean more than what is set down on paper. It
takes the human voice to infuse them with the shades of deeper meaning."

I memorized the part about the human voice infusing words. It seemed   25
so valid and poetic.

She said she was going to give me some books and that I not only must   26
read them, I must read them aloud. She suggested that I try to make a sentence sound in as many different ways as possible.

"I'll accept no excuse if you return a book to me that has been badly   27
handled." My imagination boggled at the punishment I would deserve if in
fact I did abuse a book of Mrs. Flowers's. Death would be too kind and brief.

The odors in the house surprised me. Somehow I had never connected   28
Mrs. Flowers with food or eating or any other common experience of common people. There must have been an outhouse, too, but my mind never
recorded it.

The sweet scent of vanilla had met us as she opened the door.   29

"I made tea cookies this morning. You see, I had planned to invite you   30
for cookies and lemonade so we could have this little chat. The lemonade is
in the icebox."

It followed that Mrs. Flowers would have ice on an ordinary day, when   31
most families in our town bought ice late on Saturdays only a few times
during the summer to be used in the wooden ice-cream freezers.

She took the bags from me and disappeared through the kitchen door.   32
I looked around the room that I had never in my wildest fantasies imagined
I would see. Browned photographs leered or threatened from the walls and
the white, freshly done curtains pushed against themselves and against the
wind. I wanted to gobble up the room entire and take it to Bailey, who would
help me analyze and enjoy it.

"Have a seat, Marguerite. Over there by the table." She carried a platter   33
covered with a tea towel. Although she warned that she hadn't tried her hand
at baking sweets for some time, I was certain that like everything else about
her the cookies would be perfect.

They were flat round wafers, slightly browned on the edges and butter-   34
yellow in the center. With the cold lemonade they were sufficient for childhood's lifelong diet. Remembering my manners, I took nice little lady-like
bites off the edges. She said she had made them expressly for me and that
she had a few in the kitchen that I could take home to my brother. So I
jammed one whole cake in my mouth and the rough crumbs scratched the

insides of my jaws, and if I hadn't had to swallow, it would have been a dream come true.

As I ate she began the first of what we later called "my lessons in living." 35 She said that I must always be intolerant of ignorance but understanding of illiteracy. That some people, unable to go to school, were more educated and even more intelligent than college professors. She encouraged me to listen carefully to what country people called mother wit. That in those homely sayings was couched the collective wisdom of generations.

When I finished the cookies she brushed off the table and brought a 36 thick, small book from the bookcase. I had read *A Tale of Two Cities* and found it up to my standards as a romantic novel. She opened the first page and I heard poetry for the first time in my life.

"It was the best of times and the worst of times . . ." Her voice slid in 37 and curved down through and over the words. She was nearly singing. I wanted to look at the pages. Were they the same that I had read? Or were there notes, music, lined on the pages, as in a hymn book? Her sounds began cascading gently. I knew from listening to a thousand preachers that she was nearing the end of her reading, and I hadn't really heard, heard to understand, a single word.

"How do you like that?" 38

It occurred to me that she expected a response. The sweet vanilla flavor 39 was still on my tongue and her reading was a wonder in my ears. I had to speak.

I said, "Yes, ma'am." It was the least I could do, but it was the most also. 40

"There's one more thing. Take this book of poems and memorize one for 41 me. Next time you pay me a visit, I want you to recite."

I have tried often to search behind the sophistication of years for the 42 enchantment I so easily found in those gifts. The essence escapes but its aura remains. To be allowed, no, invited, into the private lives of strangers, and to share their joys and fears, was a chance to exchange the Southern bitter wormwood for a cup of mead with Beowulf or a hot cup of tea and milk with Oliver Twist. When I said aloud, "It is a far, far better thing that I do, than I have ever done . . ." tears of love filled my eyes at my selflessness.

On that first day, I ran down the hill and into the road (few cars ever came 43 along it) and had the good sense to stop running before I reached the Store.

I was liked, and what a difference it made. I was respected not as Mrs. 44 Henderson's grandchild or Bailey's sister but for just being Marguerite Johnson.

Childhood's logic never asks to be proved (all conclusions are absolute). 45 I didn't question why Mrs. Flowers had singled me out for attention, nor did it occur to me that Momma might have asked her to give me a little talking to. All I cared about was that she had made tea cookies for *me* and read to *me* from her favorite book. It was enough to prove that she liked me.

Thinking Critically about the Text

In paragraph 44, Marguerite indicates how important it was to be respected and liked for "just being Marguerite Johnson." Why do you suppose she, in particular, feels that way? Why is it important for anyone to feel that way?

Questions on Subject

1. What is Angelou's main point in describing Sister Flowers? Why was Sister Flowers so important to her?

2. What does Angelou mean when she writes that Sister Flowers did not "encourage familiarity" (paragraph 3)?

3. Why does Sister Flowers think that reading is "good, but not good enough" for Marguerite (paragraph 24)?

4. What revelations about race relations in her community growing up does Angelou impart in this selection? What do those revelations add to the point Angelou is trying to make?

Questions on Strategy

1. What **dominant impression** of Sister Flowers does Angelou create in this selection?

2. To which of the reader's senses does Angelou appeal in describing Sister Flowers? To which senses does she appeal in describing Sister Flowers's house?

3. At the end of her description of Sister Flowers, Angelou implies that at the time it did not occur to her that Sister Flowers might have been asked to give her "a little talking to" (paragraph 45). What clues in the description suggest that Momma asked Sister Flowers to befriend and draw out Marguerite? Why do you suppose Momma didn't take on that task herself?

4. Why does Angelou have her younger self imagine the conversations that Momma and Sister Flowers have on several occasions instead of reporting them directly (paragraph 10)?

Description in Action

One of the best ways to make a description memorable is to use figurative language such as a simile (making a comparison using *like* or *as*) or a metaphor (making a comparison without the use of *like* or *as*). Create a simile or metaphor that would be helpful in describing each item in the following list. To illustrate the activity, the first one has been completed for you.

1. a pillow: To her the pillow was a huge marshmallow, soft and friendly.

2. a skyscraper:

3. a large explosion:

4. a crowded bus:

5. a narrow alley:

6. a thick milkshake:

7. the hot sun:

8. a dull knife:

Writing Suggestions

1. Sister Flowers is an excellent example of a person with grace, charm, spirit, intelligence, generosity, and high-mindedness — personality traits we ourselves might aspire to possess or admire in someone else. Describe someone you know who has similar personality traits and try to imagine what might account for such traits.

2. Sometimes as writers we need to describe a situation that is filled with actions that give rise to strong emotions. Think of such a situation — an unsuccessful attempt to have a bureaucrat understand your situation that leaves you frustrated, social injustices that cause anger, something you did or said that in retrospect seemed very callous and caused remorse, a time you helped someone reach his or her goals and gained a sense of joy and fulfilment. Write an essay in which you set the context for the description and then make the emotions in question come alive for your reader.

A Talent for Sloth

PHILIP CONNORS

Philip Connors

Born in Iowa and raised in Minnesota, essayist and author Philip Connors graduated from the University of Montana. Connors has written extensively about his professional ambitions to be a newspaper and magazine writer — and the challenges of pursuing that career. In 2002, after working as a copyeditor and writer for the *Wall Street Journal*, he left a conventional job in journalism to take a seasonal position in New Mexico as a fire lookout for the United States Forest Service. Connors has remained a prolific writer, and his essays have appeared in *Harper's, Salon,* the *London Review of Books, n+1,* and many other publications. He is also the author of two nonfiction books, *Fire Season: Field Notes from a Wilderness Lookout* (2011) and the memoir *All the Wrong Places: A Life Lost and Found* (2015). His work has received the National Outdoor Book Award and the Sigurd Olson Nature Writing Award, among other honors.

In "A Talent for Sloth," published in *Lapham's Quarterly* in 2017, Connors writes vividly and stylishly about his job as a fire lookout on a New Mexico fire tower. But his essay goes beyond rich descriptions of the natural world to address larger ideas about themes such as solitude, writing, work, and technology.

Preparing to Read

In his essay, Connors writes about swimming "languidly in the waters of solitude, unwilling to rouse myself to anything but the most basic of labors" (paragraph 7). Does this vision of life and work appeal to you? Can you imagine working alone, isolated from others for long periods of time? Explain why or why not.

The landscape where I work, in far southwest New Mexico, is one of the most fire-prone areas in America. I look out over a stretch of country with nearly a million acres of roadless wilderness, where an annual upsurge of moisture from the Gulf of Mexico combines with the summertime heat of the Chihuahuan Desert to create tens of thousands of lightning strikes. In an arid land with brief but intense storm activity, wildfire is no aberration.

My lookout tower is situated five miles from the nearest road, on a ten-thousand-foot peak in the Gila National Forest. I live here for several months each year, without electricity or running water. Although tens of thousands of acres are touched by fire here every year, I can go weeks without seeing a twist of smoke. During these lulls I simply watch and wait, my eyes becoming ever more intimate with an ecological transition zone encompassing dry grasslands, piñon-juniper foothills, ponderosa parkland, and spruce-fir high country. On clear days I can make out mountains 180 miles away. To the east extends the valley of the Rio Grande, cradled by the desert: austere, forbidding, dotted with creosote shrubs and home to a collection of horned and thorned species evolved to live in a land of little water. To the north and south, along the Black Range, a line of peaks rises and falls in timbered waves; to the west, the Rio Mimbres meanders out of the mountains, its lower valley verdant with riparian flora. Beyond it rise more mesas and mountains: the Diablos, the Jerkies, the Mogollons.

It is a world of extremes. Having spent each fire season for nearly a decade   3
in my little glass-walled perch, I've become acquainted with the look and feel of the border highlands each week of each month, from April through August: the brutal gales of spring, when a roar off the desert gusts over seventy miles an hour and the occasional snow squall turns my peak white; the dawning of summer in late May, when the wind abates and the aphids hatch and ladybugs emerge in great clouds from their hibernation; the fires of June, when dry lightning connects with the hills, sparking smokes that fill the air with the sweet smell of burning pine; the tremendous storms of July, when the thunder makes me flinch as if from the threat of a punch; and the blessed indolence of August, when the meadows bloom with wildflowers and the creeks run again, the rains having turned my world a dozen different shades of green. I've seen fires burn so hot they made their own weather; I've watched deer and elk frolic in the meadow below me and pine trees explode in a blue ball of smoke. If there's a better job anywhere on the planet, I'd like to know about it.

The work has changed remarkably little over the course of the past   4
century, except in its increasing scarcity. Ninety percent of American lookout towers have been decommissioned, and only around five hundred of us remain, mostly in the West. Nonetheless, when the last lookout tower is retired, our stories will live on. Jack Kerouac worked a summer on Desolation Peak in the North Cascades, in 1956, an experience he mined for parts of two novels, *The Dharma Bums* and *Desolation Angels*. He secured the job through a recommendation by his friend the poet Gary Snyder, who worked summers on two different lookouts in the same national forest and wrote several fine poems about that world, "up there above the clouds memorizing various peaks and watersheds." During the '60s and '70s, that old raconteur Edward Abbey worked at various postings, from Glacier National Park to the Grand Canyon. He wrote two essays on the subject and made a fire lookout the main character in his novel *Black Sun*, the book he claimed he loved most among all his works. And Norman Maclean, in his great book *A River Runs Through It*, wrote a lightly fictionalized story about his one summer as a lookout on the Selway Forest in northern Idaho, over the Bitterroot Divide from his home in Missoula.

Based on their reminiscences, I'm pretty sure the qualifications to be a 5
lookout remain the same as they ever were:

- Not blind, deaf, or mute—must be able to see fires, hear the radio, respond
  when called
- Capability for extreme patience while waiting for smokes
- One good arm to cut wood
- Two good legs for hiking to a remote post
- Ability to keep oneself amused
- Tolerance for living in proximity to rodents
- A touch of pyromania, though only of the nonparticipatory variety

Philip Connors

Twenty paces from my cabin, sixty-five more up the steps of the tower, and 6
just like that I'm on the job. After cleaning up the mess left by overwintering
rats and mice, putting up the supplies I get packed in by mule, and splitting
a good stack of firewood, I begin more or less full-time service in the sky,
9 a.m. to 6 p.m., an hour off for lunch—a schedule not unlike that of any
other runner on the hamster wheel of the eight-hour workday. For most people I know, my office, a seven-by-seven-foot box on stilts, would be a prison
cell or a catafalque. Over the years I've made some modest improvements
to it in an effort to make it slightly more functional. With a straight length
of pine limb and a square of plywood, I've fashioned a writing table wedged
into one corner of the tower, just big enough to hold my typewriter. It allows
me to write while standing; in this way I can type and look out at the same
time—the extent of my multitasking. Along the east wall of the tower I've

rebuilt a rudimentary cot, a body-sized slab of plywood perched on legs cut from an old corral post. Made up with a sleeping pad and a Forest Service bag, it offers ample comfort on which to read and allows me to look out merely by sitting up.

In quiet moments I devote my attentions to the local bird life. I listen for the call of the hermit thrush, one of the most gorgeous sounds in all of nature, a mellifluous warble beginning on a long clear note. Dark-eyed juncos hop along the ground, searching for seeds among the grass and pine litter. With no one calling on the radio, I swim languidly in the waters of solitude, unwilling to rouse myself to anything but the most basic of labors. Brush teeth. Piss in meadow. Boil water for coffee. Observe clouds. Note greening of Gambel oak. The goal, if I can be said to have one, becomes to attain that state where I'm completely in tune with cloud and light, a being of pure sensation. The cumulus build, the light shifts, and in an hour—or two—I'm looking at country made new.

How did I come upon this aptitude for idleness? I blame it on the injurious effects of my Midwestern youth. At age six I learned the logistics of cleaning manure from the family hog barns. Around the same time, I joined with my brother in plucking rocks from plowed fields and pulling weeds by hand from neat rows of soybeans. Manicured fields and well-kept barns—the whole right-angled geometry of grain farming and its attendant animal husbandry—eventually became synonymous in my mind with a kind of pointless feudal labor that condemned its practitioners to penury or government handouts. At twelve, after the bankers invited us to leave the farm, I took on odd jobs in town—mowing lawns, raking leaves, shoveling snow, gathering aluminum cans to sell at the recycling plant. At fourteen I began a short-lived career in the grocery trade, bagging foodstuffs and mopping spills in the aisles, occasionally filching a box of Little Debbie snack cakes in compensation for a paltry wage. At fifteen I learned to fry donuts in our small-town bakery, 3 a.m. to 8 a.m., six days a week, a job I held until the day I left for college. To pay tuition I painted houses, baked bread, unloaded package trailers at UPS in the middle of the night. I tended bar. I dabbled in the janitorial arts, cleaning the University of Montana fieldhouse after basketball games and circuses. I spent a summer as the least intimidating bouncer in the history of Al & Vic's Bar in Missoula. I baked more bread.

Undergraduate degree in hand at last, I ascended to the most rarefied realms of American journalism—handing out faxes and replacing empty water coolers for reporters at the *Wall Street Journal*. My tenacity and work ethic established, I was promoted to copyediting the Leisure & Arts page, a job I held for three years. I was anonymous, watchful, and discreet. Four days a week, an unblemished page was shipped electronically to seventeen printing plants across the country, and the following morning nearly two million readers held the fruits of my labor in their hands. At first I resented the lack of attention paid to my mastery of English grammar and the intricacies of the house-style book. Not once did I receive a letter from an armchair grammarian in Terre Haute or Pocatello, one of those retired English teachers who scour the daily paper with a red pen in hand, searching for evidence of American decline in the form of a split infinitive. Nor did my immediate superiors mention, even in passing, that I did my job diligently and well. Over time I began to take delight in this peculiar feature of my job — that my success was measured by how rarely people noticed what I did. I was barely noticed at all.

> " Over time I began to take delight in this peculiar feature of my job — that my success was measured by how rarely people noticed what I did. "

The essentials of my current line of work — anonymity, discretion, watchfulness — are not so different from those demanded of a copyeditor. The lookout life fell into my lap, no effort required. It came to me, in fact, while I was on vacation one summer — seemed like one long vacation itself. I had two days to decide if I wanted the job. I surveyed my past and saw only blind striving; I played out my future and saw an abyss: day after day the guillotine of an evening deadline stretching into the murky distance. How could I refuse such a sweet summer sinecure? That, at its essence, is the story of my talent for sloth. I tried it for the first time in my life. I liked it. The plague of Midwestern Catholic guilt on my conscience notwithstanding, I often feel I could work my mountain as long as I walk upright on earth.

Between five and fifteen times a year I'm the first to see a smoke, and on these occasions I use the one essential fire-spotting tool — aside, of course, from a sharp pair of eyes, augmented by fancy binoculars. That tool is the Osborne Fire Finder, which consists of a topographic map encircled by a rotating metal ring equipped with a sighting device. The sighting device allows you to discern the directional bearing of the fire from your location. The directional bearing — called an azimuth — is expressed by degree markings along the outside edge of the ring, with 360 degrees being oriented with true north. Once you have an azimuth, you must then judge the fire's distance from your perch. The easiest way to do this: alert another lookout able to spot the smoke, have her take her own azimuth reading, and triangulate your lines. We lookouts call this "a cross," as in, "Can you give me a cross on this smoke I'm seeing at my azimuth of 170 degrees and 30 minutes?" If this can't be done — the smoke is too small to be seen by another lookout or its source is hidden by a ridge—you're thrown back on your knowledge of the country. Protocol dictates that you locate each fire by its legal description, or what we in the trade simply call its "legal": ideally within one square mile, by township, range, and section, the square-ruled overlay on American property maps.

A new fire often looks beautiful, first a wisp of white like a feather, a single snag puffing a little finger of smoke in the air. I see it before it has a name. Like Adam with an animal before him, I will give it one, after I nail down its location and call it in to dispatch. We try to name the fires after a nearby landmark—a canyon, peak, or spring—but there is often a touch of poetic license involved. Some years there is more than one fire in a place called Lone Mountain; knowing this, we'll name the first the Lonesome Fire and the second the Dove Fire. Or say a fire pops up in Railroad Canyon, but there's already been a Railroad Fire that year. Something like Caboose Fire would be acceptable.   12

Once I've spotted a fire, my superiors must choose a response. For most of the twentieth century the reaction was preordained: full suppression. A military mindset prevailed in the early Forest Service, and the results for America's public lands proved disastrous. Attacking every fire the moment it was spotted warped ecosystems that had burned on a regular basis for millennia; it convinced retreating urbanites that they could build their dream homes amid the forests with impunity. Smokejumpers would float out of the sky and save the day if the call came. The fact remains that wildfire has a mind of its own, as we've learned the hard way. The lessons will only get harder in a warming world, but here on the Gila, officials are committed to making fire a part of the life of the forest again. They let certain lightning-caused fires burn for weeks at a time, over tens of thousands of acres, making the Gila healthier than it would be otherwise: more diverse in the mosaic of its flora, more open in its ponderosa savannah, with less of the brushy ladder fuels that now make the American West an almost annual show of extreme fire behavior. With crews on the ground monitoring big blazes, we are their eyes in the sky, watching their weather when they sleep outdoors, letting them know when lightning is coming or the wind has changed. Such information, relayed in timely fashion, can mean the difference between life and death.   13

Still, there's little doubt I'm practicing a vocation in its twilight. Some in the Forest Service have predicted our impending obsolescence, due to more powerful radios, more sophisticated satellites, even drone airplanes—the never-ending dreams of the technofetishists. If there's one axiom of the world we've made for ourselves, it's that technology will always find ways to replace the inefficient human hand. But in a place like the Gila—where so much of the country remains off limits to vehicles and industrial logging—lookouts are sometimes the only link to the outside world for backcountry crews of all   14 kinds: fire, trails, game and fish, law enforcement. We are also much cheaper than aerial surveillance. Safety and fiscal prudence — these will be the saving graces of the lookouts who manage to hang on.

Even for those of us who do, it's not difficult to imagine a future in which our most important task is to maintain a set of panoramic high-resolution cameras with live feeds to distant offices. Someday, no doubt, we'll be equipped with laptop computers and sophisticated mapping software with 3D graphics. Instead of learning the lay of the land the old-fashioned way, by walking its contours and staring at it for hours upon hours from above, we'll become on-site caretakers for an array of gadgets that render an intimate human knowledge of the country superfluous. Or so we'll be told. The lookouts of old, who not only kept watch over the forests but saddled their horses with tools at the ready to put out a smoke the moment it showed, will surely spin in their graves. As for the smokejumpers and hotshot crews who once relied on lookouts to know the condition of trails and the density of fuels in a specific locale, they'll have to discern what information they can from their handheld GPS units. For anything else, they'll be on their own. 15

Aldo Leopold, the man who drafted the plan to preserve the Gila Wilderness in 1922, a plan that made the headwaters of the Gila River the first piece of land in the world to be consciously protected from industrial machines, once wrote, "I am glad I shall never be young without wild country to be young in. Of what avail are forty freedoms without a blank spot on the map?" Survey the Lower Forty-eight on a coast-to-coast flight, and the most interesting country never fails to be that without roads. Down there amid one of those fragments of our natural heritage is a forest that burns and a desert that dances, 20,000 square miles of cruel and magnificent country visible from a tower nearly two miles above sea. The view some days cannot be fathomed, so I turn back to the earth beneath my feet. Wild candytuft bloom under the pine and fir, followed later by wallflowers, paintbrush, mountain wood sorrel, Mexican silene. On my evening rambles I find stellar's jay and wildturkey feathers, snake skins and mule-deer bones. Now and then an hour of hunting turns up a relic in the dirt, not far from the base of my tower: a turquoise bead or a Mogollon potsherd, white with black pattern, well more than eight hundred years old. I am given to understand these people once gathered in the high places and brought with them their crockery. They sacrificed their pots by smashing them to earth in hopes the sky gods granted rain. I am not alone in my communion here with sky. Far from it. The ravens and the vultures have me beat by two hundred feet, the Mogollons by most of a millennium. And who's to say the dust motes off the desert don't feel joy, if only for a moment, as they climb up into sky and ride the transport winds? 16

Thinking Critically about the Text

Connors's essay is perceptive and highly descriptive. What are the parallels between being a good fire lookout and being a good reader and writer? What kinds of skills and habits apply to all of these activities?

Questions on Subject

1. Why does Connors love his job so much? Summarize his reasons in your own words.

2. Why did Connors come to dislike his work as a copyeditor? How was the copyediting job similar to his job at the fire tower?

3. According to Connors, he is "practicing a vocation in its twilight" (paragraph 14). What does he mean by this? What evidence does he use to support the claim?

4. This essay is called "A Talent for Sloth." Connors claims to have an "aptitude for idleness," yet he also recounts a long list of jobs that demonstrate a willingness to work hard and even refers to his own "tenacity and work ethic" (paragraph 9). Does Connors seem like a naturally lazy or idle person, or is he a hard worker? Does the essay resolve this seeming paradox? Explain.

Questions on Strategy

1. Where in his essay does Connors use **objective** description? Where does he use **subjective** description? Is the distinction between them always clear? Why, or why not?

2. While this is a highly descriptive essay, Connors also tells a story. What elements of **narration** does the writer incorporate into "A Talent for Sloth"? Why are they necessary? How do they support his overall **purpose?**

3. How does Connors use strong, sharp, and specific nouns and verbs in his descriptions? How do they contribute to the **dominant impression** of the essay? Point to examples and explain.

4. Study the photo taken by Philip Connors on page 144. In what ways does the text complement the photo — especially the sense of isolation and peace? In what ways do the details of the photo complement Connors's text? Does knowing that Connors was the photographer change the way you read his essay?

Description in Action

Choose one well-known location, object, or physical element on your campus. Working in small groups, list the important details, elements, descriptors, and sensory impressions associated with this campus feature. Then, with the group, try to link your descriptions of this topic with an idea or even a thesis: What does the feature suggest, represent, or even assert? When groups are ready, share your ideas on the board with the whole class. Did others choose the same campus feature or the same details? Did they link the campus feature to the same ideas?

Writing Suggestions

1. Connors's description of the border highlands, beginning in paragraph 3, supports the two larger ideas that the writer notes in the opening and closing sentences of this paragraph: first, that his New Mexico landscape is a "world of extremes" and second, that he thinks that his position is the best job on the planet. Think about a region or landscape that you are familiar with, particularly as it changes from month to month or season to season. Then, write a long, descriptive paragraph about this place, using details and vivid description. As Connors does, use your description to introduce and support larger ideas or claims in the opening and concluding sentences of the paragraph.

2. Among his other aims in "A Talent for Sloth," Connors tries to answer the question "How did I come upon this aptitude for idleness?" (paragraph 8). As the essay reveals, this "aptitude" is reflected in his life, his work, his choices, and his way of looking at the world. Think about one of your own qualities, tendencies, or "aptitudes," and then write a brief descriptive essay titled "A Talent for _____." How is your aptitude or talent reflected in the details of your life? In what ways has it shaped your choices? Where did the talent come from? Choose specific examples and details to illuminate your particular talent, while limiting your use of narration.

Mike Flanagan / CartoonStock.com

CHAPTER 6

Illustration

WHAT IS ILLUSTRATION?

THE STRATEGY OF ILLUSTRATION USES EXAMPLES — FACTS, OPINIONS, samples, and anecdotes or stories — to make a general observation, assertion, or claim more vivid, understandable, and persuasive. We use examples all the time in everyday life to make our points clearer. How often have we asked for or given an example or two when something was not evident or clear?

VISUALIZING ILLUSTRATION

This cartoon uses illustration to answer the question, "What happens when you bite your nails?" Consider how the cartoonist uses the armless bust as an example to create humor. How would you characterize the speaker? The one being spoken to? How do the visual appearances of these two subjects (the speaker and his audience) contribute to the joke? Think of other directives that you heard while you were growing up. Pick one, such as "brush your teeth," "clean your plate," or "wash your hands," and explain how you might visually present the consequences of not following the directive. Your visual will likely change depending on your purpose — do you want to be informative or humorous? What examples will you use?

UNDERSTANDING ILLUSTRATION AS A WRITING STRATEGY

Illustrating a point with examples serves several purposes for writers. First, examples make writing more vivid and interesting. Writing that consists of loosely strung-together generalizations is lifeless and difficult to read, regardless of the believability of the generalizations or our willingness to accept them. Good writers try to provide just the right kind and number of examples to make their ideas clear and convincing.

In the following paragraph from "Wandering through Winter," notice how naturalist Edwin Way Teale uses examples to illustrate his generalization that "country people" have many superstitions about how harsh the coming winter will be:

Topic sentence about weather superstitions frames entire paragraph

Series of examples amplify and clarify topic sentence

In the folklore of the country, numerous superstitions relate to winter weather. Back-country farmers examine their husks — the thicker the husk, the colder the winter. They watch the acorn crop — the more acorns, the more severe the season. They observe where white-faced hornets place their paper nests — the higher they are, the deeper will be the snow. They examine the size and shape and color of the spleens of butchered hogs for clues to the severity of the season. They keep track of the blooming of the dogwood in the spring — the more abundant the blooms, the more bitter the cold in January. When chipmunks carry their tails high and squirrels have heavier fur, the superstitious gird themselves for a long, hard winter. Without any specific basis, a wider-than-usual black band on a woolly-bear caterpillar is accepted as a sign that winter will arrive early and stay late. Even the way a cat sits beside the stove carries its message to the credulous. According to the belief once widely held in the Ozarks, a cat sitting with its tail to the fire indicates very cold weather is on the way.

Teale uses nine separate examples to illustrate and explain his topic sentence about weather-related superstitions. These examples both demonstrate his knowledge of folk traditions and entertain us. As readers, we come away from Teale's paragraph thinking that he is an authority on his subject.

Teale's examples are a series of related but varied illustrations of his main point. Sometimes, however, just one sustained example can be equally effective if the example is representative and the writer develops it well. Here is one such example by basketball legend Bill Russell from his autobiographical *Second Wind*:

Topic sentence focuses on athletes slipping into a new gear

Extended example of Beamon's record exemplifies topic sentence

Every champion athlete has a moment when everything goes so perfectly for him he slips into a gear that he didn't know was there. It's easy to spot that perfect moment in a sport like track. I remember watching the 1968 Olympics in Mexico City, where the world record in the long jump was just under 27 feet. Then Bob Beamon flew down the chute and leaped out over the pit in a majestic jump that I have seen replayed many times. There was an awed silence when the announcer said that Beamon's jump measured 29 feet 2¼ inches. Generally world records are broken by fractions of inches, but Beamon had exceeded the existing record by more than two feet. On learning what he had done, Beamon slumped down on the ground and cried. Most viewers' image of

Example illustrates that even Beamon did not anticipate his own performance	Beamon ends with the picture of him weeping on the ground, but in fact he got up and took some more jumps that day. I like to think that he did so because he had jumped for so long at his best that *even then* he didn't know what might come out of him. At the end of the day he wanted to be absolutely sure that he'd had his perfect day.

Few readers have experienced that "extra gear" that Russell describes, so he illustrates what he means with a single, extended example — in this case, an anecdote that gives substance to the idea he wants his readers to understand. Russell's example of Bob Beamon's record-breaking jump is not only concrete and specific; it is also memorable because it so aptly captures the essence of his topic sentence about athletic perfection. Without this extended example, Russell's claim that every great athlete "slips into a gear that he didn't know was there" would be a hollow statement.

Illustration is so useful and versatile a strategy that it is found in many different kinds of writing, such as reports, cover letters, editorials, applications, proposals, law briefs, and reviews. In fact, there is hardly an essay in this book that does not use illustration in one way or another.

USING ILLUSTRATION ACROSS THE DISCIPLINES

When writing essays in the academic disciplines, you will have many opportunities to use the strategy of illustration to both organize and strengthen the presentation of your ideas. To determine whether illustration is the right strategy for you in a particular paper, review the guidelines described in Chapter 2, "Determining a Strategy for Developing Your Essay" (pages 34-35). Consider the following examples.

American Literature

1. **MAIN IDEA:** Mark Twain uses irony to speak out against racism in *The Adventures of Huckleberry Finn*.
2. **QUESTION:** Where does Mark Twain use irony to combat racism in *The Adventures of Huckleberry Finn*?
3. **STRATEGY:** Illustration. The direction words *uses* and *where* say "show me," and what better way to show than with solid, representative examples from the novel of Twain's use of irony to speak out against racism?
4. **SUPPORTING STRATEGY:** Argument. The examples can be used to argue in favor of a particular interpretation of Twain's work.

Criminal Justice

1. **MAIN IDEA:** America's criminal justice system neglects the families of capital offenders.
2. **QUESTION:** How has America's criminal justice system neglected the families of capital offenders?
3. **STRATEGY:** Illustration. Both the statement of the main idea and the question cry out for proof or evidence, and the best evidence would be a series of examples of the claimed neglect.
4. **SUPPORTING STRATEGY:** Process analysis. The paper might conclude with a possible remedy or solution—a step-by-step process for eliminating the current neglect.

Biology

1. **MAIN IDEA:** Cloning and other biotechnical discoveries give rise to serious moral and ethical issues that need our attention.
2. **QUESTION:** What are some of the moral and ethical issues raised by recent biotechnical discoveries that we need to address?
3. **STRATEGY:** Illustration. The direction words *what* and *some* call for examples of the moral and ethical issues raised by biotechnical discoveries.
4. **SUPPORTING STRATEGY:** Argument. The direction word *need* suggests that the examples should be both compelling and persuasive so that readers will want to address these issues.

PRACTICAL ADVICE FOR WRITING AN ESSAY OF ILLUSTRATION

As you plan, write, and revise your illustration essay, be mindful of the writing process guidelines described in Chapter 2. Pay particular attention to the basic requirements and essential ingredients for this writing strategy.

▶ Planning Your Essay of Illustration

Planning is an essential part of writing a good illustration essay. You can save yourself a great deal of effort by taking the time to think about the key building blocks of your essay before you actually begin to write.

Focus on Your Thesis or Main Idea.   Begin by thinking of how you can make your ideas clearer and more persuasive by illustrating them with examples—facts, anecdotes, and specific details. Once you have established your thesis—the main point that you will develop in your essay—you should find examples that add clarity, color, and authority.

Consider the following thesis:

> Americans are a pain-conscious people who would rather get rid of pain than seek and cure its root causes.

This assertion is broad; it cries out for evidence or support. You could make it stronger and more meaningful through illustration. You might, for example, point to the sheer number of over-the-counter painkillers available and the different types of pain they address, or you might cite specific situations in which people you know have gone to a drugstore instead of to a doctor. In addition, you might cite sales figures for painkillers in the United States and compare them with sales figures in other countries.

Gather More Examples Than You Can Use.   Before you begin to write, bring together as many examples as you can that are related to your subject—more than you can possibly use. An example may be anything from a fact or a statistic to an anecdote or a story; it may be stated in a few words—"India's population is now near 1.3 billion people"—or it may go on for several pages of elaborate description or explanation.

The kinds of examples you look for and where you look for them will depend, of course, on your subject and the point you want to make about it. If you plan to write about all the quirky, fascinating people who make up your family, you can gather your examples without leaving your room: descriptions of their habits and clothing, stories about their strange adventures, facts about their backgrounds, quotations from their conversations. If, however, you are writing an essay on book censorship in American public schools, you will need to do research in the library or on the Internet and read many sources to supply yourself with examples. Your essay might include accounts drawn from newspapers; statistics published by professional organizations; judicial opinions on censorship; and interviews with school board members, parents, publishers, and even the authors whose work has been pulled off library shelves or kept out of the classroom.

Choose Relevant Examples.   You must make sure that your examples are relevant. Do they clarify and support the points you want to make? Suppose the main point of your planned essay is that censorship currently runs rampant in American public education. A newspaper story about the banning of *The Catcher in the Rye* and *The Merchant of Venice* from the local high school's English curriculum would clearly be relevant because it concerns book censorship at a public school. The fact that James Joyce's novel *Ulysses* was once banned as obscene and then vindicated in a famous trial, although a landmark case of censorship in American history, has nothing to do with book censorship in contemporary public schools. While the case of *Ulysses* might be a useful example for other discussions of censorship, it would not be relevant to your essay.

Sometimes more than one of your examples will be relevant. In such cases, choose the examples that are most closely related to your thesis. If you were working on an essay on how Americans cope with pain, a statistic indicating the sales of a particular drug in a given year might be useful; however, a statistic showing that over the past ten years painkiller sales in America have increased more rapidly than the population has would be directly relevant to the idea that Americans are a pain-conscious people and would therefore be a more effective example.

Be Sure Your Examples Are Representative.   Besides being relevant, your examples should also be representative—that is, they should be typical of the main point or concept, indicative of a larger pattern rather than an uncommon or isolated occurrence. If, while working on the censorship paper, you found reports on a dozen quiet administrative hearings and orderly court cases, but only one report of a sensational incident in which books were actually burned in a school parking lot, the latter incident, however dramatic, is clearly not a representative example. You might want to mention the book burning in your essay as an extreme example, but you should not present it as typical.

❱ Organizing Your Essay of Illustration

Sequence Your Examples Logically.   It is important to arrange your examples in an order that serves your purpose, is easy for readers to follow, and will have maximum effect. Some possible patterns of organization include chronological order and spatial order. Others include moving from broad examples to personal examples, as in Tim Kreider's "The 'Busy' Trap," or from briefer examples to longer, more detailed ones, as in Jennifer Ackerman's "The Genius of Birds." Or you may hit on an order that "feels right" to you, as Edwin Way Teale did in his paragraph about winter superstitions (page 154).

How many examples you include depends, of course, on the length and nature of the assignment. Before starting the first draft, you may find it helpful to work out your organization in a rough outline, using only enough words so that you can tell which example each entry refers to.

Use Transitions.   While it is important to give the presentation of your examples an inherent logic, it is also important to link your examples to the topic sentences in your paragraphs and, indeed, to the thesis of your entire essay by using transitional words and expressions such as *for example, for instance, therefore, afterward, in other words, next,* and *finally.* Such structural devices will make the sequencing of the examples easy to follow.

▶ Revising and Editing Your Essay of Illustration

You may find it particularly helpful to share the drafts of your essays with other students in your writing class. To maximize the effectiveness of peer conferences, utilize the suggestions in the "Brief Guide to Peer Critiquing" box in Chapter 2 (pages 38–39). Feedback from these conferences often provides one or more places where you can start writing. Then, review Chapter 16 and the following questions to give your essay its final polish.

Questions for Revising and Editing: Illustration

1. Is my topic well focused?
2. Does my thesis statement clearly identify my topic and make an assertion about it?
3. Are my examples well chosen to support my thesis? Are there other examples that might work better?
4. Are my examples representative? That is, are they typical of the main point or concept rather than bizarre or atypical?
5. Do I have enough examples to be convincing? Do I have too many examples?
6. Have I developed my examples in enough detail to be clear to readers?
7. Have I organized my examples in some logical pattern, and is that pattern clear to readers?
8. Does the essay accomplish my purpose?
9. Are my topic sentences strong? Are my paragraphs unified?
10. Does my paper contain any errors in grammar, punctuation, or mechanics? Is my sentence style as clear, smooth, and persuasive as possible?

STUDENT ESSAY USING ILLUSTRATION AS A WRITING STRATEGY

Diets and dieting fascinated Paula Kersch, especially because she and her friends were constantly trying out the popular plans. Eventually, however, Paula began wondering: If these diets really worked, why were people always looking for new ones to try? She also wondered if these diets posed any real risks, especially when she started thinking about the more extreme ones. She made a list of the various diets she and her friends had tried and then did some research on the Internet to see what she could learn about the history of dieting. On the basis of what she discovered, she developed a thesis arguing for weight-management plans over quick fixes.

Before drafting her essay, Paula familiarized herself with the materials found in Chapter 14, "Writing with Sources," and Chapter 15, "A Brief Guide to Researching and Documenting Essays." What follows is the final draft of her essay. Notice how she uses examples of specific diet plans to explain her key points.

Weight Management:
More Than a Matter of Good Looks
Paula Kersch

Title introduces paper topic

Beginning engages reader by referring to common experience and observation

Americans are obsessed with their weight. Most Americans consider themselves in need of some type of diet. In 2017, the U.S. Centers for Disease Control and Prevention reported that "all 50 states had more than 1 in 5 adults (20 percent) with obesity" (United States, "New CDC Data"). Whether people are looking to lose those extra holiday pounds or the accumulation of a lifetime, there's plenty of help out there. Bookstore owners, for example, often stock an entire section of their stores with the latest diet books, and a quick search of the Internet reveals over 250 trendy diets that are currently in vogue. This help is there because dieting is big business in America. In fact, Melinda Parrish points out that currently "Americans spend north of $60 billion annually on diet and weight loss products" (1). Ironically, most nutritionists agree that fad diets simply don't work.

Thesis announces essay's focus: Trendy diets can be dangerous

In the face of the staggering failure rate for most fad diets, why do these quick weight loss plans remain so popular? Colorado State University Professor of Food Science and Human Nutrition Melissa Wdowik believes that when it comes to diets "vanity outweighs common sense" (1). If Americans knew more about the risks that accompany trendy diets and the seriousness of our obesity problem, perhaps they would not be so quick to look for a quick fix but instead would adopt a weight-management plan that would help them achieve the desired results without compromising their health and their pocketbooks.

3

Most of the currently popular quick-weight-loss schemes appeal to Americans' desire for instant gratification. Who wants to look forward to a year of losing a pound or less a week? Most of these diets fall into one of several categories: (1) fasts and detox cleanses, (2) plans that emphasize one food group while eliminating or minimizing others, and (3) diet pills and supplements. All of these crash-dieting methods produce immediate results. People who try them lose pounds quickly just as the advertisements promise—the South Beach Diet boasts seven pounds in seven days and Dr. Simeons's HCG Weight Loss Protocol, thirty-four pounds in forty-three days. Sadly, however, these results are short term. In addition to compromising their health, virtually all of these dieters gain back the weight they lose—and then some.

Organization: Numbers signal order in which schemes will be discussed

4

People have been using water and juice fasts and cleanses since biblical times for both spiritual and physical reasons. Many regimens last only a few days, resulting in the loss of five to seven pounds in some cases. One of the most popular was the Master Cleanse—also known as the Lemonade Diet—developed by alternative health enthusiast Stanley Burroughs. "To eliminate cravings for junk food, alcohol, tobacco, and drugs," all someone had to do with this plan, according to one nutritionist, was "consume a mixture of lemon or lime juice, maple syrup, water, and cayenne pepper six times a day for at least 10 days" (Wdowik 2). Because humans can go without food for longer periods of time if they have water, this regimen is not necessarily dangerous. However, some people push fasts and cleanses to unhealthy extremes. Even apart from any health risks, fasts and cleanses in general fail to produce the desired long-term weight loss desired.

Examples of first category of trendy diets — fasts and cleanses — illustrate dangers and problems

Parenthetical in-text citation documents information about Master Cleanse

5

Although there is a technical difference between fasting and starving, metabolically the human body does not differentiate between the two. When a person fasts, the body has to rely on burning its own reserves for energy. Because the body does not know when its next meal might be coming, the body lowers its metabolism in order to conserve fuel, thus slowing weight loss. Also, while fasting may produce lost pounds on the scale, usually it is not the fat loss most dieters aim

Explains in detail what happens during a fast

for. Short-term fasts result in large water losses, which are almost immediately regained once the fast is over.

The longer a fast or cleanse continues, the greater the serious risk for muscle damage in the body because the body is not getting the nutrients it needs. Additionally, people are at risk of gaining even more weight than they lost after coming off a fast because their bodies will still be functioning at a slower metabolic rate, allowing more rapid weight gain on fewer calories. Most importantly, repeated fasting can permanently alter the body's base metabolic rate. 6

One does not have to be a nutritionist to understand that if people eat only foods from one food group and do not eat from others, their bodies will not be able to function correctly. Over the years there have been a number of high-protein low-carb diets that promise quick weight loss by emphasizing foods high in protein, while excluding most carbohydrates. The infamous Last-Chance Diet of the 1970s, with its emphasis on a liquid protein drink and the exclusion of all other food, led to numerous heart attacks and over sixty deaths among users. The Atkins Diet, an enormously popular diet first developed in the 1970s and later updated in *Dr. Atkins's New Diet Revolution*, is another prime example of a diet that excludes large groups of foods. Meat and fat are emphasized to the exclusion of other foods, making the diet high in cholesterol. Neither medically sound nor nutritionally safe, this diet results in a rapid and dangerous drop in weight. 7

Introduces second category of trendy diets—plans that emphasize one food group while eliminating or minimizing others

In spite of the fact that this and other low-carb diets—like the popular Dr. Arthur Agatston's *The South Beach Diet Supercharged* and *Dr. Gott's No Flour, No Sugar Diet*—can compromise a person's health, many people continue to follow these diets to shed their excess pounds. While the Internet has made these and other diets that emphasize single foods or food groups, like the Cabbage Soup Diet, the Grapefruit Diet, and the Apple Cider Vinegar Diet, easier to share and kept them in fashion (Wdowik 4), they have all been debunked as unhealthy and unrealistic solutions to a very real problem. 8

Relevant and representative examples illustrate the range of "one food group" diets

America's search for a quick, easy solution to the weight problem is perhaps epitomized best in the 9

Introduces third category of trendy

diets — pills and supplements — and provides historical perspective

popularity of diet pills and supplements. In years gone by, dieters have used thyroid hormone injections, amphetamines, Hydroxycut, and fen-phen—a combination of fenfluramine or dextenfluramine and phentermine—among other things. At the request of the Food and Drug Administration (FDA), manufacturers took most of these products off the market when doctors linked their usage to heart valve and liver damage and in some cases even death (Kolata).

Nevertheless, the search for a magic bullet to combat excess weight continued, spurred on by the public's desire for more attractive and healthy bodies and corporate America's pursuit of unimaginable profits if they are able to hit on the right formula. In June of 2008, GlaxoSmithKline first marketed Alli (pronounced "ally," as in supporter or friend), an over-the-counter version of the prescription-strength Xenical. Alli promises to increase weight loss by up to 50% over what might normally be lost by most people following a healthy diet and a regular exercise program. Alli also has some annoying side effects, among them "excessive flatulence, oily bowel movements which can be difficult to control, and anal leakage" (Baldwin). Some may find these side effects minor deterrents, but others may not be willing to endure the embarrassment and inconvenience associated with them. Critics, like Dr. Sidney Wolfe, director of Public Citizen's Health Research Group in Washington, DC, see no reason to take Alli because "there are demonstrable short-term risks and no possibility of long-term benefit" (qtd. in Mann).

Example explores promise of diet pill Alli in detail

Discusses the drawbacks of using Alli

Quotation from medical authority supports reservations about using Alli

Additional examples of diet drugs and supplements

One competitor for Alli is Qsymia, a prescription-strength drug designed to help chronically overweight and obese adults manage their weight along with a balanced diet and regular exercise routine. Like Alli, Qsymia has a long list of undesirable side effects, which make taking it for any length of time difficult. On the supplement front, garcinia cambogia is being touted as a natural fat burner, appetite suppressant, and mood enhancer. Since being featured on *The Dr. Oz Show* in 2012 as a breakthrough, revolutionary weight-loss supplement, products containing garcinia cambogia have flooded the market. Unfortunately, many of these products do not contain the amount of the active ingredient

10

11

hydroxycitric acid (HCA) that they advertise. When properly dosed, garcinia cambogia does show some promise as a weight-loss supplement.

It is obvious from even this cursory examination of trendy dieting practices that "get-thin-quick" schemes typically offer little more than empty promises. According to experts, the key to real weight loss is not dieting: The best results come from long-term changes in lifestyle habits. As nutritionist Melissa Wdowik reminds us, "there's no simple secret to losing weight. Achieving sustained weight loss and maintenance requires reducing your calorie intake and increasing your activity levels" (5). While this kind of commonsense weight control cannot offer fast results, it usually proves successful where diets ultimately fail.

Here's why. Losing weight in a healthy manner is a slow process. Most nutritionists suggest that a sensible goal is 2–4 pounds per month. When a person follows a sustainable eating and exercise program, that person's body will naturally start to slim down over time. Eating a well-balanced diet with foods from the four food groups gives the body all the essentials it needs. The high amounts of fiber in fruits, vegetables, and whole grains make the stomach feel full and satisfied. When the body receives the nutrients it needs, it functions better as well. It is common knowledge that depression, migraine headaches, and lethargy are often triggered by overindulgence or nutritional deficiencies. Once moderation is achieved and any deficiencies eliminated, ailments tend to disappear (United States, "Nutrition").

Many trendy diets do not advocate exercise; some even claim that exercise is unnecessary. But working out is an essential ingredient in any good weight-management program. Exercise tones up the body and gives people more energy and a sense of well-being. Moderate exercise such as rapid walking can rev up the metabolism and help the body burn calories more efficiently. Regular exercise has the additional benefit of increasing over time the body's base metabolic rate so that more food may be eaten with no weight gain (United States, "Physical").

Trendy dieting as practiced during the past two or three decades just has not worked. Fasting,

Weight management introduced as healthy alternative to "get-thin-quick" schemes

Emphasis on eating well-balanced diet and exercising regularly

Benefits of exercise explained

Conclusion explains that trendy

12

13

14

15

diets will not solve America's problem with obesity

one-food-group dieting, and diet pills and supplements often do more harm than good in terms of nutrition and general well-being. As a society, Americans must face the obesity problem head-on. If we do not, the consequences will be dire. Dr. David L. Katz,

Quotation emphasizes gravity of the problem, lending support to the writer's position

nutrition and weight-control expert and director of the Yale Prevention Research Center, warns that by "2018 more than 100 million Americans will be obese, and we will be spending roughly $340 billion annually on obesity, a tripling of current levels that are already breaking the bank" (Katz B3). Long-term weight-management programs that incorporate healthy lifestyle habits offer a real solution where trendy diets fail. When overweight Americans forsake the lure of quick weight loss and understand all the negatives associated with these trendy diets, they will begin to get a handle on what they must do to tackle their weight problems. It worked for me; it can work for you as well.

Works Cited

Writer uses MLA style for works cited

Baldwin, Donovan. "Pros and Cons of the New Alli Diet Pill." *SearchWarp.com*, 20 June 2007, searchwarp.com/ swa224916.htm.

Katz, David. "The Compelling Case for Obesity Control." *Naples Daily News*, 3 Jan. 2010, pp. B1+.

Kolata, Gina. "2 Top Diet Drugs Are Recalled amid Reports of Heart Defects." *New York Times*, 16 Sept. 1997. General OneFile, link.galegroup.com.ezproxy.bpl.org/ apps/doc/A150292680/ITOF?u.

Mann, Denise. "All about Alli, the Weight Loss Pill." *WebMD*, 2007, www.webmd.com/diet/obesity/weight -loss-prescription-weight-loss-alli.

Parrish, Melinda. "Time to Defund the Diet Industry?" *HuffingtonPost.com*, 17 Mar. 2017, www.huffingtonpost .com/entry/time-to-defund-the-diet-industry_us _58c2b63ee4b0c3276fb783c7.

See Chapter 15, List of Works Cited on pages 552–59, for more models of MLA entries.

United States, Department of Health and Human Services, Centers for Disease Control and Prevention. "New CDC Data Shows US Adults Still Struggling with Obesity." 8 Aug. 2017, www.cdc.gov/media/releases/ 2017/20831-obesity-data-maps.html.

———, ———, ———. "Nutrition for Everyone." 14 Sept. 2009, www.cdc.gov/nutrition/general.

———, ———, ———. "Physical Activity for Everyone." 14 Sept. 2009, www.cdc.gov/physicalactivity/success/index.htm.

Wdowik, Melissa. "The Long, Strange History of Dieting Fads." *The Conversation*, 6 Nov. 2017, www.theconversation.com/the-long-strange-history-of-dieting-fads-82294.

Student Reflection
Paula Kersch

Q. How did you happen to come up with diets as a topic?
A. I had originally wanted to do a paper on world hunger—I was interested in what was happening in war-torn areas like the Middle East, the Sudan, and Haiti. While researching this topic in the library, I discovered an abundance of material on eating disorders, and, on a broader scale, dieting. I discovered that dieting was nothing new—people have been trying to lose weight for a long time, and some of the diet routines that they were willing to try fascinated me.

Q. So diets turned out to be a subject that was more interesting to you?
A. Yes, the topic interested me because I'm trying to lose some weight. I want to feel healthier and to look better. It was a subject I felt comfortable with, but I must admit there were some students in class who did not feel all that comfortable talking about food, dieting, and body image. But you've got to admit that it was more manageable than world hunger. A lot of my friends were talking about quick and easy ways to lose those extra pounds. My friends proved to be a valuable resource as I started my paper. Not only did they tell me about diets that I'd never heard about, but they also shared their experiences—both pleasant and unpleasant—with these plans.

Q. Well, what do you mean by "valuable resource"?
A. My friends were a valuable resource in the sense that collectively they had tried a variety of diets with varying degrees of success. Some of the diets they had learned about on the Internet and others had been prescribed by their doctors. I started to wonder if any of these diet programs posed any special risks, especially when my friends told me about the crazy regimens they were on.

Q. Let's get back to the examples. How did you come up with them?
A. Actually, that wasn't so hard. After talking with my friends, I googled the various diet plans they had told me about and discovered a wealth of material in newspapers, magazines, and government studies. I did a lot of reading before I selected the examples that seemed best suited to illustrate what I wanted to say and chose quotations from authorities who supported my position.

Q. As you were writing this paper, did you share your drafts with other students in the class?
A. Yes. In total, I probably wrote at least five different versions of this essay. I shared each draft with several members of the class, and they were extremely helpful. I remember one student's questions in particular, because she really got me to focus on the problems with fad diets, especially the sometimes nasty side effects associated with Alli. Other classmates helped me see places in my essay where I needed additional examples to be more convincing. I'm amazed at how different my final draft is from the very first draft I wrote.

Q. So, while you needed a number of drafts to get your essay right, the assignment went smoothly for the most part?
A. Well, not exactly. I had a difficult time writing the essay at first. After finding so much material on diets in the library and online, I felt a bit overwhelmed. I knew that I needed to get my head around my subject, but I just couldn't take in all the information at one time. Once I kind of decided what I wanted to say, things started to come into focus. Another issue was audience—it always felt like I was writing an article for a women's magazine even though I thought I was gearing my essay toward a more general college audience.

Your Response

What did you learn from Paula's essay and reflection? What challenges do you expect to face as you write your own illustration essay? Based on Paula's experiences and the practical advice discussed earlier in this chapter (pages 156–59), how will you overcome those challenges?

Be Specific

NATALIE GOLDBERG

Ritch Davidson

Author Natalie Goldberg has made a specialty of writing about writing. Her first and best-known work, *Writing Down the Bones: Freeing the Writer Within*, was published in 1986. Goldberg's advice to would-be writers is, on the one hand, practical and pithy; on the other, it is almost mystical in its call to know and appreciate the world. In a 2007 interview with Shara Stewart for *Ascent* magazine, Goldberg remarked that "[w]riting and Zen for me are completely interconnected. The relationship is seamless for me. . . . Writing is a practice for me, like someone else would do sitting or walking. Writing is a true spiritual practice." "Be Specific," the excerpt that appears here, is representative of the book as a whole. Amid widespread acclaim for the book, one critic commented, "Goldberg teaches us not only how to write better, but how to live better." *Writing Down the Bones* was followed by four more books about writing: *Wild Mind: Living the Writer's Life* (1990), *Living Color: A Writer Paints Her World* (1996), *Thunder and Lightning: Cracking Open the Writer's Craft* (2000), and *The Essential Writer's Notebook* (2001). Goldberg has also written fiction; her first novel, *Banana Rose*, was published in 1994. Her most recent books are *Old Friend from Far Away: The Practice of Writing Memoir* (2008), *The True Secret of Writing: Connecting Life with Language* (2013), and *The Great Spring* (2016), a collection of personal stories.

Notice the way in which Goldberg demonstrates her advice to be specific in the following selection.

Preparing to Read

Suppose someone says to you, "I walked in the woods." What do you envision? Write down what you see in your mind's eye. Now suppose someone says, "I walked in the redwood forest." Again, write what you see. What's different about your two descriptions, and why?

B e specific. Don't say "fruit." Tell what kind of fruit—"It is a pomegranate." Give things the dignity of their names. Just as with human beings, it is rude to say, "Hey, girl, get in line." That "girl" has a name. (As a matter of fact, if she's at least twenty years old, she's a woman, not a "girl" at all.) Things, too, have names. It is much better to say "the geranium in the window" than "the flower in the window." "Geranium"—that one word gives us a much more specific picture. It penetrates more deeply

1

into the beingness of that flower. It immediately gives us the scene by the window—red petals, green circular leaves, all straining toward sunlight.

> **Don't say 'fruit.' Tell what kind of fruit — 'It is a pomegranate.' Give things the dignity of their names.**

About ten years ago I decided I had to learn the names of plants and flowers in my environment. I bought a book on them and walked down the tree-lined streets of Boulder, examining leaf, bark, and seed, trying to match them up with their descriptions and names in the book. Maple, elm, oak, locust. I usually tried to cheat by asking people working in their yards the names of the flowers and trees growing there. I was amazed how few people had any idea of the names of the live beings inhabiting their little plot of land.

When we know the name of something, it brings us closer to the ground. It takes the blur out of our mind; it connects us to the earth. If I walk down the street and see "dogwood," "forsythia," I feel more friendly toward the environment. I am noticing what is around me and can name it. It makes me more awake.

If you read the poems of William Carlos Williams, you will see how specific he is about plants, trees, flowers—chicory, daisy, locust, poplar, quince, primrose, black-eyed Susan, lilacs—each has its own integrity. Williams says, "Write what's in front of your nose." It's good for us to know what is in front of our noses. Not just "daisy," but how the flower is in the season we are looking at it—"The dayseye hugging the earth / in August . . . brownedged, / green and pointed scales / armor his yellow."[1] Continue to hone your awareness: to the name, to the month, to the day, and finally to the moment.

Williams also says: "No idea, but in things." Study what is "in front of your nose." By saying "geranium" instead of "flower," you are penetrating more deeply into the present and being there. The closer we can get to what's in front of our nose, the more it can teach us everything. "To see the World in a Grain of Sand, and a heaven in a Wild Flower . . ."[2]

In writing groups and classes, too, it is good to quickly learn the names of all the other group members. It helps to ground you in the group and make you more attentive to each other's work.

Learn the names of everything: birds, cheese, tractors, cars, buildings. A writer is all at once everything—an architect, French cook, farmer—and at the same time, a writer is none of these things.

---

[1] William Carlos Williams, "Daisy," in *The Collected Earlier Poems* (New York: New Directions, 1938).
[2] William Blake, "The Auguries of Innocence."

Thinking Critically about the Text

Natalie Goldberg found that she wasn't the only one in her neighborhood who didn't know the names of local trees and flowers. Would you be able to name many? How might you go about learning them? (Consider why Goldberg says it was "cheating" to ask people the names of their flowers and trees.) What would you gain by knowing them?

Questions on Subject

1. Goldberg says that to name an object gives it dignity (paragraph 1) and integrity (paragraph 4). What does she mean in each case?

2. In paragraphs 3, 5, and 6, Goldberg cites a number of advantages to be gained by knowing the names of things. Review these advantages. What are they? Do they ring true?

3. Throughout the essay, Goldberg instructs readers to be specific and to be aware of the world around them. Of what besides names are the readers advised to be aware? Why?

Questions on Strategy

1. How does Goldberg "specifically" follow the advice she gives writers in this essay?

2. Goldberg makes several lists of the names of things. What purpose do these lists serve? How does she use these specifics to illustrate her point?

3. What specific **audience** is Goldberg addressing in this essay? How do you know?

4. The strategies of **definition** and illustration are closely intertwined in this essay; to name a thing precisely, after all, is to take the first step in defining it. What central concept is defined by Goldberg's many illustrations of naming? How might a writer use illustration to make definitions richer and more meaningful?

Illustration in Action

Specific examples are always more effective and convincing than general ones. A useful exercise in learning to be specific is to see the words we use for people, places, objects, and ideas as being positioned somewhere on a continuum of specificity. In the following chart, notice how the words become more specific as you move from left to right:

More General	General	Specific	More Specific
Organism	Reptile	Snake	Coral snake
Food	Sandwich	Corned beef sandwich	Reuben

Fill in the missing part for each of the following lists:

More General	General	Specific	More Specific
Writing instrument		Fountain pen	Waterman fountain pen
Vehicle	Car		1958 Chevrolet Impala
Book	Reference book	Dictionary	
American		Navaho	Laguna Pueblo
	Oral medicine	Gel capsule	Tylenol Gel Caps
School	High school	Technical high school	

Writing Suggestions

1. Write a brief essay advising your readers of something they should do. Title your essay, as Goldberg does, with a directive ("Be Specific"). Tell your readers how they can improve their lives by taking your advice, and give strong examples of the behavior you are recommending.

2. Goldberg likes William Carlos Williams's statement "No idea, but in things" (paragraph 5). Using this line as both a title and a thesis, write your own **argument** for the use of the specific over the general in a certain field — journalism, history, political science, biology, or literature, for example. Be sure to support your argument with relevant, representative examples.

The Genius of Birds

JENNIFER ACKERMAN

Science, nature, and health writer Jennifer Ackerman was born in 1959 and educated at Yale University. Her books include *The Curious Naturalist* (1991), *Sex Sleep Eat Drink Dream: A Day in the Life of Your Body* (2007), and *Ah-Choo! The Uncommon Life of Your Common Cold* (2010). As these books suggest, Ackerman follows her curiosities wherever they lead her as a writer. But even when she writes about complex topics, she does so with a general audience in mind, aiming to, as she writes on her Web site, "explain and interpret

Robert Llewellyn

science for a lay audience and to explore the riddle of humanity's place in the natural world, blending scientific knowledge with imaginative vision." In addition to authoring books, Ackerman has written for many different publications, including the *New York Times, National Geographic, Scientific American,* and *Wilderness*. She has also held fellowships and lectured at several universities, including the Bunting Institute at Radcliffe College, Harvard University, Brown University, and the Massachusetts Institute of Technology.

The following selection was first published in Ackerman's most recent book, *The Genius of Birds* (2016). As you read, be aware of Ackerman's sense of audience and how she uses examples in ways that are both sophisticated and accessible.

Preparing to Read

Many books have been written about the animals that, traditionally, people have singled out and praised for their intelligence or even seemingly human qualities. When you think of intelligent or clever animals, which ones come to mind? Where do those perceptions and stereotypes come from?

For a long time, the knock on birds was that they're stupid. Beady eyed and nut brained. Reptiles with wings. Pigeon heads. Turkeys. They fly into windows, peck at their reflections, buzz into power lines, blunder into extinction. 1

Our language reflects our disrespect. Something worthless or unappealing is "for the birds." An ineffectual politician is a "lame duck." To "lay an egg" is to flub a performance. To be "henpecked" is to be harassed with persistent nagging. "Eating crow" is eating humble pie. The expression "bird brain," for a stupid, foolish, or scatterbrained person, entered the English language in the early 1920s because people thought of birds as mere flying, pecking automatons, with brains so small they had no capacity for thought at all. 2

That view is a gone goose. In the past two decades or so, from fields and ₃
laboratories around the world have flowed examples of bird species capable of mental feats comparable to those found in primates. There's a kind of bird that creates colorful designs out of berries, bits of glass, and blossoms to attract females, and another kind that hides up to thirty-three thousand seeds scattered over dozens of square miles and remembers where it put them months later. There's a species that solves a classic puzzle at nearly the same pace as a five-year-old child, and one that's an expert at picking locks. There are birds that can count and do simple math, make their own tools, move to the beat of music, comprehend basic principles of physics, remember the past, and plan for the future.

In the past, other animals have gotten all the publicity for their near- ₄
human cleverness. Chimps make stick spears to hunt smaller primates and dolphins communicate in a complex system of whistles and clicks. Great apes console one another and elephants mourn the loss of their own.

> " A flood of new research has overturned the old views, and people are finally starting to accept that birds are far more intelligent that we ever imagined. "

Now birds have joined the party. A ₅
flood of new research has overturned the old views, and people are finally starting to accept that birds are far more intelligent than we ever imagined—in some ways closer to our primate relatives than to their reptilian ones.

Beginning in the 1980s, the charm- ₆
ing and cunning African grey parrot named Alex partnered with scientist Irene Pepperberg to show the world that some birds appear to have intellectual abilities rivaling those of primates. Before Alex died suddenly at the age of thirty-one (half his expected life span), he had mastered a vocabulary of hundreds of English labels for objects, colors, and shapes. He understood the categories of same and different in number, color, and shape. He could look at a tray holding an array of objects of various colors and materials and say how many there were of a certain type. "How many green keys?" Pepperberg would ask, displaying several green and orange keys and corks. Eight out of ten times, Alex got it right. He could use numbers to answer questions about addition. Among his greatest triumphs, says Pepperberg, were his knowledge of abstract concepts, including a zerolike concept; his capacity to figure out the meaning of a number label from its position in the number line; and his ability to sound out words the way a child does: "N-U-T." Until Alex, we thought we were alone in our use of words, or almost alone. Alex could not only comprehend words, he could use them to talk back with cogency, intelligence, and perhaps even feeling. His final words to Pepperberg as she put him back in his

cage the night before he died were his daily refrain: "You be good, see you tomorrow. I love you."

In the 1990s, reports began to roll in from New Caledonia, a small [7] island in the South Pacific, of crows that fashion their own tools in the wild and appear to transmit local styles of toolmaking from one generation to the next—a feat reminiscent of human culture and proof that sophisticated tool skills do not require a primate brain.

When scientists presented these crows with puzzles to test their problem- [8] solving abilities, the birds astonished them with their crafty solutions. In 2002, Alex Kacelnik and his colleagues at Oxford University "asked" a captive New Caledonian crow named Betty, "Can you get the food that's out of reach in a little bucket at the bottom of this tube?" Betty blew away the experimenters by spontaneously bending a piece of wire into a hook tool to pull up the little bucket.

Among the published studies tumbling from scientific journals are some [9] with titles that lift the brows: "Have we met before? Pigeons recognize familiar human faces"; "The syntax of gargles in the chickadee"; "Language discrimination by Java sparrows"; "Chicks like consonant music"; "Personality differences explain leadership in barnacle geese"; and "Pigeons on par with primates in numerical competence."

BIRD BRAIN: The slur came from the belief that birds had brains so dimin- [10] utive they had to be devoted only to instinctual behavior. The avian brain had no cortex like ours, where all the "smart" stuff happens. Birds had minimal noggins for good reason, we thought: to allow for airborne ways; to defy gravity; to hover, arabesque, dive, soar for days on end, migrate thousands of miles, and maneuver in tight spaces. For their mastery of air, it seemed, birds paid a heavy cognitive penalty.

A closer look has taught us otherwise. Birds do indeed have brains very [11] different from our own—and no wonder. Humans and birds have been evolving independently for a very long time, since our last common ancestor more than 300 million years ago. But some birds, in fact, have relatively large brains for their body size, just as we do. Moreover, when it comes to brainpower, size seems to matter less than the number of neurons, where they're located, and how they're connected. And some bird brains, it turns out, pack very high numbers of neurons where it counts, with densities akin to those found in primates, and links and connections much like ours. This may go a long way toward explaining why certain birds have such sophisticated cognitive abilities.

Like our brains, the brains of birds are lateralized; they have "sides" that [12] process different kinds of information. They also have the ability to replace old brain cells with new ones just when they're needed most. And although avian brains are organized in an entirely different way from our brains, they share similar genes and neural circuits, and are capable of feats of quite extraordinary mental power. To wit: Magpies can recognize their own image in a mirror, a grasp of "self" once thought limited to humans, great apes, elephants, and dolphins and linked to highly developed social understanding. Western scrub jays use Machiavellian tactics to hide their food caches from other jays—but only if they've stolen food themselves. These birds seem to have a rudimentary ability to know what other birds are "thinking" and, perhaps, to grasp their perspective. They can also remember what kind of food they buried in a particular place—and when—so they can retrieve the morsel before it spoils. This ability to remember the what, where, and when of an event, called episodic memory, suggests to some scientists the possibility that these jays may be able to travel back into the past in their own minds—a key component of the kind of mental time travel once vaunted as uniquely human.

13 News has arrived that songbirds learn their songs the way we learn languages and pass these tunes along in rich cultural traditions that began tens of millions of years ago, when our primate ancestors were still scuttling about on all fours.

14 Some birds are born Euclideans, capable of using geometric clues and landmarks to orient themselves in three-dimensional space, navigate through unknown territory, and locate hidden treasures. Others are born accountants. In 2015 researchers found that newborn chicks spatially "map" numbers from left to right, as most humans do (left means less; right means more). This suggests that birds share with us a left-to-right orientation system—a cognitive strategy that underlies our human capacity for higher mathematics. Baby birds can also understand proportion and can learn to choose a target from an array of objects on the basis of its ordinal position (third, eighth, ninth). They can do simple arithmetic, as well, such as addition and subtraction.

15 Bird brains may be little, but it's plain they punch well above their weight.

Thinking Critically about the Text

Ackerman makes some extraordinary claims about the intellectual abilities of birds. Do any of her claims make you skeptical? Why, or why not?

Questions on Subject

1. According to Ackerman, how have our views of birds changed over the past several decades?

2. The writer refers to chimps, apes, and elephants in the fourth paragraph. What larger point is she making with these examples?

3. What have studies shown to be remarkable about the crows in New Caledonia?

4. Where did the insult "bird brain" come from? What incorrect assumptions was it based on, according to Ackerman?

Questions on Strategy

1. Ackerman opens her essay by focusing on the view that birds are stupid, noting that even "[o]ur language reflects our disrespect" (paragraph 2). Why do you think she chose to begin this way? How do her examples help her set up her argument?

2. In paragraph 12, the writer argues that birds are self-conscious animals, with high-level cognitive abilities. Do you find her **examples** convincing? Why, or why not?

3. The writer uses many different examples, often including several within a single paragraph. But she spends all of paragraph 6 describing a "charming and cunning African grey parrot named Alex." Why do you think she devotes this long paragraph to one example? How is it related to her overall **argument**?

4. Where in the essay does Ackerman use **comparison and contrast** in the context of birds and humans? How does it support her main **purpose** in the essay?

Illustration in Action

Writers use examples to support claims, provide specific evidence, and clarify ideas. In small groups, consider one of the following general assertions:

- Many of the most important lessons in college occur outside the classroom.
- While social media may make them feel connected, today's college students are actually more isolated, disconnected, and anxious than they've ever been.
- More than any other quality, an effective teacher or professor must have sincere compassion for students.
- While a traditional college education is valuable for many people, not everyone needs to get a four-year degree.
- While STEM fields are important, students still need the skills and knowledge that comes from a broader liberal arts background.
- Overall, the technological progress of the last thirty years has improved education.

With members of your group, choose and discuss the examples you might use to support or clarify this claim and idea. You might also discuss *how* you would use the examples. For example, would it make sense to choose several examples, or would one extended illustration be sufficient? Alternatively, for some of these generalizations, you might consider identifying examples that suggest counterarguments.

Writing Suggestions

1. After showing how birds were traditionally seen as "stupid" and "nut brained," Ackerman writes that our view of these animals has changed dramatically. Her essay helps correct a misunderstanding. Write about a topic that has been misunderstood, and then use illustration to lead your readers to a better

understanding of the topic. You might use a basic template (or variation on it) such as: *For years, people believed that _____, but a closer look [or more recent evidence or example] reveals that _____.* As Ackerman does, you might want to begin by using examples to establish the previous, erroneous view.

2. Ackerman considers some parallels between the cognitive skills of birds and those of humans. For instance, she writes that some birds may have "episodic memory," which she describes as a "key component of the kind of mental time travel once vaunted as uniquely human" (paragraph 12). From your perspective, what abilities or qualities make humans "uniquely human" and distinct from other animals? Write a brief essay on this topic, and support your claims with specific examples.

If You Had One Day with Someone Who's Gone

MITCH ALBOM

Rob Kim/Getty Images

Journalist and author Mitch Albom was born in Passaic, New Jersey, in 1958. He earned a degree in sociology from Brandeis University in 1979 and master's degrees in journalism and business admin- istration from Columbia University in 1981 and 1982. Starting in 1985, after working for newspapers in New York and Florida, Albom landed a staff position at the *Detroit Free Press*, where he writes a regular sports column. Over the years he has earned a loyal following of Detroit sports fans both as a columnist and as a host of radio and television sports talk shows. His reputation as a sportswriter blossomed with the publication of *The Live Albom: The Best of* Detroit Free Press *Sports* (1988–1995), four volumes of his sports column. With the University of Michigan's legendary football coach Bo Schembechler, he wrote *Bo: The Bo Schembechler Story* (1989) and, when Michigan won the national championship in basketball, he authored *Fab Five: Basketball, Trash Talk, and the American Dream* (1993). But it was the publication of *Tuesdays with Morrie: An Old Man, a Young Man, and Life's Greatest Lesson* (1997), the story of Albom's weekly visits with his former sociology professor Morrie Schwartz, that catapulted Albom onto the national stage. Albom followed this work of nonfiction with *Have a Little Faith: A True Story* (2009) and the novels *The Five People You Meet in Heaven* (2003), *The Time Keeper* (2012), and *The First Phone Call from Heaven* (2014), all of which have been national best sellers. His most recent novel, *The Magic Strings of Frankie Presto*, came out in 2015.

In "If You Had One Day with Someone Who's Gone," an essay first published in *Parade* magazine on September 17, 2006, Albom uses the illustrative stories of five people to find out what they would do if they were granted one more day with a loved one. His examples led him to a surprising life lesson.

Preparing to Read

Have you ever lost or become disconnected from someone you loved or were close to — a family member or childhood friend? What were the circumstances that separated you? What would you most like to do with this person if you could be reconnected for a whole day?

Her world shattered in a telephone call. My mother was fifteen years old. "Your father is dead," her aunt told her.   1

Dead? How could he be dead? Hadn't she seen him the night before, when she kissed him goodnight? Hadn't he given her two new words to look up in the dictionary? Dead?   2

"You're a liar," my mother said.

But it wasn't a lie. Her father, my grandfather, had collapsed that morning from a massive heart attack. No final hugs. No goodbye. Just a phone call. And he was gone.

Have you ever lost someone you love and wanted one more conversation, one more day to make up for the time when you thought they would be here forever? I wrote that sentence as part of a new novel. Only after I finished did I realize that, my whole life, I had wondered this question of my mother.

> " **Have you ever lost someone you love and wanted one more conversation, one more day to make up for the time when you thought they would be here forever?** "

So, finally, I asked her.

"One more day with my father?" she said. Her voice seemed to tumble back into some strange, misty place. It had been six decades since their last day together. Murray had wanted his little girl, Rhoda, to be a doctor. He had wanted her to stay single and go to medical school. But after his death, my mother had to survive. She had to look after a younger brother and a depressed mother. She finished high school and married the first boy she ever dated. She never finished college.

"I guess, if I saw my father again, I would first apologize for not becoming a doctor," she answered. "But I would say that I became a different kind of doctor, someone who helped the family whenever they had problems.

"My father was my pal, and I would tell him I missed having a pal around the house after he was gone. I would tell him that my mother lived a long life and was comfortable at the end. And I would show him my family—his grandchildren and his great-grandchildren—of which I am the proudest. I hope he'd be proud of me, too."

My mother admitted that she cried when she first saw the movie *Ghost*, where Patrick Swayze "comes back to life" for a few minutes to be with his girlfriend. She couldn't help but wish for time like that with her father. I began to pose this scenario to other people—friends, colleagues, readers. How would they spend a day with a departed loved one? Their responses said a lot about what we long for.

Almost everyone wanted to once again "tell them how much I loved them"—even though these were people they had loved their whole lives on Earth.

Others wanted to relive little things. Michael Carroll, from San Antonio, Texas, wrote that he and his departed father "would head for the racetrack, then off to Dad's favorite hamburger place to eat and chat about old times."

Cathy Koncurat of Bel Air, Maryland, imagined a reunion with her best friend, who died after mysteriously falling into an icy river. People had always wondered what happened. "But if I had one more day with her, those questions wouldn't be important. Instead, I'd like to spend it the way we did when we were girls — shopping, seeing a movie, getting our hair done."

Some might say, "That's such an ordinary day." 14

Maybe that's the point. 15

Rabbi Gerald Wolpe has spent nearly fifty years on the pulpit and is a 16 senior fellow at the University of Pennsylvania's Center for Bioethics. Yet, at some moment every day, he is an eleven-year-old boy who lost his dad to a sudden heart attack in 1938.

"My father is a prisoner of my memory," he said. "Would he even recog- 17 nize me today?" Rabbi Wolpe can still picture the man, a former vaudevillian, taking him to Boston Braves baseball games or singing him a bedtime prayer.

Help me always do the right 18

Bless me every day and night. 19

If granted one more day, Rabbi Wolpe said, he "would share the good 20 and the bad. My father needed to know things. For example, as a boy, he threw a snowball at his brother and hit him between the eyes. His brother went blind. My father went to his death feeling guilty for that.

"But we now know his brother suffered an illness that made him suscep- 21 tible to losing his vision. I would want to say, 'Dad, look. It wasn't your fault.'"

At funerals, Rabbi Wolpe often hears mourners lament missed moments: 22 "I never apologized. My last words were in anger. *If only I could have one more chance.*"

Maury De Young, a pastor in Kentwood, Michigan, hears similar 23 things in his church. But De Young can sadly relate. His own son, Der- rick, was killed in a car accident a few years ago, at age sixteen, the night before his big football game. There was no advance notice. No chance for goodbye.

"If I had one more day with him?" De Young said, wistfully. "I'd start it 24 off with a long, long hug. Then we'd go for a walk, maybe to our cottage in the woods."

De Young had gone to those woods after Derrick's death. He'd sat under 25 a tree and wept. His faith had carried him through. And it eases his pain now, he said, "because I know Derrick is in heaven."

Still, there are questions. Derrick's football number was 42. The day after his 26 accident, his team, with heavy hearts, won a playoff game by scoring 42 points. And the next week, the team won the state title by scoring — yes — 42 points.

"I'd like to ask my son," De Young whispered, "if he had something to 27 do with that."

We often fantasize about a perfect day — something exotic and far away. 28 But when it comes to those we miss, we desperately want one more familiar meal, even one more argument. What does this teach us? That the ordinary is precious. That the normal day is a treasure.

Think about it. When you haven't seen a loved one in a long time, the 29 first few hours of catching up feel like a giddy gift, don't they? That's the gift we wish for when we can't catch up anymore. That feeling of connection. It could be a bedside chat, a walk in the woods, even a few words from the dictionary.

I asked my mother if she still recalled those two words her father had 30 assigned her on the last night of his life.

"Oh, yes," she said quickly. "They were 'detrimental' and 'inculcate.' I'll 31 never forget them."

Then she sighed, yearning for a day she didn't have and words she never 32 used. And it made me want to savor every day with her even more.

Thinking Critically about the Text

Albom shares with us the stories of five people who lost a loved one. In each case, the loss was sudden and unexpected. How did the suddenness of the loss affect each of the survivors? In what ways do you think sudden loss is different from losing someone to a terminal illness or old age? Explain.

Questions on Subject

1. Why did Albom's mother cry when she first viewed the movie *Ghost*?

2. When asked how they would spend a day with a departed loved one — if that were possible — how did people respond? What life lesson does Albom draw from these responses in his conclusion?

3. What do you think Rabbi Wolpe meant when he said, "My father is a prisoner of my memory" (paragraph 17)?

4. What does it say about Albom's mother and the relationship she had with her father when it's revealed that she still remembers the two vocabulary words her father gave her the night before he died six decades ago? Explain.

Questions on Strategy

1. Albom opens his essay with the story of his mother losing her father when she was fifteen years old. How effective did you find this **beginning**? How is Albom's **conclusion** connected to this beginning?

2. Paragraph 5 starts with the **rhetorical question** "Have you ever lost someone you love and wanted one more conversation, one more day to make up for the time when you thought they would be here forever?" How does this question function in the context of Albom's essay?

3. How did Albom find the examples he uses in this essay? In what ways are Albom's examples both relevant and representative?

4. Albom often repeats key words or ideas to make the **transition** from one paragraph to the next. Identify several places where he has done this particularly well. What other transitional devices or expressions does he use?

Illustration in Action

Suppose you are writing an essay about the career choices that members of your extended family have made to see what trends or influences you could discover. Using your own extended family (great-grandparents, grandparents, parents, aunts and uncles, siblings) as potential material, make several lists of examples — for instance, one for family members who worked in agriculture, a second for those who worked in education, a third for those who worked at an office job, a fourth for those who worked in the service sector, and a fifth for those who worked in the medical or legal fields. Reflect on the ways you could use these examples in an essay.

Writing Suggestions

1. Has someone close to you — a parent, grandparent, relative, or friend — died, or has someone moved away whom you would like to see again, if only for a day? Write an essay in which you first share something about your relationship with the person you are missing and then describe what you would do with that person for one whole day.

2. Study the following photograph of a ballet rehearsal in a dance studio. (For a discussion of how to analyze photographs and other visual texts, see "Reading Photographs and Visual Texts" in Chapter 1, pages 17–21.) What, if anything, in the photograph jumps out at you? What do you think is the relationship between the man dressed in black and the others in the photograph? What or who do you think the other people are looking at? In what ways does the physical setting enhance or influence the action that is taking place here? How does this photograph depict illustration?

Thomas Barwick/Getty Images

The "Busy" Trap

TIM KREIDER

Tim Kreider was born in Baltimore in 1967, went to Johns Hopkins University, and worked primarily as a cartoonist until 2009. His strip "The Pain — When Will It End?" ran in the *Baltimore City Paper* and other alternative publications for twelve years. His writing has appeared in a wide variety of publications and online venues, including the *New York Times*, the *Baltimore Sun*, *Al Jazeera*, the *Huffington Post*, the *New Yorker*'s "Page-Turner" blog, *Film Quarterly*, *Men's Journal*, and *Modern Farmer.*

Noah Sheppard

He has published three collections of cartoons and two collections of essays, *We Learn Nothing* (2012) and *I Wrote This Book Because I Love You* (2018).

He divides his time between Brooklyn and a cabin in Maryland, referred to in this essay as an "Undisclosed Location." In a "self-interview" Kreider did for the Web site *The Nervous Breakdown*, he describes his work as follows: "I'm not an especially brilliant thinker or keen observer of the human condition or a great prose stylist; my only meager strength as a writer is to be as honest as I can." This essay was originally published in the *New York Times*'s *Anxiety* blog in 2015. As you read, watch how Kreider uses examples to make his point about what it really means when people claim to be "too busy" and what we can do about it.

Preparing to Read

Do you consider yourself too busy, or do you think you've struck a good balance of work and relaxation in your life? If you feel too busy, do you have any ideas about how to solve this problem?

f you live in America in the twenty-first century you've probably had to   1
listen to a lot of people tell you how busy they are. It's become the default response when you ask anyone how they're doing: "Busy!" "*So* busy." "*Crazy* busy." It is, pretty obviously, a boast disguised as a complaint. And the stock response is a kind of congratulation: "That's a good problem to have," or "Better than the opposite."

Notice it isn't generally people pulling back-to-back shifts in the I.C.U.   2
or commuting by bus to three minimum-wage jobs who tell you how busy they are; what those people are is not busy but *tired. Exhausted. Dead on their feet.* It's almost always people whose lamented busyness is purely self-imposed: work and obligations they've taken on voluntarily, classes and activities they've "encouraged" their kids to participate in. They're busy because of their own ambition or drive or anxiety, because they're addicted to busyness and dread what they might have to face in its absence.

Almost everyone I know is busy. They feel anxious and guilty when they   3
aren't either working or doing something to promote their work. They schedule
in time with friends the way students with 4.0 G.P.A.'s make sure to sign up for
community service because it looks good on their college applications. I recently wrote a friend to ask if he wanted to do something this week, and he answered that he didn't have a lot of time but if something was going on to let him know and maybe he could ditch work for a few hours. I wanted to clarify that my question had not been a preliminary heads-up to some future invitation; this was the invitation. But his busyness was like some vast churning noise through which he was shouting out at me, and I gave up trying to shout back over it.

> **They're busy because of their own ambition or drive or anxiety, because they're addicted to busyness and dread what they might have to face in its absence.**

Even *children* are busy now, scheduled down to the half-hour with   4
classes and extracurricular activities. They come home at the end of the day
as tired as grown-ups. I was a member of the latchkey generation and had
three hours of totally unstructured, largely unsupervised time every afternoon, time I used to do everything from surfing the *World Book Encyclopedia*
to making animated films to getting together with friends in the woods to
chuck dirt clods directly into one another's eyes, all of which provided me
with important skills and insights that remain valuable to this day. Those
free hours became the model for how I wanted to live the rest of my life.

The present hysteria is not a necessary or inevitable condition of life;   5
it's something we've chosen, if only by our acquiescence to it. Not long ago
I Skyped with a friend who was driven out of the city by high rent and now
has an artist's residency in a small town in the south of France. She described
herself as happy and relaxed for the first time in years. She still gets her work
done, but it doesn't consume her entire day and brain. She says it feels like
college—she has a big circle of friends who all go out to the cafe together
every night. She has a boyfriend again. (She once ruefully summarized dating
in New York: "Everyone's too busy and everyone thinks they can do better.")
What she had mistakenly assumed was her personality—driven, cranky, anxious and sad—turned out to be a deformative effect of her environment. It's
not as if any of us wants to live like this, any more than any one person wants
to be part of a traffic jam or stadium trampling or the hierarchy of cruelty in
high school—it's something we collectively force one another to do.

Busyness serves as a kind of existential reassurance, a hedge against   6
emptiness; obviously your life cannot possibly be silly or trivial or meaningless if you are so busy, completely booked, in demand every hour of the day. I
once knew a woman who interned at a magazine where she wasn't allowed to

take lunch hours out, lest she be urgently needed for some reason. This was an entertainment magazine whose raison d'être was obviated when "menu" buttons appeared on remotes, so it's hard to see this pretence of indispensability as anything other than a form of institutional self-delusion. More and more people in this country no longer make or do anything tangible; if your job wasn't performed by a cat or a boa constrictor in a Richard Scarry book I'm not sure I believe it's necessary. I can't help but wonder whether all this histrionic exhaustion isn't a way of covering up the fact that most of what we do doesn't matter.

I am not busy. I am the laziest ambitious person I know. Like most writers, I feel like a reprobate who does not deserve to live on any day that I do not write, but I also feel that four or five hours is enough to earn my stay on the planet for one more day. On the best ordinary days of my life, I write in the morning, go for a long bike ride and run errands in the afternoon, and in the evening I see friends, read or watch a movie. This, it seems to me, is a sane and pleasant pace for a day. And if you call me up and ask whether I won't maybe blow off work and check out the new American Wing at the Met or ogle girls in Central Park or just drink chilled pink minty cocktails all day long, I will say, what time? 7

But just in the last few months, I've insidiously started, because of professional obligations, to become busy. For the first time I was able to tell people, with a straight face, that I was "too busy" to do this or that thing they wanted me to do. I could see why people enjoy this complaint; it makes you feel important, sought-after and put-upon. Except that I hate actually being busy. Every morning my in-box was full of e-mails asking me to do things I did not want to do or presenting me with problems that I now had to solve. It got more and more intolerable until finally I fled town to the Undisclosed Location from which I'm writing this. 8

Here I am largely unmolested by obligations. There is no TV. To check e-mail I have to drive to the library. I go a week at a time without seeing anyone I know. I've remembered about buttercups, stink bugs and the stars. I read. And I'm finally getting some real writing done for the first time in months. It's hard to find anything to say about life without immersing yourself in the world, but it's also just about impossible to figure out what it might be, or how best to say it, without getting the hell out of it again. 9

Idleness is not just a vacation, an indulgence or a vice; it is as indispensable to the brain as vitamin D is to the body, and deprived of it we suffer a mental affliction as disfiguring as rickets. The space and quiet that idleness provides is a necessary condition for standing back from life and seeing it whole, for making unexpected connections and waiting for the wild summer lightning strikes of inspiration — it is, paradoxically, necessary to getting any work done. "Idle dreaming is often of the essence of what we do," wrote Thomas Pynchon in 10 his essay on sloth. Archimedes' "Eureka" in the bath, Newton's apple, Jekyll & Hyde and the benzene ring: history is full of stories of inspirations that come in idle moments and dreams. It almost makes you wonder whether loafers, goldbricks and no-accounts aren't responsible for more of the world's great ideas, inventions and masterpieces than the hardworking.

"The goal of the future is full unemployment, so we can play. That's why we have to destroy the present politico-economic system." This may sound like the pronouncement of some bong-smoking anarchist, but it was actually Arthur C. Clarke, who found time between scuba diving and pinball games to write "Childhood's End" and think up communications satellites. My old colleague Ted Rall recently wrote a column proposing that we divorce income from work and give each citizen a guaranteed paycheck, which sounds like the kind of lunatic notion that'll be considered a basic human right in about a century, like abolition, universal suffrage and eight-hour workdays. The Puritans turned work into a virtue, evidently forgetting that God invented it as a punishment. 11

Perhaps the world would soon slide to ruin if everyone behaved as I do. But I would suggest that an ideal human life lies somewhere between my own defiant indolence and the rest of the world's endless frenetic hustle. My role is just to be a bad influence, the kid standing outside the classroom window making faces at you at your desk, urging you to just this once make some excuse and get out of there, come outside and play. My own resolute idleness has mostly been a luxury rather than a virtue, but I did make a conscious decision, a long time ago, to choose time over money, since I've always understood that the best investment of my limited time on earth was to spend it with people I love. I suppose it's possible I'll lie on my deathbed regretting that I didn't work harder and say everything I had to say, but I think what I'll really wish is that I could have one more beer with Chris, another long talk with Megan, one last good hard laugh with Boyd. Life is too short to be busy. 12

Thinking Critically about the Text

"Almost everyone I know is busy," Kreider writes. "They feel anxious and guilty when they aren't either working or doing something to promote their work" (paragraph 3). Does this accurately describe people you know, and if so, do you think they should feel and behave differently? Or do you think they have good reasons to work all the time?

Questions on Subject

1. Kreider writes that people who complain about being busy "dread what they might have to face" (paragraph 2) in the absence of busyness. What does he think they might have to face if they weren't so busy?

2. Kreider says that as a child, his daily hours of free time after school "provided him with important skills and insights that remain valuable to this day" (paragraph 4). What skills and insights do you think he is talking about?

3. In paragraph 9, Kreider writes "I'm finally getting some real writing done for the first time in months." What do you think he means by "real writing"? What has been keeping him from doing this real writing? How does this statement connect to the overall message of his essay? Do you think he would count this essay as "real writing"?

4. In his final paragraph, Kreider writes that his "role is just to be a bad influence, . . . urging you to just this once make some excuse and get out of there, come outside and play" (paragraph 12). Does he literally consider himself a "bad" influence? Explain.

Questions on Strategy

1. How does Kreider use **comparison** in paragraph 2, and what is the effect of this comparison?

2. Kreider uses a **simile** at the end of paragraph 3, describing his friend's busyness as "some vast churning noise through which he was shouting out at me." Where else does he use figurative language, and to what effect?

3. Who is Kreider's **audience**, and how do you know? Pay special attention to the first sentence in paragraph 2 and the last sentence in paragraph 7.

4. Consider the **allusions** Kreider provides in the second half of paragraph 10: Thomas Pynchon, Archimedes, Newton, and Jekyll & Hyde. Do you understand all of these references? Would more information have been helpful here, or can you infer their importance from the surrounding context?

Illustration in Action

Make a chart with seven columns, one for each day of the week, and twenty-four rows, one for each hour of the day. To the best of your memory, fill in what you did every hour this past week. Are there activities you don't want to be doing? Are there some things you must do but could do more quickly? Are there things you can eliminate altogether? Finally, are there things you want to be doing that are not represented in the chart? Now create a revised chart, illustrating your ideal way to spend these hours. Consider whether your ideal schedule seems possible. Is there a reasonable compromise you could reach, making some, if not all, of these changes?

Writing Suggestions

1. "More and more people in this country no longer make or do anything tangible," Kreider writes in paragraph 6. "I can't help but wonder whether all this histrionic exhaustion isn't a way of covering up the fact that most of what we do doesn't matter." What relationship is Kreider suggesting between making or

doing something "tangible" and whether what we do matters? Do you believe that work must be tangible in order to matter? What does it mean for work to be tangible? Does the product have to be something physical we can pick up or handle in some way, something concrete we can use? What other kinds of work are there? Write an essay about the kinds of work that you think matter, making sure to provide examples of both the jobs in question and the impact they make.

2. **Writing with Sources.** Write an essay on one of the following statements, using examples to illustrate your ideas. Draw your examples from a variety of sources: your library's print and Internet resources, interviews, and information gathered from lectures and the media. As you plan your essay, consider whether you will want to use a series of short examples or one or more extended examples.

- Much has been (*or* should still be) done to eliminate barriers for the physically disabled.
- Nature's oddities are numerous.
- Throughout history, dire predictions have been made about the end of the world.
- The past predictions of science fiction are today's realities.
- The world has not seen an absence of warfare since World War II.
- Young executives have developed many innovative management strategies.
- A great work of art may come out of an artist's most difficult period.
- Genius is 10 percent talent and 90 percent hard work.

For models of and advice on integrating sources in your essay, see Chapters 14 and 15.

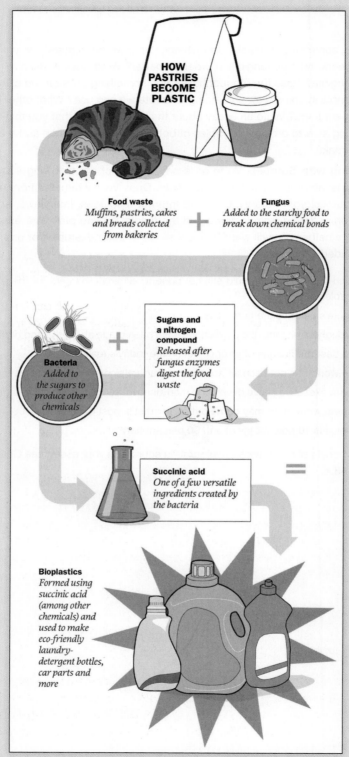

Heather Jones

CHAPTER 7

Process Analysis

WHAT IS PROCESS ANALYSIS?

THE STRATEGY OF PROCESS ANALYSIS INVOLVES SEPARATING AN EVENT, AN operation, or a cycle of development into distinct steps, describing each step precisely, and arranging the steps in their proper order.

Whenever you explain how something occurs or how it can (and should) be done—how plants create oxygen, how to make ice cream, or merely how to get to your house—you are using process analysis. Recipes are a form of process analysis; so are the instruction and assembly manuals for the many technological devices we use around the house; and so are posters telling us what to do in case of fire, choking, or other emergency.

VISUALIZING PROCESS ANALYSIS

This graphically illustrated explanation shows the process whereby stale and unused baked goods collected from bakeries are turned into plastics. Rather than provide a recipe for how specifically to make it happen, the presentation explains how the process is carried out. Using the visual, do you understand how the process takes place? What visual details in the graphic help you understand the process? How do the visual cues help you retain the information it provides? Could the flowchart be improved to help you better understand the process? If so, how?

UNDERSTANDING PROCESS ANALYSIS AS A WRITING STRATEGY

Each year, thousands of books and articles tell us how to make home repairs, how to lose weight and get physically fit, how to improve our memories, how to play better tennis, how to manage our money. They try to satisfy our curiosity about how television shows are made, how jet airplanes work, and how monkeys, bees, or whales find food. People simply want to know how things work and how to do things for themselves, so it's not surprising that process analysis is one of the most widespread and popular forms of writing today.

Here is a process analysis written by Bernard Gladstone to explain how to light a fire in a fireplace:

First sentence establishes purpose: how to build a fire in a fireplace

First paragraph takes us through six steps

Though "experts" differ as to the best technique to follow when building a fire, one generally accepted method consists of first laying a generous amount of crumpled newspaper on the hearth between the andirons. Kindling wood is then spread generously over this layer of newspaper and one of the thickest logs is placed across the back of the andirons. This should be as close to the back of the fireplace as possible, but not quite touching it. A second log is then placed an inch or so in front of this, and a few additional sticks of kindling are laid across these two. A third log is then placed on top to form a sort of pyramid with air space between all logs so that flames can lick freely up between them.

Next three paragraphs present three common mistakes

A mistake frequently made is in building the fire too far forward so that the rear wall of the fireplace does not get properly heated. A heated back wall helps increase the draft and tends to suck smoke and flames rearward with less chance of sparks or smoke spurting out into the room.

Another common mistake often made by the inexperienced fire-tender is to try to build a fire with only one or two logs, instead of using at least three. A single log is difficult to ignite properly, and even two logs do not provide an efficient bed with adequate fuel burning capacity.

Conclusion reinforces his directions for building a fire

Use of too many logs, on the other hand, is also a common fault and can prove hazardous. Building too big a fire can create more smoke and draft than the chimney can safely handle, increasing the possibility of sparks or smoke being thrown out into the room. For best results, the homeowner should start with three medium-sized logs as described above, then add additional logs as needed if the fire is to be kept burning.

Process analysis resembles narration because both strategies present a series of events occurring over time. But a narration is the story of how things happened in a particular way, during one particular period of time; process analysis relates how things always happen—or always should happen—in essentially the same way time after time.

▶ Types of Process Analysis

There are essentially two major reasons for writing a process analysis: to give directions, known as *directional process analysis*, and to inform, known as *informational process analysis*. Writers often combine one of these methods with other rhetorical strategies to evaluate the process in question; this is known as *evaluative process analysis*. Let's take a look at each of these forms more closely.

Directional Process Analysis.   Writers use directional process analysis to provide readers with the necessary steps to achieve a desired result. The directions may be as simple as the instructions on a frozen-food package ("Heat in microwave on high for six to eight minutes. Rotate one-quarter turn halfway through cooking time, stir, and serve.") or as complex as the operator's manual for a personal computer. Mortimer Adler proposes a method for getting the most out of reading in his essay "How to Mark a Book." First he compares what he sees as the "two ways in which one can own a book" and classifies book lovers into three categories. Then he presents his directions for how one should make marginal comments to get the most out of a book. In the brief selection on page 192, Bernard Gladstone explains step-by-step how to build a fire in a fireplace. Whatever their length or complexity, however, all directions have the same purpose: to guide the reader through a clear and logically ordered series of steps toward a particular goal.

Informational Process Analysis.   This strategy deals not with processes that readers are able to perform for themselves but with processes that readers are curious about or would like to understand better: how presidents are elected, how plants reproduce, how an elevator works, how the brain processes and generates language. In the following selection from *Lives around Us*, Alan Devoe explains what happens to an animal when it goes into hibernation:

> When the temperature of the September days falls below 50 degrees or so, the woodchuck becomes too drowsy to come forth from his burrow in the chilly dusk to forage. He remains in the deep nest-chamber, lethargic, hardly moving. Gradually, with the passing of hours or days, his coarse-furred body curls into a semicircle, like a fetus, nose-tip touching tail. The small legs are tucked in, the hand-like clawed forefeet folded. The woodchuck has become a compact ball. Presently the temperature of his body begins to fall.

In normal life the woodchuck's temperature, though fluctuant, averages about 97 degrees. Now, as he lies tight-curled in a ball with the winter sleep stealing over him, this body heat drops ten degrees, twenty degrees, thirty. Finally, by the time the snow is on the ground and the woodchuck's winter dormancy has become complete, his temperature is only 38 or 40. With the falling of the body heat there is a slowing of his heartbeat and his respiration. In normal life he breathes thirty or forty times each minute; when he is excited, as many as a hundred times. Now he breathes slower and slower: ten times a minute, five times a minute, once a minute, and at last only ten or twelve times in an hour. His heartbeat is a twentieth of normal. He has entered fully into the oblivion of hibernation.

The process Devoe describes is natural to woodchucks but not to humans, so obviously he cannot be giving instructions. Rather, he has created an informational process analysis to help us understand what happens during the remarkable process of hibernation. Using transitional expressions and time markers, Devoe shows us that the process lasts for weeks, even months. He connects the progress of hibernation with changes in the weather because the woodchuck's body responds to the dropping temperature as autumn sets in rather than to the passage of specific periods of time.

Evaluative Process Analysis. People often want to understand processes in order to evaluate and improve them by making them simpler, quicker, safer, or more efficient. They may also wish to analyze processes to understand them more deeply or accurately. For instance, in explaining how to build a fire in a fireplace, Bernard Gladstone presents three common mistakes to avoid when trying to make a fire.

USING PROCESS ANALYSIS ACROSS THE DISCIPLINES

When writing essays in the academic disciplines, you will have many opportunities to use process analysis to both organize and strengthen the presentation of your ideas. To determine whether process analysis is the right strategy for you in a particular paper, review the guidelines described in Chapter 2, "Determining a Strategy for Developing Your Essay" (pages 34–35). Consider the following examples:

Psychology

1. MAIN IDEA: Most people go through a predictable grief process when a friend or loved one dies.
2. QUESTION: What are the steps in the grieving process?

3. **STRATEGY:** Process analysis. The word *steps* signals the need to list the stages of the grieving process.

4. **SUPPORTING STRATEGY:** Description. Each step might be described and be accompanied by descriptions of the subject's behavior throughout the process.

Biology

1. **MAIN IDEA:** Human blood samples can be tested to determine their blood groups.

2. **QUESTION:** What steps are followed in typing human blood?

3. **STRATEGY:** Process analysis. The word *steps* suggests a sequence of activities that is to be followed in testing blood.

4. **SUPPORTING STRATEGIES:** Comparison and contrast; classification. Comparison and contrast might be used to differentiate blood characteristics and chemistry. Classification might be used to place samples in various categories.

Anthropology

1. **MAIN IDEA:** Anthropologists use several main methods for gathering their data.

2. **QUESTION:** How do anthropologists go about collecting data?

3. **STRATEGY:** Process analysis. The words *how do* and *go about* suggest process analysis.

4. **SUPPORTING STRATEGIES:** Illustration; argumentation. Illustration can give examples of particular data and how it is collected. Argumentation might support one method over others.

PRACTICAL ADVICE FOR WRITING AN ESSAY OF PROCESS ANALYSIS

As you plan and revise your process analysis essay, be mindful of the writing guidelines described in Chapter 2. Pay particular attention to the basic requirements and essential ingredients of this strategy.

▶ Planning Your Essay of Process Analysis

Know the Process You Are Writing About. Be sure that you have more than a vague or general grasp of the process you are writing about: Make sure you can analyze it fully, from beginning to end. You can sometimes convince yourself that you understand an entire process when, in fact, your under-standing is somewhat superficial. If you do outside research, it's a good idea to read explanations by several authorities on the subject. If you were analyz-ing the process by which children learn language, for example, you wouldn't want to rely on only one expert's account. Turning to more than one account reinforces your understanding of key points in the process, and it also points out various ways the process is performed; you may want to consider these alternatives in your writing.

Have a Clear Purpose.   Giving directions for administering cardiopulmonary resuscitation and explaining how the El Niño phenomenon unfolds are worthy purposes for writing a process analysis. Many process analysis papers go beyond these fundamental purposes, however. They lay out processes to evaluate them, to suggest alternative steps, to point out shortcomings in generally accepted practices, and to suggest improvements. In short, process analysis papers are frequently persuasive or argumentative. Be sure to decide what you want your writing to do before you begin.

▶ **Organizing Your Essay of Process Analysis**

Organize the Process into Steps.   As much as possible, make each step a sim-ple and well-defined action, preferably a single action. To guide yourself in doing so, write a scratch outline listing the steps. Here, for example, is an outline of Bernard Gladstone's directions for building a fire.

Process Analysis of Building a Fire in a Fireplace

1. Put down crumpled newspaper.
2. Lay kindling.
3. Place back log near rear wall but not touching.
4. Place next log an inch forward from the first one.
5. Bridge logs with kindling.
6. Place third log on top of kindling bridge.

Next, check your outline to make sure that the steps are in the right order and that none has been omitted. Then analyze your outline more carefully. Are any steps so complex that they need to be described in some detail—or perhaps divided into more steps? Will you need to explain the purpose of a certain step because the reason for it is not obvious? Especially in an infor-mational process analysis, two steps may take place at the same time; perhaps they are performed by different people or different parts of the body. Does your outline make this clear? (One solution is to assign both steps the same number but divide them into substeps by labeling one of them "A" and the other "B.") When you feel certain that the steps of the process are complete and correct, ask yourself two more questions. Will the reader need any other information to understand the process—definitions of unusual terms, for example, or descriptions of special equipment? Should you anticipate common mistakes or misunderstandings and discuss them, as Gladstone does? If so, be sure to add an appropriate note or two to your scratch outline as a reminder.

Use Transitions to Link the Steps.   Transitional words and phrases like *then*, *next*, *after doing this*, and *during the summer months* can both emphasize and clarify the sequence of steps in your process analysis. The same is true of sequence markers like *first*, *second*, *third*, and so on. Devoe uses such words to make clear which stages in the hibernation process are simultaneous and which are not; Gladstone includes an occasional *first* or *then* to alert us to shifts from one step to the next.

▶ Revising and Editing Your Essay of Process Analysis

Energize Your Writing: Use the Active Voice and Strong Action Verbs.   Writers prefer the active voice because it stresses the doer of an action, is lively and emphatic, and uses strong descriptive verbs. The passive voice, on the other hand, stresses what was done rather than who did it and uses forms of the weak verb *to be*.

> **active**   The coaches analyzed the game film, and the fullback decided to rededicate herself to playing defense.

> **passive**   A game film analysis was performed by the coaches, and a rededication to playing defense was decided on by the fullback.

Sometimes, however, the doer of an action is unknown or less important than the recipient of an action. In this case, it is acceptable to use the passive voice.

> The Earth's moon was formed more than 4 billion years ago.

When you revise your drafts, scan your sentences for passive constructions and weak verbs. Put your sentences into the active voice and find strong action verbs to replace weak verbs. (For more information and practice with using active verbs, see the following sections in Chapter 16, "Weak Nouns and Verbs" on pages 572–73 and "Wordiness" on pages 574–75.)

Use Consistent Verb Tense.   A verb's tense indicates when an action is taking place: some time in the past, right now, or in the future. Using verb tense consistently helps your readers understand time changes in your writing.

Inconsistent verb tenses—or *shifts*—within a sentence confuse readers and are especially noticeable in narration and process analysis writing, which are oriented toward sequence and time. Generally, you should write in the past or present tense and maintain that tense throughout your sentence.

> **inconsistent** I mixed the eggs and sugar and then add the flour.

Mixed is past tense; *add* is present tense.

> **corrected** I mix the eggs and sugar and then add the flour.

The sentence is now consistently in the present tense. The sentence can also be revised to be consistently in the past tense.

> **corrected** I mixed the eggs and sugar and then added the flour.

After you are confident that you have selected strong verbs in a consistent tense, consider sharing your draft with others to get some additional feedback. The "Brief Guide to Peer Critiquing" box in Chapter 2 (pages 38–39) will give you some helpful guidelines for peer review, and the following box will help to steer your own self-critique. Review Chapter 16 to give your essay its final polish.

Questions for Revising and Editing: Process Analysis

1. Do I have a thorough knowledge of the process I chose to write about?

2. Have I clearly informed readers about how to perform the process (directional process analysis), or have I explained how a process occurs (informational process analysis)? Does my choice reflect the overall purpose of my process analysis paper?

3. Have I divided the process into clear, readily understandable steps?

4. Did I pay particular attention to transitional words to take readers from one step to the next?

5. Are all my sentences in the active voice? Have I used strong action verbs?

6. Is my tense consistent?

7. Have I succeeded in tailoring my diction to my audience's familiarity with the subject?

8. Are my pronoun antecedents clear?

9. How did readers of my draft respond to my essay? Did they find any confusing passages or any missing steps?

10. Have I avoided errors in grammar, punctuation, and mechanics? Is my sentence style as clear, smooth, and persuasive as possible?

STUDENT ESSAY USING PROCESS ANALYSIS AS A WRITING STRATEGY

William Peterson wrote the following informative and playful essay while he was a student at the University of Vermont majoring in business. In the following set of directions he explains the three-step process of learning to juggle. In addition, he tells of some of the problems readers may encounter and gives sound advice on how to deal with each separate one.

Juggling Is Easier Than You Think
William Peterson

Context-setting introduction invites reader to learn how to juggle

The first time I went to the circus I was fascinated by the jugglers, clowns, and acrobats who juggled everything from bowling pins and burning batons to sharp swords. I never thought of myself as a juggler, however, until that night in college when I watched some comedian on "Saturday Night Live" telling jokes while nonchalantly juggling. When his act ended I went out to my garage and started to experiment with some tennis balls. At first, I felt helpless after tossing and chasing the balls for what seemed like countless hours. However, I actually did start to learn how to juggle. To my surprise I discovered that juggling is much easier than it had at first appeared. If you'd like to learn how to juggle, I recommend that you find some tennis balls or lacrosse balls and continue reading.   1

Transition links to next section

First step in process is introduced: the simple toss

Step one is the simple toss. Stand erect and hold one ball in your right hand. Carefully toss the ball up to approximately an inch above your head and to about half an arm's length in front of you. The ball should arch from your right hand across to your left. This step should now be repeated, starting with your left hand and tossing to your right. Be sure that the ball reaches the same height and distance from you and is not simply passed from your left hand to your right. Keep tossing the ball back and forth until you have become thoroughly disgusted with this step. If you have practiced this toss enough, we can now call this step "the perfect toss." If it is not quite perfect, then you have not become disgusted enough with the step. We'll assume that you've perfected it. Now you're ready to take a little breather and move on.   2

Recommendation is given to practice first step until it is perfected

Writer labels step one as "the perfect toss"

Writer describes the second step in process: the toss and return

Step two is the toss and return. Get back on your feet and this time hold a ball in each hand. Take a deep breath and make a perfect toss with the ball in your right hand. As that ball reaches its peak make another perfect toss with the ball in your left hand. The second ball should end up passing under the first one and reaching approximately the same height. When the second ball peaks, you should be grabbing—or already have grabbed, depending on timing—the first ball. The second ball should then gently drop into your awaiting right hand. If it was not that easy, then don't worry about the "gently" bit. Most people do not achieve perfection at first. Step two is the key factor in becoming a good juggler and should be practiced at least five times as much as step one.

Writer emphasizes the need to practice step two

3

Don't deceive yourself after a few successful completions. This maneuver really must be perfected before step three can be approached. As a way to improve dexterity, you should try several tosses and returns starting with your left hand. Let's call step two "the exchange." You're now ready for another well-deserved breather before you proceed.

A helpful suggestion is provided

Writer labels step two as "the exchange"

4

Ready or not, here it goes. Step three is merely a continuum of "the exchange" with the addition of a third ball. Don't worry if you are confused—I will explain. Get back up again, and now hold two balls in your right hand and one in your left. Make a perfect toss with one of the balls in your right hand and then an exchange with the one in your left hand. The ball coming from your left hand should now be exchanged with the, as of now, unused ball in your right hand. This process should be continued until you find yourself reaching under nearby chairs for bouncing tennis balls. It is true that many persons' backs and legs become sore when learning how to juggle because they've been picking up balls that they've inadvertently tossed around the room. Try practicing over a bed; you won't have to reach down so far. Don't get too upset if things aren't going well; you're probably keeping the same pace as everyone else at this stage. You're certainly doing better than I was because you've had me as a teacher.

Writer labels third step in process: "addition of a third ball"

5

Don't worry, this teacher is not going to leave you stranded with hours of repetition of the basic steps.

Transitional paragraph links to next section

6

I am sure that you have already run into some basic problems. I will now try to relate some of my beginner's trou-
bles and some of the best solutions you can try for them.

Writer discusses problem one and its solutions

Problem one, you are getting nowhere after the 7
simple toss. This requires a basic improvement of hand
to eye coordination. Solution one is to just go back and
practice the simple toss again and again. Unfortunately,
this becomes quite boring. Solution two is not as tedious
and involves quite a bit more skill. Try juggling two
balls in one hand. Some people show me this when
I ask them if they can juggle—they're not fooling anyone. Real juggling is what you're here to learn. First try
circular juggling in one hand. This involves tosses similar to "the perfect toss." They differ in that the balls go
half as far towards the opposite hand, are tossed and
grabbed by the same hand, and end up making their
own circles (as opposed to going up and down in upside
down V's like exchanges). Then try juggling the balls in
the same line style. I think this is harder. You have to
keep two balls traveling in their own vertical paths (the
balls should go as high as they do in a "perfect toss")
with only one hand. I think this is harder than the circular style because my hands normally tend to make
little circles when I juggle.

Writer discusses problem two and its solution

Problem two, you can make exchanges but you just 8
can't accomplish step three. The best solution to this is
to just continue practicing step two, but now add a twist.
As soon as the first ball is caught by the left hand in our
step two, throw it back up in another perfect toss for
another exchange. Continue this and increase speed up
to the point where two balls just don't seem like enough.
You should now be ready to add the third ball and
accomplish what you couldn't before—real juggling.

Writer discusses problem three and its solutions

Problem three, you have become the "runaway 9
juggler." This means you can successfully achieve
numerous exchanges but you're always chasing after
balls tossed too far in front of you. The first solution
is to stand in front of a wall. This causes you to end
up catching a couple of balls bouncing off the wall or
else you'll end up consciously keeping your tosses in
closer to your body. The second solution is you put your
back up against a wall. This will tend to make you toss
in closer to yourself because you will be restricted to

keeping your back up against the wall. This solution can work, but more often than not you'll find yourself watching balls fly across the room in front of you! I've told you about the back-on-the-wall method because some people find it effective. As you can tell, I don't.

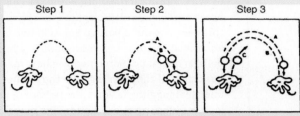

Figure 1. Illustration of the Three Steps of Juggling

Writer concludes with a visual presentation of three-step process

Juggling is a simple three-step process (see Figure 1). 10 Following my routine is the easiest way to get from being a spastic ball chaser to an accomplished juggler. Patience and coordination are really not required. The only requirements are a few tennis balls, the ability to follow some basic instructions, and the time to have some fun.

Next time you're out with friends and conversation 11 lags, you just might be surprised where your new-found juggling skills will take you.

Student Reflection
William Peterson

Q. What made you do a paper on juggling?
A. Well, I've been juggling for almost ten years, and in that time I've taught many people how to juggle. It's very easy to teach another person, especially one-on-one. All I need is a set of tennis balls. It's just something that comes easily to most people once they are shown how to do it. And my friends tell me that I'm pretty successful at showing others just how to do it. As a result, I thought I'd try to explain the process on paper.

Q. Did you start with a process analysis paper in mind?
A. In all honesty, I'd done a speech on juggling before writing this essay. In class, I discovered that the neat three-step process fit perfectly into the process analysis category. It's natural. I started by making a thorough outline of the process. That made the rough draft relatively easy.

Q. I hear you actually gave your essay to some friends to have them test your directions. What happened?

A. Yes, I gave it to people who had never tried juggling to see if there were any "bugs" or unclear sections in my instructions. This helped me a lot as a writer because they told me where certain things were not clear or outright confusing. This enabled me to go back and revise, knowing exactly what the problem was.

Q. Did any part give you trouble, Bill?

A. I had trouble with paragraph 2, the explanation of the simple toss. In my rough draft I just couldn't get detailed enough. See what I mean:

> Step one is a simple toss. Stand erect and hold one object (we'll call it a ball from now on) in your most adroit hand (we'll say the right). Toss the ball into the air to approximately an inch above your head and to about half an arm's length in front of you. The ball should take an arched path traveling from your right hand to your left. This step should now be repeated using your left hand first and returning it to your right hand. Repeat this until completely proficient. We'll now call this action the "perfect toss." Take a breather and then move on.

After several drafts, I finally felt satisfied. You can see my final version in paragraph 2.

Your Response

What did you learn from William Peterson's essay and reflection on the process of writing the essay? What challenges do you expect to face as you write your own process analysis essay? Based on William's composing strategies and the practical advice discussed earlier in this chapter (pages 195–98), what writing choices will you make?

How to Mark a Book

MORTIMER ADLER

Writer, editor, and educator Mortimer Adler was born in New York City in 1902 and passed away in 2001. A high school dropout, Adler completed the undergraduate program at Columbia University in three years, but he did not graduate because he refused to take the mandatory swimming test. Adler is recognized for his editorial work on the *Encyclopaedia Britannica* and for his leadership of the Great Books Program at the University of Chicago, where adults from all walks of life gathered twice a month to read and discuss the classics.

Alfred Eisenstaedt/Pix Inc./The LIFE Picture Collection/Getty Images

In the following essay, which first appeared in the *Saturday Review of Literature* in 1940, Adler offers a timeless lesson: He explains how to take full ownership of a book by marking it up, by making it "a part of yourself."

Preparing to Read

When you read a book that you must understand thoroughly and remember for a class or for your own purposes, what techniques do you use to help understand what you are reading? What helps you remember important parts of the book and improve your understanding of what the author is saying?

You know you have to read "between the lines" to get the most out of anything. I want to persuade you to do something equally important in the course of your reading. I want to persuade you to "write between the lines." Unless you do, you are not likely to do the most efficient kind of reading.

I contend, quite bluntly, that marking up a book is not an act of mutilation but of love.

You shouldn't mark up a book which isn't yours. Librarians (or your friends) who lend you books expect you to keep them clean, and you should. If you decide that I am right about the usefulness of marking books, you will have to buy them. Most of the world's great books are available today in reprint editions.

There are two ways in which one can own a book. The first is the property right you establish by paying for it, just as you pay for clothes and furniture. But this act of purchase is only the prelude to possession. Full ownership comes only when you have made it a part of yourself, and the best way to make yourself a part of it is by writing in it. An illustration may make the point clear. You buy a beefsteak and transfer it from the butcher's icebox to your own. But you do not own the beefsteak in the most important sense until you consume it and get it into your bloodstream. I am arguing that books, too, must be absorbed in your bloodstream to do you any good.

Confusion about what it means to *own* a book leads people to a false reverence for paper, binding, and type—a respect for the physical thing—the craft of the printer rather than the genius of the author. They forget that it is possible for a man to acquire the idea, to possess the beauty, which a great book contains, without staking his claim by pasting his bookplate inside the cover. Having a fine library doesn't prove that its owner has a mind enriched by books; it proves nothing more than that he, his father, or his wife, was rich enough to buy them. [5]

> **Marking up a book is not an act of mutilation but of love.**

There are three kinds of book owners. The first has all the standard sets and best-sellers—unread, untouched. (This deluded individual owns wood-pulp and ink, not books.) The second has a great many books—a few of them read through, most of them dipped into, but all of them as clean and shiny as the day they were bought. (This person would probably like to make books his own, but is restrained by a false respect for their physical appearance.) The third has a few books or many—every one of them dog-eared and dilapidated, shaken and loosened by continual use, marked and scribbled in from front to back. (This man owns books.) [6]

Is it false respect, you may ask, to preserve intact and unblemished a beautifully printed book, an elegantly bound edition? Of course not. I'd no more scribble all over a first edition of *Paradise Lost* than I'd give my baby a set of crayons and an original Rembrandt! I wouldn't mark up a painting or a statue. Its soul, so to speak, is inseparable from its body. And the beauty of a rare edition or of a richly manufactured volume is like that of a painting or a statue. [7]

But the soul of a book *can* be separated from its body. A book is more like the score of a piece of music than it is like a painting. No great musician confuses a symphony with the printed sheets of music. Arturo Toscanini reveres Brahms, but Toscanini's score of the C-minor Symphony is so thoroughly marked up that no one but the maestro himself can read it. The reason why a great conductor makes notations on his musical scores—marks them up again and again each time he returns to study them—is the reason why you should mark your books. If your respect for magnificent binding or typography gets in the way, buy yourself a cheap edition and pay your respects to the author. [8]

Why is marking up a book indispensable to reading? First, it keeps you awake. (And I don't mean merely conscious; I mean wide awake.) In the [9] second place, reading, if it is active, is thinking, and thinking tends to express itself in words, spoken or written. The marked book is usually the thought-through book. Finally, writing helps you remember the thoughts you had, or the thoughts the author expressed. Let me develop these three points.

If reading is to accomplish anything more than passing time, it must be active. You can't let your eyes glide across the lines of a book and come up with an understanding of what you have read. Now an ordinary piece of light fiction, like say, *Gone with the Wind*, doesn't require the most active kind of reading. The books you read for pleasure can be read in a state of relaxation, and nothing is lost. But a great book, rich in ideas and beauty, a book that raises and tries to answer great fundamental questions, demands the most active reading of which you are capable. You don't absorb the ideas of John Dewey[1] the way you absorb the crooning of Mr. Vallee.[2] You have to reach for them. That you cannot do while you're asleep.

If, when you've finished reading a book, the pages are filled with your notes, you know that you read actively. The most famous active reader of great books I know is President Hutchins, of the University of Chicago. He also has the hardest schedule of business activities of any man I know. He invariably reads with a pencil, and sometimes, when he picks up a book and pencil in the evening, he finds himself, instead of making intelligent notes, drawing what he calls "caviar factories" on the margins. When that happens, he puts the book down. He knows he's too tired to read, and he's just wasting time.

But, you may ask, why is writing necessary? Well, the physical act of writing, with your own hand, brings words and sentences more sharply before your mind and preserves them better in your memory. To set down your reaction to important words and sentences you have read, and the questions they have raised in your mind, is to preserve those reactions and sharpen those questions.

Even if you wrote on a scratch pad, and threw the paper away when you had finished writing, your grasp of the book would be surer. But you don't have to throw the paper away. The margins (top and bottom, as well as side), the end-papers, the very space between the lines, are all available. They aren't sacred. And, best of all, your marks and notes become an integral part of the book and stay there forever. You can pick up the book the following week or year, and there are all your points of agreement, disagreement, doubt, and inquiry. It's like resuming an interrupted conversation with the advantage of being able to pick up where you left off.

---

[1]John Dewey (1859–1952) was an educational philosopher who had a profound influence on learning through experimentation. — Eds.

[2]Rudy Vallee (1901–1986) was a popular singer of the 1920s and 1930s, famous for his crooning high notes. — Eds.

And that is exactly what reading a book should be: a conversation 14
between you and the author. Presumably he knows more about the subject
than you do; naturally, you'll have the proper humility as you approach him.
But don't let anybody tell you that a reader is supposed to be solely on the
receiving end. Understanding is a two-way operation; learning doesn't consist in being an empty receptacle. The learner has to question himself and
question the teacher. He even has to argue with the teacher, once he understands what the teacher is saying. And marking a book is literally an expression of your differences, or agreements of opinion, with the author.

There are all kinds of devices for marking a book intelligently and fruit- 15
fully. Here's the way I do it:

1. *Underlining*: of major points, of important or forceful statements. 16
2. *Vertical lines at the margin*: to emphasize a statement already underlined. 17
3. *Star, asterisk, or other doo-dad at the margin*: to be used sparingly, to 18
   emphasize the ten or twenty most important statements in the book.
   (You may want to fold the bottom corner of each page on which you
   use such marks. It won't hurt the sturdy paper on which most modern
   books are printed, and you will be able to take the book off the shelf
   at any time and, by opening it at the folded-corner page, refresh your
   recollection of the book.)
4. *Numbers in the margin*: to indicate the sequence of points the author 19
   makes in developing a single argument.
5. *Numbers of other pages in the margin*: to indicate where else in the book 20
   the author made points relevant to the point marked; to tie up the ideas
   in a book, which, though they may be separated by many pages, belong
   together.
6. *Circling*: of key words or phrases. 21
7. *Writing in the margin, or at the top or bottom of the page, for the sake of*: 22
   recording questions (and perhaps answers) which a passage raised in
   your mind; reducing a complicated discussion to a simple statement;
   recording the sequence of major points right through the book. I use
   the end-papers at the back of the book to make a personal index of the
   author's points in the order of their appearance.

The front end-papers are, to me, the most important. Some people 23
reserve them for a fancy bookplate. I reserve them for fancy thinking. After
I have finished reading the book and making my personal index on the back
end-papers, I turn to the front and try to outline the book, not page by page,
or point by point (I've already done that at the back), but as an integrated
structure, with a basic unity and an order of parts. This outline is, to me, the
measure of my understanding of the work.

If you're a die-hard anti-book-marker, you may object that the margins, 24 the space between the lines, and the end-papers don't give you room enough. All right. How about using a scratch pad slightly smaller than the page-size of the book—so that the edges of the sheets won't protrude? Make your index, outlines, and even your notes on the pad, and then insert these sheets permanently inside the front and back covers of the book.

Or, you may say that this business of marking books is going to slow up 25 your reading. It probably will. That's one of the reasons for doing it. Most of us have been taken in by the notion that speed of reading is a measure of our intelligence. There is no such thing as the right speed for intelligent reading. Some things should be read quickly and effortlessly, and some should be read slowly and even laboriously. The sign of intelligence in reading is the ability to read different things differently according to their worth. In the case of good books, the point is not to see how many of them you can get through, but rather how many can get through you—how many you can make your own. A few friends are better than a thousand acquaintances. If this be your aim, as it should be, you will not be impatient if it takes more time and effort to read a great book than it does a newspaper.

You may have one final objection to marking books. You can't lend them 26 to your friends because nobody else can read them without being distracted by your notes. Furthermore, you won't want to lend them because a marked copy is a kind of intellectual diary, and lending it is almost like giving your mind away.

If your friend wishes to read your *Plutarch's Lives*, *Shakespeare*, or *The* 27 *Federalist Papers*, tell him gently but firmly to buy a copy. You will lend him your car or your coat—but your books are as much a part of you as your head or your heart.

Thinking Critically about the Text

After you have read Adler's essay, compare your answer to the Preparing to Read prompt with Adler's guidelines for reading. What are the most significant differences between Adler's guidelines and your own? How can you better make the books you read part of yourself?

Questions on Subject

1. What are the three kinds of book owners Adler identifies? What are their differences?

2. According to Adler, why is marking up a book indispensable to reading? Do you agree with his three **arguments**? Why, or why not?

3. Adler says that reading a book should be a conversation between the reader and the author. What characteristics does he say the conversation should have? How does marking a book help in carrying on and preserving the conversation?

4. What kinds of devices do you use for "marking a book intelligently and fruit-fully" (paragraph 15)? How useful do you find these devices?

Questions on Strategy

1. In the first paragraph, Adler writes, "I want to persuade you to do something equally important in the course of your reading. I want to persuade you to 'write between the lines.'" What assumptions does Adler make about his **audience** when he chooses to use the **parallel** structure of "I want to per-suade you . . ."? Is stating his intention so blatantly an effective way of pre-senting his **argument**? Why, or why not?

2. Adler expresses himself very clearly throughout the essay, and his **topic sen-tences** are carefully crafted. Reread the topic sentences for paragraphs 3–6 and identify how each introduces the main idea for the paragraph and unifies it.

3. Throughout the essay, Adler provides the reader with a number of verbal cues ("There are two ways," "Let me develop these three points"). What do these verbal cues indicate about the organizational connections of the essay? Explain how Adler's **organization** creates an essay that logically follows from sentence to sentence and from paragraph to paragraph.

4. Adler's process analysis is also a description of an event or a sequence of events (how to read). Does he claim that his recommended reading process will aid the reader's understanding, increase the reader's interest, or both?

Process Analysis in Action

This exercise requires that you work in pairs. Draw a simple geometric design, such as the following, without letting your partner see your drawing.

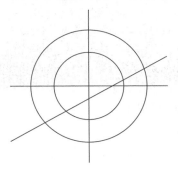

With the finished design in front of you, write a set of directions that will allow your partner to reproduce it accurately. Before writing your directions, ask your-self how you will convey the context for your instructions, where you will begin, and how what you write may help your partner or lead your partner astray. As your partner attempts to draw the design from your instructions, do not offer any verbal advice. Let your directions speak for themselves. Once you have finished, compare your drawing to the one your partner has produced. Discuss the results with your partner and, if time allows, with the entire class.

Writing Suggestions

1. Write a directional process analysis in which you present your techniques for getting the most enjoyment out of a common activity. For example, perhaps you have a set routine you follow for spending an evening watching television — preparing popcorn, checking what's on, clearing off the coffee table, finding the remote control, settling into your favorite chair, and so on. Choose from the following topics or select one of your own:

   • how to listen to music
   • how to eat an ice-cream cone
   • how to reduce stress
   • how to wash a dog

2. Adler devotes a large portion of his essay to persuading his audience that marking books is a worthwhile task. Write an essay in which you instruct your audience about how to do something they do not necessarily wish to do or they do not think they need to do. For instance, before explaining how to buy the best robot vacuum, you may need to convince readers that they *should* buy a robot vacuum. Write your directional process analysis after making a convincing argument for the validity of the process you wish to present.

What Would Happen If You Were Attacked by a Great White Shark?

CODY CASSIDY AND PAUL DOHERTY

Image courtesy of Cody Cassidy

Cody Cassidy is a writer and editor. He graduated from the University of Oregon in 2006 with a bachelor's degree in journalism and then wrote and edited for a series of online publications before becoming a full-time author. Currently he is at work on his next book, *Who Ate the First Oyster?* (2019). Paul Doherty (1948–2017) was a scientist, author, and educator. He received his doctorate from the Massachusetts Institute of Technology and for nearly thirty years was a scientist at the San Francisco Exploratorium, a science museum that also focuses on education and teacher training. Together, Cassidy and Doherty are the authors of *And Then You're Dead: The World's Most Interesting Ways to Die* (2017), which the book's publishers describe as a "gleefully gruesome look at the actual science behind the most outlandish, cartoonish, and impossible deaths you can imagine."

Courtesy of the Estate of Paul Doherty

In the following selection from that book, Cassidy and Doherty consider the process of being attacked by a great white shark — both the chain of events and why they would happen. As you read, pay attention to how the authors approach seemingly dark material in a way that is funny and engaging.

Preparing to Read

Have you ever thought about what it would be like to be attacked by a shark? Is it something you fear if you go to the beach? Why do you think people are often preoccupied by — and afraid of — being harmed in ways that are statistically unlikely?

Like all predators, sharks are not interested in fair fights. Even for the winners, fair fights lead to injuries, and injuries mean a slow and hungry animal. So predators prefer devastating blowouts with as little risk as possible, which makes you the perfect opponent: You're slow, weak, and completely oblivious in the water. Fortunately, you don't taste very good. You're the squirrel of the ocean, too much bone and not enough fat. Still, sharks are curious creatures and attacks happen—usually from the smaller species that aren't as dangerous.

But not always. Big sharks *can* attack. The great white can grow to 2 twenty feet, and even its exploratory nibbles are devastating. Why might the shark go for a bite?

It probably would not be for food. Researchers have stitched shark vic- 3 tims back together and discovered not a single morsel missing. When great white sharks bite a human, they are like children scrambling peas on their plate. Careful reconstruction reveals nary a pea eaten. We must taste so terrible to sharks that, frankly, we should be a little insulted.

So if we taste so horrible, why bite us at all? One popular explanation 4 is that it's a case of mistaken identity. The theory goes that sharks mistake human swimmers for normal seal prey and take a bite, only then realizing their error and spitting the person out like a diner mistaking the salt for the sugar. It is plausible, but there is little science to back up this theory. There are visual similarities between a surfer and a seal from a shark's point of view, but that does not explain important differences in the way a shark attacks a swimmer versus the way it strikes a seal.

Researchers placed dummies in chummed water to observe the way 5 sharks approached them. Unlike seal attacks, in which the shark comes from below and hits the animal with one devastating surprise attack, the sharks swam in circles around the dummies—checking them out with multiple passes before striking. The nature of the bite was also a more exploratory, open-bite slash as opposed to the full-gusto chomping bite a shark uses with a seal—like the difference in how you approach a carton of fresh milk as opposed to one close to its expiration date.

So far the evidence suggests that it is not confusion at work when a 6 great white shark attacks, but mere curiosity. Sharks can sense movement by detecting small changes in water pressure, and swimmers are moving, particularly if they have just spotted a fin. This motion can pique a great white's interest, and sharks seem to operate under a "when in doubt, bite it" policy.*

> " **Sharks seem to operate under a 'when in doubt, bite it' policy.** "

---

*It's important to note that we're talking about great white sharks here—which kill the most people but don't appear to do it out of hunger. Another breed of shark, called the oceanic whitetip, has intentionally killed and eaten humans. However, attacks from whitetips are uncommon (usually survivors of shipwrecks) because they frequent open ocean, far away from people, whereas great whites often patrol beaches.

The most famous oceanic whitetip attack occurred in 1945 just before Japan's surrender when a navy ship, the USS *Indianapolis*, was torpedoed near the Philippines. Nine hundred men hit the water alive, but because of a miscommunication they weren't rescued for four days. Oceanic whitetip sharks, attracted to all the commotion, began feeding on the sailors. By the time the survivors were rescued, the sharks had killed and eaten as many as 150 men.

Incidentally, this is common behavior for many predators — if you have ⁊
a cat you may have seen this explore-the-world-via-biting behavior. But
exploratory biting by sharks significantly differs from your cat's. There aren't
any reliable measurements of exactly how strong a great white's bite is, but
the few experiments that have been done all come to the same general conclusion: It's strong enough. In at least one instance a great white bit a man in
half as clean as any guillotine.

So let's say you're splashing about in the waves and, unbeknownst to you, 8
you attract the attention of a curious great white.

First of all, you would have every right to be upset. Not because you could 9
be slashed to death in a moment, but because the odds of this happening are
infinitesimal. If you're headed for a day at the beach, you're ten times more
likely to fall down your stairs and die on your way to your car. Once you get in
your car you're way more likely to die in an accident driving to the beach, and
once you get to the beach you're far more likely to die in a collapsing sand pit
on your way to the water. And even if you avoid those sand pits and make it to
the waves, you face the greatest threat of all: drowning. Once you hit the waves,
you're a hundred times more likely to drown than die from a shark attack.

But let's say you're lucky and dodge all these bullets. And then you get 10
really unlucky and a great white decides to go for a nibble.

Sharks like to attack from below and behind, so you would probably be 11
struck in the legs. They also have bad table manners: They don't chew. They
tear and rip by thrashing their heads from side to side and rolling their bodies. From spiral teeth markings on bone we can see that sharks like to saw
flesh off and then swallow it whole.

The good news is that 70 percent of attacks are one bite only. The bad 12
news is that a single bite and rip from a great white shark is more than
enough to remove your leg. However, that can actually work *for* you.

The great danger in a leg chomping is a cut to your femoral artery. In 13
general, injuries to arteries are more dangerous than those to veins because
arteries carry blood *from* your heart and are under pressure, so when they're
severed they squirt — as opposed to veins, which just drool.

The femoral is one of the worst arteries to sever. It's responsible for oxy- 14
genating your entire leg, and nearly 5 percent of your blood volume passes
through it every minute.

Exactly how the shark bites your leg would determine whether you have 15
any chance at all. The human body cannot afford to lose 5 percent of its
blood volume per minute — that equates to death in four minutes — so you
would think that if your femoral artery was severed, your story would be a
short one. But that's not always the case.

Right now, as you read these words, your femoral artery is under a small 16
bit of tension, like a stretched rubber band. If it were severed *cleanly* by the

shark, it would snap back into the stump of your leg, where your muscles could pinch it shut—slowing the leak and giving you time to get a tourniquet on. But if it were slashed *unevenly,* or at an angle, it wouldn't recede correctly—that's bad. You would black out in thirty seconds. From there you would go into circulatory shock—a deadly positive feedback loop wherein your tissues die from lack of blood, swell up, and compound the problem by blocking blood flow elsewhere in the body.

Four minutes after the attack, if your femoral was cut unevenly, you would have lost 20 percent of your blood and you would enter a critical stage. Your heart needs a minimum blood pressure to keep beating, and once you lost 20 percent of your blood volume you would drop below that threshold. After that it would only be a few minutes until complete brain death. 17

All of this assumes you were lucky and the shark did the expected and attacked from behind. A frontal attack on your head and torso is less likely but worse. Losing your head is bad because, one, your brain is in it and, two, tourniquets are far less effective on your neck than they are on your legs (for details, see Wikipedia for "Hanging"). 18

Lawyer's note: Seriously — do not put a tourniquet around your neck. 19

Thinking Critically about the Text

The writers point out that "the odds of [being attacked by a shark] are *infinitesimal*" (paragraph 9) and that people are far more likely to drown or even die in a car accident on the way to the beach than be killed by a shark. How does this concession align with their overall purpose in writing about shark attacks? Does it undermine it in any way?

Questions on Subject

1. Who are Cassidy and Doherty's readers? What is the authors' attitude toward their **audience**? How can you tell?

2. According to the writers, why would a shark bite you? What different theories are there? What does the authors' evidence suggest would be the real reason?

3. In paragraph 11, Cassidy and Doherty note that sharks have "bad table manners." What do they mean?

4. Cassidy and Doherty write, "Exactly how the shark bites your leg would determine whether you have any chance at all" (paragraph 15). How would you summarize the different factors and processes that would decide the fate of someone bitten in the leg by a shark?

Questions on Strategy

1. Throughout this excerpt, the writers use the second person **point of view**. That is, they address the reader as "you." What is the effect of writing in

the second person? How does this influence the **tone** of the writing and the writers' relationship with their audience? How would the excerpt be different if it was written in the first or third person?

2. Where do the writers use **analogies** and **similes**? What is your reaction to them? What do you think the writers are trying to achieve with them?

3. How do the writers use **transitional words** and phrases to clarify and sequence the process of shark attacks? Point to specific examples.

4. Is this essay a directional process analysis, an informational process analysis, or an evaluative process analysis? Explain your answer.

Process Analysis in Action

Based on an idea similar to the one contained in the following cartoon, work with a small group to write a humorous process analysis essay or create a presentation with the thesis "Nothing is ever as simple as it looks."

"And that's how you make a peanut butter sandwich."

Tom Cheney/The New Yorker Collection/The Cartoon Bank

Writing Suggestions

1. In this essay, Cassidy and Doherty write a process analysis about a terrifying experience that is highly unlikely to happen to any of their readers. Nevertheless, many people fear being attacked by sharks. Following the lead of the authors, write your own process analysis of a situation, experience, or threat

that you (or others) fear. But as with Cassidy and Doherty, choose a danger that is statistically improbable. As they do, try to identify and examine the key elements of the process, as well as its causal factors.

2. **Writing with Sources.** Although each of us hopes never to be in a natural disaster such as an earthquake or a major flood (or attacked in nature, as in Cassidy and Doherty's account of a shark attack), many of us have been or could be, and it is important that people know what to do. Do some research on the topic, and then write an essay in which you explain the steps that a person should follow to protect life and property during and in the aftermath of a particular natural disaster. For models of and advice on integrating sources in your essay, see Chapters 14 and 15.

Why We All Scream When We Get Ice Cream Brain Freeze

ASHLIE STEVENS

Courtesy of Ashlie Stevens

Ashlie Stevens was born in St. Charles, Illinois, in 1993. She grew up near Chicago, Illinois, before moving to Louisville, Kentucky, to finish high school. She earned her undergraduate degree from Bellarmine University and is currently pursuing a master of fine arts degree in creative writing at the University of Kentucky. In addition to her academic pursuits, Stevens is also an arts and culture reporter for public radio station WFPL in Louisville. Her print and audio work has been featured in the *Atlantic, Eater, Here & Now, National Geographic*'s "The Plate," and NPR's *The Salt*.

In this post, which appeared on National Public Radio's food and science blog, *The Salt*, Stevens investigates the science and physiology behind a common and painful summer phenomenon: the ice cream headache. The piece also brings together two of the writer's passions: "When growing up, I really wanted to be a scientist," Stevens says. "But during school, my love of writing won out. Now, I count myself lucky to be able to write about anatomy and food science for a living." As you read, notice the writing choices Stevens makes as she writes about a biological process for her nonscientific audiences.

Preparing to Read

Have you ever had the experience of "brain freeze" or wondered about why it happens? Does it seem important? What other everyday physical experiences and sensations do you wonder about?

Ah, the brain freeze—the signature pain of summer experienced by anyone who has eaten an ice cream cone with too much enthusiasm or slurped down a slushie a little too quickly. But have you ever stopped mid-freeze to think about why our bodies react like this? Well, researchers who study pain have, and some, like Dr. Kris Rau of the University of Louisville in Kentucky, say it's a good way to understand the basics of how we process damaging stimuli.

But first, a lesson in terminology. "There's a scientific medical term for ice cream headaches which is sphenopalatine ganglion neuralgia," Rau says.

Try breaking that out at your next ice cream social. Anyway, to understand how brain freeze happens, it helps to think of your body and brain as a big computer where everything is hooked together.

> ❝ **In this case, you see an ice cream truck. You get some ice cream. And then your brain gives you the go-ahead and you dive face-first into a double-scoop of mint chocolate chip.** ❞

In this case, you see an ice cream truck. You get some ice cream. And then your brain gives you the go-ahead and you dive face-first into a double-scoop of mint chocolate chip. "Now on the roof of your mouth there are a lot of little blood vessels, capillaries," Rau says. "And there's a lot of nerve fibers called nociceptors that detect painful or noxious stimuli." The rush of cold causes those vessels to constrict. "And when that happens, it happens so quickly that all of those little pain fibers in the roof of your mouth—they interpret that as being a painful stimulus," Rau says. A message is then shot up to your brain via the trigeminal nerve, one of the major nerves of the facial area.

The brain itself doesn't have any pain-sensing fibers, but its covering—called the meninges—does. "And of course all of those little pain-sensing fibers are hooked up to your trigeminal nerve," Rau says. "So the brain is trying to figure out what is going on. It knows there is something wrong, something that is painful and they don't know exactly where it is." And the pain message finally registers at the top of your head, which seems kind of random. "But it's a very similar phenomenon to the referred pain that is experienced by people who have heart attacks," Rau says. "You don't feel like your heart is hurting itself; it's your shoulder that is starting to hurt on your left side." And most importantly, it's enough to get most people to stop eating the ice cream. Crisis averted.

After a minute or two, the brain and body go back to normal. "The brain is what actually interprets all those signals that are coming in and determines whether it is painful or not painful," Rau says. "So without the brain there would be no pain." Knowing the mechanisms behind how your brain processes those signals—and how factors like genetics, race or sex impact those—is a crucial area of research for Rau. Rau says there is anecdotal evidence suggesting that ice cream headaches might be an effective treatment for migraines. It does not work for everyone, and the reasons why it might be effective are unclear, but for those who have to deal with the debilitating effects of migraines, he says it might be worth a tasty shot.

Thinking Critically about the Text

While Stevens writes in an informal and conversational style, she also manages to include scientific terms, scientific concepts, and a scientific explanation. How does she reconcile these two aspects of her essay? Do you think she's successful?

Questions on Subject

1. If the brain has no "pain-sensing fibers" (paragraph 5), why do we get a headache from eating ice cream too quickly, according to Stevens? Explain.

2. In paragraph 3, what **analogy** does Stevens use? Why is it important for her overall **purpose**?

3. According to the researcher Stevens interviews, the ice cream headache is similar to the pain experienced by people who have heart attacks. What is the similarity?

4. Why are ice cream headaches a useful topic for researchers? What are the practical implications of this research and questions about ice cream headaches, according to Stevens?

Questions on Strategy

1. Stevens uses several sentence fragments in this blog post, including in her opening sentence. What other fragments can you find? What effect does Stevens hope to achieve by writing with them?

2. How does Stevens **organize** this essay? Do you find the organization effective? Why, or why not?

3. Where in the essay does Stevens use **definition**? How are the definitions related to her overall process analysis?

4. Find specific examples of strong, descriptive verbs in the essay. How do these contribute to your experience reading the essay?

Process Analysis in Action

Before class, find a how-to article that interests you at the Web site www.wikihow .com. Read the article and bring it to class. Then, be prepared to discuss the article's strengths and weaknesses as a directional process analysis. For example, is it accurate and complete? How would you revise it?

Writing Suggestions

1. In this blog post, the writer moves from an ordinary experience to a relatively simple question, and then to a complex scientific answer. Most of us are not working scientists or researchers. As nonspecialists, how do we write about and explain scientific topics? Write a brief directional process analysis that provides instructions for researching and writing about specialized or scientific topics. For example, where should writers begin? What order should the steps take?

2. Stevens writes about a common sensation that many people have experienced. In the process, she provides a process explanation, a research summary, and even some practical benefits from exploring this question. Following her example, research another everyday phenomenon, and then write an informational process analysis that explains it clearly. You might want to begin with a question, as Stevens does. Here are some possible topics and processes, if you need suggestions: bumping your funny bone, falling asleep, cooking with a microwave, recycling plastic, connecting to a wireless network, brewing coffee.

How Do Spiders Make Their Webs?

ALICIA AULT

Courtesy of Alicia Ault

Journalist Alicia Ault graduated from Boston University and later earned a CASE journalism fellowship to study at the University of Pittsburgh's School of Medicine. Ault specializes in science, medicine, and health policy, covering everything from the Affordable Care Act to the National Institutes of Health and the Food and Drug Administration. She also writes about art, business, real estate, food, and adventure sports, including races in Borneo, Patagonia, and the Sierra Nevada mountains. She worked as associate editor for Frontline Medical Communications and has written for the *New York Times*, the *Washington Post*, the *Wall Street Journal*, Reuters, *Wired*, the *Miami Herald*, *Science*, *Nature*, the Discovery Channel, and Sirius Radio. Ault now divides her time between Washington, D.C., and New Orleans.

Ault is currently a contributing writer for both Medscape Medical News and Smithsonian.com, where she writes the "Ask Smithsonian" column. This essay appeared in that column in December 2015. As you read, notice how Ault explores how spiders do what they do and suggests what scientists might accomplish with that knowledge.

Preparing to Read

Is there a process, natural or otherwise, that has always intrigued you? Perhaps you wonder how a tadpole turns into a frog, or how the electoral college works, or how a wireless router transmits a signal. Consider what you know about the process and where you might turn to learn more.

Spiders are skillful engineers, gifted with amazing planning skills and 1 a material that allows them to precisely design rigorous and functional webs.

The material — spider silk — has chemical properties that make it lustrous, 2 strong and light. It's stronger than steel and has impressive tensile strength, meaning it can be stretched a lot before it snaps. Scientists have been trying for decades to decode exactly what gives the silk both strength and elasticity, but so far they have found only clues.

Any individual spider can make up to seven different types of silk, but 3 most generally make four to five kinds, says Jonathan Coddington, director of the Global Genome Initiative and senior scientist at the Smithsonian's National Museum of Natural History.

> Scientists have been trying for decades to decode exactly what gives the silk both strength and elasticity, but so far they have found only clues.

Spiders use their silk for several purposes, including web-building. That diversity is not hard to imagine, given that Earth hosts 45,749 species of spiders, according to the World Spider Catalog. The number is changing constantly with the frequent discovery of new species.

4

Why build webs? They serve as "pretty much offense and defense," says Coddington. "If you're going to live in a web, it's going to be a defensive structure," he says, noting that vibrations in the strands can alert the spiders to predators. Webs are also used to catch prey, says Coddington, whose research has focused in part on spider evolution and taxonomy. Scientists have been trying for decades to decode exactly what gives the silk both strength and elasticity, but so far they have found only clues.

5

Sometimes spiders eat their own webs when they are done with them, as a way to replenish the silk supply.

6

Spider silk is made of connected protein chains that help make it strong, along with unconnected areas that give it flexibility. It is produced in internal glands, moving from a soluble form to a hardened form and then spun into fiber by the spinnerets on the spider's abdomen.

7

Spiders' multiple spinnerets and eight legs come in handy for web-building. The architecture of a web is very species-specific, says Coddington. "If you show me a web, I can tell you what spider made it," he says, adding that spiders "are opinionated" about where they will make a web. Some might be at home in the bottom of a paper cup, while others wouldn't touch that space.

8

Most web-building happens under the cover of darkness.

9

The typical orb weaver spider (the group that's most familiar to Americans) will build a planar orb web, suspended by seven guy lines attached to leaves, twigs, rocks, telephone poles or other surfaces. Hanging from a leaf or some other object, the spider must get its silk from that point to the other surfaces.

10

The spider starts by pulling silk from a gland with its fourth leg. The opposite fourth leg is used to pull out multiple strands of silk from about 20 additional silk glands, creating a balloon-like structure. The spider sits patiently, knowing that eventually a warm breeze will take up the balloon, which carries away the first line of silk.

11

Eventually the balloon's trailing silk strand snags—and, like an angler with a fish on the line, the spider can feel the hit. It tugs to make sure the silk strand is truly attached, then it pulls out new silk and attaches the strand to whatever it is perched on and starts gathering up the snagged strand, pulling itself towards the endpoint, all the while laying out new silk behind it. That

12

new silk is the first planar line. The spider may do this 20 times, creating a network of dry (not sticky) silk lines arcing in all directions.

The spider then has to determine which of those lines constitute seven good attachment points—they must be in a plane and "distributed usefully around the circle the web will occupy," says Coddington. The spider cuts away the 13 lines that it won't use. "Now that you have the seven attachments you need, you no longer need to touch the ground, leaves, twigs, anything . . . you are in your own, arguably solipsistic, world." 13

Then the spider starts to spin its web, a relatively simple and predictable process. It begins at the outside and works its way in, attaching segment by segment with its legs, creating concentric circles and ending with a center spiral of sticky silk that traps much-needed prey—all the energy invested in making the web depletes protein stores. 14

The sticky stuff merely immobilizes the prey. The coup de grâce comes from the spider's jaws. "Most spiders attack with their teeth," says Coddington. "They just wade in and bite the thing to death." That's a risky proposition, though, because the prey might not be entirely stuck. 15

A few families of spiders have developed an alternative mode of offense: the sticky-silk wrap attack. Those spiders lay a strand of sticky silk across the ground. When an insect crosses, the vibration alerts the spider, which then attacks, flicking lines of sticky, strong silk around the insect and wrapping it up until it is fully immobilized. The spider then moves in for the death bite. But this is more of a rarity than a rule in the spider world. 16

Many researchers are studying spider behavior and spider silk in the hopes of someday being able to farm the material or perhaps replicate it through genetic engineering. The silk could be used, for instance, to increase the strength of body armor, or to create skin grafts. "That would be a great thing for the human race," says Coddington. 17

A handful of companies are currently invested in spider silk, including Ann Arbor, Michigan–based Kraig Biocraft Laboratories, a Swedish biotech firm, Spiber Technologies, and a German company, AMSilk, which says it has genetically engineered a protein that is similar to spider silk that is currently being used in shampoos and other cosmetics. 18

Thinking Critically about the Text

Ault mentions two possible uses for spider silk: body armor and skin grafts. Based on the information provided in this article, can you think of other potential uses for spider silk?

Questions on Subject

1. What purposes do spider webs serve? Where do you find this information?

2. What are the qualities of spider silk? Why do scientists consider it valuable?

3. Paragraph 4 begins "Spiders use their silk for several purposes, including web-building." What other purposes do spiders use their silk for?

4. Ault writes, "Most web-building happens under the cover of darkness" (paragraph 9). Why do you think Ault includes this information? What significance does it have?

Questions on Strategy

1. What is Ault's **purpose** in this essay? Where is it stated?

2. Ault relies heavily on description. What dominant impression does she create of spiders and of their webs? Locate the details she uses to do this.

3. How many experts has Ault cited in this essay? Is her research adequate and convincing? Would you like to have heard **evidence** from additional scientists? Why, or why not?

4. How is this selection organized? What **transitional** expressions and time markers are used to help create a logical flow of ideas?

Process Analysis in Action

Draw the process Ault describes in paragraphs 10–15. You don't need to be an artist for this activity: The spider can be an oval with eight lines representing legs. Create at least one image for each paragraph; you'll probably need several images for the more complex steps. Work in pencil so you can adjust your drawing as you proceed. Does the act of drawing the process help you more clearly understand it? Why do you think that is?

Writing Suggestions

1. Ault tells us that researchers hope they may one day be able to "replicate [spider silk] through genetic engineering" (paragraph 17). According to the Union of Concerned Scientists, "Genetic engineering is a set of technologies used to change the genetic makeup of cells, including the transfer of genes within and across species boundaries to produce improved or novel organisms." Both genetically modified food and human genetic engineering are highly controversial. What do you know about genetic engineering, and how do you feel about it? Are the uses mentioned in this article (strengthening body armor and skin grafts) legitimate? What concerns do you have about genetic engineering? Write an essay exploring the pros and cons of genetic engineering, providing detailed examples to support your claims.

2. Think about a process all students have to go through at your college, or a process that you anticipate doing in the near future. For example, all college students have to register for courses each term. What is the registration process like at your college? Do you find any part of the process unnecessarily frustrating or annoying? Or, most students rent an apartment for the first time in college. Have you experienced this process, or will you soon? What steps does a first-time renter need to take to have the best outcome? In a letter to your campus newspaper or a prospective renter, evaluate the current or common procedure for registration or renting and offer suggestions for making the process more efficient and pleasurable.

Nick Vedros/Getty Images

CHAPTER 8

Comparison and Contrast

WHAT ARE COMPARISON AND CONTRAST?

A COMPARISON PRESENTS TWO OR MORE SUBJECTS (PEOPLE, IDEAS, OR OBJECTS), considers them together, and shows in what ways they are alike; a contrast shows how they differ. These two perspectives, apparently in contradiction to each other, actually work so often in conjunction that they are commonly considered a single strategy, called *comparison and contrast* or simply *comparison* for short.

Comparison and contrast are so much a part of daily life that we are often not aware of using them. Whenever you make a choice — what to wear, where to eat, what college to attend, what career to pursue — you implicitly use comparison and contrast to evaluate your options and arrive at your decision.

VISUALIZING COMPARISON AND CONTRAST

Photographs of people with their pets often bring smiles to viewers' faces, especially when the pet and the pet owner look alike. What facial feature(s) do this owner and pet share? What other similarities in appearance or expression do you see between the pet owner and his Shar-Pei? What differences? Which do you find more interesting — the similarities or the differences? Explain why. What do you think a photograph like this could be used to illustrate or sell? Could it be made into a meme?

UNDERSTANDING COMPARISON AND CONTRAST AS A WRITING STRATEGY

To compare one thing or idea with another, to discover the similarities and differences between them, is one of the most basic human strategies for learning, evaluating, and making decisions. Because it serves so many fundamental purposes, using comparison and contrast is a particularly strong strategy for the writer. It may be the primary mode for essay writers who seek to educate or persuade the reader; to evaluate things, people, or events; and to differentiate between apparently similar subjects or to reconcile the differences between dissimilar ones.

The strategy of comparison and contrast is most commonly used in writing when the subjects under discussion belong to the same class or general category: four makes of car, for example, or two candidates for Senate. (See Chapter 9, "Division and Classification," for a more complete discussion of classes.) Such subjects are said to be *comparable*, or to have a strong basis for comparison.

▶ Types of Comparison and Contrast

Point-by-Point and Block Comparison.   There are two basic ways to organize comparison and contrast essays. In the first, *point-by-point comparison*, the author starts by comparing both subjects in terms of a particular point, moves on to a second point and compares both subjects, moves on to a third point, and so on. The other way to organize a comparison is called *block comparison*. In this pattern, the information about one subject is gathered into a block, which is followed by a block of comparable information about the second subject.

Each pattern of comparison has advantages and disadvantages. Point-by-point comparison allows the reader to grasp fairly easily the specific points of comparison the author is making; it may be harder, though, to pull together the details and convey a distinct impression of what each subject is like. The block comparison guarantees that each subject will receive a more unified discussion; however, the points of comparison between them may be less clear.

The first of the following two annotated passages illustrates a point-by-point comparison. This selection, a comparison of President Franklin Roosevelt and his vice-presidential running mate Harry Truman of Missouri, is from historian David McCullough's Pulitzer Prize–winning biography *Truman* (1992):

Point-by-point comparison identifies central similarities	Both were men of exceptional determination, with great reserves of personal courage and cheerfulness. They were alike, too, in their enjoyment of people. (The human race, Truman once told a reporter, was an "excellent outfit.") Each had an active sense of humor and was inclined to be dubious of those who did not. But Roosevelt, who loved stories, loved also to laugh at his own, while Truman was more of a listener and laughed best when somebody else told "a good one."
Point-by-point contrast introduces differences	Roosevelt enjoyed flattery, Truman was made uneasy by it. Roosevelt loved the subtleties of human relations. He was a master of the circuitous solution to problems, of the pleasing if ambiguous answer to difficult questions. He was sensitive to nuances in a way Harry Truman

<table>
<tr><td>

Development of key difference

</td><td>

never was and never would be. Truman, with his rural Missouri background, and partly, too, because of the limits of his education, was inclined to see things in far simpler terms, as right or wrong, wise or foolish. He dealt little in abstractions. His answers to questions, even complicated questions, were nearly always direct and assured, plainly said, and followed often by a conclusive "And that's all there is to it," an old Missouri expression, when in truth there may have been a great deal more "to it."

</td></tr>
</table>

Point-by-point comparison and contrast of each man's life struggles and experiences

Each of them had been tested by his own painful struggle, Roosevelt with crippling polio, Truman with debt, failure, obscurity, and the heavy stigma of the Pendergasts. Roosevelt liked to quote the admonition of his old headmaster at Groton, Dr. Endicott Peabody: "Things in life will not always run smoothly. Sometimes we will be rising toward the heights — then all will seem to reverse itself and start downward. The great fact to remember is that the trend of civilization is forever upward. ..." Assuredly Truman would have subscribed to the same vision. They were two optimists at heart, each in his way faithful to the old creed of human progress. But there had been nothing in Roosevelt's experience like the night young Harry held the lantern as his mother underwent surgery, nothing like the Argonne, or Truman's desperate fight for political survival in 1940.

In the following example from *Harper's* magazine, Otto Friedrich uses a block format to contrast a newspaper story with a newsmagazine story:

Subjects of comparison: Newspaper story and magazine story belong to the same class

There is an essential difference between a news story, as understood by a newspaperman or a wire-service writer, and a newsmagazine story. The chief purpose of the conventional news story is to tell what happened. It starts with the most important information and continues into increasingly inconsequential details, not only because the reader may not read beyond the first paragraph, but because an editor working on galley proofs a few minutes before press time likes to be able to cut freely from the end of the story.

Block comparison: Each paragraph deals with one type of story

A newsmagazine is very different. It is written to be read consecutively from beginning to end, and each of its stories is designed, following the critical theories of Edgar Allan Poe, to create one emotional effect. The news, what happened that week, may be told in the beginning, the middle, or the end; for the purpose is not to throw information at t he reader but to seduce him into reading the whole story, and into accepting the dramatic (and often political) point being made.

In this selection, Friedrich has two purposes: to offer information that explains the differences between a newspaper story and a newsmagazine story and to persuade readers that magazine stories tend to be more biased than newspaper stories.

Analogy: A Special Form of Comparison and Contrast. When the subject under discussion is unfamiliar, complex, or abstract, the resourceful writer may use a special form of comparison called *analogy* to help readers understand the difficult subject. Whereas most comparisons analyze items within the same class, analogies compare two largely dissimilar subjects to look for illuminating similarities. In addition, while the typical comparison seeks to illuminate specific features of both subjects, the primary purpose of analogy is to clarify one subject that is complex or unfamiliar by pointing out its similarities to a more familiar or concrete subject.

If, for example, your purpose were to explain the craft of fiction writing, you might note its similarities to the craft of carpentry. In this case, you would be drawing an analogy because the two subjects clearly belong to different classes. You would be using the concrete work of the carpenter to help readers understand the more abstract work of the novelist. You can use analogy in one or two paragraphs to clarify a particular aspect of the larger topic, or you can use it as the organizational strategy for an entire essay.

In the following example from *The Mysterious Sky* (1960), observe how Lester Del Rey explains the functions of Earth's atmosphere (a subject that people have difficulty with because they can't "see" it) by making an analogy to an ordinary window:

> The atmosphere of Earth acts like any window in serving two very important functions. It lets light in and it permits us to look out. It also serves as a shield to keep out dangerous or uncomfortable things. A normal glazed window lets us keep our houses warm by keeping out cold air, and it prevents rain, dirt, and unwelcome insects and animals from coming in. As we have already seen, Earth's atmospheric window also helps to keep our planet at a comfortable temperature by holding back radiated heat and protecting us from dangerous levels of ultraviolet light.

You'll notice that Del Rey's analogy establishes no direct relationship between the subjects under comparison. The analogy is effective precisely because it enables the reader to visualize the atmosphere, which is unobservable, by comparing it to something quite different—a window—that is familiar and concrete.

USING COMPARISON AND CONTRAST ACROSS THE DISCIPLINES

When writing essays in the academic disciplines, you will have many opportunities to use the strategy of comparison and contrast to both organize and strengthen the presentation of your ideas. To determine whether comparison and contrast is the right strategy for you in a particular paper, review the guidelines described in Chapter 2, "Determining a Strategy for Developing Your Essay" (pages 34–35). Consider the following examples:

Music

1. MAIN IDEA: The music of the Romantic period sharply contrasts with the music of the earlier Classical period.
2. QUESTION: What are the key differences between the music of the Romantic and the Classical periods?
3. STRATEGY: Comparison and contrast. The direction words *contrasts* and *differences* call for a discussion that distinguishes characteristics of the two periods in music history.
4. SUPPORTING STRATEGIES: Definition and illustration. It might be helpful to define the key terms *Romanticism* and *Classicism* and to illustrate each of the differences with examples from representative Romantic composers (Brahms, Chopin, Schubert, and Tchaikovsky) and Classical composers (Beethoven, Haydn, and Mozart).

Political Science

1. MAIN IDEA: Though very different people, Franklin D. Roosevelt and Winston Churchill shared many larger-than-life leadership qualities during World War II, a period of doubt and crisis.
2. QUESTION: What are the similarities between Winston Churchill and Franklin D. Roosevelt as world leaders?
3. STRATEGY: Comparison and contrast. The direction words *shared* and *similarities* require a discussion of the leadership traits displayed by both men.
4. SUPPORTING STRATEGY: Definition. It might prove helpful to define *leader* and/or *leadership* to establish a context for this comparison.

Physics

1. MAIN IDEA: Compare and contrast the three classes of levers—simple machines used to amplify force.

2. **QUESTION:** What are the similarities and differences among the three classes of levers?

3. **STRATEGY:** Comparison and contrast. The direction words *compare, contrast, similarities,* and *differences* say it all.

4. **SUPPORTING STRATEGY:** Illustration. Readers will certainly appreciate familiar examples — pliers, nutcrackers, and tongs — of the three classes of levers, examples that both clarify and emphasize the similarities and differences.

PRACTICAL ADVICE FOR WRITING AN ESSAY OF COMPARISON AND CONTRAST

As you plan, write, and revise your comparison and contrast essay, be mindful of the writing process guidelines described in Chapter 2. Also, pay particular attention to the basic requirements and essential ingredients for this writing strategy.

▶ Planning Your Essay of Comparison and Contrast

Planning is an essential part of writing a good comparison and contrast essay. You can save yourself a great deal of aggravation by taking the time to think about the key components of your essay before you actually begin to write.

Many college assignments ask you to use the strategy of comparison and contrast. As you read an assignment, look for one or more of the words that suggest the use of this strategy. When you are asked to identify the *similarities* and *differences* between two items, you should use comparison and contrast. Other assignments might ask you to determine which of two options is *better* or to select the *best* solution to a particular problem. Again, the strategy of comparison and contrast will help you make this evaluation and arrive at a sound, logical conclusion.

As you start planning and writing a comparison and contrast essay, keep in mind the basic requirements of this writing strategy.

Compare Subjects from the Same Class. Remember that the subjects of your comparison should be in the same class or general category so that you can establish a clear basis for comparison. (There are any number of possible classes, such as particular types of persons, places, and things, as well as occupations, activities, philosophies, points in history, and even concepts and ideas.) If your subject is difficult, complex, or unobservable, you may find that analogy, a special form of comparison, is the most effective strategy to explain that subject. Remember, also, that if the similarities and differences between the subjects are too obvious, your reader is certain to lose interest quickly.

Determine Your Purpose and Focus on It. Suppose you choose to compare and contrast solar energy with wind energy. It is clear that both are members of the same class—energy—so there is a basis for comparing them; there also seem to be enough interesting differences to make a comparison and contrast possible. But before going any further, you must ask yourself why you want to compare and contrast these particular subjects. What audience do you seek to address? Do you want to inform, to emphasize, to explain, to evaluate, to persuade? Do you have more than one purpose? Whatever your purpose, it will influence the content and organization of your comparison.

In comparing and contrasting solar and wind energy, you will certainly provide factual information, and you will probably also want to evaluate the two energy sources to determine whether either is a practical means of producing energy. You may also want to persuade your readers that one technology is superior to the other.

Formulate a Thesis Statement. Once you have your purpose clearly in mind, formulate a preliminary thesis statement. At this early stage in the writing process, the thesis statement is not cast in stone; you may well want to modify it later on, as a result of research and further consideration of your subject. A preliminary thesis statement has two functions: First, it fixes your direction so that you will be less tempted to stray into byways while doing research and writing drafts; second, establishing the central point of the essay makes it easier for you to gather supporting material and to organize your essay.

Choose the Points of Comparison. *Points of comparison* are the qualities and features of your subjects on which you base your comparison. For some comparisons, you will find the information you need in your own head; for others, you will have to search for information in the library or on the Internet.

At this stage, if you know only a little about the subjects of your comparison, you may have only a few hazy ideas for points of comparison. Perhaps wind energy means no more to you than an image of giant windmills lined up on a California ridge, and solar energy brings to mind only the reflective, glassy roof on a Colorado ski lodge. Even so, it is possible to list points of comparison that will be relevant to your subjects and your purpose. Here, for example, are important points of comparison in considering energy sources:

Cost

Efficiency

Convenience

Environmental impact

A tentative list of points will help you by suggesting the kind of information you need to gather for your comparison and contrast. You should always remain alert, however, for other factors you may not have thought of. For example, as you conduct research, you may find that maintenance requirements are another important factor in considering energy systems, and thus you might add that point to your list.

▎ **Organizing Your Essay of Comparison and Contrast**

Choose an Organizational Pattern That Fits Your Material.   Once you have gathered the necessary information, you should decide which organizational pattern, block or point-by-point, will best serve your purpose. In deciding which pattern to use, you may find it helpful to jot down a scratch outline before beginning your draft.

Block organization works best when the two objects of comparison are relatively straightforward and when the points of comparison are rather general, are few in number, and can be stated succinctly. As a scratch outline illustrates, block organization makes for a unified discussion of each object, which can help your readers understand the information you have for them:

Block Organization

BLOCK ONE   **Solar Energy**
   Point 1. Cost
   Point 2. Efficiency
   Point 3. Convenience
   Point 4. Maintenance requirements
   Point 5. Environmental impact

BLOCK TWO   **Wind Energy**
   Point 1. Cost
   Point 2. Efficiency
   Point 3. Convenience
   Point 4. Maintenance requirements
   Point 5. Environmental impact

If your essay will be more than two or three pages long, however, block organization may be a poor choice: By the time your readers come to your discussion of the costs of wind energy, they may well have forgotten what you had to say about solar energy costs several pages earlier. In this case, you would do better to use point-by-point organization:

Point-by-Point Organization

POINT ONE   **Cost**
   Subject 1. Solar energy
   Subject 2. Wind energy

Point Two   **Efficiency**
   Subject 1. Solar energy
   Subject 2. Wind energy

Point Three   **Convenience**
   Subject 1. Solar energy
   Subject 2. Wind energy

Point Four   **Maintenance Requirements**
   Subject 1. Solar energy
   Subject 2. Wind energy

Point Five   **Environmental Impact**
   Subject 1. Solar energy
   Subject 2. Wind energy

Draw a Conclusion from Your Comparison.   Only after you have gathered your information and made your comparisons will you be ready to decide on a conclusion. When drawing your essay to its conclusion, remember your purpose in writing, the claim made in your thesis statement, and your audience and emphasis.

Perhaps, having presented information about both technologies, your comparison shows that solar and wind energy are both feasible, with solar energy having a slight edge on most points. If your purpose has been evaluation for a general audience, you might conclude, "Both solar and wind energy are practical alternatives to conventional energy sources." If you asserted in your thesis statement that one of the technologies is superior to the other, your comparison will support a more persuasive conclusion. For the general audience, you might say, "While both solar and wind energy are practical technologies, solar energy now seems the better investment." However, for a readership made up of residents of the cloudy northwest United States, you might conclude, "While both solar and wind energy are practical technologies, wind energy makes more economic sense for investors in Oregon and Washington."

▶ Revising and Editing Your Essay of Comparison and Contrast

Careful rereading, or even reading aloud to yourself, will help you catch missing or unequal points of comparison. You may also want to ask a friend or fellow students to read through your draft, using the guidelines presented in the "Brief Guide to Peer Critiquing" box in Chapter 2 (pages 38–39). A fresh pair of eyes is always helpful, and they may give you a head start in catching grammatical inconsistencies as well (see Chapter 16).

Questions for Revising and Editing: Comparison and Contrast

1. Are the subjects of my comparison comparable; that is, do they belong to the same class of items (for example, two cars, two advertisements, two landscape paintings) so that there is a clear basis for comparison?

2. Are there any complex or abstract concepts that might be clarified by using an analogy?

3. Is the purpose of my comparison clearly stated?

4. Have I presented a clear thesis statement?

5. Have I chosen my points of comparison well? Have I avoided obvious points of comparison, concentrating instead on similarities between obviously different items or differences between essentially similar items?

6. Have I developed my points of comparison in sufficient detail so that my readers can appreciate my thinking?

7. Have I chosen the best pattern — block or point-by-point — to organize my information?

8. Have I drawn a conclusion that is in line with my thesis and purpose?

9. Have I used parallel constructions correctly in my sentences?

10. Have I avoided other errors in grammar, punctuation, and mechanics? Is my sentence style as clear, smooth, and persuasive as possible?

STUDENT ESSAY USING COMPARISON AND CONTRAST AS A WRITING STRATEGY

A studio art major from Pittsburgh, Pennsylvania, Barbara Bowman loved photography. In her writing courses, Bowman discovered many similarities between the writing process and the process that an artist follows. Her essay "Guns and Cameras," however, explores similarities of another kind: those between hunting with a gun and hunting with a camera.

Guns and Cameras
Barbara Bowman

Introduces objects being compared

With a growing number of animals heading toward extinction and with the idea of protecting such animals on game reserves increasing in popularity, photographic safaris are replacing hunting safaris. This may seem odd because of the obvious differences between guns and cameras. Shooting is aggressive, photography is passive; shooting eliminates, photography preserves.

Brief point-by-point contrast

Thesis

However, some hunters are willing to trade their guns

1

for cameras because of similarities in the way the equipment is used, as well as in the relationship among equipment, user, and "prey."

Block organization: first block about the hunter

The hunter has a deep interest in the apparatus he uses to kill his prey. He carries various types of guns, different kinds of ammunition, and special sights and telescopes to increase his chances of success. He knows *Point A: equipment* the mechanics of his guns and understands how and why they work. This fascination with the hardware of his sport is practical—it helps him achieve his goal—but it frequently becomes an end, almost a hobby in itself.

Point B: stalking

Not until the very end of the long process of stalking an animal does a game hunter use his gun. First he enters into the animal's world. He studies his prey, its habitat, its daily habits, its watering holes and feeding areas, its migration patterns, its enemies and allies, its diet and food chain. Eventually the hunter himself becomes animal-like, instinctively sensing the habits and moves of his prey. Of course, this instinct gives the hunter a better chance of killing the animal; he knows where and when he will get the best shot. But it gives him more than that. Hunting is not just pulling the trigger and killing the prey. Much of it is a multifaceted and ritualistic identification with nature.

Point C: the result

After the kill, the hunter can do a number of things with his trophy. He can sell the meat or eat it himself. He can hang the animal's head on the wall or lay its hide on the floor or even sell these objects. But any of these uses is a luxury, and its cost is high. An animal has been destroyed; a life has been eliminated.

Second block about the photographer

Like the hunter, the photographer has a great interest in the tools he uses. He carries various types of cameras, lenses, and film to help him get the picture *Point A: equipment* he wants. He understands the way cameras work, the uses of telephoto and micro lenses, and often the technical procedures of printing and developing. Of course, the time and interest a photographer invests in these mechanical aspects of his art allow him to capture and produce the image he wants. But as with the hunter, these mechanics can and often do become fascinating in themselves.

Point B: stalking

The wildlife photographer also needs to stalk his "prey" with knowledge and skill in order to get an

2

3

4

5

6

accurate "shot." Like the hunter, he has to understand the animal's patterns, characteristics, and habitat; he must become animal-like in order to succeed. And like the hunter's, his pursuit is much more prolonged and complicated than the shot itself. The stalking processes are almost identical and give many of the same satisfactions.

Point C: the result

The successful photographer also has something tangible to show for his efforts. A still picture of an animal can be displayed in a home, a gallery, a shop; it can be printed in a publication, as a postcard, or as a poster. In fact, a single photograph can be used in all these ways at once; it can be reproduced countless times. And despite all these ways of using his "trophies," the photographer continues to preserve his prey.

7

Conclusion: The two activities are similar and give the same satisfaction, so why kill?

Photography is obviously the less violent and to many the more acceptable method for obtaining a trophy of a wild animal. People no longer need to hunt in order to feed or clothe themselves, and hunting for "sport" seems to be barbaric. Luckily, the excitement of pursuing an animal, learning its habits and patterns, outsmarting it on its own level, and finally "getting" it can all be done with a camera. So why use guns?

8

Student Reflection
Barbara Bowman

Q. Tell me something about yourself.
A. Photography is a big part of my life right now. I'm a studio art major, and this summer I'll be an intern with the local weekly newspaper, their only staff photographer. So you can see why my bias is toward cameras instead of guns.

Q. How did you think of comparing them?
A. I was reading a photography book and it mentioned a safari in Africa that used cameras instead of guns. I thought that was very interesting, so I thought I'd use it for a writing subject. I don't know that much about guns, but there's a guy in my English class who's a big hunter—he wrote a paper for the class about hunting—so I asked him about it. I could tell from what he said that he got the same gratification from it that a nature photographer would. Other people I know who hunt do it mostly for the meat and for the adventure of stalking the prey. So that's how I got what I needed to know about hunting. Photography I knew lots about already, of course.

Q. Why did you use block comparison?
A. Well, the first draft was a point-by-point comparison, and it was very bumpy, shifting back and forth between the hunter and the photographer, and I thought it was probably confusing. As I kept developing the paper, it just made more sense to switch to block comparison. Unfortunately this meant that I had to throw out some paragraphs in the first draft that I liked. That's hard for me—to throw out some writing that seems different and new—but it wasn't fitting right, so I had to make the cuts.

Q. Did you make any other large-scale changes as you revised?
A. Nothing in particular, but each time I revised I threw things out that I didn't need, and now the essay is only half as long as it used to be. For example, here's a sentence from the next to last draft: "Guns kill, cameras don't; guns use ammunition, cameras use film; shooting eliminates, photography preserves." Everybody knows this, and the first and last parts say the same thing. I liked the last part, the way the words go together, so I kept that, but I cut out the rest. I did a lot of that.

Q. You use your comparison to support a particular point of view . . .
A. I don't like the idea of killing things for sport. I can see the hunter's argument that you've got to keep the animals' numbers under control, but I still would rather they weren't shot to death. That was the point of the comparison right from the first draft.

Your Response

What did you learn from Barbara Bowman's essay and reflection on the process of writing the essay? What challenges do you expect to face as you write your own comparison and contrast essay? Based on Barbara's composing strategies and on the practical advice discussed earlier in this chapter (pages 230–34), what writing choices will you make?

Neat People vs.
Sloppy People

SUZANNE BRITT

Courtesy of Suzanne Britt

Born in Winston-Salem, North Carolina, Suzanne Britt now makes her home in Raleigh. She graduated from Salem College and Washington University, where she received an M.A. in English. A poet and essayist, Britt has been a columnist for the Raleigh *News and Observer* and *Stars and Stripes*, European edition. Her work appears regularly in *North Carolina Gardens and Homes*, the *New York Times*, *Newsweek*, and the *Boston Globe*. Her essays have been collected in two books, *Skinny People Are Dull and Crunchy Like Carrots* (1982) and *Show and Tell* (1983). She is the author of *A Writer's Rhetoric* (1988), a college textbook; and *Images: A Centennial Journey* (1991), a history of Meredith College, the small independent women's college in Raleigh where Britt teaches English and continues to write.

The following essay was taken from *Show and Tell*, a book Britt humorously describes as a report on her journey into "the awful cave of self: You shout your name and voices come back in exultant response, telling you their names." Here, mingling humor with a touch of seriousness, Britt examines the differences between neat and sloppy people and gives us some insights about several important personality traits.

Preparing to Read

Many people in our society are fond of comparing people, places, and things. Often, these comparisons are premature and even damaging. Consider the ways people judge others based on clothes, appearance, or hearsay. Write about a time in your life when you made such a comparison about someone or something. Did your initial judgment hold up? If not, why did it change?

'Ve finally figured out the difference between neat people and sloppy people. The distinction is, as always, moral. Neat people are lazier and meaner than sloppy people. 1

Sloppy people, you see, are not really sloppy. Their sloppiness is merely the unfortunate consequence of their extreme moral rectitude. Sloppy people carry in their mind's eye a heavenly vision, a precise plan, that is so stupendous, so perfect, it can't be achieved in this world or the next. 2

Sloppy people live in Never-Never Land. Someday is their métier.[1] Someday they are planning to alphabetize all their books and set up home catalogs. 3

---

[1] Activity or work for which a person is especially suited. — Eds.

Someday they will go through their wardrobes and mark certain items for tentative mending and certain items for passing on to relatives of similar shape and size. Someday sloppy people will make family scrapbooks into which they will put newspaper clippings, postcards, locks of hair, and the dried corsage from their senior prom. Someday they will file everything on the surface of their desks, including the cash receipts from coffee purchases at the snack shop. Someday they will sit down and read all the back issues of *The New Yorker*.

> " I've finally figured out the difference between neat people and sloppy people. The distinction is, as always, moral. "

For all these noble reasons and more, 4 sloppy people never get neat. They aim too high and wide. They save everything, planning someday to file, order, and straighten out the world. But while these ambitious plans take clearer and clearer shape in their heads, the books spill from the shelves onto the floor, the clothes pile up in the hamper and closet, the family mementos accumulate in every drawer, the surface of the desk is buried under mounds of paper and the unread magazines threaten to reach the ceiling.

Sloppy people can't bear to part with anything. They give loving attention 5 to every detail. When sloppy people say they're going to tackle the surface of the desk, they really mean it. Not a paper will go unturned; not a rubber band will go unboxed. Four hours or two weeks into the excavation, the desk looks exactly the same, primarily because the sloppy person is meticulously creating new piles of papers with new headings and scrupulously stopping to read all of the old book catalogs before he throws them away. A neat person would just bulldoze the desk.

Neat people are bums and clods at heart. They have cavalier attitudes 6 toward possessions, including family heirlooms. Everything is just another dust-catcher to them. If anything collects dust, it's got to go and that's that. Neat people will toy with the idea of throwing the children out of the house just to cut down on the clutter.

Neat people don't care about process. They like results. What they want 7 to do is get the whole thing over with so they can sit down and watch the rasslin' on TV. Neat people operate on two unvarying principles: Never handle any item twice, and throw everything away.

The only thing messy in a neat person's house is the trash can. The minute 8 something comes to a neat person's hand, he will look at it, try to decide if it has immediate use and, finding none, throw it in the trash.

Neat people are especially vicious with mail. They never go through 9 their mail unless they are standing directly over a trash can. If the trash can is beside the mailbox, even better. All ads, catalogs, pleas for charitable contributions, church bulletins, and money-saving coupons go straight into the trash can without being opened. All letters from home, postcards from Europe, bills, and paychecks are opened, immediately responded to, then dropped in the trash can. Neat people keep their receipts only for tax purposes. That's it. No sentimental salvaging of birthday cards or the last letter a dying relative ever wrote. Into the trash it goes.

Neat people place neatness above everything, even economics. They are 10 incredibly wasteful. Neat people throw away several toys every time they walk through the den. I knew a neat person once who threw away a perfectly good dish drainer because it had mold on it. The drainer was too much trouble to wash. And neat people sell their furniture when they move. They will sell a La-Z-Boy recliner while you are reclining in it.

Neat people are no good to borrow from. Neat people buy everything in 11 expensive little single portions. They get their flour and sugar in two-pound bags. They wouldn't consider clipping a coupon, saving a leftover, reusing plastic nondairy whipped cream containers, or rinsing off tin foil and draping it over the unmoldy dish drainer. You can never borrow a neat person's newspaper to see what's playing at the movies. Neat people have the paper all wadded up and in the trash by 7:05 A.M.

Neat people cut a clean swath through the organic as well as the inor- 12 ganic world. People, animals, and things are all one to them. They are so insensitive. After they've finished with the pantry, the medicine cabinet, and the attic, they will throw out the red geranium (too many leaves), sell the dog (too many fleas), and send the children off to boarding school (too many scuff marks on the hardwood floors).

Thinking Critically about the Text

Suzanne Britt reduces people to two types: sloppy and neat. What does she see as the defining characteristics of each type? Do you consider yourself a sloppy or a neat person? Perhaps you are neither. If this is the case, make up your own category and explain why Britt's categories are not broad enough.

Questions on Subject

1. Why do you suppose Britt characterizes the distinction between sloppy and neat people as a "moral" one (paragraph 1)? What is she really poking fun at with this reference? (Glossary: **Irony**)

2. In your own words, what is the "heavenly vision," the "precise plan," Britt refers to in paragraph 2? How does Britt use this idea to explain why sloppy people can never be neat?

3. Exaggeration, as Britt uses it, is only effective if it is based on some shared idea of the truth. What commonly understood ideas about sloppy and neat people does Britt rely on? Do you agree with her? Why, or why not?

Questions on Strategy

1. Note Britt's use of **transitions** as she moves from trait to trait. How well does she use transitions to achieve **unity** in her essay? Explain.

2. Britt uses block comparison to point out the differences between sloppy and neat people. Make a side-by-side list of the traits of sloppy and neat people. After reviewing your list, determine any ways in which sloppy and neat people may be similar. Why do you suppose Britt does not include any of the ways in which they are the same?

3. Why do you think Britt has chosen to use a block comparison? What would have been gained or lost had she used a point-by-point system of contrast?

4. Throughout the essay, Britt uses numerous examples to show the differences between sloppy and neat people. Cite five examples that Britt uses to exemplify these points. How effective do you find Britt's use of **illustration**? What do they add to her comparison and contrast essay?

Comparison and Contrast in Action

Using the sample outlines on pages 232-33 as models, prepare both block and point-by-point outlines for one of the following topics:

- dogs and cats as pets
- print media and electronic media
- an economy car and a luxury car
- your local newspaper and the *New York Times*
- a high school teacher and a college teacher

Explain any advantages of one organizational plan over the other.

Writing Suggestions

1. Write an essay in which you describe yourself as either sloppy or neat. In what ways does your behavior compare or contrast with the traits Britt offers? You may follow Britt's definition of sloppy and neat, or you may come up with your own.

2. **Writing in the Workplace.** Imagine that you were recently hired to work in a small insurance business that employs five people. Your boss asks you to research and make a recommendation about the purchase of a new photo-editing program for the office. Explore different programs online or visit an office equipment store and talk with a salesperson about what programs or devices might be appropriate for a five-person office. Decide which two or three programs best fill the bill and then write a memo to your boss in which you compare and contrast the features of the top candidates, concluding with your recommendation of which program to purchase. For models of and advice on integrating sources in your essay, see Chapters 14 and 15.

Two Ways to Belong in America

BHARATI MUKHERJEE

Reagan Louie

The prominent Indian American writer and university professor Bharati Mukherjee (1940–2017) was born into a wealthy family in Calcutta (now Kolkata), India. Shortly after India gained its independence, her family relocated to England. In the 1950s, she returned to India, where she earned her bachelor's degree at the University of Calcutta in 1959 and a master's degree from the University of Baroda in 1961. Later she pursued her long-held desire to become a writer by earning a master of fine arts degree at the University of Iowa and eventually a doctorate in English and comparative literature. After marrying Canadian-American Clark Blaise, she moved with her husband to Canada, where they lived for fourteen years until legislation there against South Asians led them to move back to the United States.

Before joining the faculty at the University of California–Berkeley, Mukherjee taught at McGill University, Skidmore College, Queens College, and the City University of New York. Her work centered on writing and the theme of immigration, particularly as it concerned women, immigration policy, and cultural alienation. With her husband, she authored *Days and Nights in Calcutta* (1977) and *The Sorrow and the Terror: The Haunting Legacy of the Air India Tragedy* (1987). In addition, she published eight novels, including *The Tiger's Daughter* (1971), *Jasmine* (1989), *The Holder of the World* (1993), and *Miss New India* (2011); two collections of short stories, *Darkness* (1985) and *The Middleman and Other Stories* (1988), for which she won the National Book Critics Circle Award; and two works of nonfiction, *Political Culture and Leadership in India* (1991) and *Regionalism in Indian Perspective* (1992).

The following essay was first published in the *New York Times* in 1996, in response to new legislation championed by then–vice president Al Gore that provided for expedited routes to citizenship for legal immigrants living in the United States. As you read Mukherjee's essay, notice the way she has organized the contrasting views she and her sister have toward various aspects of living as either a legal immigrant or a citizen.

Preparing to Read

The word *immigrant* has many connotations. What associations does the word have for you? If you were to move to another country, how do you think it would feel to be considered an immigrant? If you are considered an immigrant now, what has been your experience since arriving in this country?

This is a tale of two sisters from Calcutta, Mira and Bharati, who have 1
lived in the United States for some thirty-five years, but who find themselves on different sides in the current debate over the status of immigrants. I am an American citizen and she is not. I am moved that thousands of
long-term residents are finally taking the oath of citizenship. She is not.

Mira arrived in Detroit in 1960 to study child psychology and pre- 2
school education. I followed her a year later to study creative writing at the
University of Iowa. When we left India, we were almost identical in appearance and attitude. We dressed alike, in saris; we expressed identical views on
politics, social issues, love, and marriage in the same Calcutta convent-school
accent. We would endure our two years in America, secure our degrees, then
return to India to marry the grooms of our father's choosing.

Instead, Mira married an Indian student in 1962 who was getting 3
his business administration degree at Wayne State University. They soon
acquired the labor certifications necessary for the green card of hassle-free
residence and employment.

Mira still lives in Detroit, works in the Southfield, Michigan, school sys- 4
tem, and has become nationally recognized for her contributions in the fields
of preschool education and parent-teacher relationships. After thirty-six
years as a legal immigrant in this country, she clings passionately to her
Indian citizenship and hopes to go home to India when she retires.

In Iowa City in 1963, I married a fellow student, an American of 5
Canadian parentage. Because of the accident of his North Dakota birth,
I bypassed labor-certification requirements and the race-related "quota"
system that favored the applicant's country of origin over his or her merit.
I was prepared for (and even welcomed) the emotional strain that came
with marrying outside my ethnic community. In thirty-three years of marriage, we have lived in every part of North America. By choosing a husband
who was not my father's selection, I was opting for fluidity, self-invention,
blue jeans, and T-shirts, and renouncing three thousand years (at least)
of caste-observant, "pure culture" marriage in the Mukherjee family. My
books have often been read as unapologetic (and in some quarters overen-
thusiastic) texts for cultural and psychological "mongrelization." It's a word
I celebrate.

Mira and I have stayed sisterly close by phone. In our regular Sunday 6
morning conversations, we are unguardedly affectionate. I am her only blood
relative on this continent. We expect to see each other through the looming
crises of aging and ill health without being asked. Long before Vice President
Gore's "Citizenship USA" drive, we'd had our polite arguments over the ethics
of retaining an overseas citizenship while expecting the permanent protection
and economic benefits that come with living and working in America.

Like well-raised sisters, we never said what was really on our minds, but 7 we probably pitied one another. She, for the lack of structure in my life, the erasure of Indianness, the absence of an unvarying daily core. I, for the narrowness of her perspective, her uninvolvement with the mythic depths or the superficial pop culture of this society. But, now, with the scapegoating of "aliens" (documented or illegal) on the increase, and the targeting of long-term legal immigrants like Mira for new scrutiny and new self-consciousness, she and I find ourselves unable to maintain the same polite discretion. We were always unacknowledged adversaries, and we are now, more than ever, sisters.

"I feel used," Mira raged on the phone the other night. "I feel manip- 8 ulated and discarded. This is such an unfair way to treat a person who was invited to stay and work here because of her talent. My employer went to the INS and petitioned for the labor certification. For over thirty years, I've invested my creativity and professional skills into the improvement of *this* country's preschool system. I've obeyed all the rules, I've paid my taxes, I love my work, I love my students, I love the friends I've made. How dare America now change its rules in midstream? If America wants to make new rules curtailing benefits of legal immigrants, they should apply only to immigrants who arrive after those rules are already in place."

To my ears, it sounded like the description of a long-enduring, comfort- 9 able yet loveless marriage, without risk or recklessness. Have we the right to demand, and to expect, that we be loved? (That, to me, is the subtext of the arguments by immigration advocates.) My sister is an expatriate, professionally generous and creative, socially courteous and gracious, and that's as far as her Americanization can go. She is here to maintain an identity, not to transform it.

I asked her if she would follow the example of others who have decided 10 to become citizens because of the anti-immigration bills in Congress. And here, she surprised me. "If America wants to play the manipulative game, I'll play it, too," she snapped. "I'll become a U.S. citizen for now, then change back to Indian when I'm ready to go home. I feel some kind of irrational attachment to India that I don't to America. Until all this hysteria against legal immigrants, I was totally happy. Having my green card meant I could visit any place in the world I wanted to and then come back to a job that's satisfying and that I do very well."

In one family, from two sisters alike as peas in a pod, there could not be a 11 wider divergence of immigrant experience. America spoke to me—I married it—I embraced the demotion from expatriate aristocrat to immigrant nobody, surrendering those thousands of years of "pure culture," the saris, the delightfully accented English. She retained them all. Which of us is the freak?

Mira's voice, I realize, is the voice not just of the immigrant South Asian 12 community but of an immigrant community of the millions who have stayed rooted in one job, one city, one house, one ancestral culture, one cuisine, for the entirety of their productive years. She speaks for greater numbers than I possibly can. Only the fluency of her English and the anger, rather than fear, born of confidence from her education, differentiate her from the seamstresses, the domestics, the technicians, the shop owners, the millions of hardworking but effectively silenced documented immigrants as well as their less fortunate "illegal" brothers and sisters.

> **I embraced the demotion from expatriate aristocrat to immigrant nobody, surrendering those thousands of years of 'pure culture,' the saris, the delightfully accented English.**

Nearly twenty years ago, when I was living in my husband's ancestral homeland of Canada, I was always well-employed but never allowed to feel part of the local Quebec or larger Canadian society. Then, through a Green Paper that invited a national referendum on the unwanted side effects of "nontraditional" immigration, the government officially turned against its immigrant communities, particularly those from South Asia.

I felt then the same sense of betrayal that Mira feels now. I will never forget the pain of that sudden turning, and the casual racist outbursts the Green Paper elicited. That sense of betrayal had its desired effect and drove me, and thousands like me, from the country.

Mira and I differ, however, in the ways in which we hope to interact with the country that we have chosen to live in. She is happier to live in America as an expatriate Indian than as an immigrant American. I need to feel like a part of the community I have adopted (as I tried to feel in Canada as well). I need to put roots down, to vote and make the difference that I can. The price that the immigrant willingly pays, and that the exile avoids, is the trauma of self-transformation.

Thinking Critically about the Text

What do you think Mukherjee's sister means when she says in paragraph 10, "If America wants to play the manipulative game, I'll play it, too"? How do you react to her plans? Explain.

Questions on Subject

1. What is Mukherjee's **thesis**? Where does she present it?

2. What arguments does Mukherjee make for becoming an American citizen? What arguments does her sister make for retaining Indian citizenship?

3. At the end of paragraph 11, Mukherjee asks a question. How does she answer it? How would you answer it?

4. What does Mukherjee mean when she says, "The price that the immigrant willingly pays, and that the exile avoids, is the trauma of self-transformation" (paragraph 15)?

Questions on Strategy

1. How has Mukherjee organized her essay? Is it block comparison, point-by-point comparison, or some combination of the two?

2. Why is the pattern of organization that Mukherjee uses appropriate for her **subject** and **purpose**?

3. Mukherjee chooses to let her sister, Mira, speak for herself in this essay. What do you think would have been lost had Mukherjee simply reported what Mira felt and believed? Explain.

Comparison and Contrast in Action

Why do you think people in general find the unexpected "interesting"? Do you, for example, find it interesting that two people with similar backgrounds could have completely different views about or interpretations of something? And why are we so fascinated by differences when we were expecting similarities or by similarities when we were expecting differences? Why is this important to know when using comparison and contrast as a strategy? Take a minute to write down some quick answers to these questions (and examples to support your answers, if you can), and then discuss your ideas with a classmate.

Writing Suggestions

1. Mukherjee writes about her relationship with her sister, saying, "[W]e never said what was really on our minds, but we probably pitied one another" (paragraph 7). Such differences are often played out on a larger scale when immigrants who assimilate into American life are confronted by those who choose to retain their ethnic identity; these tensions can lead to name-calling and even aggressive prejudice within immigrant communities. Write an essay about an ethnic or cultural community you are familiar with, comparing and contrasting lifestyle choices its members make as they try to find a comfortable place in American society.

2. Mukherjee presents her sister's reasons for not becoming a citizen and supports them with statements that her sister has made. Imagine that you are Mira Mukherjee. Write a counterargument to the argument presented by Bharati, giving your reasons for remaining an Indian citizen. Remember that you have already broken with tradition by marrying a man not of your "father's choosing" and that the "trauma of self-transformation" that Bharati raises in the conclusion of her essay is much deeper and more complicated than she has represented it to be. Can you say that you are holding to tradition when you are not? Can you engage in a challenging self-transformation if it is not genuinely motivated?

The Difference between "Sick" and "Evil"

ANDREW VACHSS

AP Photo Mark Lennihan

Andrew Vachss, attorney and author, was born in New York City in 1942. Before graduating from the New England School of Law in 1975, Vachss held a number of positions related to child protection, ranging from a New York City social services caseworker to director of a maximum-security prison for aggressive, violent juvenile offenders. As a lawyer, he exclusively represents children and youths and serves as a child protection consultant. Vachss has written more than twenty-five novels, three collections of short stories, three plays, and two works of nonfiction. He is perhaps best known as the author of the award-winning Burke series of hard-boiled crime mysteries. Vachss lectures widely on issues relating to child protection and has written for *Esquire*, *Playboy*, the *New York Times*, and *Parade*, among others.

In the following article, which first appeared in *Parade* on July 14, 2002, Andrew Vachss issues a call to action to protect America's children in the wake of the so-called pedophile priest scandal. Here he asks the fundamental question: "Are those who abuse their positions of trust to prey upon children—a category certainly not limited to those in religious orders—sick … or are they evil?" To answer this question, Vachss believes that we need to establish a clear understanding of the differences between the words *sick* and *evil*, two words that the public often uses synonymously.

Preparing to Read

How do you define *evil*? What kinds of behavior or things do you use the word *evil* to describe? Identify several historical figures whom you consider evil and briefly describe what makes them evil.

The shock waves caused by the recent exposures of so-called "pedophile priests" have reverberated throughout America. But beneath our anger and revulsion, a fundamental question pulsates: Are those who abuse their positions of trust to prey upon children—a category certainly not limited to those in religious orders—sick … or are they evil?

We need the answer to that fundamental question. Because, without the truth, we cannot act. And until we act, nothing will change.

My job is protecting children. It has taken me from big cities to rural outposts, from ghettos to penthouses, and from courtrooms to genocidal battlefields. But whatever the venue, the truth remains constant: Some humans intentionally hurt children. They commit unspeakable acts—for their pleasure, their profit, or both.

Many people who hear of my cases against humans who rape, torture, and package children for sale or rent immediately respond with, "That's sick!" Crimes against children seem so grotesquely abnormal that the most obvious explanation is that the perpetrator must be mentally ill—helpless in the grip of a force beyond his or her control. 4

> **" Sickness is a condition. Evil is a behavior. Evil is always a matter of choice. "**

But that very natural reaction has, inadvertently, created a special category of "blameless predator." That confusion of "sick" with "sickening" is the single greatest barrier to our primary biological and ethical mandate: the protection of our children. 5

The difference between sick and evil cannot be dismissed with facile eye-of-the-beholder rhetoric. There are specific criteria we can employ to give us the answers in every case, every time. 6

Some of those answers are self-evident and beyond dispute: A mother who puts her baby in the oven because she hears voices commanding her to bake the devil out of the child's spirit is sick; and a mother who sells or rents her baby to child pornographers is evil. But most cases of child sexual abuse—especially those whose "nonviolent" perpetrators come from within the child's circle of trust—seem, on their surface, to be far more complex. 7

That complexity is an illusion. The truth is as simple as it is terrifying: 8

Sickness is a condition. 9

Evil is a behavior. 10

Evil is always a matter of choice. Evil is not thought; it is conduct. And that conduct is always volitional. 11

And just as evil is always a choice, sickness is always the absence of choice. Sickness happens. Evil is inflicted. 12

Until we perceive the difference clearly, we will continue to give aid and comfort to our most pernicious enemies. We, as a society, decide whether something is sick or evil. Either decision confers an obligation upon us. Sickness should be treated. Evil must be fought. 13

If a person has desires or fantasies about sexually exploiting children, that individual may be sick. (Indeed, if such desires are disturbing, as opposed to gratifying, to the individual, there may even be a "cure.") But if the individual chooses to act upon those feelings, that conduct is evil. People are not what they think; they are what they do. 14

Our society distrusts the term *evil*. It has an almost biblical ring to it—something we believe in (or not), but never actually understand. 15

We prefer scientific-sounding terms, such as *sociopath*. But sociopathy is not a mental condition; it is a specific cluster of behaviors. The diagnosis is only made from actual criminal conduct.

No reputable psychiatrist claims to be able to cure a sociopath—or, for that matter, a predatory pedophile. Even the most optimistic professionals do not aim to change such a person's thoughts and feelings. What they hope is that the predator can learn self-control, leading to a change in behavior.

Such hopes ignore the inescapable fact that the overwhelming majority of those who prey upon children don't want to change their behavior—they want only to minimize the consequences of being caught at it.

In the animal kingdom, there is a food chain—predators and prey. But among humans, there is no such natural order. Among our species, predators select themselves for that role.

Psychology has given us many insights of great value. But it has also clouded our vision with euphemisms. To say a person suffers from the "disease" of pedophilia is to absolve the predator of responsibility for his behavior.

Imagine if an attorney, defending someone accused of committing a dozen holdups, told the jury his poor client was suffering from "armed-robberia." That jury would decide that the only crazy person in the courtroom was the lawyer.

When a perpetrator claims to be sick, the *timing* of that claim is critical to discovering the truth. Predatory pedophiles carefully insinuate themselves into positions of trust. They select their prey and approach cautiously. Gradually, sometimes over a period of years, they gain greater control over their victims. Eventually, they leave dozens of permanently damaged children in their wake.

But only when they are caught do predatory pedophiles declare themselves to be sick. And the higher the victim count, the sicker (and, therefore less responsible), they claim to be.

In too many cases, a veil of secrecy and protection then descends. The predator's own organization appoints itself judge and jury. The perpetrator is deemed sick, and sent off for in-house "treatment." The truth is never made public. And when some secret tribunal decides a cure has been achieved, the perpetrator's rights and privileges are restored, and he or she is given a new assignment.

In fact, such privileged predators actually are assisted. They enter new communities with the blessing of their own organization, their history and propensities kept secret. As a direct result, unsuspecting parents entrust their children to them. Inevitably, the predator eventually resumes his or her conduct and preys upon children again. And when that conduct comes to light, the claim of "sickness" re-emerges as well.

Too often, our society contorts itself to excuse such predators. We are so eager to call those who sexually abuse children "sick," so quick to understand their demons. Why? Because sickness not only offers the possibility of finding a cure but also assures us that the predator didn't really mean it. After all, it is human nature to try to understand inhuman conduct.

Conversely, the concept of evil terrifies us. The idea that some humans *choose* to prey upon our children is frightening, and their demonstrated skill at camouflage only heightens this fear. 26

For some, the question, "Does evil exist?" is philosophical. But for those who have confronted or been victimized by predatory pedophiles, there is no question at all. We are what we do. 27

Just as conduct is a choice, so is our present helplessness. We may be powerless to change the arrogance of those who believe they alone should have the power to decide whether predatory pedophiles are "sick," or when they are "cured." But, as with the perpetrators themselves, we do have the power to change their behavior. 28

In every state, laws designate certain professions that regularly come into contact with children—such as teachers, doctors, social workers, and day-care employees—as "mandated reporters." Such personnel are required to report reasonable suspicion of child abuse when it comes to their attention. Failure to do so is a crime. 29

Until now, we have exempted religious organizations from mandated-reporter laws. Recent events have proven the catastrophic consequences of this exemption. We must demand—now—that our legislators close this pathway to evil. 30

A predatory pedophile who is recycled into an unsuspecting community enters it cloaked with a protection no other sex offender enjoys. If members of religious orders were mandated reporters, we would not have to rely on their good-faith belief that a predator is cured. We could make our own informed decisions on this most vital issue. 31

Modifying the law in this way would not interfere with priest–penitent privileges: When child victims or their parents disclose abuse, they are not confessing, they are crying for help. Neither confidentiality nor religious freedom would in any way be compromised by mandatory reporting. 32

Changing the laws so that religious orders join the ranks of mandated reporters is the right thing to do. And the time is right now. 33

Thinking Critically about the Text

Vachss believes that "our society distrusts the term *evil*" (paragraph 15). Do you agree? Why is the concept of evil such a difficult one to understand when it comes to human behavior?

Questions on Subject

1. What question does Vachss ask in his opening paragraph? What for Vachss is the essential difference between "sick" and "evil"? What criteria does he offer to help his readers understand the difference?

2. What does Vachss mean when he says that "psychology has given us many insights of great value. But it has also clouded our vision with euphemisms" (paragraph 19)?

3. Why does Vachss believe that people are so willing to call sex offenders sick instead of evil? Do you agree? What is the danger of letting evil pass as a sickness?

4. What action does Vachss want his readers to take after reading his article? Did you find Vachss's argument compelling? Why, or why not?

Questions on Strategy

1. What is Vachss's **thesis**, and where is it stated?

2. What experience or expertise qualifies Vachss to write about this subject?

3. How does Vachss develop the essential differences between "sick" and "evil" in paragraphs 6 through 14? How effectively does he use examples to **illustrate** these differences?

4. In paragraph 20, Vachss uses the analogy of a lawyer defending a robber to give his readers insight into the "'disease' of pedophilia" presented in the previous paragraph. How effective or convincing do you find his **analogy**?

Comparison and Contrast in Action

After reviewing the discussion of analogy in the introduction to this chapter (page 228) and Vachss's analogy in paragraphs 18–20, create an analogy to explain one of the following:

- your relationship with one of your teachers or coaches
- the essence of a game that you enjoy playing
- a scientific or sociological principle or idea
- a creative activity such as writing, weaving, painting, or composing music

Share your analogy with other members of your class and discuss how well the analogies work.

Writing Suggestions

1. As Vachss demonstrates in his discussion of "sick" and "evil," important decisions and actions hinge on establishing a clear understanding of the similarities and/or differences in the terminology that we use. Using his essay as a model, write an essay in which you compare and contrast one of the following pairs of terms or a pair of your own choosing:

   smart and intelligent   professional and amateur   normal and abnormal

   weird and eccentric   manager and leader   public and private

2. What is your position on capital punishment? Who has the right to take the life of another? Ideally, knowing what the punishment will be should deter people

from doing the wrong thing in the first place, but does the death penalty really act as a deterrent? Are certain punishments more effective as deterrents than others? In this context, consider the message in the following cartoon, which highlights the great irony that is inherent in capital punishment. Write an essay in which you compare and contrast the arguments for and against the death penalty.

"Maybe this will teach you that it's morally wrong to kill people!"

Harley Schwadron/CartoonStock.com

3. **Writing with Sources.** For more than four decades, lawyer Andrew Vachss has advocated for children victimized by adult predators. His article in *Parade* on July 14, 2002, was written in response to the handling of the so-called pedophile priests in America. However, as Vachss points out, there are other instances of people who intentionally hurt children, people who "rape, torture, and package children for sale or rent." In your library or online, research one such case that has been in the news. What was the nature of the crime against the children? Would you label the perpetrator "sick" or "evil"? Why? How was the perpetrator of the crime punished? Do you agree with the way the perpetrator was handled? Write an essay in which you report your findings. For models of and advice on integrating sources in your essay, see Chapters 14 and 15.

America Made Me a Feminist

PAULINA PORIZKOVA

Rabbani and Solimene Photography/ Getty Images

As she notes in her essay, Paulina Porizkova was born in Czechoslovakia, now the Czech Republic, in 1965. She grew up in Sweden and, as a teenager, began a celebrated modeling career in Paris and then the United States. Porizkova became a pop culture icon in the 1980s. She participated in advertising campaigns for fashion brands such as Hermes, Versace, and Christian Dior and posed in swimwear for *Sports Illustrated* magazine. She appeared in a famous music video by the American rock band The Cars and later married the band's lead singer, Ric Ocasek. Porizkova joined *America's Next Top Model* as a judge in its tenth through twelfth seasons and also appeared in numerous film and television roles. In addition to her modeling and acting, Porizkova is an author, having written a children's book, *The Adventures of Ralphie the Roach* (1992), and a novel, *A Model Summer* (2007). She has also contributed to the *Huffington Post*.

In the following essay, which appeared in the June 10, 2017, issue of the *New York Times*, Porizkova offers a sharp, provocative account of how she became a feminist. Notice especially how she compares and contrasts her experiences as a woman in four distinctive national cultures.

Preparing to Read

What does the word *feminist* mean to you? What connotations does it have? Do you think feminism should be embraced, celebrated, and practiced by women and men? Is it important? Necessary? Counterproductive? Confusing?

I used to think the word "feminist" reeked of insecurity. A woman who needed to state that she was equal to a man might as well be shouting that she was smart or brave. If you were, you wouldn't need to say it. I thought this because back then, I was a Swedish woman. 1

I was 9 when I first stepped into a Swedish school. Freshly arrived from Czechoslovakia, I was bullied by a boy for being an immigrant. My one friend, a tiny little girl, punched him in the face. I was impressed. In my former country, a bullied girl would tattle or cry. I looked around to see what my new classmates thought of my friend's feat, but no one seemed to have noticed. It didn't take long to understand that in Sweden, my power was suddenly equal to a boy's. 2

In Czechoslovakia, women came home from a long day of work to cook, clean, and serve their husbands. In return, those women were cajoled, ignored, and occasionally abused, much like domestic animals. But they were mentally unstable domestic animals, like milk cows that could go berserk if you didn't know exactly how to handle them.

In Sweden, the housekeeping tasks were equally divided. Soon my own father was cleaning and cooking as well. Why? He had divorced my mother and married a Swedish woman.

> **In America, important men were desirable. Important women had to *be* desirable. That got to me.**

As high school approached, the boys wanted to kiss us and touch us, and the girls became a group of benevolent queens dispensing favors. The more the boys wanted us, the more powerful we became. When a girl chose to bestow her favors, the lucky boy was envied and celebrated. Slut shaming? What's a slut?

Condoms were provided by the school nurse without question. Sex education taught us the dangers of venereal diseases and unwanted pregnancy, but it also focused on fun stuff like masturbation. For a girl to own her sexuality meant she owned her body, she owned herself. Women could do anything men did, but they could also — when they chose to — bear children. And that made us more powerful than men. The word "feminist" felt antiquated; there was no longer a use for it.

When I moved to Paris at 15 to work as a model, the first thing that struck me was how differently the men behaved. They opened doors for me, they wanted to pay for my dinner. They seemed to think I was too delicate, or too stupid, to take care of myself.

Instead of feeling celebrated, I felt patronized. I claimed my power the way I had learned in Sweden: by being sexually assertive. But Frenchmen don't work this way. In discos, I'd set my eye on an attractive stranger, and then dance my way over to let him know he was a chosen one. More often than not, he fled. And when he didn't run, he asked how much I charged.

In France, women did have power, but a secret one, like a hidden stiletto knife. It was all about manipulation: the sexy vixen luring the man to do her bidding. It wasn't until I reached the United States, at 18, and fell in love with an American man that I truly had to rearrange my cultural notions.

It turned out most of America didn't think of sex as a healthy habit or a bargaining tool. Instead, it was something secret. If I mentioned masturbation, ears went red. Orgasms? Men made smutty remarks, while women went silent. There was a fine line between the private and the shameful. A former gynecologist spoke of the weather when doing a pelvic exam, as if I were a Victorian maiden who'd rather not know where all my bits were.

In America, a woman's body seemed to belong to everybody but herself. 11
Her sexuality belonged to her husband, her opinion of herself belonged to
her social circles, and her uterus belonged to the government. She was
supposed to be a mother and a lover and a career woman (at a fraction
of the pay) while remaining perpetually youthful and slim. In America,
important men were desirable. Important women had to *be* desirable. That
got to me.

In the Czech Republic, the nicknames for women, whether sweet or bit- 12
ter, fall into the animal category: little bug, kitten, old cow, swine. In Sweden,
women are rulers of the universe. In France, women are dangerous objects
to treasure and fear. For better or worse, in those countries, a woman knows
her place.

But the American woman is told she can do anything and then is 13
knocked down the moment she proves it. In adapting myself to my new
country, my Swedish woman power began to wilt. I joined the women
around me who were struggling to do it all and failing miserably. I now
have no choice but to pull the word "feminist" out of the dusty drawer and
polish it up.

My name is Paulina Porizkova, and I am a feminist. 14

Thinking Critically about the Text

Historically, America has often defined itself against Europe as a place that celebrates freedom, individualism, and progress, as opposed to "old world" traditions
and hierarchies. How does Porizkova complicate or problematize this view of the
United States? What burdens and restraints does American society seem to place
on women, in her view?

Questions on Subject

1. After Porizkova moves from Sweden to Paris, she notices that men behave
   differently toward her. How does she adjust her own behavior in response? Is
   she successful? Explain.

2. Porizkova writes that most Americans consider sex "something secret," rather
   than a "healthy habit" or a "bargaining tool" (paragraph 10). Do you agree with
   this and other generalizations she makes about America? Why, or why not?

3. According to Porizkova, "It wasn't until I reached the United States, at 18,
   and fell in love with an American man that I truly had to rearrange my cultural
   notions" (paragraph 9). How do you interpret the meaning of this claim?

4. For the writer, what is the key difference between the role of women in the
   Czech Republic, Sweden, and France (on the one hand) and their role in the
   United States (on the other hand)? Why is this difference important to her
   overall **purpose**?

Questions on Strategy

1. How does the writer organize the comparison and contrast? Does she primarily use a point-by-point comparison, or does she use block comparison? Why do you think she chose this way of organizing her argument?

2. Throughout the essay, the writer uses **parallelism**—the repetition of word order or grammatical form within a single sentence or several sentences—to develop ideas, as well as to emphasize similarities and differences. Find a specific example and explain how it helps clarify her point or highlight a contrast.

3. What is Porizkova's **thesis**? Where does she state it? Why do you think she places it in this section of the essay?

4. How does Porizkova use both definition and cause and effect analysis to clarify her comparison and contrast of feminism and gender relations in four different countries?

Comparison and Contrast in Action

Carefully read the following paragraphs from Stephen E. Ambrose's book *Crazy Horse and Custer: The Parallel Lives of Two American Warriors* (1975), and then answer the questions that follow.

It was bravery, above and beyond all other qualities, that Custer and Crazy Horse had in common. Each man was an outstanding warrior in war-mad societies. Thousands upon thousands of Custer's fellow whites had as much opportunity as he did to demonstrate their courage, just as all of Crazy Horse's associates had countless opportunities to show that they equaled him in bravery. But no white warrior, save his younger brother, Tom, could outdo Custer, just as no Indian warrior, save his younger brother, Little Hawk, could outdo Crazy Horse. And for both white and red societies, no masculine virtue was more admired than bravery. To survive, both societies felt they had to have men willing to put their lives on the line. For men who were willing to do so, no reward was too great, even though there were vast differences in the way each society honored its heroes.

Beyond their bravery, Custer and Crazy Horse were individualists, each standing out from the crowd in his separate way. Custer wore outlandish uniforms, let his hair fall in long, flowing golden locks across his shoulders, surrounded himself with pet animals and admirers, and in general did all he could to draw attention to himself. Crazy Horse's individualism pushed him in the opposite direction — he wore a single feather in his hair when going into battle, rather than a war bonnet. Custer's vast energy set him apart from most of his fellows; the Sioux distinguished Crazy Horse from other warriors because of Crazy Horse's quietness and introspection. Both men lived in societies in which drugs, especially alcohol, were widely used, but neither Custer nor Crazy Horse drank. Most of all, of course, each man stood out in battle as a great risk taker.

What is Ambrose's point in these two paragraphs? How does he use comparison and contrast to make this point? How has he organized his paragraphs?

Writing Suggestions

1. Porizkova compares and contrasts roles and views of women in different countries. But at the same time, she is also comparing her early views of feminism with her views of it after coming to America. Think of an idea, issue, person, place, or problem that you have changed your mind about over the years. Then, write an essay comparing and contrasting your earlier views with your current views. How have they changed? What caused the change? What points of comparison will help focus the essay? What key insight would you like to communicate to your readers about your topic?

2. Porizkova considers how views of women and their status differ across different countries and societies. Have you observed this phenomenon in your own life or personal experience? You may consider these differences in the context of two different countries, but you can also consider them at a more local, regional, or cultural level. Choose a topic: political opinions, perspectives on women, perceptions of masculinity, attitudes toward money, attitudes toward sex, views of religion, views of family, or another subject of your choice. Then, write a comparison and contrast essay that explores similarities or differences in points of view between two regions, cultures, or groups of people. As Porizkova does, make sure your essay has a clear thesis and a purpose.

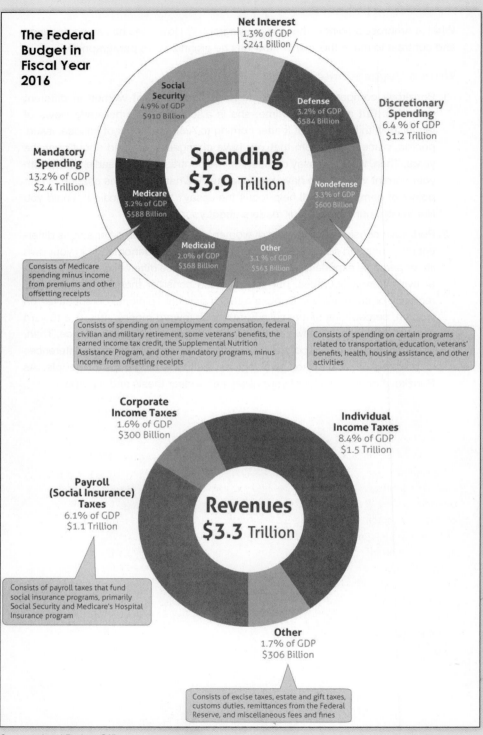

The Federal Budget in Fiscal Year 2016

Net Interest
1.3% of GDP
$241 Billion

Social Security
4.9% of GDP
$910 Billion

Defense
3.2% of GDP
$584 Billion

Discretionary Spending
6.4 % of GDP
$1.2 Trillion

Mandatory Spending
13.2% of GDP
$2.4 Trillion

Medicare
3.2% of GDP
$588 Billion

Spending $3.9 Trillion

Nondefense
3.3% of GDP
$600 Billion

Medicaid
2.0% of GDP
$368 Billion

Other
3.1 % of GDP
$563 Billion

Consists of Medicare spending minus income from premiums and other offsetting receipts

Consists of spending on unemployment compensation, federal civilian and military retirement, some veterans' benefits, the earned income tax credit, the Supplemental Nutrition Assistance Program, and other mandatory programs, minus income from offsetting receipts

Consists of spending on certain programs related to transportation, education, veterans' benefits, health, housing assistance, and other activities

Corporate Income Taxes
1.6% of GDP
$300 Billion

Individual Income Taxes
8.4% of GDP
$1.5 Trillion

Payroll (Social Insurance) Taxes
6.1% of GDP
$1.1 Trillion

Revenues $3.3 Trillion

Consists of payroll taxes that fund social insurance programs, primarily Social Security and Medicare's Hospital Insurance program

Other
1.7% of GDP
$306 Billion

Consists of excise taxes, estate and gift taxes, customs duties, remittances from the Federal Reserve, and miscellaneous fees and fines

Congressional Budget Office

Division and Classification

WHAT ARE DIVISION AND CLASSIFICATION?

LIKE COMPARISON AND CONTRAST, DIVISION AND CLASSIFICATION ARE separate yet closely related operations. Division involves breaking down a single large unit into smaller subunits or separating a group of items into discrete categories. Classification, on the other hand, entails placing individual items into established categories. To put it another way, division takes apart, whereas classification groups together. But even though the two processes can operate separately, they tend to be used together.

VISUALIZING DIVISION AND CLASSIFICATION

Pie charts are one of the best ways to visualize division and classification. Together these charts represent the Spending and Revenues of the federal government in 2016. The Spending chart indicates the total amount the federal government spent ($3.9 trillion) and the categories that total amount was divided into. These categories are also classified, or grouped together, into Mandatory Spending (what the government is committed to spend by law) and Discretionary Spending (how much and on what the government has the freedom to spend). The same principles of division can be seen in the Revenues pie chart. How are these pie charts helpful to anyone quickly trying to understand how the federal government both collected and spent our federal dollars in 2016? What visual cues help you see to what categories the money went? What does this division and classification tell you about the government's priorities in 2016? Find an updated spending and revenue budget for the current year, make a pie chart, and compare the use of federal funds.

UNDERSTANDING DIVISION AND CLASSIFICATION AS A WRITING STRATEGY

In writing, division can be the most effective method for making sense of one large, complex, or multifaceted entity. Consider, for example, the following passage from E. B. White's *Here Is New York,* in which he discusses New Yorkers and their city:

<table>
<tr>
<td>Division into categories occurs in opening sentence</td>
<td>There are roughly three New Yorks. There is, first, the New York of the man or woman who was born here, who takes the city for granted and accepts its size and its turbulence as natural and inevitable. Second, there is the New York of the commuter—the city that is devoured by locusts each day and spat out each night. Third, there is the New York of the person who was born somewhere else and came to New York in quest of something. Of these three trembling cities the greatest is the last—the city of final destination, the city that is a goal. It is this third city that accounts for New York's highstrung disposition, its poetical deportment, its dedication to the arts, and its</td>
</tr>
<tr>
<td>Author explains the nature of people in each category</td>
<td>incomparable achievements. Commuters give the city its tidal restlessness; natives give it solidarity and continuity; but the settlers give it passion. And whether it is a farmer arriving from Italy to set up a small grocery store in a slum, or a young girl arriving from a small town in Mississippi to escape the indignity of being observed by her neighbors, or a boy arriving from the Corn Belt with a manuscript in his suitcase and a pain in his heart, it makes no difference: each embraces New York with the intense excitement of first love, each absorbs New York with the fresh eyes of an adventurer, each generates heat and light to dwarf the Consolidated Edison Company.</td>
</tr>
</table>

In his opening sentences, White suggests a principle for dividing the population of New York, establishing his three categories on the basis of a person's relationship to the city. There is the New York of the native, the New York of the commuter, and the New York of the immigrant. White's divisions help him make a point about the character of New York City, depicting its restlessness, its solidarity, and its passion.

In contrast to breaking a large idea into parts, classification can be used to draw connections between disparate elements based on a common category—such as price, for example. Often, classification is used in conjunction with another rhetorical strategy, such as comparison and contrast. Consider, for example, how in the following passage from Toni Cade Bambara's "The Lesson" she classifies a toy in F.A.O. Schwarz and other items in the thirty-five-dollar category to compare the relative values of things in the life of two girls, Sylvia and Sugar.

> Me and Sugar at the back of the train watchin the tracks whizzin by large then small then getting gobbled up in the dark. I'm thinkin about this tricky toy I saw in the store. A clown that somersaults on a bar then does chin-ups just cause you yank lightly at his leg. Cost $35. I could see me askin my mother for a $35 birthday clown. "You wanna who that costs what?" she'd say, cocking her head to the side to get a better view of the hole in my head. Thirty-five dollars could buy new bunk beds for Junior and Gretchen's boy. Thirty-five dollars and the whole household could go visit Grand-daddy Nelson in the country. Thirty-five dollars would pay for the rent and the piano bill, too. Who are these people that spend that much for performing clowns and $1000 for toy sailboats? What kinda work they do and how they live and how come we ain't in on it?

Classification used along with comparison and contrast

Another example may help clarify how division and classification work hand in hand. Suppose a sociologist wants to determine whether the socioeconomic status of the people in a particular neighborhood has any influence on their voting behavior. Having decided on her purpose, the sociologist chooses as her subject the fifteen families living on Maple Street. Her goal then becomes to group these families in a way that will be relevant to her purpose: (1) according to socioeconomic status (low-income earners, middle-income earners, and high-income earners) and (2) according to voting behavior (voters and nonvoters).

In confidential interviews with each family, the sociologist begins to classify each family according to her established categories. Her work leads her to construct the following diagram, which allows her to visualize her division and classification system and its essential components: the subject, her bases or principles of division, the subclasses or categories that derive from these principles, and her conclusion.

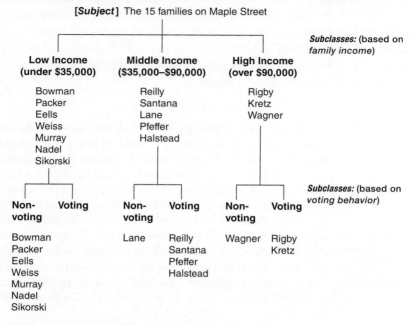

Purpose: To study the relationship between socioeconomic status and voting behavior

[Subject] The 15 families on Maple Street

Subclasses: (based on family income)

Low Income (under $35,000)	Middle Income ($35,000–$90,000)	High Income (over $90,000)
Bowman	Reilly	Rigby
Packer	Santana	Kretz
Eells	Lane	Wagner
Weiss	Pfeffer	
Murray	Halstead	
Nadel		
Sikorski		

Subclasses: (based on voting behavior)

Non-voting	Voting	Non-voting	Voting	Non-voting	Voting
Bowman		Lane	Reilly	Wagner	Rigby
Packer			Santana		Kretz
Eells			Pfeffer		
Weiss			Halstead		
Murray					
Nadel					
Sikorski					

Conclusion: On Maple Street there seems to be a relationship between socioeconomic status and voting behavior: The low-income families are nonvoters.

Division and classification are used primarily to demonstrate a particular point about the subject under discussion. In a paper about the emphasis a television network places on reaching various audiences, you could begin by dividing prime-time programming into suitable subclasses: shows primarily for adults, shows for families, shows for children, and so forth. You could then classify each of that network's programs into one of these categories, analyze these data, and draw your conclusions about which audiences the network tries hardest to reach.

Another purpose of division and classification is to help writers and readers make choices. A voter may classify politicians on the basis of their attitudes toward nuclear energy or abortion; the technology magazine *Wired* classifies smartphones on the basis of available memory, screen size, processor speed, camera pixels, and carrier availability; high school seniors classify colleges and universities on the basis of prestige, geographic location, programs available, and tuition fees. In such cases, division and classification have an absolutely practical end: making a decision about whom to vote for, which smartphone to buy, and where to apply for admission to college.

USING DIVISION AND CLASSIFICATION ACROSS THE DISCIPLINES

When writing essays in the academic disciplines, you will have many opportunities to use the strategy of division and classification to both organize and strengthen the presentation of your ideas. To determine whether division and classification is the right strategy to use in a particular paper, review the guidelines described in Chapter 2, "Determining a Strategy for Developing Your Essay" (pages 34–35). Consider the following examples:

Earth Sciences

1. **MAIN IDEA:** Pollution is a far-reaching and unwieldy subject.
2. **QUESTION:** What kinds of pollution are there, and what examples of pollution can we place into each category?
3. **STRATEGY:** Division and classification. This strategy involves two activities: dividing into categories and placing items in their appropriate categories. The word *kinds* signals the need to separate pollution into manageable groupings. The word *examples* and the phrase *place into each category* signal the need to classify types of pollution into appropriate categories.
4. **SUPPORTING STRATEGY:** Argumentation is often used to support both the rationale for categorization and classification itself.

Education

1. **MAIN IDEA:** Children's learning disabilities fall into three major groups.
2. **QUESTION:** What are the major types of learning disabilities into which children fall?
3. **STRATEGY:** Division and classification. The words *major types* suggest the need to divide learning problems into major categories. The words *fall into* suggest that every learning disability can be classified into one of the three categories.
4. **SUPPORTING STRATEGY:** Argumentation could be used to persuade readers that the categories of problems discussed are major and to persuade them that a knowledge of these three major types of problems can be useful to teachers and parents in helping a child.

Political Science

1. **MAIN IDEA:** There are four types of U.S. presidents.
2. **QUESTION:** On what basis or bases do we group U.S. presidents?
3. **STRATEGY:** Division and classification. The words *basis* and *bases* signal the need to establish criteria for dividing all our presidents. The word *group* suggests the need to classify the presidents according to the established groupings.
4. **SUPPORTING STRATEGY:** Illustration can be used to provide examples of various presidents.

PRACTICAL ADVICE FOR WRITING AN ESSAY OF DIVISION AND CLASSIFICATION

As you plan, write, and revise your division and classification essay, be mindful of the writing process guidelines described in Chapter 2. Pay particular attention to the basic requirements and essential ingredients of this writing strategy.

▌ Planning Your Essay of Division and Classification

Planning is an essential part of writing a good division and classification essay. You can save yourself a great deal of trouble by taking the time to think about the key building blocks of your essay before you actually begin to write.

Determine Your Purpose and Focus on It.   The principle you use to divide your subject into categories depends on your larger purpose. It is crucial, then, that you determine a clear purpose for your division and classification before you begin to examine your subject in detail. Let's say, for example, that you are in charge of writing an editorial for your school newspaper that will make people aware of how they might reduce the amount of trash going to the landfill. Having established your purpose, your next task might be to identify the different ways objects could be handled to avoid sending them to the landfill. For instance, you might decide that there are four basic ways to prevent things from ending up in the trash. Then, you could establish a sequence or an order of importance in which they should be addressed. Your first draft might start something like the following:

> Over the course of the last semester, more trash was removed from our campus than in any semester in history. But was it all trash that had to go to the landfill? For example, many of us love to wear fleece vests, but did you know that they are made from recycled plastic bottles? Much of what is considered trash need not go to the landfill at all. There are four ways we can prevent trash from being sent to the landfill. I call them the four R's. First, we can all reduce the amount of individually packaged

goods that we send to the landfill by buying frequently used items in family-size or bulk containers. Next, we can reuse those containers, as well as other items, either for their original purpose or for another. Be creative. After a while, though, things will wear out after repeated use. Then it's a good time to try to restore them. If that, too, can no longer be done, then they should be recycled. Only after these options have failed should items be considered "real" trash and be removed to the landfill. Using the four R's—Reduce, Reuse, Restore, Recycle—we can reduce the amount of trash our campus sends to the landfill every semester.

This introduction clearly expresses the purpose of the editorial: to change readers' behavior regarding the amount of "trash" they throw out.

Formulate a Thesis Statement. When writing a division and classification essay, be sure that your thesis statement clearly presents the categories that you will be using to make your point. Here is an example:

> Because girls' social hierarchies are complicated, I'm going to take you through a general breakdown of the different positions in the clique.

This thesis statement is from a chapter by Rosalind Wiseman entitled "The Queen Bee and Her Court" about the cliques that teenage girls form in school. From this opening statement, the reader knows exactly what Wiseman intends to discuss and how.

You could also look for examples of thesis statements in the essays throughout this book. As you begin to develop your thesis statement, ask yourself the following questions:

1. "What is my point?"
2. "What categories will be most useful in making my point?"

If you can't answer these questions, write down some ideas and try to determine your main point from these ideas.

Once you have settled on an idea, go back to the two questions above and write down your answers to them. Then combine the answers into a single thesis statement. Your thesis statement does not necessarily have to be one sentence; making it one sentence, though, can be an effective way of focusing both your point and your categories.

▶ Organizing Your Essay of Division and Classification

Establish Valid Categories. When establishing categories, make sure that they meet three criteria:

- *The categories must be appropriate to your purpose.* In determining the factors affecting financial aid distribution among students at a particular school,

you might consider family income, academic major, and athletic participation, but obviously you would not consider style of dress or preferred
brand of toothpaste.

- *The categories must be consistent and mutually exclusive.* For example, dividing the student body into the classes on-campus students, commuter students, and athletes would be illogical because athletes can live either on
or off campus. Instead, you could divide the student body into on-campus
athletes, commuter athletes, on-campus nonathletes, and commuter
nonathletes.

- *The categories must be complete, and they must account for all the members or
aspects of your subject.* In dividing the student body according to place of
birth, it would be inaccurate to consider only states in the United States;
such a division would not account for foreign students or citizens born
outside the country.

You may often find that a diagram (such as the one of families on Maple
Street, shown on page 262), a chart, or a table can help you visualize your organization and help you make sure that your categories are appropriate, mutually
exclusive, and complete.

Division and classification essays, when sensibly planned, can generally be organized with little trouble; an essay's chief divisions will reflect the
classes into which you have divided the subject. A scratch outline can help
you see those divisions and plan your presentation. For example, here is an
outline of student Katie Angeles's essay "The Forgotten Personality Type"
(pages 268–71) about how one personality type gets lost among all the others:

Four Personality Types

1. Sanguine
   a. Popular
   b. "Life of the party"
   c. yellow bile

2. Melancholic
   a. Perfect
   b. "Busy bee"
   c. black bile

3. Choleric
   a. Powerful
   b. "Leader"
   c. blood

4. Phlegmatic
   a. Peaceful
   b. "Forgotten"
   c. phlegm

Such an outline clearly reveals the essay's overall structure.

State Your Conclusion.   Your essay's purpose will determine the kinds of conclusions you reach. For example, a study of the student body of your college might show that 35 percent of male athletes are receiving scholarships, compared with 20 percent of female athletes, 15 percent of male nonathletes, and 10 percent of female nonathletes. These facts could provide a conclusion in themselves, or they might be the basis for a more controversial assertion about your school's athletic program. A study of dorm-room decor might conclude with the observation that juniors and seniors tend to have more elaborate rooms than first-year students. Your conclusion will depend on the way you work back and forth between the various classes you establish and the individual items available for you to classify.

▶ Revising and Editing Your Essay of Division and Classification

Revision is best done by asking yourself (and others) key questions about what you have written. Along with the questions in the following box, try reading your essay aloud or asking a classmate to read through your writing, following the guidelines in the "Brief Guide to Peer Critiquing" box in Chapter 2 (pages 38–39). If you or your classmate find any problems that you cannot think of a solution for, take a look at Chapter 16, which offers help for twelve common writing problems.

Questions for Revising and Editing: Division and Classification

1. Does the manner in which I divide my subject into categories help me achieve my purpose in writing the essay?
2. Does my thesis statement clearly identify the number and type of categories I will be using in my essay?
3. Do I stay focused on my subject and stay within the limits of my categories throughout my essay?
4. Are my categories appropriate to my purpose, consistent and mutually exclusive, and complete?
5. Have I organized my essay in a way that makes it easy for the reader to understand my categories and how they relate to my purpose?
6. Are there other rhetorical strategies that I can use to help achieve my purpose?
7. Does my paper contain any errors in grammar, punctuation, or mechanics? Is my sentence style as clear, smooth, and persuasive as possible?

STUDENT ESSAY USING DIVISION AND CLASSIFICATION AS A WRITING STRATEGY

The Forgotten Personality Type
Katie Angeles

Division into categories occurs in second, third, and fourth sentences

The next time you're at a party or any other type of social gathering, look around. Some people are telling stories and making everyone laugh, others are making sure everything is running smoothly and perfectly, and a few individuals are the bold ones who liven things up and "get the party started." These are the obvious personalities—the "life of the party," the "busy bee," and the "leader." Personality experts call these personalities sanguine (the popular one), the melancholic (the perfect one), and choleric (the powerful one).

Thesis: The phlegmatic personality is easy to overlook

However, there's one personality that's not so easy to spot, and therefore is usually forgotten—the peaceful phlegmatic.

Author introduces history of the concept of personality types

What makes people the way they are? Why do some people command the spotlight, while others are experts at fading into the background? Personality types were first identified around 400 BC, when the Greek physician Hippocrates noticed that people not only looked different, but also acted differently. He believed that each person's personality type was related to a particular body fluid they had in excess: yellow bile, black bile, blood, or phlegm. These were classified as the "four humors" (Funder 203). Around AD 149, a Greek physiologist named Galen built on Hippocrates's theory, stating that sanguines had an excess amount of yellow bile, melancholics had extra black bile, cholerics had more blood than others, and phlegmatics had an extraordinary amount of phlegm (Littauer 16). In later years, more theories evolved—American scientist William Sheldon believed that personality was related to body type, while people in India said that metabolic body type contributed to the way people behave (Funder 373). Ultimately, these theories were proven incorrect; but we still recognize different personality types. Today, what do we think determines personality?

1

2

As *Time* magazine reported on January 15, 1996, D4DR, a gene that regulates dopamine, is usually found in people who are risk takers (Toufexis par. 2). However, researchers suspected that the gene itself wasn't the only cause of risktaking and that other genes, as well as upbringing, contributed to this phenomenon (Toufexis par. 3). At the time the report appeared, people were worried that parents would use prenatal testing to weed out certain genes that invoked undesirable personality traits (Toufexis par. 6). Since all personalities have their good and bad sides, this would have been a controversial development. Thankfully, parents are not yet able to test for their child's future personality.

3

Moreover, we know that even though people may be born with a certain personality, the way they are brought up can also contribute to how they relate to others later in life. For example, birth order has been shown to affect personality type (Franco par. 1). Firstborn children tend to be choleric since they have the job of leading their siblings; middle children are usually phlegmatic since they're in a prime negotiating spot; and the youngest are generally sanguine because they're used to being spoiled (Franco par. 2-4). Parents can also influence the way a child's personality turns out.

4

Point-by-point comparison of birth order

Each personality type has its strength, but a strength taken to an extreme can become a weakness. While sanguines love to talk, sometimes they may talk too much. Although cholerics are born leaders, they may use their influence in negative ways. Melancholics are perfectionists, but they may prefer being right to being happy, and phlegmatics tend to be easygoing and agreeable, but they may be too passive and have a fear of conflict. Their laid-back attitude can be very frustrating to the most fast-paced personalities, such as cholerics and melancholics.

5

Point-by-point comparison of weaknesses

Phlegmatic people can be hard to notice because they're usually not doing anything to call attention to themselves. While the sanguines are talking and loving life, the cholerics are getting things done, and the melancholics are taking care of the little details,

6

Paragraph devoted entirely to the essay's main topic: phlegmatics

the phlegmatics distinguish themselves by simply being laid-back and easygoing. Even though phlegmatic people tend to fly under the radar, it's very noticeable when they're not around, because they are the peacemakers of the world and the glue that holds everyone together. They are low-maintenance, adaptable, even-keeled, calm, cool, and collected individuals. They are usually reserved, yet they love being around people, and they have a knack for saying the right thing at the right time. Phlegmatics also work well under pressure. However, they hate change, they avoid taking risks, they are extremely stubborn, and it's very hard to get them motivated or excited, which can translate into laziness (Littauer 21). Aside from these traits, the phlegmatic's characteristics are hard to define, because phlegmatics tend to adopt the traits of either the sanguine personality or the melancholy personality.

Most people are a combination of personalities—they have a dominant and a secondary personality that combine the traits of the personalities. For example, some phlegmatics are phlegmatic-sanguine, making them more talkative, while others are phlegmatic-melancholy, causing them to be more introverted. It's not possible to be phlegmatic-choleric, since phlegmatics avoid conflict and cholerics are fueled by it (Littauer 24, 25). People who try to resist their natural personality type can wind up unhappy, since they are trying to be someone they are not.

All personalities have emotional needs. The sanguine needs attention, affection, approval, and activity; the melancholic needs space, support, silence, and stability; the choleric needs action, appreciation, leadership, and control; and the phlegmatic needs peace, self-worth, and significance (Littauer 22). If people don't have their emotional needs met, their worst sides tend to emerge. For example, if a phlegmatic, easygoing, type B personality is in a family of all cholerics, or "go-getter," type A personalities, the phlegmatics may find themselves masking their true personality in order to survive. This can be very draining for phlegmatics, and sooner or later, their negative side will emerge.

Examples of how personality types may be combined

7

8

Phlegmatics are very adaptable—they get along with everyone because they are able to meet the emotional needs of all the individual personalities. They listen to the sanguine, they follow the choleric, and they support the melancholic. In return, the sanguine entertains them, the choleric motivates them, and the melancholic listens to them. However, if phlegmatics feel like they're being taken for granted, they will become resentful. Since they have an innate need for peace, they won't say anything, and people won't know that there's a problem (Littauer 125).

Conclusion: The purpose and usefulness of the classification are explained

Even though phlegmatics are often overlooked, they have a lot to contribute with their ability to work under pressure, their diplomatic skill, and their contagious contentment. So the next time you're checking out personalities at a party, try looking for the phlegmatic first. The forgotten personality might just be the most interesting person in the room.

Works Cited

Franco, Virginia. "Siblings Birth Order and Personality Types." Essortment. Pagewise, 2002, il.essortment .com/birthordersibl_rbay.htm.

Funder, D.C. *The Personality Puzzle.* 2nd ed., W.W. Norton, 2001.

Littauer, Florence. *Personality Plus for Couples: Understanding Yourself and the One You Love.* Baker Publishing Group, 2001.

Toufexis, Anastasia. "What Makes Them Do It." *Time,* 15 Jan. 1996, www.time.com/time/magazine/ article/0,9171,983955,00.html.

Student Reflection
Katie Angeles

Q. How did you decide on your topic, or was your essay written in response to an assignment?
A. When I wrote this essay, I was in my first quarter of college and missing my high school friends terribly. In high school we had taken personality tests for our marriage and family class and my three best friends and I made up what we called the "square," because we each had one of the four different personality types classified in the

essay. After that class, personalities became a topic of interest to me, so when my English professor asked us to write an essay that explained a concept in detail, writing about personality types was a no-brainer. I chose to focus on the phlegmatic because that was my personality type, and it still flies under the radar.

Q. **How did you organize your paper? Did you order the four categories in the way you did for a particular reason?**
A. When organizing my paper, I decided to focus first on the background of the personality types so that readers would have a history to draw from regarding the topic. I didn't want to bore readers with medical terminology so I tried to simplify the explanation by using lay terms. I knew I wanted to end with the phlegmatic type because it was the most interesting to me and I figured to most readers as well. Introducing it last helped emphasize it and led to my thesis.

Q. **What's the purpose of your paper? What did you hope readers got from reading your essay?**
A. The purpose of my essay was to introduce readers to the different personality types and get them thinking about how personalities interact with and influence one another. Learning about your personality type gives you a lot of insight into your thoughts and actions. Since my essay focused mainly on the phlegmatic personality, I wanted readers to be able to identify and appreciate their phlegmatic friends and family members. However, the take-home message of the essay was for readers to start reflecting on their own personality types and begin to understand how this knowledge contributes to who they are.

Your Response

What did you learn from Katie Angeles's essay and reflection on the process of writing the essay? What challenges do you expect to face as you write your own division and classification essay? Based on Katie's composing strategies and the practical advice discussed earlier in this chapter (pages 264–67), what writing choices will you make?

The Truth about Lying

JUDITH VIORST

Judith Viorst, poet, journalist, author of children's books, and novelist, was born in 1931 in Newark, New Jersey. She has chronicled her life in such books as *It's Hard to Be Hip over Thirty and Other Tragedies of Married Life* (1968), *How Did I Get to Be Forty and Other Atrocities* (1976), and *When Did I Stop Being Twenty and Other Injustices: Selected Prose from Single to Mid-Life* (1987). In 1981, she went back to school, taking courses at the Washington Psychoanalytic Institute. This study, along with her personal experience of psychoanalysis, helped to inspire *Necessary Losses*

Brendan Smialowski/The New York Times/Redux

(1986), a popular and critical success. Combining theory, poetry, interviews, and anecdotes, Viorst approaches personal growth as a shedding of illusions. She is also the author of the acclaimed children's book *Alexander and the Terrible, Horrible, No Good, Very Bad Day* (1972).

In this essay, first published in the March 1981 issue of *Redbook*, the author approaches lying with delicacy and candor as she carefully classifies the different types of lies we all encounter.

Preparing to Read

Lying happens every day in our society, whether it is a politician hiding behind a subtly worded statement or a guest fibbing to a host about the quality of a meal. What, for you, constitutes lying? Are all lies the same? In other words, are there different degrees or types of lying?

''ve been wanting to write on a subject that intrigues and challenges me: the   1
subject of lying. I've found it very difficult to do. Everyone I've talked to has a quite intense and personal but often rather intolerant point of view about what we can — and can never *never* — tell lies about. I've finally reached the conclusion that I can't present any ultimate conclusions, for too many people would promptly disagree. Instead, I'd like to present a series of moral puzzles, all concerned with lying. I'll tell you what I think about them. Do you agree?

SOCIAL LIES

Most of the people I've talked with say that they find social lying acceptable   2
and necessary. They think it's the civilized way for folks to behave. Without these little white lies, they say, our relationships would be short and brutish

and nasty. It's arrogant, they say, to insist on being so incorruptible and so brave that you cause other people unnecessary embarrassment or pain by compulsively assailing them with your honesty. I basically agree. What about you?

Will you say to people, when it simply isn't true, "I like your new hairdo," 3 "You're looking much better," "It's so nice to see you," "I had a wonderful time"?

Will you praise hideous presents and homely kids? 4

Will you decline invitations with "We're busy that night — so sorry we 5 can't come," when the truth is you'd rather stay home than dine with the So-and-sos?

And even though, as I do, you may prefer the polite evasion of "You 6 really cooked up a storm" instead of "The soup" — which tastes like warmed-over coffee — "is wonderful," will you, if you must, proclaim it wonderful?

There's one man I know who absolutely refuses to tell social lies. "I can't 7 play that game," he says; "I'm simply not made that way." And his answer to the argument that saying nice things to someone doesn't cost anything is, "Yes, it does — it destroys your credibility." Now, he won't, unsolicited, offer his views on the painting you just bought, but you don't ask his frank opinion unless you want *frank*, and his silence at those moments when the rest of us liars are muttering, "Isn't it lovely?" is, for the most part, eloquent enough. My friend does not indulge in what he calls "flattery, false praise, and mellifluous comments." When others tell fibs he will not go along. He says that social lying is lying, that little white lies are still lies. And he feels that telling lies is morally wrong. What about you?

PEACE-KEEPING LIES

Many people tell peace-keeping lies; lies designed to avoid irritation or argu- 8 ment; lies designed to shelter the liar from possible blame or pain; lies (or so it is rationalized) designed to keep trouble at bay without hurting anyone.

I tell these lies at times, and yet I always feel they're wrong. I under- 9 stand why we tell them, but still they feel wrong. And whenever I lie so that someone won't disapprove of me or think less of me or holler at me, I feel I'm a bit of a coward, I feel I'm dodging responsibility, I feel . . . guilty. What about you?

Do you, when you're late for a date because you overslept, say that you're 10 late because you got caught in a traffic jam?

Do you, when you forget to call a friend, say that you called several times 11 but the line was busy?

Do you, when you didn't remember that it was your father's birthday, say 12 that his present must be delayed in the mail?

And when you're planning a weekend in New York City and you're not   13
in the mood to visit your mother, who lives there, do you conceal—with a
lie, if you must—the fact that you'll be in New York? Or do you have the
courage—or is it the cruelty?—to say, "I'll be in New York, but sorry—I
don't plan on seeing you"?

(Dave and his wife Elaine have two quite different points of view on this   14
very subject. He calls her a coward. She says she's being wise. He says she
must assert her right to visit New York sometimes and not see her mother.
To which she always patiently replies: "Why should we have useless fights?
My mother's too old to change. We get along much better when I lie to her.")

Finally, do you keep the peace by telling your husband lies on the subject   15
of money? Do you reduce what you really paid for your shoes? And in general do you find yourself ready, willing and able to lie to him when you make
absurd mistakes or lose or break things?

"I used to have a romantic idea that part of intimacy was confessing   16
every dumb thing that you did to your husband. But after a couple of years
of that," says Laura, "have I changed my mind!"

And having changed her mind, she finds herself telling peace-keeping   17
lies. And yes, I tell them, too. What about you?

PROTECTIVE LIES

Protective lies are lies folks tell—often quite serious lies—because they're   18
convinced that the truth would be too damaging. They lie because they feel
there are certain human values that supersede the wrong of having lied. They
lie, not for personal gain, but because they believe it's for the good of the
person they're lying to. They lie to those they love, to those who trust them
most of all, on the grounds that breaking this trust is justified.

They may lie to their children on money or marital matters.   19

They may lie to the dying about the state of their health.   20

They may lie about adultery, and not—or so they insist—to save their   21
own hide, but to save the heart and the pride of the men they are married to.

They may lie to their closest friend because the truth about her talents or   22
son or psyche would be—or so they insist—utterly devastating.

I sometimes tell such lies, but I'm aware that it's quite presumptuous   23
to claim I know what's best for others to know. That's called playing God.
That's called manipulation and control. And we never can be sure, once we
start to juggle lies, just where they'll land, exactly where they'll roll.

And furthermore, we may find ourselves lying in order to back up the   24
lies that are backing up the lie we initially told.

And furthermore—let's be honest—if conditions were reversed, we   25
certainly wouldn't want anyone lying to us.

Yet, having said all that, I still believe that there are times when protec- 26
tive lies must nonetheless be told. What about you?

If your Dad had a very bad heart and you had to tell him some bad fam- 27
ily news, which would you choose: to tell him the truth or lie?

If your former husband failed to send his monthly child-support 28
check and in other ways behaved like a total rat, would you allow your
children—who believed he was simply wonderful—to continue to believe
that he was wonderful?

If your dearly beloved brother selected a wife whom you deeply disliked, 29
would you reveal your feelings or would you fake it?

And if you were asked, after making love, "And how was that for you?" 30
would you reply, if it wasn't too good, "Not too good"?

Now, some would call a sex lie unimportant, little more than social lying, 31
a simple act of courtesy that makes all human intercourse run smoothly. And
some would say all sex lies are bad news and unacceptably protective. Because,
says Ruth, "a man with an ego that fragile doesn't need your lies—he needs a
psychiatrist." Still others feel that sex lies are indeed protective lies, more serious than simple social lying, and yet at times they tell them on the grounds that
when it comes to matters sexual, everybody's ego is somewhat fragile.

"If most of the time things go well in sex," says Sue, "I think you're 32
allowed to dissemble when they don't. I can't believe it's good to say, 'Last
night was four stars, darling, but tonight's performance rates only a half.'"

I'm inclined to agree with Sue. What about you? 33

TRUST-KEEPING LIES

Another group of lies are trust-keeping lies, lies that involve triangulation, 34
with *A* (that's you) telling lies to *B* on behalf of *C* (whose trust you'd promised to keep). Most people concede that once you've agreed not to betray a
friend's confidence, you can't betray it, even if you must lie. But I've talked
with people who don't want you telling them anything that they might be
called on to lie about.

"I don't tell lies for myself," says Fran, "and I don't want to have to tell 35
them for other people." Which means, she agrees, that if her best friend is
having an affair, she absolutely doesn't want to know about it.

"Are you saying," her best friend asks, "that if I went off with a lover and 36
I asked you to tell my husband I'd been with you, that you wouldn't lie for
me, that you'd betray me?"

Fran is very pained but very adamant. "I wouldn't want to betray you, 37
so . . . don't ask me."

Fran's best friend is shocked. What about you? 38

Do you believe you can have close friends if you're not prepared to 39
receive their deepest secrets?

Do you believe you must always lie for your friends? 40

Do you believe, if your friend tells a secret that turns out to be quite 41 immoral or illegal, that once you've promised to keep it, you must keep it?

And what if your friend were your boss — if you were perhaps one of the 42 President's men — would you betray or lie for him over, say, Watergate?

As you can see, these issues get terribly sticky. 43

It's my belief that once we've promised to keep a trust, we must tell lies 44 to keep it. I also believe that we can't tell Watergate lies. And if these two statements strike you as quite contradictory, you're right — they're quite contradictory. But for now they're the best I can do. What about you?

Some say that truth will out and thus you might as well tell the truth. 45 Some say you can't regain the trust that lies lose. Some say that even though the truth may never be revealed, our lies pervert and damage our relationships. Some say . . . well, here's what some of them have to say.

"I'm a coward," says Grace, "about telling close people important, dif- 46 ficult truths. I find that I'm unable to carry it off. And so if something is bothering me, it keeps building up inside till I end up just not seeing them anymore."

"I lie to my husband on sexual things, but I'm furious," says Joyce, "that 47 he's too insensitive to know I'm lying."

"I suffer most from the misconception that children can't take the truth," 48 says Emily. "But I'm starting to see that what's harder and more damaging for them is being told lies, is not being told the truth."

"I'm afraid," says Joan, "that we often wind up feeling a bit of contempt 49 for the people we lie to."

And then there are those who have no talent for lying. 50

"Over the years, I tried to lie," a friend of mine explained, "but I always 51 got found out and I always got punished. I guess I gave myself away because I feel guilty about any kind of lying. It looks as if I'm stuck with telling the truth."

> " I'm willing to lie.
> But just as a last
> resort — the truth's
> always better. "

For those of us, however, who are 52 good at telling lies, for those of us who lie and don't get caught, the question of whether or not to lie can be a hard and serious moral problem. I liked the remark of a friend of mine who said, "I'm willing to lie. But just as a last resort — the truth's always better."

"Because," he explained, "though others may completely accept the lie 53 I'm telling, I don't."

I tend to feel that way, too. 54

What about you? 55

Thinking Critically about the Text

The title of the essay plays with the relationship between lies and the truth. Viorst discusses lies that help to conceal the truth, but she's quick to point out that not all lies are malicious. Look at her subsections about "protective lies" (paragraphs 18–33) and "trust-keeping lies" (paragraphs 34–44). Do you think these lies are necessary, or would it be easier to tell the truth? Explain.

Questions on Subject

1. Why is Viorst wary of giving advice on the subject of lying?

2. Viorst admits to contradicting herself in her section on "trust-keeping lies." Where else do you see her contradicting herself?

3. In telling a "protective lie," what assumption about the person hearing the lie does Viorst make? Would you make the same assumption? Why, or why not?

4. What's the difference between a "peace-keeping lie" and a "protective lie"?

Questions on Strategy

1. Into what main categories does Viorst divide lying? Do you agree with her division, or do some of her categories seem to overlap? Explain.

2. Viorst recognizes that many people have steadfast views on lying. What accommodations does she make for this **audience**? How does she challenge this audience?

3. Viorst chooses an unconventional way to conclude her essay, by showing different people's opinions of lying. What do you think she's doing in this last section, beginning in paragraph 45? Does this ending intensify any of the points she has made? Explain.

4. Viorst wants us to see that a lie is not a lie is not a lie is not a lie (i.e., that not all lies are the same). To clarify the various types of lies, she uses division and classification. She also uses **illustration** to show the reasons people lie. Using several of the examples that work best for you, discuss how Viorst's use of illustration strengthens and enhances her classification.

Division and Classification in Action

Consider the following classes of items:

> movies
> college professors
> social sciences
> roommates
> professional sports

Determine at least two principles of division that could be used for each class. Then write a paragraph or two in which you classify one of the groups of items according to a single principle of division. For example, in discussing crime, one could use the seriousness of the crime or the type of crime as principles of division. If the seriousness of the crime were used, this might yield two categories: felonies and misdemeanors. If the types of crime were used, this would yield categories such as burglary, murder, arson, fraud, rape, and drug dealing.

Writing Suggestions

1. Viorst wrote this essay for *Redbook*, which is usually considered a women's magazine. If you were writing this essay for a male audience, would you change the examples? If so, how would you change them? If not, why not? Do you think men are more likely to tell lies of a certain category? Explain. Write an essay in which you discuss whether men and women share similar perspectives about lying. (For more help with this writing strategy, see Chapter 8, Comparison and Contrast.)

2. Write an essay on the subject of friends using division and classification. How many different types of friends do you recognize? On what basis do you differentiate them? Are some friends more important, more useful, more intimate, more convenient, more trustworthy, more reliable, more supportive, more lasting than others? Are you more willing to share your most personal thoughts and feelings with some friends than with others? Be sure to establish a context for why you are writing about friends and putting forth an essay that divides and classifies them. Conclude with an insightful statement drawn from your thesis, the division and classification you establish, and the examples you provide.

The Different Ways of Being Smart

SARA GILBERT

Maggie Benmour

Sara Dulaney Gilbert is a writer, educator, and counselor. The daughter of two journalists, Gilbert was born and grew up in Washington, D.C., and is a graduate of both Barnard College and New York University. Building off her expertise in counseling, Gilbert's writing specializes in life management, education, careers, and family relationships. She is the author of over thirty useful nonfiction books, including *What Happens in Therapy* (1982), *Get Help: Solving the Problems in Your Life* (1989), *The Complete Idiot's Guide to Single Parenting* (1998), and *The Unofficial Guide to Managing Eating Disorders* (2000). Her work has also appeared in *Ms.* magazine, the *New York Times*, *Modern Maturity*, *Scholastic*, and *Good Housekeeping*. She now lives in the Hudson Highlands of New York.

In the following essay, excerpted from her book *Using Your Head: The Many Ways of Being Smart* (1984), Gilbert classifies different types of intelligence. As you read, consider how these categories challenge the conventional idea that intelligence or "IQ" is a single, unified, and testable ability.

Preparing to Read

How would you define "intelligence"? What does it mean to be "smart"? Do you consider yourself smarter in some ways than in others?

B ook smarts, art smarts, body smarts, street smarts, and people smarts: 1
These labels describe the various forms of intelligence and their use. As you might imagine, psychologists and other researchers into the nature of intelligence have come up with more formal terms for the types that they have isolated. One set of labels in common use is convergent, divergent, assimilating, and accommodating. The converger and assimilator are like our book-smart person; the diverger, like our art-smart; and the accommodator, like our street-smart and people-smart.

Whatever categorization we use, we will find some overlap within 2
any individual. In fact, there are probably as many answers to the question "What are the different ways of being smart?" as there are people in the universe, because each of us is unique. We can't be typecast; we each have a wide spectrum of special talents.

Still, you probably know well at least one person whose talents gener- 3
ally fall into each of our categories. Keep those people in mind as you read
through the detailed descriptions of them.

At first, it might seem that each of those types must call on very different 4
sorts of abilities to be smart in his or her own ways. But in fact, each of the
categories of intelligence on our list must use the same ingredients: learning
ability, memory, speed, judgment, problem-solving skill, good use of language
and other symbols, and creativity. Also, the thought processes that go on inside
the heads of people with those varying kinds of smarts include the same steps:
planning, perceiving, imaging, remembering, feeling, and acting.

> **Intelligence expresses itself in different forms, in part because of the different physical qualities born and built into each person's body and brain, and in part because of the values and motivations that each person has learned.**

Intelligence expresses itself in 5
different forms, in part because of
the differing physical qualities born
and built into each person's body and
brain, and in part because of the values and motivations that each person
has learned.

However, the fact that each kind 6
of smarts makes use of the same
steps means that anyone can learn
or develop skills in any or all of the
categories. Let's take a closer look at
the many ways of being smart.

A *book-smart* person is one who 7
tends to do well in school, to score
high on tests, including intelligence tests. He or she is likely to be well organized, to go about solving problems in a logical, step-by-step fashion, and
to have a highly developed language ability. Another label for a book-smart
person is "intellectual," meaning someone who uses the mind more to know
than to feel or to control, and a book-smart person is especially proud of having knowledge. That knowledge may range from literature through science
to math, but it is probable that it is concentrated in one area. Research shows
that different knowledge areas occupy different clusters in the brain, so that
someone whose connections for complicated calculations are highly developed may have less development in the areas controlling speech and writing.

Although, as we've said, current brain research indicates that learning 8
centers may be scattered throughout both hemispheres of the brain, the
activities of the "logical" left side are probably most important in the lives
of book-smart people. Book-smart people may also be quite creative: Many
mathematical or scientific problems could not be solved, for instance, without creative insights, but the primary focus of a book-smart person is the
increase of knowledge.

Art-smart people, on the other hand, rely primarily on creativity. They 9 create music, paintings, sculpture, plays, photographs, or other forms of art often without being able to explain why or how they chose a particular form or design. They are said to be "right-brained" people, because it appears that the control centers for such skills as touch perception and intuition — the formation of ideas without the use of words — lie in the right hemisphere. Artistic people tend to take in knowledge more often by seeing, hearing, and feeling than by conscientious reading and memorizing.

An art-smart person may not do too well in school, not because he or 10 she is not bright, but because of an approach to problem solving that does not fit in well with the formats usually used by teachers and tests. A book-smart person might approach a problem on a math test logically, working step-by-step toward the right answer, while an art-smart person may simply "know" the answer without being able to demonstrate the calculations involved. On a social studies exam, the book-smart person will carefully recount all the facts while the more artistic one may weave stories and fantasies using the facts only as a base. In both cases, it's a good bet that the book-smart student will get the higher grade.

People who are serious about becoming artists, of course, may need to 11 absorb a great deal of "book knowledge" in order to develop a solid background for their skills. There are other overlaps, as well: People with great musical ability, for instance, also tend to be skilled at mathematics, perhaps because of brain-cell interactions that are common to both processes. And in order to make use of any talent, art-smart people must have good body control as well.

The people we're calling *body-smart* have a lot of that kind of body control. 12 Most of them start out with bodies that are well put together for some kind of athletics — they may have inherited good muscular development for a sport like football, or loose and limber joints for gymnastic-style athletics. Or they may be people whose hands are naturally well coordinated for performing intricate tasks.

But although the physical basis for their talent may come from their 13 genes and from especially sensitive brain centers for motor control, to make use of their "natural" skills they must bring higher levels of brain function into action. They must be able to observe accurately — to figure out how a move is made or an object is constructed — and they must think about how to do it themselves. This thinking involves a complex use of symbols that enables the brain to "tell" another part of itself what to do. In other situations, such as school, a body-smart person is probably best able to learn through some physical technique: In studying for an exam, for instance, he or she will retain information by saying it out loud, acting out the facts, or counting them off with finger taps. Although athletes or the manually talented are often teased as being "dumb" in schoolwork, that is not necessarily an accurate picture. To be good in using physical talents, a person must put in a lot of practice, be able to concentrate intently, and be stubbornly persistent in achieving a goal. And those qualities of will and self-control can also be put to good use in more "intellectual" achievements.

Persistence is also an important quality of *street-smart* people. They are   14
the ones who are able to see difficulties as challenges, to turn almost any situation to advantage for themselves. As young people, they are the ones who are able to make the most money doing odd jobs, or who can get free tickets to a concert that others believe is completely sold out. As adults, they are the business tycoons, for instance, or the personalities who shoot to stardom no matter how much or little talent they have. A street-smart student may do well in the school subjects that he or she knows count for the most and will all but ignore the rest. When taking exams, street-smart people are likely to get better grades than their knowledge merits because they can "psych out" the test and because, when facing a problem or question they can't answer, they are skilled at putting on the paper something that looks good.

To be street-smart in these ways — to be able to achieve highly indi-   15
vidualistic goals and to be able to get around obstacles that totally stump others — a person must draw on a wide scope of mental powers. It takes excellent problem-solving ability, creative thought, good planning and goal setting, accurate perception, persistent effort, skill with language, quick thinking, and a strong sense of intuition.

Intuition plays a major role in *people smarts* as well. This kind of intel-   16
ligence allows a person to sense what others are thinking, feeling, wanting, and planning. Although we might tend to put this sort of skill down as basic "instinct," it actually relies on higher activities of the brain. People smarts rely on very accurate and quick perceptions of clues and relationships that escape the notice of many, and they include the ability to analyze the information taken in. A people-smart student can do well in school simply by dealing with individual teachers in the most productive way: Some can be charmed, some respond well to special requests for help, some reward hard work no matter what the results, and so forth. The people-smart student figures out easily what is the best approach to take. People with these talents also achieve well in other activities, of course — they become the leaders in clubs and organizations, and they are able to win important individuals, like potential employers, over to their side. They would probably be typed as right-brained people, like artists, but their skill with language, both spoken and unspoken, is one that draws heavily on the left side.

Have you been able to compare these types with people you know in   17
your class, family, or neighborhood? Of course, no individual is actually a type: People with any one of the kinds of smarts that we've described also

have some of the others. Skill in using one part of the brain does not mean that the other parts stay lazy.

Rather, some people are able to develop one set of brain-powered skills 18 to a higher degree than others who are able to strengthen other talents.

One person's choice of which skills to develop results from the rewards 19 that he or she receives from the family and the larger environment.

Thinking Critically about the Text

In her first paragraph, Gilbert notes that "psychologists and other researchers into the nature of intelligence have come up with more formal terms for the types [of intelligence] that they have isolated." If a variety of categories and labels already exists, why is Gilbert writing this essay? What do you think it adds to the conversation about intelligence?

Questions on Subject

1. Gilbert writes that regardless of the specific categories used to classify intelligence, "we will find some overlap within any individual" (paragraph 2). Does this "overlap" undermine her purpose or her argument? Why, or why not?

2. In paragraph 2, Gilbert writes, "[w]e can't be typecast." In paragraph 17, she writes, "Of course, no individual is actually a type." What does she mean by this — and why does she choose to repeat the same basic **claim**?

3. What point does the writer make in paragraph 4? Why is it important for her **purpose**? How is it important to the basis of her classification?

4. According to Gilbert, how are the talents and skills used for athletic achievement similar to the skills used for intellectual and academic achievement? Do you find her claims convincing? Why, or why not?

Questions on Strategy

1. Where in the essay does Gilbert use **illustration** and **comparison and contrast**? How do they support her main idea and argument? Point to a specific example of each and explain.

2. Consider the order that Gilbert uses to structure her essay: She begins with "book smarts" and concludes with "people smarts." Why do you think she chose this sequence?

3. How does Gilbert shift from one category to the next in this essay? Look at the **transitions**, which usually begin new paragraphs. What point does this strategy reinforce? Point to specific examples.

4. Look at the essay's three concluding paragraphs. How are they related to her initial question, "What are the different ways of being smart" (paragraph 2)? What other questions does she try to answer in her conclusion?

Division and Classification in Action

In pairs or small groups, choose one of the following questions about a general subject:

- What is the benefit of a college education?
- What does "friendship" mean in different contexts?
- What is the value of playing sports?
- How should we use technology in the college classroom?

Then, decide how to divide the general subject into specific categories or types, such as "There are four different kinds of friendship" or "Technology can be used in the classroom in three different ways," and make a diagram, chart, or outline. Discuss and establish categories that are consistent, mutually exclusive, and account for all aspects of your subject. Then, in your discussion, identify examples to support each category.

Writing Suggestions

1. Near the end of her essay, Gilbert asks, "Have you been able to compare these types with people you know in your class, family, or neighborhood?" (paragraph 17). Write an essay in which you answer her question by using examples of people in your life to support her types. Alternatively, you may use examples of well-known figures to illustrate her categories.

2. The following photograph depicts a common scene of a group of girls passing the time together. How do you "read" this photograph? What might the girls' facial expressions, body language, hairstyles, and dress tell you about them as individuals? As members of the group? About the kind of "smarts" they have? Write an essay in which you analyze the photograph and speculate about this group of girls and the dynamics that may hold them together as well as separate them.

Nick David/Getty Images

All-American Dialects

RICHARD LEDERER

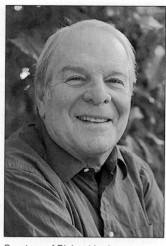

Richard Lederer is a linguist, writer, speaker, and teacher. He was born in Philadelphia in 1938 and graduated from Haverford College and Harvard University's Teaching Program before earning a doctorate degree from the University of New Hampshire. He also taught at St. Paul's School in New Hampshire. Lederer is the author of over thirty books, including *Anguished English: An Anthology of Accidental Assaults upon Our Language* (1987), *Crazy English: The Ultimate Joy Ride through Our Language* (1989), *Adventures of a Verbivore* (1995), *Word Wizard: Super Bloopers, Rich Reflections, and Other Acts of Word Magic* (2006), and *Challenging Words for Smart People: Bringing Order to the English Language* (2016). He has been a cohost of the public radio show *A Way with Words*, as well as a newspaper and magazine columnist for various publications.

Courtesy of Richard Lederer

    Lederer has described English as "the most cheerfully democratic and hospitable language that ever existed." In this essay, which originally appeared in *USA Today* in 2009, he dives deeply and playfully into the regional dialects, accents, and expressions that make American English so rich and various.

Preparing to Read

Do you have a regional accent? Could someone guess your hometown or region from your pronunciation or style of speech? Do you use specific terms, phrases, expressions, or idioms that are distinctive to your region?

have tongue and will travel, so I run around the country speaking to groups of teachers, students, librarians, women's clubbers, guild professionals, and corporate clients. These good people go to all the trouble of putting together meetings and conferences, and I walk in, share my thoughts about language in their lives, and imbibe their collective energy and synergy. I will go anywhere to spread the word about words and, in venturing from California to Manhattan Island, from the redwood forest to the Gulf Stream waters, I hear America singing. We are teeming nations within a nation, a country that is like a world. We talk in melodies of infinite variety; we dance to their sundry measure and lyrics.

    Midway through John Steinbeck's epic *The Grapes of Wrath*, young Ivy observes, "Ever'body says words different. Arkansas folks says 'em different, and Oklahomy folks says 'em different, and we seen a lady from

Massachusetts, an' she said 'em differentest of all. Couldn't hardly make out what she was sayin'."

One aspect of American rugged individualism is that not all of us say the same word in the same way. Sometimes, we do not even use the same name for the same object. I was born and grew up in Philadelphia a coon's age, a blue moon, a month of Sundays ago—when Hector was a pup. Phillufia, or Philly, which is what we kids called the city, was where the epicurean delight made with cold cuts, cheese, tomatoes, pickles, and onions stuffed into a long, hard-crusted Italian bread loaf was invented. The creation of that sandwich took place in the Italian pushcart section of the city, known as Hog Island. Some linguists contend that it was but a short leap from Hog Island to hoagie, while others claim that the label hoagie arose because only a hog had the appetite or technique to eat one properly.

As a young man, I moved to northern New England (N'Hampsha, to be specific), where the same sandwich designed to be a meal in itself is called a grinder—because you need a good set of grinders to chew it. Yet, my travels around the country have revealed that the hoagie or grinder is called at least a dozen other names—a bomber, Garibaldi (after the Italian liberator), hero, Italian sandwich, rocket, sub, submarine (which is what they call it in California, where I now live), torpedo, wedge, wedgie, and, in the deep South, a poor-boy (usually pronounced poh-boy).

In Philadelphia, we washed down our hoagies with soda. In New England, we did it with tonic and, by that word, I do not mean medicine. Soda and tonic in other parts are known as pop, soda pop, a soft drink, Coke, and quinine.

In northern New England, they take the term milk shake quite literally. To many residing in that corner of the country, a milk shake consists of milk mixed with flavored syrup—and nothing more—shaken up until foamy. If you live in Rhode Island or in southern Massachusetts and you want ice cream in your milk drink, you ask for a cabinet (named after the square wooden cabinet in which the mixer was encased). If you live farther north, you order a velvet or a frappe (from the French *frapper*, "to ice").

Clear—or is it clean or plumb?—across the nation, Americans sure do talk different. What do you call those flat, doughy things you often eat for breakfast—battercakes, flannel cakes, flapjacks, fritters, griddle cakes, or pancakes? Is that simple strip of grass between the street and the sidewalk a berm, boulevard, boulevard strip, city strip, devil strip, green belt, the parking, the parking strip, parkway, sidewalk plot, strip, swale, tree bank, or tree lawn? Is the part of the highway that separates the northbound from the southbound lanes the centerline, center strip, mall, medial strip, median strip, medium strip, or neutral ground? Is it a cock horse, dandle, hicky horse, horse, horse tilt, ridy horse, seesaw, teeter, teeterboard, teetering board, teetering horse, teeter-totter, tilt, tilting board, tinter, tinter board, or tippity bounce? Do fishermen employ an angledog, angleworm, baitworm, earthworm, eaceworm, fishworm, mudworm, rainworm, or redworm? Is a larger worm a dew worm, night crawler, night walker, or town worm? Is it a crabfish, clawfish, craw, crawdab, crawdad, crawdaddy, crawfish, crawler, crayfish, creekcrab, crowfish, freshwater lobster, ghost shrimp, mudbug, spiny lobster, or yabby? Depends where you live and who or whom it is you are talking to.

I figger, figure, guess, imagine, opine, reckon, and suspect that my being   8 bullheaded, contrary, headstrong, muley, mulish, ornery, otsny, pigheaded, set, sot, stubborn, or utsy about this whole matter of dialects makes you sick to, in, or at your stomach. I assure you, though, that when it comes to American dialects, I'm not speaking fahdoodle, flumadiddle, flummydiddle, or flurriddiddle — translation, nonsense. I am no all-thumbs-and-no-fingers, all-knees-and-elbows, all-left-feet, antigoddling, bumfuzzled, discombobulated, flusterated, or foozled bumpkin, clodhopper, country jake, hayseed, hick, hillbilly, hoosier, jackpine savage, mossback, mountain-boomer, pumpkin-husker, rail-splitter, rube, sodbuster, stump farmer, swamp angel, yahoo, or yokel.

The biblical book of Judges tells of how one group of speakers used the   9 word *shibboleth*, Hebrew for "stream," as a military password. The Gileadites had defeated the Ephraimites in battle and were holding some narrow places on the Jordan River that the fleeing Ephraimites had to cross to get home. In those days, it was hard to tell one kind of soldier from another because they did not wear uniforms. The Gileadites knew that the Ephraimites spoke a slightly different dialect of Hebrew and could be recognized by their inability to pronounce an initial "sh" sound. Thus, each time a soldier wanted to cross the river, "the men of Gilead said unto him, Art thou an Ephraimite? If he said, Nay, then they said unto him, Say now Shibboleth, and he said Sibboleth: for he could not frame to pronounce it right. Then they took him and slew him at the passages of Jordan: and there fell at that time of the Ephraimites forty and two thousand."

During World War II, some American officers adapted the strategy of   10 the Old Testament Gileadites. Knowing that many Japanese have difficulty pronouncing the letter "L," these officers instructed their sentries to use only passwords that had L's in them, such as lallapalooza. The closest the Japanese got to the sentries was rarraparooza.

These days, English speakers do not get slaughtered for pronouncing   11 their words differently from other English speakers, but the way those words sound can be labeled "funny" or "quaint" or "out of touch." In the George Bernard Shaw play "Pygmalion," Prof. Henry Higgins rails at Liza Doolittle and her cockney accent: "A woman who utters such depressing and disgusting sounds has no right to be anywhere—no right to live. Remember that you are a human being with a soul and the divine gift of articulate speech: that your native language is the language of Shakespeare and Milton and the Bible; and don't sit there crooning like a bilious pigeon!"

Most of us are aware that large numbers of people in the U.S. speak very 12 differently than we do. Most of us tend to feel that the way "we" talk is right, and the way "they" talk is weird. "They," of course, refers to anyone who differs from "us." If you ask most adults what a dialect is, they will tell you it is what somebody else in another region passes off as English. These regions tend to be exotic places like Mississippi or Texas—or Brooklyn, where oil is a rank of nobility and earl is a black, slippery substance.

It is reported that many Southerners reacted to the elections of Jimmy 13 Carter (Georgia) and Bill Clinton (Arkansas) by saying, "Well, at last we have a president who talks without an accent." Actually, Southerners, like everyone else, do speak with an accent, as witness these tongue-in-cheek entries in our Dictionary of Southernisms: ah (organ for seeing); are (60 minutes); arn (ferrous metal); ass (frozen water); ast (questioned); bane (small, kidney-shaped vegetable); bar (seek and receive a loan); bold (heated in water); card (one who lacks courage); farst (a lot of trees); fur (distance); har (to employ); hep (to assist); hire yew (a greeting); paw tree (verse); rat (opposite of lef); reckanize (to see); tarred (exhausted); t'mar (the day following t'day); thang (item); thank (to cogitate); and y'all (a bunch of "you's").

When I visited Alexandria, Louisiana, a local pastor offered me proof 14 that y'all has biblical origins, especially in the letters of the apostle Paul: "We give thanks to God always for you all, making mention of you in our prayers" (First Epistle to the Thessalonians, 1:2) and "First, I thank my God through Jesus Christ for you all" (First Epistle to the Romans, 1:8). "Obviously," the good reverend told me, "Saint Paul was a Southerner," before adding, "Thank you, Yankee visitor, for appreciating our beloved Southernspeak. We couldn't talk without it."

An anonymous poem that I came upon in Louisville, Kentucky, clarifies 15 the plural use of the one-syllable pronoun y'all:

> Y'all gather 'round from far and near,
> Both city folk and rural,
> And listen while I tell you this:
> The pronoun y'all is plural.
>
> If I should utter, "Y'all come down,
> Or we-all shall be lonely,"
> I mean at least a couple of folks
> And not one person only.

If I should say to Hiram Jones,
"I think that y'all are lazy,"
Or "Will y'all let me use y'all's knife?"
He'd think that I was crazy.

Don't think I mean to criticize
Or that I'm full of gall,
But when we speak of one alone,
We all say "you," not "y'all."

We all have accents. Many New Englanders drop the r in cart and   16
farm and say "caht" and "fahm." Thus, the Midwesterner's "park the car in
Harvard Yard" becomes the New Englander's "pahk the cah in Hahvahd
Yahd." Those r's, though, are not lost. A number of upper Northeasterners,
including the famous Kennedy family of Massachusetts, add "r" to words,
such as "idear" and "Cuber," when those words come before a vowel or at
the end of a sentence.

I.D. BY SPEECH PATTERN

When an amnesia victim appeared at a truck stop in Missouri in the fall of   17
1987, authorities tried in vain to discover her identity. Even after three months,
police "ran into a brick wall," according to the *Columbia Daily Tribune.* Then,
linguist Donald Lance of the University of Missouri–Columbia was called
in to analyze her speech. After only a few sentences, Lance recognized the
woman's West Pennsylvania dialect, and, within one month, police in Pittsburgh located her family. Among the clues used to pinpoint the woman's
origin was the West Pennsylvanian use of "greezy" instead of "greasy," and
"teeter-totter" rather than "seesaw." Dialectologists know that people who
pronounce the word as "greezy" usually live south of a line that wiggles across
the northern parts of New Jersey, Pennsylvania, Ohio, Indiana, and Illinois.

Linguist Roger Shuy writes about the reactions of Illinois residents in a   18
1962 survey of regional pronunciations, including the soundings of "greasy":
"The northern Illinois informants felt the southern pronunciation was crude
and ugly; it made them think of a very messy, dirty, sticky, smelly frying pan.
To the southern and midland speakers, however, the northern pronunciation
connoted a messy, dirty, sticky, smelly skillet."

Using the tools of his trade, Shuy was able to profile accurately Ted   19
Kaczynski, the elusive Unabomber who terrorized the nation through the
1990s. Culling linguistic evidence from Kaczynski's "Manife   sto," published in *The New York Times*, and the notes and letters accompanying the
bombs, Shuy deduced the Unabomber's geographical origin, religious background, age, and education level.

Among the clues were the Unabomber's use of "sierras" to mean 20
"mountains," an indication that the writer had spent some time living in
Northern California. In his manifesto, Kaczynski used expressions common
to a person who was a young adult in the 1960s—"Holy Robots," "working
stiff," and "playing footsy." His employment of sociological terms, such as
"other directed," and his many references to "individual drives" suggested an
acquaintance with the sociology in vogue during that decade, particularly
that of David Reisman. The complexity of Kaczynski's sentence structure,
including the subjunctive mood, and the learned-ness of his vocabulary, such
as the words "surrogate," "sublimate," "overspecialization," and "tautology,"
pointed to someone highly educated.

> 66 **When you learn
> language, you learn it
> as a dialect; if you do
> not speak a dialect,
> you do not speak.** 99

All these conclusions were verified 21
when Kaczynski was captured: He was in
his early 50s, had grown up in Chicago and
lived for a time in Northern California,
and was well educated, having once been a
university professor.

Face facts; we all speak some sort of 22
dialect. When you learn language, you
learn it as a dialect; if you do not speak a dialect, you do not speak. Dialect
is not a label for careless, unlettered, nonstandard speech. A dialect is not
something to be avoided or cured. Each language is a great pie. Each slice of
that pie is a dialect, and no single slice is the language. Do not try to change
your language into the kind of English that nobody really speaks. Be proud
of your slice of the pie.

In the early 1960s, writer John Steinbeck decided to rediscover America 23
in a camper with his French poodle, Charley. He reported on his observations in a book called *Travels with Charley* and included these thoughts on
dialects: "One of my purposes was to listen, to hear speech, accent, speech
rhythms, overtones, and emphasis. For speech is so much more than words
and sentences. I did listen everywhere. It seemed to me that regional speech
is in the process of disappearing, not gone but going. Forty years of radio
and twenty years of television must have this impact. Communications must
destroy localness by a slow, inevitable process."

I can remember a time when I almost could pinpoint a man's place of 24
origin by his speech. That is growing more difficult and, in some foresee-
able future, will become impossible. It is a rare house or building that is not
rigged with spiky combers of the air. Radio and television speech becomes
standardized, perhaps better English than we ever have used. Just as our
bread—mixed and baked, packaged, and sold without benefit of accident
or human frailty—is uniformly good and uniformly tasteless, so will our
speech become one speech.

Forty years have passed since Steinbeck's trip, and the hum and buzz 25
of electronic voices have since permeated almost every home across our
nation. Formerly, the psalmist tells us, "The voice of the turtle was heard in
the land"—now, though, it is the voice of the broadcaster, with his or her
immaculately groomed diction. Let us hope that American English does not
turn into a bland, homogenized, pasteurized, assembly line product. May our
bodacious language remain tasty and nourishing—full of flavor, variety, and
local ingredients.

Thinking Critically about the Text

Lederer argues that people should "[b]e proud of [their] slice of the pie" (paragraph 22). Do you agree? Are there any advantages to language becoming more
uniform and (in Lederer's phrase) "immaculately groomed" (paragraph 25)?

Questions on Subject

1. How would you state Lederer's **thesis** in your own words? Do you agree
   with it?

2. In paragraph 3, the writer refers to "American rugged individualism." What
   does he mean by that phrase? What does "individualism" have to do with his
   main idea?

3. In paragraphs 9 and 10, he discusses **examples** of pronunciation in a wartime
   context from the Bible and World War II. What points do these examples make?

4. According to Lederer, regional expressions, along with other aspects of speech
   and writing, can reveal personal identity. How does he support this claim?

Questions on Strategy

1. The writer packs his sentences with regional terms and expressions, even
   when doing so leads him to make grammatical errors ("Americans sure do talk
   different" [paragraph 7]). How does this stylistic approach help reinforce the
   claims in his essay?

2. Lederer uses division and classification in conjunction with other strategies,
   including **comparison and contrast** and **definition**. Find specific examples
   of one of these strategies (or all three), and explain how it supports the writer's
   overall purpose.

3. At several points during his essay, Lederer explains his points by using
   figures of speech. Do you find this use of figurative language persuasive and
   effective? How do the similes, metaphors, and analogies help him to make an
   abstract topic such as dialects more realizable?

4. The writer includes a variety of cultural references in "All-American Dialects,"
   including songs, novels, poems, and plays. Why do you think he does this?
   What do these references suggest about his **audience**?

Division and Classification in Action

Be prepared to discuss in class why you believe division and classification are important strategies or ways of thinking in everyday life. Explain, for example, how useful the two complementary strategies are for you as you go shopping in the supermarket for items on your shopping list or look for particular textbooks in your college bookstore.

Writing Suggestions

1. According to Lederer, we all use language in ways that are influenced by region and other factors: "When you learn language, you learn it as a dialect; if you do not speak a dialect, you do not speak" (paragraph 22). What are the characteristics and examples of your dialect? Using Lederer's essay as a starting point, create basic classifications for your own speech. For example, you may use categories like "regional accent," "regional words," and "regional expressions." Then, support each category with examples. Keep in mind that factors other than region may influence your speech, including aspects that are ethnic, cultural, social, or personal. What do these categories and examples reveal about your identity?

2. **Writing from Sources**. Lederer quotes the writer John Steinbeck from his famous 1960 travelogue, *Travels with Charley: In Search of America*. According to Steinbeck, local accents and speech patterns were disappearing: "Forty years of radio and twenty years of television must have this impact. Communications must destroy localness by a slow, inevitable process" (paragraph 23). Lederer seems to agree, although he hopes that American speech will keep its "tasty" local flavors. Do you agree with them, or are they overstating the problem? Have entertainment and media changed the way we speak? What other factors may lead to speech becoming more "standardized"? What factors may help different dialects survive? Research current reports or think-pieces on the topic from areas such as sociology, linguistics, literature, or history, and write an essay that addresses these and other related issues. You may structure it as a direct response to Lederer, or to even a specific claim in "All-American Dialects."

Mother Tongue

AMY TAN

Amy Tan was born in Oakland, California, in 1952, to Chinese immigrant parents. After studying English and linguistics at San Jose State University, she earned her master's degree in linguistics and worked as a language development specialist for children with developmental disabilities. After a stint as a business writer, she turned to fiction. Her first book, *The Joy Luck Club* (1989), became a best seller and was nominated for the National Book Award and the National Book Critics Circle Award, and it was selected for the National Endowment for the Arts' Big Read program. Her

Mireya Acierto/Getty Images

other books include the novels *The Kitchen God's Wife* (1991), *The Bonesetter's Daughter* (2000), and *The Valley of Amazement* (2013) and the children's books *The Moon Lady* (1992) and *The Chinese Siamese Cat* (1994); the latter was adapted into an internationally popular television series for children. Her work has appeared in the *New Yorker*, the *Atlantic*, *Grand Street*, *National Geographic*, and other publications, and has been translated into thirty-five languages.

"Mother Tongue" first appeared in the *Threepenny Review* and was reprinted in *The Best American Essays* (1991). In this essay, Tan examines the way context shapes how we use and understand language. As you read, notice the different categories she creates and how she illustrates them.

Preparing to Read

Think about the different languages you know. Perhaps English was not the first language you spoke, or maybe you grew up with a family who spoke another language. Even if the only language you know is English, do you speak more than one kind of English? Are there things you say at home that you would say differently at school or at work? Are there things you say to your friends that you wouldn't say at home? Do you consciously adjust how you speak in different circumstances, or do you think this happens naturally?

I am not a scholar of English or literature. I cannot give you much more 1 than personal opinions on the English language and its variations in this country or others.

I am a writer. And by that definition, I am someone who has always 2 loved language. I am fascinated by language in daily life. I spend a great deal of my time thinking about the power of language — the way it can evoke an emotion, a visual image, a complex idea, or a simple truth. Language is the tool of my trade. And I use them all — all the Englishes I grew up with.

Recently, I was made keenly aware of the different Englishes I do use. I   3
was giving a talk to a large group of people, the same talk I had already given to
half a dozen other groups. The nature of the talk was about my writing, my life,
and my book, *The Joy Luck Club*. The talk was going along well enough, until I
remembered one major difference that made the whole talk sound wrong. My
mother was in the room. And it was perhaps the first time she had heard me
give a lengthy speech, using the kind of English I have never used with her.
I was saying things like "The intersection of memory upon imagination" and
"There is an aspect of my fiction that relates to thus-and-thus"—a speech filled
with carefully wrought grammatical phrases, burdened, it suddenly seemed to
me, with nominalized forms, past perfect tenses, conditional phrases, all the
forms of standard English that I had learned in school and through books, the
forms of English I did not use at home with my mother.

Just last week, I was walking down the street with my mother, and I   4
again found myself conscious of the English I was using, the English I do
use with her. We were talking about the price of new and used furniture and
I heard myself saying this: "Not waste money that way." My husband was
with us as well, and he didn't notice any switch in my English. And then I
realized why. It's because over the twenty years we've been together I've often
used that same kind of English with him, and sometimes he even uses it with
me. It has become our language of intimacy, a different sort of English that
relates to family talk, the language I grew up with.

So you'll have some idea of what this family talk I heard sounds like,   5
I'll quote what my mother said during a recent conversation which I video-
taped and then transcribed. During this conversation, my mother was talking
about a political gangster in Shanghai who had the same last name as her
family's, Du, and how the gangster in his early years wanted to be adopted by
her family, which was rich by comparison. Later, the gangster became more
powerful, far richer than my mother's family, and one day showed up at my
mother's wedding to pay his respects. Here's what she said in part:

"Du Yusong having business like fruit stand. Like off the street kind. He   6
is Du like Du Zong—but not Tsung-ming Island people. The local people
call putong, the river east side, he belong to that side local people. That man
want to ask Du Zong father take him in like become own family. Du Zong
father wasn't look down on him, but didn't take seriously, until that man
big like become a mafia. Now important person, very hard to inviting him.
Chinese way, came only to show respect, don't stay for dinner. Respect for
making big celebration, he shows up. Mean gives lots of respect. Chinese
custom. Chinese social life that way. If too important won't have to stay too
long. He come to my wedding. I didn't see, I heard it. I gone to boy's side,
they have YMCA dinner. Chinese age I was nineteen."

You should know that my mother's expressive command of English   7
belies how much she actually understands. She reads the *Forbes* report, listens

to *Wall Street Week*, converses daily with her stockbroker, reads all of Shirley MacLaine's books with ease—all kinds of things I can't begin to understand. Yet some of my friends tell me they understand 50 percent of what my mother says. Some say they understand 80 to 90 percent. Some say they understand none of it, as if she were speaking pure Chinese. But to me, my mother's English is perfectly clear, perfectly natural. It's my mother tongue. Her language, as I hear it, is vivid, direct, full of observation and imagery. That was the language that helped shape the way I saw things, expressed things, made sense of the world.

Lately, I've been giving more thought to the kind of English my mother 8 speaks. Like others, I have described it to people as "broken" or "fractured" English. But I wince when I say that. It has always bothered me that I can think of no other way to describe it other than "broken," as if it were damaged and needed to be fixed, as if it lacked a certain wholeness and soundness. I've heard other terms used, "limited English," for example. But they seem just as bad, as if everything is limited, including people's perceptions of the limited English speaker.

> **" I believed that her English reflected the quality of what she had to say. "**

I know this for a fact, because when 9 I was growing up, my mother's "limited" English limited *my* perception of her. I was ashamed of her English. I believed that her English reflected the quality of what she had to say. That is, because she expressed them imperfectly her thoughts were imperfect. And I had plenty of empirical evidence to support me: the fact that people in department stores, at banks, and at restaurants did not take her seriously, did not give her good service, pretended not to understand her, or even acted as if they did not hear her.

My mother has long realized the limitations of her English as well. 10 When I was fifteen, she used to have me call people on the phone to pretend I was she. In this guise, I was forced to ask for information or even to complain and yell at people who had been rude to her. One time it was a call to her stockbroker in New York. She had cashed out her small portfolio and it just so happened we were going to go to New York the next week, our very first trip outside California. I had to get on the phone and say in an adolescent voice that was not very convincing, "This is Mrs. Tan."

And my mother was standing in the back whispering loudly, "Why he 11 don't send me check, already two weeks late. So mad he lie to me, losing me money."

And then I said in perfect English, "Yes, I'm getting rather concerned. 12 You had agreed to send the check two weeks ago, but it hasn't arrived."

Then she began to talk more loudly. "What he want, I come to New 13
York tell him front of his boss, you cheating me?" And I was trying to calm
her down, make her be quiet, while telling the stockbroker, "I can't tolerate
any more excuses. If I don't receive the check immediately, I am going to
have to speak to your manager when I'm in New York next week." And sure
enough, the following week there we were in front of this astonished stockbroker, and I was sitting there red-faced and quiet, and my mother, the real
Mrs. Tan, was shouting at his boss in her impeccable broken English.

We used a similar routine just five days ago, for a situation that was far 14
less humorous. My mother had gone to the hospital for an appointment, to
find out about a benign brain tumor a CAT scan had revealed a month ago.
She said she had spoken very good English, her best English, no mistakes.
Still, she said, the hospital did not apologize when they said they had lost
the CAT scan and she had come for nothing. She said they did not seem to
have any sympathy when she told them she was anxious to know the exact
diagnosis, since her husband and son had both died of brain tumors. She said
they would not give her any more information until the next time and she
would have to make another appointment for that. So she said she would not
leave until the doctor called her daughter. She wouldn't budge. And when the
doctor finally called her daughter, me, who spoke in perfect English—lo and
behold—we had assurances the CAT scan would be found, promises that a
conference call on Monday would be held, and apologies for any suffering
my mother had gone through for a most regrettable mistake.

I think my mother's English almost had an effect on limiting my pos- 15
sibilities in life as well. Sociologists and linguists probably will tell you that
a person's developing language skills are more influenced by peers. But I do
think that the language spoken in the family, especially in immigrant families which are more insular, plays a large role in shaping the language of the
child. And I believe that it affected my results on achievement tests, IQ tests,
and the SAT. While my English skills were never judged as poor, compared
to math, English could not be considered my strong suit. In grade school I
did moderately well, getting perhaps B's, sometimes B-pluses, in English and
scoring perhaps in the sixtieth or seventieth percentile on achievement tests.
But those scores were not good enough to override the opinion that my true
abilities lay in math and science, because in those areas I achieved A's and
scored in the ninetieth percentile or higher.

This was understandable. Math is precise; there is only one correct 16
answer. Whereas, for me at least, the answers on English tests were always
a judgment call, a matter of opinion and personal experience. Those tests
were constructed around items like fill-in-the-blank sentence completion,
such as "Even though Tom was _____, Mary thought he was _____." And
the correct answer always seemed to be the most bland combinations of

thoughts, for example, "Even though Tom was shy, Mary thought he was charming," with the grammatical structure "even though" limiting the correct answer to some sort of semantic opposites, so you wouldn't get answers like, "Even though Tom was foolish, Mary thought he was ridiculous." Well, according to my mother, there were very few limitations as to what Tom could have been and what Mary might have thought of him. So I never did well on tests like that.

The same was true with word analogies, pairs of words in which you were supposed to find some sort of logical, semantic relationship—for example, "*Sunset* is to *nightfall* as _____ is to _____." And here you would be presented with a list of four possible pairs, one of which showed the same kind of relationship: *red* is to *stoplight*, *bus* is to *arrival*, *chills* is to *fever*, *yawn* is to *boring*. Well, I could never think that way. I knew what the tests were asking, but I could not block out of my mind the images already created by the first pair, "*sunset* is to *nightfall*"—and I would see a burst of colors against a darkening sky, the moon rising, the lowering of a curtain of stars. And all the other pairs of words—red, bus, stoplight, boring—just threw up a mass of confusing images, making it impossible for me to sort out something as logical as saying: "A sunset precedes nightfall" is the same as "a chill precedes a fever." The only way I would have gotten that answer right would have been to imagine an associative situation, for example, my being disobedient and staying out past sunset, catching a chill at night, which turns into feverish pneumonia as punishment, which indeed did happen to me.

I have been thinking about all this lately, about my mother's English, about achievement tests. Because lately I've been asked, as a writer, why there are not more Asian Americans represented in American literature. Why are there few Asian Americans enrolled in creative writing programs? Why do so many Chinese students go into engineering? Well, these are broad sociological questions I can't begin to answer. But I have noticed in surveys—in fact, just last week—that Asian students, as a whole, always do significantly better on math achievement tests than in English. And this makes me think that there are other Asian-American students whose English spoken in the home might also be described as "broken" or "limited." And perhaps they also have teachers who are steering them away from writing and into math and science, which is what happened to me.

Fortunately, I happen to be rebellious in nature and enjoy the challenge of disproving assumptions made about me. I became an English major my first year in college, after being enrolled as pre-med. I started writing nonfiction as a freelancer the week after I was told by my former boss that writing was my worst skill and I should hone my talents toward account management.

But it wasn't until 1985 that I finally began to write fiction. And at 20 first I wrote using what I thought to be wittily crafted sentences, sentences that would finally prove I had mastery over the English language. Here's an example from the first draft of a story that later made its way into *The Joy Luck Club*, but without this line: "That was my mental quandary in its nascent state." A terrible line, which I can barely pronounce.

Fortunately, for reasons I won't get into today, I later decided I should 21 envision a reader for the stories I would write. And the reader I decided upon was my mother, because these were stories about mothers. So with this reader in mind—and in fact she did read my early drafts—I began to write stories using all the Englishes I grew up with: the English I spoke to my mother, which for lack of a better term might be described as "simple"; the English she used with me, which for lack of a better term might be described as "broken"; my translation of her Chinese, which could certainly be described as "watered down"; and what I imagined to be her translation of her Chinese if she could speak in perfect English, her internal language, and for that I sought to preserve the essence, but neither an English nor a Chinese structure. I wanted to capture what language ability tests can never reveal: her intent, her passion, her imagery, the rhythms of her speech, and the nature of her thoughts.

Apart from what any critic had to say about my writing, I knew I had 22 succeeded where it counted when my mother finished reading my book and gave me her verdict: "So easy to read."

Thinking Critically about the Text

Tan writes that she "succeeded where it counted when my mother finished reading my book and gave me her verdict: 'So easy to read'" (paragraph 22). If someone told you this about your own writing, would you feel you had succeeded? What are your goals for your writing? Do you want it to be easy to read, no matter what? Are there types of writing that should be difficult?

Questions on Subject

1. What is the **thesis** of Tan's essay, and where do you find it?

2. What are the different Englishes Tan examines in this essay? Define each one, using evidence from the essay to support your answer.

3. In paragraph 9, Tan writes that as a child, she was "ashamed of" her mother's English. Why did she feel this way? Now, as an adult, does she feel the same way?

4. Tan writes that in school, she did better in math than in English because "math is precise; there is only one correct answer." Do you agree with her that the

answers on English tests are "always a judgment call, a matter of opinion and personal experience" (paragraph 16)? Why, or why not?

Questions on Strategy

1. What is Tan's **purpose** in this essay? Where is it stated?

2. How does the author organize her classification of the different "Englishes" she has come to know?

3. In paragraph 6, Tan shares a story her mother told, recording the exact words her mother used. Could you follow what Tan's mother said? Do you think you would have been able to understand it as well without Tan's explanation in the preceding paragraph? Why do you think Tan included paragraph 6?

4. Tan hears her mother's language as "vivid, direct, full of observation and imagery" (paragraph 7). Yet she spends much of the essay discussing the limitations of her mother's English. How does this apparent contradiction contribute to the overall message of Tan's essay?

Division and Classification in Action

Categorize the kinds of television programs you watch or the kinds of music you listen to. Think not only of classes but also of subclasses. For example, you may claim that the only types of programs you watch are documentaries, situation comedies, and sports, but within the sports category, you realize you watch only NFL games and not college games. Perhaps you watch basketball, but only college games and not NBA games. By looking at subclasses as well as classes, you will come to a much more detailed understanding of your viewing or listening habits.

Writing Suggestions

1. Using the Preparing to Read prompt as a springboard, write an essay in which you create a classification system for the different types of language you use. Consider the language you use with your family, your friends, your teachers, and at work. Remember that there may be subclasses, such as different parts of your family (your siblings versus your parents or grandparents) or different groups of friends (your school friends versus your neighborhood friends). How and why do your languages differ? Have you ever felt ignored or invisible because you are being misunderstood? Have you ever dismissed someone because you couldn't understand that person or the person couldn't understand you? Be sure to provide examples, with dialogue, to illustrate your understanding of the way you use, and react to, your different types of language.

2. Richard Lederer's "All-American Dialects" and Amy Tan's "Mother Tongue" both explore dialects and language communities: Lederer focuses on American regional dialects, and Tan focuses on the various subsets of one's personal language experience. Write an essay in which you reflect on how each author has chosen to analyze through division and classification the various Englishes he or she finds most interesting in the American experience. What are the larger implications or practical consequences of their findings? How do their ideas intersect with your own experiences and ideas about language?

Lokesh Dhakar

CHAPTER 10

Definition

WHAT IS DEFINITION?

IF YOU HAVE EVER USED A DICTIONARY, YOU ARE ALREADY FAMILIAR WITH the concept of definition. We use definition all the time in our everyday lives to make our points clearer. How often have you been asked what you mean when a word or phrase you're using is ambiguous, unusual, or simply unfamiliar to your listener? We can only communicate with one another clearly and effectively when we all understand the words we use in the same way—and that is not always easy.

VISUALIZING DEFINITION

Consider the chart that one specialty coffee shop prominently displayed at its order counter. According to the chart, what are the essential components of coffee drinks? Would you find a chart like this helpful if you were ordering a specialty coffee? Why, or why not? What advantages, if any, does a chart like this have over a menu that presents a simple list by name of the various coffee drinks available? Does it help you understand better what "coffee" is? How?

UNDERSTANDING DEFINITION AS A WRITING STRATEGY

Unlike showing the relative proportions of coffee, milk, and water to define various *coffee* drinks, understanding and explaining complex concepts is often impossible without using precise, detailed, verbal definitions. These definitions can take on many different forms, depending, in part, on their purpose and on what is being defined.

For example, let's look at how Robert Keith Miller attempts to define *discrimination* in his essay "Discrimination Is a Virtue," which first appeared in *Newsweek*:

<table>
<tr>
<td>Establishes issue: *dis-crimination* misused</td>
<td>We have a word in English which means "the ability to tell differences." That word is *discrimination*. But within the last [sixty] years, this word has been so frequently misused that an entire generation has grown up believing that "discrimination" means "racism." People are always proclaiming that "discrimination" is something that should be done away with. Should that ever happen, it would prove to be our undoing.</td>
</tr>
<tr>
<td>Provides dictionary definition and history of usage</td>
<td>Discrimination means discernment; it means the ability to perceive the truth, to use good judgment and to profit accordingly. The *Oxford English Dictionary* traces this meaning of the word back to 1648 and demonstrates that for the next 300 years, "discrimination" was a virtue, not a vice. Thus, when a character in a nineteenth-century novel makes a happy marriage, Dickens has another character remark, "It does credit to your discrimination that you should have found such a very excellent young woman."</td>
</tr>
<tr>
<td>Shows how compound discriminate against has led to misuse</td>
<td>Of course, "the ability to tell differences" assumes that differences exist, and this is unsettling for a culture obsessed with the notion of equality. The contemporary belief that discrimination is a vice stems from the compound "discriminate against." What we need to remember, however, is that some things deserve to be judged harshly: We should not leave our kingdoms to the selfish and the wicked.</td>
</tr>
<tr>
<td>Reiterates main point: discrimination is a virtue, not a vice</td>
<td>Discrimination is wrong only when someone or something is discriminated against because of prejudice. But to use the word in that sense, as so many people do, is to destroy its true meaning. If you discriminate against something because of general preconceptions rather than particular insights, then you are not discriminating—bias has clouded the clarity of vision that discrimination demands.</td>
</tr>
</table>

How does Miller define *discrimination*? He mainly uses a technique called *extended definition*, a definition that requires a full discussion. This is only one of many types of definition that you could use to explain what a word or an idea means to you. The following section identifies and explains several other types.

▶ Types of Definition

A *formal definition* — a definition such as that found in a dictionary — explains the meaning of a word by assigning it to a class and then differentiating it from other members of that class.

TERM		CLASS	DIFFERENTIATION
Music	is	sound	made by voices or instruments and characterized by melody, harmony, or rhythm.

Note how crucial the differentiation is here: There are many sounds — from the roar of a passing jet airplane to the fizz of soda in a glass — that must be excluded for the definition to be precise and useful. Dictionary entries often follow the class-differentiation pattern of the formal definition.

A *synonymous definition* explains a word by pairing it with another word of similar but perhaps more limited meaning:

Music is melody.

Synonymous definition is almost never as precise as formal definition because few words share exactly the same meaning. But when the word being defined is reasonably familiar and somewhat broad, a well-chosen synonym can provide readers with a surer sense of its meaning in context.

A *negative definition* explains a word by saying what it does not mean:

Music is not silence, and it is not noise.

Such a definition must obviously be incomplete: There are sounds that are neither silence nor noise and yet are not music — quiet conversation, for example. But specifying what something is *not* often helps to clarify other statements about what it *is*.

An *etymological definition* also seldom stands alone, but by tracing a word's origins it helps readers understand its meaning. *Etymology* itself is defined as the study of the history of a linguistic form — the history of words.

Music is descended from the Greek word *mousikē*, meaning literally "the art of the Muse."

The Muses, according to Greek mythology, were deities and the sources of inspiration in the arts. Thus the etymology suggests why we think of music as an art and as the product of inspiration. Etymological definitions often reveal surprising sources that suggest new ways of looking at ideas or objects.

A *stipulative definition* is a definition invented by a writer to convey a special or unexpected sense of an existing and often familiar word:

> Music is a language, but a language of the intangible, a kind of soul-language.
> —EDWARD MACDOWELL

> Music is the arithmetic of sounds.
> —CLAUDE DEBUSSY

Although these two examples seem to disagree with each other, and perhaps also with your idea of what music is, note that neither is arbitrary. (That is, neither assigns to the word *music* a completely foreign meaning.) The stipulative definitions by MacDowell and Debussy help explain each composer's conception of the subject and can lead, of course, to further elaboration. Stipulative definitions almost always provide the basis for a more complex discussion. These definitions are often the subjects of an extended definition.

Extended definition, like the definition of *discrimination* given by Robert Keith Miller on page 304, is used when a word, or the idea it stands for, requires more than a sentence of explanation. *Extended definition* may employ any of the definition techniques already mentioned, as well as the strategies discussed in other chapters. For example, an extended definition of music might provide *examples*, ranging from African drumming to a Bach fugue to a Bruce Springsteen song, to develop a fuller and more vivid sense of what music is. A writer might *describe* music in detail by showing its characteristic features, or explain the *process* of composing music, or *compare and contrast* music with language (according to MacDowell's stipulative definition) or arithmetic (according to Debussy's). Each of these strategies helps make the meaning of a writer's words and ideas clear.

In his extended definition of the word *discrimination*, Miller uses a very brief formal definition of *discrimination* [term]: "the ability [class] to tell differences [differentiation]." He then offers a negative definition (discrimination is not racism) and a synonymous definition (discrimination is discernment). Next he cites the entry in a great historical dictionary of English to support his claim, and he quotes an example to illustrate his definition. He concludes by contrasting the word *discrimination* with the compound *discriminate against*. Each of these techniques helps make the case that the most precise meaning of *discrimination* is in direct opposition to its common usage today and that readers should make an effort to use the word correctly.

USING DEFINITION ACROSS THE DISCIPLINES

When writing essays in the academic disciplines, you will have many opportunities to use the strategy of definition to both organize and strengthen the presentation of your ideas. To determine whether definition is the right strategy for you in a particular paper, use the guidelines described in Chapter 2,

"Determining a Strategy for Developing Your Essay" (pages 34–35). Consider the following examples:

Philosophy

1. MAIN IDEA: A person of integrity is more than just an honest person.
2. QUESTION: What does it mean to have *integrity*?
3. STRATEGY: Definition. The direction words *mean* and *is more than* call for a complete explanation of the meaning of the word *integrity*.
4. SUPPORTING STRATEGY: Comparison and contrast. To clarify the definition of *integrity*, it might be helpful to differentiate a person of integrity from a moral person or an ethical person. ,

Economics ·

1. MAIN IDEA: One way to understand the swings in the U.S. economy is to know the meaning of inflation.
2. QUESTION: What is inflation?
3. STRATEGY: Definition. The direction words *meaning* and *is* point us toward the strategy of definition; the word *inflation* needs to be explained.
4. SUPPORTING STRATEGY: Cause and effect analysis. In explaining the meaning of *inflation*, it would be interesting to explore economic factors that cause inflation as well as the effects of inflation on the economy.

Astronomy

1. MAIN IDEA: With the demotion of Pluto from planet to "dwarf planet" or plutoid, astronomers have given new attention to the definition of *planet*.
2. QUESTION: What is a planet?
3. STRATEGY: Definition. The direction words *definition* and *is* call for an extended definition of the word *planet*. For clarification purposes, it would be helpful to define *asteroid* as well.
4. SUPPORTING STRATEGIES: Illustration; cause and effect analysis. The definition of *planet* could be supported with several concrete examples of planets as well as an explanation of why astronomers thought a new definition was necessary.

PRACTICAL ADVICE FOR WRITING AN ESSAY OF DEFINITION

As you plan, write, and revise your definition essay, be mindful of the writing process guidelines described in Chapter 2. Also, pay particular attention to the basic requirements and essential ingredients for this writing strategy.

▶ Planning Your Essay of Definition

Planning is an essential part of writing a good definition essay. You can save yourself a great deal of work by taking the time to think about the key components of your essay before you actually begin to write.

Determine Your Purpose.   Whatever your subject, make sure you have a clear sense of your purpose. Why are you writing a definition? If it's only to explain what a word or phrase means, you'll probably run out of things to say in a few sentences, or you'll find that a good dictionary has already said them for you. An effective extended definition should attempt to explain the essential nature of a thing or an idea—whether it be *photosynthesis* or *spring fever* or *Republicanism* or *prison* or *common sense*—or to persuade readers to change their thinking or take a particular action.

When you decide on your topic, consider an idea or a term that you would like to clarify or explain to someone. At the beginning, you should have at least a general idea of what your subject means to you, as well as a sense of the audience you are writing your definition for and the impact you want your definition to achieve. The following advice will guide you as you plan and draft your essay.

Formulate a Thesis Statement.   A strong, clear thesis statement is critical in any essay. When writing an essay using extended definition, you should formulate a thesis statement that states clearly both the word or idea that you want to define or explain and the way in which you are going to present your thoughts. Here is an example from this chapter:

> We have a word in English which means "the ability to tell differences." That word is *discrimination*. But within the last [sixty] years, this word has been so frequently misused that an entire generation has grown up believing that "discrimination" means "racism."

Robert Keith Miller's thesis statement tells us that he will be discussing the word *discrimination* and how it is not the same as racism.

As you begin to develop your thesis statement, ask yourself, "What is my point?" Next, ask yourself, "What types of definitions will be most useful in making my point?" If you can't answer these questions yet, make a list of some ideas and try to determine your main point from the items on your list. Then write down your answers to the two original questions. Next, combine your answers into a single-sentence thesis statement. Your eventual thesis statement does not have to be one sentence, but this exercise can help you focus your point.

Consider Your Audience.   What do your readers know? If you're an economics major in an undergraduate writing course, you can safely assume that you know economics as a subject better than most of your readers do, and so you will have to explain even very basic terms and ideas. If, however, you're writing a paper for your course in econometrics, your most important reader—the one who grades your paper—won't even slow down at your references to *monetary aggregates* and *Philips curves*—provided, of course, that you use the terms correctly, showing that you know what they mean.

Choose a Type of Definition That Fits Your Subject. How you choose to develop your definition depends on your subject, your purpose, and your readers. Many inexperienced writers believe that any extended definition, no matter what the subject, should begin with a formal "dictionary" definition. This is not necessarily so; you will find that few of the essays in this chapter include formal definitions. Instead, their authors assume that their readers have dictionaries and know how to use them.

If, however, you think your readers do require a formal definition at some point, don't simply quote from a dictionary. (Certainly, in an essay about photosynthesis, nonscientists would be baffled by an opening such as this: "The dictionary defines *photosynthesis* as 'the process by which chlorophyll-containing cells in green plants convert incident light to chemical energy and synthesize organic compounds from inorganic compounds, especially carbohydrates from carbon dioxide and water, with the simultaneous release of oxygen.'") Unless you have some very good reason for doing otherwise, put the definition into your own words—words that suit your approach and the probable readers of your essay. There's another advantage to using your own words: You won't have to write "The dictionary defines . . ." or "According to *Webster's* . . ."; stock phrases like these almost immediately put the reader's mind to sleep.

Certain concepts, such as *liberalism* and *discrimination*, lend themselves to different interpretations, depending on the writer's point of view. While readers may agree in general about what such subjects mean, there will be much disagreement over particulars and therefore room for you to propose and defend your own definitions.

▶ Organizing Your Essay of Definition

Develop an Organizational Plan. Once you have gathered all the information you will need for your extended definition essay, you will want to settle on an organizational plan that suits your purpose and your materials. If you want to show that one definition of *family* is better than others, for example, you might want to lead with the definitions you plan to discard and end with the one you want your readers to accept.

Use Other Rhetorical Strategies to Support Your Definition. Although definition can be used effectively as a separate rhetorical strategy, it is generally used alongside other writing strategies. *Photosynthesis*, for example, is a natural process, so one logical strategy for defining it would be *process analysis*; readers who know little about biology may better understand photosynthesis if you draw an *analogy* with the eating and breathing of human beings. *Common sense* is an abstract concept, so its meaning could certainly be *illustrated* with concrete *examples*; in addition, its special nature might emerge more sharply through *comparison and contrast* with other ways of thinking. To define a salt marsh, you might choose a typical marsh and *describe* it. To define economic inflation or a particular disease, you might discuss its *causes and effects*. In the end, only one requirement limits your choice of supporting strategy: The strategy must help you define your term.

▌ Revising and Editing Your Essay of Definition

Begin your revision by reading aloud what you have written. This will help you to hear any lapses in the logical flow of thought and makes it easier to catch any words that have been accidentally left out. Once you have caught any major errors, use Chapter 16 along with the following guidelines and questions to help you make your corrections.

Select Words That Accurately Denote and Connote What You Want to Say.   The denotation of a word is its literal meaning or dictionary definition. Most of the time you will have no trouble with denotation, but problems can occur when words are close in meaning or sound a lot alike.

accept	*v.*, to receive
except	*prep.*, to exclude
affect	*v.*, to influence
effect	*n.*, the result; *v.*, to produce, bring into existence
anecdote	*n.*, a short narrative
antidote	*n.*, a medicine for countering effects of poison
coarse	*adj.*, rough; crude
course	*n.*, a route, a program of instruction
disinterested	*adj.*, free of self-interest or bias
uninterested	*adj.*, without interest
eminent	*adj.*, outstanding, as in reputation
immanent	*adj.*, remaining within, inherent
imminent	*adj.*, about to happen

| **principal** | *n.*, a school official; in finance, a capital sum; *adj.*, most important |
| **principle** | *n.*, a basic law or rule of conduct |

| **than** | *conj.*, used in comparisons |
| **then** | *adv.*, at that time |

Consult a dictionary if you are not sure you are using the correct word.

Words have connotative values as well as denotative meanings. *Connotations* are the associations or emotional overtones that words have acquired. For example, the word *hostage* denotes a person who is given or held as security for the fulfillment of certain conditions or terms, but it connotes images of suffering, loneliness, torture, fear, deprivation, starvation, or anxiety, as well as other images based on our individual associations. Because many words in English are synonyms or have the same meanings — *strength*, *potency*, *force*, and *might* all denote *power* — your task as a writer in any given situation is to choose the word with the connotations that best suit your purpose.

Use Specific and Concrete Words.   Words can be classified as relatively general or specific, abstract or concrete. *General words* name groups or classes of objects, qualities, or actions. *Specific words* name individual objects, qualities, or actions within a class or group. For example, *dessert* is more specific than *food* but more general than *pie*, and *pie* is more general than *blueberry pie*.

Abstract words refer to ideas, concepts, qualities, and conditions — *love*, *anger*, *beauty*, *youth*, *wisdom*, *honesty*, *patriotism*, and *liberty*, for example. *Concrete words*, on the other hand, name things you can see, hear, taste, touch, or smell. *Corn bread*, *rocking chair*, *sailboat*, *nitrogen*, *computer*, *rain*, *horse*, and *coffee* are all concrete words.

General and abstract words generally fail to create in the reader's mind the kind of vivid responses that concrete, specific words do, as Natalie Goldberg memorably notes in "Be Specific" (page 168). Always question the words you choose. Notice how Jo Goodwin Parker uses concrete, specific diction in the opening sentences of many paragraphs in her essay "What Is Poverty?" (page 317) to paint a powerful verbal picture of what poverty is:

> Poverty is getting up every morning from a dirt- and illness-stained mattress. . . .
> Poverty is being tired. . . .
> Poverty is dirt. . . .
> Poverty is staying up all night on cold nights to watch the fire, knowing one spark on the newspaper covering the walls means your sleeping children die in flames.

Collectively, these specific and concrete words create a memorable definition of the abstraction *poverty*.

STUDENT ESSAY USING DEFINITION AS A WRITING STRATEGY

A native of New York City, Howard Solomon Jr. studied in France as part of the American Field Services Intercultural Program in high school, and he majored in French in college. For the following essay, Solomon interviewed twenty students in his dormitory, collecting information and opinions that he eventually brought together with his own experiences to develop a definition of *best friends*.

Best Friends
Howard Solomon Jr.

Introduction: brief definition of *best friend*

Purpose: In defining *best friend*, writer comes to new understanding of self and relationships

Best friends, even when they are not a part of people's day-to-day lives, are essential to their well-being. They supply the companionship, help, security, and love that all people need. It is not easy to put into words exactly what a best friend is, because the matter is so personal. People can benefit, however, from thinking about their best friends—who they are, what characteristics they share, and why they are so important—in order to

1

gain a better understanding of themselves and their relationships.

When interviewed for their opinions about the qualities they most valued in their own best friends, twenty people in a University of Vermont dormitory agreed on three traits: reciprocity, honesty, and love.

Reciprocity means that one can always rely on a best friend in times of need. A favor doesn't necessarily have to be returned, but best friends will return it anyway, because they want to. Best friends are willing to help each other for the sake of helping and not just for personal gain. One woman interviewed said that life seemed more secure because she knew her best friend was there if she ever needed help.

Honesty in a best friendship is the sharing of feelings openly and without reserve. All people interviewed said they could rely on their best friends as confidants: They could share problems with their best friends and ask for advice. They also felt that, even if best friends were critical of each other, they would never be hurtful or spiteful.

Love is probably the most important quality of a best friend relationship, according to the interview group. They very much prized the affection and enjoyment they felt in the company of their best friends. One man described it as a "gut reaction," and all said it was a different feeling from being with other friends. Private jokes, looks, and gestures create personal communication between best friends that is at a very high level—many times one person knows what the other is thinking without anything being said. The specifics differ, but almost everyone agreed that a special feeling exists, which is best described as love.

When asked who could be a best friend and who could not, most of those interviewed stated that it was impossible for parents, other relatives, and people of the opposite sex (especially husbands or wives) to be best friends. One woman said such people were "too inhibitive." Only two of those interviewed, both of whom were men, disagree—each had a female best friend. However, they seem to be an exception. Most of the people interviewed thought that their best friends were not demanding, while relatives and partners of the opposite sex can be very demanding.

Answers to question 3: How many best friends can a person have?

To the question of how many best friends one can have, about half of the sample responded that it is possible to have several best friends, although very few people can do so; others said it was possible to have only a very few best friends; and still others felt they could have just one. It was interesting to see how ideas varied on this question. Although best friends may be no less special for one person than another, people do define the concept differently.

6

Answers to question 4: How long does it take to become a best friend?

Quotes sources to capture their thoughts and feelings accurately

Regarding how long it takes to become best friends and how long the relationship lasts, all were in agreement. "It is a long hard process which takes a lot of time," one woman explained. "It isn't something that can happen overnight," suggested another. One man said, "You usually know the person very well before you consider him your best friend. In fact you know everything about him, his bad points as well as his good points, so there is little likelihood that you can come into conflict with him." In addition, everyone thought that once a person has become a best friend, he or she remains so for the rest of one's life.

7

Highlights an important difference in responses from men and women

During the course of the interviews one important and unexpected difference emerged between men and women. The men all said that a best friend usually possessed one quality that stood out above all others—an easygoing manner or humor or sympathy, for example. One of them said that he looked not for loyalty but for honesty, for someone who was truthful, because it was so rare to find this quality in anyone. The women, however, all responded that they looked for a well-rounded person who had many good qualities. One woman said that a person who had just one good quality and not several would be "too boring to associate with." If this difference holds true beyond my sample, it means that men and women have quite different definitions of their best friends.

8

Personal example: tells what he learned about best friends at the time of his father's death

On a personal note, I have always wondered why my own best friends were so important to me; it wasn't until recently that something happened to make me really understand my relationship with them. My father died, and this was a crisis for me. Most of my friends gave me their condolences, but my best friends did more than that: They actually supported me. They called long distance to see how I was and what I needed, to try to help me work out my problems, or

9

simply to talk. Two of my best friends even took time from their spring break and, along with two other best friends, attended my father's memorial service. None of my other friends came. Since then, these are the only people who have continued to worry about me and talk to me about my father. I know that whenever I need someone they will be there and willing to help me. I know also that whenever they need help I will be ready to do the same for them.

Conclusion: personal definition of *best friend*

Yet, like the people I interviewed, I don't value my best friends just for what they do for me. I simply enjoy their company more than anyone else's. We talk, joke, play sports, and do all kinds of things when we are together. I never feel ill at ease with them, even after we've been apart for a while. As with virtually all of those I interviewed, the most important thing for me about best friends is the knowledge that I am never alone, that there are others in the world who care about

Thesis

my well-being as much as I do about theirs. Viewed in this light, having a best friend seems more like a necessity than it does a luxury reserved for the lucky few.

10

Student Reflection
Howard Solomon Jr.

Q. How did you hit on the idea of defining what a best friend is?
A. A friend of mine had become a best friend—we're like brothers almost—and I was trying to figure out what had happened, what was the difference. So I decided to explore what was on my mind. Of course, I shared the paper with the other students in my class, because that's what we do, but I think I was really writing for myself, not for them.

Q. How did you feel about getting feedback from your classmates?
A. The first time I had to read a paper, I was afraid and embarrassed because I didn't know how it was going to be received, so I got someone to read it aloud for me. Everybody liked the paper, so the next time it was better. The other students showed me I was doing better than I thought I was, and that helped my confidence.

Q. Friendship is a very personal topic, but I see that you've gone beyond your own opinions and experiences.
A. In fact, the first drafts didn't have anything personal in them at all. I've not written a personal paper since maybe sixth grade—my high

school teachers made me show evidence for what I had to say, and my opinion wasn't evidence. The teacher would tell me that I wasn't an authority. So even though I was writing on a very personal kind of topic, I still kept thinking that I wasn't an authority. Fortunately, my college writing teacher told me that sometimes teachers are wrong and that on certain subjects like this you can write from your own experiences and beliefs. But that didn't come in until a late draft.

Q. What led you to interview other people about their ideas of best friendship?
A. The first draft I wrote was nothing. I tried to get a start with the dictionary definition, but it didn't help—they try to put into two words what really needs hundreds of words to explain, and the words they use have to be defined too. My teacher suggested I might get going better if I talked about my topic with other people. I decided to make it semi-formal, so I made up a list of a few specific questions—five questions—and went to about a dozen people I knew and asked them. Questions like, "What qualities do your best friends have?" and "What are some of the things they've done for you?" And I took notes on the answers. I was surprised when so many of them agreed. It isn't a scientific sampling, but the results helped get me started.

Q. So the hard part of the paper was past.
A. Not exactly! Doing this paper showed me that writing isn't all that easy. Boy, I went through so many copies—adding some things, taking out some things, reorganizing. At one point half the paper was a definition of *friends*, so I could contrast them with *best friends*. That wasn't necessary. Then, I've said that the personal stuff came in late. In fact, my father died after I'd begun writing the paper, so that paragraph came in almost last of all. On the next-to-last draft everything was there, but it was put together in a sort of random way — not completely random, one idea would lead to the next and then the next, but there was a lot of circling around. My teacher pointed this out and suggested I outline what I'd written and work on the outline. So I tried it and I saw what the problem was and what I had to do. It was just a matter of getting things into the right order, and finally everything clicked into place.

Your Response

What did you learn from Howard Solomon Jr.'s essay and reflection on his experience writing the essay? What challenges do you expect to face as you write your own essay of definition? Based on Howard's composing strategies and the practical advice discussed earlier in this chapter (pages 307–12), what writing decisions do you anticipate making?

What Is Poverty?

JO GOODWIN PARKER

Everything we know about Jo Goodwin Parker comes from the account of Dr. George Henderson, Professor Emeritus at the University of Oklahoma, who received the following essay from Parker while he was compiling a selection of readings intended for future educators planning to teach in rural communities. This selection, which Henderson subsequently included in *America's Other Children: Public Schools outside Suburbs* (1971), has been identified as the text of a speech given in De Land, Florida, on December 27, 1965. Although Henderson has not shared any biographical information about the author, it may be useful to consider her identity. While Parker may be who she claims to be — one of the rural poor who eke out a difficult living just beyond the view of America's middle-class majority — it is also possible that she is instead a spokesperson for these individuals, families, and communities, writing not from her own experience but from long and sympathetic observation. In either case, her definition of *poverty* is so detailed and forceful that it conveys, even to those who have never known it, the nature of poverty.

Preparing to Read

What does it mean to you to be poor? What do you see as some of the effects of poverty on people?

You ask me what is poverty? Listen to me. Here I am, dirty, smelly, and with no "proper" underwear on and with the stench of my rotting teeth near you. I will tell you. Listen to me. Listen without pity. I cannot use your pity. Listen with understanding. Put yourself in my dirty, worn-out, ill-fitting shoes, and hear me.

Poverty is getting up every morning from a dirt- and illness-stained mattress. The sheets have long since been used for diapers. Poverty is living in a smell that never leaves. This is a smell of urine, sour milk, and spoiling food sometimes joined with the strong smell of long-cooked onions. Onions are cheap. If you have smelled this smell, you did not know how it came. It is the smell of the outdoor privy. It is the smell of young children who cannot walk the long dark way in the night. It is the smell of the mattresses where years of "accidents" have happened. It is the smell of the milk which has gone sour because the refrigerator long has not worked, and it costs money to get it fixed. It is the smell of rotting garbage. I could bury it, but where is the shovel? Shovels cost money.

Poverty is being tired. I have always been tired. They told me at the hospital when the last baby came that I had chronic anemia caused from poor diet, a bad case of worms, and that I needed a corrective operation. I listened politely — the poor are always polite. The poor always listen. They don't say that there is no money for iron pills, or better food, or worm medicine. The idea of an operation is frightening and costs so much that, if I had dared, I would have laughed. Who takes care of my children? Recovery from an operation takes a long time. I have three children. When I left them with "Granny" the last time I had a job, I came home to find the baby covered with fly specks, and a diaper that had not been changed since I left. When the dried diaper came off, bits of my baby's flesh came with it. My other child was playing with a sharp bit of broken glass, and my oldest was playing alone at the edge of a lake. I made twenty-two dollars a week, and a good nursery school costs twenty dollars a week for three children. I quit my job.

> " Poverty is getting up every morning from a dirt- and illness-stained mattress. The sheets have long since been used for diapers. Poverty is living in a smell that never leaves. "

Poverty is dirt. You say in your 4 clean clothes coming from your clean house, "Anybody can be clean." Let me explain about housekeeping with no money. For breakfast I give my children grits with no oleo or cornbread without eggs and oleo. This does not use up many dishes. What dishes there are, I wash in cold water and with no soap. Even the cheapest soap has to be saved for the baby's diapers. Look at my hands, so cracked and red. Once I saved for two months to buy a jar of Vaseline for my hands and the baby's diaper rash. When I had saved enough, I went to buy it and the price had gone up two cents. The baby and I suffered on. I have to decide every day if I can bear to put my cracked, sore hands into the cold water and strong soap. But you ask, why not hot water? Fuel costs money. If you have a wood fire it costs money. If you burn electricity, it costs money. Hot water is a luxury. I do not have luxuries. I know you will be surprised when I tell you how young I am. I look so much older. My back has been bent over the wash tubs for so long, I cannot remember when I ever did anything else. Every night I wash every stitch my school-age child has on and just hope her clothes will be dry by morning.

Poverty is staying up all night on cold nights to watch the fire, knowing 5 one spark on the newspaper covering the walls means your sleeping children die in flames. In summer poverty is watching gnats and flies devour your baby's tears when he cries. The screens are torn and you pay so little rent you know they will never be fixed. Poverty means insects in your food, in your nose, in your eyes, and crawling over you when you sleep. Poverty is hoping it never rains because diapers won't dry when it rains and soon you are using newspapers. Poverty is seeing your children forever with runny noses. Paper handkerchiefs cost money and all your rags you need for other things. Even more costly are antihistamines. Poverty is cooking without food and cleaning without soap.

Poverty is asking for help. Have you ever had to ask for help, knowing 6 your children will suffer unless you get it? Think about asking for a loan from a relative, if this is the only way you can imagine asking for help. I will tell you how it feels. You find out where the office is that you are supposed to visit. You circle that block four or five times. Thinking of your children, you go in. Everyone is very busy. Finally, someone comes out and you tell her that you need help. That never is the person you need to see. You go see another person, and after spilling the whole shame of your poverty all over the desk between you, you find that this isn't the right office after all—you must repeat the whole process, and it never is any easier at the next place.

You have asked for help, and after all it has a cost. You are again told to 7 wait. You are told why, but you don't really hear because of the red cloud of shame and the rising black cloud of despair.

Poverty is remembering. It is remembering quitting school in junior 8 high because "nice" children had been so cruel about my clothes and my smell. The attendance officer came. My mother told him I was pregnant. I wasn't but she thought that I could get a job and help out. I had jobs off and on, but never long enough to learn anything. Mostly I remember being married. I was so young then. I am still young. For a time, we had all the things you have. There was a little house in another town, with hot water and everything. Then my husband lost his job. There was unemployment insurance for a while and what few jobs I could get. Soon, all our nice things were repossessed and we moved back here. I was pregnant then. This house didn't look so bad when we first moved in. Every week it gets worse. Nothing is ever fixed. We now had no money. There were a few odd jobs for my husband, but everything went for food then, as it does now. I don't know how we lived through three years and three babies, but we did. I'll tell you something, after the last baby I destroyed my marriage. It had been a good one, but could you keep on bringing children in this dirt? Did you ever think how much it costs for any kind of birth control? I knew my husband was leaving the day he left, but there were no good-byes between us. I hope he has been able to climb out of this mess somewhere. He never could hope with us to drag him down.

That's when I asked for help. When I got it, you know how much it was? 9 It was, and is, seventy-eight dollars a month for the four of us; that is all I ever can get. Now you know why there is no soap, no needles and thread, no hot water, no aspirin, no worm medicine, no hand cream, no shampoo. None of these things forever and ever and ever. So that you can see clearly, I pay twenty dollars a month rent, and most of the rest goes for food. For grits and cornmeal, and rice and milk and beans. I try my best to use only the minimum electricity. If I use more, there is that much less for food.

Poverty is looking into a black future. Your children won't play with my 10 boys. They will turn to other boys who steal to get what they want. I can already see them behind the bars of their prison instead of behind the bars of my poverty. Or they will turn to the freedom of alcohol or drugs, and find themselves enslaved. And my daughter? At best, there is for her a life like mine.

But you say to me, there are schools. Yes, there are schools. My children 11 have no extra books, no magazines, no extra pencils, or crayons, or paper and the most important of all, they do not have health. They have worms, they have infections, they have pinkeye all summer. They do not sleep well on the floor, or with me in my one bed. They do not suffer from hunger, my seventy-eight dollars keeps us alive, but they do suffer from malnutrition. Oh yes, I do remember what I was taught about health in school. It doesn't do much good. In some places there is a surplus commodities program. Not here. The county said it cost too much. There is a school lunch program. But I have two children who will already be damaged by the time they get to school.

But, you say to me, there are health clinics. Yes, there are health clinics and 12 they are in the towns. I live out here eight miles from town. I can walk that far (even if it is sixteen miles both ways), but can my little children? My neighbor will take me when he goes; but he expects to get paid, *one way or another.* I bet you know my neighbor. He is that large man who spends his time at the gas station, the barbershop, and the corner store complaining about the government spending money on the immoral mothers of illegitimate children.

Poverty is an acid that drips on pride until all pride is worn away. Poverty 13 is a chisel that chips on honor until honor is worn away. Some of you say that you would do *something* in my situation, and maybe you would, for the first week or the first month, but for year after year after year?

Even the poor can dream. A dream of a time when there is money. 14 Money for the right kinds of food, for worm medicine, for iron pills, for toothbrushes, for hand cream, for a hammer and nails and a bit of screening, for a shovel, for a bit of paint, for some sheeting, for needles and thread. Money to pay *in money* for a trip to town. And, oh, money for hot water and money for soap. A dream of when asking for help does not eat away the last bit of pride. When the office you visit is as nice as the offices of other governmental agencies, when there are enough workers to help you quickly, when workers do not quit in defeat and despair. When you have to tell your story to only one person, and that person can send you for other help and you don't have to prove your poverty over and over and over again.

I have come out of my despair to tell you this. Remember I did not come 15 from another place or another time. Others like me are all around you. Look at us with an angry heart, anger that will help you help me. Anger that will let you tell of me. The poor are always silent. Can you be silent, too?

Thinking Critically about the Text

Throughout the essay, Parker describes the feelings and emotions associated with her poverty. Have you ever witnessed or observed people in Parker's situation? What was your reaction? What are the chances that the dreams described in paragraph 14 will come true? What do you think Parker would say?

Questions on Subject

1. Why didn't Parker have the operation that was recommended for her? Why did she quit her job?

2. In Parker's view, what makes asking for help such a difficult and painful experience? What compels her to do so anyway?

3. Why did Parker's husband leave her? How does she justify her **attitude** toward his leaving?

4. In paragraph 12, Parker says the following about a neighbor giving her a ride to the nearest health clinic: "My neighbor will take me when he goes; but he expects to get paid, *one way or another*. I bet you know my neighbor." What is she implying in these sentences and in the rest of the paragraph?

Questions on Strategy

1. What is Parker's **purpose** in defining poverty as she does? Why has she cast her essay in the form of an extended definition? What effect does this have on the reader?

2. What techniques of definition does Parker use? What is missing that you would expect to find in a more general and impersonal definition of poverty? Why does Parker leave out such information?

3. In depicting poverty, Parker uses **description** to create vivid verbal pictures, and she **illustrates** the various aspects of poverty with examples drawn from her experience. What are the most striking details she uses? How do you account for the emotional impact of the details and images she has selected? In what ways do description and illustration enhance her definition of poverty?

4. Although her essay is written for the most part in simple, straightforward language, Parker does use an occasional striking **figure of speech**. Identify at least three such figures — you might begin with those in paragraph 13 (for example, "Poverty is an acid") — and explain their effect on the reader.

Definition in Action

Without consulting a dictionary, try writing a formal definition for one of the following terms by putting it in a class and then differentiating it from other words in the class. (See pages 305–6 for a discussion of formal definitions together with examples.)

tortilla chips	trombone
psychology	*Fixer Upper*
robin	Catholicism
anger	secretary

Once you have completed your definition, compare it with the definition found in a dictionary. What conclusions can you draw? Explain.

Writing Suggestions

1. Using Parker's essay as a model, write an extended definition of a topic about which you have some expertise. Choose as your subject a particular environment (suburbia, the inner city, a dormitory, a shared living area), a way of living (as the child of divorce, as a person with a disability, as a working student), or a topic of your own choosing. If you prefer, you can adopt a persona instead of writing from your own perspective.

2. **Writing with Sources.** Write a proposal or a plan of action that will make people aware of poverty or some other social problem in your community. How do you define the problem? What needs to be done to increase awareness of it? What practical steps would you propose be undertaken once the public is made aware of the situation? You will likely need to do some research in the library or online in order to garner support for your proposal. For models of and advice on integrating sources in your essay, see Chapters 14 and 15.

What Does "Boys Will Be Boys" Really Mean?

DEBORAH M. ROFFMAN

Courtesy of Deborah Roffman

A nationally certified sexuality and family life edu-cator, Deborah M. Roffman was born in 1948 in Baltimore, Maryland. She graduated from Goucher College in 1968 and later received an M.S. in community health education from Towson University. Since 1975, Roffman has worked with scores of public and private schools on curric-ulum, faculty development, and parent education issues. Her work in health and sex education has been featured in the *New York Times*, *Baltimore Sun*, *Chicago Tribune*, *Los Angeles Times*, *Education Week*, and *Parents* magazine. A former asso-ciate editor of the *Journal of Sex Education and Therapy*, she has appeared on an HBO special on parenting, on National Public Radio, on *The Early Show*, and on *The O'Reilly Factor*. In 2001 Roffman published her first book, *Sex and Sensibility: The Thinking Parent's Guide to Talking Sense about Sex*. Her most recent book is *Talk to Me First: Everything You Need to Know to Become Your Kids' "Go-To" Person about Sex* (2012). Currently Roffman lives in Baltimore, where she teaches human sexuality education in grades 4 through 12.

The following essay was first published in the *Washington Post* on February 5, 2006. Roffman reports that the reaction to this article was overwhelming. "Many people thanked me for underscoring the point that boys and men are also treated disrespectfully in our culture and in some ways even more disrespectfully than girls and women, because of the gender-role stereotyping that defines them in even ani-malistic terms." Here she takes a common expression — "boys will be boys" — and asks us to think about what it really means and how that message affects boys in our society.

Preparing to Read

When you hear the expression "boys will be boys," what comes to mind? What traits or characteristics about boys and men does the expression imply for you?

Three of my seventh-grade students asked the other week if we might   1
view a recent episode of the Fox TV cartoon show *Family Guy* in our
human sexuality class. It's about reproduction, they said, and besides,
it's funny. Not having seen it, I said I'd have to check it out.

Well, there must be something wrong with my sense of humor because   2
most of the episode made me want to alternately scream and cry.

It centers on Stewie, a sexist, foul-mouthed preschooler who hates his 3
mother, fantasizes killing her off in violent ways, and wants to prevent his
parents from making a new baby—until he realizes that he might get to
have a sibling as nasty as he is. Then he starts encouraging his parents' love-
making. At one point he peers into their room and tells his dad to "Give it to
her good, old man." When his father leaves the bed he orders him to "Come
here this instant you fat [expletive] and do her!"

Of course I know that this is farce, but I announced the next day that 4
no, we wouldn't be taking class time to view the episode, titled "Emission
Impossible." When I asked my students why they thought that was, they
guessed: The language? The women dressed like "bimbos"? The implied sexual acts? The mistreatment of the mother?

Nope, nope, nope, I replied. I didn't love any of that, either, but it was the 5
less obvious images and messages that got my attention, the ones that kids
your age *are* less likely to notice. It's not
so much that the boy is always *being*
bad—sometimes that sort of thing can
seem so outrageous it's funny. It's the
underlying assumption in the show,
and often in our society, that boys, by
nature, are bad.

> **It's not so much that the boy is always *being* bad — sometimes that sort of thing can seem so outrageous it's funny. It's the underlying assumption . . . that boys, by nature, are bad.**

I said I thought the "boys will be 6
bad" message of the show was a terribly
disrespectful one, and I wouldn't use my
classroom in any way to reinforce it. It
was a good moment: Recognizing for
the first time the irony that maybe it
was they who were really being demeaned, some of the boys got mad, even
indignant.

You can hear and see evidence of this long-standing folk "wisdom" about 7
boys almost everywhere, from the gender-typed assumptions people make
about young boys to the resigned attitude or blind eye adults so often turn to
disrespectful or insensitive male behavior. Two years ago, when Justin Tim-
berlake grabbed at Janet Jackson's breast during the Super Bowl halftime,
he got a free pass while she was excoriated. As the mother of two sons and
teacher of thousands of boys, the reaction to that incident made me furious,
but perhaps not for the reason you may think: I understood it paradoxically as a twisted kind of compliment to women and a hidden and powerful
indictment of men. Is the female in such instances the only one from whom
we think we can expect responsible behavior?

That incident and so many others explain why, no matter how demean- 8
ing today's culture may seem toward girls and women, I've always understood it to be fundamentally more disrespectful of boys and men—a point

that escapes many of us because we typically think of men as always having the upper hand.

Consider, though, what "boys will be boys" thinking implies about the true nature of boys. I often ask groups of adults or students what inherent traits or characteristics the expression implies. The answers typically are astonishingly negative: Boys are messy, immature, and selfish; hormone-driven and insensitive; irresponsible and troublemaking; rebellious, rude, aggressive, and disrespectful—even violent, predatory, and animal-like.

Is this a window into what we truly think, at least unconsciously, of the male of the species? Is it possible that deep inside we really think they simply can't be expected to do any better than this? How else to explain the very low bar we continue to set for their behavior, particularly when it comes to girls, women, and sex? At a talk I gave recently, a woman in the audience asked, only half in jest, "Is it okay to instruct my daughters that when it comes to sex, teenage boys are animals?" Do we stop to think how easily these kinds of remarks can become self-fulfilling prophecies or permission-giving of the worst kind?

Thanks to popular culture, unfortunately, it only gets worse. Not too long ago, I confiscated a hat from a student's head that read, "I'm a Pimp." This once-derogatory term is a complimentary handle these days for boys whom girls consider "hot." I asked the boy whether he would wear a hat that said "I'm a Rapist." Totally offended, he looked at me as if I had three heads. "Duh," I said. "Do you have any idea what real pimps do to keep their 'girls' in line?" Yet the term—like "slut" for girls—has been glamorized and legitimized by TV, movies, and popular music to such an extent that kids now bandy it about freely.

Just as fish don't know they're in water, young people today, who've been swimming all their formative years in the cesspool that is American popular culture, are often maddeningly incapable of seeing how none of this is in their social, sexual, or personal best interest.

Adults I work with tend to be a lot less clueless. They are sick and tired of watching the advertising and entertainment industries shamelessly pimp the increasingly naked bodies of American women and girls to sell everything from Internet service to floor tiles (I've got the ads to prove it).

Yet from my perspective, these same adults aren't nearly as clued in about how destructive these ubiquitous images and messages can be for boys. It, too, often takes patient coaching for them to see "boys will be boys" for what it is—an insidious and long-neglected character issue: People who think of and treat others as objects, in any way, are not kind, decent people. It's bad enough that boys are being trained by the culture to think that behaving in these ways is "cool"; it's outrageous and much more disturbing that many of the immediate adults in their lives can't see it, and may even buy into it.

The "boys will be bad" stereotype no doubt derives from a time when 15 men were the exclusively entitled gender: Many did behave badly, simply because they could. (Interestingly, that's pretty much how Bill Clinton in hindsight ultimately explained his poor behavior in the Lewinsky affair.) For today's boys, however, the low expectations set for them socially and sexually have less to do with any real entitlement than with the blinders we wear to these antiquated and degrading gender myths.

I think, too, that the staying power of these myths has to do with the fact 16 that as stereotypes go, they can be remarkably invisible. I've long asked students to bring in print advertisements using sex to sell products or showing people as sex objects. No surprise that in the vast majority of ads I receive, women are the focus, not men.

And yet, as I try to teach my students, there's always at least one invisible 17 man present — looking at the advertisement. The messages being delivered to and/or about him are equally if not more powerful.

In one of my least favorite examples, a magazine ad for a video game 18 (brought to me by a sixth-grade boy) depicts a highly sexualized woman with a dominatrix air brandishing a weapon. The heading reads, "Bet you'd like to get your hands on these!," meaning her breasts, er, the game controllers. And the man or boy not in the picture but looking on? The ad implies that he's just another low-life guy who lives and breathes to ogle and grab every large-breasted woman he sees.

Many boys I've talked with are pretty savvy about the permission-giving 19 that "boys will be bad" affords and use it to their advantage in their relationships with adults. "Well, they really don't expect as much from us as they do from girls," said one tenth-grade boy. "It makes it easier to get away with a lot of stuff."

Others play it sexually to their advantage, knowing that in a system 20 where boys are expected to want sex but not necessarily to be responsible about it, the girl will probably face the consequences if anything happens. As long as girls can still be called sluts, the sexual double standard — and its lack of accountability for boys — will rule.

Most boys I know are grateful when they finally get clued in to all this. A 21 fifth-grade boy once told me that the worst insult anyone could possibly give him would be to call him a girl. When I walked him through what he seemed to be saying — that girls are inferior to him — he was suddenly ashamed that he could have thought such a thing. "I'm a better person than that," he said.

Just as we've adjusted the bar for girls in academics and athletics, we 22 need to let boys know that, in the sexual and social arenas, we've been short-changing them by setting the bar so low. We need to explain why the notion that "boys will be boys" embodies a bogus and ultimately corrupting set of expectations that are unacceptable.

We'll know we've succeeded when girls and boys better recognize sexual 23
and social mistreatment and become angry and personally offended whenever anyone dares use the word *slut* against any girl, call any boy a *pimp*, or
suggest that anyone reduce themselves or others to a sexual object.

We'll also know when boys call one another more often on disrespect- 24
ful behavior, instead of being congratulatory, because they will have the
self-respect and confidence that comes with being held to and holding
themselves to high standards.

Thinking Critically about the Text

Why is it important that Roffman ask her readers to think about what the expression "boys will be boys" really means? What does she mean when she says, "We
need to explain why the notion that 'boys will be boys' embodies a bogus and
ultimately corrupting set of expectations that are unacceptable" (paragraph 22)?

Questions on Subject

1. Roffman opens her essay with an anecdote about seventh-graders asking
   to view and discuss an episode of *Family Guy* in their human sexuality class.
   Why did Roffman's students think she did not want to show the episode in
   class? How does she respond to their answers? What about the show does
   Roffman find objectionable?

2. How did some of the boys react when Roffman revealed her reason for not
   viewing the show in class? In what ways was it "a good moment" (paragraph 6)?

3. What about America's advertising and entertainment industries does Roffman
   find objectionable? What does she find disturbing about adult responses to
   the images and messages in so much current advertising and entertainment?

4. What does Roffman see as the source of the "boys will be bad" stereotype?
   Why does she believe this stereotype has such staying power?

Questions on Strategy

1. What is Roffman's **purpose** in writing this essay?

2. Who is Roffman's intended **audience**? To whom do the pronouns *you* in paragraph 7 and *us* and *we* in paragraph 8 refer? What other evidence in Roffman's
   diction do you find to support your conclusion about her audience?

3. In paragraph 10, Roffman asks a series of questions. How do these questions
   function in the context of her essay? How did you answer these questions
   when you first read them?

4. Identify the **analogy** that Roffman uses in paragraph 12. How does this strategy help her explain the plight of today's young people? Explain.

Definition in Action

Consider the following *Grand Avenue* strip by Steve Breen and Mike Thompson.

GRAND AVENUE © 2009 Steve Breen and Mike Thompson. Reprinted by permission of
UNIVERSAL UCLICK for UFS. All rights reserved.

What insights into the nature of definition does the cartoon give you? If you were
asked to help Michael, what advice or suggestions would you give him?

Writing Suggestions

1. Some of the most pressing social issues in American life today are further
   complicated by imprecise definitions of critical terms. Various medical cases,
   for example, have brought worldwide attention to the legal and medical definitions of the word *death*. Debates continue about the meanings of other controversial words, such as these:

values	censorship	success
alcoholism	remedial	happiness
cheating	insanity	life
kidnapping	forgiveness	equality
lying	sex	

   Select one of these words and write an essay in which you discuss not only
   the definition of the term but also the problems associated with defining it.

2. **Writing with Sources.** In analyzing "print advertisements using sex to sell
   products or showing people as sex objects" (paragraph 16), Roffman recounts
   how she and her students discovered that, while most of the ads focused on
   women, "there's always at least one invisible man present — looking at the
   advertisement" (paragraph 17). They conclude that what these ads say or imply
   about this invisible man is not very flattering. Collect several print advertisements that use sex to promote products or show women or men as sex objects
   and analyze one of them. What insights, if any, do these advertisements offer
   about how popular culture portrays and defines both men and women? How
   do you think Roffman would interpret or analyze your advertisement? Write a
   paper in which you report your findings and conclusions. For models of and
   advice on integrating sources in your essay, see Chapters 14 and 15.

The Company Man

ELLEN GOODMAN

Journalist, public speaker, and commentator Ellen Goodman was born in Newton, Massachusetts, in 1941. After graduating from Radcliffe College, she worked as a researcher at *Newsweek* magazine and a reporter at the *Detroit Free Press*. She next moved to the *Boston Globe*, where she wrote an extremely popular and widely syndicated column for over thirty years. In 1980, Goodman won the Pulitzer Prize for Distinguished Commentary. Other awards include the American Society of Newspaper Editors Distinguished Writing Award, the Hubert H. Humphrey Civil Rights Award from

D Dipasupil/Getty Images

the Leadership Conference on Civil Rights, the President's Award by the National Women's Political Caucus, a Nieman Fellowship at Harvard, and the Ernie Pyle Award for Lifetime Achievement from the National Society of Newspaper Columnists. Her books include *Close to Home* (1979), *Value Judgments* (1993), *I Know Just What You Mean: The Power of Friendship in Women's Lives* (2000), and *Paper Trail: Common Sense in Uncommon Times* (2004). In 2012, Goodman founded the Conversation Project, "a public health campaign that aims to change the way people talk about, and prepare for, death — across the nation and beyond."

In this selection, published in her collection *Close to Home*, Goodman chronicles a man's work history, defining a certain type of person and a certain type of career. As you read, pay close attention to the way she uses repetition to reinforce her meaning.

Preparing to Read

What is your concept of a good job? What career path are you interested in? Do you imagine it will involve sacrifices and, if so, what kind? If not, how do you hope to accomplish your professional goals?

H e worked himself to death, finally and precisely, at 3:00 a.m. Sunday 1 morning.

The obituary didn't say that, of course. It said that he died of a 2 coronary thrombosis — I think that was it — but everyone among his friends and acquaintances knew it instantly. He was a perfect Type A, a workaholic, a classic, they said to each other and shook their heads — and thought for five or ten minutes about the way they lived.

This man who worked himself to death finally and precisely at 3 3:00 a.m. Sunday morning — on his day off — was fifty-one years old and a vice-president. He was, however, one of six vice-presidents, and one of three who might conceivably — if the president died or retired soon enough — have moved to the top spot. Phil knew that.

He worked six days a week, five of them until eight or nine at night, during ⁴ a time when his own company had begun the four-day week for everyone but the executives. He worked like the Important People. He had no outside "extracurricular interests," unless, of course, you think about a monthly golf game that way. To Phil, it was work. He always ate egg salad sandwiches at his desk. He was, of course, overweight, by twenty or twenty-five pounds. He thought it was okay, though, because he didn't smoke.

> ❝ **He worked like the Important People.** ❞

On Saturdays, Phil wore a sports ⁵ jacket to the office instead of a suit, because it was the weekend.

He had a lot of people working for him, maybe sixty, and most of them ⁶ liked him most of the time. Three of them will be seriously considered for his job. The obituary didn't mention that.

But it did list his "survivors" quite accurately. He is survived by his wife, ⁷ Helen, forty-eight years old, a good woman of no particular marketable skills, who worked in an office before marrying and mothering. She had, according to her daughter, given up trying to compete with his work years ago, when the children were small. A company friend said, "I know how much you will miss him." And she answered, "I already have."

"Missing him all those years," she must have given up part of herself ⁸ which had cared too much for the man. She would be "well taken care of."

His "dearly beloved" eldest of the "dearly beloved" children is a ⁹ hard-working executive in a manufacturing firm down South. In the day and a half before the funeral, he went around the neighborhood researching his father, asking the neighbors what he was like. They were embarrassed.

His second child is a girl, who is twenty-four and newly married. She ¹⁰ lives near her mother and they are close, but whenever she was alone with her father, in a car driving somewhere, they had nothing to say to each other.

The youngest is twenty, a boy, a high-school graduate who has spent the ¹¹ last couple of years, like a lot of his friends, doing enough odd jobs to stay in grass and food. He was the one who tried to grab at his father, and tried to mean enough to him to keep the man at home. He was his father's favorite. Over the last two years, Phil stayed up nights worrying about the boy.

The boy once said, "my father and I only board here." ¹²

At the funeral, the sixty-year-old company president told the forty- ¹³ eight-year-old widow that the fifty-one-year-old deceased had meant much to the company and would be missed and would be hard to replace. The widow didn't look him in the eye. She was afraid he would read her bitterness and, after all, she would need him to straighten out her finances — the stock options and all that.

Phil was overweight and nervous and worked too hard. If he wasn't at   14
the office, he was worried about it. Phil was a Type A, a heart-attack natural.
You could have picked him out in a minute from a lineup.

So when he finally worked himself to death, at precisely 3:00 a.m.   15
Sunday morning, no one was really surprised.

By 5:00 p.m. the afternoon of the funeral, the company president had   16
begun, discreetly of course, with care and taste, to make inquiries about his
replacement. One of three men. He asked around: "Who's been working
the hardest?"

Thinking Critically about the Text

Goodman tells us that Phil was "overweight, by twenty or twenty-five pounds. He
thought it was okay, though, because he didn't smoke" (paragraph 4). Why do
you think she includes these details? Is Phil's employer in any way responsible
for Phil's being overweight? Was Phil responsible for knowing the risks of being
overweight, or stressed, whether or not he smoked? Do you think social values
and expectations contributed to Phil's death?

Questions on Subject

1. What is a Type A personality? Where does Goodman define this phrase?

2. What does Goodman mean when she writes that Phil "worked himself to
   death"? How did his job as an executive who sat at a desk **cause** him to die
   at 3 a.m. on a Sunday when he was not even at the office?

3. According to Goodman, why did Phil work as hard as he did? Are there other
   explanations you can imagine?

4. Goodman tells us Phil was an executive but does not tell us what he actually
   did, what kind of job he had. Why do you think Goodman did not include Phil's
   specific profession?

Questions on Strategy

1. What is Goodman's **purpose** in this essay? How do you know?

2. Why do you think Goodman waits till the end of her third paragraph to use the
   name of the man she is writing about (Phil)? What is the effect of referring to
   him as "he" or "the man" until that point?

3. What **evidence** does Goodman use to develop her definition of a *company
   man*? Make a list and then describe the overall picture these examples paint.

4. Goodman uses a lot of numbers in this essay: For example, Phil was one
   of "six vice presidents" (paragraph 3); "maybe sixty" people worked for him
   (paragraph 6); and "the sixty-year-old company president told the forty-eight-
   year-old widow that the fifty-one-year-old deceased . . . would be hard to
   replace" (paragraph 13). What do all these numbers add to the selection?

Definition in Action

Definitions are often dependent on one's perspective. Discuss with your classmates other words or terms — such as *success*, *failure*, *wealth*, *poverty*, *cheap*, *expensive*, *happiness*, *loneliness*, *want*, *need* — whose definitions often are dependent on one's perspective. Write brief definitions for several of these words from *your* perspective. Share your definitions with other members of your class. What differences in perspective, if any, are apparent in the definitions?

Writing Suggestions

1. When discussing people, we often resort to personality labels to identify or define them — *leader*, *procrastinator*, *workaholic*, *obsessive-compulsive*, *liar*, *addict*, *athlete*, *genius*, *mentor*, and so on. But such labels can be misleading because one person's idea of what a leader or a workaholic is doesn't necessarily match another person's idea. Write an essay in which you explain the defining characteristics for one of these personality types or for one personality type of your own choosing. Be sure to use examples to illustrate each of the defining characteristics.

2. **Writing with Sources.** Does working extremely hard and striving to excel *require* neglecting one's mental and physical health? Research the connection between the Type A personality and stress, and write an essay reporting your findings. What strategies and attitudes can be used to help manage stress, and how effective are they? What other precautions can highly driven and competitive people take to ensure their well-being? Be sure to consult scholarly scientific resources (for example, the *New England Journal of Medicine*, the American Psychological Association, or the Centers for Disease Control and Prevention) as well as popular journals. Also consider field research; you might interview some highly successful professionals to learn their perspectives on this issue. For models of and advice on integrating sources into your essay, see Chapters 14 and 15.

Virtue Signaling and Other Inane Platitudes

MARK PETERS

Mark Peters

Mark Peters is a writer, lexicographer, and humor- ist based in Chicago, Illinois. He is a graduate of the Second City Writing Program and a member of the American Dialect Society. Unsurprisingly, one of his favorite topics to write about is lan- guage and the curious — and humorous — ways we use it. Currently, Peters writes the Best Joke Ever column for *McSweeney's*, an online humor publication and part of a literary publishing company, as well as a regular column on euphemisms at Thinkmap's *Visual Thesaurus*. His work has also appeared in *Esquire*, *New Scientist, Psychology Today*, and *Slate*, among other publications. In 2015, Three Rivers Press published his book *Bullshit: A Lexicon*.

In this essay, which was published in the *Boston Globe* in 2015, Peters unpacks the term "virtue signaling" and its use in online writing. As you read, make note of the different strategies Peters uses to provide a thorough, clear, and precise definition of "virtue signaling," including examples and a brief history of how the concept gained attention in the media.

Preparing to Read

Do you ever use online social media to raise awareness of issues, share your political opinions, or show solidarity with others over social and political causes? For exam- ple, have you ever changed your Facebook avatar to express sympathy for victims or support an organization? Do you think these individual and collective actions make a difference?

H ave you changed your Facebook avatar to support a cause? Did you 1 take the ice bucket challenge? Have you ever offered your thoughts and prayers in the aftermath of a disaster? Do you express your beliefs through hashtags?

There's actually a name for that: virtue signaling. This newly promi- 2 nent phrase sums up actions (mostly online) that send the message "I'm a good person"—though they might not be accompanied by doing anything good at all. Since the only thing people seem to like more than virtue sig- naling is judging other people, this term has caught on like, well, the ice bucket challenge.

> " Since the only thing people seem to like more than virtue signaling is judging other people, this term has caught on like, well, the ice bucket challenge. "

James Bartholomew appeared to have 3 coined the term in an April 18, 2015, article in The (London) Spectator called "Hating the Daily Mail is a substitute for doing good." In that article, Bartholomew discussed pretentious signs at Whole Foods, outrage at cheesecake pictures of women, and comedians attacking bankers as examples of virtue signaling. The common denominator is the emptiness of the gestures. As Bartholomew puts it, "No one actually has to do anything. Virtue comes from mere words or even from silently held beliefs." While Bartholomew can be thanked for repopularizing virtue signaling, he didn't coin it. Paul McFedries's terrific Word Spy site records a message board use from 2004 that discussed "Virtue signaling at its most pedestrian."

Since April, the phrase "virtue signaling" has turned up in a variety of 4 publications. Most often, it's used by conservatives to slam liberals, as in this comment on a Breitbart article: "The progressives ruin everything they touch with their endless virtue signaling and smug illusion of preening moral superiority." That type of insulting generalization is discussed in The (Scotland) Herald, where Catriona Stewart wrote, "The charge of virtue-signalling is a lazy tool of those on the right to condemn the left as woolly-thinking and naïve."

Sometimes conservatives use the phrase to criticize each other, too. In 5 an interview with The Daily Beast, Ann Coulter blasted, "this whole culture of virtue-signaling where debates are about nothing. Look, Republicans all agree 100 percent that we are pro-Israel, pro-life, pro-gun. So why do we spend so much time on these issues? It's just pandering, so who are they pandering to?" Pandering, whether for the approval of voters or friends, is a major ingredient of virtue signaling.

Though virtue signaling has a form that is quite common in insults used 6 by the right to mock the left, it is a bit different. Geoffrey Nunberg—a linguist who teaches at the University of California Berkeley School of Information and is author of "Talking Right: How Conservatives Turned Liberalism into a Tax-Raising, Latte-Drinking, Sushi-Eating, Volvo-Driving, New York Times-Reading, Body-Piercing, Hollywood-Loving, Left-Wing Freak Show"—said via e-mail that this term is a departure from previous insults: "Like 'latte-sipping,' 'Volvo-driving' and the rest, 'virtue signaling' belongs chiefly to the right. But it's not really comparable. For one thing, it's a gerund, not a participle—that is, it functions as a noun and not an adjective. Second, it's a clunky mouthful—it doesn't trip off the tongue, it stumbles. And it's abstract. It doesn't bring a vivid image to mind—a car, a drink, a dish, a sport—but only describes the vague object of a certain kind of behavior, which the right believes is exclusive to the left."

Clunky or not, virtue signaling has proven useful in discussing   7 self-glorifying online behavior, regardless of politics. As lexicographer Orin Hargraves pointed out by e-mail, "It aptly describes what a lot of people's Facebook status updates are about (probably mine, too)." Hargraves called the term "an artifact of the profusion of social media, especially Facebook and Twitter in which there is no barrier to entry for anyone who wants to broadcast a sentiment (or 'send a message,' to use the familiar cliché)." Therefore "we need new terms to characterize the quality, content, or intent of such messages, and virtue-signaling falls right into that category. Another bunch of related and productive neologisms are the -shaming compounds: slut-shaming, fat-shaming, pet-shaming, and now prayer-shaming."

Prayer shaming has a very close relationship to virtue signaling in that it   8 shares a lexical form but has an opposite meaning. When people are scolded for offering their thoughts and prayers after a tragedy instead of actually doing something helpful—classic value signaling—the scolding is called prayer shaming. Comedian Anthony Jeselnik was ahead of the curve in prayer shaming, as his most recent standup special, "Thoughts and Prayers," called out people who write inane, unoriginal platitudes on the day of a tragedy. Emily Brewster, an associate editor at Merriam-Webster, mentions another related word: "I like the academic—or even clinical—ring virtue-signaling has to it. It reminds me of the more quotidian humblebrag, which has done pretty well since it came on the scene in 2011. Both refer so efficiently to especially social media behavior that we encounter (or find ourselves engaging in) so often."

Humblebrag was coined by the late comedian Harris Wittels, and it   9 is the closest lexical relation to virtue signaling. Wittels's coinage highlighted self-aggrandizement cloaked in humility, such as when zillionaire Mark Cuban tweeted, "It was right around this date in November when I was 27 years old that I remember looking at a 0 dollar bank balance at the ATM. . ." While Cuban likely meant to portray himself as someone who understands hard times and was once broke, the message that actually registers is how impressive it is that he became rich. Humblebragging and virtue signaling both involve a certain kind of social media post that says one thing on the surface ("I'm no big deal!" or "What is wrong with the world?") but also say another ("I'm a very big deal!" or "I'm the last decent person left in the world"). It's likely we'll see more such words over time, as the free-for-all of online discourse gets fully described.

Virtue signaling is likely to be a top contender for the American Dialect   10 Society's Word of the Year award, since it's so applicable to the endless stream of social media chatter that few of us can resist. It's also a great reminder that doing stuff is more important than saying stuff, and that we are all united—conservative or liberal, young or old—in finding our Facebook friends annoying.

Thinking Critically about the Text

Peters suggests that supporting causes online, expressing beliefs in hashtags, and participating in social media events such as the ice bucket challenge are mere "virtue signaling." Do you agree with this judgment? Are there ways to interpret these activities in a more positive light?

Questions on Subject

1. How does Peters define "virtue signaling"? What is the problem with it, according to the writer?

2. What is the partisan and political context for virtue signaling? For example, who are usually targets of the term? Why is that context important for Peters's definition?

3. What is a "humblebrag," and how is it related to virtue signaling? What message does a "humblebrag" convey?

4. In his conclusion, Peters suggests that "doing stuff is better than saying stuff" (paragraph 10). Do you agree with his distinction between posting online and taking action? Why, or why not?

Questions on Strategy

1. The writer begins this essay with a series of **rhetorical questions** for his readers. How are these questions related to his definition? Do you find this **beginning** effective? If not, how else could he have begun the essay?

2. In the essay, Peters cites several authorities on language, including a linguist and a lexicographer. Why do you think he does this? What does this expert testimony add to his discussion? Point to a specific example and explain.

3. Where does Peters incorporate **comparison and contrast** into this essay? How does this strategy help support his purpose?

4. What do you think is Peters's **purpose** in this essay? Does he assume that his readers are familiar with the practice of virtue signaling, or does he want to inform them of the practice? Or, do you think he wants to change the attitudes or behavior of his **audience**? Explain.

Definition in Action

In small groups, brainstorm a list of general or abstract terms whose meaning is open to interpretation, such as *liberty*, *success*, or *genius*. After choosing one (or more) of these to define, write down a brief stipulative definition of the term from your perspective. Then, discuss your different definitions as a class. How do the different definitions reflect different viewpoints and values? How might disagreements over definitions lead to other, larger arguments that impact your education, career, school, or community?

Writing Suggestions

1. Peters concludes by claiming that "we are all united . . . in finding our Facebook friends annoying" (paragraph 10). What online social media behaviors do you find especially annoying? Briefly define and explain one of the more annoying characteristics, activities, or behaviors that you have observed. Make sure to provide **description** and **illustration** to help make your definition clear and concrete.

2. As Peters's essay shows, the term "virtue signaling" has a negative **connotation**, particularly in the context of our polarized political discourse. His definition and examples mostly reinforce that negative view, as when he implies that the practice is "annoying" (paragraph 10). But does Peters provide a fair interpretation and a reasonable definition of these online behaviors? Can social media be used for good, perhaps to raise awareness or money for causes or to show solidarity? Using Peters's essay as a model, write an essay that redeems, reframes, and perhaps renames "virtue signaling" to defend these online activities — and to respond to the use of the term as an insult.

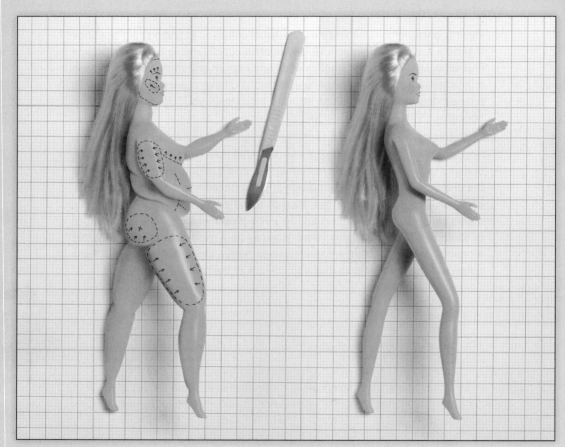

Peter Dazeley/Getty Images

CHAPTER 11

Cause and Effect Analysis

WHAT IS CAUSE AND EFFECT ANALYSIS?

PEOPLE EXHIBIT THEIR NATURAL CURIOSITY ABOUT THE WORLD BY asking questions. These questions represent a fundamental human need to find out how things work. Whenever a question asks *why*, answering it will require discovering a *cause* or a series of causes for a particular *effect*; whenever a question asks *what if*, its answer will point out the effect or effects that can result from a particular cause. Cause and effect analysis, then, explores the relationship between events or circumstances and the outcomes that result from them.

VISUALIZING CAUSE AND EFFECT ANALYSIS

The image that opens this chapter depicts a "before and after" scenario in which a female doll has plastic surgery to transform it into an "ideal" Barbie shape. Can you identify from the various visual cues what specific procedures need to be done? How do the position and framing of the subjects in the image create a cause and effect strategy? What are some of the cultural and social implications suggested by the image? What is your opinion of those implications? Is the figure on the left a cause or an effect, or both? Is the figure on the right a cause or an effect, or both? Explain.

UNDERSTANDING CAUSE AND EFFECT ANALYSIS AS A WRITING STRATEGY

You will have frequent opportunity to use cause and effect analysis in your college writing. For example, a history instructor might ask you to explain the causes of the Six-Day War between Israel and its neighbors. In a paper for an American literature course, you might try to determine why *Huckleberry Finn* has sparked so much controversy in a number of schools and communities. On an environmental studies exam, you might have to speculate about the long-term effects acid rain will have on the ecology of northeastern Canada and the United States. Demonstrating an understanding of cause and effect is crucial to the process of learning.

One common use of the strategy is for the writer to identify a particular causal agent or circumstance and then discuss the consequences or effects it has had or may have. In the following passage from *Telephone* by John Brooks, it is clear from the first sentence that the author is primarily concerned with the effects that the telephone has had or may have had on modern life:

<table>
<tr>
<td>**First sentence establishes purpose in the form of a question**</td>
<td>What has the telephone done to us, or for us, in the hundred years of its existence? A few effects suggest themselves at once. It has saved lives by getting rapid word of illness, injury, or famine from remote places. By joining with the elevator to make possible the multistory residence or office building, it has made possible — for better or worse — the modern city. By bringing about a quantum leap in the speed and ease with which information moves from place to place, it has greatly accelerated the rate of scientific and technolog-</td>
</tr>
<tr>
<td>**A series of negative effects with the telephone as cause**</td>
<td>ical change and growth in industry. Beyond doubt it has crippled if not killed the ancient art of letter writing. It has made living alone possible for persons with normal social impulses; by so doing, it has played a role in one of the greatest social changes of this century, the breakup of the multigenerational household. It has made the waging of war chillingly more efficient than formerly. Perhaps (though not provably) it has prevented wars that might have arisen out of international misunderstanding caused by written communication. Or perhaps — again not provably — by magnifying and extending irrational personal conflicts based on voice contact, it has caused wars. Certainly it has extended the scope of human conflicts, since it impartially disseminates the useful knowledge of scientists and the babble of bores, the affection of the affectionate and the malice of the malicious.</td>
</tr>
</table>

The bulk of Brooks's paragraph is devoted to answering the very question he poses in his opening sentence: "What has the telephone done to us, or for us, in the hundred years of its existence?" Notice that even though many of the effects Brooks discusses are verifiable or probable, he is willing to admit that he is speculating about those effects that he cannot prove.

A second common use of the strategy is to reverse the forms by first examining the effect; the writer describes an important event or problem (effect) and then examines the possible reasons (causes) for it. For example, experts might trace the causes of poverty to any or all of the following: poor education, a nonprogressive tax system, declining commitment to social services, inflation, discrimination, or even the welfare system that is designed to help those most in need.

A third use of the strategy is for the writer to explore a complex causal chain. In this selection from his book *The Politics of Energy*, Barry Commoner examines the series of malfunctions that led to the near disaster at the Three Mile Island nuclear facility in Harrisburg, Pennsylvania:

> On March 28, 1979, at 3:53 a.m., a pump at the Harrisburg plant failed. Because the pump failed, the reactor's heat was not drawn off in the heat exchanger and the very hot water in the primary loop overheated. The pressure in the loop increased, opening a release valve that was supposed to counteract such an event. But the valve stuck open and the primary loop system lost so much water (which ended up as a highly radioactive pool, six feet deep, on the floor of the reactor building) that it was unable to carry off all the heat generated within the reactor core. Under these circumstances, the intense heat held within the reactor could, in theory, melt its fuel rods, and the resulting "meltdown" could then carry a hugely radioactive mass through the floor of the reactor. The reactor's emergency cooling system, which is designed to prevent this disaster, was then automatically activated, but when it was, apparently, turned off too soon, some of the fuel rods overheated. This produced a bubble of hydrogen gas at the top of the reactor. (The hydrogen is dissolved in the water in order to react with oxygen that is produced when the intense reactor radiation splits water molecules into their atomic constituents. When heated, the dissolved hydrogen bubbles out of the solution.) This bubble blocked the flow of cooling water so that despite the action of the emergency cooling system the reactor core was again in danger of melting down. Another danger was that the gas might contain enough oxygen to cause an explosion that could rupture the huge containers that surround the reactor and release a deadly cloud of radioactive material into the surrounding countryside.

Tracing a causal chain, as Commoner does here, is similar to narration. The writer must organize the events sequentially to show clearly how each event leads to the next.

In a causal chain, an initial cause brings about a particular effect, which in turn becomes the immediate cause of a further effect, and so on, bringing about a series of effects that also act as new causes. The so-called domino effect is a good illustration of the idea of a causal chain; the simple tipping over of a domino (initial cause) can result in the toppling of any number of dominoes down the line (series of effects). For example, before a salesperson approaches an important client about a big sale, she prepares extensively for the meeting (initial cause). Her preparation causes her to impress the client (effect A), which guarantees her the big sale (effect B), which in turn results in her promotion to district sales manager (effect C). The sale she made is the most immediate and most obvious cause of her promotion, but it is possible to trace the chain back to its more essential cause: her hard work preparing for the meeting.

While the ultimate purpose of cause and effect analysis may seem simple — to know or to understand why something happens — determining causes and effects is often a thought-provoking and complex exercise. One reason for this complexity is that some causes are less obvious than others. *Immediate causes* are readily apparent because they are closest in time to the effect; the immediate cause of a flood, for example, may be the collapse of a dam. However, *remote causes* may be just as important, even though they are not as apparent and are perhaps even hidden. The remote (and, in fact, primary) cause of the flood might have been an engineering error or the use of substandard building materials or the failure of personnel to relieve the pressure on the dam caused by unseasonably heavy rains. In many cases, it is necessary to look beyond the most immediate causes to discover the true underlying sources of an event.

A second reason for the complexity of this strategy is the difficulty of distinguishing between possible and actual causes, as well as between possible and actual effects. An upset stomach may be caused by spoiled food, but it may also be caused by overeating, by flu, by nervousness, by pregnancy, or by a combination of factors. Similarly, an increase in the cost of electricity may have multiple effects: higher profits for utility companies, fewer sales of electrical appliances, higher prices for other products that depend on electricity in their manufacture, and even the development of alternative sources of energy. Making reasonable choices among the various possibilities requires thought and care.

▶ Purposes of Cause and Effect Analysis

Writers may use cause and effect analysis for three essential purposes: to inform, to speculate, and to argue.

1. Most commonly, writers will want to *inform* — to help their readers understand some identifiable fact. A state wildlife biologist, for example, might wish to tell the public about the effects severe winter weather has had on the state's deer herds. Similarly, in a newsletter, a member of Congress might explain to his or her constituency the reasons changes are being made in the federal tax system.

2. Cause and effect analysis may also allow writers to *speculate* — to consider what might be or what might have been. Pollsters estimate the effects that various voter groups will have on future elections, and historians evaluate how the current presidency will continue to influence American government in the coming decades.

3. Finally, cause and effect analysis provides an excellent basis from which to *argue* a given position or point of view. An editorial writer, for example, could argue that bringing a professional basketball team into the area would have many positive effects on the local economy and on the community as a whole.

USING CAUSE AND EFFECT ANALYSIS ACROSS THE DISCIPLINES

When writing essays in the academic disciplines, you will have many opportunities to use the strategy of cause and effect analysis to both organize and strengthen the presentation of your ideas. To determine whether cause and effect analysis is the right strategy for you in a particular paper, use the guidelines described in Chapter 2, "Determining a Strategy for Developing Your Essay" (pages 34–35). Consider the following examples:

Native American History

1. **MAIN IDEA:** Treaties between Native American groups and the U.S. government had various negative impacts on the Native Americans involved.
2. **QUESTION:** What have been some of the most harmful results for Native Americans of treaties between Native American groups and the U.S. government?
3. **STRATEGY:** Cause and effect analysis. The word *results* signals that this study needs to examine the harmful effects of the provisions of the treaties.
4. **SUPPORTING STRATEGY:** Illustration. Examples need to be given of both treaties and their consequences.

Nutrition

1. **MAIN IDEA:** A major factor to consider when examining why people suffer from poor nutrition is poverty.
2. **QUESTION:** What is the relationship between poverty and nutrition?
3. **STRATEGY:** Cause and effect analysis. The word *relationship* signals a linkage between poverty and nutrition. The writer has to determine what is meant by poverty and poor nutrition in this country or in the countries examined.
4. **SUPPORTING STRATEGY:** Definition. Precise definitions of *nutrition* and *poverty* will first be necessary in order for the writer to make valid judgments concerning the causal relationship in question.

Nursing

1. **MAIN IDEA:** Alzheimer's disease is the progressive loss of brain nerve cells caused by an overproductive protein, leading to gradual loss of memory, concentration, understanding, and in some cases sanity.

2. **QUESTION:** What role does the overproduction of a protein that destroys nerve cells play in the development of Alzheimer's disease, and what causes the overproduction in the first place?

3. **STRATEGY:** Cause and effect analysis. The words *role*, *play*, and *causes* signal that the issue here is determining and explaining how Alzheimer's disease originates.

4. **SUPPORTING STRATEGY:** Process analysis describing how Alzheimer's operates will be essential to making the reader understand its cause and effects.

PRACTICAL ADVICE FOR WRITING AN ESSAY OF CAUSE AND EFFECT ANALYSIS

As you plan, write, and revise your cause and effect analysis, be mindful of the writing process guidelines described in Chapter 2. Pay particular attention to the basic requirements and essential ingredients of this writing strategy.

▶ Planning Your Essay of Cause and Effect Analysis

Establish Your Focus.   Decide whether your essay will propose causes, talk about effects, or analyze both causes and effects. Any research you do and any questions you ask will depend on how you wish to concentrate your attention. For example, let's say that as a reporter for the local news web site, you are writing a story about a fire that destroyed an apartment building in the neighborhood, killing four people. In planning your story, you might focus on the cause of the fire: Was there more than one cause? Was carelessness to blame? Was the fire of suspicious origin? You might focus on the effects of the fire: How much damage was done to the building? How many people had to find housing? What was the impact on the families of the four victims? Or you might cover both the reasons for this tragic event and its ultimate effects, setting up a sort of causal chain. Such focus is crucial as you gather information.

Determine Your Purpose.   Once you begin to draft your essay and as you continue to refine it, make sure your purpose is clear. Do you wish your cause and effect analysis to be primarily informative, speculative, or argumentative? An informative essay allows readers to say, "I learned something from this. I didn't know that the fire was caused by faulty wiring." A speculative essay suggests to readers new possibilities: "That never occurred to me before. The apartment house could indeed be replaced by an office building." An argumentative essay convinces readers that some sort of action should be taken: "I have to agree: Fire inspections should occur more regularly in our neighborhood."

Formulate a Thesis Statement. Every essay needs a strong, clear thesis statement. When you are writing an essay using cause and effect analysis, your thesis statement should clearly present either a cause and its effect(s) or an effect and its cause(s). As a third approach, your essay could focus on a complex causal chain of events. Here are a couple of examples from this chapter:

- "*What has the telephone done to us, or for us, in the hundred years of its existence?*" (page 340) This opening sentence signals that the essay will explore the effects of a single cause, the telephone.
- "*On March 28, 1979, at 3:53 a.m., a pump at the Harrisburg plant failed.*" (page 341) Here, the pump failure introduces a causal chain of events leading to the disaster at Three Mile Island.

When you begin to formulate your thesis statement, keep these examples in mind. You can find other examples of thesis statements in the essays throughout this book. As you begin to develop your thesis statement, ask yourself, "What is my point?" Next, ask yourself, "What approach to a cause and effect essay will be most useful in making my point?" If you can't answer these questions yet, write down some ideas and try to determine your main point from those ideas.

▶ Organizing Your Essay of Cause and Effect Analysis

Avoid Oversimplification and Errors of Logic. Sound and thoughtful reasoning, while present in all good writing, is central to any analysis of cause and effect. Writers of convincing cause and effect analysis must examine their material objectively and develop their essays carefully, taking into account any potential objections that readers might raise. Therefore, do not jump to conclusions or let your prejudices interfere with the logic of your interpretation or the completeness of your presentation.

Be sure that you do not oversimplify the cause and effect relationship you are writing about. A good working assumption is that most important matters cannot be traced to a single verifiable cause; similarly, a cause or set of causes rarely produces a single isolated effect. To be believable, your analysis of your topic must demonstrate a thorough understanding of the surrounding circumstances; readers are unlikely to be convinced by a single-minded determination to show one particular connection. For example, someone writing about how the passage of a tough new crime bill (cause) has led to a decrease in arrests in a particular area (effect) will have little credibility unless other possible causes—socioeconomic conditions, seasonal fluctuations in crime, the size and budget of the police force, and so on—are also examined and taken into account. Of course, to achieve coherence, you will want to emphasize the important causes or the most significant effects. Just be careful not to lose your reader's trust by insisting on an oversimplified "X leads to Y" relationship.

The other common problem in cause and effect analysis is lack of evidence in establishing a cause or an effect. This error is known as the "after this, therefore because of this" fallacy (in Latin, *post hoc, ergo propter hoc*). In attempting to discover an explanation for a particular event or circumstance, a writer may point to something that merely preceded it in time, assuming a causal connection where none has in fact been proven. For example, if you have dinner out one evening and the next day come down with stomach cramps, you may blame your illness on the restaurant where you ate the night before; you do so without justification, however, if your only proof is the fact that you ate there beforehand. More evidence would be required to establish a causal relationship. The *post hoc, ergo propter hoc* fallacy is often harmlessly foolish ("I failed the exam because I lost my lucky key chain"). It can, however, lead writers into serious errors of judgment and blind them to more reasonable explanations of cause and effect. And, like oversimplification, such mistakes in logic can undercut a reader's confidence. Make sure that the causal relationships you cite are, in fact, based on demonstrable evidence and not merely on a temporal connection.

Use Other Rhetorical Strategies.   Although cause and effect analysis can be used effectively as a separate writing strategy, it is more common for essays to combine different strategies. For example, in an essay about a soccer team's victories, you might use comparison and contrast to highlight the differences between the team's play in two losses and in five victories. Narration from interviews might also be used to add interest and color. An essay about social media might incorporate the strategy of argumentation as well as definition to defend the openness and effectiveness of a particular social network. The argument could analyze exactly how the benefits outweigh the drawbacks, while definition could be used to focus the subject matter to better achieve your purpose. By combining strategies, you can gain both clarity and forcefulness in your writing. (For more on combining strategies, see Chapter 13.)

▶ Revising and Editing Your Essay of Cause and Effect Analysis

Revision is best done by asking yourself key questions about what you have written. Begin by reading, preferably aloud, what you have written. Reading aloud forces you to pay attention to every word, and you are more likely to catch lapses in the logic. Once you have caught any major errors, use

Chapter 16 along with the following guidelines and questions to help you make your corrections.

Select Words That Strike a Balanced Tone. Be careful to neither overstate nor understate your position. Avoid exaggerations like "there can be no question" and "the evidence speaks for itself." Such diction is usually annoying and undermines your interpretation. Instead, allow your analysis of the facts to convince readers of the cause and effect relationship you wish to suggest. At the same time, no analytical writer convinces by continually understating or qualifying information with words and phrases such as *it seems that, perhaps, maybe, I think, sometimes, most often, nearly always,* or *in my opinion.* While it may be your intention to appear reasonable, overusing such qualifying words can make you sound unclear or indecisive, and it renders your analysis less convincing. Present your case forcefully, but do so honestly and sensibly.

Share Your Draft with Others. Ask a fellow student to look over your draft. Have the student tell you what he or she thinks is the point of your analysis, and whether your causal relationship seems reasonable. The guidelines in the "Brief Guide to Peer Critiquing" box in Chapter 2 (pages 38–39) will help make the peer review more effective. After getting feedback from a classmate, answer the questions in the box that follows and see Chapter 16 for advice on solving common writing problems.

Questions for Revising and Editing: Cause and Effect Analysis

1. Why do I want to use cause and effect analysis: to inform, to speculate, or to argue? Does my analysis help me achieve my purpose?

2. Is my topic manageable for the essay I wish to write? Have I effectively established my focus?

3. Does my thesis statement clearly state either the cause and its effects or the effect and its causes?

4. Is there a causal chain? Have I identified immediate and remote causes? Have I distinguished between possible and actual causes and effects?

5. Have I been able to avoid oversimplifying the cause and effect relationship I am writing about? Are there any errors in my logic?

6. Is there another rhetorical strategy that I can use with cause and effect analysis to assist me in achieving my purpose? If so, have I been able to implement it with care so that I have not altered either the direction or the tone of my essay?

7. Is my tone balanced, neither overstating nor understating my position?

8. Have I taken every opportunity to use words and phrases that signal cause and effect relationships?

9. Have I used *affect* and *effect* properly?

10. Have I avoided errors in grammar, punctuation, and mechanics? Is my sentence style as clear, smooth, and persuasive as possible?

STUDENT ESSAY USING CAUSE AND EFFECT ANALYSIS AS A WRITING STRATEGY

While he was a student at the University of Vermont, Kevin Cunningham shared an apartment near the Burlington waterfront with several other students. There he became interested in the effects that upscale real estate development—or gentrification—would have on his neighborhood. After gathering information by talking with people who lived in his neighborhood, Cunningham found it useful to discuss both the causes and the effects of gentrification in his well-unified essay.

Gentrification
Kevin Cunningham

Epigraph sets the theme

> I went back to Ohio, and my city was gone. . . .
> —Chrissie Hynde, of the Pretenders

My city is in Vermont, not Ohio, but soon my city might be gone, too. Or maybe it's I who will be gone. My street, Lakeview Terrace, lies unobtrusively in the old northwest part of Burlington and is notable, as its name suggests, for spectacular views of Lake Champlain framed by the Adirondacks. It's not that *Thesis* the neighborhood is going to seed, though — quite the contrary. Recently it has been discovered, and now it is on the verge of being gentrified. For some of us who live here, that's bad.   1

Well-organized and unified paragraph: describes life cycle of city neighborhoods

Cities are often assigned human characteristics, one of which is a life cycle: They have a birth, a youth, a middle age, and an old age. A neighborhood is built and settled by young, vibrant people, proud of their sturdy new homes. Together, residents and houses mature, as families grow larger and extensions get built on. Eventually, though, the neighborhood begins to show its age. Buildings sag a little, houses aren't repainted as quickly, and maintenance slips. The neighborhood may grow poorer, as the young and upwardly mobile find new jobs and move away, while the older and less successful inhabitants remain.   2

Lists possible results when neighborhoods age

One of three fates awaits the aging neighborhood. Decay may continue until the neighborhood becomes a slum. It may face urban renewal, with old buildings being razed and ugly, new apartment houses taking their place. Finally, it may undergo redevelopment,   3 in which government encourages the upgrading of existing housing stock by offering low-interest loans or outright grants. This last possibility would mean that the original character of the neighborhood may be retained or restored, allowing the city to keep part of its identity.

Supporting strategy (illustration): example of Hoboken

An example of redevelopment at its best is Hoboken, New Jersey. In the early 1970s Hoboken was a dying city, with rundown housing and many abandoned buildings. However, low-interest loans enabled some younger residents to begin to refurbish their homes, and soon the area began to show signs of renewed vigor. Outsiders moved in and rebuilt some of the abandoned houses. Today, whole blocks have been restored, and neighborhood life is active again. The city does well, too, because property values are higher and so are property taxes. There, at least for my neighborhood, is the rub.

Effects of redevelopment on Hoboken

Transition: writer moves from example of Hoboken to his Lakeview Terrace neighborhood

Lakeview Terrace is a demographic potpourri of students and families, young professionals and elderly retirees, homeowners and renters. It's a quiet street where kids can play safely and the neighbors know each other. Most of the houses are fairly old and look it, but already some redevelopment has begun. Recently, several old houses were bought by a real estate company, rebuilt, and sold as condominiums; the new residents drive BMWs and keep to themselves. The house where I live is owned by a young professional couple, and they have renovated the place to what it must have looked like when it was new. They did a nice job, too. These two kinds of development are the main forms of gentrification, and so far they have done no real harm.

Describes "gentrification" to date

Writer describes chain of events

The city is about to start a major property tax reappraisal, however. Because of the renovations, the houses on Lakeview Terrace are currently worth more than they used to be; soon there will be a big jump in property taxes. That's when a lot of people will be hurt — possibly even evicted from their own neighborhood.

Organization: effects of gentrification on local property owners

Clem is a retired General Electric employee who has lived on Lakeview for over thirty years and who owns his home. About three years ago some condos were built on the lot next door, which didn't please Clem — he says they just don't fit in. With higher property taxes, however, it may be Clem who no longer fits in. At the very least, since he's on a fixed income, he will have to make sacrifices in order to stay. Ryan works as a mailman and also owns his Lakeview Terrace home, which is across the street from the houses that were converted into condos: same cause, same effect.

Organization: effects of gentrification on renters

Then there are those who rent. As landlords have to pay higher property taxes, they will naturally raise rents at least as much (and maybe more, if they've spent money on renovations of their own). Some renters won't be able to afford the increase and will have to leave. "Some renters" almost certainly includes me, as well as others who have lived on Lakeview Terrace much longer than I have. In fact, the exodus has already begun, with the people who were displaced by the condo conversions.

8

Conclusion

Of course, many people would consider what's happening on Lakeview Terrace a genuine improvement in every way, resulting not only in better-looking houses but also in a better class of people. I dispute that. The new people may be more affluent than those they displace, but certainly not "better," not by any standard that matters. Gentrification may do wonders for a neighborhood's aesthetics, but it certainly can be hard on its soul.

9

Restatement of thesis

Student Reflection
Kevin Cunningham

Q. I know that you are a relaxed, fluent talker: Is writing as easy for you?

A. I don't mind writing at all, but I hate doing rewrites. Actually, I always have trouble getting started, and I can spend a lot of time trying to get the first couple of paragraphs or the first page down, but once I get started I can roar right along to the end. In fact, I need to, because if I stop to think too much about any part I can lose the thread. After I finish a draft I let it sit and then go back to it, and that's when I can see what works and what doesn't. I enjoy the second draft because I can see the paper as a whole, but the third draft is just torture. I guess I don't have the patience—it's like I've done this twice already. But I see that it has to be done again.

Q. So it's the revision that makes writing harder than talking.

A. That's part of it. But the two tie in. When I write, even if it's on a dry topic, I like to write the way I talk, in a conversational tone. Even recently when I was writing a paper for business, I found myself writing that way. I hate formal, pretentious prose.

Q. But your gentrification essay, when I read it, doesn't "sound" to me quite the same as your conversation.

A. Yeah, in writing you have to finish your sentences, specify your nouns, make sure you're understood. It has to be more precise. You'll have to fix up this interview if you're going to print it. [Editor's note: Kevin was right.]

Q. In gathering information for your paper, did you distinguish between cause and effect and mere coincidence?

A. You have to know your subject, and you have to be honest. For example, my downstairs neighbors moved out last month because the rent was raised. Somebody who didn't know the situation might say, "See? Gentrification." But that wasn't the reason—it's that heating costs went up. This is New England, and we have had a cold winter; gentrification had nothing to do with it. It's something that's just beginning to happen and it's going to have a big effect, but we haven't actually felt many of its effects here yet.

Q. So, are you using cause and effect analysis to predict the future?

A. Is there any other way?

Q. Tell me more about your revisions.

A. In my first draft, I strung things together almost on a geographical basis, as if I were walking down Lakeview Terrace talking with my neighbors—which is actually one of the things I did. For my second draft, to show my professor, I was just polishing the writing. Then he showed me the logic wasn't quite there—it jumped around from one idea to another, and I took some stuff for granted that needed explaining. Also, I used to think of a cause and effect paper as just an explanation of why something happens; but I was writing about a subject that affects me, so part of me wanted to keep it objective and part of me was trying to say what I feel. My professor said, "Look, if you want to say something, just use this as your vehicle for saying it." So I felt much freer when I went back to revise again, because I could say what I wanted to say.

Your Response

What did you learn from Kevin Cunningham's essay and reflection on the writing process of writing the essay? What challenges do you expect to face as you write your own cause and effect analysis essay? Based on Kevin's composing strategies and the practical advice discussed earlier in this chapter (pages 344–47), what writing choices will you make?

How Boys Become Men

JON KATZ

Journalist and novelist Jon Katz was born in 1947. He writes with a keen understanding of life in contemporary suburban America. Each of his four mystery novels is a volume in the Suburban Detective Mystery series: *The Family Stalker* (1994), *Death by Station Wagon* (1994), *The Father's Club* (1996), and *The Last Housewife* (1996). The best known of these novels, *The Last Housewife*, won critical praise for its insights into the pressures and conflicts experienced by

James Lattanzo

young professional couples in their efforts to achieve the American dream. Katz is also the author of *Media Rants: Post-politics in the Digital Nation* (1997), a collection of his newspaper columns dealing primarily with the role and influence of the media in the public life of modern America; *Virtuous Reality: How Americans Surrendered Discussion of Moral Values to Opportunists, Nitwits, and Blockheads Like William Bennett* (1998); and *Geeks: How Two Lost Boys Rode the Internet Out of Idaho* (2000). *The Second-Chance Dog: A Love Story* (2013) and *Talking to Animals: How You Can Understand Animals and They Can Understand You* (2017) continue his recent focus on writing fiction and nonfiction about dogs.

In the following essay, first published in January 1993 in *Glamour*, Katz explains why many men appear to be insensitive.

Preparing to Read

How important are childhood experiences to the development of identity? How do the rituals of the playground, the slumber party, and the neighborhood gang help mold us as men and women? Write about one or two examples from your own experience.

Two nine-year-old boys, neighbors and friends, were walking home from school. The one in the bright blue windbreaker was laughing and swinging a heavy-looking book bag toward the head of his friend, who kept ducking and stepping back. "What's the matter?" asked the kid with the bag, whooshing it over his head. "You chicken?"

His friend stopped, stood still, and braced himself. The bag slammed into the side of his face, the thump audible all the way across the street where I stood watching. The impact knocked him to the ground, where he lay mildly stunned for a second. Then he struggled up, rubbing the side of his head. "See?" he said proudly. "I'm no chicken."

No. A chicken would probably have had the sense to get out of the way. 3
This boy was already well on the road to becoming a *man*, having learned one
of the central ethics of his gender: Experience pain rather than show fear.

Women tend to see men as a giant problem in need of solution. They tell 4
us that we're remote and uncommunicative, that we need to demonstrate less
machismo and more commitment, more humanity. But if you don't understand something about boys, you can't understand why men are the way we
are, why we find it so difficult to make friends or to acknowledge our fears
and problems.

Boys live in a world with its own Code of Conduct, a set of ruthless, 5
unspoken, and unyielding rules:

> Don't be a goody-goody.
> Never rat. If your parents ask about bruises, shrug.
> Never admit fear. Ride the roller coaster, join the fistfight, do what you
> have to do. Asking for help is for sissies.
> Empathy is for nerds. You can help your best buddy, under certain cir-
> cumstances. Everyone else is on his own.
> Never discuss anything of substance with anybody. Grunt, shrug, dump
> on teachers, laugh at wimps, talk about comic books. Anything else is risky.

Boys are rewarded for throwing hard. Most other activities—reading, 6
befriending girls, or just thinking—are considered weird. And if there's one
thing boys don't want to be, it's weird.

More than anything else, boys are supposed to learn how to handle 7
themselves. I remember the bitter fifth-grade conflict I touched off by
elbowing aside a bigger boy named Barry and seizing the cafeteria's last carton of chocolate milk. Teased for getting aced out by a wimp, he had to
reclaim his place in the pack. Our fistfight, at recess, ended with my knees
buckling and my lip bleeding while my friends, sympathetic but out of range,
watched resignedly.

When I got home, my mother took one look at my swollen face and 8
screamed. I wouldn't tell her anything, but when my father got home I cracked
and confessed, pleading with them to do nothing. Instead, they called Barry's
parents, who restricted his television for a week.

The following morning, Barry and six of his pals stepped out from 9
behind a stand of trees. "It's the rat," said Barry.

I bled a little more. *Rat* was scrawled in crayon across my desk. 10

They were waiting for me after school for a number of afternoons to 11
follow. I tried varying my routes and avoiding bushes and hedges. It usually
didn't work.

I was as ashamed for telling as I was frightened. "You did ask for it," said 12
my best friend. Frontier Justice has nothing on Boy Justice.

In panic, I appealed to a cousin who was several years older. He followed [13]
me home from school, and when Barry's gang surrounded me, he came
barreling toward us. "Stay away from my cousin," he shouted, "or I'll kill you."

After they were gone, however, my cousin could barely stop laughing. [14]
"You were afraid of *them*?" he howled. "They barely came up to my waist."

Men remember receiving little mercy as boys; maybe that's why it's [15]
sometimes difficult for them to show any.

> " Men remember
> receiving little mercy
> as boys; maybe that's
> why it's sometimes
> difficult for them to
> show any. "

"I know lots of men who had happy [16]
childhoods, but none who have happy
memories of the way other boys treated
them," says a friend. "It's a macho mara-
thon from third grade up, when you start
butting each other in the stomach."

"The thing is," adds another friend, [17]
"you learn early on to hide what you feel.
It's never safe to say, 'I'm scared.' My girl-
friend asks me why I don't talk more about what I'm feeling. I've gotten
better at it, but it will *never* come naturally."

You don't need to be a shrink to see how the lessons boys learn affect their [18]
behavior as men. Men are being asked, more and more, to show sensitivity,
but they dread the very word. They struggle to build their increasingly uncertain work lives but will deny they're in trouble. They want love, affection, and
support but don't know how to ask for them. They hide their weaknesses
and fears from all, even those they care for. They've learned to be wary of
intervening when they see others in trouble. They often still balk at being
stigmatized as weird.

Some men get shocked into sensitivity—when they lose their jobs, their [19]
wives, or their lovers. Others learn it through a strong marriage, or through
their own children.

It may be a long while, however, before male culture evolves to the point [20]
that boys can learn more from one another than how to hit curve balls. Last
month, walking my dog past the playground near my house, I saw three boys
encircling a fourth, laughing and pushing him. He was skinny and rumpled,
and he looked frightened. One boy knelt behind him while another pushed
him from the front, a trick familiar to any former boy. He fell backward.

When the others ran off, he brushed the dirt off his elbows and walked [21]
toward the swings. His eyes were moist and he was struggling for control.

"Hi," I said through the chain-link fence. "How ya doing?" [22]

"Fine," he said quickly, kicking his legs out and beginning his swing. [23]

Thinking Critically about the Text

Do you agree with Katz that men in general are less communicative, less sensitive, and less sympathetic in their behavior than women? Why or why not? Where does "Boy Justice" originate?

Questions on Subject

1. Why, according to Katz, do "women tend to see men as a giant problem in need of solution" (paragraph 4)?

2. In paragraph 3, Katz states that one of the "central ethics" of his gender is "Experience pain rather than show fear." Would you agree with Katz?

3. What is it that boys are supposed to learn "more than anything else" (paragraph 7)? What do you think girls are supposed to learn more than anything else?

4. How, according to Katz, do some men finally achieve sensitivity? Can you think of other softening influences on adult males?

Questions on Strategy

1. This essay was originally published in *Glamour* magazine. Can you find any places where Katz addresses himself specifically to an **audience** of young women? Where? Why?

2. Early in the essay, Katz refers to men as "we," but later he refers to men as "they." What is the purpose of this change?

3. Notice that in paragraphs 16 and 17, Katz quotes two friends on the nature of male development. Why is the location of these quotes crucial to the structure of the essay?

4. Katz illustrates his thesis with three anecdotes. Identify each of them. Where in the essay is each located? How do they differ? How does each enhance the author's message?

Cause and Effect Analysis in Action

Think about what might be necessary to write an essay similar to Katz's that explores how children grow to adulthood in a specific country (for instance, "How Americans Become Adults"). If we assume, as Katz does, that who we are is the product of our early experiences, what aspects of national cultures might shape us? How might they do so? Share your thoughts with others in your class.

Writing Suggestions

1. Write an essay patterned on "How Boys Become Men," showing the causes and effects surrounding females growing up in American culture. In preparing to write, it may be helpful to review your response to the Preparing to Read

prompt as well as ideas generated by the Cause and Effect Analysis in Action activity for this selection. You might come to the conclusion that women do not have a standard way of growing up; you could also write a cause and effect essay supporting this idea. Either way, be sure to include convincing examples. (You might also draw connections with Paulina Porizkova's essay "America Made Me a Feminist.")

2. **Writing with Sources.** The subject of the differences between men and women perpetually spawns discussion and debate, much of it finding its way into lectures, articles, and even books. Research the types of gender roles that Katz discusses in his essay, or responses to those gender roles, perhaps from writers who argue for a different or changing **definition** of gender. Write an essay explaining the causes and/or effects of gender roles as you see them today. Try to incorporate visuals as sources to analyze, respond to, and use to support your thesis. For example, how does the following image challenge or reinforce gender stereotypes? You may wish to work this image into your discussion, or find other images. As with any source, be sure to properly cite your use of any image (see Chapter 15, "List of Works Cited").

Westend61 GmbH / Alamy

The Downside of Diversity

MICHAEL JONAS

Michael Jonas, who has been a journalist since the early 1980s, is an executive editor of *CommonWealth* magazine, a quarterly focused on politics, ideas, and civic life in Massachusetts. Jonas was born in 1959 in Ann Arbor, Michigan, and received his bachelor's degree in history from Hampshire College in 1981. Before joining the *CommonWealth* staff in 2001, Jonas was a contributing writer for the magazine. His cover story for *CommonWealth*'s Fall 1999 issue on youth

Mary Beth Meehan

antiviolence workers was selected for a PASS (Prevention for a Safer Society) Award from the National Council on Crime and Delinquency. His 2009 article on the centralization of power in the Massachusetts House of Representatives won an award for commentary and analysis from Capitolbeat, the national organization of state capitol reporters and editors.

In the following article, first published August 5, 2007, on the web site of the *Boston Globe*, Jonas reports on a Harvard political scientist who finds that diversity hurts civic life. "Be fearless in your willingness to probe difficult questions and write uncomfortable truths," comments Jonas. "Not only do I hope my article does this, but it is, in many ways, what Robert Putnam, the Harvard scholar whose study I write about, confronted himself in publishing research results that are at odds with what he would have hoped to find."

Preparing to Read

Do you think that people who live in ethnically diverse communities demonstrate stronger or weaker civic engagement and interconnectedness than people who live in homogeneous communities? What are your reasons for thinking as you do?

It has become increasingly popular to speak of racial and ethnic diversity as a civic strength. From multicultural festivals to pronouncements from political leaders, the message is the same: Our differences make us stronger.

But a massive new study, based on detailed interviews of nearly 30,000 people across America, has concluded just the opposite. Harvard political scientist Robert Putnam—famous for *Bowling Alone*, his 2000 book on declining civic engagement—has found that the greater the diversity in a community, the fewer people vote and the less they volunteer, the less they give to charity and work on community projects. In the most diverse communities, neighbors trust one another about half as much as they do in the most homogeneous settings. The study, the largest ever on civic engagement in America, found that virtually all measures of civic health are lower in more diverse settings.

"The extent of the effect is shocking," says Scott Page, a University of 3 Michigan political scientist.

The study comes at a time when the future of the American melting 4 pot is the focus of intense political debate, from immigration to race-based admissions to schools, and it poses challenges to advocates on all sides of the issues. The study is already being cited by some conservatives as proof of the harm large-scale immigration causes to the nation's social fabric. But with demographic trends already pushing the nation inexorably toward greater diversity, the real question may yet lie ahead: how to handle the unsettling social changes that Putnam's research predicts.

"We can't ignore the findings," says Ali Noorani, executive director of 5 the Massachusetts Immigrant and Refugee Advocacy Coalition. "The big question we have to ask ourselves is, what do we do about it; what are the next steps?"

The study is part of a fascinating new portrait of diversity emerging 6 from recent scholarship. Diversity, it shows, makes us uncomfortable—but discomfort, it turns out, isn't always a bad thing. Unease with differences helps explain why teams of engineers from different cultures may be ideally suited to solve a vexing problem. Culture clashes can produce a dynamic give-and-take, generating a solution that may have eluded a group of people with more similar backgrounds and approaches. At the same time, though, Putnam's work adds to a growing body of research indicating that more diverse populations seem to extend themselves less on behalf of collective needs and goals.

His findings on the downsides of diversity have also posed a chal- 7 lenge for Putnam, a liberal academic whose own values put him squarely in the pro-diversity camp. Suddenly finding himself the bearer of bad news, Putnam has struggled with how to present his work. He gathered the initial raw data in 2000 and issued a press release the following year outlining the results. He then spent several years testing other possible explanations.

When he finally published a detailed scholarly analysis in June in the 8 journal *Scandinavian Political Studies*, he faced criticism for straying from data into advocacy. His paper argues strongly that the negative effects of diversity can be remedied and says history suggests that ethnic diversity may eventually fade as a sharp line of social demarcation.

"Having aligned himself with the central planners intent on sustaining 9 such social engineering, Putnam concludes the facts with a stern pep talk," wrote conservative commentator Ilana Mercer, in a recent *Orange County Register* op-ed titled "Greater diversity equals more misery."

Putnam has long staked out ground as both a researcher and a civic   10
player, someone willing to describe social problems and then have a hand in
addressing them. He says social science should be "simultaneously rigorous
and relevant," meeting high research standards while also "speaking to concerns of our fellow citizens." But on a topic as charged as ethnicity and race,
Putnam worries that many people hear only what they want to.

"It would be unfortunate if a politically correct progressivism were to   11
deny the reality of the challenge to social solidarity posed by diversity," he
writes in the new report. "It would be equally unfortunate if an ahistorical
and ethnocentric conservatism were to deny that addressing that challenge is
both feasible and desirable."

Putnam is the nation's premier guru of civic engagement. After studying   12
civic life in Italy in the 1970s and 1980s, Putnam turned his attention to
the United States, publishing an influential journal article on civic engagement in 1995 that he expanded five years later into the best-selling *Bowling
Alone*. The book sounded a national wake-up call on what Putnam called a
sharp drop in civic connections among Americans. It won him audiences
with presidents Bill Clinton and George W. Bush and made him one of the
country's best-known social scientists.

> " Birds of different feathers may sometimes flock together, but they are also less likely to look out for one another. "

Putnam claims the United States has   13
experienced a pronounced decline in
social capital, a term he helped popu-
larize. Social capital refers to the social
networks—whether friendships or religious congregations or neighborhood
associations—that he says are key indicators of civic well-being. When social
capital is high, says Putnam, communi-
ties are better places to live. Neighborhoods are safer; people are healthier;
and more citizens vote.

The results of his new study come from a survey Putnam directed   14
among residents in forty-one U.S. communities, including Boston.
Residents were sorted into the four principal categories used by the U.S.
Census: black, white, Hispanic, and Asian. They were asked how much they
trusted their neighbors and those of each racial category and questioned
about a long list of civic attitudes and practices, including their views on
local government, their involvement in community projects, and their
friendships. What emerged in more diverse communities was a bleak picture of civic desolation, affecting everything from political engagement to
the state of social ties.

Putnam knew he had provocative findings on his hands. He worried   15
about coming under some of the same liberal attacks that greeted Daniel
Patrick Moynihan's landmark 1965 report on the social costs associated with

the breakdown of the black family. There is always the risk of being pilloried as the bearer of "an inconvenient truth," says Putnam.

After releasing the initial results in 2001, Putnam says he spent time 16 "kicking the tires really hard" to be sure the study had it right. Putnam realized, for instance, that more diverse communities tended to be larger, have greater income ranges, higher crime rates, and more mobility among their residents — all factors that could depress social capital independent of any impact ethnic diversity might have.

"People would say, 'I bet you forgot about X,'" Putnam says of the string 17 of suggestions from colleagues. "There were twenty or thirty Xs."

But even after statistically taking them all into account, the connection 18 remained strong: Higher diversity meant lower social capital. In his findings, Putnam writes that those in more diverse communities tend to "distrust their neighbors, regardless of the color of their skin, to withdraw even from close friends, to expect the worst from their community and its leaders, to volunteer less, give less to charity and work on community projects less often, to register to vote less, to agitate for social reform more but have less faith that they can actually make a difference, and to huddle unhappily in front of the television."

"People living in ethnically diverse settings appear to 'hunker down' — that 19 is, to pull in like a turtle," Putnam writes.

In documenting that hunkering down, Putnam challenged the two 20 dominant schools of thought on ethnic and racial diversity, the "contact" theory and the "conflict" theory. Under the contact theory, more time spent with those of other backgrounds leads to greater understanding and harmony between groups. Under the conflict theory, that proximity produces tension and discord.

Putnam's findings reject both theories. In more diverse communities, he 21 says, there were neither great bonds formed across group lines nor heightened ethnic tensions, but a general civic malaise. And in perhaps the most surprising result of all, levels of trust were not only lower between groups in more diverse settings, but even among members of the same group.

"Diversity, at least in the short run," he writes, "seems to bring out the 22 turtle in all of us."

The overall findings may be jarring during a time when it's become 23 commonplace to sing the praises of diverse communities, but researchers in the field say they shouldn't be.

"It's an important addition to a growing body of evidence on the challenges 24 created by diversity," says Harvard economist Edward Glaeser.

In a recent study, Glaeser and colleague Alberto Alesina demonstrated 25 that roughly half the difference in social welfare spending between the United States and Europe — Europe spends far more — can be attributed to the greater ethnic diversity of the U.S. population. Glaeser says lower national social welfare spending in the United States is a "macro" version of the decreased civic engagement Putnam found in more diverse communities within the country.

Economists Matthew Kahn of UCLA and Dora Costa of MIT 26 reviewed fifteen recent studies in a 2003 paper, all of which linked diversity with lower levels of social capital. Greater ethnic diversity was linked, for example, to lower school funding, census response rates, and trust in others. Kahn and Costa's own research documented higher desertion rates in the Civil War among Union Army soldiers serving in companies whose soldiers varied more by age, occupation, and birthplace.

Birds of different feathers may sometimes flock together, but they are 27 also less likely to look out for one another. "Everyone is a little self-conscious that this is not politically correct stuff," says Kahn.

So how to explain New York, London, Rio de Janeiro, Los Angeles— 28 the great melting-pot cities that drive the world's creative and financial economies?

The image of civic lassitude dragging down more diverse communities 29 is at odds with the vigor often associated with urban centers, where ethnic diversity is greatest. It turns out there is a flip side to the discomfort diversity can cause. If ethnic diversity, at least in the short run, is a liability for social connectedness, a parallel line of emerging research suggests it can be a big asset when it comes to driving productivity and innovation. In high-skill workplace settings, says Scott Page, the University of Michigan political scientist, the different ways of thinking among people from different cultures can be a boon.

"Because they see the world and think about the world differently than 30 you, that's challenging," says Page, author of *The Difference: How the Power of Diversity Creates Better Groups, Firms, Schools, and Societies.* "But by hanging out with people different than you, you're likely to get more insights. Diverse teams tend to be more productive."

In other words, those in more diverse communities may do more bowl- 31 ing alone, but the creative tensions unleashed by those differences in the workplace may vault those same places to the cutting edge of the economy and of creative culture.

Page calls it the "diversity paradox." He thinks the contrasting positive 32 and negative effects of diversity can coexist in communities, but "there's got to be a limit." If civic engagement falls off too far, he says, it's easy to imagine the positive effects of diversity beginning to wane as well. "That's what's unsettling about his findings," Page says of Putnam's new work.

Meanwhile, by drawing a portrait of civic engagement in which more 33 homogeneous communities seem much healthier, some of Putnam's worst fears about how his results could be used have been realized. A stream of conservative commentary has begun—from places like the Manhattan Institute and the *American Conservative*—highlighting the harm the study suggests will come from large-scale immigration. But Putnam says he's also received hundreds of complimentary e-mails laced with bigoted language. "It certainly is not pleasant when David Duke's Web site hails me as the guy who found out racism is good," he says.

In the final quarter of his paper, Putnam puts the diversity challenge in 34 a broader context by describing how social identity can change over time. Experience shows that social divisions can eventually give way to "more encompassing identities" that create a "new, more capacious sense of 'we,'" he writes.

Growing up in the 1950s in a small midwestern town, Putnam knew 35 the religion of virtually every member of his high school graduating class because, he says, such information was crucial to the question of "who was a possible mate or date." The importance of marrying within one's faith, he says, has largely faded since then, at least among many mainline Protestants, Catholics, and Jews.

While acknowledging that racial and ethnic divisions may prove more 36 stubborn, Putnam argues that such examples bode well for the long-term prospects for social capital in a multiethnic America.

In his paper, Putnam cites the work done by Page and others, and 37 uses it to help frame his conclusion that increasing diversity in America is not only inevitable, but ultimately valuable and enriching. As for smoothing over the divisions that hinder civic engagement, Putnam argues that Americans can help that process along through targeted efforts. He suggests expanding support for English-language instruction and investing in community centers and other places that allow for "meaningful interaction across ethnic lines."

Some critics have found his prescriptions underwhelming. And in offering 38 ideas for mitigating his findings, Putnam has drawn scorn for stepping out of the role of dispassionate researcher. "You're just supposed to tell your peers what you found," says John Leo, senior fellow at the Manhattan Institute, a conservative think tank. "I don't expect academics to fret about these matters."

But fretting about the state of American civic health is exactly what 39 Putnam has spent more than a decade doing. While continuing to research questions involving social capital, he has directed the Saguaro Seminar, a project he started at Harvard's Kennedy School of Government that promotes efforts throughout the country to increase civic connections in communities.

"Social scientists are both scientists and citizens," says Alan Wolfe, direc- 40 tor of the Boisi Center for Religion and American Public Life at Boston

College, who sees nothing wrong in Putnam's efforts to affect some of the phenomena he studies.

Wolfe says what is unusual is that Putnam has published findings as 41 a social scientist that are not the ones he would have wished for as a civic leader. There are plenty of social scientists, says Wolfe, who never produce research results at odds with their own worldview.

"The problem too often," says Wolfe, "is people are never uncomfortable 42 about their findings."

Thinking Critically about the Text

If ethnic diversity seems to be a liability, at least in the short term, why does Putnam think it's "ultimately valuable and enriching" (paragraph 37)?

Questions on Subject

1. What are the effects of greater social diversity that Putnam's research reveals? What's being lost and gained? How serious are the losses, as Putnam sees them?

2. Why did Putnam worry about the effects that his research might have on his fellow social scientists and on the public at large?

3. What **evidence** related to the world's most vibrant cities seems to contradict the findings in Putnam's study?

4. What are Putnam's suggestions for increasing social capital within diverse ethnic communities? Do you think those efforts are worthwhile? Why, or why not?

Questions on Strategy

1. How does cause and effect analysis work in Jonas's essay? Does it work only on the level of diversity and its effects?

2. In paragraph 38, conservative think-tank fellow John Leo is scornful of Putnam's role as an advocate for diversity. Do you agree with Leo's criticism of Putnam? Why, or why not?

3. Examine Jonas's essay for examples of his use of outside authorities and evidence. How has this **evidence** from outside sources helped him to provide perspective on the issues he discusses?

4. Is Jonas objective about the results and implications of Putnam's research, or does he reveal his own **attitude** about them? Explain.

Cause and Effect Analysis in Action

Determining causes and effects requires careful thought. Establishing a causal chain of events is no less demanding, but it can also bring clarity and understanding to many complex issues. Consider the following example involving the H1N1 virus, or swine flu:

ultimate cause According to the Centers for Disease Control (CDC), this virus was originally referred to as "swine flu" because laboratory testing showed that many of the genes in this new virus were very similar to influenza viruses that normally occur in pigs (swine) in North America. But further study has shown that this new virus is very different from what normally circulates in North American pigs. It has two genes from flu viruses that normally circulate in pigs in Europe and Asia, bird (avian) genes, and human genes. Scientists call this a "quadruple reassortant" virus.

immediate cause Contact with surfaces that have the flu virus on them and then touching the mouth or nose or eyes

effect Influenza (fever, cough, sore throat, runny or stuffy nose, body aches, headache, chills and fatigue, possible vomiting and diarrhea)

effect Possible death; possible pandemic

Develop a causal chain for each of the following cause and effect pairs. Then mix two of the pairs (for example, develop a causal chain for vacation/anxiety). Be prepared to discuss your answers with the class.

terror/alert   making a speech/anxiety

vacation/relaxation   climate change/technological innovation

Writing Suggestions

1. In the note that precedes this selection, Jonas suggests that you "be fearless in your willingness to probe difficult questions and write uncomfortable truths." Write an essay in which you examine more deeply the implications of Jonas's advice. Why does he consider it good and necessary advice to follow? What might be the difficult-to-deal-with effects of following that advice?

2. **Writing with Sources.** Write an essay in which you examine your own ideas about diversity at all levels. What do you think are its benefits and its negative aspects? How might we as Americans work to achieve more social integration and understanding? In thinking about your topic, you might want to consider the lessons that American history has taught us about how waves of immigrants gradually learned to live in mutually beneficial settings. Do some research to consider also the measures that have been taken legally, socially, economically, and in other ways to maintain respect for diversity as well as social cohesion.

Coca-Cola Funds Scientists' Effort to Alter Obesity Battle

ANAHAD O'CONNOR

Anahad O'Connor was born as the second youngest in a family of seven children in New York City in 1981. As a high school senior, he was selected as a *New York Times* College Scholar, and he went on to receive a bachelor's degree in psychology from Yale University. He began his writing career at the *New York Times* in 2003, writing for the weekly Tuesday science section. Since then, he has expanded his coverage to include politics, metropolitan and breaking news, and consistent contributions to the paper's Health and Wellness blog. He is the author of four books, including *Never Shower in a Thunderstorm: Surprising Facts and Misleading Myths about Our Health and the World We Live In* (2007) and *Lose It! The Personalized Weight Loss Revolution* (2010).

This article appeared on the *New York Times* Health and Wellness blog on August 9, 2015. Consider the cause that Coca-Cola is attributing to obesity. Does O'Connor agree with the company's assessment? How does he make his case, and what other causes — and potential effects — does he bring to the reader's attention?

Preparing to Read

What is your relationship with your weight? Has a doctor ever advised you to lose or gain weight? Have you tried to address the issues with diet, exercise, or a combination of the two? How successful have you been? If you have always maintained a healthy weight, why do you think that is the case?

Coca-Cola, the world's largest producer of sugary beverages, is backing a new "science-based" solution to the obesity crisis: To maintain a healthy weight, get more exercise and worry less about cutting calories.

The beverage giant has teamed up with influential scientists who are advancing this message in medical journals, at conferences and through social media. To help the scientists get the word out, Coke has provided financial and logistical support to a new nonprofit organization called the Global Energy Balance Network, which promotes the argument that weight-conscious Americans are overly fixated on how much they eat and drink while not paying enough attention to exercise.

"Most of the focus in the popular media and in the scientific press is, 'Oh they're eating too much, eating too much, eating too much'—blaming fast food, blaming sugary drinks and so on," the group's vice president, Steven N. Blair, an exercise scientist, says in a recent video announcing the new organization. "And there's really virtually no compelling evidence that that, in fact, is the cause."

> **Funding from the food industry is not uncommon in scientific research. But studies suggest that the funds tend to bias findings.**

Health experts say this message is misleading and part of an effort by Coke to deflect criticism about the role sugary drinks have played in the spread of obesity and Type 2 diabetes. They contend that the company is using the new group to convince the public that physical activity can offset a bad diet despite evidence that exercise has only minimal impact on weight compared with what people consume.

This clash over the science of obesity comes in a period of rising efforts to tax sugary drinks, remove them from schools and stop companies from marketing them to children. In the last two decades, consumption of full-calorie sodas by the average American has dropped by 25 percent.

"Coca-Cola's sales are slipping, and there's this huge political and public backlash against soda, with every major city trying to do something to curb consumption," said Michele Simon, a public health lawyer. "This is a direct response to the ways that the company is losing. They're desperate to stop the bleeding."

Coke has made a substantial investment in the new nonprofit. In response to requests based on state open records laws, two universities that employ leaders of the Global Energy Balance Network disclosed that Coke had donated $1.5 million last year to start the organization.

Since 2008, the company has also provided close to $4 million in funding for various projects to two of the organization's founding members: Blair, a professor at the University of South Carolina whose research over the past 25 years has formed much of the basis of federal guidelines on physical activity, and Gregory A. Hand, dean of the West Virginia University School of Public Health.

Records show that the network's website, gebn.org, is registered to Coca-Cola headquarters in Atlanta, and the company is also listed as the site's administrator. The group's president, James O. Hill, a professor at the University of Colorado School of Medicine, said Coke had registered the website because the network's members did not know how.

"They're not running the show," he said. "We're running the show."

Coca-Cola's public relations department repeatedly declined requests for an interview with its chief scientific officer, Rhona Applebaum. In a statement, the company said it had a long history of supporting scientific research related to its beverages and topics such as energy balance.

"We partner with some of the foremost experts in the fields of nutrition and physical activity," the statement said. "It's important to us that the researchers we work with share their own views and scientific findings, regardless of the outcome, and are transparent and open about our funding."

Blair and other scientists affiliated with the group said that Coke had   13
no control over its work or message and that they saw no problem with the
company's support because they had been transparent about it.

But as of last week, the group's Twitter and Facebook pages, which   14
promote physical activity as a solution to chronic disease and obesity
while remaining largely silent on the role of food and nutrition, made no
mention of Coca-Cola's financial support. The group's website also omitted
mention of Coke's backing until Yoni Freedhoff, an obesity expert at the
University of Ottawa, wrote to the organization to inquire about its funding.
Blair said this was an oversight that had been quickly corrected.

"As soon as we discovered that we didn't have not only Coca-Cola but   15
other funding sources on the website, we put it on there," Blair said. "Does
that make us totally corrupt in everything we do?"

Funding from the food industry is not uncommon in scientific research.   16
But studies suggest that the funds tend to bias findings. A recent analysis of
beverage studies, published in the journal *PLOS Medicine*, found that those
funded by Coca-Cola, PepsiCo, the American Beverage Association and the
sugar industry were five times more likely to find no link between sugary drinks
and weight gain than studies whose authors reported no financial conflicts.

The group says there is "strong evidence" that the key to preventing   17
weight gain is not reducing food intake—as many public health experts
recommend—"but maintaining an active lifestyle and eating more calories."
To back up this contention, the group provides links on its website to two
research papers, each of which contains this footnote: "The publication of
this article was supported by The Coca-Cola Company."

Hill said he had sought money from Coke to start the nonprofit because   18
there was no funding available from his university. The group's website says
it is also supported by a few universities and ShareWIK Media Group, a
producer of videos about health. Hill said that he had also received a commitment of help from General Mills, as well as promises of support from
other businesses, which had not formally confirmed their offers.

He said he believed public health authorities could more easily change   19
the way people eat by working with the food industry instead of against it.

On its website, the group recommends combining greater exercise and   20
food intake because, Hill said, "'Eat less' has never been a message that's been
effective. The message should be 'Move more and eat smarter.'"

He emphasized that weight loss involved a combination of complex fac-   21
tors and that his group's goal was not to play down the role of diet or to
portray obesity as solely a problem of inadequate exercise.

"If we are out there saying it's all about physical activity and it's not about   22
food, then we deserve criticism," he said. "But I think we haven't done that."

While people can lose weight in several ways, many studies suggest that   23
those who keep it off for good consume fewer calories. Growing evidence

also suggests that maintaining weight loss is easier when people limit their intake of high glycemic foods such as sugary drinks and other refined carbohydrates, which sharply raise blood sugar.

Physical activity is important and certainly helps, experts say. But studies show that exercise increases appetite, causing people to consume more calories. Exercise also expends far fewer calories than most people think. A 12-ounce can of Coca-Cola, for example, contains 140 calories and roughly 10 teaspoons of sugar. "It takes 3 miles of walking to offset that one can of Coke," said Barry M. Popkin, a professor of global nutrition at the University of North Carolina at Chapel Hill.   24

Kelly D. Brownell, dean of the Sanford School of Public Policy at Duke University, said that as a business, Coke "focused on pushing a lot of calories in, but then their philanthropy is focused on the calories out part, the exercise."   25

In recent years, Coke has donated money to build fitness centers in more than 100 schools across the country. It sponsors a program called "Exercise Is Medicine" to encourage doctors to prescribe physical activity to patients. And when Chicago's City Council proposed a soda tax in 2012 to help address the city's obesity problem, Coca-Cola donated $3 million to establish fitness programs in more than 60 of the city's community centers.   26

The initiative to tax soda ultimately failed.   27

"Reversing the obesity trend won't happen overnight," Coca-Cola said in an ad for its Chicago exercise initiative. "But for thousands of families in Chicago, it starts now, with the next pushup, a single situp or a jumping jack."   28

Thinking Critically about the Text

O'Connor points out that the scientists backed by Coca-Cola "promote physical activity as a solution to chronic disease and obesity while remaining largely silent on the role of food and nutrition" (paragraph 14). Why does he feel this message is misleading and potentially harmful? Do you agree? Why, or why not?

Questions on Subject

1. Explain the title of O'Connor's article: "Coca-Cola Funds Scientists' Effort to Alter Obesity Battle." How does this title prepare the reader for the argument that is to follow? Be specific.

2. What does O'Connor think is the main cause of obesity?

3. O'Connor says that "Coke has provided financial and logistical support" (paragraph 2) to the Global Energy Balance Network. According to O'Connor, what is the mission of this network, and why is Coca-Cola's support relevant?

4. O'Connor writes, "In recent years, Coke has donated money to build fitness centers in more than 100 schools across the country" (paragraph 26). What does this have to do with the "Exercise Is Medicine" campaign and Coke's financing of the Global Energy Balance Network?

Questions on Strategy

1. How does O'Connor use cause and effect analysis in his essay? Cite several examples.

2. O'Connor ends the fifteenth paragraph with a citation from Global Energy Balance Network's vice president Steven N. Blair: "Does that [neglecting to list Coca-Cola as a sponsor, allegedly by accident] make us totally corrupt in everything we do?" How would O'Connor answer this question? How can you tell? What is the stylistic effect of including this question in the text?

3. According to O'Connor, how might Coca-Cola's prescription for fighting obesity — "To maintain a healthy weight, get more exercise and worry less about cutting calories" (paragraph 1) — ultimately serve the soda company's interests? How do you know?

4. Characterize O'Connor's use of quotations. Select three of the quotations O'Connor uses, from three different sources. Determine what purpose they serve in developing his argument by analyzing how he integrates them into the piece.

Cause and Effect Analysis in Action

In preparation for writing a cause and effect analysis, list at least two effects on society and two effects on personal behavior for one of the following: television talk shows, online shopping, all-sports channels, reality television programs, television advertising, Internet advertising, fast food, or another item of your choosing. For example, a cell phone could be said to have the following effects:

Society

* Fewer highway fatalities due to quicker response to accidents
* Expansion of the economy

Personal Behavior

* Higher personal phone bills
* Risks to users, other drivers, and pedestrians' safety

Writing Suggestions

1. **Writing with Sources.** Research has shown that children and adolescents are extremely susceptible to ads in all media directed at them, ads that often alter their minds, appetites, behaviors, and health. In addition to soft drinks, such as Coca-Cola, ads promote candy; sugar-laden cereals; artificially sweetened foods; and a wide variety of unhealthy snacks that can cause obesity, diabetes, and heart trouble. It's no wonder that some countries have gone so far as to ban all advertising directed at children. Write an essay in which you

research and analyze how cause and effect works in the advertisement world with respect to children. Are there any solutions short of totally banning such ads? Have they been tried, and with what results?

2. Write a cause and effect analysis on one of the following topics or on one of your own choosing. Consider the causal chains that might have led to one of the following situations:

- a ban on bottled water in your community
- a car that won't start
- an increase (or decrease) in voter participation in local elections
- the approval of hydraulic fracturing (fracking) in your state
- the crash of the real estate market in 2008

What questions need to be asked and answered? For example, if math scores on standardized tests have improved recently in your local high school, was it the school board, the parents, the teachers, the students, or someone else who asked for changes to be made? Was more time allotted to the teaching of math? Were new teaching materials provided? What other causes might have been in play, and in what order might they have occurred? Make sure to do research as needed to support your claims.

Save Your Sanity, Downgrade Your Life

PAMELA PAUL

Pamela Paul was born in 1971 and graduated from Brown University with a bachelor's degree in history. She is currently the editor of the *New York Times Book Review* and hosts the weekly podcast *The Book Review*. Previously, Paul was the *Times*'s children's books editor. She has also written for the *Atlantic*, the *Economist*, *Slate*, *Worth*, and many other publications. Paul is the author of several books, including *The Starter Marriage and the Future of Matrimony* (2002) and *Pornified*: *How Pornography Is Damaging Our Lives, Our Relationships, and Our Families* (2005).

Erwin Wilson/© 2017 The New York Times

In this 2017 essay, which originally appeared in the *New York Times Sunday Review*, Paul writes about her desire to simplify and detechnologize her life, even as the pace of technological progress keeps moving faster.

Preparing to Read

How do you manage technology in your life? Do you ever use certain strategies to control the time you spend online or on your devices?

Recently, I gave up my electric toothbrush. There was nothing wrong 1 with it. It was, in fact, an upscale model, and when I used it, I felt certain my teeth were not only getting cleaner and whiter but also perhaps even better aligned. And yet, my old manual toothbrush, poking out of a mug on the vanity, beckoned. One night, as I wearily approached the sink, I realized the last thing I wanted to experience was the frantic whir of yet another spinning gizmo. I plucked out the old-timey toothbrush instead, and never looked back.

I deliberately downgraded. 2

Over the past few years, as my work life has accelerated at boggling 3 speed, my personal life has begun creeping backward toward the 20th century. Like carbon offsets, each decision to remove a technology at home makes the corresponding upgrade at work feel more acceptable. Work: Slack, our latest instant-messaging program, replaces conversation as a way of conveying simple queries. Home: Devices are banned from bedrooms. Work: Upgrade to new "content management system." Home: Netflix account to remain stubbornly DVD-based.

Disruption can be a positive force in the office, but at home it feels the way disruption has always felt: intrusive and annoying. At home, at least, we have the power to pace the change, to choose the old over the new. These incremental lifestyle downgrades help calibrate a rate of technological change that might otherwise produce a resting state of whiplash. They let me catch my breath. 4

Even the highest-tech among us seem to feel this need: Digital tweens lust after manual typewriters while techies embrace Maker culture on weekends. People want to use more of their hands than just their thumbs, to get them dirty and scrub them clean afterward. 5

> **People want to use more of their hands than just their thumbs, to get them dirty and scrub them clean afterward. This requires occasionally putting down the smartphone.**

This requires occasionally putting down the smartphone. According to a 2017 study by the American Psychological Association, more Americans are employing "technology usage management strategies" such as banning cellphones from the dinner table (depressingly, only 28 percent of people do this), taking occasional "digital detoxes" and forbidding devices during family time. 6

My personal mode of self-restraint is to always carry my phone when I'm not with my kids and always leave it in another room when I am. The kids themselves don't get phones at all. When my 12-year-old daughter walks home from school without one, I intentionally have no idea where she is, just like nobody knew where kids were when I was growing up. How rare it is these days not to be able to know something. 7

Though we are a forward-looking people, Americans are also quite good at nostalgia. We understand that the economy, the technology, the culture, the media are relentlessly pushing forward ("The March of Time!"), yet a streak of Luddite backwardness persists. This tendency is aided and abetted by an ancient technology, the book. Each season seems to have its stop-the-world best seller. In the mid-1990s it was Elaine St. James's "Simplify Your Life." In the mid-aughts, "The Paradox of Choice: Why More Is Less." At the end of the last decade, it was the sweaty toolbox of "Shop Class as Soulcraft." Most recently, it was the minimalist Marie Kondo's book about tidying and the sensibly titled "Overwhelmed: How to Work, Love, and Play When No One Has the Time," a book I may one day have time to read. 8

Why this yearning? In recent years, a number of studies have documented the effects of techno-stress—the psychological and physical impact of spending countless hours staring at a screen. According to the 2017 A.P.A. study, on a typical workday, 85 percent of people are constantly or often 9 digitally connected (by email, text and social media). On their days "off"? It's nearly the same: 81 percent.

This turns out not to be soothing. According to the A.P.A. study, nearly half of millennials worry about the negative effects of social media on their physical and mental health. Often for good reason. A 2017 survey by the Pew Internet and American Life Project found that 66 percent of Americans have witnessed online harassment and 41 percent have experienced it themselves.

When I watch kids giggling at their phones rather than at one another or families in the local diner silently sitting together in front of their respective devices, I can't help thinking of Pixar's post-apocalyptic "WALL-E," a nightmare vision in which earthlings, stripped of their musculature and humanity, recline blobbily in automated loungers, affixed to portable screens whose animated features are all they know of human interaction.

And so, I resist. I downgrade, I discard, I decline to upgrade. More than a decade ago, I got rid of cable TV, then network TV. I cut out personal phone calls (unless the person is a continent away), then anything other than businesslike emails. If I want to catch up with a good friend or a family member, I wait until we actually see each other.

When the pop-up window on my computer asks if I'd like to install the latest version of this or that, unless it's for security reasons, my response is, "No, thank you." Nor do I want that "amazing" new app. My mother—yes, my mother—knew about Lyft before I did. I've never tried whatever Spotify is, preferring the radio and ye olde compact discs. I'm sure I'd still be using a CD Walkman if I'd ever gotten one to begin with.

Never got a Nook, a Kindle, an iPad, don't want them. Until quite recently, I thought Alexa was a joke, a wild, hypothetical Orwellian item that might one day be foisted upon the world, not something that anyone might actually desire, pay for and willingly allow into her home.

Forced to buy a laptop in order to work on the train, I had to consider the latest models, so swift, so dynamic, they might leap into your backpack lest you accidentally forget to tuck one in yourself. In the end, I let my husband pick out the sleekest, most enlightened version for himself, while I took his four-year-old model, one his own mother had rejected as a relic from another geological age.

Do I slip up? Do I email unnecessarily? Have I found myself frantically texting something inconsequential from a beautiful outdoor setting surrounded by impatient children and adults making the same judgy how-could-you-be-doing-that face I so often make myself? I have. But I feel bad about it.

Thinking Critically about the Text

Do you find Paul's perspective accurate and fair-minded? Does she seem even-handed in her evaluation of technology and its role in our lives? How does she leave herself open to counterarguments and criticisms?

Questions on Subject

1. What primary cause and effect relationship does Paul present and explore in this essay?

2. What negative effects do contemporary devices and other technologies have, according to Paul? Identify as many as you can from her essay.

3. In paragraph 4, Paul writes, "Disruption can be a positive force in the office, but at home it feels the way disruption has always felt: intrusive and annoying." What contrast does she make here? Why would disruption be a "positive force" in a professional, business, or "office" context?

4. What "yearning" is Paul referring to in paragraph 9? What evidence does she provide that it exists? How does she answer the question?

Questions on Strategy

1. What is Paul's **purpose** in this essay? How do you think she wants her readers to react? For example, does she want to change their behavior? Their attitudes? Their views of her? Their understanding of technology? Explain.

2. Why do you think Paul chose to make paragraph 2 only one sentence long? What does she gain by making this stylistic choice?

3. Where does Paul use other strategies, such as **illustration** and **definition**? Point to specific examples. How do they support her main claims?

4. How would you describe the author's **attitude** and **tone** toward both her subject and herself? What specific words or phrases would you cite to support your answer?

Cause and Effect Analysis in Action

With a partner or small group, choose a common piece of technology or some relatively recent innovation (such as smartphones, digital printing, or online retail shopping). Then, brainstorm and list its positive and negative effects. What causal chains can you establish? These chains might include the factors that led to the development of the device or innovation. Do you all agree about the benefits and drawbacks? Do its upsides outweigh its downsides? If you disagree, identify what values lie behind your individual positions. Are these additional causes?

Writing Suggestions

1. According to Paul, many people are now drawn to earlier and even archaic technologies: "People want to use more of their hands than just their thumbs, to get them dirty and scrub them clean afterward" (paragraph 5). Do you agree? Are you drawn to any older devices, objects, or hobbies that require you to use "more than just [your] thumbs"? Write an essay in which you describe the object or activity and explain its appeal for you. Do you see the impulse to work with one's hands as a backlash against recent technological innovations, as a way of returning to meaningful human involvement? Is it a way of putting humans back in the center of things? Are there other examples of backlash in today's society?

2. Paul's essay is autobiographical, but it also reflects wider concerns and comments on a broader issue. Following her model, write an essay that considers the role of technology in your own life. Focus on cause and effect relationships. What drives your use of devices and different technologies? What effects do these technologies have? Do you find yourself needing management strategies to control them? Given your own experiences and perspectives, can you make any recommendations to others, as Paul does?

I AM NOT A RUG

As few as 3,890 wild tigers remain. Poaching for their skins, bones and other parts is the greatest immediate threat to their survival.

Find out what you can do to stop wildlife crime.

STOP WILDLIFE CRIME
IT'S DEAD SERIOUS

worldwildlife.org/wildlifecrime

2014 WWF-US Stop Wildlife Crime PSA

CHAPTER 12

Argumentation

WHAT IS ARGUMENTATION?

THE WORD *ARGUMENT* PROBABLY FIRST BRINGS TO MIND DISAGREEMENTS and disputes. Occasionally, such disputes are constructive. More often, though, disputes like these are inconclusive and result only in anger over your opponent's stubbornness or in the frustration of realizing that you have failed to make your position understood.

Reasoned argument is something else again entirely. In reasoned argument, we attempt to convince listeners or readers to agree with a particular point of view, to make a particular decision, or to pursue a particular course of action. Such arguments involve the presentation of well-chosen evidence and the artful control of language or other persuasive tools. Arguments need not be written to be effective, however; oral argument, if well planned and well delivered, can be equally effective, as can primarily visual arguments.

VISUALIZING ARGUMENTATION

For an example of argument that combines text and visuals, consider this antipoaching public service announcement (PSA). What argument does this ad, created by the World Wildlife Fund, make? How does the use of a photograph and an emphatic text headline make its argument? How do the visual and the text complement each other? What figure of speech does the headline rely upon to drive home the message? Is the PSA effective? That is, does it encourage viewers to act or behave differently? If so, how?

UNDERSTANDING ARGUMENTATION AS A WRITING STRATEGY

Written arguments must be carefully planned. The writer must settle in advance on a specific thesis or proposition rather than grope toward one, as in a dispute. There is a greater need for organization, for choosing the most effective types of evidence from all that are available, and for determining the strategies of rhetoric, language, and style that will best suit the argument's subject, purpose, thesis, and effect on the intended audience.

Reasoned arguments are limited to assertions about which there is a legitimate and recognized difference of opinion. It is unlikely that anyone will ever need to convince a reader that falling in love is a rare and intense experience, that crime rates should be reduced, or that computers are changing the world. Not everyone would agree, however, that women experience love more intensely than men do, that the death penalty reduces the incidence of crime, or that computers are changing the world for the worse; these assertions are arguable and admit differing perspectives.

No matter what forum it uses and no matter what its structure, an argument has as its chief purpose the detailed setting forth of a particular point of view and the rebuttal of any opposing views. Therefore, most strong arguments are constructed around an effective thesis statement. Take, for example, the following opening to the essay "The Case for Short Words" by Richard Lederer:

> **Thesis statement** When you speak and write, there is no law that says you have to use big words. Short words are as good as long ones, and short, old words—like *sun* and *grass* and *home*—are best of all. A lot of small words, more than you might think, can meet your needs with a strength, grace, and charm that large words do not have.
>
> **Several examples support the thesis** Big words can make the way dark for those who read what you write and hear what you say. Small words cast their clear light on big things—night and day, love and hate, war and peace, and life and death. Big words at times seem strange to the eye and the ear and the mind and the heart. Small words are the ones we seem to have known from the time we were born, like the hearth fire that warms the home.

Note how Lederer uses examples to support his thesis statement. A strong argument will be not only well reasoned and carefully organized but logical and persuasive as well.

▶ The Rhetorical Situation

Classical thinkers believed that there are three key components in all rhetorical situations or attempts to communicate: the *speaker* (and, for us, the *writer*) who comments about a *subject* to an *audience*. For purposes of discussion, we can isolate each of these three entities, but in actual rhetorical situations, they are inseparable, each inextricably tied to and influencing the other two.

The ancients also recognized the importance of three elements of argumentation: *ethos*, which is related to the speaker or writer; *logos*, which is related to the subject; and *pathos*, which is related to the audience. Let's look a little closer at each of these.

Ethos.   *Ethos* (Greek for "character") has to do with the authority, the credibility, and, to a certain extent, the morals of the speaker or writer. In other words, *ethos* is the speaker's character as perceived by the audience, often based on shared values. Aristotle and Cicero, classical rhetoricians, believed that it was important for the speaker to be credible and to argue for a worthwhile cause. Putting one's argumentative skills in the service of a questionable cause was simply not acceptable. But how did one establish credibility? Sometimes it was gained through achievements outside the rhetorical arena—that is, the speaker had experience with an issue, had argued the subject before, and had been judged to be sincere and honest.

In the case of your own writing, establishing such credentials is not always possible, so you will need to be more concerned than usual with presenting your argument reasonably, sincerely, and in language untainted by excessive emotionalism. Finally, it is well worth remembering that you should always show respect for your audience—as well as your critics—in your writing.

Logos.   *Logos* (Greek for "word"), related as it is to the subject, is the effective presentation of the argument itself. It refers to the speaker's grasp of the subject—his or her knowledge. Is the thesis or claim worthwhile? Is it logical, consistent, and well buttressed by supporting evidence? Is the evidence itself factual, reliable, and convincing? Finally, is the argument so thoughtfully organized and so clearly presented that it has an impact on the audience and could change opinions? Indeed, this aspect of argumentation is the most difficult to accomplish but is, at the same time, the most rewarding.

Logical argument appeals primarily to the mind—to the audience's intellectual faculties, understanding, and knowledge. Such appeals depend on the reasoned movement from assertion to evidence to conclusion and on an almost mathematical system of proof and counterproof. Logical argument is commonly found in scientific or philosophical articles, in legal decisions, and in technical proposals, but also in many disciplines in which writers use rational thought or hard evidence such as statistics.

Pathos.   *Pathos* (Greek for "emotion") has the most to do with the audience and appeals to emotion, to the subconscious, even to bias and prejudice. The essential question is, How does the speaker or writer present an argument or a persuasive essay to maximize its appeal for a given audience? One way, of course, is to appeal to the audience's emotions through the artful and strategic use of well-crafted language. Certain buzzwords, slanted diction, or emotionally loaded language may become either rallying cries or causes of resentment in an argument. Examples of persuasive appeals are found in the claims of advertisers and in the speech making of politicians and social activists who try to convince an audience to buy a product, support a bill, or join a protest by appealing to their values, beliefs, and emotions.

Persuasive arguments can be especially effective but should not be used without a strong logical backing. Indeed, this is the only way to use emotional persuasion ethically. Emotional persuasion, when not in support of a logical point, can be dangerous in that it can make an illogical point sound appealing to a listener or reader.

▶ Considering Audience

It is worth remembering at this point that you can never be certain who your audience is; readers range along a spectrum from extremely friendly and sympathetic to extremely hostile and resistant, with a myriad of possibilities in between. A friendly audience will welcome new information and support the writer's position; a hostile audience will look for just the opposite—flaws in logic and examples of dishonest manipulation. With many arguments, there is the potential for a considerable audience of interested parties who are uncommitted. If the targeted audience is judged to be friendly, the writer needs to be logical but should feel free to use emotional appeals. If the audience is thought to be hostile, presenting a logical argument must be the writer's immediate concern, and the language should be straightforward and objective. The greatest caution, subtlety, and critical thinking must be applied to the attempt to win over an uncommitted audience.

▶ Types of Argument

People who specialize in the study of argument often identify two essential categories: persuasion and logic. Most arguments are neither purely persuasive nor purely logical in nature. A well-written newspaper editorial that supports a controversial piece of legislation or that proposes a solution to a local problem, for example, will rest on a logical arrangement of assertions and evidence but will use striking diction and other persuasive patterns of language to make it more effective. Thus the kinds of appeals a writer emphasizes depend on the nature of the topic, the thesis or proposition of the argument, the various kinds of support (e.g., evidence, opinions, examples, facts, statistics) offered, and a thoughtful consideration of the audience. Knowing the differences between types of arguments is, then, helpful in understanding this strategy and in learning both to read and to write arguments.

Informational, or Exploratory, Argument.   It is often useful to provide a comprehensive review of the various facets of an issue. This is done to inform an audience, especially one that may not understand why the issue is controversial in the first place, and to help that audience take a position. The writer of this type of argument does not take a position but aims, instead, to render the positions taken by the various sides in accurate and clear language. Your instructors may occasionally call for this kind of argumentative writing as a way of teaching you to explore the complexity of a particular issue. This type of argument may also be helpful in establishing and understanding the similarities and differences that may exist among opposing sides in an argument in order to understand how the conversation around the issue has developed.

Focused Argument.   This kind of argument has only one objective: to change the audience's mind about a controversial issue. An example of this kind of argument is Nancy Armour's "Participation Awards Do Disservice" (pages 402–4), which argues firmly against the notion of participation awards and points out the negative precedent they establish. Being comprehensive or taking the broad view is not the objective here. If opposing viewpoints are considered, it is usually to show their inadequacies and thereby to strengthen the writer's own position. This kind of argument is what we usually think of when we think of traditional argument.

Action-Oriented Argument.   This type of argument is highly persuasive and attempts to accomplish a specific task. This is the loud car salesperson on your television, the over-the-top subscription solicitation in your mail, the vote-for-me-because-I-am-the-only-candidate-who-can-lower-your-taxes type of argument. The language is emotionally charged, and buzzwords designed to arouse the emotions of the audience may even be used, along with such propaganda devices as glittering generalities (broad, sweeping statements) and bandwagonism ("Everyone else is voting for me — don't be left out").

Quiet, or Subtle, Argument.   Some arguments do not immediately appear to the audience to be arguments at all. They set out to be informative and objective, but when closely examined, they reveal that the author has consciously, or perhaps subconsciously, shaped and slanted the evidence in such a manner as to favor a particular position. Such shaping may be the result of choices in diction that bend the audience to the writer's perspective, or they may be the result of decisions not to include certain types of evidence while admitting others. Such arguments can, of course, be quite convincing, as there are always those who distrust obvious efforts to convince them, preferring to make their own decisions on the issues.

Reconciliation Argument.   Increasingly popular today is a form of argument in which the writer attempts to explore all facets of an issue to find common ground or areas of agreement. Of course, one way of viewing that common ground is to see it as a new argument, a new assertion, about which there may yet be more debate. But the object is to tone down harshness and hard positions and to mediate opposing views into a rational and, where appropriate, even practical outcome. Martin Luther King Jr.'s speech "I Have a Dream" is perhaps the greatest example of a reconciliation argument of the past century.

▌ Inductive and Deductive Reasoning

There are two basic patterns of thinking and of presenting our thoughts that are followed in argumentation: *induction* and *deduction*.

Inductive reasoning moves from a set of specific examples to a general statement or principle. As long as the evidence is accurate, pertinent, complete, and sufficient to represent the assertion, the conclusion of an inductive argument can be regarded as valid; if, however, you can spot inaccuracies in the evidence or can point to contrary evidence, you have good reason to doubt the assertion as it stands. Inductive reasoning is the most common of argumentative structures.

Deductive reasoning, more formal and complex than inductive reasoning, moves from an overall premise, rule, or generalization to a more specific conclusion. Deductive logic follows the pattern of the *syllogism*, a simple three-part argument consisting of a major premise, a minor premise, and a conclusion. For example, notice how the following syllogism works:

 a. All humans are mortal. (*Major premise*)
 b. Catalina is a human. (*Minor premise*)
 c. Catalina is mortal. (*Conclusion*)

The conclusion here is true because both premises are true, and the logic of the syllogism is valid.

Obviously, a syllogism fails to work if either of the premises is untrue, as in this example:

 a. All living creatures are mammals. (*Major premise*)
 b. A lobster is a living creature. (*Minor premise*)
 c. A lobster is a mammal. (*Conclusion*)

The problem is immediately apparent. The major premise is obviously false: There are many living creatures that are not mammals, and a lobster happens to be one of them. Consequently, the conclusion is invalid.

Syllogisms, however, can fail even if both premises are objectively true. Such failures occur most often when the arguer jumps to a conclusion without taking into account obvious exceptions, as in this example:

a. All college students read books. (*Major premise*)

b. Larry reads books. (*Minor premise*)

c. Larry is a college student. (*Conclusion*)

Both of the premises in this syllogism are true, but the syllogism is invalid because it does not take into account that other people besides college students read books. The problem is in the way the major premise has been interpreted: If the minor premise were instead "Larry is a college student," then the valid conclusion "Larry reads books" would logically follow.

It is fairly easy to see the problems in a deductive argument when its premises and conclusion are rendered in the a-b-c form of a syllogism. It is often more difficult to see errors in logic when the argument is presented discursively, or within the context of a long essay. If you can reduce the argument to its syllogistic form, however, you will have much less difficulty testing its validity. Similarly, if you can isolate and examine out of context the evidence provided to support an inductive assertion, you can more readily evaluate the written inductive argument.

Consider this excerpt from "The Draft: Why the Country Needs It," an article by James Fallows that first appeared in the *Atlantic* in 1980:

> The Vietnam draft was unfair racially, economically, educationally. By every one of those measures, the volunteer Army is less representative still. Libertarians argue that military service should be a matter of choice, but the plain fact is that service in the volunteer force is too frequently dictated by economics. Army enlisted ranks E1 through E4, the privates and corporals, the cannon fodder, the ones who will fight and die, are 36 percent black now. By the Army's own projections, they will be 42 percent black in three years. When other "minorities" are taken into account, we will have, for the first time, an army whose fighting members are mainly "non-majority," or more bluntly, a black and brown army defending a mainly white nation. The military has been an avenue of opportunity of many young blacks. They may well be first-class fighting men. They do not represent the nation.
>
> Such a selective sharing of the burden has destructive spiritual effects in a nation based on the democratic creed. But its practical implications can be quite as grave. The effect of a fair, representative draft is to hold the public hostage to the consequences of its decisions, much as the children's presence in the public schools focuses parents' attention on the quality of the schools. If the citizens are willing to countenance a decision that means that someone's child may die, they may contemplate more deeply if there is the possibility that the child will be theirs. Indeed, I would like to extend this

principle even further. Young men of nineteen are rightly suspicious of the congressmen and columnists who urge them to the fore. I wish there were a practical way to resurrect provisions of the amended Selective Service Act of 1940, which raised the draft age to forty-four.

Here Fallows presents an inductive argument against the volunteer army and in favor of reinstating a draft. His argument can be summarized as follows:

Assertion: The volunteer army is racially and economically unfair.

Evidence: He points to the disproportionate percentage of blacks in the army, as well as to projections indicating that, within three years of the article's publication, more than half of the army's fighting members would be nonwhite.

Conclusion: "Such a selective sharing of the burden has destructive spiritual effects in a nation based on the democratic creed." Not until there is a fair, representative draft will the powerful majority be held accountable for any decision to go to war.

Fallows's inductive scheme here is, in fact, very effective. The evidence is convincing, and the conclusion is strong. But his argument also depends on a more complicated deductive syllogism:

a. The democratic ideal requires equal representation in the responsibilities of citizenship. (*Major premise*)
b. Military service is a responsibility of citizenship. (*Minor premise*)
c. The democratic ideal requires equal representation in military service. (*Conclusion*)

To attack Fallows's argument, it would be necessary to deny one of his premises.

Fallows also uses a number of other persuasive techniques, including an analogy: "The effect of a fair, representative draft is to hold the public hostage to the consequences of its decisions, much as the children's presence in the public schools focuses parents' attention on the quality of the schools." The use of such an analogy proves nothing, but it can force readers to reconsider their viewpoint and can make them more open-minded. Like most writers, Fallows uses persuasive arguments to complement his more important logical ones.

USING ARGUMENTATION ACROSS THE DISCIPLINES

When writing essays in the academic disciplines, you will have many opportunities to use the strategy of argumentation to both organize and strengthen the presentation of your ideas. To determine whether argumentation is the right strategy for you in a particular paper, use the guidelines described in Chapter 2, "Determining a Strategy for Developing Your Essay" (pages 34–35). Consider the following examples:

Ethics

1. **MAIN IDEA:** Suicide is an end-of-life option.
2. **QUESTION:** Should a person be allowed to end his or her life when no longer able to maintain an acceptable quality of life?
3. **STRATEGY:** Argumentation. The question "Should a person be allowed?" triggers a debate. The writer argues for or against laws that allow physician-assisted suicide, for example.
4. **SUPPORTING STRATEGIES:** Definition should be used to clarify what is meant by the expression "quality of life." Cause and effect analysis should be used to determine, for example, at what point a person has lost a desirable "quality of life."

Environmental Studies

1. **MAIN IDEA:** The burning of fossil fuels is creating greenhouse gas emissions that are, in turn, causing global warming.
2. **QUESTION:** What can we do to reduce emissions from the burning of fossil fuels?
3. **STRATEGY:** Argumentation. The question "What can we do?" suggests an answer in the form of an argument. The writer might want to argue for higher taxes on fossil fuels or for the installation of smokestack scrubbers.
4. **SUPPORTING STRATEGY:** Cause and effect analysis will be necessary to show how burning fossil fuels increases greenhouse emissions and how higher taxes and smokestack scrubbers will work to reduce harmful gases.

Biology

1. **MAIN IDEA:** The use of animals in biomedical research is crucial.
2. **QUESTION:** Should there be a ban on the use of animals in biomedical research?
3. **STRATEGY:** Argumentation. The word *should* signals a debate: Animals should/should not be used in biomedical research, or used only under particular circumstances.
4. **SUPPORTING STRATEGIES:** Comparison and contrast might be used to help make the case that alternatives to the use of animals are better/worse than using animals. Description could be used to identify any particular circumstances that may be exceptions to the rule.

PRACTICAL ADVICE FOR WRITING AN ESSAY OF ARGUMENTATION

As you plan, write, and revise your argumentation essay, be mindful of the writing process guidelines described in Chapter 2. Pay particular attention to the basic requirements and essential ingredients of this writing strategy.

▸ Planning Your Essay of Argumentation

Writing an argument can be very rewarding. By its nature, an argument must be carefully reasoned and thoughtfully structured to have maximum effect. In other words, the *logos* of the argument must be carefully tended. Allow yourself, therefore, enough time to think about your thesis, to gather the evidence you need, and to draft, revise, edit, and proofread your essay. Sloppy thinking, confused expression, and poor organization will be immediately evident to your reader and will make for weaker arguments.

For example, you might be given an assignment in your history class to write a paper explaining what you think was the main cause of the Civil War. How would you approach this topic? First, it would help to assemble a number of possible interpretations of the causes of the Civil War and to examine them closely. Once you have determined what you consider to be the main cause, you will need to develop points that support your position. Then you will need to explain why you did not choose other possibilities, and you will have to assemble reasons that refute them. For instance, you might write an opening similar to this example:

The Fugitive Slave Act Forced the North to Go to War

While the start of the Civil War can be attributed to many factors—states' rights, slavery, a clash between antithetical economic systems, and westward expansion—the final straw for the North was the Fugitive Slave Act. This act, more than any other single element of disagreement between the North and the South, forced the North into a position in which the only option was to fight.

Certainly, slavery and the clash over open lands in the West contributed to the growing tensions between the two sides, as did the economically incompatible systems of production—plantation and manufacture—but the Fugitive Slave Act required the North either to actively support slavery or to run the risk of becoming a criminal in defiance of it. The North chose not to support the Fugitive Slave Act and was openly angered by the idea that it should be required to do so by law. This anger and open defiance led directly to the Civil War.

In these opening paragraphs, the author states the main argument for the cause of the Civil War and sets up, in addition, the possible alternatives to this view. The points outlined in the introduction would lead, one by one, to a logical argument asserting that the Fugitive Slave Act was responsible for the onset of the Civil War and refuting the other interpretations.

Determine Your Thesis or Proposition.   Begin by determining a topic that interests you and about which there is some significant difference of opinion or about which you have a number of questions. Find out what's in the news, what people are talking about, what authors and instructors are emphasizing as important intellectual arguments. As you pursue your research, consider what assertion you can make about the topic you chose. The more specific this thesis or proposition, the more directed your research can become and the more focused your ultimate argument will be. While researching your topic, however, be aware that the information may point you in new directions. Don't hesitate at any point to modify or even reject an initial or preliminary thesis as continued research warrants.

A thesis can be placed anywhere in an argument, but it is probably best while learning to write arguments to place the statement of your controlling idea somewhere near the beginning of your composition. Explain the importance of the thesis and make clear to your reader that you share a common concern or interest in this issue (if your audience is a friendly one). You may wish to state your central assertion directly in your first or second paragraph so that there is no possibility for your reader to be confused about your position.

Consider Your Audience.   In no other type of writing is the question of audience more important than in argumentation. Here again, the *ethos* and *pathos* aspects of argumentation come into play. The tone you establish, the type of diction you choose, the kinds of evidence you select to buttress your assertions, and indeed the organizational pattern you design and follow will all influence your audience's perception of your trustworthiness and believability. If you make good judgments about the nature of your audience, respect its knowledge of the subject, and correctly envision whether it is likely to be hostile, neutral, complacent, or receptive, you will be able to tailor the various aspects of your argument appropriately.

Gather Supporting Evidence.   For each point of your argument, be sure to provide appropriate and sufficient supporting evidence: verifiable facts and statistics, illustrative examples and narratives, or quotations from authorities. Don't overwhelm your reader with evidence but don't skimp either; it is important to demonstrate your command of the topic and your control of the thesis by choosing carefully from all the evidence at your disposal. If there are strong arguments on both sides of the issue, you will need to take this into account while making your choices. (See the "Consider Refutations to Your Argument" section below.)

▌ Organizing Your Essay of Argumentation

Choose an Organizational Pattern.   Once you think that you have sufficient evidence to make your assertion convincing, consider how best to organize your argument. To some extent, your organization will depend on your method of reasoning: inductive, deductive, or a combination of the two. As you present your primary points, you may find it effective to move from those that are least important to those that are most important or from those that are least familiar to those that are most familiar. A scratch outline can help, but often a writer's most crucial revisions in an argument involve rearranging its components into a sharper, more coherent order. It is often difficult to tell what that order should be until the revision stage of the writing process.

Consider Refutations to Your Argument.   As you proceed with your argument, you may wish to take into account well-known and significant opposing arguments. To ignore them would be to suggest to your readers any one of the following: You don't know about them, you know about them and are obviously and unfairly weighting the argument in your favor, or you know about them and have no reasonable answers to them. Grant the validity of the opposing argument or refute it, but respect your readers' intelligence by addressing the problems. Your readers will in turn respect you for doing so.

To avoid weakening your thesis, you must be very clear in your thinking and presentation. It must remain apparent to your readers why your argument is superior to opposing points of view. If you feel that you cannot introduce opposing arguments because they will weaken rather than strengthen your thesis, you should probably reassess your thesis and the supporting evidence.

Use Other Writing Strategies.   Although argument is one of the most powerful single rhetorical strategies, it is almost always strengthened by incorporating other strategies. In every professional selection in this chapter, you will find a number of rhetorical strategies at work.

Combining strategies is probably not something you want to think about when you first try to write an argument. Instead, let the strategies develop naturally as you organize, draft, and revise your essay. As you draft your essay, look for places where you can use other strategies to strengthen your argument. For example, do you need a more convincing example, a term defined, a process explained, or the likely effects of an action detailed?

Conclude Forcefully.   In the conclusion of your essay, be sure to restate your position in different language, at least briefly. Besides persuading your reader to accept your point of view, you may also want to encourage some specific course of action. Above all, your conclusion should not introduce new information that may surprise your reader; it should seem to follow naturally, almost seamlessly, from the series of points that have been carefully established in the body of the essay.

▌ Revising and Editing Your Essay of Argumentation

Avoid Faulty Reasoning.   Have someone read your argument, checking sentences for errors in judgment and reasoning. Sometimes others can see easily what you can't because you are so intimately tied to your assertion. Review the following list of errors in reasoning and make sure you have not committed any of them:

Logical Fallacy	Definition	Example
Oversimplification	A foolishly simple solution to what is clearly a complex problem	The reason we have a balance-of-trade deficit is that other countries make better products than we do.
Hasty generalization	In inductive reasoning, a generalization that is based on too little evidence or on evidence that is not representative	My friend and I both took Uber rides in Boston this weekend, and both drivers were friendly. Uber drivers in Boston are all friendly.
Post hoc, ergo propter hoc ("after this, therefore because of this")	Confusing chance or coincidence with causation; the fact that one event comes after another does not necessarily mean that the first event caused the second	Every time I wear my orange Syracuse sweater to a game, we win.
Begging the question	Assuming in a premise something that needs to be proven	Parking fines work because they keep people from parking illegally.
False analogy	Assuming that because two things are similar in some respects they are necessarily similar in others	Of course he'll make a fine coach. He was an all-star basketball player.
Either/or thinking	Seeing only two alternatives when there may in fact be other possibilities	Either you love your job or you hate it.

(continued on next page)

Logical Fallacy	Definition	Example
Non sequitur ("it does not follow")	An inference or conclusion that is not clearly related to the established premises or evidence	She is very sincere; she must know what she is talking about.
Name-calling	Linking a person to a negative idea or symbol; the hope is that by invoking the name, the user will elicit a negative reaction without the necessary evidence	Senator Jones is a bleeding heart.

It is important to have a firm grasp of what logical fallacies are and how they can mislead both listeners and readers. False logic, both intentional and inadvertent, denies and obscures the truth and weakens or nullifies arguments. While always a danger, logical fallacies are more of a threat today than ever before because of the powerful impact of mass media and the increasingly manipulative rhetorical strategies employed by politicians, ideologues, advertisers, and a host of others who wish to gain your support for their views. Only by approaching critically everything we read and understanding how messages can be manipulated—not just by lies, half-truths, and omissions, but by the employment of age-old persuasive techniques—can we discern the truth and protect ourselves.

Questions for Revising and Editing: Argumentation

1. Is my thesis or proposition focused? Do I state my thesis well?

2. Am I using the right type of argument to argue my thesis? Does my strategy fit my subject matter and audience?

3. Does my presentation include enough evidence to support my thesis? Do I acknowledge opposing points of view in a way that strengthens, rather than weakens, my argument?

4. In what ways have I made appeals to *ethos*, *logos*, and/or *pathos* in my argument? Have I chosen the best appeals for my intended audience?

5. Have I chosen an appropriate organizational pattern that makes it easy to support my thesis?

6. Have I avoided faulty reasoning within my essay? Have I had a friend read the essay to help me find problems in my logic?

7. Is my conclusion forceful and effective?

8. Have I thought about or attempted to combine rhetorical strategies to strengthen my argument? If so, is the combination of strategies effective? If not, what strategy or strategies would help my argument?

9. Have I used a variety of sentences to enliven my writing? Have I avoided wordiness?

10. Have I avoided errors in grammar, punctuation, and mechanics?

STUDENT ESSAY USING ARGUMENTATION AS A WRITING STRATEGY

Mundy Wilson-Piper wrote the following essay when she was a student at the University of Vermont, where she earned a degree in English with a coordinate major in Environmental Studies. In this essay, Wilson-Piper humorously tries to persuade meat eaters to be more tolerant of vegetarians by recounting her own experiences as a vegetarian amongst a family of "non-veggies."

The State of My Plate
Mundy Wilson-Piper

Writer explains personal experience to establish context for her argument

The holiday that I dread the most is fast approaching. The relatives will gather to gossip and bicker, the house will be filled with the smells of onions, giblets, and allspice, and I will be pursuing trivial conversations in the hopes of avoiding any commentaries upon the state of my plate. 1

Writer anticipates and deflects ad hominem attack

Do not misunderstand me: I am not a scrooge. I enjoy the idea of Thanksgiving—the giving of thanks for blessings received in the past year and the opportunity to share an unhurried day with family and friends. The problem for me is that I am one of those freaky, misunderstood dampers on the party—a vegetarian. Since all traditional Western holidays revolve around food and more specifically around the ham, turkey, lamb, or roast beef and their respective starchy accompaniments, it's no picnic for we "rabbit food" people. The mention of the word "vegetarian" has, on various similar occasions, caused Great-Aunt Bertha to rant and rave for what seems like hours about "those communist conspirators." Other relations cough or groan or simply stare, change the subject or reminisce about somebody they used to know who was "into that," and some proceed either to demand that I defend my position or try to talk me out of it. That is why I try to avoid the subject at all times, but especially during the holidays. 2

Description helps reader visualize and empathize with the scene, appealing to emotion (pathos)

In years past I have had about as many successes as failures in steering comments about my food toward other topics. Politics and religion are the easiest outs, guaranteed to immerse the family into a heated debate lasting until the loudest shouter has been abandoned amidst empty pie plates, wine corks, and rumpled linen napkins. I prefer, however, to use this tactic as a last resort. Holidays are supposed to be for relaxing. 3

Narration of the
scene contributes
to the appeal to
emotion *pathos*

I can already picture the scenario. Narration of the
scene contributes to the appeal to emotion. As plates,
platters, and bowls holding the traditional fixings of
the Thanksgiving feast are passed around the table,
two or three I transfer immediately from the person on
my right to the one on my left. Seldom is this noticed
since everyone from Uncle Fred to little Ely is engrossed
in what is happening on their own plates. After our
traditional secular prayer (supposedly designed to keep
the peace) and about five minutes of horse-like chomping mingled with contented moans and groans, my
observant Aunt Nancy will usually say something like,
"Why M.L., you don't have any turkey or duck on your
plate! Let me help you to some."

"Thanks, Nance, but I'm fine," I say, grinding my
teeth.

"But how can you have a Thanksgiving meal without
turkey? You're not still one of those vegetarians, are you?"

I try an avoidance maneuver. "So Uncle Russ, how's
life in Florida?" Not a chance this time. All eyes are on
me waiting for the response they do not wish to hear.
Why is it such a big deal for my family to swallow that
I do not eat meat? I hardly ever encounter such resistance to the way I choose to nourish my body outside of
my relatives. They seem to take it as a personal affront,
a betrayal, and an undermining of, God forbid, tradition. They want to understand, in a patronizing way. My
brother was a vegetarian for ten years until the recent
birth of his second child caused his wife to declare she
was no longer going to spend her precious time preparing meals of complementary proteins. The relatives
gave him a hard time too, but with less vigor. It may
have something to do with my being the only female
of the younger generation; what will happen when my
mother relinquishes the "Dinner Rights"? Tofu turkey,
granola stuffing, and yogurt pie for Thanksgiving???

I close my eyes tightly and concentrate on controlling the pitch of my voice. "Do we have to go
through this again? I have been a vegetarian through
the last six Thanksgivings and I am tired of this new
tradition of having a conversation about it every year.
You must grasp the idea that I am not crazy, fanatical,
unhealthy, or unhappy. I just do not like to eat meat."

Silence. I pray for someone to change the subject.

4

5

6

7

8

9

Though the thesis remains unstated, the writer shows through dialogue how her argument to coexist peacefully during holidays changes the family dynamic

"We're only concerned about you, dear. You're so thin and meat is so good for you."   10

"Hey, leave her alone," my brother chimes in. "She simply feels that eating meat is unnecessary, irrational, anatomically unsound, unhealthy, unhygienic, uneconomic, unecological, unaesthetic, unkind, and unethical. Right, M.L.? Now let's talk about really important things—like football."   11

Student Reflection
Mundy Wilson-Piper

Q. How did you find the topic for your essay?

A. It was November. My mother had just telephoned to finalize our plans for Thanksgiving—immediately I recalled past holidays and the frustration I felt about my relatives' attitudes toward my vegetarianism. All of my writing topics come from my life experiences. I especially enjoy relating everyday types of events from a humorous perspective. Usually when I'm in the midst of writing a piece I'll find several or a dozen other related topics in which I'm interested. I keep a topic notebook—a three-by-five-inch pad—with me at all times so I can jot down my ideas. When I feel like writing and can't think of a topic, I flip through my notebook and one always jumps out at me.

Q. Did any parts of your essay prove more difficult than you had expected? If so, explain the problem and how you resolved it.

A. Yes, I had a difficult time with the ending. I wanted it to be meaningful but not heavy, and it took a long time to achieve some satisfaction. Actually, I'm still not completely satisfied with it, but I've yet to come up with anything else. I can only rethink a piece so many times before I get frustrated with it and have to move on. I finally decided on this ending after remembering all the arguments my brother and I made to defend our choice of not eating meat. Then I remembered nothing is more important to my brother than football (at least during the winter holidays). I think it made for an ironic resolution because in many ways vegetarianism and football are completely incongruous.

Q. Who is your audience for this essay? What did you want them to do or think as a result of reading your piece?

A. When I first started it I thought of my family as my audience. Later I realized I was perhaps speaking for and to vegetarians and to meat eaters who have close relationships with "veggies." Then it dawned on me that I was really trying to persuade anyone who is intolerant of other people's different choices and lifestyles to be more accepting instead of resistant and antagonistic. I've always found it amazing that when a person makes a decision to improve his or her well-being, people surrounding that person often make it difficult. I hoped that after reading this essay people might think twice about giving anyone—perhaps especially relatives—a hard time about their choices.

Q. How many drafts do you usually write?
A. Not nearly enough on paper. I do a lot of writing and rewriting in my head before I'm able to put anything on paper. I think it's left over from my sixth-grade teacher who *insisted* we do a lot of thinking before picking up the pen. Lately, I've been doing some freewriting to get loosened up before I allow myself to work on a piece.

Q. What do you enjoy most about writing?
A. Writing's an outlet for me. By changing the form or style or perspective to suit my topic, I learn things about myself, other people, and the world. And this gives me a fresh outlook on life. Also, I have always expressed myself better in writing than orally. I always feel rushed in conversations whereas when writing I can take time to think things through and to get closer to what I really want to say.

Q. I understand that you had this essay published in the local newspaper just before Thanksgiving. What did that feel like?
A. Fantastic! I was so surprised and elated that the newspaper published it. It's funny—even though I've had several more articles published in local papers since then, it feels the same every time. I hope I never lose the feeling of "success" because it really helps my confidence—it spurs me on to write more and more.

Your Response

What did you learn from Mundy Wilson-Piper's essay and her reflection on the writing process of writing the essay? What challenges do you expect to face as you write your own argumentative essay? Based on Mundy's composing strategies and the practical advice discussed earlier in this chapter (pages 386–90), what writing choices will you make?

Ain't I a Woman?

SOJOURNER TRUTH

Sojourner Truth was born into slavery and named Isabella in Ulster County, New York, in 1797. After her escape from slavery in 1827, she went to New York City and underwent a profound religious transformation. She worked as a domestic servant, and as an evangelist she tried to reform prostitutes. Adopting the name Sojourner Truth in 1843, she became a traveling preacher and abolitionist, frequently appearing with Frederick Douglass. Although she never learned to write, Truth's compelling presence gripped her audience as she spoke eloquently about emancipation and women's rights. After the Civil War and until her death in 1883, she worked to provide education and employment for emancipated slaves.

Library of Congress

At the Women's Rights Convention in Akron, Ohio, in May 1851, Truth extemporaneously delivered the following speech to a nearly all-white audience. The version we reprint was transcribed by Elizabeth Cady Stanton.

Preparing to Read

What comes to mind when you hear the word *speech*? Have you ever attended a rally or convention and heard speeches given on behalf of a social cause or political issue? What were your impressions of the speakers and their speeches?

Well, children, where there is so much racket there must be some- 1 thing out of kilter. I think that 'twixt the Negroes of the South and the women of the North, all talking about rights, the white men will be in a fix pretty soon. But what's all this here talking about?

That man over there says that women need to be helped into carriages, 2 and lifted over ditches, and to have the best place everywhere. Nobody ever helps me into carriages, or over mud-puddles, or gives me any best place! And ain't I a woman? Look at me! Look at my arm! I have ploughed and planted, and gathered into barns, and no man could head me! And ain't I a woman? I could work as much and eat as much as a man — when I could get it — and bear the lash as well! And ain't I a woman? I have borne thirteen children, and seen them most all sold off to slavery, and when I cried out with my mother's grief, none but Jesus heard me! And ain't I a woman?

Then they talk about this thing in the head; what's this they call it? [Intellect, 3 someone whispers.] That's it, honey. What's that got to do with women's rights or negro's rights? If my cup won't hold but a pint, and yours holds a quart, wouldn't you be mean not to let me have my little half-measure full?

> **❝ Nobody ever helps me into carriages, or over mud-puddles, or gives me any best place! ❞**

Then that little man in black there, he says women can't have as much rights as men, 'cause Christ wasn't a woman! Where did your Christ come from? Where did your Christ come from? From God and a woman! Man had nothing to do with Him. 4

If the first woman God ever made was strong enough to turn the world upside down all alone, these women together ought to be able to turn it back, and get it right side up again! And now they is asking to do it, the men better let them. 5

Obliged to you for hearing me, and now old Sojourner ain't got nothing more to say. 6

Thinking Critically about the Text

What are your immediate impressions of Truth's speech? Now take a minute to read her speech again, this time aloud. What are your impressions now? Are they different, and if so, how and why? What aspects of her speech are memorable?

Questions on Subject

1. What does Truth mean when she says "Where there is so much racket there must be something out of kilter" (paragraph 1)? Why does Truth believe that white men are going to find themselves in a "fix" (paragraph 1)?

2. What does Truth put forth as her "credentials" as a woman?

3. What does Truth mean with her metaphor of the cup in paragraph 3? How is she accusing her audience of being "mean"?

4. How does Truth counter the argument that "women can't have as much rights as men, 'cause Christ wasn't a woman" (paragraph 4)?

Questions on Strategy

1. What is Truth's **purpose** in this essay? Why is it important for her to define what a woman is for her **audience**?

2. How does Truth use the comments of "that man over there" (paragraph 2) and "that little man in black" (paragraph 4) to help her establish her definition of *woman*?

3. What, for you, is the effect of Truth's repetition of the question "And ain't I a woman?" four times? What other questions does she ask? Why do you suppose Truth doesn't provide answers to the questions in paragraph 3 but does for the question in paragraph 4?

4. How would you characterize Truth's **tone** in this speech? What phrases in the speech suggest that tone to you?

Argumentation in Action

In a letter to the editor of the *New York Times*, Nancy Stevens, president of a small New York City advertising agency, argues against using the word *guys* to address women. She believes that the "use of *guy* to mean 'person' is so insidious that I'll bet most women don't notice they are being called 'guys,' or, if they do, find it somehow flattering to be one of them." Do you find such usage objectionable? Why, or why not? How is the use of *guy* to mean "person" different from using *gal* to mean "person"? How do you think Truth would react to the use of the word *guys* to refer to women? What light does your dictionary shed on this issue of definition?

Writing Suggestions

1. Sojourner Truth spoke out against the injustice she saw around her. In arguing for the rights of women, she found it helpful to define *woman* in order to make her point. What social cause do you find most compelling today? Human rights? Climate change? Domestic abuse? Alcoholism? Racism? Immigration reform? Select an issue about which you have strong feelings. Now carefully identify all key terms that you must define before arguing your position. Write an essay in which you use definition to make your point convincingly.

2. Sojourner Truth's speech holds out hope for the future. She envisions a future in which women join together to take charge and "turn [the world] back, and get it right side up again" (paragraph 5). What she envisioned has, to some extent, come to pass. For example, today the distinction between "women's work" and "men's work" has blurred or even vanished in some fields. Write an essay in which you speculate about how Truth would react to the world as we know it. What do you think would please her? What would disappoint her? What do you think she would want to change about our society? Explain your reasoning.

Second Inaugural Address

ABRAHAM LINCOLN

John Parrot/Stocktrek Images/Getty Images

Born in Hodgenville, Kentucky, in 1809, Abraham Lincoln grew up on what was our country's western frontier in Kentucky and Indiana. Largely self-educated, he went on to become a successful lawyer, politician, and the sixteenth president of the United States before he was assassinated in 1865. He remains a towering figure in America's history. Indeed, more books have been written about him than any other American. Lincoln held the presidency during America's greatest crisis, the Civil War. That was also the occasion and the context for the following speech, which he delivered after his reelection, as the war was coming to an end. After the Gettysburg Address, this is probably Lincoln's most famous public oration. At the time, however, his second inaugural address received mixed reviews. Lincoln thought he knew why some disliked his speech, noting that people "are not flattered by being shown that there has been a difference of purpose between the Almighty and them."

Preparing to Read

Do you watch or listen to political speeches to the public, such as the State of the Union address? What role do these play in American society? Do they influence your opinion on issues or make you more or less favorable to the politician speaking?

Fellow-Countrymen: 1

At this second appearing to take the oath of the Presidential 2 office there is less occasion for an extended address than there was at the first. Then a statement somewhat in detail of a course to be pursued seemed fitting and proper. Now, at the expiration of four years, during which public declarations have been constantly called forth on every point and phase of the great contest which still absorbs the attention and engrosses the energies of the nation, little that is new could be presented. The progress of our arms, upon which all else chiefly depends, is as well known to the public as to myself, and it is, I trust, reasonably satisfactory and encouraging to all. With high hope for the future, no prediction in regard to it is ventured.

On the occasion corresponding to this four years ago all thoughts were 3 anxiously directed to an impending civil war. All dreaded it, all sought to avert it. While the inaugural address was being delivered from this place, devoted altogether to saving the Union without war, insurgent agents were in the city seeking to destroy it without war—seeking to dissolve the Union and divide effects by negotiation. Both parties deprecated war, but one of them would make war rather than let the nation survive, and the other would accept war rather than let it perish, and the war came.

One-eighth of the whole population were colored slaves, not distrib-   4
uted generally over the Union, but localized in the southern part of it. These slaves constituted a peculiar and powerful interest. All knew that this interest was somehow the cause of the war. To strengthen, perpetuate, and extend this interest was the object for which the insurgents would rend the Union even by war, while the Government claimed no right to do more than to restrict the territorial enlargement of it. Neither party expected for the war the magnitude or the duration which it has already attained. Neither anticipated that the cause of the conflict might cease with or even before the conflict itself should cease. Each looked for an easier triumph, and a result less fundamental and astounding. Both read the same Bible and pray to the same God, and each invokes His aid against the other. It may seem strange that any men should dare to ask a just God's assistance in wringing their bread from the sweat of other men's faces, but let us judge not, that we be not judged. The prayers of both could not be answered. That of neither has been answered fully. The Almighty has His own purposes. "Woe unto the world because of offenses; for it must needs be that offenses come, but woe to that man by whom the offense cometh." If we shall suppose that American slavery is one of those offenses which, in the providence of God, must needs come, but which, having continued through His appointed time, He now wills to remove, and that He gives to both North and South this terrible war as the woe due to those by whom the offense came, shall we discern therein any departure from those divine attributes which the believers in a living God always ascribe to Him? Fondly do we hope, fervently do we pray, that this mighty scourge of war may speedily pass away. Yet, if God wills that it continue until all the wealth piled by the bondsman's two hundred and fifty years of unrequited toil shall be sunk, and until every drop of blood drawn with the lash shall be paid by another drawn with the sword, as was said three thousand years ago, so still it must be said "the judgments of the Lord are true and righteous altogether."

With malice toward none, with charity for all, with firmness in the right   5
as God gives us to see the right, let us strive on to finish the work we are in, to bind up the nation's wounds, to care for him who shall have borne the battle and for his widow and his orphan, to do all which may achieve and cherish a just and lasting peace among ourselves and with all nations.

Thinking Critically about the Text

This is a speech, not an essay. It was written to be spoken aloud. How do you think that purpose shapes the substance and form of the writing? How would you describe Lincoln's tone as you read it? Is it conciliatory? Confident? Angry? Weary? Sarcastic?

Questions on Subject

1. What is the main idea of Lincoln's first paragraph? What is the context for the speech?

2. What is Lincoln's view of slavery, as suggested by the speech?

3. How does Lincoln interpret the war's purpose and meaning? For example, what does he think caused the war? When does he think it will end?

4. Lincoln says of the Confederacy's motives, "let us judge not, that we be not judged" (paragraph 4). Does he follow this principle in his speech, or does he cast a negative judgment on the South? Point to specific examples to support your position.

Questions on Strategy

1. What examples of *logos*, *pathos*, and *ethos* can you find in Lincoln's speech? Point to specific examples.

2. How does Lincoln use **parallelism** in paragraphs 3 and 4? In what way does doing so reinforce the point he is making?

3. Where does Lincoln use **deduction**, or deductive reasoning, to further his argument? (Refer to the "Inductive and Deductive Reasoning" section on pages 382–84 for help.)

4. In what way is this speech an action-oriented argument? What is Lincoln's **purpose** in delivering his speech? Is he trying to convince his audience to change their opinion on an issue? To pursue a particular course of action? Something else?

Argumentation in Action

In class, search online for a short political speech in writing or as an audio or video clip. Read, listen, or watch the speech, and be prepared to summarize your example and discuss its purpose and its appeals. Does it use deductive reasoning? Inductive reasoning? Both? How does it rely on *logos, pathos*, or *ethos*? Are there any examples of unsupported claims or fallacious reasoning?

Writing Suggestions

1. **Writing with Sources.** Lincoln's speech attempted to reconcile a nation at war and try to find a common way forward as a united body. Write an essay in which you identify an area in today's society where people at odds would benefit from uniting. What are their respective arguments? What common ground can you find between them? Why should they unite, and how do you propose they would join together and see progress? Read some articles in the editorial section of different newspapers or news sites to gather ideas on divisive topics and to support your points with sources.

2. In this speech, Lincoln works through the causes and meaning of the Civil War, as when he claims that the "interest" of slavery was "somehow the cause of the war" (paragraph 2). Today, people still argue about the meaning of the war and the war's legacy. For example, we have seen heated debates and controversies around statues of Confederate political and military leaders and the lingering presence of the Confederate national flag. Why do you think Americans are still arguing about the meaning of the war and its aftermath? What issues does the topic raise? How do opposing arguments reflect different assumptions, values, and viewpoints?

Participation Awards Do Disservice

NANCY ARMOUR

Nancy Armour began her career as the Associated Press correspondent in South Bend, Indiana, before moving to Chicago and making a name for herself as a sports writer. In two consecutive years, 2006 and 2007, Armour won the Will Grimsley Award for Outstanding Body of Work. She is currently writing for the USA Today Sports Media group, where she regularly covers major events such as the Olympics and the World Cup.

AP Photo/Ted S. Warren, File

In the following article, published in *USA Today Sports* in August 2015, Armour points out the long-term consequences of what she calls the "youth sports trophy culture."

Preparing to Read

Did you ever receive a participation award growing up? Did it make you feel accomplished, or did you dismiss it as meaningless? Do you think these sorts of awards made a lasting impression on you or anyone you know?

L ife isn't always fair. 1

You can work your hardest, try your best, expend every ounce of 2 energy you have and sometimes things just don't work out the way you hoped or imagined. That's just the way things go.

Yet somewhere along the way, someone had the misguided notion that 3 kids should live in a la-la land where everything is perfect, there are no hardships or heartbreaks, and you get a shiny trophy or a pretty blue ribbon just for being you.

There's time enough to get acquainted with reality, the thinking goes. 4 In the meantime, children should be praised and encouraged, reminded at every turn how wonderful they are.

No wonder study after study has shown that millennials, the first of the 5 trophy generations, are stressed out and depressed. They were sold a bill of goods when they were kids, and discovering that the harsh realities of life apply to them, too, had to have been like a punch to the gut.

Pittsburgh Steelers linebacker James Harrison may be the last person 6 you want to take life lessons from, given his history of violence on and off the field. But his announcement Sunday that he was giving back his 8- and

6-year-old sons'"participation" trophies because they hadn't earned them was dead on, and that message shouldn't be discounted simply because he was the one delivering it.

"While I am very proud of my boys for everything they do and will 7 encourage them till the day I die, these trophies will be given back until they EARN a real trophy," Harrison said in a post on Instagram. "I'm sorry I'm not sorry for believing that everything in life should be earned and I'm not about to raise two boys to be men by making them believe that they are entitled to something just because they tried their best."

Amen. 8

Everybody-gets-a-trophy proponents say children should be rewarded 9 for their efforts, that the prizes give kids incentive to always try their best and persevere. But isn't that what the orange slices and cookies are for? By handing out trophies and medals at every turn, it actually sends the *opposite* message, essentially telling kids it's enough just to show up.

Why should a kid strive to improve or put in the extra effort when he 10 or she is treated no differently than the kid who sits in the outfield picking dandelions? Or, as NFL MVP Kurt Warner said on Twitter on Monday, "They don't let kids pass classes 4 just showing up!"

"The whole idea is to protect that kid and, ultimately, it's a huge dis- 11 service. What kids need is skill-building. Help them do what they're doing and do it better," said Ashley Merryman, co-author of *Top Dog: The Science of Winning and Losing.*

> **❝ If we're honest with ourselves, the trophies, ribbons and medals we hand out so willingly are more about us than the children getting them. ❞**

"The benefit of competition 12 isn't actually winning. The benefit is improving," Merryman added. "When you're constantly giving a kid a trophy for everything they're doing, you're saying, 'I don't care about improve- ment. I don't care that you're learning from your mistakes. All we expect is that you're always a winner.'"

And if you've taken a peek at any 9-year-old's room recently, you'll see 13 how much those precious trophies and ribbons really mean. Most are either coated in dust or buried in the back of a closet.

If we're honest with ourselves, the trophies, ribbons and medals we hand 14 out so willingly are more about us than the children getting them. It's affir- mation that our kids are as wonderful as we think they are. It's also a way to fool ourselves into thinking that we're sheltering them, at least temporarily, from the cold, cruel world.

But real life is hard, and no amount of trophies can shield kids from the 15 disappointments and challenges they'll eventually face.

"I like kids. I want them to be happy and do well," said Merryman, who 16
has mentored Olympic athletes. "But I'd much rather have a 6-year-old cry
because he didn't get a medal than have a 26-year-old lose it because they
realized they weren't as special as they thought they were."

Learning the true values of hard work, perseverance and resilience, that's 17
the real reward. All other trophies pale in comparison.

Thinking Critically about the Text

Armour anticipated that readers might refute her argument on the grounds that
linebacker James Harrison is not an ideal role model. How does she address this
potential concern? Do you think her position is reasonable? What does the inclusion of Harrison's announcement contribute to her argument?

Questions on Subject

1. According to Armour, what is the central problem with participation trophies?
   Where does she state her **thesis**?

2. Where does Armour address the views of those in favor of participation
   awards? What does she identify as the reasoning behind this practice?

3. In paragraph 5, Armour calls millennials "the first of the trophy generations"
   and characterizes them as stressed out and depressed. Does she provide
   sufficient evidence for this claim? Why, or why not?

4. The author suggests in paragraph 14 that the participation trophies are actually for adults rather than children. Why does she think so? What does she
   believe that adults get out of giving awards to their children?

Questions on Strategy

1. The article begins with the declarative sentence "Life isn't always fair." How
   does this **cliché** set the **tone** for Armour's entire argument?

2. Armour says that millennials were "sold a bill of goods" when they were
   children (paragraph 5). What does she mean by this? How does her use of
   this **metaphor** contribute to her argument?

3. In paragraph 16, the author quotes Ashley Merryman, the coauthor of a book
   on winning and losing. What does this quotation add to her argument?

4. After pointing out the potential harm of participation trophies, Armour adds
   that most nine-year-olds don't actually value them anyway (paragraph 13).
   How does this statement contribute to her thesis? How might it weaken her
   argument?

Argumentation in Action

It can be challenging to make an argument using sources that might not have the best reputations, as Armour did in quoting James Harrison. Generally, it is advisable to simply find a source with stronger appeal to *ethos*, but occasionally you may encounter important quotes or evidence that come from controversial sources. Select some quotes from a source that others might view as suspect (for instance, a convict speaking on prison reform or a discredited politician) and brainstorm ways to incorporate their message without weakening your argument. If you get stuck, revisit Armour's article and note how she addresses the flaws in her source directly and supplements Harrison's quotes with a tweet from NFL MVP Kurt Warner.

Writing Suggestions

1. Armour is primarily a sports writer, and she examines the issue of participation awards through the lens of athletics. Select another activity where participation might be rewarded, such as learning in a classroom or entering a costume contest or a painting contest. Do you think Armour's argument is valid in the activity you have chosen? Write a brief essay arguing why or why not.

2. **Writing from Sources.** Football has come under fire for causing brain damage in players, and doctors have expressed concerns that even children and young adults who play football in school are at risk. Do some research into concussions caused by sports and write a paper arguing for or against dramatic changes in youth athletics.

Telling Americans to Vote, or Else

WILLIAM GALSTON

William Galston was born in 1946 and served as a
sergeant in the Marine Corps before receiving his
doctorate from the University of Chicago in 1973.
He taught government at the University of Texas
before becoming a policy advisor under President
Clinton. He is the author of eight books on politics
and governance, including *The Practice of Liberal
Pluralism* (2004) and *Public Matters* (2005). He
has also written numerous articles and has a
weekly column in the *Wall Street Journal*.

Scott J. Ferrell/Congressional
Quarterly/Getty Images

The following article first appeared in the
New York Times in November 2011. Galston lays
out a series of arguments in favor of mandatory voting. He points to the success of
similar programs in Australia and other countries and suggests that a mandatory vote
might be the remedy to the increasingly polarized politics in the United States.

Preparing to Read

Did you vote in the last presidential election? Have you ever voted in a local election?
What motivated your decision to vote, or not to vote? How would you solve the problem of poor voter turnout?

J ury duty is mandatory; why not voting? The idea seems vaguely 1
un-American. Maybe so, but it's neither unusual nor undemocratic.
And it would ease the intense partisan polarization that weakens our
capacity for self-government and public trust in our governing institutions.

Thirty-one countries have some form of mandatory voting, according 2
to the International Institute for Democracy and Electoral Assistance. The
list includes nine members of the Organization for Economic Cooperation
and Development and two-thirds of the Latin American nations. More than
half back up the legal requirement with an enforcement mechanism, while
the rest are content to rely on the moral force of the law.

Despite the prevalence of mandatory voting in so many democracies, 3
it's easy to dismiss the practice as a form of statism that couldn't work in
America's individualistic and libertarian political culture. But consider
Australia, whose political culture is closer to that of the United States than
that of any other English-speaking country. Alarmed by a decline in voter
turnout to less than 60 percent in 1922, Australia adopted mandatory voting in 1924, backed by small fines (roughly the size of traffic tickets) for

nonvoting, rising with repeated acts of nonparticipation. The law established permissible reasons for not voting, like illness and foreign travel, and allows citizens who faced fines for not voting to defend themselves.

The results were remarkable. In the 1925 election, the first held under the new law, turnout soared to 91 percent. In recent elections, it has hovered around 95 percent. The law also changed civic norms. Australians are more likely than before to see voting as an obligation. The negative side effects many feared did not materialize. For example, the percentage of ballots intentionally spoiled or completed randomly as acts of resistance remained on the order of 2 to 3 percent.

> " A democracy can't be strong if its citizenship is weak. "

Proponents offer three reasons in favor of mandatory voting. The first is straightforwardly civic. A democracy can't be strong if its citizenship is weak. And right now American citizenship is attenuated—strong on rights, weak on responsibilities. There is less and less that being a citizen requires of us, especially after the abolition of the draft. Requiring people to vote in national elections once every two years would reinforce the principle of reciprocity at the heart of citizenship.

The second argument for mandatory voting is democratic. Ideally, a democracy will take into account the interests and views of all citizens. But if some regularly vote while others don't, officials are likely to give greater weight to participants. This might not matter much if nonparticipants were evenly distributed through the population. But political scientists have long known that they aren't. People with lower levels of income and education are less likely to vote, as are young adults and recent first-generation immigrants.

Changes in our political system have magnified these disparities. During the 1950s and '60s, when turnout rates were much higher, political parties reached out to citizens year-round. At the local level these parties, which reformers often criticized as "machines," connected even citizens of modest means and limited education with neighborhood institutions and gave them a sense of participation in national politics as well. (In its heyday, organized labor reinforced these effects.) But in the absence of these more organic forms of political mobilization, the second-best option is a top-down mechanism of universal mobilization.

Mandatory voting would tend to even out disparities stemming from income, education and age, enhancing our system's inclusiveness. It is true, as some object, that an enforcement mechanism would impose greater burdens on those with fewer resources. But this makes it all the more likely that these citizens would respond by going to the polls, and they would stand to gain far more than the cost of a traffic ticket.

The third argument for mandatory voting goes to the heart of our current ills. Our low turnout rate pushes American politics toward increased polarization. The reason is that hard-core partisans are more likely to dominate lower-turnout elections, while those who are less fervent about specific issues and less attached to political organizations tend not to participate at levels proportional to their share of the electorate.

A distinctive feature of our constitutional system — elections that are 10 quadrennial for president but biennial for the House of Representatives — magnifies these effects. It's bad enough that only three-fifths of the electorate turns out to determine the next president, but much worse that only two-fifths of our citizens vote in House elections two years later. If events combine to energize one part of the political spectrum and dishearten the other, a relatively small portion of the electorate can shift the system out of all proportion to its numbers.

Some observers are comfortable with this asymmetry. But if you think 11 that today's intensely polarized politics impedes governance and exacerbates mistrust — and that is what most Americans firmly (and in my view rightly) believe — then you should be willing to consider reforms that would strengthen the forces of conciliation.

Imagine our politics with laws and civic norms that yield near-universal 12 voting. Campaigns could devote far less money to costly, labor-intensive get-out-the-vote efforts. Media gurus wouldn't have the same incentive to drive down turnout with negative advertising. Candidates would know that they must do more than mobilize their bases with red-meat rhetoric on hot-button issues. Such a system would improve not only electoral politics but also the legislative process. Rather than focusing on symbolic gestures whose major purpose is to agitate partisans, Congress might actually roll up its sleeves and tackle the serious, complex issues it ignores.

The United States is not Australia, of course, and there's no guarantee 13 that the similarity of our political cultures would produce equivalent political results. For example, reforms of general elections would leave untouched the distortions generated by party primaries in which small numbers of voters can shape the choices for the entire electorate. And the United States Constitution gives the states enormous power over voting procedures. Mandating voting nationwide would go counter to our traditions (and perhaps our Constitution) and would encounter strong state opposition. Instead, a half-dozen states from parts of the country with different civic traditions should experiment with the practice, and observers — journalists, social scientists, citizens' groups and elected officials — would monitor the consequences.

We don't know what the outcome would be. But one thing is clear: 14 If we do nothing and allow a politics of passion to define the bounds of the electorate, as it has for much of the last four decades, the prospect for a less polarized, more effective political system that enjoys the trust and confidence of the people is not bright.

Thinking Critically about the Text

Galston believes that voting should be mandatory nationwide, even though he acknowledges that this is likely to go against the Constitution. Why does he feel that voting is of such great importance? What type of argument is he making, and how does he support it?

Questions on Subject

1. What does Galston mean when he says that America is "strong on rights, weak on responsibilities" (paragraph 5)?
2. What three arguments does Galston present in favor of mandatory voting?
3. Where does Galston address opposing arguments? Does he make any rebuttal? How would you address the concerns he raises?
4. How does Galston think that mandatory voting would benefit citizens who have fewer resources?

Questions on Strategy

1. The **title** for this piece, "Telling Americans to Vote, or Else," is effective at capturing the attention of readers. How does the **tone** of the title relate to the tone of the article itself? Why might Galston have made this choice?
2. The article opens with a brief comparison between voting and jury duty. What is the impact of this comparison? Why is it located at the **beginning**?
3. Throughout the article, Galston compares the success of the Australian voting laws with a projection of how those same laws would play out in the United States. What is the effect of this **comparison**? Why is it convincing?
4. Galston labels the three central arguments for mandatory voting. How do these **transitions** help you to follow his argument? How might they be improved?

Argumentation in Action

Organizing your argument effectively can be the key to persuading your audience. Depending on the complexity of the argument you are making, as well as your audience, you could present the same set of information and order it in different ways. Suppose, for example, you wanted to make the case that fracking is harmful to the environment. You could present the risks from least hazardous to most hazardous, or you could describe the process of hydraulic fracturing, noting areas for concern along the way.

In order to see how this works, first make a list of supporting details on the topic of your choice. Then organize them according to any two of the following principles:

- Best to worst
- By process

- Least important to most important
- Simplest to most complicated
- General to specific

Writing Suggestions

1. **Writing from Sources.** Visit the Web site for the International Institute for Democracy and Electoral Assistance (www.idea.int). Spend some time on the site, exploring the trending news. Select a region or topic that interests you and write an exploratory argument on the subject. Don't forget to cite any facts that are not common knowledge. For advice on integrating sources in your essay, see Chapters 14 and 15.

2. **Writing in the Workplace.** Imagine that you are working on a political campaign. You are in charge of writing scripts for the call center that the volunteers will use when they contact potential voters. You will need to write two scripts. The first will be for voters who are believed to be in favor of your candidate. This script should encourage the person to vote, inform him or her of the date of the election, and provide advice on registering in the area. The second should be aimed at voters who may be neutral or hostile. This script should offer evidence on why your candidate is preferable and list some quick responses to frequently asked questions your volunteers may receive. Remember that people are often impatient on the phone, so be concise in delivering your information.

The Organic Fable

ROGER COHEN

Roger Cohen was born in London in 1955. He received his master's degrees in history and French in 1977 from Oxford University before moving to Paris to teach English. While there, he became a contributor to *Paris Metro*. In 1983, Cohen began writing for the *Wall Street Journal* in Rome, before being transferred to Beirut. He became a foreign correspondent for the *New York Times* in 1990, covering the Bosnian War and winning the Burger Human Rights Award for

Gilbert Carrasquillo/FilmMagic/
Getty Images

a piece on a Serbian-run concentration camp. He currently writes a biweekly column for the *New York Times* and has written a number of books, including, most recently, *The Girl from Human Street: Ghosts of Memory in a Jewish Family* (2015).

In "The Organic Fable," an op-ed that first appeared in the *New York Times* on September 6, 2012, Cohen compares the realities of organic food with the romanticized marketing messages. He concludes that while there are some benefits to the concept of organic eating, the practice is not sustainable on a global level.

Preparing to Read

Where do you buy your food? Does it come mostly from a dining hall, a grocery store, or a specialty store? Why do you choose that location: convenience, cost, quality, or a combination of those reasons? What qualities in a store or brand would make you willing to pay more for its food?

At some point—perhaps it was gazing at a Le Pain Quotidien 1 menu offering an "organic baker's basket served with organic butter, organic jam and organic spread" as well as seasonally organic orange juice—I found I just could not stomach the "O" word or what it stood for any longer.

Organic has long since become an ideology, the romantic back-to-nature 2 obsession of an upper middle class able to afford it and oblivious, in their affluent narcissism, to the challenge of feeding a planet whose population will surge to 9 billion before the middle of the century and whose poor will get a lot more nutrients from the two regular carrots they can buy for the price of one organic carrot.

An effective form of premium branding rather than a science, a slogan 3 rather than better nutrition, "organic" has oozed over the menus, markets and malls of the world's upscale neighborhood at a remarkable pace. In 2010, according to the Organic Trade Association, organic food and drink sales totaled $26.7 billion in the United States, or about 4 percent of the overall market, having grown steadily since 2000. The British organic market is also large; menus like to mention that bacon comes from pampered pigs at the Happy Hog farm down the road.

In the midst of the fad few questions have been asked. But the fact is that buying organic baby food, a growing sector, is like paying to send your child to private school: It is a class-driven decision that demonstrates how much you love your offspring but whose overall impact on society is debatable.

So I cheered this week when Stanford University concluded, after examining four decades of research, that fruits and vegetables labeled organic are, on average, no more nutritious than their cheaper conventional counterparts. The study also found that organic meats offered no obvious health advantages. And it found that organic food was not less likely to be contaminated by dangerous bacteria like E. coli.

> **The takeaway from the study could be summed up in two words: Organic, schmorganic.**

The takeaway from the study could be summed up in two words: Organic, schmorganic. That's been my feeling for a while.

Now let me say three nice things about the organic phenomenon. The first is that it reflects a growing awareness about diet that has spurred quality, small-scale local farming that had been at risk of disappearance.

The second is that even if it's not better for you, organic farming is probably better for the environment because less soil, flora and fauna are contaminated by chemicals (although of course, without fertilizers, you have to use more land to grow the same amount of produce or feed the same amount of livestock). So this is food that is better ecologically even if it is not better nutritionally.

The third is that the word "organic"—unlike other feel-good descriptions of food like "natural"—actually means something. Certification procedures in both the United States and Britain are strict. In the United States, organic food must meet standards ensuring that genetic engineering, synthetic fertilizers, sewage and irradiation were not used in the food's production. It must also be produced using methods that, according to the Department of Agriculture, "foster cycling of resources, promote ecological balance and conserve biodiversity."

Still, the organic ideology is an elitist, pseudoscientific indulgence shot through with hype. There is a niche for it, if you can afford to shop at Whole Foods, but the future is nonorganic.

To feed a planet of 9 billion people, we are going to need high yields not low yields; we are going to need genetically modified crops; we are going to need pesticides and fertilizers and other elements of the industrialized food processes that have led mankind to be better fed and live longer than at any time in history.

Logically, the organic movement should favor genetically modified pro- 12 duce. If you cannot use pesticides or fertilizers, you might at least want to modify your crops so they are more resilient and plentiful. But that would go against the ideology and romance of a movement that says: We are for nature, everyone else is against nature.

I'd rather be against nature and have more people better fed. I'd rather 13 be serious about the world's needs. And I trust the monitoring agencies that ensure pesticides are used at safe levels—a trust the Stanford study found to be justified.

Martin Orbach, the co-founder and program director of the Aber- 14 gavenny Food Festival in Britain, owns a company called Shepherds that produces a superb sheep's milk ice-cream sold at a store in Hay-on-Wye. It has a cult following at the Hay literary festival and beyond. Journalists, Orbach told me, regularly report that they have eaten an "organic sheep's milk ice cream."

The only catch is this is not true. "We have never said it's organic because 15 it would be illegal for us to do so," Orbach said. "But it fits with the story of a small sheep's milk ice-cream maker."

Organic is a fable of the pampered parts of the planet—romantic and 16 comforting. Now, thanks to Stanford researchers, we know just how replete with myth the "O" fable is.

Thinking Critically about the Text

If Cohen is correct, and the benefits of organic food are largely a myth, what do you think it would take to convince others to stop purchasing specifically organic food? What does Cohen believe is the potential impact if this trend continues?

Questions on Subject

1. What type of argument is Cohen making? (See "Types of Argument," pages 380–82, for a discussion of the different types of argument.) How do you know?

2. Cohen describes the term *organic* as "an effective form of premium branding rather than a science" (paragraph 3). What does he mean? How does this idea support his thesis?

3. Why does Cohen say that the organic movement will not "favor genetically modified produce" (paragraph 12)? Why does he believe it should?

4. What does Cohen mean when he says that he would rather be "against nature and have more people better fed" (paragraph 13)? Why is this a potentially controversial statement, given his likely readership?

Questions on Strategy

1. Where does Cohen state his **thesis**? Why do you think he expresses it as he does?

2. Find moments in the piece where Cohen incorporates quotes from outside sources. Select three and explain how they contribute to Cohen's argument.

3. Why, after agreeing with a Stanford University study that organic food is not any better, does Cohen go on to "say three nice things about the organic phenomenon" (paragraph 7)?

4. Cohen is actually making two connected arguments in his essay: that organic food is not any better for you and that we need pesticides and other chemicals to grow enough food to feed the world. How does Cohen connect these two ideas? Does he spend more time on either argument, or does he spend equal time on both?

Argumentation in Action

In the process of arguing against organic foods, Cohen makes an argument about what the term *organic* actually means, particularly in terms of the health of consumers. Write your own definition of one of the following food-related words and explain how the term is more complicated — or means something different — than most people realize.

Artisanal	Light	Natural
Free	Local	Sustainable
Lean		

Writing Suggestions

1. Write a rebuttal addressing Cohen's points and arguing for the importance of having an organic food option.

2. **Writing from Sources.** One of the benefits Cohen mentions for organic food is the resurgence of small-scale local farms. Do some research into this sort of farm and make an argument for or against the need to develop more of them. What are the benefits of local farms? What are the benefits of large, corporate food organizations? Which benefits, in your opinion, are the most important? For models of and advice on integrating sources in your essay, see Chapters 14 and 15.

Campus Racism 101

NIKKI GIOVANNI

Yolanda Cornelia "Nikki" Giovanni was born in Knoxville, Tennessee, in 1943 and raised in Ohio. After graduating from Fisk University, she organized the Black Arts Festival in Cincinnati and then entered graduate school at the University of Pennsylvania. Her first book of poetry, *Black Feeling, Black Talk*, was published in 1968 and began a lifetime of writing that reflects on the African American identity. Recent books of poetry include the anthologies *Selected Poems by Nikki Giovanni* (1996), *Blues for All the Changes: New*

Courtesy of Nikki Giovanni

Poems (1999), *Quilting the Black-Eyed Pea: Poems and Not Quite Poems* (2002), *Bicycles: Love Poems* (2009), and *Chasing Utopia: A Hybrid* (2013). Her honors include the Langston Hughes Award for Distinguished Contributions to Arts and Letters in 1996, seven NAACP Image awards, and Woman of the Year awards from several magazines, including *Essence*, *Mademoiselle*, and *Ladies' Home Journal*. She is currently professor of English and Gloria D. Smith Professor of Black Studies at Virginia Tech.

The following selection, taken from her nonfiction work *Racism* (1995), instructs black students about how to succeed at predominantly white colleges.

Preparing to Read

How would you characterize race relations at your school? How much do white and minority students interact, and what, in your experience, is the tone of those interactions? What is being done within the institution to address any problems or to foster greater respect and understanding?

There is a bumper sticker that reads: TOO BAD IGNORANCE ISN'T PAIN- 1
FUL. I like that. But ignorance is. We just seldom attribute the pain to it or even recognize it when we see it. Like the postcard on my corkboard. It shows a young man in a very hip jacket smoking a cigarette. In the background is a high school with the American flag waving. The caption says: "Too cool for school. Yet too stupid for the real world." Out of the mouth of the young man is a bubble enclosing the words "Maybe I'll start a band." There could be a postcard showing a jock in a uniform saying, "I don't need school. I'm going to the NFL or NBA." Or one showing a young man or woman studying and a group of young people saying, "So you want to be white." Or something equally demeaning. We need to quit it.

I am a professor of English at Virginia Tech. I've been here for four years, 2
though for only two years with academic rank. I am tenured, which means I have

a teaching position for life, a rarity on a predominantly white campus. Whether from malice or ignorance, people who think I should be at a predominantly Black institution will ask, "Why are you at Tech?" Because it's here. And so are Black students. But even if Black students weren't here, it's painfully obvious that this nation and this world cannot allow white students to go through higher education without interacting with Blacks in authoritative positions. It is equally clear that predominantly Black colleges cannot accommodate the numbers of Black students who want and need an education.

Is it difficult to attend a predominantly white college? Compared with what? Being passed over for promotion because you lack credentials? Being turned down for jobs because you are not college-educated? Joining the armed forces or going to jail because you cannot find an alternative to the streets? Let's have a little perspective here. Where can you go and what can you do that frees you from interacting with the white American mentality? You're going to interact; the only question is, will you be in some control of yourself and your actions, or will you be controlled by others? I'm going to recommend self-control.

What's the difference between prison and college? They both prescribe your behavior for a given period of time. They both allow you to read books and develop your writing. They both give you time alone to think and time with your peers to talk about issues. But four years of prison doesn't give you a passport to greater opportunities. Most likely that time only gives you greater knowledge of how to get back in. Four years of college gives you an opportunity not only to lift yourself but to serve your people effectively. What's the difference when you are called nigger in college from when you are called nigger in prison? In college you can, though I admit with effort, follow procedures to have those students who called you nigger kicked out or suspended. You can bring issues to public attention without risking your life. But mostly, college is and always has been the future. We, neither less nor more than other people, need knowledge. There are discomforts attached to attending predominantly white colleges, though no more so than living in a racist world. Here are some rules to follow that may help:

> **There are discomforts attached to attending predominantly white colleges, though no more so than living in a racist world.**

Go to class. No matter how you feel. No matter how you think the professor feels about you. It's important to have a consistent presence in the classroom. If nothing else, the professor will know you care enough and are serious enough to be there.

Meet your professors. Extend your hand (give a firm handshake) and tell them your name. Ask them what you need to do to make an A. You may never make an A, but you have put them on notice that you are serious about getting good grades.

Do assignments on time. Typed or computer-generated. You have the 7 syllabus. Follow it, and turn those papers in. If for some reason you can't complete an assignment on time, let your professor know before it is due and work out a new due date — then meet it.

Go back to see your professor. Tell him or her your name again. If an assign- 8 ment received less than an A, ask why, and find out what you need to do to improve the next assignment.

Yes, your professor is busy. So are you. So are your parents who are working 9 to pay or help with your tuition. Ask early what you need to do if you feel you are starting to get into academic trouble. Do not wait until you are failing.

Understand that there will be professors who do not like you; there may even 10 be professors who are racist or sexist or both. You must discriminate among your professors to see who will give you the help you need. You may not simply say, "They are all against me." They aren't. They mostly don't care. Since you are the one who wants to be educated, find the people who want to help.

Don't defeat yourself. Cultivate your friends. Know your enemies. You can- 11 not undo hundreds of years of prejudicial thinking. Think for yourself and speak up. Raise your hand in class. Say what you believe no matter how awkward you may think it sounds. You will improve in your articulation and confidence.

Participate in some campus activity. Join the newspaper staff. Run for 12 office. Join a dorm council. Do something that involves you on campus. You are going to be there for four years, so let your presence be known, if not felt.

You will inevitably run into some white classmates who are troubling 13 because they often say stupid things, ask stupid questions — and expect an answer. Here are some comebacks to some of the most common inquiries and comments:

Q: What's it like to grow up in a ghetto?
A: I don't know.

Q: (from the teacher) Can you give us the Black perspective on Toni Morrison, Huck Finn, slavery, Martin Luther King Jr., and others?
A: I can give you *my* perspective. (Do not take the burden of 22 million people on your shoulders. Remind everyone that you are an individual, and don't speak for the race or any other individual within it.)

Q: Why do all the Black people sit together in the dining hall?
A: Why do all the white students sit together?

Q: Why should there be an African American studies course?
A: Because white Americans have not adequately studied the contributions of Africans and African Americans. Both Black and white students need to know our total common history.

Q: Why are there so many scholarships for "minority" students?
A: Because they wouldn't give my great-grandparents their forty acres and the mule.

Q: How can whites understand Black history, culture, literature, and so forth?
A: The same way we understand white history, culture, literature, and so forth. That is why we're in school: to learn.

Q: Should whites take African American studies courses?
A: Of course. We take white-studies courses, though the universities don't call them that.

Comment: When I see groups of Black people on campus, it's really intimidating.
Comeback: I understand what you mean. I'm frightened when I see white students congregating.

Comment: It's not fair. It's easier for you guys to get into college than for other people.
Comeback: If it's so easy, why aren't there more of us?

Comment: It's not our fault that America is the way it is.
Comeback: It's not our fault, either, but both of us have a responsibility to make changes.

It's really very simple. Educational progress is a national concern; education is a private one. Your job is not to educate white people; it is to obtain an education. If you take the racial world on your shoulders, you will not get the job done. Deal with yourself as an individual worthy of respect, and make everyone else deal with you the same way. College is a little like playing grown-up. Practice what you want to be. You have been telling your parents you are grown. Now is your chance to act like it. 14

Thinking Critically about the Text

Giovanni concludes her essay by pointing out the nature of the "job" black students have undertaken, focusing on what it does *not* involve for them. For you, does the "job" of being a student involve more than just getting an education? If so, what other priorities do you have, and what additional challenges do they present? If not, explain your situation. How well are you able to put other things aside to achieve your educational goals?

Questions on Subject

1. Who is Giovanni's **audience**? When does the intended audience first become clear?

2. Why does Giovanni dismiss the notion that it is difficult being a black student at a predominantly white college? What contexts does she use to support her contention?

3. The rules Giovanni presents to help black students succeed at white colleges offer a lot of sound advice for any student at any college. Why does Giovanni use what could be considered general information in her essay?

4. On what topic does Giovanni provide sample questions and answers for her readers? Why is the topic important to her readers?

Questions on Strategy

1. What is Giovanni arguing for in this essay? What is her **thesis**?

2. Giovanni begins her essay with staccato rhythm. Short sentences appear throughout the essay, but they are emphasized in the **beginning**. Reread paragraph 1. What does Giovanni accomplish with her rapid-fire delivery? Why is it appropriate for the subject matter?

3. What does Giovanni gain by including her short personal narrative in paragraph 2? Why is it necessary to know her personal history and current situation?

4. After beginning her essay with straight prose, Giovanni uses a list with full explanations and a series of Q&A examples to outline strategies to help black students cope at predominantly white colleges. Why did Giovanni use these techniques to convey her material? How might they add to the usefulness of the essay for the reader?

Argumentation in Action

One strategy in developing a strong argument that most people find convincing is illustration. As Giovanni demonstrates, an array of examples, both brief and extended, real and hypothetical, have a remarkable ability to convince readers of the truth of a proposition. While it is possible to argue a case with one specific example that is both appropriate and representative, most writers find that a varied set of examples often makes a more convincing case. Therefore, it is important to identify your examples before starting to write.

As an exercise in argumentation, choose one of the following position statements:

- More parking spaces should be provided on campus for students.
- Capital punishment is a relatively ineffective deterrent to crime.
- More computer stations should be provided on campus for students.
- In-state residency requirements for tuition are unfair at my school.

Make a list of the examples — types of information and evidence — you would need to write an argumentative essay on the topic you choose. Indicate where and how you might obtain this information. Finally, share your list of examples with other students in your class who chose the same topic.

Writing Suggestions

1. What specific strategies do you employ to do well in your classes? Do you ask the professor what is needed for an A and make sure you attend every class, as Giovanni suggests in her essay? Do you take meticulous notes, study every day, just cram the night before exams, or have a lucky shirt for test days? Write an essay in which you present your argument for how to succeed in college in a way that others could emulate.

2. **Writing with Sources.** The battle over education rights became one of the most important components of the civil rights movement and led to some of the most contentious showdowns. The following photograph shows James Meredith as he attempts to become the first African American to enter the University of Mississippi on October 1, 1962. His efforts resulted in riots that

Flip Schulke/CORBIS/Corbis via Getty Images

caused two deaths and 160 injuries. Meredith graduated from Ole Miss in 1964 and then went on to Columbia University and earned a degree in law.

What evidence of determination do you see on the faces and in the body language of both those who wished to keep James Meredith from entering the university and those who were his supporters? What do you learn from the posture and expression of Meredith himself? Notice that the photograph reveals a sort of mirror image, with the opposing sides reflecting each other's confrontational attitudes.

Research the background and precipitating circumstances of Meredith's admittance to the University of Mississippi, and write an essay explaining the process he went through to make his case heard and accepted by authorities in the civil rights movement, the federal government, the state of Mississippi, and the university. You might also research the Black Lives Matter movement and student protests on college campuses to make an argument about current tensions surrounding race and higher education. For models of and advice on integrating sources in your essay, see Chapters 14 and 15.

On the Subject of Trigger Warnings

SIOBHAN CROWLEY

Siobhan Crowley is a teaching assistant who has requested that her school remain anonymous. She is currently pursuing a graduate degree in English literature and teaches first-year writing and literature. She grew up in rural Missouri.

The following essay was written in response to a call for writing on the topic of education and safe spaces. In it, Crowley expresses her mixed feelings about avoiding triggering issues in her own classroom.

Preparing to Read

Do you think instructors should be required to warn students that readings, lectures, and other teaching materials may include troubling ideas for some students? For example, if someone close to you has committed suicide, should you be required to relive memories of that incident and consider it in an educational setting? On the other hand, might the more objective and intellectual analysis of painful subjects in a supportive educational setting actually lead to understanding and healing? Explain.

A college president at a Midwestern school recently took issue with 1 the idea of "triggers" and "safe zones." He remarked vividly that his school "is not a daycare. [It] is a university." While I can appreciate the snarkiness of his comments, and the frustration with yet another roadblock to effectively teaching students, I have to disagree with his stance that there is anything infantile about dealing with triggering experiences. The trauma involved can be very real, and I think student concerns need to be met with serious reflection. I have concerns, however, over whether they can be met with equally serious action, if not for the reasons that a certain president mentions.

Let's start with the easy part of the argument: If a student has experiences 2 that impede their ability to approach certain subject matter, then allowances absolutely need to be made. Alternative assignments might be created, for instance, or a student might be excused from multiple class sessions. Final tests might be adapted for the one or two students who have come privately to express their inability to address certain topics.

From there, however, the question gets more difficult. Let's say you study 3 literature. Or sociology. And you can't read certain selections because the idea of imperialism or slavery is a trigger for you. Or the concept of sexual assault is a trigger for you. So you don't study *Huckleberry Finn* or *Othello* or read Marx or chunks of Weber. And then you go out into the world to use your degree and you have these glaring blind spots. You won't have been prepared adequately in the field you said you studied. Let's say you want to be a teacher (as many TAs in English go on to do). Are you going to *not* teach *Romeo and Juliet* because someone in your family committed suicide? Or not teach *Huck Finn* because you can't address the issue of race? That would be a criminal neglect to students who need to learn this material, if only so that they can address *exactly these issues*. Will your papers ever be accepted in a sociological journal if you skip obvious references to canon theorists?

I appreciate the validity of trigger-warnings and other accommodations as a theory, but I think that they can only apply to non-major courses. Someone majoring in math certainly doesn't need to know *Othello* (though they might benefit from doing so). But someone who majors in English really ought to. Not even *Othello* specifically, but you just can't get away from race or sexual violence, or suicide, or any triggering issue in literature because these are the very meat of what authors are trying to address.

The other concern, of course, is that great literature is great *because* it tackles these painful topics. *Beloved* and *Sula* were difficult books to read, but there is power in tapping into that artistic expression of pain. Power that I worry my students will need when they leave school behind and enter a culture that does not make the allowances that college professors can make. A world full of triggering episodes. I would hate for students to miss an opportunity to work through their trauma in my classroom, where I can mediate discussions to ensure that comments are not hurtful. Particularly if that student makes me aware of their fears and I can work with them in conjunction with a university counselor. There is so much to be gained from the study of literature, including the ability to address and mediate the very triggering issues that students want to avoid. It makes me sad to think that students will blindly turn away from that power and that opportunity. Even for the very best of reasons.

Thinking Critically about the Text

This message was written by a graduate student and teaching assistant at a four-year college. How do you think Crowley's teaching experience has influenced her stance on trigger warnings? Do you think that experience strengthens or undermines her perspective?

Questions on Subject

1. What is Crowley trying to convince her readers of in this argument? Were you convinced? Why, or why not?

2. If Crowley is saying she agrees with her college president's remarks about "'triggers' and 'safe zones,'" is she doing so for the same reason he has? Explain.

3. Crowley identifies two central concerns with not teaching triggering content. What are they?

4. In paragraph 5, Crowley argues that there is "power in tapping into that artistic expression of pain." What do you think that power might be? Do you agree with Crowley that it exists?

Questions on Strategy

1. On the basis of what authority does Crowley make her argument? (Glossary: *ethos*) Does her position make you more or less likely to be convinced by her argument? Why?

2. What distinction does Crowley make between majors and non-majors? Why is it important to her argument?

3. Does Crowley argue **inductively** or **deductively**, or use some combination of both approaches? How do you know?

4. How effective is the author's conclusion? Explain.

Argumentation in Action

A good argument relies on the reasoned refutation of counterarguments. Yet, counterarguments are difficult to see when you're writing because you may be so invested in your position that opposing views simply don't enter into your thinking. Work in groups of three and have each member of the group briefly present a thesis. Have the other two members of the group present realistic counterarguments. Each presenter should then offer ways of rebutting the counterarguments to his or her position. The object of this exercise is to become more familiar with counterarguments and how you as a writer might answer them.

Here is an example of how this might work in your group.

> **Presenter offers a thesis:** "The opioid crisis can best be solved by having tighter controls on the pharmaceutical industry."
>
> **Opponents offer counterarguments:** "Big pharmaceutical companies have a lot of power and money and are difficult to regulate because of powerful lobbies working on their behalf."
>
> **Presenter gives rebuttals:** "We can fight the big drug companies with new legislation to stop the senseless overproduction of opioid medications; we can mount powerful public service announcements that bring pressure to bear on the ethics of those drug companies and their lobbyists; we can use advertising, such as was done with cigarette smoking, that makes the public more aware of the dangers of opioids."

Writing Suggestions

1. While Crowley "appreciates" the college president's "snarkiness" in responding to threats to students' mental health, she says he does not take the need for "'triggers' and 'safe zones'" seriously or in an educationally sound manner.

Write an argumentative essay in which you take the college president's position but argue the issues responsibly and in a positive manner. Offer an intelligent response to the legitimate concerns of students who are shaken by speakers, written documents, graphic images, frightening audio and television presentations, and classroom environments that raise anxiety levels. You may, of course, include Crowley's own approach to the problem as an opposing source.

2. Write an argumentative essay in which you agree or disagree with the approach your school has taken in dealing with issues involving "triggers" and "microaggressions." What is free speech, and what is hate speech? Who gets to make the decision about which is which? Are some forms of discomfort and trauma healing necessary? Or should students be protected from ideas that conflict with their foundational beliefs? Where do we draw the line? Has your school made a difficult situation better or worse?

I Invested Early in Google and Facebook. Now They Terrify Me.

ROGER MCNAMEE

Rob Kim/Getty Images

Investor and venture capitalist Roger McNamee was born in 1956 in Albany, New York, and graduated from Yale University and Dartmouth's Tuck School of Business. He cofounded Elevation Partners, an investment firm focused on media, entertainment content, and consumer technology, and now serves as the company's managing director. Previously, McNamee worked at the global financial services company T. Rowe Price and cofounded the private equity firm Silver Lake Partners.

McNamee has a long history of working (and investing) in technology, as he notes in the introduction of this opinion column, which appeared in *USA Today* on August 8, 2017. (This piece published before the Cambridge Analytica scandal, where Facebook data from 50 million users was used to inform the 2016 United States presidential election.) Despite his early investments, McNamee is now deeply concerned that our technologies and devices have become a "menace to public health and to democracy." As you read, consider what changed his mind, as well as the ways in which technology can threaten the ideals, customs, and conventions of our political system.

Preparing to Read

Do you find technologies and devices addictive? Do you find it difficult to disengage from them? Have you witnessed other people struggle to "unplug" themselves? Do companies like Netflix, Facebook, and others bear any blame for the dangers of addictive behaviors, or should all the responsibility be placed on individual users and consumers?

invested in Google and Facebook years before their first revenue and profited enormously. I was an early adviser to Facebook's team, but I am terrified by the damage being done by these internet monopolies.   1

Technology has transformed our lives in countless ways, mostly for   2
the better. Thanks to the now ubiquitous smartphone, tech touches us from the moment we wake up until we go to sleep. While the convenience of smartphones has many benefits, the unintended consequences of well-intentioned product choices have become a menace to public health and to democracy.

Facebook and Google get their revenue from advertising, the effec- 3
tiveness of which depends on gaining and maintaining consumer attention. Borrowing techniques from the gambling industry, Facebook, Google
and others exploit human nature, creating addictive behaviors that compel
consumers to check for new messages, respond to notifications and seek
validation from technologies whose only goal is to generate profits for
their owners.

The people at Facebook and Google believe that giving consumers more 4
of what they want and like is worthy of praise, not criticism. What they fail
to recognize is that their products are not making consumers happier or
more successful. Like gambling, nicotine, alcohol or heroin, Facebook and
Google—most importantly through its YouTube subsidiary—produce short-
term happiness with serious negative consequences in the long term. Users fail
to recognize the warning signs of addiction until it is too late. There are only
24 hours in a day, and technology companies are making a play for all of them.
The CEO of Netflix recently noted that his company's primary competitor
is sleep.

How does this work? A 2013 study found that average consumers check 5
their smartphones 150 times a day. And that number has probably grown.
People spend 50 minutes a day on Facebook. Other social apps such as
Snapchat, Instagram and Twitter combine to take up still more time. Those
companies maintain a profile on every user, which grows every time you
like, share, search, shop or post a photo. Google also is analyzing credit card
records of millions of people.

> **The big internet companies know more about you than you know about yourself, which gives them huge power to influence you, to persuade you to do things that serve their economic interests.**

As a result, the big internet com- 6
panies know more about you than you
know about yourself, which gives them
huge power to influence you, to persuade you to do things that serve their
economic interests. Facebook, Google
and others compete for each consumer's
attention, reinforcing biases and reducing the diversity of ideas to which each
is exposed. The degree of harm grows
over time.

Consider a recent story from 7
Australia, where someone at Facebook told advertisers that they had the
ability to target teens who were sad or depressed, which made them more
susceptible to advertising. In the United States, Facebook once demonstrated
its ability to make users happier or sadder by manipulating their news feed.
While it did not turn either capability into a product, the fact remains that
Facebook influences the emotional state of users every moment of every day.
Former Google design ethicist Tristan Harris calls this "brain hacking."

The fault here is not with search and social networking, per se. Those 8 services have enormous value. The fault lies with advertising business models that drive companies to maximize attention at all costs, leading to ever more aggressive brain hacking.

The Facebook application has 2 billion active users around the world. 9 Google's YouTube has 1.5 billion. These numbers are comparable to Christianity and Islam, respectively, giving Facebook and Google influence greater than most First World countries. They are too big and too global to be held accountable. Other attention-based apps—including Instagram, WhatsApp, WeChat, SnapChat and Twitter—also have user bases between 100 million and 1.3 billion. Not all their users have had their brains hacked, but all are on that path. And there are no watchdogs.

Anyone who wants to pay for access to addicted users can work with 10 Facebook and YouTube. Lots of bad people have done it. One firm was caught using Facebook tools to spy on law-abiding citizens. A federal agency confronted Facebook about the use of its tools by financial firms to discriminate based on race in the housing market. America's intelligence agencies have concluded that Russia interfered in our election and that Facebook was a key platform for spreading misinformation. For the price of a few fighter aircraft, Russia won an information war against us.

Incentives being what they are, we cannot expect internet monopolies to 11 police themselves. There is little government regulation and no appetite to change that. If we want to stop brain hacking, consumers will have to force changes at Facebook and Google.

Thinking Critically about the Text

As both his biography and his opinion column suggest, McNamee has benefited financially from companies such as Google, Facebook, and others. How does his background shape your view of his argument? Do you see his position as hypocritical in any way?

Questions on Subject

1. What is "brain hacking"?

2. McNamee notes, "The CEO of Netflix recently noted that his company's primary competitor is sleep" (paragraph 4). What does this suggest about the appeal of our technologies?

3. When assessing responsibility for the "menace" of new technologies, McNamee writes, "The fault here is not with search and social networking, per se" (paragraph 8). Who or what does he find at fault?

4. In the conclusion, McNamee argues that "incentives" have created this situation with Internet monopolies. What incentives does he mean? What solution does he propose?

Questions on Strategy

1. How would you define the rhetorical appeal in the first paragraph? Is it *ethos*, *pathos*, or *logos*? Explain.

2. How does McNamee incorporate **cause and effect analysis** into his argument? Point to specific examples. Why is this strategy so important to his **purpose**?

3. What **analogy** does McNamee use in paragraph 4? Do you find it accurate and persuasive? Why, or why not?

4. Who is McNamee's intended **audience**? Do you think he sees his readers as friendly, uncommitted, skeptical, or hostile? How does his sense of audience shape his writing strategy?

Argument in Action

The Socratic Method, named after the Greek philosopher Socrates's approach to teaching, involves asking and answering questions to help develop a student's thinking skills. Try it in class. In groups of three, begin with a broad question from the following list and take turns asking and answering questions until you have narrowed the issue into a useful argumentative thesis.

- Is fracking good or bad for the environment?
- Does democracy work?
- Should everyone study a foreign language?
- What does country matter?
- Is philosophy still a useful field of study?

Writing Suggestions

1. After having invested in companies such as Google and Facebook, McNamee has now changed his mind about them. Have you ever changed your mind about an issue, topic, or controversy? What led you to do so? What was your original perspective? What factors caused you to change your mind? For example, did new evidence emerge? Did your more general premises or assumptions change? Did a well-presented argument invite you to see a different side of the issue? In an essay, explain how and why you changed your mind, taking care to analyze any arguments you found effective in making you think differently.

2. McNamee makes a provocative argument: one that seeks not only to change people's views, but perhaps change their behaviors. How do you respond to his column? Do you agree or disagree with his stances on the influence of big Internet companies or the effects of social media? Are you "on the path" to having your brain hacked? Write a response to his argument that evaluates its strengths and weaknesses as it applies to your own experiences and viewpoints. What does McNamee get right? What does he get wrong? Will you change your behaviors? Why, or why not?

ARGUMENT CLUSTER

Race and Privilege: How Do We Address a System of Bias?

JONATHAN BACHMAN/REUTERS/Newscom

VISUALIZING THE ISSUE: RACE AND PRIVILEGE

This photo of a young woman facing a trio of police officers represents the dramatic confrontation that has been taking place between the Black Lives Matter protesters and police in recent years. One particular flashpoint, captured during a demonstration protesting the death of Alton Sterling in Baton Rouge, Louisiana, is highlighted by the many stark contrasts in this particular photo. How many of those contrasting details can you identify? How do those details, and others in the photo, affect the audience or contribute to the effect of the photo? Why do you think this photo went viral, becoming a symbol for the Black Lives Matter cause?

Intolerance and racism have sadly been a part of the United States since it was established a few centuries ago. As a society, we have celebrated movement toward equality, holding up leaders of the civil rights movement as the social heroes they were. And, as a society, we have felt the shame and regret of our many missteps. Social scientists are coming to realize, however, that the problem of racism does not have clear, obvious definitions and boundaries. In 1999, an investigation was made into the brutal, racially motivated murder of Stephen Lawrence, a resident of London. The public investigation into his death revealed an as-yet-undefined threat: institutional racism. This is a form of discrimination practiced not by individuals but openly or subtly by political entities, organizations, and companies.

The term *institutional racism* has been embraced by activists and social scientists in the United States as a valuable tool for understanding — and hopefully counteracting — this pervasive and damaging prejudice. Conversations and controversy arose around well-publicized instances of police violence against African American men such as Trayvon Martin, Michael Brown, and Eric Gardner, leading to the Black Lives Matter movement. But there is also a subtle form of racism. Research at Teachers College, Columbia University, led Derald Wing Sue to classify some of what scholars in the field term *microaggressions*, or "the brief and everyday slights, insults, indignities and denigrating messages sent to people of color by well-intentioned White people who are unaware of the hidden messages being communicated." Sue goes on to note that these actions are not a part of conscious behaviors and hopes that by raising awareness and making "the 'invisible' visible," people might help to eradicate this form of racism.

All of the authors in this cluster attempt to delve beyond the obvious expressions of racism in our society to explore the subtle aggressions and systematic disadvantages that are so divisive, and all of them do so with an eye toward both self-improvement and creating a culture of change. In addition to Sue's essay, "Racial Microagressions in Everyday Life: Is Subtle Bias Harmless?," John Metta explains why he hesitates to talk about race with "White people" and shares his resolution to speak up in the future in his essay "I, Racist." Finally, in "No, I Won't Be Writing about Black-on-Black Crime," Shaun King answers critics who want him to redirect his social criticism on police brutality in the United States.

Preparing to Read

What role does race play in your life? Is it something that impacts you on a daily basis or something that you seldom consider? Do you think it's possible to address the subtle biases and institutional prejudices that plague our society? How might we do so? Is awareness enough of a first step, as some of the authors in this cluster propose? How does social change happen?

I, Racist

JOHN METTA

John Metta studied anthropology and geology at the College of Charleston before earning master's degrees in ecological engineering and resource geography. A programmer and integrations specialist in the software industry, he has also worked as a teacher, cook, clerk, and park ranger. His work has appeared in the *San Francisco Chronicle*, the *Huffington Post*, Al Jazeera, and Medium.

Jessica Metta

Metta describes this selection as "the text of 'a sermon' he gave" to an all-white audience at the Bethel Congregational Church of Christ. He began with this quote from Chimamanda Ngozi Adichie's *Americanah*:

> The only reason you say that race was not an issue is because you wish it was not. We all wish it was not. But it's a lie. I came from a country where race was not an issue; I did not think of myself as black and I only became black when I came to America. When you are black in America and you fall in love with a white person, race doesn't matter when you're alone together because it's just you and your love. But the minute you step outside, race matters. But we don't talk about it. We don't even tell our white partners the small things that piss us off and the things we wish they understood better, because we're worried they will say we're overreacting, or we're being too sensitive. And we don't want them to say, Look how far we've come, just forty years ago it would have been illegal for us to even be a couple blah blah blah, because you know what we're thinking when they say that? We're thinking why the fuck should it ever have been illegal anyway? But we don't say any of this stuff. We let it pile up inside our heads and when we come to nice liberal dinners like this, we say that race doesn't matter because that's what we're supposed to say, to keep our nice liberal friends comfortable. It's true. I speak from experience.

Consider how this quotation relates to Metta's argument.

A couple weeks ago, I was debating what I was going to talk about 1
in this sermon. I told Pastor Kelly Ryan I had great reservations talking about the one topic that I think about every single day.

Then, a terrorist massacred nine innocent people in a church that I went 2
to, in a city that I still think of as home. At that point, I knew that despite any misgivings, I needed to talk about race.

You see, I don't talk about race with White people. 3

To illustrate why, I'll tell a story: 4

It was probably about 15 years ago when a conversation took place 5
between my aunt, who is White and lives in New York State, and my sister,

who is Black and lives in North Carolina. This conversation can be distilled to a single sentence, said by my Black sister:

"The only difference between people in the North and people in the 6 South is that down here, at least people are honest about being racist."

> **❝ You see, I don't talk about race with White people. ❞**

There was a lot more to that conversation, obviously, but I suggest that it can be distilled into that one sentence because it has been, by my White aunt. Over a decade later, this sentence is still what she talks about. It has become the single most important aspect of my aunt's relationship with my Black family. She is still hurt by the suggestion that people in New York, that she, a northerner, a liberal, a good person who has Black family members, is a racist.

This perfectly illustrates why I don't talk about race with White people. 8 Even—or rather, especially—my own family.

I love my aunt. She's actually my favorite aunt, and believe me, I have *a* 9 *lot* of awesome aunts to choose from. But the facts are actually quite in my sister's favor on this one.

New York State is one of the most segregated states in the country. 10 Buffalo, New York, where my aunt lives, is one of the 10 most segregated school systems in the country. The racial inequality of the area she inhabits is so bad that it has been the subject of reports by the Civil Rights Action Network and the NAACP.

Those, however, are facts that my aunt does not need to know. She does 11 not need to live with the racial segregation and oppression of her home. As a white person with upward mobility, she has continued to improve her situation. She moved out of the area I grew up in—she moved to an area with better schools. She doesn't have to experience racism, and so it is not real to her.

Nor does it dawn on her that the very fact that she moved away from an 12 increasingly Black neighborhood to live in a White suburb might itself be an aspect of racism. She doesn't need to realize that "better schools" exclusively means "whiter schools."

I don't talk about race with White people because I have so often seen it 13 go nowhere. When I was younger, I thought it was because all white people are racist. Recently, I've begun to understand that it's more nuanced than that.

To understand, you have to know that Black people think in terms of 14 Black *people.*

We don't see a shooting of an innocent Black child in another state as 15 something separate from us because we know viscerally that it could be our child, our parent, or us, that is shot.

The shooting of Walter Scott in North Charleston resonated with 16 me because Walter Scott was portrayed in the media as a deadbeat and a criminal—but when you look at the facts about the actual man, he was nearly indistinguishable from my own father.

Racism affects us directly because the fact that it happened at a geographically remote location or to another Black person is only a coincidence, an accident. It could just as easily happen to us—right here, right now. 17

Black people think in terms of *we* because we live in a society where the social and political structures interact with us *as Black people.* 18

White people do not think in terms of *we.* White people have the privilege to interact with the social and political structures of our society *as individuals.* You are "you," I am "one of them." Whites are often not directly affected by racial oppression even in their own community, so what does not affect them locally has little chance of affecting them regionally or nationally. They have no need, nor often any real desire, to think in terms of a group. They are supported by the system, and so are mostly unaffected by it. 19

What they are affected by are attacks on their own character. To my aunt, the suggestion that "people in the North are racist" is an attack on her *as a racist.* She is unable to differentiate her participation *within* a racist system (upwardly mobile, not racially profiled, able to move to White suburbs, etc.) from an accusation that she, individually, is *a racist.* Without being able to make that differentiation, White people in general decide to vigorously defend their own personal non-racism, or point out that it doesn't exist because they don't see it. 20

The result of this is an incessantly repeating argument where a Black person says "Racism still exists. It is real," and a white person argues "You're wrong, I'm not racist at all. I don't even see any racism." My aunt's immediate response is not "that is wrong, we should do better." No, her response is self-protection: "That's not my fault, I didn't do anything. You are wrong." 21

Racism is not slavery. As President Obama said, it's not avoiding the use of the word Nigger. Racism is not white water fountains and the back of the bus. Martin Luther King did not end racism. Racism is a cop severing the spine of an innocent man. It is a 12 year old child being shot for playing with a toy gun in a state where it is legal to openly carry firearms. 22

But racism is even more subtle than that. It's more nuanced. Racism is the fact that "White" means "normal" and that anything else is different. Racism is our acceptance of an all white Lord of the Rings cast because of "historical accuracy," ignoring the fact that this is a world with an *entirely fictionalized history.* 23

Even when we make shit up, we want it to be white. 24

And racism is the fact that we all *accept* that it *is* white. Benedict Cumberbatch playing Khan in Star Trek. Khan, who is from India. Is there anyone Whiter than Benedict fucking Cumberbatch? What? They needed a "less racial" cast because they already had the Black Uhura character? 25

That is racism. Once you let yourself see it, it's there all the time. 26

Black children learn this when their parents give them "The Talk." 27
When they are sat down at the age of 5 or so and told that their best friend's
father is not sick, and not in a bad mood—he just doesn't want his son playing with you. Black children grow up early to life in The Matrix. We're not
given a choice of the red or blue pill. Most white people, like my aunt, never
have to choose. The system was made for White people, so White people
don't have to think about living in it.

But we can't point this out. 28

Living every single day with institutionalized racism and then having 29
to argue its very existence, is tiring, and saddening, and angering. Yet if we
express any emotion while talking about it, we're tone policed, told we're
being angry. In fact, a key element in any racial argument in America is
the Angry Black person, and racial discussions shut down when that person speaks. The Angry Black person invalidates any arguments about racism
because they are "just being overly sensitive," or "too emotional," or—playing
the race card. Or even worse, we're told that *we* are being racist. (Does any
intelligent person actually believe a systematically oppressed demographic
has the ability to oppress those in power?)

But here is the irony, here's the thing that all the angry Black people 30
know, and no calmly debating White people want to admit: The entire discussion of race in America centers around the protection of White feelings.

Ask any Black person and they'll tell you the same thing. The reality of 31
thousands of innocent people raped, shot, imprisoned, and systematically
disenfranchised are less important than the suggestion that a single White
person might be complicit in a racist system.

This is the country we live in. Millions of Black lives are valued less than 32
a single White person's hurt feelings.

White people and Black people are not having a discussion about race. 33
Black people, thinking as a group, are talking about *living in a racist system*.
White people, thinking as individuals, refuse to talk about "I, racist" and
instead protect their own individual and personal goodness. In doing so, they
reject the existence of racism.

But arguing about personal non-racism is missing the point. 34

Despite what the Charleston Massacre makes things look like, people 35
are dying not because individuals are racist, but because individuals are
helping support a racist system by wanting to protect their own non-racist
self beliefs.

People are dying because we are supporting a racist system that justifies 36
White people killing Black people.

We see this in how one Muslim killer is Islamic terror; how one Mexican 37
thief points to the need for border security; in one innocent, unarmed Black
man shot in the back by a cop, then sullied in the media as a thug and criminal.

And in the way a white racist in a state that still flies the confederate flag 38
is seen as "troubling" and "unnerving." In the way people "can't understand
why he would do such a thing."

A white person smoking pot is a "hippie" and a Black person doing it is a 39
"criminal." It's evident in the school to prison pipeline and the fact that there
are close to 20 people of color in prison for every white person.

There's a headline from *The Independent* that sums this up quite nicely: 40
"Charleston shooting: Black and Muslim killers are 'terrorists' and 'thugs'.
Why are white shooters called 'mentally ill'?"

I'm gonna read that again: "Black and Muslim killers are 'terrorists' and 41
'thugs'. Why are white shooters called 'mentally ill'?"

Did you catch that? It's beautifully subtle. This is an article talking spe- 42
cifically about the different way we treat people of color in this nation and
even in this article's headline, the white people are "shooters" and the Black
and Muslim people are "killers."

Even when we're talking about racism, we're using racist language to 43
make people of color look dangerous and make White people come out as
not so bad.

Just let that sink in for a minute, then ask yourself why Black people are 44
angry when they talk about race.

The reality of America is that White people are fundamentally good, 45
and so when a white person commits a crime, it is a sign that they, *as an
individual*, are bad. Their actions as a person are not indicative of any broader
social construct. Even the fact that America has a growing number of violent hate groups, populated mostly by white men, and that nearly *all* serial
killers are white men cannot shadow the fundamental truth of white male
goodness. In fact, we like White serial killers so much, we make mini-series
about them.

White people are good as a whole, and only act badly as individuals. 46

People of color, especially Black people (but boy we can talk about "The 47
Mexicans" in this community) are seen as fundamentally bad. There might be
a good one—and we are always quick to point them out to our friends, show
them off as our Academy Award for "Best Non-Racist in a White Role"—but
when we see a bad one, it's just proof that the rest are, as a rule, bad.

This, all of this, expectation, treatment, thought, the underlying social 48
system that puts White in the position of Normal and good, and Black in the
position of "other" and "bad," all of this, is racism.

And White people, every single one of you, are complicit in this racism 49
because *you benefit directly from it.*

This is why I don't like the story of the good Samaritan. Everyone likes 50
to think of themselves as the person who sees someone beaten and bloodied
and helps him out.

That's too easy. 51

If I could rewrite that story, I'd rewrite it from the perspective of Black 52
America. What if the person wasn't beaten and bloody? What if it wasn't
so obvious? What if they were just systematically challenged in a thousand
small ways *that actually made it easier for you to succeed in life*?

Would you be so quick to help then? 53

Or would you, like most White people, stay silent and let it happen? 54

Here's what I want to say to you: Racism is so deeply embedded in this 55
country not because of the racist right-wing radicals who practice it openly,
it exists because of the silence and hurt feelings of liberal America.

That's what I want to say, but really, I can't. I can't say that because I've 56
spent my life not talking about race to White people. In a big way, it's my
fault. Racism exists because I, as a Black person, don't challenge you to look
at it.

Racism exists because I, not you, am silent. 57

But I'm caught in the perfect Catch 22, because when I start pointing 58
out racism, I become the Angry Black Person, and the discussion shuts down
again. So I'm stuck.

All the Black voices in the world speaking about racism all the time 59
do not move White people to think about it — but one White Jon Stewart
talking about Charleston has a whole lot of White people talking about it.
That's the world we live in. Black people can't change it while White people
are silent and deaf to our words.

White people are in a position of power in this country *because of racism*. 60
The question is: Are they brave enough to use that power to speak against
the system that gave it to them?

So I'm asking you to help me. Notice this. Speak up. Don't let it slide. 61
Don't stand watching in silence. Help build a world where it never gets to the
point where the Samaritan has to see someone bloodied and broken.

As for me, I will no longer be silent. 62

I'm going to *try* to speak kindly, and softly, but that's gonna be hard. 63
Because it's getting harder and harder for me to think about the protection
of White people's feelings when White people don't seem to care at all about
the loss of so many Black lives.

Thinking Critically about the Text

After reading this selection, do you better understand why minorities are often
angry or frustrated when talking about race? How closely do your own experiences match those of Metta?

Examining the Issue

1. Metta writes, "I had great reservations talking about the one topic that I think about every single day" (paragraph 1). What is this topic, and why might someone feel this way? Why wouldn't someone want to talk about a topic he thinks about all the time?

2. Do you believe you are complicit in racism? Explain.

3. Do you agree that "the entire discussion of race in America centers around the protection of White feelings" (paragraph 30)?

4. What does "tone policed" (paragraph 29) mean?

5. Metta writes that "Black people think in terms of *we*" and "White people do not think in terms of *we*" (paragraphs 18 and 19). Do these statements match your experience? Have you ever thought of yourself as part of a "we" because of the color of your skin, your ethnicity, your religion, your sexual orientation, or for any other reason? Do you have the option of defining yourself as belonging to more than one group?

6. Where does Metta use definition in this essay?

7. Metta writes that the fact that his aunt "moved away from an increasingly Black neighborhood to live in a White suburb might itself be an aspect of racism" (paragraph 12). What do you think he means by this?

8. Why does Metta believe that racism exists?

Racial Microaggressions in Everyday Life: Is Subtle Bias Harmless?

Derald Wing Sue

DERALD WING SUE

Derald Wing Sue is a professor at Columbia University, where he teaches psychology and education courses. He has written extensively on race, including articles in *American Psychologist* and *Cultural Diversity and Ethnic Minority Psychology*. He published his first book, *Counseling the Culturally Diverse: Theory and Practice*, in 1981 and has since published more than a half dozen others, including the textbook *Understanding Abnormal Behavior*, which went into its tenth edition in 2013. In 1996, Wing Sue served on the President's Advisory Board on Race under President Bill Clinton.

The following exploration was published as a blog post on PsychologyToday .com in October 2010. In it, Sue addresses the question of whether subconscious racial discrimination — even in its most subtle forms — is harmful.

Not too long ago, I (Asian American) boarded a small plane with an African American colleague in the early hours of the morning. As there were few passengers, the flight attendant told us to sit anywhere, so we choose seats near the front of the plane and across the aisle from one another. 1

At the last minute, three White men entered the plane and took seats in front of us. Just before takeoff, the flight attendant, who is White, asked if we would mind moving to the back of the aircraft to better balance the plane's weight. We grudgingly complied but felt singled out as passengers of color in being told to "move to the back of the bus." When we expressed these feelings to the attendant, she indignantly denied the charge, became defensive, stated that her intent was to ensure the flight's safety, and wanted to give us some privacy. 2

Since we had entered the plane first, I asked why she did not ask the White men to move instead of us. She became indignant, stated that we had misunderstood her intentions, claimed she did not see "color," suggested that we were being "oversensitive," and refused to talk about the matter any further. 3

Were we being overly sensitive, or was the flight attendant being 4 racist? That is a question that people of color are constantly faced with in their day-to-day interactions with well-intentioned White folks who experience themselves as good, moral, and decent human beings.

The Common Experience of Racial Microaggressions

Such incidents have become a common-place experience for many people of 5 color because they seem to occur constantly in our daily lives.

- When a White couple (man and woman) passes a Black man on the sidewalk, the woman automatically clutches her purse more tightly, while the White man checks for his wallet in the back pocket. (Hidden Message: Blacks are prone to crime and up to no good.)

- A third generation Asian American is complimented by a taxi cab driver for speaking such good English. (Hidden Message: Asian Americans are perceived as perpetual aliens in their own country and not "real Americans.")

- Police stop a Latino male driver for no apparent reason but to subtly check his driver's license to determine immigration status. (Hidden Message: Latinas/os are illegal aliens.)

- American Indian students at the University of Illinois see Native American symbols and mascots—exemplified by Chief Illiniwek dancing and whooping fiercely during football games. (Hidden Message: American Indians are savages, blood-thirsty, and their culture and traditions are demeaned.)

> " Were we being overly sensitive, or was the flight attendant being racist? "

In our 8-year research at Teachers 6 College, Columbia University, we have found that these racial microaggressions may on the surface appear like a compliment or seem quite innocent and harmless, but nevertheless, they contain what we call demeaning meta-communications or hidden messages.

What Are Racial Microaggressions?

The term racial microaggressions was first coined by psychiatrist Chester 7 Pierce, MD, in the 1970s. But the concept is also rooted in the work of Jack Dovidio, Ph.D. (Yale University) and Samuel Gaertner, Ph.D. (University of Delaware) in their formulation of aversive racism—many well-intentioned

Whites consciously believe in and profess equality, but unconsciously act in a racist manner, particularly in ambiguous situations.

Racial microaggressions are the brief and everyday slights, insults, indig- 8 nities and denigrating messages sent to people of color by well-intentioned White people who are unaware of the hidden messages being communicated. These messages may be sent verbally ("You speak good English."), nonverbally (clutching one's purse more tightly) or environmentally (symbols like the confederate flag or using American Indian mascots). Such communications are usually outside the level of conscious awareness of perpetrators. In the case of the flight attendant, I am sure that she believed she was acting with the best of intentions and probably felt aghast that someone would accuse her of such a horrendous act.

Our research and those of many social psychologists suggest that most 9 people, like the flight attendant, harbor unconscious biases and prejudices that leak out in many interpersonal situations and decision points. In other words, the attendant was acting with bias — she just didn't know it. Getting perpetrators to realize that they are acting in a biased manner is a monumental task because (a) on a conscious level they see themselves as fair minded individuals who would never consciously discriminate, (b) they are genuinely not aware of their biases, and (c) their self image of being "a good moral human being" is assailed if they realize and acknowledge that they possess biased thoughts, attitudes and feelings that harm people of color.

To better understand the type and range of these incidents, my research 10 team and other researchers are exploring the manifestation, dynamics and impact of microaggressions. We have begun documenting how African Americans, Asian Americans, American Indians and Latina(o) Americans who receive these everyday psychological slings and arrows experience an erosion of their mental health, job performance, classroom learning, the quality of social experience, and ultimately their standard of living.

Classifying Microaggressions

In my book, *Racial Microaggressions in Everyday Life: Race, Gender and Sexual* 11 *Orientation* (John Wiley & Sons, 2010), I summarize research conducted at Teachers College, Columbia University which led us to propose a classification of racial microaggressions. Three types of current racial transgressions were described:

- Microassaults: Conscious and intentional discriminatory actions: using racial epithets, displaying White supremacist symbols — swastikas — or preventing one's son or daughter from dating outside of their race.

- Microinsults: Verbal, nonverbal, and environmental communications that subtly convey rudeness and insensitivity that demean a person's racial heritage or identity. An example is an employee who asks a co-worker of color how he/she got his/her job, implying he/she may have landed it through an affirmative action or quota system.
- Microinvalidations: Communications that subtly exclude, negate or nullify the thoughts, feelings, or experiential reality of a person of color. For instance, White people often ask Latinos where they were born, conveying the message that they are perpetual foreigners in their own land.

Our research suggests that microinsults and microinvalidations are 12 potentially more harmful because of their invisibility, which puts people of color in a psychological bind: While people of color may feel insulted, they are often uncertain why, and perpetrators are unaware that anything has happened and are not aware they have been offensive. For people of color, they are caught in a catch-22. If they question the perpetrator, as in the case of the flight attendant, denials are likely to follow. Indeed, they may be labeled "oversensitive" or even "paranoid." If they choose not to confront perpetrators, the turmoil stews and percolates in the psyche of the person, taking a huge emotional toll. In other words, they are damned if they do and damned if they don't.

Note that the denials by perpetrators are usually not conscious attempts 13 to deceive; they honestly believe they have done no wrong. Microaggressions hold their power because they are invisible, and therefore they don't allow Whites to see that their actions and attitudes may be discriminatory. Therein lays the dilemma. The person of color is left to question what actually happened. The result is confusion, anger and an overall draining of energy.

Ironically, some research and testimony from people of color indicate 14 they are better able to handle overt, conscious and deliberate acts of racism than the unconscious, subtle and less obvious forms. That is because there is no guesswork involved in overt forms of racism.

Harmful Impact

Many racial microaggressions are so subtle that neither target nor perpe- 15 trator may entirely understand what is happening. The invisibility of racial microaggressions may be more harmful to people of color than hate crimes or the overt and deliberate acts of White supremacists such as the Klan and Skinheads. Studies support the fact that people of color frequently experience microaggressions, that it is a continuing reality in their day-to-day interactions with friends, neighbors, co-workers, teachers, and employers in academic, social and public settings.

They are often made to feel excluded, untrustworthy, second-class 16 citizens, and abnormal. People of color often describe the terrible feeling of being watched suspiciously in stores, that any slipup they make would negatively impact every person of color, that they felt pressured to represent the group in positive ways, and that they feel trapped in a stereotype. The burden of constant vigilance drains and saps psychological and spiritual energies of targets and contributes to chronic fatigue and a feeling of racial frustration and anger.

Space does not allow me to elaborate the harmful impact of racial 17 microaggressions, but I summarize what the research literature reveals. Although they may appear like insignificant slights, or banal and trivial in nature, studies reveal that racial microaggressions have powerful detrimental consequences to people of color. They have been found to: (a) assail the mental health of recipients, (b) create a hostile and invalidating work or campus climate, (c) perpetuate stereotype threat, (d) create physical health problems, (e) saturate the broader society with cues that signal devaluation of social group identities, (f) lower work productivity and problem solving abilities, and (g) be partially responsible for creating inequities in education, employment and health care.

Future Blogs

I realize that I have left many questions unanswered with this posting, but 18 my research team and I plan to continue updating our findings for readers to consider. For readers who desire a more thorough understanding of microaggressions, I recommend two major sources on the topic published this year (2010): *Microaggressions in Everyday Life: Race, Gender, and Sexual Orientation* and *Microaggressions and Marginality: Manifestation, Dynamics and Impact*. Both can be accessed through the John Wiley & Sons, publisher's website.

Future blogs will deal with questions such as: How do people of color 19 cope with the daily onslaught of racial microaggressions? Are some coping strategies better than others? How do we help perpetrators to become aware of microaggressions? What are the best ways to prevent them at an individual, institutional and societal level? Do other socially marginalized groups like women, LGBTs, those with disabilities, and religious minorities experience microaggressions? In what ways are they similar or different? Is it possible for any of us to be born and raised in the United States without inheriting the racial, gender and sexual orientation biases of our ancestors? Are you personally a racist, sexist, or heterosexist? What is the best way for the average U.S. citizen to overcome these biases?

The first step in eliminating microaggressions is to make the "invisi- 20
ble" visible. I realize how controversial topics of race and racism, gender and
sexism and sexual orientation and heterosexism push emotional hot buttons
in all of us. I am hopeful that our blogs will stimulate discussion, debate,
self-reflection, and helpful dialogue directed at increasing mutual respect and
understanding of the multiple social identities we all possess.

Thinking Critically about the Text

Sue writes in his final sentence of his hope that his work will "stimulate discussion,
debate, self-reflection, and helpful dialogue." Do you think these things are sufficient to address the concerns he raises about microaggressions? What are some
of the questions that Sue acknowledges he has left unanswered (paragraph 18)?

Examining the Issue

1. What is a microaggression? Why does Sue find microinvalidations concerning?

2. Why does Sue reiterate throughout his piece that microaggressions are
   unconscious actions? How does this strengthen or weaken his argument?

3. Compare and contrast the three types of "racial transgressions" Sue identifies. How are they similar? How are they different? What is most significant
   about the differences?

4. Why does Sue believe that microinsults and microinvalidations have the
   potential to be more harmful than microassaults?

5. Sue opens his piece with a brief **narrative** of his own experience. How does
   this contribute to his argument?

6. Why does Sue include the history of the term *microaggression* in paragraph 7?

7. Why does Sue call microaggressions both *brief* and *everyday* (paragraph 8)?

No, I Won't Be Writing about Black-on-Black Crime

SHAUN KING

Courtesy of Shaun King

Writer, entrepreneur, and activist Shaun King was born in 1979 and grew up in Versailles, Kentucky. He graduated from Morehouse College, where he majored in history. Before becoming a writer, King worked as a high school teacher, motivational speaker, and pastor. He also founded the Courageous Church in Atlanta, Georgia, where he became known for using social media to attract people to his congregation — as well as to raise money for philanthropic causes such as aid for the devastating 2010 earthquake in Haiti. He helped launch similar online charity platforms like TwitChange.com and HopeMob.org.

King regularly uses social media to write about race, social justice, and his activism as part of the Black Lives Matter movement. He began writing regularly for the liberal blog *The Daily Kos* in 2014, and then became the senior social justice writer for the *New York Daily News* in 2015. Currently, King is the writer-in-residence at the Fair Punishment Project at Harvard Law School. He is also author of the book *The Power of 100!: Kickstart Your Dreams, Build Momentum, and Discover Unlimited Possibility* (2015). In the following 2017 column from the *New York Daily News*, King addresses his critics, who want him to spend less time focused on Black Lives Matter and police brutality, and more time writing about "black-on-black" violence.

E very 10 minutes or so, I get an email, or a tweet, or a Facebook message showing me some genuinely horrific story of a violent crime committed by black folk. Invariably, the hateful messages accompanying the stories go something like this (an actual message by the way): 1

"Shaun — you race baiting piece of s–t. If you cared so much about injustice like you say you do, why aren't you talking about this? Seems you only care about violence when it's from white people. F–k you." 2

That person, like every person before them, and every person on schedule to send me their own version of that same email, then pastes a link to a story of a random assault committed by young black teens. 3

I loathe violence of all kinds. I've been a victim of violence. But I won't be writing or tweeting or Facebooking about what those black teenagers did for one simple reason. They've already been arrested. They've already been charged. The bail was already set higher than their family could ever afford. 4

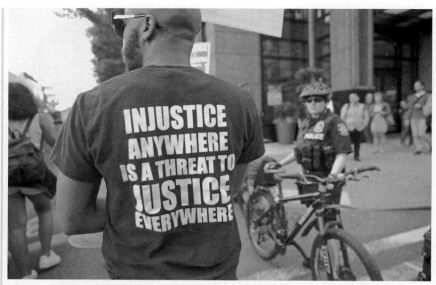

When I write about police brutality in America, it's because the perpetrators of it aren't being held responsible in any meaningful way whatsoever.
AFP Contributor/Getty Images

They will, in all likelihood, be found guilty. And, as sure as the sun will set today, they will be sent to prison. Press repeat.

My mission in life is to call out injustice so that those who are not being held accountable for the crimes they commit against vulnerable people may actually go to jail or lose their jobs or pay the restitution their victims deserve. When I write about police brutality in America, it's because the perpetrators of it aren't being held responsible in any meaningful way whatsoever.

Right now, without Googling it, can you name even one white officer in jail for killing somebody on the job? Just one. I've asked that same question on college campuses across America and have never had a single person yell back an answer. Justice is so outrageously rare in cases of police violence that we can't name a single person being held responsible for it. Who? Where? When?

> " When I write about police brutality in America, it's because the perpetrators of it aren't being held responsible in any meaningful way whatsoever. "

Naming a white cop in jail right now for killing a person of color is as hard as naming an African-American who killed or even seriously injured somebody who isn't in jail. To be black in America and commit a crime means automatic justice. Juries don't struggle to convict a black man or woman for assaulting or killing someone. The wheels on that machine move swiftly and quietly and efficiently.

I don't write about the brutal cop who choked Eric Garner because he's white.
REUTERS/Eduardo Munoz

An article or social media post from me is not needed to help bring a conviction. The entire system was built to make sure that happens without ever needing outside help from anyone. Nobody is held more responsible for their mistakes or crimes in this country more than black folk. Our jails and prisons are overflowing with African-Americans who've been held super responsible for every single infraction under the sun.

I don't write about the brutal cop who choked Eric Garner because he's 8 white. I write about Daniel Pantaleo because he still has his job and never served a day in jail for what he did to a nonviolent man who was minding his own business.

I don't write about the cops who shot and killed John Crawford in the 9 middle of a Walmart because they are white. I write about those men because John was peaceful, harmless, nonviolent, and had not even broken a law when they shot and killed him.

I don't write about the cop who shot and killed 12-year-old Tamir Rice 10 because he's white. I write about Timothy Loehmann because he should've never been a cop in the first place. He was forced to resign from his previous police job, and his previous supervisors recommended that he never serve in law enforcement again because of his emotional instability. I write about him because his justifications for the shooting aren't adequate.

I don't write about the cops who killed Amadou Diallo, Rekia Boyd, Terence 11 Crutcher or Ramarley Graham because they were white. I write about those cops because they each shot and killed unarmed people who did not deserve any violence—and none of the cops served a day in jail for what they did.

I write about Daniel Pantaleo because he still has his job and never served a day in jail for what he did to a nonviolent man who was minding his own business.

I don't write about the cop who arrested Sandra Bland after pulling her over because she didn't use a turn signal because he was white. I write about him because Sandra Bland should've never been arrested and sent to jail in the first place. I write about Brian Encinia because he was charged with lying under oath about the arrest, but still found a way to have the perjury charge dropped.

The overwhelming majority of cops who kill people are white. They are almost never held accountable. These are facts. I didn't create them. I don't want them. But they are real. I don't write about these cops because of their whiteness, but because of the glaring lack of accountability that accompanies almost every single act of violence from police in America.

I also won't be writing about black-on-black crime, because most local news outlets from coast to coast seem absolutely obsessed with it. They lead their television broadcast with it. They tweet about it. They put it in the headlines of their local papers—so much so that the stereotypes of drug dealers or thugs in America are young black men—when the truth is that a higher percentage of white people sell drugs than black people. None of us would know that from watching the news, though, because again, black people are not only held super responsible for their mistakes by law enforcement, but by the media as well.

This country doesn't need a single journalist to fight for the criminalization of African-Americans. Those jobs are already filled and have been in abundance for a few hundred years. What I'm doing by fighting for police to be held accountable, on the other hand, is a completely different story.

I write about Timothy Loehmann, the cop who killed Tamir
Rice (pictured), because he should've never been a cop in
the first place.
AP Photo/Jose Luis Magana

Thinking Critically about the Text

King quotes one of his critics directly in the second paragraph. What does he
gain by including the actual message, rather than simply saying that he receives
responses from readers and that these messages can be offensive and hateful? Is
King choosing to ignore one important social problem in favor of another? In your
opinion, is this a proper approach for a social commentator to take?

Examining the Issue

1. What is King's self-described mission in life? How is it related to the **thesis** of
   this essay?

2. Where does King use **examples** to support his thesis?

3. In paragraph 6, what question does King ask his readers? How does it support
   his argument and purpose?

4. How does the writer use **parallelism** in his argument? How does it add
   emphasis and help reinforce his thesis?

5. King asserts, "Nobody is held more responsible for their mistakes or crimes in this
   country more than black folk" (paragraph 7). How does he support this claim?

6. In his conclusion, King writes, "This country doesn't need a single journalist to fight for the criminalization of African-Americans." What does he mean by the phrase "the criminalization of African-Americans"? Do you agree with his claim? Why, or why not?

7. Do King's critics seem to be committing any **logical fallacies** in their arguments? Which examples of faulty reasoning can you identify?

8. Where in this essay does King appeal to *ethos*? Why is this appeal important to his argument?

MAKING CONNECTIONS

Writing and Discussion Suggestions on Race and Privilege

1. Each of the authors in this cluster addresses an aspect of *privilege*. Combining the thoughts of all three authors, write your own brief definition of the term. How is your definition similar to that of each of the authors in this cluster? How does it differ?

2. Both John Metta and Derald Wing Sue use the term *catch-22*, a reference to the book by Joseph Heller. (Glossary: **Allusion**) Explain the concept of a catch-22. What does this reference add to Metta's and Sue's arguments?

3. Derald Wing Sue argues that subtle instances of racial aggression are potentially more damaging than overt racism. Use examples from your own life to support or refute this claim.

4. How might companies — like the airline in Derald Wing Sue's piece — help to address our current systems of racial bias? What types of training or guidelines would help employees to better interact with the public? Might this be more difficult in some industries than in others?

5. Other authors in this book address issues of race and privilege, as well. Choose another selection from a different chapter or section and compare and contrast the author's exploration of the topic with the selections in this section. (Pieces by Toni Morrison, Maya Angelou, Nikki Giovanni, and Issa Rae may be especially suitable.) Do the authors recognize race and privilege in the same areas of their lives? Do they use different rhetorical writing strategies? If so, how do their chosen strategies suit their different purposes?

6. Shaun King explains his reasons for not wanting to write about black-on-black crime. Do you think that John Metta and Derald Wing Sue will agree with his argument? Can an author reasonably decide what aspects of an argument can be included or ignored? Why, or why not?

7. **Writing with Sources.** Write a letter to your state or local representative with suggestions for raising public awareness of institutional racism. Use information and arguments from the three essays in this cluster as well as articles and

books you find on the Internet and in the library to help build a case for why this is necessary. For models of and advice on integrating sources in your essay, see Chapters 14 and 15.

8. **Writing with Sources.** Do some research online or in your school library about racially motivated violence, such as the incidents that motivated the creation of the Black Lives Matter movement, several of which Shaun King mentions in "No, I Won't Be Writing about Black-on-Black Crime." Have there been more of these incidents in the past five years than in prior decades, or have there been fewer? Do you think such incidents may have been prompted, in some way, by the more subtle forms of racism addressed in this chapter? Why, or why not? Be sure to cite specific examples and integrate material from your sources. For models of and advice on integrating sources in your essay, see Chapters 14 and 15.

ARGUMENT CLUSTER

The Changing Nature of Work: What Is the Value of a Career — Now and in the Future?

SM/AIUEO/Getty Images

VISUALIZING THE ISSUE: THE CHANGING NATURE OF WORK

The rapid rate of change throughout the nineteenth and twentieth centuries in how workers work — and in how machines complement or replace that work — has raised concerns about the job security of humans in the workforce. As you examine this photograph of robots working alongside food service employees in a Tokyo restaurant, what evidence can you find of such concerns? What evidence do you find to the contrary? What message, if any, do you think the photographer is sending concerning an evolving workplace environment? Do you think robots should be allowed to work in certain job roles, such as food service or medicine? Should they be barred from any jobs? Why, or why not?

The nature of work is always evolving. There are many circumstances that account for changes, including the type of work (agriculture, service, manufacturing, artistic, scientific, academic, and so forth), the emergence of new technologies, and developing and changing markets. Factor in how workers regard their careers, their specific jobs, their relationships with employers and coworkers, the level of job satisfaction they have and perhaps seek, how they define themselves by the work they do, and how they see the trajectory of their work experiences and careers unfolding before them, and you have a vibrant and complicated set of dynamic conditions. Whether or not you already have a job or are just beginning to think about entering the workforce and how your education will lead toward a particular career, we think the arguments put forth in the following articles should be of interest to you.

Arguments in this cluster reflect three different time frames: the recent past, the present, and the not too distant future. We begin with an essay by Caitlin McCormick in which she reflects on her work in the hospitality industry and what it taught her about sexism, racism, ableism, imbalances of power, and the need to have trust in humanity. In Ilana Gershon's "The Quitting Economy," we are introduced to a present-day workplace phenomenon, the argument that a job is only as good as it allows one to acquire a new skillset useful for climbing to the next rung on the employment ladder. Finally, in "Don't Assume Robots Will Be Our Future Coworkers," Noah Smith looks to a pressing question for the near future: Will robots take over our jobs? The standard argument against robots putting us out of work is that it hasn't happened yet. But just because it hasn't happened yet doesn't mean that it won't.

Preparing to Read

Reflect on the job you now have or have had in the past. What's attractive about it? What were the challenges you faced? If you do not have work experience, what are some of the ideas you have about what it is like to be employed? What benefits would you like your future job(s) to provide for you? How does your career future and the pathway to success in the workplace compare to your parents' or grandparents' generations — or to your peers who have different socioeconomic backgrounds? What ideas do you have about the future of employment? Do you think technological advances in the workplace will help or hinder your job satisfaction?

The Gingham Apron

"Slowly, my mother's gingham apron began to look more like metal armor."

CAITLIN MCCORMICK

Courtesy of Caitlin McCormick

Caitlin McCormick was born in 1999 in Alexandria, Virginia, but grew up in Tucson, Arizona. She attended the Gregory School, a private college preparatory school in Tucson. Since graduating, she has attended Barnard College, Columbia University, in New York City, where she lives. Currently, McCormick is an associate in the Opinion section for the *Columbia Daily Spectator*, the university's newspaper. McCormick's work has also appeared in the *Arizona Daily Star*, the *Barnard Bulletin*, the *Kenyon Review Young Writers Workshop Anthology* (2015), the *University of Iowa between the Lines Anthology* (2016), and other places.

In the following essay, featured by the *New York Times* in its 2017 series of standout college application essays on work, money, and class, McCormick shows how her personal experiences growing up in her parents' bed and breakfast provided insight into power and injustice. They also illustrated the importance of serving and trusting others.

W hen it comes to service workers, as a society we completely dis- 1 regard the manners instilled in us as toddlers.

For seventeen years, I have awoken to those workers, to 2 clinking silverware rolled in cloth and porcelain plates removed from the oven in preparation for breakfast service. I memorized the geometry of place mats slid on metal trays, coffee cups turned downward, dirtied cloth napkins disposed on dining tables.

I knew never to wear pajamas outside in the public courtyard, and years 3 of shushing from my mother informed me not to speak loudly in front of a guest room window. I grew up in the swaddled cacophony of morning chatter between tourists, professors, and videographers. I grew up conditioned in excessive politeness, fitted for making small talk with strangers.

I grew up in a bed and breakfast, in the sticky thickness of the hospitality 4 industry. And for a very long time I hated it.

I was late to my own fifth birthday party in the park because a guest 5 arrived five hours late without apology. Following a weeklong stay in which someone specially requested her room be cleaned twice a day, not once did she leave a tip for housekeeping. Small-business scammers came for a stop at the inn several times. Guests stained sheets, clogged toilets, locked themselves out of their rooms, and then demanded a discount.

There exists between service workers and their customers an inherent imbalance of power: We meet sneers with apologies. At the end of their meal, or stay, or drink, we let patrons determine how much effort their server put into their job.

For most of my life I believed my parents were intense masochists for devoting their existences to the least thankful business I know: the very business that taught me how to discern imbalances of power. Soon I recognized this stem of injustice in all sorts of everyday interactions. I came to understand how latent racism, sexism, classism and ableism structure our society—how tipping was only a synonym for "microaggression."

> **There exists between service workers and their customers an inherent imbalance of power: We meet sneers with apologies.**

I became passionate. Sometimes enraged. I stumbled upon nonprofits, foundations, and political campaigns. I canvassed for Senate candidates, phone-banked for grass-roots action groups, served as a board member for the Women's Foundation of Southern Arizona, reviewed grant applications for nonprofits and organized events for the nearby children's hospital.

I devoted my time to the raw grit of helping people, and in the process I fell irrevocably in love with a new type of service: public service. At the same time, I worked midnight Black Friday retail shifts and scraped vomit off linoleum. When I brought home my first W-2, I had never seen my parents so proud.

The truth, I recently learned, was that not all service is created equal. Seeing guests scream at my parents over a late airport taxi still sickens me even as I spend hours a week as a volunteer. But I was taught all work is noble, especially the work we do for others. Slowly, my mother's gingham apron began to look more like metal armor. I learned how to worship my parents' gift for attentive listening, easily hearing the things guests were incapable of asking for—not sugar with their tea, but somebody to talk with while they waited for a conference call. I envied their ability to wear the role of self-assured host like a second skin, capable of tolerating any type of cruelty with a smile.

Most of all, I admired my parents' continuous trust in humanity to not abuse their help. I realized that learning to serve people looks a lot like learning to trust them.

Thinking Critically about the Text

McCormick originally wrote this article as an essay for her college application. In what ways might that context and writing situation have influenced her argument or the way she presented it? Why do you think it was appealing to her university admissions officers? Or to the *New York Times*, who featured her essay as one of the best of the year?

Examining the Issue

1. McCormick writes that she grew up in the hospitality industry, and that "for a very long time [she] hated it" (paragraph 4). How does she illustrate her reasons for that hatred?

2. In paragraphs 6 and 7, she claims that her childhood among service workers gave her an awareness of injustice. What did her experiences and observations teach her?

3. What do you think McCormick means by the phrase "the raw grit of helping people" (paragraph 9)?

4. McCormick sees tipping as "only a synonym for 'microaggression'" (paragraph 7). How do you make sense of her claim here? What is she referring to?

5. How does this essay combine elements of **logical reasoning** with elements of **persuasion**? Does the writer achieve an effective balance of the two?

6. What other rhetorical strategies does McCormick incorporate here? For example, how does she rely on **narration** and **cause and effect**, in particular?

7. Has McCormick effectively blurred the line between what we normally think of as work and education? Is the dichotomy between work and education a false one? Explain.

8. Does physical work in some ways activate the mind? If so, what might be the reasons for this? Have you had any work/thought experiences that might shed some light on this ironic twist?

The Quitting Economy

ILANA GERSHON

Ilana Gershon was born in 1971 in Philadelphia, Pennsylvania, where she grew up. She earned her bachelor's degree in history and philosophy of the social sciences at Stanford University, her master's degree in social anthropology from Cambridge University, and her doctorate in cultural anthropology from the University of Chicago. Currently, Gershon is an associate professor of anthropology at Indiana University in Bloomington. While Gershon's research interests are various, much of

Courtesy of Ilana Gershon

her recent work has focused on jobs, new media, and democracy. Her books include *The Breakup 2.0: Disconnecting over New Media* (2012) and *Down and Out in the New Economy: How People Find (or Don't Find) Work* (2017), and she edited *A World of Work: Imagined Manuals for Real Jobs* (2015). In addition to publishing in academic journals, Gershon has written for the *Harvard Business Review*, the *Atlantic*, and *Aeon*, where the following essay appeared on July 26, 2017.

In "The Quitting Economy," Gershon explores the ways in which the dominance of neoliberalism — that is, profit-focused, free-market values — over the past several decades has radically reshaped the way employees and employers view their jobs, their companies, their colleagues, and themselves.

I n the early 1990s, career advice in the United States changed. A new social philosophy, neoliberalism, was transforming society, including the nature of employment, and career counsellors and business writers had to respond. The Soviet Union had recently collapsed, and much as communist thinkers had tried to apply Marxist ideas to every aspect of life, triumphant US economic intellectuals raced to implement the ultra-individualist ideals of Friedrich Hayek, Milton Friedman and other members of the Mont Pelerin Society, far and wide. In doing so for work, they developed a metaphor — that every person should think of herself as a business, the CEO of Me, Inc. The metaphor took off, and has had profound implications for how workplaces are run, how people understand their jobs, and how they plan careers, which increasingly revolve around quitting. 1

Hayek (1899–1992) was an influential Austrian economist who operated from the core conviction that markets provided the best means to order the world. Today, many people share this conviction, and that is in part because of the influence of Hayek and his cohort. At the time that Hayek and his circle began making their arguments, it was an eccentric and minority position. 2

For Hayek and the Mount Pelerin group, the centralized economic planning that characterized both communism and fascism was a recipe for disaster. Hayek held that humans are too flawed to successfully undertake the planning of a complex modern economy. A single human being, or even group of human beings, could never competently handle the informational complexities of modern economic systems. Given humans' limitations in the face of modern economic complexity, freeing the market to organize large-scale production and distribution was the best possible course.

Hayek understood that markets do not emerge naturally, that traders, consumers and laws construct markets. Once established, markets have tendencies toward monopoly and other business practices that could undercut forming an even playing field. So markets can't be entirely left to self-regulate; laws and governments are necessary. Indeed, this is the primary reason why governments should exist—to ensure that markets function well. Governments should not be providing services to its citizenry such as public transportation or a postal service—Hayek believed that private interests most efficiently manage these services. Also governments should not be providing forms of welfare to its citizens, since welfare undercuts how the market allocates value and introduces too much centralized planning. Instead, what governments should focus upon is organizing markets well, keeping them functioning to promote competition, and thus also promoting innovation. Because market competition is the goal, arbitrarily curtailing this competition through tariffs or other nationalist strategies for undercutting a global market was also deeply undesirable. Hayek wanted a global market.

This approach to markets and governments, commonly called neoliberalism by its critics, has grown increasingly dominant. As this theory moved off the page and the blackboard, people who wanted to live according to neoliberal principles ran into a basic problem. This is a specific way of dealing with markets, even for those committed in principle to capitalism. So, as more governments and businesses adopted market measures as often as possible, new ways of talking about many aspects of life, including work and careers, arose. Every total way of life, after all, requires its own vocabulary.

Predictably, saying that "the market is the best way to organize or determine value" overlooks many sorts of life dilemmas. Hayek did understand that his model of making the market so foundational would require a specific kind of person, a new kind of person. But he never developed an effective model for making complicated decisions such as deciding whom to hire for a job opening, or how to fashion a career over a lifetime. Others, the Nobel Prize-winner Gary Becker for example, who coined the idea of human capital, had to come up with concrete models for how people should, in market terms, understand everyday interactions. Inspired by Becker in adopting the market idiom, business writers began to talk about how people need to think about *investing* in themselves, and viewing themselves as an *asset* whose *value* only the market could effectively determine. Over time, a whole body of literature emerged advocating that people should view themselves as a business — a bundle of skills, assets, qualities, experiences and relationships to be managed and continually enhanced.

The change that saw business writers, career counsellors and others adopting the view that individual employees, or potential employees, should think of themselves as businesses occurred at the same time that the way the value of a company was assessed also changed. Not so long ago, business people thought that companies provided a wide variety of benefits to a large number of constituents — to upper management, to employees, to the local community, as well as to shareholders. Many of these benefits were long-term. 6

But as market value overtook other measures of a company's value, maximizing the short-term interests of shareholders began to override other concerns, other relationships. Quarterly earnings reports and stock prices became even more important, the sole measures of success. How companies treated employees changed, and has not changed back. A recent illustration of the ethos came when American Airlines, having decided that its current levels of compensation were not competitive, announced an increase to its staff salaries. The company was, in fact, funnelling money to workers instead of to its shareholders. Wall Street's reaction was immediate: American Airlines' stock price plummeted. 7

In general, to keep stock prices high, companies not only have to pay their employees as little as possible, they must also have as temporary a workforce as their particular business can allow. The more expendable the workforce, the easier it is to expand and contract in response to short-term demands. These are market and shareholder metrics. Their dominance diminished commitment to employees, and all other commitments but to shareholders, as much as the particular industry requirements of production allow. With companies so organized, the idea of loyalty receded. 8

Companies now needed to free themselves as much as possible of long-term obligations, such as pensions and other worker incentives. Employees who work long, and in many cases, intense hours to finish short-term projects, became more valuable. While companies rarely say so explicitly, in practice they often want employees who can be let go easily and with little fuss, employees who do not expect long-term commitments from their employer. But, like employment, loyalty is a two-way street — making jobs short-term, commitment-free enterprises leads to workers who view temporary work contracts as also desirable. You start hiring job-quitters. 9

The CEO of Me, Inc is a job-quitter for a good reason — the business world has come to agree with Hayek that market value is the best measure 10 of value. As a consequence, a career means a string of jobs at different companies. So workers respond in kind, thinking about how to shape their career in a world where you can expect so little from employers. In a society where market rules rule, the only way for an employee to know her value is to look for another job and, if she finds one, usually to quit.

If you are a white-collar worker, it is simply rational to view yourself first and foremost as a job quitter—someone who takes a job for a certain amount of time when the best outcome is that you quit for another job (and the worst is that you get laid off). So how does work change when everyone is trying to become a quitter? First of all, in the society of perpetual job searches, different criteria make a job good or not. Good jobs used to be ones with a good salary, benefits, location, hours, boss, co-workers, and a clear path toward promotion. Now, a good job is one that prepares you for your next job, almost always with another company.

> **In a society where market rules rule, the only way for an employee to know her value is to look for another job and, if she finds one, usually to quit.**

Your job might be a space to learn skills that you can use in the future. Or, it might be a job with a company that has a good-enough reputation that other companies are keen to hire away its employees. On the other hand, it isn't as good a job if everything you learn there is too specific to that company, if you aren't learning easily transferrable skills. It isn't a good job if it enmeshes you in local regulatory schemes and keeps you tied to a particular location. And it isn't a good job if you have to work such long hours that you never have time to look for the next job. In short, a job becomes a good job if it will lead to another job, likely with another company or organization. You start choosing a job for how good it will be for you to quit it.

In significant ways, the calculus of quitting changes workplace dynamics. Being a good manager now means helping those whom you manage acquire the skills that will help them to leave for a better job at another company. Good managers know this. I observed a Berkeley continuing education workshop for new managers, and one speaker described her strategies for behaving well to her team. She explained that she did this from the outset by clarifying what she understood their implicit business contract to be. She takes each new member of her team out to lunch in the week they start: "So I always say things like: 'You don't work for me, I work for you... My job is to make sure you can do your job well. And one day, you are going to leave this job, right, our careers are long, and we will have many jobs along the way. When you want to leave this job, I hope to be here to help you move on to this next job.'" From the outset, managers say that they will help those who work under them become job-quitters—to find the next best stepping stone in their career.

The calculus of quitting also changes what it means to have a good division of labor at work. If your goal is to get a job somewhere else, not all work projects are equally valuable. Workers must jockey for the tasks and projects that might lead to a job elsewhere. They must try to avoid tasks that, either due to intellectual property issues or for other reasons, are too company-specific. Linus Huang, a sociologist at Berkeley, saw this happening in the Silicon Valley startup where he was working when Java was first becoming a popular programming language. There was quite a bit of work in his company involving the general-purpose programming language, C++, and for many of the company's needs, it was sufficient. Employees wanted to have practice with Java, however, because Java would make them more marketable in the future. Workers began to evaluate projects in terms of whether they would improve their Java skills. The managers began to struggle to find people who would do the day-to-day programming work, mostly in C++, upon which the company depended. They had no trouble, on the other hand, finding people to work on the few Java projects. When you work a job that presumes you will quit before too long, the tasks that are good for the company might not be good for you.

The calculus of quitting also changes the nature of being co-workers, and not just because they are jockeying over who does which tasks in a new way. While you might always have wanted to get along with your co-workers, the quitting economy introduced a new instrumental reason why collegiality is especially important. Now that people aren't supposed to stay all that long at a company, you experience a regular turnover in your workplace. Workers who used to get ahead by impressing their managers by being steady, self-effacing and conscientious no longer have the time to establish the appreciative audience they used to within a company. As a result, these types of workers might no longer be steadily promoted. If their co-workers appreciate them, however, then they might, when it comes time for them to look for their next job, have supporters at other companies. After all, everyone works in the quitting economy, and everyone knows it, creating a different incentive for people to get along with their co-workers. Today, when every job opening has too many applicants, having an insider in the company who can be an ally can make all the difference.

The environment of the quitting economy also brings about a change in the emotional life of the worker and workplace. When you start imagining yourself as always on the verge of quitting, the emotions you feel for your work change. When companies decided to do away with company loyalty, businesses had to find a new way to help workers foster an emotional connection to work. In the US especially, there is a strong cultural consensus that people should feel passion for their work, and work hard. One hiring manager explained to me that he always chose people who seemed passionate about their work over someone who seemed to have the most experience. He could teach them any necessary skills, he explained, but his need for them to work very long hours meant that he needed people with passion. Since company loyalty is no longer around to guarantee committed workers, passion is now supposed to be the driving force.

Intriguingly, this passion that workers are supposed to feel is restricted to the tasks at work or to learning certain skills. People are not supposed to feel passion for working with particular people. Nor do workers talk about having passion for augmenting the reputation of the company for which they work. Passion is reserved for the tasks that they do or learn to do, for the solutions that they might develop for the company's market-specific problems. Not surprisingly, the market-specific problems for which workers feel a passion for solving are usually the problems that a range of companies might face. They aren't specific to that particular company. In the quitting economy, you have to work for passion, and working for passion means focusing on the task, not the company.

Cultivating their feelings of passion for tasks that bring market remuneration makes workers more mobile. It is easier for them to consider moving to another company where they can still do the work about which they feel passionately. One executive recruiter told me she used this focus on passion to help convince executives to leave, regardless of the financial incentives put in place by their current company. She would tell an executive she was trying to recruit that if they no longer felt any passion for their work, then they were harming all their colleagues at work, who now had to work with someone who no longer enjoyed work to its utmost. In short, when one of the main reasons to work somewhere is because you feel passion, when you stop feeling that passion, it is easier to quit.

In a way new to the world, and begun by the re-orientation of companies to maximize shareholder value, quitting work is now central to what it means to have a job in the first place. People apply for jobs with the conscious plan to quit, with an eye toward what other jobs the job for which they are applying might help them get. Managers welcome new employees by promising to position them as advantageously as possible to quit in a few years. Co-workers, the ones who like you, are now hoping you will quit—since if you do, you might help them get a good job somewhere else. As is often the case, history brings unintended consequences, even to doctrinaire and theoretical ideas. Hayek's philosophy has led to workers thinking of themselves as the CEO of Me, Inc; and to survive in the neoliberal world of work, the CEO of Me, Inc must be a quitter.

Thinking Critically about the Text

After reading Gershon's essay, have you changed your ideas about the economics of the workplace and how changes in it will affect your own employment decisions going forward? How so?

Examining the Issue

1. What key **metaphor** does Gershon discuss in her introduction? Why is it important to her argument?

2. What is Gershon's **thesis**?

3. What was Friedrich Hayek's "core conviction" (paragraph 2)? Why did he oppose the government providing services to its citizens?

4. In paragraph 4, Gershon refers to neoliberalism as a "total way of life." What do you think she means by this?

5. What claim does Gershon support with the example from American Airlines in paragraph 7?

6. How has the definition of a "good job" changed (paragraph 11)? How might the new understanding of a "good job" be beneficial to employees? That is, what counterarguments could you make to Gershon's argument that suggest that the new kind of job is a "good job" worth having?

7. What replaced company loyalty as a driver of employee commitment, according to Gershon?

8. How (and where) does Gershon use **cause and effect analysis** as a supporting strategy?

Don't Assume Robots Will Be Our Future Coworkers

NOAH SMITH

Economist Noah Smith earned his bachelor's degree in physics from Stanford University and his Ph.D. in economics from the University of Michigan. He is a *Bloomberg View* columnist and a blogger at *Noahpinion*, his personal blog site. Previously, he was an assistant professor of finance at Stony Brook University, New York. In addition to his regular postings on *Bloomberg View*, Smith's work has appeared in publications and news Web sites such as the *Business Times*, *RealClearPolitics*, the *Pittsburgh Post-Gazette*, and *LiveMint*.

Courtesy of Noah Smith

In the following 2016 column published on *Bloomberg View*, Smith considers the future of automation and its impact on our jobs and our economy, an issue equally important for both long-term employees and those about to enter the workplace. Note: We have set Smith's original hyperlinks to sources as works cited in MLA style.

O f all the economic questions being debated today, the most frightening one is "Will the robots take our jobs?" This nightmare scenario comes in several flavors. The extreme version is that automation simply makes human workers obsolete, just as cars made horses redundant. A less apocalyptic possibility is what economists call "skill-biased technological change" (Autor)—people who are technically savvy, mentally flexible and educated will reap greater and greater rewards while everyone else sees their wages decline. These two scenarios might look different on paper, but the net result is largely the same—a very big portion of humanity would be either be impoverished or reduced to living off of the government dole. Books like "The Wealth of Humans," by economics writer Ryan Avent, explore this frightening possibility.

So far, the robot revolution hasn't happened, or at least not very much— if it had, we'd be seeing faster productivity growth and higher unemployment. A few papers have claimed to see evidence of companies substituting machines for humans more than in the past, but so far the evidence remains scant (Chui et al.). The robot revolution is more of a long-term concern, driven by the rapid advances in machine learning and other technologies that seem to allow machines to mimic or even surpass human cognition (Chui et al.). If computers can do mental tasks better and machines can do physical tasks better than humans, what special skills do we have left?

Predicting whether machines will make the bulk of humans useless is 3 beyond my capability. The future of technology is much too hard to predict. But I can say this: one of the main arguments often used to rule out this worrisome possibility is very shaky. If you think that history proves that humans can't be replaced, think again.

> **❝ If you think that history proves that humans can't be replaced, think again. ❞**

I see this argument all the time. 4 Because humans have never been replaced before, people say, it can't happen in the future. Many cite the example of the Luddites, British textile workers in the early 19th century who protested against the introduction of technologies that could do their jobs more cheaply. In retrospect, the Luddites look foolish. As industrial technology improved, skilled workers were not impoverished— instead, they found ever-more-lucrative jobs that made use of new tools. As a result, "Luddite" is now a term of derision for those who doubt the power of technology to improve the world.

A more sophisticated version of this argument is offered by John Lewis 5 of the Bank of England, in a recent blog post. Reviewing economic history, he shows what most people intuitively understand—new technology has *complemented* human labor rather than *replacing* it. Indeed, as Lewis points out, most macroeconomic models assume that the relationship between technology and humans is basically fixed.

That's the problem, though — economic assumptions are right, until they're 6 not. The future isn't always like the past. Sometimes it breaks in radical ways.

The clearest, most important example is the Industrial Revolution itself. 7 For thousands of years before 1800, the wealth of the average human was almost constant. New technologies were invented—steel, the horse collar, plumbing, the compass, paper. But per capita output barely went up. Most people were still indigent farmers.

Imagine an economist or pundit in 1780, observing the new industrial 8 technologies that were popping up in the U.K. Imagine him scoffing at the entrepreneurs and visionaries who predicted that the power loom and the steam engine heralded the dawn of a new era of abundance for humanity. "Nonsense," the skeptic would say. "Technologies of the past have never allowed the mass of the species to escape from poverty, so why should this new crop be any different?"

We all know what happened next. The new technologies were qualita-   9
tively different. And that resulted in an abrupt acceleration of wealth generation the likes of which the world had never seen. Via Derek Thompson of
the *Atlantic*, here is a graph of per capita gross domestic product for various
regions since the beginning of the first millennium A.D.:

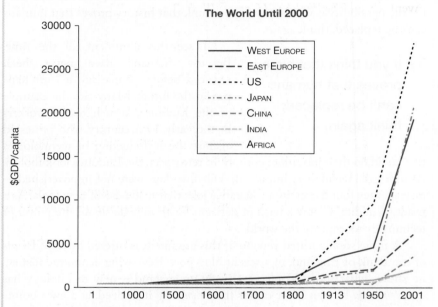

Data from Michael Cembalest, "HS–8: The World Economy, 1–2001 AD," cdn.theatlantic.com/
static/mt/assets/business/HS-8_2003.pdf

What happened in 1800 and afterward utterly defied all of the lessons   10
of history up until that point.

And automation could now do the same. There is no fundamental law of   11
economics that says that technology must always complement human labor. In
fact, the math of how robots could replace humans is simple and well understood (Rognlie). If the elasticity of substitution between capital and labor—
basically, jargon for "how easy it is to replace humans with machines"—goes
up, labor's share of income can go down and down. Skill-biased technological
change, which rewards the top workers while punishing everyone else, has also
been modeled by economic theorists for decades (Acemoglu).

So there is no deep, abiding reason why the future will look like the   12
past. Machines have never replaced humans before, and they probably
aren't doing so right now. But that says very little about whether they will
in the future. The nature of technology is that it changes the world in ways
that are totally new and unanticipated. For all we know, this time really
might be different.

Works Cited

Acemoglu, Daron. "Labor-Augmenting and Skill-Biased Technical Change." Massachusetts Institute of Technology, economics.mit.edu/files/967.

Autor, David H. "Skill Biased Technical Change and Rising Inequality: What Is the Evidence? What Are the Alternatives?" Massachusetts Institute of Technology, economics.mit.edu/files/559.

Avent, Ryan. *The Wealth of Humans: Work, Power, and Status in the Twenty-first Century*. St. Martin's Press, 2016.

Chui, Michael, et al. "Where Machines Could Replace Humans—and Where They Can't Yet." *McKinsey Quarterly*, July 2016, www.mckinsey.com/business-functions/digital-mckinsey/our-insights/where-machines-could-replace-humans-and-where-they-cant-yet/.

Lewis, John. "Robot Macroeconomics: What Can Theory and Several Centuries of Economic History Teach Us?" *Bank Underground*, Bank of England, 6 Sept. 2016, bankunderground.co.uk/2016/09/06/robot-macroeconomics-what-can-theory-and-several-centuries-of-economic-history-teach-us/.

Rognlie, Matthew. "A Note on Piketty and Diminishing Returns to Capital." *Tematic Contexpert*, 15 June 2014, www.conta-conta.ro/economisti/Thomas_Piketty_file%2030_.pdf.

Thompson, Derek. "The Economic History of the Last 2000 Years: Part II." *The Atlantic*, 20 June 2012, www.theatlantic.com/business/archive/2012/06/the-economic-history-of-the-last-2000-years-part-ii/258762/.

Thinking Critically about the Text

Smith writes that the most frightening economic question is 'Will the robots take our jobs?' (paragraph 1). Do you agree that this is the most frightening economic question right now? Why, or why not? Do you hear about this fear from the people around you? What has been — or should be — their response?

Examining the Issue

1. What does "skill-biased technological change" mean (paragraph 1)? What are its effects?

2. How do we know the "robot revolution" has not happened yet, according to Smith?

3. What is a "Luddite" (paragraph 4)? How does the name become a "term of derision," according to Smith?

4. According to Smith, how do economists generally view the relationship between technology and humans?

5. Discussing the future implications of automation, Smith writes that "economic assumptions are right, until they're not" (paragraph 6). What historical example does he use to **illustrate** this point? Is it effective?

6. In paragraph 9, Smith includes a chart. What does the chart illustrate? Why does Smith include the chart instead of simply listing or describing its contents?

7. What is the "nature of technology," according to Smith?

MAKING CONNECTIONS

Writing and Discussion Suggestions on the Changing Nature of Work

1. In "The Gingham Apron," Caitlin McCormick makes a powerful argument for what a job can teach you. What examples from your own experience can you offer that give further evidence for this argument? Perhaps you would like to argue just the opposite: Some jobs have no redeeming value and are just pure drudgery. Explain.

2. Caitlin McCormick argues that jobs in the service industry set up a class-based power dynamic. Are there other jobs or careers that create similar power structures? How? What other factors may contribute to "power struggles" in the workplace?

3. In "The Quitting Economy," Ilana Gershon addresses a relatively new phenomenon: workers taking jobs to acquire certain skills and then moving on to market those skills to other employers. Why is this practice occurring, and what concerns from employees does it address? What connections can you draw between Gershon's argument and the worries Noah Smith describes in "Don't Assume Robots Will Be Our Future Coworkers"?

4. Do employers and workers owe each other any degree of loyalty, or are the stipulations of an employment contract the limits of the relationship between employers and workers? Do employers owe anything to workers beyond what is stated in a contract?

5. What argument would you make for being self-employed as a business owner or freelance professional? What problems would you face? What benefits might you enjoy in terms of job satisfaction?

6. Are you worried about robots taking over the job you have now, or could have in the future? What evidence have you seen that automation is becoming an increasing problem? Have family members or friends been replaced by machines? What have been the consequences of such displacement?

7. **Writing with Sources**. Argue for the benefits of automation. Do research about areas in our economy (for example, surgical procedures or the handling of hazardous materials) where you could argue that automation and the use of robotics are having a profoundly beneficial effect on our quality of life.

8. **Writing with Sources**. Do some research on the changing nature of work today in your intended profession. Based on what you read (secondary research) and the discussions you have with both your peers and people you know in the workforce (primary research), what actions should you take to ensure job security and satisfaction in the future? What recommendations would you make for others? For models of and advice on integrating sources in your essay, see Chapters 14 and 15.

60 Minutes or More a Day
Where Kids Live, Learn, and Play

Inform

Enable

Health Care
92% of youth saw a health care provider last year

Preschool
4.2 million youth attend center-based preschools

24 minutes of physical activity are added for youth who walk to school

Youth are **65%** more likely to join organized physical activities when encouraged by their parents

95% of youth are in school for 6-7 hours per day

Community
Build

School
Integrate

Home
Support

Physical activity is critical for overall health.

Learn more: www.health.gov/paguidelines

Sources: Synder T, Dillow S. Digest of education statistics 2010. Washington, DC: National Center for Education Statistics, Institute of Education Sciences, US Department of Education; 2011. Federal Interagency Forum on Child and Family Statistics. America's children in brief: key national indicators of well-being, 2006. Washington, DC: US Government Printing Office; 2006. Sirard JR, Riner WF, McIver KL, Pate RR. Physical activity and active commuting to elementary school. Med Sci Sports Exerc. 2005;37(12):2062–9. J Pediatr. 1991;118(2):215–9. Bloom B, Cohen RA, Freeman G. Summary health statistics for U.S. children: National Health Interview Survey, 2011. Vital Health Stat 10. 2012 Dec;(254):1–148. Heitzler CD, Martin SL, Duke J, et al. Correlates of physical activity in a national sample of children aged 9-13 years. Prev Med. 2006;42(4):254–60.

Office of Disease Prevention and Health Promotion,
https://health.gov/paguidelines/blog/post/60-Minutes-or-More-a-Day-Where-Kids-Live-Learn-and-Play.aspx

Combining Strategies

WHAT DOES IT MEAN TO COMBINE STRATEGIES?

EACH OF THE PRECEDING CHAPTERS OF *SUBJECT & STRATEGY* EMPHASIZES a particular writing strategy: narration, description, illustration, process analysis, and so forth. The essays and selections within each of these chapters use the given strategy as the dominant method of development. It is important to remember, however, that the *dominant* strategy is rarely the *only* one used to develop a piece of writing. To fully explore their topics, writers often use other strategies in combination with the dominant strategy. In each of the introductions for Chapters 4 through 12, for example, we show how writers use one or more supporting strategies in combination with a dominant strategy to write about topics across the disciplines. To highlight and reinforce this point, we focus on the use of multiple strategies in the "Questions on Strategy" sections following each of the professional selections in this chapter.

VISUALIZING COMBINING STRATEGIES

Infographics use a combination of visual strategies to communicate data. Carefully analyze the infographic from the Office of Disease Prevention and Health Promotion. What, if anything, jumped out at you when you first looked at the infographic? What were you drawn to, and why? How does the "60 Minutes" headline help to introduce the organizational design of this chart? What is the main point or argument of this infographic? Explain how the designer uses division and classification, illustration, and cause and effect analysis to both support and develop the central argument.

UNDERSTANDING A COMBINATION OF STRATEGIES IN WRITTEN TEXTS

In this chapter on combining strategies, we offer a collection of essays that make notable use of several different strategies. You will encounter such combinations of strategies in the reading and writing you do in other college courses. Beyond the classroom, you might write a business proposal using both description and cause and effect to make an argument for a new marketing plan, or you might use narration, description, and illustration to write a news story for a company blog or a letter to the editor of your local newspaper.

The following essay by Sydney Harris reveals how several strategies can be used effectively, even in a brief piece of writing. Although primarily a work of definition, notice how "A Jerk" also uses illustration and personal narrative to engage the reader and achieve Harris's purpose.

A JERK

Uses narration to introduce central question: What's a jerk?

I don't know whether history repeats itself, but biography certainly does. The other day, Michael came in and asked me what a "jerk" was—the same question Carolyn put to me a dozen years ago.

At that time, I fluffed her off with some inane answer, such as "A jerk isn't a very nice person," but both of us knew it was an unsatisfactory reply. When she went to bed, I began trying to work up a suitable definition.

Uses comparison to show what a jerk is not

It is a marvelously apt word, of course. Until it was coined, not more than twenty-five years ago, there was really no single word in English to describe the kind of person who is a jerk—"boob" and "simp" were too old hat, and besides they really didn't fit, for they could be lovable, and a jerk never is.

Begins developing definition of jerk

Thinking it over, I decided that a jerk is basically a person without insight. He is not necessarily a fool or a dope, because some extremely clever persons can be jerks. In fact, it has little to do with intelligence as we commonly think of it; it is, rather, a kind of subtle but persuasive aroma emanating from the inner part of the personality.

Uses example of college president to illustrate "a person without insight"

I know a college president who can be described only as a jerk. He is not an unintelligent man, nor unlearned, nor even unschooled in the social amenities. Yet he is a jerk cum laude, because of a fatal flaw in his nature—he is totally incapable of looking into the mirror of his soul and shuddering at what he sees there.

Uses comparison to support thoughtful definition

A jerk, then, is a man (or woman) who is utterly unable to see himself as he appears to others. He has no grace, he is tactless without meaning to be, he is a bore even to his best friends, he is an egotist without charm. All of us are egotists to some extent, but most of us—unlike the jerk—are perfectly and horribly aware of it when we make asses of ourselves. The jerk never knows.

Essays that use thoughtful combinations of rhetorical strategies have some obvious advantages for the writer and the reader. By reading the work of professional writers, you can learn how multiple strategies can be used to your advantage—how a paragraph of narration, a vivid description, a clarifying instance of comparison and contrast, or a clear definition can help convey your purpose and thesis.

For example, let's suppose you wanted to write an essay on the slang you hear on campus. You might find it helpful to use a variety of strategies:

Definition—to explain what slang is

Illustration—to give examples of slang

Comparison and contrast—to differentiate slang from other types of speech, such as idioms or technical language

Division and classification—to categorize different types of slang or different topics that slang terms are used for, such as courses, students, food, grades

Or let's say you wanted to write a paper on the Japanese Americans who were sent to internment camps during World War II while the United States was at war with Japan. The following strategies would be available to you:

Illustration—to illustrate several particular cases of families that were sent to internment camps

Narration—to tell the stories of former camp residents, including their first reaction to their internment and their actual experiences in the camps

Cause and effect—to examine the reasons the United States government interned Japanese Americans and the long-term effects of this policy

When you rely on a single mode or approach to an essay, you lose the opportunity to come at your subject from a number of different angles, all of which complete the picture and any one of which might be the most insightful or engaging and, therefore, the most memorable for the reader. This is particularly the case with essays that attempt to persuade or argue. The task of changing readers' beliefs and thoughts is so difficult that writers look for any combination of strategies that will make their arguments more convincing. For more examples of how you can us strategies in combination, review Chapter 2, "Choosing Strategies Across the Disciplines" (pages 35–36), as well as the section "Using [the Strategy] Across the Disciplines" in each of the introductions for Chapters 4 through 12.

PRACTICAL ADVICE FOR USING A COMBINATION OF STRATEGIES IN AN ESSAY

As you plan, write, and revise your essay using a combination of strategies, be mindful of the writing process guidelines described in Chapter 2. Pay particular attention to the basic requirements and essential ingredients of each writing strategy you choose.

▶ Planning Your Essay Using a Combination of Strategies

Planning is an essential part of writing any good essay. You can save yourself a great deal of trouble by taking the time to think about the key building blocks of your essay before you actually begin to write. Before you can start combining strategies in your writing, it's essential that you know what you want to say and have a firm understanding of the purposes and workings of each strategy. Once you become familiar with how the strategies work, you should be able to recognize ways to use and combine them in your writing.

Sometimes you will find yourself using a particular strategy almost intuitively. When you encounter a difficult or abstract term or concept — *liberal*, for example — you will define it almost as a matter of course. If you become perplexed because you are having trouble getting your readers to appreciate the severity of a problem, a quick review of the strategies will remind you that you could also use description and illustration.

Knowledge of the individual strategies is crucial because there are no formulas or prescriptions for combining strategies. The more you write and the more aware you are of the options available to you, the more skillful you will become at thinking critically about your topic, developing your ideas, and conveying your thoughts to your readers.

Determine Your Purpose.   The most common purposes in nonfiction writing are (1) to express your thoughts and feelings about a life experience, (2) to inform your readers by explaining something about the world around them, and (3) to persuade readers to embrace some belief or action. Your purpose will determine the dominant strategy you use in your essay.

Formulate a Thesis Statement.   Regardless of the purpose you have set for yourself in writing an essay, it is essential that you commit to a thesis statement, usually a one- or two-sentence statement giving the main point of your essay.

> Party primaries are an indispensable part of the American political process.

> Antibiotic use must be curtailed. Antibiotics have been overprescribed and are not nearly as effective as they once were at combating infections among humans.

A question is not a thesis statement. If you find yourself writing a thesis statement that asks a question, answer the question first and then turn your answer into a thesis statement. A thesis statement can be presented anywhere in an essay, but usually it is presented at the beginning of a composition, sometimes after a few introductory sentences that set a context for it.

❱ Organizing Your Essay Using a Combination of Strategies

Determine Your Dominant Strategy. Depending on your purpose for writing, your thesis statement, and the kinds of information you have gathered in preparing to write your essay, you may use any of the following strategies as the dominant strategy for your essay: narration, description, illustration, process analysis, comparison and contrast, division and classification, definition, cause and effect analysis, or argumentation.

If your major purpose is to tell a story of a river-rafting trip, for example, you will primarily use narration. If you wish to re-create the experience of seeing a famous landmark for the first time, you may find description most helpful. If you wish to inform your readers, you may find definition, cause and effect, process analysis, comparison and contrast, and/or division and classification to be best suited to your needs. If you wish to convince your readers of a certain belief or course of action, argumentation is an obvious choice.

Determine Your Supporting Strategies. The following questions—organized by rhetorical strategy—will help you decide which strategies will be most helpful in the service of the dominant strategy you have chosen for your essay and in achieving your overall purpose.

Questions for Determining Your Rhetorical Strategy	
Narration	Are you trying to report or recount an anecdote, an experience, or an event? Does any part of your essay include the telling of a story (something that happened to you or to a person you include in your essay)?
Description	Does a person, a place, or an object play a prominent role in your essay? Would the tone, pacing, or overall purpose of your essay benefit from sensory details?
Illustration	Are there examples — facts, statistics, cases in point, personal experiences, interview quotations — that you could add to help achieve the purpose of your essay?
Process analysis	Would any part of your essay be clearer if you included concrete directions about a certain process? Are there processes that readers would like to understand better? Are you evaluating any processes?

(continued on next page)

Comparison and contrast	Does your essay contain two or more related subjects? Are you evaluating or analyzing two or more people, places, processes, events, or things? Do you need to establish the similarities and differences between two or more elements?
Division and classification	Are you trying to explain a broad and complicated subject? Would it benefit your essay to reduce this subject to more manageable parts to focus your discussion?
Definition	Who is your audience? Does your essay focus on any abstract, specialized, or new terms that need further explanation so readers understand your point? Does any important word in your essay have many meanings and need to be clarified?
Cause and effect analysis	Are you examining past events or their outcomes? Is your purpose to inform, speculate, or argue about why an identifiable fact happens the way it does?
Argumentation	Are you trying to explain aspects of a particular subject, and are you trying to advocate a specific opinion on this subject or issue in your essay?

❿ Revising and Editing Your Essay Using a Combination of Strategies

Listen to What Your Classmates Have to Say. The importance of student peer conferences cannot be stressed enough, particularly as you revise and edit your essay. Others in your class will often see, for example, that the basis for your classification needs adjustment or that there are inconsistencies in your division categories that can easily be corrected — problems that you may not be able to see yourself because you are too close to your essay. To maximize the effectiveness of working with your classmates, use the guidelines in the "Brief Guide to Peer Critiquing" box on pages 38–39. Take advantage of suggestions when you know them to be valid and make revisions accordingly.

Question Your Own Work While Revising and Editing. Revision is best done by asking yourself key questions about what you have written. Begin by reading, preferably aloud, what you have written. Reading aloud forces you to pay attention to every single word, and you are more likely to catch lapses in the logical flow of thought. After you have read your paper through, answer the following questions for revising and editing and make the necessary changes.

For help with twelve common writing problems, see Chapter 16.

> ## Questions for Revising and Editing: Combining Strategies
>
> 1. Do I have a purpose for my essay?
> 2. Is my thesis statement clear?
> 3. Does my dominant strategy reflect my purpose and my thesis statement?
> 4. Do my supporting strategies effectively support the dominant strategy of my essay?
> 5. Are my supporting strategies woven into my essay in a natural manner?
> 6. Have I revised and edited my essay to avoid wordiness?
> 7. Have I used a variety of sentences to enliven my writing?
> 8. Have I avoided errors in grammar, punctuation, and mechanics?

STUDENT ESSAY USING A COMBINATION OF STRATEGIES

LeeLee Goodson was born in Burlington, Vermont, but grew up in Stowe, Vermont, a popular ski town. An English major in college, she studied writing and literature. In her essay "The Ducks on Corrigan's Pond," LeeLee uses an analogy to help explain the way she feels about her hometown and the people who live there.

The Ducks on Corrigan's Pond
LeeLee Goodson

Description: depicts the wooden decoys on the pond from memory

1   I used to see them every morning from the school bus. They were decoys—three wooden mallards, anchored to the bottom. I watched them move across the surface of the pond. On windy days they were blown toward the reeds, where they stopped and leaned against their tethers. On calmer days they floated in the center, bobbing and changing their position in relation to one another. I never understood why they were there, for they never drew other ducks to the pond—they just turned in the breeze and weathered.

Narration: recounts recent visit to the pond

2   Driving by the other day, I noticed that the reeds had grown and the ducks were gone. No one was around, so I got out of my car and circled the pond to search for them. I found them anchored on the far side, water-heavy and stripped of their paint, but floating still. I could see their age in the cracks and the moss on their backs. As I sat on the bank and watched them bobbing purposelessly, my thoughts turned to the past, to growing up in this town.

Illustration: provides examples of what it was like growing up in a small town

I remembered the summers I spent riding my bike on the hot sidewalk under the storefront awnings on Main Street. Mr. Adams always waved from his egg truck, and I always waved back. Mrs. Wilkins was usually in her garden. I remembered the candy counter at Lackey's, the Reverend Hall, the Junior Prom. I remembered, also, every Memorial Day when I marched in the high school band down Maple Street. A few people stood on the sidewalk to watch, but most just fell in behind as we turned down Old Cemetery Road. Every year we went the same route, wore the same uniforms, played the same songs. We were always impatient to be done, to have the rest of the day off. But the veterans led the march, and they were old and walked slowly. We listened to the speech that we knew by heart, and watched while the old men stood as straight as they could when the guns were fired. 3

Feeling like a stuck decoy, writer decides to take wing

Somehow, I felt like one of those decoys on the pond. I was floating on the surface, yet anchored to the mud on the bottom. I wanted to escape the smallness here. I wanted more. When Andy Lockwood proposed marriage to me in the first grade, I accepted. When Heather Adams proposed that we run away in the sixth grade, I also accepted. Not until I was twenty, however, did I really leave. I took my car, my clothes, and four hundred dollars, and I escaped with my first serious boyfriend. 4

Analogy: explains why childhood friends stayed by comparing them to the decoys

In those days, I felt such contempt for my friends who stayed. Beth had Scott's child, and Laura had twins. Will worked in his father's store, and Larry worked the family farm. Ann and Dean were married; Bobby drove the school bus; Randy fixed the streets. Like the ducks, they were anchored here. They seemed mindlessly content to repeat their parents' lives, and I couldn't understand why they stayed. 5

Writer begins to understand why people stayed at home

But the longer I was away, the more I began to understand. They stayed for the same reason that eventually brought me back: they needed the comfort of the familiar, the security of everyday ritual. They wanted to raise their children the way they had been raised because they found satisfaction in the regularity of life here. 6

Conclusion: writer goes beyond analogy to understand herself better

7

I finally saw what I had missed before—that the ducks are here because they have to be, but the people are here by choice. Once I thought the people were as mindless as the ducks. Going away made me recognize that they are not. The ducks were anchored by someone else; the people have anchored themselves. I've come back—back home—because I realize that I need Lackey's store and the Memorial Day parade. I need this town and the security of my past.

Student Reflection
LeeLee Goodson

Q. How did you hit on the analogy between the decoys and the townspeople?

A. The essay is about feelings that I had had for a long time and wanted to write about. I started with a different analogy, though. Near the highway I pass along every day, there's a rock that dangles from a string tied to the limb of an elm tree—maybe it has to do with the wind, or it's someone's idea of art—and its flat side catches the sun when you drive by. I thought that would make for an effective analogy, how I felt tied to Vermont and could turn like the rock to see all those vistas but not really be able to go anywhere. But being suspended like that had a real negative connotation for me. Then I drove by the duck decoys and they seemed to be a way of describing what I felt. I didn't have anything handy to write with at the time, but all the way home I was thinking about it. Even sentences—I had "written" the entire opening before I actually started a draft.

Q. So it all actually happened.

A. Yes, it actually happened. I've no idea what the man's name was—it wasn't actually Corrigan—this old man who lived in a trailer across the street and actually moved the decoys around. It just struck me as odd when I was a little kid. The decoys were exactly what I was looking for to write the paper: anchored, able to move around a little bit on the surface. When I moved away I was homesick the entire time; I wanted to come back and I couldn't put into words why, and I didn't understand being tied to a place.

Q. Once you had your object and the opening, did the rest come easily?

A. The essay went through about four drafts. I started out on a couple of different tacks and had to change them. For example, I first included the old man who had moved the ducks around, but my analogy would have made me provide something or someone to move the people around; I didn't want to do that because they were there by choice. So I cut out the old man. I wanted to include the Memorial Day parade, but I wasn't sure where, so I tried a couple of different ways. I moved paragraphs around—that kind of thing. And there were a lot of smaller revisions. But I'd say that I had the overall content and shape about right in the first draft.

Q. Why an analogy?

A. It helped me to objectify my feelings, and maybe clarify them. Making a comparison between the townspeople and the decoys, listing points they did and didn't have in common, helped me to think. I don't think I could have written about these feelings in a different way. I might have done it as a narration, but I don't think it would have been as effective and I don't think it would have made my emotions and thoughts as clear to the reader.

Q. You sound as though you like to write.

A. Writing is a way of dealing with a strong emotion, at least for me. For instance, last summer I drove by an auction on a country road and I stopped and went in. All the possessions were being auctioned off. The family wasn't there, but their personal things were being sold—I saw photographs being pulled out of their albums—and I felt so strongly that I needed to write about it to help vent the emotions. I write to communicate too, of course, and I'd like to be a writer—some fiction, some nonfiction. I do some writing at least every other day, but I don't usually finish it; who has time?

Your Response

What did you learn from LeeLee Goodson's essay and reflection about the experience of writing the essay? What challenges do you expect to face as you write your own essay using a combination of strategies? Based on LeeLee's composing strategies and the practical advice discussed earlier in this chapter (pages 474–77), how will you address those challenges? What writing choices will you make?

On Dumpster Diving

LARS EIGHNER

By permission of Lars Eighner

Born in Corpus Christi, Texas, in 1948, Lars Eighner grew up in Houston and attended the University of Texas–Austin. After graduation, he wrote essays and fiction, and several of his articles were published in magazines like *Threepenny Review*, the *Guide*, and *Inches*. A volume of short stories, *Bayou Boy and Other Stories*, was published in 1985. Eighner became homeless in 1988 when he left his job as an attendant at a mental hospital. The following piece, which appeared in the *Utne Reader*, is an abridged version of an essay that first appeared in *Threepenny Review*. The piece eventually became part of Eighner's startling account of the three years he spent with his dog as a homeless person, *Travels with Lizbeth* (1993). His publications include the novel *Pawn to Queen Four* (1995), the short story collection *Whispered in the Dark* (1996), and the nonfiction book of essays *Gay Cosmos* (1995).

Eighner uses a number of rhetorical strategies in "On Dumpster Diving" but pays particular attention to how his process analysis of the "stages that a person goes through in learning to scavenge" contributes to the success of the essay as a whole.

Preparing to Read

Are you a pack rat, or do you get rid of what is not immediately useful to you? Outside of the usual kitchen garbage and empty toothpaste tubes, how do you make the decision to throw something away?

I began Dumpster diving about a year before I became homeless. 1

I prefer the term *scavenging*. I have heard people, evidently meaning 2 to be polite, use the word *foraging*, but I prefer to reserve that word for gathering nuts and berries and such, which I also do, according to the season and opportunity.

I like the frankness of the word *scavenging*. I live from the refuse of 3 others. I am a scavenger. I think it a sound and honorable niche, although if I could I would naturally prefer to live the comfortable consumer life, perhaps — and only perhaps — as a slightly less wasteful consumer owing to what I have learned as a scavenger.

Except for jeans, all my clothes come from Dumpsters. Boom boxes, 4 candles, bedding, toilet paper, medicine, books, a typewriter, a virgin male love doll, coins sometimes amounting to many dollars: All came from Dumpsters. And, yes, I eat from Dumpsters, too.

There is a predictable series of stages that a person goes through in learning to scavenge. At first the new scavenger is filled with disgust and self-loathing. He is ashamed of being seen.

This stage passes with experience. The scavenger finds a pair of running shoes that fit and look and smell brand-new. He finds a pocket calculator in perfect working order. He finds pristine ice cream, still frozen, more than he can eat or keep. He begins to understand: People do throw away perfectly good stuff, a lot of perfectly good stuff.

At this stage he may become lost and never recover: All the Dumpster divers I have known come to the point of trying to acquire everything they touch. Why not take it, they reason, it is all free. This is, of course, hopeless, and most divers come to realize that they must restrict themselves to items of relatively immediate utility.

" **I live from the refuse of others. I am a scavenger.** " The finding of objects is becoming something of an urban art. Even respectable, employed people will sometimes find something tempting sticking out of a Dumpster or standing beside one. Quite a number of people, not all of them of the bohemian type, are willing to brag that they found this or that piece in the trash.

But eating from Dumpsters is the thing that separates the dilettanti from the professionals. Eating safely involves three principles: using the senses and common sense to evaluate the condition of the found materials; knowing the Dumpsters of a given area and checking them regularly; and seeking always to answer the question "Why was this discarded?"

Yet perfectly good food can be found in Dumpsters. Canned goods, for example, turn up fairly often in the Dumpsters I frequent. I also have few qualms about dry foods such as crackers, cookies, cereal, chips, and pasta if they are free of visible contaminants and still dry and crisp. Raw fruits and vegetables with intact skins seem perfectly safe to me, excluding, of course, the obviously rotten. Many are discarded for minor imperfections that can be pared away.

A typical discard is a half jar of peanut butter—though nonorganic peanut butter does not require refrigeration and is unlikely to spoil in any reasonable time. One of my favorite finds is yogurt—often discarded, still sealed, when the expiration date has passed—because it will keep for several days, even in warm weather.

No matter how careful I am I still get dysentery at least once a month, oftener in warm weather. I do not want to paint too romantic a picture. Dumpster diving has serious drawbacks as a way of life.

I find from the experience of scavenging two rather deep lessons. The first is to take what I can use and let the rest go. I have come to think that there is no value in the abstract. A thing I cannot use or make useful, perhaps by trading, has no value, however fine or rare it may be.

The second lesson is the transience of material being. I do not suppose 14 that ideas are immortal, but certainly they are longer-lived than material objects.

The things I find in Dumpsters, the love letters and rag dolls of so many 15 lives, remind me of this lesson. Now I hardly pick up a thing without envisioning the time I will cast it away. This, I think, is a healthy state of mind. Almost everything I have now has already been cast out at least once, proving that what I own is valueless to someone.

I find that my desire to grab for the gaudy bauble has been largely 16 sated. I think this is an attitude I share with the very wealthy — we both know there is plenty more where whatever we have came from. Between us are the rat-race millions who have confounded their selves with the objects they grasp and who nightly scavenge the cable channels for they know not what.

I am sorry for them. 17

Thinking Critically about the Text

In paragraph 15, Eighner writes, "I hardly pick up a thing without envisioning the time I will cast it away. This, I think, is a healthy state of mind." React to this statement. Do you think such an attitude is healthy or defeatist? If many people thought this way, what impact would it have on our consumer society?

Questions on Subject

1. What stages do beginning Dumpster divers go through before they become what Eighner terms "professionals" (paragraph 9)? What examples does Eighner use to illustrate the passage through these stages?

2. What three principles does one need to follow to eat safely from Dumpsters? What foods are best to eat from Dumpsters? What are the risks?

3. What two lessons has Eighner learned from his Dumpster diving experiences? Why are they significant to him?

4. Dumpster diving has had a profound effect on Eighner and the way he lives. How do his explanations of choices he makes, such as deciding which items to keep, enhance his presentation of the practical art of Dumpster diving?

Questions on Strategy

1. Eighner's essay deals with both the immediate, physical aspects of Dumpster diving, such as what can be found in a typical Dumpster and the physical price one pays for eating out of Dumpsters, and the larger, abstract issues that Dumpster diving raises, such as materialism and the transience of material

objects. Why does he describe the **concrete** things before he discusses the **abstract** issues raised by their presence in Dumpsters? What does he achieve by using both types of elements?

2. Eighner's account of Dumpster diving focuses primarily on the odd appeal and interest inherent in the activity. Paragraph 12 is his one disclaimer, in which he states, "I do not want to paint too romantic a picture." Why does Eighner include this disclaimer? How does it add to the effectiveness of his piece? Why do you think it is so brief and abrupt?

3. Eighner uses many rhetorical techniques in his essay, but its core is a fairly complete **process analysis** of how to Dumpster dive. Summarize this process analysis. Why do you think Eighner did not title the essay "How to Dumpster Dive"?

4. Discuss how Eighner uses **illustration** to bring the world of Dumpster diving to life. What characterizes the examples he uses?

Combining Strategies in Action

As a class, discuss the strategies that Eighner uses in his essay: narration, process analysis, cause and effect, illustration, and definition, for example. Where in the essay has he used each strategy and to what end? Has he used any other strategies not mentioned above? Explain.

Writing Suggestions

1. In paragraph 3, Eighner states that he "live[s] from the refuse of others." How does his confession affect you? Do you think that we have become a throwaway society? If so, how? How do Eighner's accounts of homelessness and Dumpster diving make you feel about your own consumerism and trash habits? Write an essay in which you examine the things you throw away in a single day. What items did you get rid of? Why? Could those items be used by someone else? Have you ever felt guilty about throwing something away? If so, what was it, and why did you feel guilty?

2. One person's treasure is another person's trash. In the following photograph, young adults in their early twenties explore what's available inside a Dumpster near a supermarket in Charlotte, North Carolina. Stephanie Braun, in plaid, hands a fruit to Kaitlyn Tokay, pictured in front. Choose a theme derived from the photograph and Eighner's essay — for example, the treasure/trash statement above or whether this sort of Dumpster diving is the purest form of recycling — and write an essay that includes at least three different strategies used in combination.

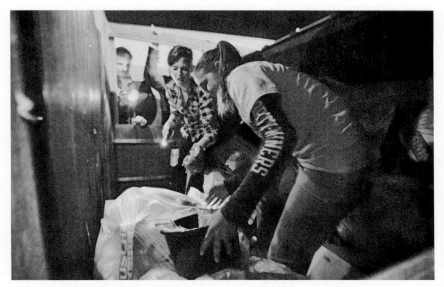

Gary O'Brien/Charlotte Observer/MCT via Getty Images

The Struggle

ISSA RAE

Issa Rae was born in 1985 and grew up in Potomac, Maryland; Dakar, Senegal; and Los Angeles, California. After graduating with a bachelor's degree in African and African American Studies from Stanford University, where she produced a popular "mockumentary" video series called "Dorm Diaries," Rae received a fellowship to the Public Theater in New York City. She found networking and social life difficult in New York, which inspired her to create and star in the YouTube comedy Web series *The Mis-Adventures of Awkward Black Girl* in 2011. The show became a viral sensation on social media and ultimately evolved into the HBO comedy drama *Insecure*, which Rae co-created with comedian, writer, and producer Larry Wilmore. Among other honors, she has won an African American Film Critics Association Award and a Vision Award from the National Association for Multi-Ethnicity in Communications.

MediaPunch Inc. / Alamy Stock Photo

In her work, Rae is often preoccupied with the difficulties of fitting in, particularly in the context of her racial identity. That theme is evident in the following selection, which is taken from her best-selling memoir, *The Misadventures of Awkward Black Girl* (2015). As you read Rae's essay, notice how she uses a combination of strategies to advance her argument about being black.

Preparing to Read

Do you have a collective identity as well as an individual identity? In other words, do you identify as a member of a religious, racial, ethnic, or other group? Do other people judge you according to that group identity? How do you negotiate the relationship between these two forms of identity?

I don't remember the exact day I demilitarized from my blackness. It's all a blur and since I'm fairly certain that militants never forget, and I forget stuff *all* the time, I guess I wasn't meant to be one. 1

I love being black; that's not a problem. The problem is that I don't 2 want to always *talk* about it because honestly, talking about being "black" is extremely tiring. I don't know how Al Sharpton and Jesse Jackson do it. I know why Cornel West and Tavis Smiley do it. They *love* the attention and the groupies. But the rest of these people who talk, think, and breathe race every single day—how? Just how? Aren't they exhausted?

The pressure to contribute to these conversations now that we have a 3 black president is even more infuriating.

"What do you think about what's going on in the world? And how our ⁴ black president is handling it?" asks a race baiter.

"It's all good, I guess," I want to answer, apathetically, with a Kanye ⁵ shrug. "I'm over it." But am I really? Could I be even if I wanted to?

> ❝ **I love being black; that's not a problem. The problem is that I don't want to always *talk* about it because honestly, talking about being 'black' is extremely tiring.** ❞

Even now, I feel obligated to write ⁶ about race. It's as though it's expected of me to acknowledge what we all already know. The truth is, I slip in and out of my black consciousness, as if I'm in a racial coma. Sometimes, I'm so deep in my anger, my irritation, my need to stir change, that I can't see anything outside of the lens of race.

At other times I feel guilty about my ⁷ apathy. But then I think, *isn't this what those who came before me fought for?* The right *not* to have to deal with race? If faced with a choice between fighting until the death for freedom and civil rights and living life without any acknowledgment of race, they'd choose the latter.

Growing up as a young black girl in Potomac, Maryland, was easy. I ⁸ never really had to put much thought into my race, and neither did anybody else. I had a Rainbow Coalition of friends of all ethnicities, and we would carelessly skip around our elementary school like the powerless version of Captain Planet's Planeteers. I knew I was black. I knew there was a history that accompanied my skin color and my parents taught me to be proud of it. End of story.

All that changed when my family moved to Los Angeles and placed me ⁹ in a middle school where my blackness was constantly questioned—and not even necessarily in the traditional sense, i.e. "You talk white, Oreo girl" or "You can't dance, white girl." Those claims were arguable, for the most part. My biggest frustration in the challenge to prove my "blackness" usually stemmed from two very annoying, very repetitive situations:

SITUATION #1: "I'm not even black, and I'm blacker than you." It's ¹⁰ one thing when other African Americans try to call me out on my race card, but when people outside my ethnicity have the audacity to question how "down" I am because of the bleak, stereotypical picture pop culture has painted of black women, it's a whole other thing. Unacceptable. I can recall a time when I was having a heated discussion with a white, male classmate of mine. Our eighth-grade class was on a museum field trip as the bus driver blasted Puff Daddy's "Been Around the World" to drown us out.

It began as a passive competition of lyrics, as we each silently listened ¹¹ for who would mess up first. By the second verse, our lazy rap-whispers escalated to an aggressive volume, accompanied by rigorous side-eyes by the time we got to, "Playa please, I'm the macaroni with the cheese," and I felt threatened. Was this fool seriously trying to outrap me? And why did I care? After the song ended, he offered his opinion: "Puff Daddy is wack, yo." How dare he? Not only was I pissed, but I felt as if he had insulted my own father (who did I think I was? Puff Daughter?).

"Puff Daddy is tight," I retorted. He rolled his eyes and said, "Have you heard of [insert Underground rapper]? Now, *he's* dope." I hadn't heard of him, but I couldn't let this white boy defeat me in rap music knowledge, especially as others started to listen. "Yeah, I know him. He's not dope," I lied, for the sake of saving face. Perhaps because he saw through me or because he actually felt strongly about this particular artist, he asked me to name which songs I thought were "not dope." Panic set in as I found myself exposed, then — "You don't even know him, huh? Have you even heard of [insert Random Underground rapper]?" 12

As he continued to rattle off the names of make-believe-sounding MCs, delighted that he had one-upped me, he managed to make me feel as though my credibility as a black person relied on my knowledge of hip-hop culture. My identity had been reduced to the Bad Boy label clique as this boy seemingly claimed my black card as his own. 13

Of course, as I grew older and Ma$e found his calling as a reverend, I realized there was more to being black than a knowledge of rap music, and that I didn't have to live up to this pop cultural archetype. I began to take pride in the fact that I couldn't be reduced to a stereotype and that I didn't have to be. This leads me to my next situation: 14

SITUATION #2: "Black people don't do that." Or so I'm told by a black person. These, too, are derived from (mostly negative) stereotypes shaped by popular culture. The difference is that in these situations, we black people are the ones buying into these stereotypes. 15

When I was a teenager, for example, others questioned my blackness because some of the life choices I made weren't considered to be "black" choices: joining the swim team when it is a known fact that "black people don't swim," or choosing to become a vegetarian when blacks clearly love chicken. These choices and the various positive and negative responses to them helped to broaden my own perspective on blackness and, eventually, caused me to spurn these self-imposed limitations. But not before embarrassing the hell out of myself in a poor attempt to prove I was "down." I'll never forget submitting a school project in "Ebonics" for my seventh-grade English class, just to prove that I could talk *and* write "black." I was trying to prove it to myself just as much as I was to everyone around me. 16

Even in my early adulthood, post-college, I'd overtip to demonstrate I was one of the good ones. Only recently have I come to ask, *What am I trying to* 17 *prove and to whom am I proving it?* Today, I haven't completely rid myself of the feeling that I'm still working through Du Bois's double consciousness.

For the majority of my life I cared too much about how my blackness 18 was perceived, but *now?* At this very moment? I couldn't care less. Call it maturation or denial or self-hatred—I give no f%^&s. And it feels great. I've decided to focus only on the positivity of being black, and especially of being a black woman. Am I supposed to feel oppressed? Because I don't. Is racism supposed to hurt me? That's so 1950s. Should I feel marginalized? I prefer to think of myself as belonging to an "exclusive" club.

While experiencing both types of situations—being made to feel not 19 black enough by "down" white people on one hand and not black enough by the blacks in the so-called know on the other—has played a role in shaping a more comfortably black me, in the end, I have to ask: Who is to say what we do and don't do? What we can and can't do? The very definition of "blackness" is as broad as that of "whiteness," yet the media seemingly always tries to find a specific, limited definition. As CNN produces news specials about us, and white and Latino rappers feel culturally dignified in using the N-word, our collective grasp of "blackness" is becoming more and more elusive. And that may not be a bad thing.

Thinking Critically about the Text

Early in her essay, Rae says she finds talking about race and "blackness" tiring. Does her attitude about this change over the course of "The Struggle"?

Questions on Subject

1. In her opening paragraph, Rae writes that she "demilitarized" from her "blackness." What do "demilitarized" and "militant" mean in this context?

2. Rae reflects back on her childhood and teenage years, and points to a change in her life that complicated her relationship with her black identity. What was the change? How did it affect her?

3. What two main judgments of her racial identity does Rae encounter?

4. How does Rae try to frame her racial identity at the end of the essay? What is her relationship to oppression, racism, and marginalization? Do you find her perspective convincing?

Questions on Strategy

1. How would you describe Rae's **attitude** toward her main topic in this essay? What is her **tone**?

2. What is the dominant rhetorical strategy of "The Struggle"? What are the supporting strategies?

3. What is Rae's **purpose** in writing this essay? What is she trying to accomplish?

4. Where in the essay does Rae use examples? What broader claims or points is she trying to **illustrate**?

Combining Strategies in Action

Choose a local newspaper editorial dealing with a controversial social or educational problem. Read the text and determine the writer's purpose. Outline the issues involved. Then, identify the different rhetorical strategies used in the text and explain why you think the writer chose to use them. Is there a dominant strategy? How are each of the strategies related to the writer's purpose?

Writing Suggestions

1. In this selection, Rae narrates moments from her younger years when her identity was challenged. She recalls her reactions to those challenges at the time and reflects on how the meaning of those events has changed since she has gotten older. In a brief narrative reflection, recall a specific time in your own childhood when you were challenged or provoked in some fundamental way to "prove yourself." What happened? How did you react at the time? What was the experience like? Now that you are older, how has your interpretation of the experience changed?

2. **Writing with Sources.** In paragraph 17, Rae wonders if she is still "working through Du Bois's double consciousness." Do some research on W. E. B. Du Bois and his idea of "double consciousness." Where does it come from? How does he define it? What problems does it cause? Write an essay that explains and explores this concept, using Rae's narrative as an example. Be sure to use other examples and writing strategies to make and support your points. For models of and advice on integrating sources in your essay, see Chapters 14 and 15.

The Sad, Beautiful Fact That We're All Going to Miss Almost Everything

LINDA HOLMES

Linda Holmes was born in 1970 and grew up in Wilmington, Delaware. She graduated from Oberlin College and Lewis and Clark Law School. While she spent several years working as a lawyer, her interest in popular culture — and in writing about popular culture — slowly overtook her legal career. In 2007, she left her job as an attorney to become a writer and editor at *Television without Pity*, a Web site devoted to recaps, discussion, and criticism of television dramas, situation comedies, and reality TV shows. Currently, Holmes writes and edits National Public Radio's pop culture and entertainment blog, *Monkey See*. She also hosts NPR's successful pop culture and entertainment podcast, *Pop Culture Happy Hour*. Holmes has written for *Vulture*, *TV Guide*, and MSNBC. Her first novel, *Head Case*, is scheduled to be published in 2019.

Despite her broad and deep engagement with popular culture, Holmes knows that no one can read, watch, and listen to *everything*. As she told her law school's alumni magazine, "I read and watch the things I think I'm going to learn the most from. The other stuff will be covered by lots of other writers out there." As you read Holmes's essay, published on NPR's *Monkey See* blog in 2011, notice how she uses the strategies of illustration, comparison and contrast, definition, and process analysis to support her central argument about being "well read."

Preparing to Read

Is it important to you to be "well read"? Do you feel obligated to keep up with the latest music, movies, and television shows? Do you experience the fear of missing out? Why, or why not?

T he vast majority of the world's books, music, films, television and art, you will never see. It's just numbers. 1

Consider books alone. Let's say you read two a week, and some- 2 times you take on a long one that takes you a *whole* week. That's quite a brisk pace for the average person. That lets you finish, let's say, 100 books a year. If we assume you start now, and you're 15, and you are willing to continue at this pace until you're 80. That's 6,500 books, which really sounds like a lot.

Let's do you another favor: Let's further assume you limit yourself to 3 books from the last, say, 250 years. Nothing before 1761. This cuts out giant, enormous swaths of literature, of course, but we'll assume you're willing to write off thousands of years of writing in an effort to be reasonably well-read.

Of course, by the time you're 80, there will be 65 more years of new   4
books, so by then, you're dealing with 315 years of books, which allows you to read about 20 books from each year. You'll have to break down your 20 books each year between fiction and nonfiction—you have to cover history, philosophy, essays, diaries, science, religion, science fiction, westerns, political theory . . . I hope you weren't planning to go out very much.

You can hit the highlights, and you can specialize enough to become   5
knowledgeable in some things, but most of what's out there, you'll have to ignore. (Don't forget books not written in English! Don't forget to learn all the other languages!)

> **❝ You can hit the highlights, and you can specialize enough to become knowledgeable in some things, but most of what's out there, you'll have to ignore. ❞**

Oh, and heaven help your kid, who will   6
either have to throw out maybe 30 years of what you deemed most critical or be even more selective than you had to be.

We could do the same calculus with   7
film or music or, increasingly, television—you simply have no chance of seeing even most of what exists. Statistically speaking, you will die having missed almost everything.

Roger Ebert wrote a lovely piece   8
about the idea of being "well-read," and specifically about the way writers aren't read as much once they've been dead a long time. He worries—well, not worries, but laments a little—that he senses people don't read Henry James anymore, that they don't read Sinclair Lewis, that their knowledge of Allen Ginsberg is limited to *Howl*.

It's undoubtedly true; there are things that fade. But I can't help blaming, in   9
part, the fact that we also simply have access to more and more things to choose from more and more easily. Netflix, Amazon, iTunes—you wouldn't have to go and search dusty used bookstores or know the guy who works at a record store in order to hear most of that stuff you're missing. You'd only have to choose to hear it.

You used to have a limited number of reasonably practical choices pre-   10
sented to you, based on what bookstores carried, what your local newspaper reviewed, or what you heard on the radio, or what was taught in college by a particular English department. There was a *huge* amount of selection that took place above the consumer level. (And here, I don't mean "consumer" in the crass sense of consumerism, but in the sense of one who devours, as you do a book or a film you love.)

Now, everything gets dropped into our laps, and there are really only two   11
responses if you want to feel like you're well-read, or well-versed in music, or whatever the case may be: culling and surrender.

Culling is the choosing you do for yourself. It's the sorting of what's 12
worth your time and what's not worth your time. It's saying, "I deem *Keeping
Up With The Kardashians* a poor use of my time, and therefore, I choose not
to watch it." It's saying, "I read the last Jonathan Franzen book and fell asleep
six times, so I'm not going to read this one."

Surrender, on the other hand, is the realization that you do not have time 13
for everything that would be worth the time you invested in it if you had the
time, and that this fact doesn't have to threaten your sense that you are well-
read. Surrender is the moment when you say, "I bet every single one of those
1,000 books I'm supposed to read before I die is very, very good, but I cannot
read them all, and they will have to go on the list of things I didn't get to."

It is the recognition that well-read is not a destination; there is nowhere 14
to get to, and if you assume there is somewhere to get to, you'd have to live
a thousand years to even think about getting there, and by the time you got
there, there would be a thousand years to catch up on.

What I've observed in recent years is that many people, in cultural con- 15
versations, are far more interested in culling than in surrender. And they
want to cull as aggressively as they can. After all, you can eliminate a lot of
discernment you'd otherwise have to apply to your choices of books if you
say, "All genre fiction is trash." You have just massively reduced your effective
surrender load, because you've thrown out so much at once.

The same goes for throwing out foreign films, documentaries, classical 16
music, fantasy novels, soap operas, humor, or westerns. I see people culling by
category, broadly and aggressively: television is not important, popular fiction is not important, blockbuster movies are not important. *Don't talk about
rap; it's not important. Don't talk about anyone famous; it isn't important. And
by the way, don't tell me it is important, because that would mean I'm ignoring
something important, and that's . . . uncomfortable. That's surrender.*

It's an effort, I think, to make the world smaller and easier to manage, to 17
make the awareness of what we're missing less painful. There are people who
choose not to watch television—and plenty of people don't, and good for
them—who find it easier to declare that they don't watch television because
there is no good television (which is culling) than to say they choose to do
other things, but acknowledge that they're missing out on *Game of Thrones*
(which is surrender).

And people cull in the other direction, too, obviously, dismissing any and 18
all art museums as dull and old-fashioned because actually learning about art
is time-consuming—and admitting that you simply don't prioritize it means
you might be missing out. (Hint: You are.)

Culling is easy; it implies a huge amount of control and mastery. 19
Surrender, on the other hand, is a little sad. That's the moment you realize
you're separated from *so much.* That's your moment of understanding that
you'll miss most of the music and the dancing and the art and the books and

the films that there have ever been and ever will be, and *right now,* there's something being performed somewhere in the world that you're not seeing that you would love.

It's sad, but it's also . . . *great,* really. Imagine if you'd seen everything 20 good, or if you knew about everything good. Imagine if you really got to all the recordings and books and movies you're "supposed to see." Imagine you got through everybody's list, until everything you hadn't read didn't really need reading. That would imply that all the cultural value the world has managed to produce since a glob of primordial ooze first picked up a violin is so tiny and insignificant that a single human being can gobble all of it in one lifetime. That would make us failures, I think.

If "well-read" means "not missing anything," then nobody has a chance. 21 If "well-read" means "making a genuine effort to explore thoughtfully," then yes, we can all be well-read. But what we've seen is always going to be a very small cup dipped out of a very big ocean, and turning your back on the ocean to stare into the cup can't change that.

Thinking Critically about the Text

Who do you think is the audience for this essay? How does Holmes imagine her readers? For example, what does she assume that they care about?

Questions on Subject

1. According to Holmes, why might older books, movies, music, and other cultural products "fade" more quickly now than they did in the past?

2. Holmes argues that we can have only two responses to the oversupply of television shows, books, movies, and music that we face. What are they? Are there any other possible responses?

3. Holmes writes that being "well-read is not a destination" (paragraph 14). What do you think she means? Why is this claim important for her argument?

4. Holmes finds it "sad" that all of us will miss out on so much art, music, dancing, and other things we would love if we saw them. But she also thinks it is "great" (paragraph 20). Why? Do you agree with her reasoning?

Questions on Strategy

1. Discuss how Holmes uses **process analysis** to support the claim in the opening two sentences of the essay.

2. Where in the essay does Holmes use **definition**? Why is it important to her **purpose**?

3. How does Holmes use **comparison and contrast** in the essay? Identify specific examples.

4. How do you interpret the **metaphor** in the final sentence of the essay? Do you think this is an effective conclusion? Why, or why not?

Combining Strategies in Action

Working as a class, or in small groups, think of a conflict or problem on your campus. Identify and define the issue. Then, brainstorm possible solutions to the problem. Imagine that you have to present your explanation of the problem — and your recommendations for solving it — to students, faculty, and others. What patterns of development would you have to use and combine to make your presentation effective? For example, how would you use illustrations? Would you need to include definition, cause and effect, or other patterns?

Writing Suggestions

1. In paragraph 3, Holmes writes about the possibility of being "reasonably well-read," which would require reading thousands of books over the course of a lifetime. In your opinion, what is one book that you have read that you consider essential to being "well-read"? Why is the book so important, not just for you, but for others? How did you originally come across it? Was it assigned, or did you choose to read it on your own? What qualities does the book have that make it universal and enduring? Write an essay in which you argue for your book being one of the "essentials" for people to read. Identify appropriate supporting strategies to help persuade your audience.

2. **Writing with Sources.** Holmes writes that, unlike in the past, when our cultural choices were shaped by academic departments at colleges, bookstores, and various media filters, now "everything gets dropped into our laps" (paragraph 11). Many find the choices overwhelming, as people struggle either to "cull" or "surrender." How is the phenomenon Holmes describes related to the larger issue of "FoMo," or the "fear of missing out," which has been identified by therapists and psychologists as a problem facing people today? Do some research on this topic. What are the similarities and differences between the "missing out" in Holmes's essay and the more general problem of "FoMo"? Write an essay that explores the relationship between these two concepts, as well as your own reflections on how you deal with the problem of "missing out." For models of and advice on integrating sources in your essay, see Chapters 14 and 15.

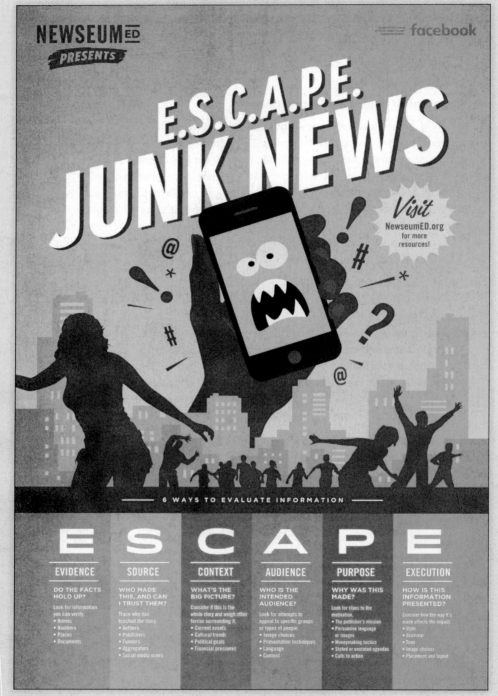

Newseum

CHAPTER 14

Writing with Sources

WHAT DOES IT MEAN TO WRITE WITH SOURCES?

MANY OF YOUR COLLEGE ASSIGNMENTS WILL CALL UPON YOU TO DO research and write using information from sources. To do this effectively, you will have to learn some basic research practices—locating and evaluating print and online sources, taking notes from those sources, and documenting those sources. (For help with research and documentation, see Chapter 15.) Even more fundamental than this, however, is to understand what it *means* to do research and to write with sources.

Your purpose in writing with sources is not to present a collection of quotations that report what others have said about your topic. Rather, your goal is to *analyze*, *evaluate*, and *synthesize* the materials you have researched so that you become a full-fledged participant in the conversation about your topic. To enter into this conversation with authority, you will have to learn how to use sources ethically and effectively. This chapter provides advice on summarizing, paraphrasing, and quoting sources; integrating sources; and avoiding plagiarism. In addition, two student papers and two professional essays model different ways of engaging meaningfully with sources and of reflecting that engagement in writing.

VISUALIZING WRITING WITH SOURCES

Do you believe everything you read or hear about in the news? Carefully analyze the Newseum's infographic about "junk news." What argument is the infographic making? What popular movie genre is the infographic referencing, and what visual details clue you in? What appears to be the source of the junk news? How, according to the infographic, does one "E.S.C.A.P.E." junk news? Think about the ways this information might be helpful as you do a research project. Is the infographic effective in conveying its message? Is the information useful? Explain.

WRITING WITH SOURCES

Outside sources can be used to:

- Support your thesis and points with statements from noted authorities
- Offer memorable wording of key terms or ideas
- Extend your ideas by introducing new information
- Articulate opposing positions for you to argue against

Consider Sharon Begley's use of an outside source in the following paragraph from her *Newsweek* essay "Praise the Humble Dung Beetle":

> Of all creatures great and small, it is the charismatic megafauna—tigers and rhinos and gorillas and pandas and other soulful-eyed, warm, and fuzzy animals—that personify endangered species. That's both a shame and a dangerous bias. "Plants and invertebrates are the silent majority which feed the entire planet, stabilize the soil, and make all life possible," says Kiernan Suckling, cofounder of the Center for Biological Diversity. They pollinate crops and decompose carcasses, filter water and, lacking weapons like teeth and claws, brew up molecules to defend themselves that turn out to be remarkably potent medicines: The breast-cancer compound taxol comes from a yew tree, and a leukemia drug from the rosy periwinkle. Those are tricks that, Suckling dryly notes, "polar bears and blue whales haven't mastered yet."

Here Begley quotes Kiernan Suckling, a biologist specializing in biodiversity, to support her contention that it's "both a shame and a dangerous bias" to have tigers, polar bears, and other photogenic mammals be the headliners for all endangered species.

Sometimes source material is too long and detailed to be quoted directly in its entirety. In such cases, a writer will choose to summarize or paraphrase the material in his or her own words before introducing it in an essay. For example, notice how Judith Newman summarizes two lengthy sleep studies for use in her essay "What's Really Going on Inside Your Teen's Head," which appeared in the November 28, 2010, issue of *Parade* magazine:

> In a pair of related studies published in 1993 and 1997 by Mary Carskadon, a professor of psychiatry at Brown University and director of the Sleep Research program at Bradley Hospital in Rhode Island, Carskadon and colleagues found that more physically mature girls preferred activities later in the day than did less-mature girls and that the sleep-promoting hormone melatonin rises later in teenagers than in children and adults. Translation: Teenagers are physically programmed to stay up later and sleep later.

Here, Newman introduces her summary with an extensive signal phrase highlighting Mary Carskadon's academic credentials, and she concludes with a pointed statement of the researchers' conclusion, information that is needed to broaden her discussion.

In the following passage from "Blaming the Family for Economic Decline," Stephanie Coontz uses outside sources to present the position that she will argue against:

> The fallback position for those in denial about the socioeconomic transformation we are experiencing is to admit that many families are in economic stress but to blame their plight on divorce and unwed motherhood. Lawrence Mead of New York University argues that economic inequalities stemming from differences in wages and employment patterns "are now trivial in comparison to those stemming from family structure." David Blankenhorn claims that the "primary fault line" dividing privileged and nonprivileged Americans is no longer "race, religion, class, education, or gender" but family structure. Every major newspaper in the country has published editorials and opinion pieces along these lines. This "new consensus" produces a delightfully simple, inexpensive solution to the economic ills of America's families. From Republican Dan Quayle to the Democratic Party's Progressive Policy Institute, we hear the same words: "Marriage is the best antipoverty program for children."
>
> Now I am as horrified as anyone by irresponsible parents who yield to the temptations of our winner-take-all society and abandon their family obligations. But we are kidding ourselves if we think the solution to the economic difficulties of America's children lies in getting their parents back together. Single-parent families, it is true, are five to six times more likely to be poor than two-parent ones. But correlations are not the same as causes. The association between poverty and single parenthood has several different sources, suggesting that the battle to end child poverty needs to be fought on a number of different fronts.

By letting the opposition articulate their own position, Coontz reduces the possibility of being criticized for misrepresenting her opponents; at the same time, she sets herself up to give strong voice to her thesis.

LEARNING TO SUMMARIZE, PARAPHRASE, AND QUOTE FROM YOUR SOURCES

Learning to summarize, paraphrase, and quote effectively and correctly is essential for the writing you'll do in school, at work, and in everyday life. The approach you take during your research and note taking largely depends on the content of the source passage and the way you envision using it in your paper. Be aware, however, that making use of all three of these techniques—rather than relying on only one or two—will keep your text varied and interesting.

The following sections will help you understand how the three techniques differ, when to use these techniques, and how to make them work within the context of your writing.

▶ Summarizing

When you *summarize* material from one of your sources, you use your own words to capture in condensed form the essential idea of a passage, an article, or an entire chapter. Summaries are particularly useful when you are working with lengthy, detailed arguments or long passages of narrative or descriptive background information. You simply want to capture the essence of the passage while dispensing with the details because you are confident that your readers will readily understand the point being made or will not need to be convinced about the validity of the point. Because you are distilling information, a summary is always shorter than the original; often a chapter or more can be reduced to a paragraph, or several paragraphs to a sentence or two. Remember, in writing a summary you should use your own words.

Consider the following paragraphs from "The Case for Short Words," in which Richard Lederer compares big words with small words:

> When you speak and write, there is no law that says you have to use big words. Short words are as good as long ones, and short, old words — like *sun* and *grass* and *home* — are best of all. A lot of small words, more than you might think, can meet your needs with a strength, grace, and charm that large words do not have.
>
> Big words can make the way dark for those who read what you write and hear what you say. Small words cast their clear light on big things — night and day, love and hate, war and peace, and life and death. Big words at times seem strange to the eye and the ear and the mind and the heart. Small words are the ones we seem to have known from the time we were born, like the hearth fire that warms the home.
>
> — RICHARD LEDERER,
> *The Miracle of Language*, page 30

A student wishing to capture the gist of Lederer's point without repeating his detail wrote the following summary:

> Lederer favors short words for their clarity, familiarity, durability, and overall usefulness (30).

▶ Paraphrasing

When you *paraphrase* a source, you restate the information in your own words instead of quoting directly. Unlike a summary, which gives a brief overview of the essential information in the original, a paraphrase seeks to maintain the same level of detail as the original to aid readers in understanding or believing the information presented. A summary, then, condenses the original material, while a paraphrase presents the original information in approximately the same number of words as the original.

Paraphrase can be thought of as a sort of middle ground between summary and quotation, but beware: While a paraphrase should closely parallel the presentation of ideas in the original, it should not use the same words or sentence structure as the original. Even though you are using your own words in a paraphrase, it's important to remember that you are borrowing ideas and therefore must acknowledge the source of these ideas with a citation.

How would you paraphrase the following passage from a speech by Martin Luther King Jr.?

> But one hundred years later [after the Emancipation Proclamation], we must face the tragic fact that the Negro is still not free. One hundred years later, the life of the Negro is still sadly crippled by the manacles of segregation and the chains of discrimination. One hundred years later, the Negro lives on a lonely island of poverty in the midst of a vast ocean of material prosperity. One hundred years later, the Negro is still languishing in the corners of American society and finds himself an exile in his own land.
>
> —MARTIN LUTHER KING JR.,
> "I Have a Dream," paragraph 3

One student paraphrased the passage from King's speech as follows:

Speaking on the one hundredth anniversary of the Emancipation Proclamation, King observed that African Americans still found themselves a marginalized people. He contended that African Americans did not experience the freedom that other Americans did—in a land of opportunity and plenty, racism and poverty affected the way they lived their lives, separating them from mainstream society (par. 3).

In most cases, it is better to summarize or paraphrase materials—which by definition means using your own words—instead of quoting verbatim (word for word). Capturing an idea in your own words ensures that you have thought about and understood what your source is saying.

▎ Using Direct Quotation

You should reserve direct quotation for important ideas stated memorably, for especially clear explanations by authorities, and for arguments by proponents of a particular position. Consider the following direct quotation from Malcolm Jones's article "Who Was More Important: Lincoln or Darwin?" that appeared in *Newsweek* on June 28, 2008. Notice how Jones captures

Charles Darwin's mixed emotions upon realizing the impact his theory of evolution would have on the world:

> As delighted as he was with his discovery, Darwin was equally horrified, because he understood the consequences of his theory. Mankind was no longer the culmination of life but merely part of it; creation was mechanistic and purposeless. In a letter to a fellow scientist, Darwin wrote that confiding his theory was "like confessing a murder." Small wonder that instead of rushing to publish his theory, he sat on it—for twenty years.
>
> —MALCOLM JONES,
> "Who Was More Important: Lincoln or Darwin?"

The skillful prose Jones uses to describe Darwin's state of mind makes this passage well worth quoting in full rather than summarizing or paraphrasing.

▶ Using Direct Quotation with Summary or Paraphrase

On occasion, you'll find a useful passage with some memorable phrases in it. Avoid the temptation to quote the whole passage; instead, you can combine summary or paraphrase with direct quotation. Consider, for example, the following paragraphs from Rosalind Wiseman's chapter "The Queen Bee and Her Court" about schoolgirls' roles in cliques:

> Information about other people is currency in Girl World—whoever has the most information has the most power. I call that girl the "Banker." She creates chaos by banking information about girls in her social sphere and dispensing it at strategic intervals.
>
> For instance, if a girl has said something negative about another girl, the Banker will casually mention it to someone in conversation because she knows it's going to cause a conflict and strengthen her status as someone in the know. She can get girls to trust her because when she pumps them for information it doesn't seem like gossip; instead, she does it in an innocent, "I'm trying to be there for you" kind of way.
>
> —ROSALIND WISEMAN,
> *Queen Bees and Wannabees*, page 35

Note how one student cited this passage using paraphrase *and* quotation:

> In Wiseman's schema, the most dangerous character in the clique is the Banker, who "creates chaos by banking information about girls in her social sphere and dispensing it at strategic intervals" (35). The Banker spreads gossip freely in order to cement her position as someone "in the know" (35).

Be sure that when you directly quote a source, you copy the words *exactly* and put quotation marks around them. Check and double-check your copy for accuracy, whether it's handwritten, transcribed, or copied and pasted from the original source.

▶ Integrating Borrowed Material into Your Text

Whenever you use borrowed material, be it a quotation, paraphrase, or summary, your goal is to integrate it smoothly and logically to avoid disrupting the flow of your paper or confusing your readers. It is best to introduce such material with a *signal phrase* that alerts readers that borrowed information is about to be presented. A signal phrase minimally consists of the author's name and a verb: *Michael Pollan contends*.

How well you integrate a quote, paraphrase, or summary into your paper depends partly on varying your signal phrases and, in particular, choosing verbs for these signal phrases that accurately convey the tone and intent of the writers you are citing. Signal phrases help readers better follow your train of thought. If a writer is arguing, use the verb *argues* (or *asserts*, *claims*, or *contends*); if the writer is contesting a particular position or fact, use the verb *contests* (or *denies*, *disputes*, *refutes*, or *rejects*). In using verbs that are specific to the situation in your paper, you bring your readers into the intellectual debate as well as avoid the monotony of repeating such all-purpose verbs as *says* or *writes*.

The following are just a few examples of how you can vary signal phrases to add interest to your paper:

Malcolm X confesses that . . .

As professor of linguistics at Georgetown University, Deborah Tannen has observed . . .

Bruce Catton, noted Civil War historian, emphasizes . . .

Rosalind Wiseman rejects the widely held belief that . . .

Robert Ramírez enriches our understanding of . . .

Jane Shaw, formerly a senior fellow at the Property and Environment Research Center, contends . . .

Here are other verbs that you might use when constructing signal phrases:

acknowledges	declares	points out
adds	endorses	reasons
admits	grants	reports
believes	implies	responds
compares	insists	suggests
confirms		

Signal phrases also let your reader know exactly where your ideas end and someone else's begin. Never confuse your reader by inserting a quotation that appears suddenly without introduction in your paper. Unannounced quotations leave your reader wondering how the quoted material relates to the point you are trying to make.

Unannounced Quotation

Television, it could be argued, presents life in tidy, almost predictable 30- and 60-minute packages. As any episode of *Twin Peaks: The Return*, *Master of None*, *Will and Grace*, or *This Is Us* demonstrates, life on television, though exciting, is relatively easy to follow. Humor, simultaneous action, and special effects cannot overshadow the fact that each show has a beginning, a middle, and an end. "Life . . . is ragged. Loose ends are the rule" (Dove 99). For many Americans, television provides an escape from the anxieties, stresses, and uncertainties of their day-to-day lives.

In the following revision, the student uses a signal phrase to integrate the quotation from Rita Dove's essay "Loose Ends," from her book *The Poet's World*, into the text of her paper. By giving the name of the writer being quoted, referring to her credentials, and noting that the writer is arguing for a difference she sees between television life and real life, the student provides more context so that readers can better understand how the quotation fits into the discussion.

Integrated Quotation

Television, it could be argued, presents life in tidy, almost predictable 30- and 60-minute packages. As any episode of *Twin Peaks: The Return*, *Master of None*, *Will and Grace*, or *This Is Us* demonstrates, life on television, though exciting, is relatively easy to follow. Humor, simultaneous action, and special effects cannot overshadow the fact that each show has a beginning, a middle, and an end. In contrast, real "life," according to Pulitzer Prize–winning poet and professor Rita Dove, "is ragged. Loose ends are the rule" (99). For many Americans, television provides an escape or time out from the anxieties, stresses, and uncertainties of their day-to-day lives.

▶ Synthesizing Several Sources to Deepen Your Discussion

Synthesis enables you to weave your ideas with the ideas of others in a single paragraph, deepening your discussion and often helping you arrive at a new interpretation or conclusion. By learning how to synthesize the results of your research from your own perspective, you can arrive at an informed opinion of your topic.

When you synthesize several sources in your writing, you get your sources to "talk" with one another. You literally create a conversation in which you take an active role. Sometimes you will find yourself discussing two or three sources together to show a range of views regarding a particular topic or issue—this is called *informational* or *explanatory synthesis*. At other times, you will have opportunities to play your sources off against one another so as to delineate the opposing positions—this is called *persuasive* or *argument synthesis*.

In the following example from her essay "The Qualities of Good Teachers," student Marah Britto uses *informational synthesis* to combine her own thoughts about good teachers with the thoughts of three other writers. In doing so, she explains the range of attributes that distinguish good teachers from their peers:

> We have all experienced a teacher who in some way stands out from all the others we have had, a teacher who has made an important difference in each of our lives. While most of us can agree on some of the character traits—dedication, love for students, patience, passion for his/her subject—that such teachers have in common, we cannot agree on that special something that sets them apart, the something that distinguishes them from the crowd. For me, it was my sixth-grade teacher Mrs. Engstrom, a teacher who motivated with her example. She never asked me to do anything that she was not willing to do herself. How many teachers show their love of ornithology by taking a student out for a bird walk at 5:30 in the morning, on a school day no less? For Thomas L. Friedman, it was his high school journalism teacher Hattie M. Steinberg. In "My Favorite Teacher," he relates how her insistence upon the importance of "fundamentals" made a lifelong impression on him, so much so that he never had to take another journalism course (12). For Carl Rowan, it was his high school English, history, and civics teacher Miss Bessie Taylor Gwynn, whose influence he captures in "Unforgettable Miss Bessie." Miss Bessie taught Rowan to hold himself to high standards, to refuse "to lower [his] standards to those of the crowd" (87). And for Joanne Lipman, it was Mr. Jerry Kupchynsky, her childhood music teacher. She remembers how tough and demanding he was on his students, how he made his students "better than we had any right to be." Ironically, Lipman muses, "I doubt any of us realized how much we loved him for it." Interestingly, isn't it mutual respect and love that is at the heart of any memorable student–teacher bond?
>
> Works Cited
>
> Friedman, Thomas L. "My Favorite Teacher." *Subject & Strategy*, edited by Paul Eschholz and Alfred Rosa, 15th ed., Bedford/St. Martin's, 2019, pp. 13–15.

Lipman, Joanne. "And the Orchestra Played On." *New York Times*, 28 Feb. 2010, www.nytimes.com/2010/02/28/opinion/28lipman.html?_r=0.

Rowan, Carl T. "Unforgettable Miss Bessie." *Reader's Digest*, Mar. 1985, pp. 87–91.

The second example is taken from student Bonnie Sherman's essay "Should Shame Be Used as Punishment?" Here she uses *argument synthesis* deftly to combine Hawthorne's use of shame in *The Scarlet Letter* with two opposing essays about shame as punishment, both of which appeared together in the *Boston Globe*. Notice how Sherman uses her own reading of *The Scarlet Letter* as evidence to ultimately side with Professor Kahan's position:

Shame has long been used as an alternative punishment to more traditional sentences of corporeal punishment, jail time, or community service. American colonists used the stocks to publicly humiliate citizens for their transgressions. In *The Scarlet Letter*, author Nathaniel Hawthorne recounts the story of how the community of Boston punished Hester Prynne for her adulterous affair by having her wear a scarlet letter "A" on her breast as a badge of shame. Such punishments were controversial then and continue to spark heated debate in today's world of criminal justice. Like June Tangney, psychology professor at George Mason University, many believe that shaming punishments—those designed to humiliate offenders—are unusually cruel and should be abandoned. In her article "Condemn the Crime, Not the Person," she argues that "shame serves to escalate the very destructive patterns of behavior we aim to curb" (34). Interestingly, Hester Prynne's post-punishment life of community service and charitable work does not seem to bear out Tangney's claim. In contrast, Yale Law School professor Dan M. Kahan believes that Tangney's "anxieties about shame . . . seem overstated," and he persuasively supports this position in his essay "Shame Is Worth a Try" by citing a study showing that the threat of public humiliation generates more compliance than does the threat of jail time (34).

Sources

Hawthorne, Nathaniel. *The Scarlet Letter*. Bantam Books, 1981.

Kahan, Dan M. "Shame Is Worth a Try." *Boston Globe*, 5 Aug. 2001, p. A34.

Tangney, June. "Condemn the Crime, Not the Person." *Boston Globe*, 5 Aug. 2001, p. A34.

In your essay, instead of simply presenting your sources with a quotation here and a summary there, look for opportunities to use synthesis, to go beyond an individual source by relating several of your sources to one another and to your own thesis. Use the following checklist to help you with synthesis in your writing.

Checklist for Writing a Synthesis

1. Start by writing a brief summary of each source that you will refer to in your synthesis.

2. Explain in your own words how your sources are related to one another and to your own ideas. For example, what assumptions do your sources share? Do your sources present opposing views? Do your sources illustrate a range or diversity of opinions? Do your sources support or challenge your ideas?

3. Have a clear idea or topic sentence for your paragraph before starting to write.

4. Combine information from two or more sources with your own ideas to support or illustrate your main idea.

5. Use signal phrases and parenthetical citations to show your readers the source of your borrowed materials.

6. Have fresh interpretations or conclusions as a goal each time you synthesize sources.

AVOIDING PLAGIARISM

The importance of honesty and accuracy in doing library research can't be stressed enough. Any material borrowed word for word must be placed within quotation marks and properly cited; any idea, explanation, or argument you have paraphrased or summarized must be documented, and it must be clear where the paraphrased material begins and ends. In short, to use someone else's ideas, whether in their original form or in an altered form, without proper acknowledgment is to be guilty of plagiarism.

You must acknowledge and document the source of your information whenever you do any of the following:

- Quote a source word for word
- Refer to information and ideas from another source that you present in your own words, as either a paraphrase or a summary
- Cite statistics, tables, charts, graphs, or other visuals

You do not need to document the following types of information:

- Your own observations, experiences, ideas, and opinions
- Factual information available in a number of sources (information known as "common knowledge")
- Proverbs, sayings, or familiar quotations

For a discussion of MLA-style in-text documentation, see Chapter 15, "Documenting Sources" (pages 550–51).

The Council of Writing Program Administrators offers the following helpful definition of *plagiarism* in academic settings for administrators, faculty, and students: "In an instructional setting, plagiarism occurs when a writer deliberately uses someone else's language, ideas, or other (not common knowledge) material without acknowledging its source." Note, however, that accusations of plagiarism can be substantiated even if plagiarism is accidental. A little attention and effort at the note-taking stage can go a long way toward eliminating the possibility of such inadvertent plagiarism. While taking notes, check all direct quotations against the wording of the original and double-check your paraphrases to be sure that you have not used the writer's wording or sentence structure. It is easy to forget to put quotation marks around material taken verbatim or to use the same sentence structure and most of the same words — substituting a synonym here and there — and record it as a paraphrase. In working closely with the ideas and words of others, intellectual honesty demands that you distinguish between what you borrow — and therefore acknowledge in a citation — and what is your own.

While writing your paper, be careful whenever you incorporate one of your notes into your paper: Make sure that you put quotation marks around material taken verbatim and double-check your text against your notes — or, better yet, against the original if you have it on hand — to make sure that your quotations are accurate and that all paraphrases and summaries are really in your own words.

▶ Using Quotation Marks for Language Borrowed Directly

Whenever you use another person's exact words or sentences, you must enclose the borrowed language in quotation marks. Without quotation marks, you give your reader the impression that the wording is your own. Even if you cite the source, you are guilty of plagiarism if you fail to use quotation marks. The following example demonstrates both plagiarism and a correct citation for a direct quotation.

Original Source

> On my father's side, I figured, high cheekbones and almond eyes probably showed evidence of native-Andean blood. The aquiline profiles and curly hair on my mother's side, on the other hand, are common on Mediterranean shores. My best guess: I was mostly European, a bit of native South American, and perhaps a dash of Middle Eastern.
>
> —Carolina A. Miranda,
> "Diving into the Gene Pool,"
> *Time*, 20 Aug. 2006, page 64

Plagiarism

> On my father's side, I figured, high cheekbones and almond eyes probably showed evidence of native-Andean blood, confesses Carolina A.

Miranda. The aquiline profiles and curly hair on my mother's side, on the other hand, are common on Mediterranean shores. My best guess: I was mostly European, a bit of native South American, and perhaps a dash of Middle Eastern (64).

Correct Citation of Borrowed Words in Quotation Marks

"On my father's side, I figured, high cheekbones and almond eyes probably showed evidence of native-Andean blood," confesses Carolina A. Miranda. "The aquiline profiles and curly hair on my mother's side, on the other hand, are common on Mediterranean shores. My best guess: I was mostly European, a bit of native South American, and perhaps a dash of Middle Eastern" (64).

▶ Using Your Own Words and Word Order When Summarizing and Paraphrasing

When summarizing or paraphrasing a source, you need to use your own language. Pay particular attention to word choice and word order, especially if you are paraphrasing. Remember, it is not enough simply to use a synonym here or there and think you have paraphrased the source; you *must* restate the idea from the original in your own words, using your own style and sentence structure. In the following example, notice how plagiarism can occur when care is not taken in the wording or sentence structure of a paraphrase. Notice that in the acceptable paraphrase, the student writer uses her own language and sentence structure.

Original Source

Stereotypes are a kind of gossip about the world, a gossip that makes us prejudge people before we ever lay eyes on them. Hence it is not surprising that stereotypes have something to do with the dark world of prejudice. Explore most prejudices (note that the word means prejudgment) and you will find a cruel stereotype at the core of each one.

—Robert L. Heilbroner,
"Don't Let Stereotypes Warp Your Judgments,"
Think, June 1961, page 43

Unacceptably Close Wording

According to Heilbroner, we prejudge other people even before we have seen them when we think in stereotypes. That stereotypes are related to the ugly world of prejudice should not surprise anyone. If you explore the heart of most prejudices, beliefs that literally prejudge, you will discover a mean stereotype lurking (43).

Unacceptably Close Sentence Structure

Heilbroner believes that stereotypes are images of people, images that enable people to prejudge other people before they have seen them. Therefore, no one should find it surprising that stereotypes are somehow related to the ugly world of prejudice. Examine most prejudices (the word literally means prejudgment) and you will uncover a vicious stereotype at the center of each (43).

Acceptable Paraphrase

Heilbroner believes that there is a link between stereotypes and the hurtful practice of prejudice. Stereotypes make for easy conversation, a kind of shorthand that enables us to find fault with people before ever meeting them. If you were to dissect most human prejudices, you would likely discover an ugly stereotype lurking somewhere inside it (43).

Preventing Plagiarism

Questions to Ask about Direct Quotations

- Do quotation marks clearly indicate the language that I borrowed verbatim?
- Is the language of the quotation accurate, with no missing or misquoted words or phrases?
- Do brackets ([ ]) or ellipsis marks (. . .) clearly indicate any changes or omissions I have introduced?
- Does a signal phrase naming the author introduce each quotation? Does the verb in the signal phrase help establish a context for each quotation?
- Does a parenthetical page citation follow each quotation?

Questions to Ask about Summaries and Paraphrases

- Is each summary and paraphrase written in my own words and style?
- Does each summary and paraphrase accurately represent the opinion, position, or reasoning of the original writer?
- Does each summary and paraphrase start with a signal phrase so that readers know where my borrowed material begins?
- Does each summary and paraphrase conclude with a parenthetical page citation?

Questions to Ask about Facts and Statistics

- Do I use a signal phrase or some other marker to introduce each fact or statistic that is not common knowledge so that readers know where the borrowed material begins?
- Is each fact or statistic that is not common knowledge clearly documented with a parenthetical page citation?

Finally, as you proofread your final draft, check all your citations one last time. If at any time while you are taking notes or writing your paper you have a question about plagiarism, consult your instructor for clarification and guidance before proceeding.

STUDENT ESSAY USING LIBRARY AND INTERNET SOURCES

Katherine Kachnowski wrote the following essay from experience. She had been witnessing firsthand her grandfather's decade-long fight with skin cancer, and she wanted to get the word out to her classmates that skin cancer is not just for old people. She decided to explore the latest research on skin cancer, especially as it pertained to people under thirty.

Kachnowski began by brainstorming her topic, listing recent news stories about the rise in melanoma cases and the need to use sunscreens. She then went to her college library and searched the Internet, where she discovered a number of credible sources for current skin cancer research and statistics.

Kachnowski's essay is annotated to highlight how she has integrated sources into her paper and has used them to establish, explore, and support her key points. Kachnowski uses MLA-style documentation.

Skin Cancer Is Not Just for Grandparents: Dispelling Widespread Misconceptions about This Disease
Katherine Kachnowski

Title indicates focus on "misconceptions"

Introductory paragraphs establish context for discussion and grab readers' attention with personal story and startling statistics

Direct quotation introduced with signal phrase

1   While we all know that cancer is a disease, the nightmare really hits home when someone you love is diagnosed. I have personal experience with cancer. My grandfather has had to endure the ordeal of twelve separate incidents of skin cancer over the past decade. Watching my grandfather fight the disease has caused me to drastically change my own skincare habits. In an effort to avoid a diagnosis for myself, I have started to educate myself about the causes.

2   As a result of my research, I discovered that most Americans are under-informed about healthy skincare habits as well as about skin cancer in general. According to the United States Centers for Disease Control and Prevention, roughly 50% of adults aged 18–29 do not regularly practice protective skin behaviors.

Additionally, in 2014 the United States Surgeon General wrote, "Skin cancer is the most commonly diagnosed cancer in the United States, and most cases are preventable" (United States, Department of Health and Human Services). While many Americans seem to be aware of the dangers of this disease, they are not taking the necessary steps to prevent a diagnosis of skin cancer. People have a variety of excuses for not being more proactive about preventing skin cancer, and some of these excuses are based on myths or misconceptions that need to be set straight.

Writer states her intention to clear up common misconceptions people have about skin cancer

Decreasing the prevalence of skin cancer begins with education and understanding how the disease develops. Everyone is at risk for skin cancer because we have all been in the presence of the sun's rays. The disease is primarily caused by long-term exposure to two rays: Ultraviolet A (UVA) and Ultraviolet B (UVB) rays. UVA rays are able to penetrate more layers of skin than UVB rays, which are the cause of sunburns, and harm the outer layers of the epidermis. The three types of skin cancer include basal cell and squamous cell, which are found on the outer layers of the skin, and melanoma, which originates in the melanin that is located in the deeper layers of the skin. (Figure 1 illustrates these differences.) Melanoma is considered the deadliest form because it develops so far from the surface

3

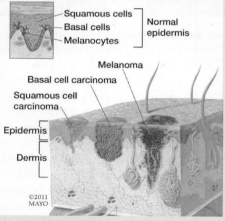

Image inserted as a figure to illustrate information for readers. The writer also provides source information near the figure as well as in the Works Cited list.

Figure 1: Where Skin Cancer Develops
© Mayo Foundation for Medical Education and Research. All Rights Reserved.

Writer uses sources to identify the basic types of skin cancer

of the skin ("Skin Cancer Facts"). Although squamous cell and basal cell cancers are not as lethal, they can require costly treatments that can leave substantial scarring. The National Cancer Institute estimates that 40–50% of Americans will experience either basal cell or squamous cell carcinoma before reaching age sixty-five ("Skin Cancer Facts").

Writer organizes her essay around four common misconceptions about skin cancer

One big misconception about skin cancer is that certain demographics don't have to worry about a cancer diagnosis. Young Americans, for example, tend to take risks with the sun because they live in the moment and perceive the risks of skin damage as being a problem for older people. It is true that the incidence of skin cancer among adults is higher, especially if you have a family history or experienced numerous blistering sunburns as a child. Unfortunately, deadly skin cancers appear more frequently than you would think among young people as well. Melanoma is the second most commonly occurring cancer for those in the 15–29 age bracket ("NAACCR Fast Stats"). Skin protection is no longer a concern for just grandparents—everyone needs to start taking action.

4

In-text citations in MLA style: in this paragraph, all begin with the author's name given in a signal phrase and the page number given in parentheses

A second misconception is that people of color do not need to use sunscreen. CDC behavioral scientist Dawn M. Holman argues that Hispanics and African Americans are significantly less likely to wear sunscreen than Caucasians (90). As a result, when cancer is detected on people of color, it is more likely to be deadly. According to Sean M. Dawes and his colleagues, melanoma incidence rates are higher in people of European-American descent, but melanoma is more likely to kill a person of color (984). The myth that sunscreen is for those with fair skin needs to be rectified.

5

Writer introduces paraphrase of survey with signal phrase and marks the end with a parenthetical citation of the source

A third common misconception is that tanned skin is beautiful, healthy skin. Dermatologist Dr. Vinh Q. Chung has shown that because darker skin is perceived as more attractive, many people are motivated to make a visit to the tanning salon (1653). In a survey done by the American Academy of Dermatology, 59% of college students and 17% of teenagers reported using a tanning bed. Tanning salons may offer a way for people to maintain a bronzed look all year long but even infrequent use drastically increases the risk of

6

Paraphrase of an
Internet source

cancer. Research has shown that women younger than thirty who use tanning beds are six times more likely to develop melanoma than those who don't tan indoors (American Academy of Dermatology). These practices may feel good in the moment but can cause lasting, often irreversible harm. Unnecessary intense exposure for the sake of a tan body should not be so commonplace. Rather, the focus should be on staying protected using daily application of sunscreen.

Finally, one of the most widespread misconceptions about skin care is that sunscreen is only needed on summer days spent outdoors. According to an article by the American Academy of Dermatology, "only 14.3 percent of men and 29.9 percent of women reported that they regularly use sunscreen on both their face and other exposed skin." The Skin Cancer Foundation reports that "regular daily use of an SPF 15 or higher sunscreen reduces the risk of developing squamous cell carcinoma by about 40 percent and the risk of developing melanoma by 50 percent" ("Skin Cancer Facts"). These statistics demonstrate that sunscreens are not just for a day at the beach. Americans need to make sunscreen part of their regular morning routine.

7

Healthy skincare habits can easily be integrated into a daily hygiene routine. Personally, I apply a moisturizer with SPF 15 every morning. In addition, I try to keep covered when I am outside by wearing hats and clothing that protects my skin or by staying in the shade. I have found that it is worth the effort; my worries are calmed by the thought that I am practicing healthy behaviors. Once a month, I inspect my skin, looking for changes to moles, new growths, or anything out of the ordinary.

8

Due to his lack of knowledge, and therefore a lack of caution, my grandfather unknowingly damaged his skin as a young man. While his skincare habits have drastically changed today, my grandfather must regularly monitor his body for any troublesome signs. I urge you to become more proactive with skincare. According to the American Melanoma Foundation, someone in the United States dies of melanoma every sixty-one

9

minutes. Why be part of that statistic when prevention is so easy? Minimal changes in routine today can save your life or prevent painful surgeries and medical procedures in the future.

Works Cited

American Academy of Dermatology. "Study: Most Americans Don't Use Sunscreen." *American Academy of Dermatology*, 19 May 2015, www.aad.org/media/news-releases/study -most-americans-don-t-use-sunscreen.

Chung, Vinh Q., et al. "Hot or Not: Evaluating the Effect of Artificial Tanning on the Public's Perception of Attractiveness." *Dermatologic Surgery*, vol. 36, no. 11, Nov. 2010, pp. 1651–55. *Academic Search Premier*, doi:10.1111/j.1524-4725.2010.01713.x.

Dawes, Sean M., et al. "Racial Disparities in Melanoma Survival." *Journal of the American Academy of Dermatology*, vol. 75, no. 5, Nov. 2016, pp. 983–91.

Holman, Dawn M., et al. "Patterns of Sunscreen Use on the Face and Other Exposed Skin among US Adults." *Journal of the American Academy of Dermatology*, vol. 73, no. 1, July 2015, pp. 83–92.

"NAACCR Fast Stats." *North American Association of Central Cancer Registries*, 2016, faststats.naaccr.org/. Accessed 4 Mar. 2018.

"Skin Cancer." *American Cancer Society*, 13 Apr. 2015, www .cancer.org/cancer/skin-cancer.html. Accessed 3 Mar. 2016.

"Skin Cancer Facts & Statistics." *SkinCancer.org*, Skin Cancer Foundation, 2 Feb. 2017, www.skincancer.org/ skin-cancer-information/skin-cancer-facts.

United States, Centers for Disease Control and Prevention. "Sunburn and Sun Protective Behaviors among Adults Aged 18–29 Years—United States, 2000–2010." *Morbidity and Mortality Weekly Report*, vol. 61, no. 18, 11 May 2012, pp. 317–22, www.cdc.gov/mmwr/preview/ mmwrhtml/mm6118a1.htm.

United States, Department of Health and Human Services, Office of the Surgeon General. *The Surgeon General's Call to Action to Prevent Skin Cancer*. 2014, www.surgeon general.gov/library/calls/prevent-skin-cancer/call-to -action-prevent-skin-cancer.pdf.

MLA style used for list of works cited. Entries are presented in alphabetical order by authors' last names (or title, if no author is listed).

The first line of each entry begins at the left margin and subsequent lines are indented

For more examples and information on correct MLA citation, see Chapter 15, "List of Works Cited," on pages 552–59

Student Reflection
Katherine Kachnowski

Q. How did you decide on the topic for your essay?

A. I guess I was thinking of my grandfather; he has had many cases of skin cancer. His battles with the disease have influenced me and the way I care for my own skin protection. At the same time I noticed that people who are my age kind of associate skin cancer with something that their older relatives get. I sensed that my generation saw skin cancer as a far-off problem, one that they won't encounter for some time. At that point, I knew I had an issue that I could write about and, funny thing, the title that I would eventually use came to me right then.

Q. How did you go about looking for sources on your topic?

A. I was looking for scholarly articles, peer-reviewed articles that would help support my argument. I'm a big fan of Google Scholar and JSTOR—those are the two databases that I use. That's where I started my research. After that I went to government Web sites like the United States Centers for Disease Control and Prevention and the United States Department of Health and Human Services. I also located articles on skin cancer at the Web sites for the Skin Cancer Foundation and the American Academy of Dermatology. These were all helpful sources because from the beginning I definitely knew there was certain information I wanted to touch on. For example, I knew I had to explain some of the basics about skin cancer, and I wanted to find out why young people were not heeding the warnings. While researching these parts of my topic, I came across the startling statistics for people of color. I had not realized that people of color were so adversely affected by not using sunscreen. The explanation seemed simple—many didn't think they had to. So in the end my paper focused on four key misconceptions about skin cancer.

But not all sources were that helpful. I found a blog post where the writer claimed that blending certain oils was better for your skin than using sunscreen. The writer also believed that people should have a certain amount of exposure to the sun each day without sunscreen; otherwise they wouldn't get the right amount of Vitamin D—obviously not very credible for me.

Q. How many drafts did you write for this essay?

A. I wrote at least four drafts of this paper. For me, revision is such a large, large part of the writing process—more than people who don't write regularly would think. While rewriting my essay I could literally see it change; I could feel it come into its own. I started my rough draft with the story about my grandfather and then went on to explain the three types of skin cancer, how to recognize a melanoma, and what to do to prevent skin cancer. When I read it over, I realized that I'd lost sight of my purpose to persuade my peers to use sunscreen.

In between drafts I definitely stepped away—sometimes for a day or two—before going back to read it over and then kind of think on it from there. So, even if I'm not still writing, even if I'm not sitting down and working on my paper, I'm thinking about it. When I do sit down to revise, I usually start by annotating my paper in the margins just to kind of play devil's advocate with myself and say, "OK, now where could it be stronger?" "Why isn't this working?" "Do I need more evidence here?" These marginal notes give me direction when I actually begin to rewrite. I've discovered that the longer I have to write something, the better. I like to dwell on it and do a little bit at a time.

Q. How did you organize your essay?
A. Well, I knew I wanted to start out by giving my readers a little background information just as a refresher—you know, types of cancer and the seriousness of melanomas. And by the third draft the organization just kind of fell into place. I presented the four myths or misconceptions about skin cancer in an order that I thought moved from the most important to the least important. My peers who read this draft agreed. When I was preparing my final draft, I remembered the story of my grandfather that I had dropped earlier and decided to reintroduce it as an interesting way to both begin my paper and conclude it.

Your Response

What did you learn from Katherine Kachnowski's essay and reflection about the experience of writing the essay? What challenges do you expect to face as you write your own essay using sources? Based on Katherine's composing strategies and the practical advice discussed earlier in this chapter, how will you address those challenges? What writing choices will you make?

How a Kids' Cartoon Created a Real-Life Invasive Army

JASON G. GOLDMAN

Courtesy of Jason Goldman

Born in 1985 and raised in Los Angeles, Jason G. Goldman earned his bachelor's, master's, and doctorate degrees in psychology at the University of Southern California. Now a prolific freelance science journalist and editor, Goldman has published articles on conservation, ecology, wildlife biology, human and animal behavior, and other topics in *Scientific American*, *Los Angeles Magazine*, the *Washington Post*, *Slate, Salon*, and *Gizmodo*, among other outlets. He is the editor of *The Open Laboratory* (2011), an anthology of online science writing, and coeditor of *Science Blogging: The Essential Guide* (2016). Goldman cofounded and directs an annual science communication retreat in Malibu, California, called SciCommCamp. He is also a founding member of the Nerd Brigade, a Los Angeles–based collective of scientists and science communicators who promote literacy in science, technology, engineering, and mathematics.

In the following blog, first posted on May 30, 2017, in the science magazine *Nautilus*, Goldman writes about how an animal "both less fearsome and more adorable than Godzilla" became a harmful, invasive species in Japan. As you read this essay, notice how Goldman uses his knowledge of Sterling North's book *Rascal: A Memoir of a Better Era* and the work of several Japanese researchers to tell the story of how raccoons came to Japan and the problems they caused.

Preparing to Read

How have your views of specific animals been influenced by images and stories from popular culture? For example, in what ways do Disney films shape our views of particular species? Have you ever wanted a particular pet because you read or watched a story about a specific animal?

Tales of monsters invading Japan are a longstanding tradition, usually involving menacing *kaiju*—literally "strange creatures"—rising from the sea to wreak havoc on a Japanese city. At this very moment, the country is engaged in just such a war, with an entire army of invasive creatures, but they're both less fearsome and more adorable than Godzilla or Mothra. And they're from North America, not the bottom of the ocean. They're common raccoons, *Procyon lotor*. Sometimes real life is stranger than fiction.

Our story begins when a young Wisconsin boy named Sterling North 2
adopts an orphaned baby raccoon and names him Rascal. The boy and the
raccoon were inseparable as best friends, and for a year they did everything together. They fished the local streams and lakes, wandered the rural
countryside together, and went for bike rides with Rascal riding in a basket attached to the handlebars. At the end of their year together, the young
North began to realize that the raccoon was truly a wild animal, and not a
pet. A critter that was once tame as a juvenile became more mischievous as
he aged. The maturing male raccoon began to draw the attention of female
raccoons and the aggression of other males. When North's neighbors could
no longer bear Rascal's incursions into their fields and chicken coops, he
knew that he would have to release his best friend. A life inside a cage—the
only safe way to keep Rascal as a pet—was no life for a raccoon. North
constructs a canoe and uses it to cross a nearby lake at the edge of a nicely
wooded forest. There, he lets his best friend go, and returns home.

The true story of Sterling North and Rascal the raccoon formed the 3
basis for North's award-winning 1963 memoir, *Rascal: A Memoir of a Better
Era.* In 1969, Disney would go on to create a feature film based on the book,
predictably called *Rascal,* and a 52-episode anime series called *Araiguma
Rasukaru,* based on the book, aired in Japan throughout 1977.

Once upon a time, raccoons were strangers to the island of Japan, save for 4
the occasional critter kept in a zoo. That all changed when *Araiguma Rasukaru*
aired and turned a nation onto raccoons' inherent charm. "Its round, funny face
with a bandit's mask across the eyes and a striped bushy tail create a humorous
impression," writes Japanese researcher Tohru Ikeda of Hokkaido University,
"and people find its habit of washing of food prior to eating curious." Suddenly,
every Japanese child wanted their own pet raccoon, like the boy hero of the
cartoon. At the peak of their popularity, Japan imported more than 1,500 North
American raccoons each year. The government eventually banned importing
them or keeping them as pets, but it was too late.

Life imitated art when some of the Japanese children who had kept pet 5
raccoons released their pets into the wilderness, like the boy in the cartoon
and the real-life Sterling North before him. Other raccoons, being wild animals and not domesticates like dogs, cats, or horses, simply escaped. Still
others were released out of frustration by their owners. Raccoons, like chimpanzees, are friendly when young, but as they age they become more aggressive, harder to control, and pose a potential threat to humans. Raccoons, like
chimpanzees, are simply not suitable pets.

Raccoons have since proliferated in Japan, where they have no natural 6
predators, and by 2004, they had spread to at least 42 of 47 prefectures. In
some parts of the country, they invade cattle farms, where they feed on the
same corn that gets fed to cows, and find safe spaces for reproduction in the

tall grasses of grazing pastures. In other places, fish farms provide them with a veritable buffet. The animals damage crops across the food pyramid: corn, melons, strawberries, rice, soybeans, potatoes, oats, and more. In 2004 Ikeda and colleagues estimated that raccoons were responsible for more than thirty million yen (approximately US $300,000) worth of agricultural damage each year on the island of Hokkaido alone. Raccoons have also adapted to city life in the more urban parts of Japan, where they nest in air vents beneath floorboards, attic spaces of older wooden houses, Buddhist temples, and Shinto shrines. In cities, raccoons forage by going through human garbage, and hunt carp and goldfish that are kept in decorative ponds.

The masked invaders have also taken a toll on the ecology of Japan,   7
preying on native mammals like the gray red-backed vole, along with snakes, frogs, dragonflies, damselflies, butterflies, bees, cicadas, and shrimp and other shellfish. They hunt the Japanese crayfish, a species classified as vulnerable by the Japanese Ministry of Environment, and the Tokyo salamander, which is threatened.

They compete both for food and for territory with the native raccoon   8
dog (*tanuki*) and the red fox, and push native owls out of nesting spots in hollow trees. Ever since raccoons attacked a reproductive colony of grey herons in Nopporo Forest Park in 1997, the grand birds have not returned to their historic breeding grounds.

Raccoons are also important vectors for the spread of infection diseases.   9
They're known to carry rabies, and a 2011 report in the *Journal of Parasitology* even found evidence for the potentially dangerous and brain-altering parasite *Toxoplasmosa gondii* in raccoon droppings.

Following the passing of a law protecting native Japanese ecosystems in   10
2004, local governments began the culling of invasive raccoon populations. That year, Reiji Yoshida wrote in the *Japan Times* that Hokkaido would kill 2,000 raccoons each year. Predictably, there was public backlash to the harming of these cute, furry animals. "When the Kanagawa prefectural government announced the raccoon eradication plan in 2005, comments from the public revealed a wide range of opinions, including preference for control over eradication, negative response to lethal methods, skepticism of success, and opposition toward using great amounts of tax revenue for the plan," said Harumi Akiba and colleagues in a 2012 paper in the journal *Human Dimensions of Wildlife*. Indeed, according to their survey of Kanagawa prefecture residents, only 31% of the population supported the complete eradication of invasive raccoons in Japan. Further, they discovered that *Araiguma Rasukaru* no longer held sway over the public perception of raccoons. More than half of the study participants had seen the series, but Akiba's statistical models showed that it didn't influence peoples' support or rejection for raccoon culls. The anime series that had originally instigated the raccoon invasion itself has lost its control over public opinion.

This is one unfortunate consequence of fame. A species once beloved by 11 a country's children thanks to a popular cartoon has in the space of just a few decades become a public nuisance, a source of significant agricultural economic losses, a possible vector for disease transmission, and a threat to other threatened and vulnerable species.

> " **A species once beloved by a country's children thanks to a popular cartoon has in the space of just a few decades become a public nuisance, a source of significant agricultural economic losses, a possible vector for disease transmission, and a threat to other threatened and vulnerable species.** "

There is no good solution to 12 the problem of invasive raccoons in Japan. Left uncontrolled, they will continue to cause problems. But the alternative — mass culls — doesn't enjoy public support, and most research indicates that culls aren't actually all that effective anyway. In the end, the best antidote against the anthropogenic origins of animal invasions is wildlife education. If more people understood that raccoons do not make good pets, no matter how adorable, Japan might not be in the unfortunate position in which they now find themselves, stuck between the rock of an invasive species, and the hard place of low public support for its eradication. Raccoons are best left in their natural North American habitats — and on TV.

Sterling North's choice of name for his pet raccoon was perhaps pro- 13 phetic, foreseeing the consequences of the mass adoption of an animal that was never meant to be a pet in the first place.

Thinking Critically about the Text

Goldman writes about a curious and highly specific problem that developed in Japan in the decades after Disney's *Rascal* and the Japanese anime series *Araiguma Rasukaru*. Does his essay have any wider significance? Are there any broader lessons or insights a reader can draw from it?

Questions on Subject

1. Raccoons are not native to Japan. How did they become popular in that country?

2. Why are raccoons not suitable as pets?

3. What problems have raccoons caused in Japan? Point to specific examples cited by Goldman.

4. What's the best solution to Japan's raccoon problem, according to Goldman?

Questions on Strategy

1. In paragraph 2, Goldman provides a summary of the story of Sterling North and his raccoon, Rascal. Is this summary necessary? Why, or why not?

2. How does Goldman use **narration** in this essay? How does he use **cause and effect analysis**? Point to specific examples of each strategy.

3. Goldman cites research from the *Journal of Parasitology* in paragraph 9. What point is he supporting with this **evidence**? Why is it important to his argument?

4. In paragraph 10, Goldman includes a quotation from the academic journal *Human Dimensions of Wildlife*. Is the quotation successfully integrated into Goldman's prose? Why, or why not? What strategy for incorporating research does he use in the sentences after the direct quotation?

Writing with Sources in Action

Using the examples in the sections "Paraphrasing" (pages 500–501) and "Using Your Own Words and Word Order When Summarizing and Paraphrasing" (pages 509–11) as models, write a *paraphrase* for each of the following paragraphs — that is, restate the original ideas in your own words, using your own sentence structure.

> The history of life on earth has been a history of interaction between living things and their surroundings. To a large extent, the physical form and the habits of the earth's vegetation and its animal life have been molded by the environment. Considering the whole span of earthly time, the opposite effect, in which life actually modifies its surroundings, has been relatively slight. Only within the moment of time represented by the present century has one species — man — acquired significant power to alter the nature of his world.
>
> — RACHEL CARSON,
> "The Obligation to Endure," *Silent Spring*

> Extroverts are energized by people, and wilt or fade when alone. They often seem bored by themselves, in both senses of the expression. Leave an extrovert alone for two minutes and he will reach for his cell phone. In contrast, after an hour or two of being socially "on," we introverts need to turn off and recharge. My own formula is roughly two hours alone for every hour of socializing. This isn't antisocial. It isn't a sign of depression. It does not call for medication. For introverts, to be alone with our thoughts is as restorative as sleeping, as nourishing as eating. Our motto: "I'm okay, you're okay — in small doses."
>
> — JONATHAN RAUCH,
> "Caring for Your Introvert"

No, the romance and beauty were all gone from the river. All the value any feature of it had for me now was the amount of usefulness it could furnish toward compassing the safe piloting of a steamboat. Since those days, I have pitied doctors from my heart. What does the lovely flush in a beauty's cheek mean to a doctor but a "break" that ripples above some deadly disease? Are not all her visible charms sown thick with what are to him the signs and symbols of hidden decay? Does he ever see her beauty at all, or doesn't he simply view her professionally, and comment upon her unwholesome condition all to himself? And doesn't he sometimes wonder whether he has gained most or lost most by learning his trade?

— MARK TWAIN,
Life on the Mississippi

Writing Suggestions

1. **Writing with Sources.** According to Goldman, Japan's raccoon problem was, among other things, a case of "life imitat[ing] art" (paragraph 5). That is, semifictional representations from popular culture strongly influenced the thinking and behavior of real people, with real-world consequences. Can you find another example of this cause and effect relationship, in which a mass media or pop culture fiction, image, or trend affected the attitudes and actions of real people? You may work from your own experiences and observations, or you may find a historical example, but in either case, make sure to include outside research. How did the process work? What were the consequences? How long did the influence last? Do not forget to use signal phrases, and remember to review the chapter for advice on smoothly integrating and synthesizing your sources.

2. **Writing with Sources.** Goldman writes about how human interaction with the natural world can have unintended consequences. Do some research and write an essay about another example of this process in the context of nature, science, or technology. For example, you might consider the unintended effects of the introduction of a species to a region where it is not native; the unintended consequences of a particular animal's extinction or overexploitation (as in the case of overfishing certain species of fish); or the unintended effects of a particular scientific development, invention, or device. For models of and advice on integrating sources into your essay, review the introduction for this chapter.

American Hookup

LISA WADE

An associate professor of sociology at Occidental College, Lisa Wade was born in 1974 in Long Beach, California, and grew up in Chico, California, and San Jose, California. She earned her bachelor's degree from the University of California, Santa Barbara, her master's from New York University, and her doctorate from the University of Wisconsin, Madison. As a researcher and scholar, she writes about sexuality and gender in a variety of contexts, including female genital mutilation, the sociology of the body, and college hookup culture. Wade's work has appeared in *Journal of Marriage and Family*; Courtesy of Lisa Wade
Gender & Society; *Social Problems*; *Journalism: Theory, Practice & Criticism*, and other scholarly publications and books. She is also the author of *American Hookup: The New Culture of Sex on Campus* (2017).

In the following essay from *American Hookup*, Wade examines the nature of "hookup culture" on college campuses. But while she is interested in the behaviors of students with regard to sex, romance, and relationships, she is equally interested in the attitudes, assumptions, and discussions about this culture. As she points out, those attitudes not only shape the experience of students but also spill over into a wider cultural debate that goes well beyond college campuses. As you read this selection, notice how adroitly Wade uses signal phrases to introduce the many participants in this conversation about hookup culture on America's college campuses.

The notes at the end of the selection appear in the style of Wade's original publication, though we have updated the page numbers to match *Subject & Strategy*.

Preparing to Read

What does the term "hooking up" mean to you? Would you say that people around your age participate in a culture of "hooking up"? Why, or why not?

O n campuses across America, students are sounding an alarm. They 1
are telling us that they are depressed, anxious, and overwhelmed.
Half of first-year students express concern that they are not emotionally healthy, and one in ten say that they frequently feel depressed. The transition from teenager to young adult is rarely easy, but this is more than just youthful angst. Students are less happy and healthy than in previous generations, less so even than just ten or twenty years ago.

One in three students say that their intimate relationships have been 2
"traumatic" or "very difficult to handle," and 10 percent say that they've been sexually coerced or assaulted in the past year. In addition, there is a persistent

malaise: a deep, indefinable disappointment. Students find that their sexual experiences are distressing or boring. They worry that they're feeling too much or too little. They are frustrated and feel regret, but they're not sure why. They consider the possibility that they're inadequate, unsexy, and unlovable. And it goes far beyond the usual suspects. [Student] Owen, for example, is not the kind of student who usually attracts concern. He's a handsome, heterosexual white guy with a healthy sex drive. He should have thrived. He didn't.

Thus far, the culprit seems to be the hookup. Sociologist Kathleen 3 Bogle sparked the conversation in 2008 with *Hooking Up: Sex, Dating, and Relationships on Campus.* She described a new norm on campus that favored casual sexual contact and argued that this was especially harmful to women. Michael Kimmel, the well-known sociologist of masculinity, agreed. Hooking up is "guys' sex," he explained in *Guyland* that year; "guys run the scene." More recently, journalist Jon Birger added math, concluding that a shortage of men in college gives them the power to dictate sexual terms, making campuses a "sexual nirvana for heterosexual men." These thinkers, and many more, argue that hooking up is just a new way for men to get what they want from women.

Journalists Hanna Rosin and Kate Taylor have countered the idea that 4 hooking up only benefits men. At the *Atlantic* and in the *New York Times,* they've suggested that casual sex allows women to put their careers and education before men. In their view, it's a way of giving the middle finger to the "Mrs. Degree," that now outdated but once quite real reason why women sought higher education. Rosin goes so far as to say that future feminist progress "depends on" hooking up, with serious relationships a "danger to be avoided at all costs." Their anecdotal evidence is backed up by social scientists like Elizabeth Armstrong and Laura Hamilton, who show in *Paying for the Party* that women with economically stable families and ambitious career plans are more likely than other women to be successful at hookup-heavy party schools.

Meanwhile, at *Rolling Stone* and *New York* magazine, the whole scene is 5 portrayed as a poly, queer, bacchanalian Utopia with lots of skin and a little light BDSM. Not only is it not sexist, it's non-binary. Maybe this is what the future looks like. At *Elle,* columnist Karley Sciortino seems to think so. She defends hooking up, but only because she thinks that worrying about it amounts to little more than old-fashioned fuddy-duddery. All this talk about young people and their sexual choices, she insists, is just "moral panic" and "reactionary hysteria." What's really harmful, she argues, is suggesting that women might not enjoy casual sex. She's not alone in expressing annoyance at the "kids these days" fretting. It can seem like a lot of hand-wringing to students, many of whom wish everyone would just mind their own business.

Hookups have been damned, praised, and dismissed in the popular and 6 academic presses, feeding a debate about whether we should applaud or condemn the "hookup generation," and drawing out prescriptions for students' sex lives from both the right and the left. But, as is so often the case, the very premise of the debate is wrong.

The idea that college students are having a lot of sex is certainly an 7 enthralling myth. Even students believe it. In Bogle's landmark study, students guessed that their peers were doing it fifty times a year. That's twenty-five times what the numbers actually show. In Kimmel's *Guyland,* young men figured that 80 percent of college guys were having sex any given weekend; they would have been closer to the truth if they were guessing the percent of men who had *ever* had sex. Students overestimate how much sex their peers are having, and by quite a lot.

> " The idea that college students are having a lot of sex is certainly an enthralling myth. Even students believe it. "

In fact, today's students boast no more 8 sexual partners than their parents did at their age. Scholars using the University of Chicago's General Social Survey have shown that they actually report slightly fewer sexual partners than Gen-Xers did. Millennials look more similar to the baby boomer generation than they do to the wild sexual cohort that they are frequently imagined to be.

There are students on campus with active sex lives, of course, but there 9 are plenty with none at all and some with sexual escapades that are, at best, only "slightly less nonexistent" than they were in high school. The average graduating senior reports hooking up just eight times in four years. That amounts to one hookup per semester. Studies looking specifically at the sexual cultures at Duke, Yale, and East Carolina universities, the universities of Georgia and Tennessee, the State University of New York at Geneseo, and UC Berkeley report similar numbers. Not all students are hooking up, and those that do aren't necessarily doing so very often. Neither are students always hopping out of one bed and into another; half of those eight hookups are with someone the student has hooked up with before. Almost a third of students will graduate without hooking up a single time.

Despite the rumors, then, there is no epidemic of casual sexual encoun- 10 ters on college campuses. So, hookups can't be blamed. There just aren't enough of them to account for the malaise. Neither does two sexual encounters every twelve months, possibly with the same person, look like either female empowerment or male domination; if so, it's quite a tepid expression of power. There certainly is no bacchanalian utopia, poly, queer, or otherwise. Students are too busy not having sex to be enacting the next revolution. The cause of students' unhappiness, then, can't be the hookup. But it *is* about hooking up. It's hookup *culture.*

* * *

Hookup culture has descended upon college campuses like a fog. It's thickest 11 on Greek row, where students hope to find wild parties, hot bodies, and easy sex. It's dense, too, in the large off-campus houses known for dirty bathrooms and high-octane drinks. It gathers and dissipates in student dorms, filling the halls as students pre-party and primp on weekend nights and emptying out as it follows them to nearby bars and clubs that flaunt laws against serving minors.

The fog of hookup culture isn't confined, though, to where students live 12 and party. It creeps through the quad and reaches into the classrooms and study halls where academics are supposed to prevail. On mornings after big parties and games, it hovers over the bright non-sexy dining halls, where students nurse hangovers over brunch and tell their stories from the previous night. By afternoon, it has occupied life online, too. Students take pictures and hookup culture blankets social media.

Hookup culture is an occupying force, coercive and omnipresent. For those 13 who love it, it's all sunshine, but it isn't for everyone else. Deep in the fog, students often feel dreary, confused, helpless. Many behave in ways they don't like, hurt other people unwillingly, and consent to sexual activity they don't desire.

Campuses of all kinds are in this fog. No matter the size of the college, 14 how heavy a Greek or athletic presence it boasts, its exclusivity, its religious affiliation, or whether it's public or private, hookup culture is there. We find it in all regions of the country, from the Sunshine State of Florida to the sunny state of California. Students all over say so. Hookups are "part of our collegiate culture," writes a representative of the American South in the University of Florida's *Alligator*. If you don't hook up, warns a woman at the University of Georgia, then you're "failing at the college experience." A woman at Tulane puts it succinctly: "Hookup culture," she says, "it's college."

Up north, a student at Cornell confirms: "We go to parties. And then after 15 we're good and drunk, we hook up. Everyone just hooks up." "At the end of the day," boasts a student at Yale, "you can get laid." Nearby, at Connecticut College, a female student describes it as the "be-all and end-all" of social life. "Oh, sure," says a guy 2,500 miles away at Arizona State, "you go to parties on the prowl." "A one-night stand," admits a student a few hundred miles north at Chico State, "is a constant possibility." Further up, at Whitman in Walla Walla, a female student calls hookup culture "an established norm."

Students like these almost certainly overestimate how much hooking up is 16 going on, but they're not wrong to feel that hookup culture is everywhere. And while the exhilaration and delight in their voices is real, so is the disappointment and trauma. In response, many students opt out of hooking up, but they can't opt out of hookup culture. It's more than just a behavior; it's the climate. It can't be wished away any more than we can wish away a foggy day.

Notes

[524] **depressed, anxious, and overwhelmed**: Eagan et al. (2014); Twenge (2000, 2006).

[524] **Half of first-year students**: Eagan et al. (2014).

[524] **One in three students**: American College Health Association (2013).

[524] **a persistent malaise**: Bersamin et al. (2013), Bogle (2008), England et al. (2008), Epstein et al. (2009), Eshbaugh and Gute (2008), Fisher et al. (2012), Flack et al. (2007), Hamilton and Armstrong

(2009), Freitas (2008, 2013), Glenn and Marquardt (2001), Grello et al. (2006), Katz et al. (2012), Lewis et al. (2012), Paul and Hayes (2002), Lewis et al. (2000), Smith et al. (2011), Smith et al. (2008), Wade and Heldman (2012).

[525] **Kathleen Bogle**: Bogle (2008).

[525] **"guys' sex"**: Kimmel (2008).

[525] **Jon Birger**: Birger (2015).

[525] **Hanna Rosin and Kate Taylor**: Rosin (2012), Taylor (2013).

[525] **the "Mrs. Degree"**: Holland and Eisenhart (1992).

[525] **women with economically stable families**: Armstrong and Hamilton (2013).

[525] ***Rolling Stone* and *New York***: Morris (2014); "Sex on Campus: The Politics of Hookups, Genders, 'Yes,'" *New York*, October 19–November 1, 2015.

[525] **At *Elle***: Sciortino (2015).

[526] **students guessed**: Bogle (2008).

[526] **young men figured that 80 percent**: Kimmel (2008).

[526] **report slightly fewer sexual partners**: Monto and Carey (2014). See also Twenge et al. (2015).

[526] **The average graduating senior**: Ford et al. (2015). See also Hoffman and Berntson (2014).

[526] **Studies looking specifically at the sexual cultures**: Abercrombie and Mays (2013), Foxhall (2010), Grello et al. (2006), Katz et al. (2012), Knox and Zusman (2009), Najmabadi (2012), Uecker et al. (2015).

[526] **Almost a third of students**: Ford et al. (2015).

[527] **a representative of the American South**: Usyk (2007).

[527] **a woman at the University of Georgia**: Abercrombie and Mays (2013).

[527] **A woman at Tulane**: Manzone (2015).

[527] **a student at Cornell**: Kimmel (2008).

[527] **a student at Yale**: Foxhall (2010).

[527] **at Connecticut College**: Yacos (2014).

[527] **at Arizona State**: Kimmel (2008).

[527] **at Chico State**: Karp (2014).

[527] **at Whitman**: Vandervilt (2012).

Thinking Critically about the Text

Wade characterizes college students as "depressed, anxious, and overwhelmed" and claims that they are "less happy and healthy" than their predecessors (paragraph 1). Do her opening generalizations match your own experiences and observations? Do you recognize the "malaise" that Wade describes? Or do you think she is overstating her case?

Questions on Subject

1. Wade cites several writers who defend hooking up, particularly in the context of female empowerment and sexual freedom. What are the defenses that she includes here? How would you summarize them in your own words?

2. According to Wade, why is the whole "premise of the debate" about hooking up wrong (paragraph 6)?

3. What's the difference between "hooking up" and "hookup culture"? Why is the distinction so important for Wade's argument?

4. One of Wade's sources dismissively refers to the concern about hookup culture as "moral panic" on the part of older generations (paragraph 5). What is a "moral panic"? What connotations does the phrase have?

Questions on Strategy

1. Wade spends much of this essay citing and summarizing the academic work and journalism of other researchers and writers. Why is this survey of *other* writers on her subject important to her main argument about hookup culture?

2. How does Wade use **cause and effect analysis** in this essay? Why is this strategy especially important for her argument?

3. What extended **simile** does Wade use to describe the descent of "hookup culture" on college campuses? Do you find it effective? Why, or why not?

4. In paragraphs 13 and 14, Wade surveys and quotes college students from geographically disparate parts of the United States. Why? What point is she trying to make?

Writing with Sources in Action

Plagiarism is a serious issue. The honest and accurate use of sources cannot be stressed enough. While academic dishonesty has long been a problem, the Internet has in many ways made it worse. Chapter 14 includes important guidelines for avoiding plagiarism, but what insight do you and other students have into the topic? How can instructors design writing assignments that limit or even eliminate opportunities for plagiarism? What steps, processes, and requirements can be built into assignments to encourage academic honesty and the ethical use of sources? As a class, brainstorm practical ideas that can be used by instructors and students to help avoid plagiarism.

Writing Suggestions

1. **Writing with Sources.** In the opening paragraphs of this excerpt, Wade focuses on the pervasive hookup culture on campuses as a significant causal factor in creating emotional problems for today's college students. But what other factors might lead students to be less happy and healthy than college students of previous generations? Accepting Wade's premise that students are more anxious and depressed than their predecessors, research and write an essay that considers other causal factors that might contribute to this problem. As Wade does, try to use a mix of research from journalistic and academic sources, as well as interviews and quotations from college students or even college health professionals and counselors.

2. **Writing with Sources.** In part, Wade is writing to correct a misunderstanding about college students and the culture of college campuses. She establishes that the inaccurate misperception is widely held, and then uses evidence and logical demonstration to show that this view is incorrect. What other things do people misunderstand about people your age or about college students? What inaccurate or false beliefs do they hold? Write an essay that analyzes a misconception and that follows Wade's basic approach: Establish that the misunderstanding or incorrect view exists, and then use research and logical argument to show that the view is incorrect. For models of and advice on integrating sources in your essay, see this chapter and Chapter 15.

The English-Only Movement
Can America Proscribe Language with a Clear Conscience?

JAKE JAMIESON

Courtesy of Jake Jamieson

An eighth-generation Vermonter, Jake Jamieson was born in the town of Berlin and grew up in nearby Waterbury, home of Ben & Jerry's Ice Cream. He graduated from the University of Vermont with a degree in elementary education and a focus in English. After graduation Jamieson "bounced around" California and Colorado before landing in the Boston area, where he directed the product innovation and training department for iProspect, a search-engine marketing company. Currently, he is living in Montpelier and works out of his house for an online marketing company with some freelancing on the side.

Jamieson wrote the following essay while he was a college student and has updated it for inclusion in this book. As one who believes in the old axiom "If it isn't broken, don't fix it," Jamieson is intrigued by the official-English movement, which advocates fixing a system that seems to be working just fine. In this essay he tackles the issue of legislating English as the official language for the United States. As you read, notice how he uses outside sources to set out the various pieces of the English-only position and then uses his own thinking and examples, as well as experts who support his side, to undercut that position. Throughout his essay, Jamieson uses MLA-style in-text citations together with a list of works cited.

Preparing to Read

It is now possible to go many places in the world and get along pretty well using English, no matter what other languages are spoken in the host country. If you were to emigrate, how hard would you work to learn the predominant language of your chosen country? What advantages would there be in learning that language, even if you could get by with English? How would you feel if the country had a law that forced you to learn and use its language as quickly as possible?

Jake Jamieson

Professor Rosa

Composition 101

May 10, 2010

The English-Only Movement:

Can America Proscribe Language with a

Clear Conscience?

Many people think of the United States as a giant cultural   1
"melting pot" where people from other countries come together
and bathe in the warm waters of assimilation. In this scenario
the newly arrived immigrants readily adopt American cultural
ways and learn to speak English. For others, however, this serene
picture of the melting pot does not ring true. These people see the
melting pot as a giant cauldron into which immigrants are tossed;
here their cultures, values, and backgrounds are boiled away in
the scalding waters of discrimination. At the center of the discussion about immigrants and assimilation is language: Should
immigrants be required to learn English or should accommodations be made so they can continue to use their native
languages?

Those who argue that the melting-pot analogy is valid believe   2
that immigrants who come to America do so willingly and should
be expected to become a part of its culture instead of hanging
on to their past. For them, the expectation that immigrants will
celebrate this country's holidays, dress as Americans dress,
embrace American values, and most importantly, speak English is
not unreasonable. They believe that assimilation offers the only way
for everyone in this country to live together in harmony and the
only way to dissipate the tensions that inevitably arise when cultures clash.

A major problem with this argument, however, is that there is no   3
agreement on what exactly constitutes the "American way" of doing
things. Not everyone in America is of the same religious persuasion
or has the same set of values, and different people affect vastly
different styles of dress. There are so many sets of variables that it
would be hard to defend the argument that there is only one culture
in the United States.

Currently, the one common denominator in America is that   4
the majority of us speak English, and because of this a major
movement is being staged in favor of making English the country's
"official" language while it is still the country's national and

common language. Making English America's official language would change the ground rules and expectations surrounding immigrant assimilation. According to the columnist and social commentator Charles Krauthammer, making English the official language has important implications:

> "Official" means the language of the government and its institutions. "Official" makes clear our expectations of acculturation. "Official" means that every citizen, upon entering America's most sacred political space, the voting booth, should minimally be able to identify the words president and vice president and county commissioner and judge. The immigrant, of course, has the right to speak whatever he wants. But he must understand that when he comes to the United States, swears allegiance, and accepts its bounty, he undertakes to join its civic culture. In English. (521)

Many reasons are given to support the notion that making English the official language of the land is a good idea and that it is exactly what this country needs, especially in the face of the growing diversity of languages in metropolitan areas. Indeed, the National Center for Education Statistics reports that in 2008, 21 percent of children ages 5–17 spoke a language other than English at home (United States, Department of Education, sec. 1).

Supporters of English-only contend that all government communication must be in English. Because communication is absolutely necessary for democracy to survive, they believe that the only way to ensure the existence of our nation is to make sure a common language exists. Making English official would ensure that all government business, from ballots to official forms to judicial hearings, would have to be conducted in English. According to former senator and presidential candidate Bob Dole, "Promoting English as our national language is not an act of hostility but a welcoming act of inclusion." He goes on to state that while immigrants are encouraged to continue speaking their native languages, "thousands of children [are] failing to learn the language, English, that is the ticket to the 'American Dream' " (qtd. in Donegan 51). Political and cultural commentator Greg Lewis echoes Dole's sentiments when he boldly states, "to succeed in America . . . it's important to speak, read, and understand English as most Americans speak it. There's nothing cruel or unfair in that; it's just the way it is" (par. 5).

Jamieson 3

For those who do not subscribe to this way of thinking, however, this type of legislation is anything but the "welcoming act of inclusion" that it is described to be. Many of them, like Myriam Marquez, readily acknowledge the importance of English but fear that "talking in Spanish—or any other language, for that matter—is some sort of litmus test used to gauge American patriotism" ("Why and When" A12). Others suggest that anyone attempting to regulate language is treading dangerously close to the First Amendment and must have a hidden agenda of some type. Why, it is asked, make a language official when it is already firmly entrenched and widely used in this country without legislation to mandate it?

7

According to language diversity advocate James Crawford, the answer is plain and simple: "discrimination." He states that "it is certainly more respectable to discriminate by language than by race" or ethnicity. He points out that "most people are not sensitive to language discrimination in this nation, so it is easy to argue that you're doing someone a favor by making them speak English" (qtd. in Donegan 51). English-only legislation has been criticized as bigoted, anti-immigrant, mean-spirited, and steeped in nativism by those who oppose it, and some go so far as to say that this type of legislation will not foster better communication, as is the claim, but will instead encourage a "fear of being subsumed by a growing 'foreignness' in our midst" (Underwood 65).

8

For example, when a judge in Texas ruled that a mother was abusing her five-year-old girl by speaking to her only in Spanish, an uproar ensued. This ruling was accompanied by the statement that by talking to her daughter in a language other than English, the mother was "abusing that child and . . . relegating her to the position of housemaid." The National Association for Bilingual Education (NABE) condemned this statement for "labeling the Spanish language as abuse." The judge, Samuel C. Kiser, subsequently apologized to the housekeepers of the country, adding that he held them "in the highest esteem," but stood firm on his ruling (qtd. in Donegan 51). One might notice that he went out of his way to apologize to the housekeepers he might have offended but saw no need to apologize to the millions of Spanish speakers whose language had just been belittled in a nationally publicized case.

9

This tendency of official-English proponents to put down other languages is one that shows up again and again, even though they maintain that they have nothing against other languages or the people who speak them. If there is no malice intended toward other

10

languages, why is the use of any language other than English so often portrayed by them as tantamount to lunacy? In a listing of the "New Year's Resolutions" of various conservative organizations, a group called U.S. English, Inc., stated that the U.S. government was not doing its job of convincing immigrants that they "must learn English to succeed in this country." Instead, according to Stephen Moore and his associates, "in a bewildering display of irrationality, the U.S. government makes it possible to vote, file a tax return, get married, obtain a driver's license, and become a U.S. citizen in many languages" (46).

Now, according to this mind-set, speaking any language other 11 than English is "abusive," "irrational," and "bewildering." What is this world coming to when people want to speak and make trans- actions in their native language? Why do they refuse to change and become more like us? Why can't immigrants see that speaking English is quite simply the right way to go? These and many other questions like them are implied by official-English proponents when they discuss the issue.

Conservative attorney David Price argues that official-English 12 legislation is a good idea because most English-speaking Americans prefer "out of pride and convenience to speak their native language on the job" (A13). Not only does this statement imply that the pride and convenience of non-English-speaking Americans is unimportant but also that their native tongues are not as important as English. The scariest prospect of all is that this opinion is quickly gaining popularity all around the country. It appears to be most prevalent in areas with high concentrations of Spanish-speaking residents.

To date a number of official-English bills and one amendment 13 to the Constitution have been proposed in the House and Senate. There are more than twenty-seven states—including Missouri, North Dakota, Florida, Massachusetts, California, Virginia, and New Hampshire—that have made English their official language, and more are debating the issue every day. An especially disturbing fact about this debate—and it was front and center in 2007 during the discus- sions and protests about what to do with America's 12.5 million illegal immigrants—is that official-English laws always seem to be linked to anti-immigration legislation, such as proposals to limit immigration or to restrict government benefits to immigrants.

Although official-English proponents maintain that their bid for 14 language legislation is in the best interest of immigrants, the facts tend to show otherwise. University of Texas professor Robert D. King strongly believes that "language does not threaten American unity." He recommends that "we relax and luxuriate in our linguistic richness and our traditional tolerance of language differences" (531). A decision has to be made in this country about what kind of message we will send to the rest of the world. Do we plan to allow everyone in this country the freedom of speech that we profess to cherish, or will we decide to reserve it only for those who speak English? Will we hold firm to our belief that everyone is deserving of life, liberty, and the pursuit of happiness in this country? Or will we show the world that we believe in these things only when they pertain to us and people like us? "The irony," as columnist Myriam Marquez observes, "is that English-only laws directed at government have done little to change the inevitable multicultural flavor of America" ("English-Only Laws").

Works Cited

Donegan, Craig. "Debate over Bilingualism: Should English Be the Nation's Official Language?" *CQ Researcher*, 19 Jan. 1996, pp. 51-71.

King, Robert D. "Should English Be the Law?" *Subject & Strategy*, edited by Alfred Rosa and Paul Eschholz, 11th ed., Bedford/St. Martin's, 2008, pp. 522-31.

Krauthammer, Charles. "In Plain English: Let's Make It Official." *Subject & Strategy*, edited by Alfred Rosa and Paul Eschholz, 11th ed., Bedford/St. Martin's, 2009, pp. 519-21.

Lewis, Greg. "An Open Letter to Diversity's Victims." *Washington Dispatch*, 12 Aug. 2003, www.washingtondispatch.com/open-letter -to-victims/.

Marquez, Myriam. "English-Only Laws Serve to Appease Those Who Fear the Inevitable." *Orlando Sentinel*, 10 July 2000, p. A10.

—. "Why and When We Speak Spanish among Ourselves in Public." *Orlando Sentinel*, 28 June 1998, p. A12.

Moore, Stephen, et al. "New Year's Resolutions." *National Review*, 29 Jan. 1996, pp. 46-48.

Price, David. "English-Only Rules: EEOC Has Gone Too Far." *USA Today*, 28 Mar. 1996, Final ed., p. A13.

Underwood, Robert L. "At Issue: Should English Be the Official Language of the United States?" *CQ Researcher*, 19 Jan. 1996, p. 65.

United States, Department of Education, Institute of Education Sciences, National Center for Education Statistics. *The Condition of Education 2010*. NCES, 2010, nces.ed.gov/pubs2010/2010028.pdf.

Thinking Critically about the Text

Jamieson claims that "there are so many sets of variables that it would be hard to defend the argument that there is only one culture in the United States" (paragraph 3). Do you agree with him, or do you see a dominant "American culture" with many regional variations? Explain.

Questions on Subject

1. What question does Jamieson seek to answer in his paper? How does he answer that question?

2. How does Jamieson counter the argument that the melting-pot analogy is valid? Do you agree with his counterargument?

3. Former senator Bob Dole believes that English "is the ticket to the 'American Dream'" (paragraph 6). In what ways can it be considered a "ticket"?

4. In his concluding paragraph, Jamieson leaves his readers with three important questions. How do you think he would answer each one? How would you answer them?

Questions on Strategy

1. What is Jamieson's **thesis**, and where does he present it?

2. How has Jamieson **organized** his argument?

3. Jamieson is careful to use signal phrases to introduce each of his quotations and paraphrases. How do these **signal phrases** help readers follow the flow of the argument in his essay?

4. In paragraph 9, Jamieson presents the example of the Texas judge who ruled that speaking to a child only in Spanish constituted abuse. What point does this example help Jamieson make?

Writing with Sources in Action

For each of the following quotations, write an acceptable paraphrase and then a paraphrase including a partial quotation that avoids plagiarism (see "Learning to Summarize, Paraphrase, and Quote from Your Sources" and "Avoiding Plagiarism" on pages 500–501 and 509–11). Pay particular attention to the word choice and the sentence structure of the original.

> A truly equal world would be one where women ran half of our countries and companies and men ran half of our homes. The laws of economics and many studies of diversity tell us that if we tapped the entire pool of human resources and talent, our performance would improve.

> — SHERYL SANDBERG,
> *Lean In*

Astronauts from over twenty nations have gone into space and they all come back, amazingly enough, saying the very same thing: The earth is a small, blue place of profound beauty that we must take care of. For each, the journey into space, whatever its original intents and purposes, became above all a spiritual one.

— AL REINHERT,
For All Mankind

One of the unusual things about education in mathematics in the United States is its relatively impoverished vocabulary. Whereas the student completing elementary school will already have a vocabulary for most disciplines of many hundreds, even thousands of words, the typical student will have a mathematics vocabulary of only a couple of dozen words.

— MARVIN MINSKY,
The Society of Mind

Writing Suggestions

1. **Writing with Sources.** While it's no secret that English is the common language of the United States, few of us know that our country has been extremely cautious about promoting a government-mandated "official language." Why do you suppose the federal government has chosen to take a hands-off position on the language issue? If it has not been necessary to mandate it in the past, why do you think that people now feel a need to declare English the "official language" of the United States? Do you think that this need is real? Write an essay articulating your position on the English-only issue. Support your position with your own experiences and observations as well as several outside sources. For models of and advice on integrating sources in your essay, see this chapter and Chapter 15.

2. **Writing with Sources.** Is the English-only debate a political issue, a social issue, an economic issue, or some combination of the three? In this context, what do you see as the relationship between language and power? After doing some research on the topic, write an essay in which you explore the relationship between language and power as it pertains to the non-English-speaking immigrants trying to live and function within the dominant English-speaking culture. For models of and advice on integrating sources in your essay, see this chapter and Chapter 15.

CHAPTER 15

A Brief Guide to Researching and Documenting Essays

IN THIS CHAPTER, YOU WILL LEARN SOME VALUABLE RESEARCH techniques:

- How to establish a realistic schedule for your research project
- How to conduct research online using directory and keyword searches
- How to evaluate sources
- How to analyze sources
- How to develop a working bibliography
- How to take useful notes
- How to acknowledge your sources using Modern Language Association (MLA) style in-text citations and a list of works cited

ESTABLISHING A REALISTIC SCHEDULE

A research project easily spans several weeks. So as not to lose track of time and find yourself facing an impossible deadline at the last moment, establish a realistic schedule for completing key tasks. By thinking of the research paper as a multistaged process, you avoid becoming overwhelmed by the size of the whole undertaking.

Your schedule should allow at least a few days to accommodate unforeseen needs and delays. Use the following template (page 540), which lists the essential steps in writing a research paper, to plan your own research schedule:

Research Paper Schedule

Task	Completion Date
1. Choose a research topic and pose a worthwhile question.	___/___/___
2. Locate print and electronic sources.	___/___/___
3. Develop a working bibliography.	___/___/___
4. Evaluate your sources.	___/___/___
5. Read your sources, taking complete and accurate notes.	___/___/___
6. Develop a preliminary thesis and make a working outline.	___/___/___
7. Write a draft of your paper, integrating sources you have summarized, paraphrased, and quoted.	___/___/___
8. Visit your college writing center for help with your revision.	___/___/___
9. Decide on a final thesis and modify your outline.	___/___/___
10. Revise your paper and properly cite all borrowed materials.	___/___/___
11. Prepare a list of works cited.	___/___/___
12. Prepare the final manuscript and proofread.	___/___/___
13. Submit your research paper.	___/___/___

FINDING AND USING SOURCES

You should use materials found through a search of your school library's holdings—including books, newspapers, journals, magazines, encyclopedias, pamphlets, brochures, and government documents—as your primary tools for research. These sources are reviewed by experts in the field before they are published, generally overseen by a reputable publishing company or organization, and examined by editors and fact checkers for accuracy and reliability. These sources are very different from "open-Internet" sources, by which we mean the vast array of resources, ranging from Library of Congress holdings to pictures of a stranger's summer vacation, available to anyone using a search engine. Because anyone with a computer and Internet access can post information online, sources found on the open Internet should be scrutinized more carefully for relevance and reliability than those found through a search of academic databases or library holdings.

The best place to start your search, in most cases, is your college library's home page (see the following image). Here you will find links to the library's computerized catalog of hard-copy holdings, online reference works, periodical databases, electronic journals, and a list of full-text databases. Most libraries also provide links to other helpful materials, including subject study guides and guides to research.

To get started, decide on some likely search terms and try them out. You might have to try a number of different terms related to your topic to generate the best results. (For tips on refining your searches, see "Conducting Keyword Searches" on pages 542–43.) Your goal is to create a preliminary listing of books, magazine and newspaper articles, public documents and reports, and other sources that may be helpful in exploring your topic. At this early stage, it is better to err on the side of listing too many sources. Then, later on, you will not have to backtrack to find sources you discarded too hastily.

You will likely find some open-Internet sources to be informative and valuable additions to your research. The Internet is especially useful in providing recent data, stories, and reports. For example, you might find a just-published article from a university laboratory or a news story in your local newspaper's online archives. Generally, however, open-Internet sources should be used

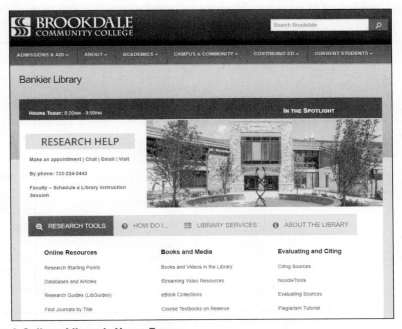

A College Library's Home Page
Courtesy of Brookdale Community College

alongside other sources and not as a replacement for them. The Internet offers a vast number of useful and carefully maintained resources, but it also contains much unreliable information. It is your responsibility to determine whether a given Internet source should be trusted. (For advice on evaluating sources, see "Evaluating Your Sources" on pages 544–46.)

▶ Conducting Keyword Searches

When searching for sources about your topic in an electronic database, in the library's computerized catalog, or on the Internet, you should start with a keyword search. To make the most efficient use of your time, you will want to know how to conduct a keyword search that is likely to yield solid sources and leads for your research project. As obvious or simple as it may sound, the key to a successful keyword search is the quality of the keywords you generate about your topic. You might find it helpful to start a list of potential keywords as you begin your research and add to it as your work proceeds. Often you will discover combinations of keywords that will lead you right to the sources you need.

Databases and library catalogs index sources by author, title, and year of publication, as well as by subject headings assigned by a cataloger who has previewed the source. In order to generate results, the keywords you

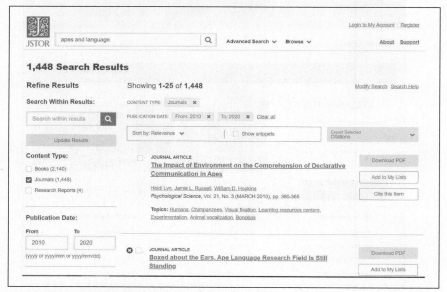

Database Search Results for a Journal Article

use will have to match words found in one or more of these categories. Once you begin to locate sources that are on your topic, be sure to note the subject headings listed for each source. You can use these subject headings as keywords to lead you to additional book sources or, later, to articles in periodicals cataloged by full-text databases like *InfoTrac*, *LexisNexis*, *Academic Search Premier*, or *JSTOR* to which your library subscribes. The figure on page 542 shows a typical search in a database for a journal article. Notice the hyperlinked topics, all of which can be used as possible keywords.

The keyword search process is somewhat different — more wide open — when you are searching on the Web. It is always a good idea to look for search tips on the help screens or advanced search instructions for the search engine you are using before initiating a keyword search. When you type in a keyword in the "Search" box on a search engine's home page, the search engine electronically scans Web sites, looking for matches to your keywords. On the Web, the quality of the keywords used determines the relevance of the hits on the first page or two that come up. While it is not uncommon for a search on the Internet to yield between 500,000 and 1,000,000 hits, the search engine's algorithm puts the best sources up front. If after scanning the first couple of pages of results you determine that these sites seem off topic, you need to refine your terms to either narrow or broaden your search.

Refining Keyword Searches on the Web

While some variation in command terms and characters exists among databases and popular search engines, the following functions are almost universally accepted. If you have a particular question about refining your keyword search, seek assistance by clicking on "Help" or "Advanced Search."

- Use quotation marks or parentheses to indicate that you are searching for words in exact sequence — e.g., "whooping cough"; (Supreme Court).
- Use AND or a plus sign (+) between words to narrow your search by specifying that all words need to appear in a document — e.g., tobacco AND cancer; Shakespeare + sonnet.
- Use NOT or a minus sign (–) between words to narrow your search by eliminating unwanted words — e.g., monopoly NOT game, cowboys – Dallas.
- Use OR to broaden your search by requiring that only one of the words need appear — e.g., buffalo OR bison.
- Use an asterisk (*) to indicate that you will accept variations of a term — e.g., "food label*" for food labels, food labeling, and so forth.

▶ Using Subject Directories to Define and Develop Your Research Topic

If you are undecided about your exact topic, general search engines might not yield the credible depth of information you need for initial research and brainstorming. Instead, explore subject directories—collections of sites and online resources organized and edited by human experts. Search *subject directories* online or try popular options like *INFOMINE: Scholarly Internet Resource Collections* and the Best of the Web Directory. Subject directories can also help if you simply want to see if there is enough material to supplement your print-source research. Once you choose a directory's subject area, you can select more specialized subcategories and eventually arrive at a list of sites closely related to your topic.

The most common question students have at this stage of a Web search is, "How can I tell if I'm looking in the right place?" There is no straight answer; if more than one subject area sounds plausible, you will have to dig more deeply into each of their subcategories, using logic and the process of elimination to determine which one is likely to produce the best leads for your topic. In most cases, it doesn't take long—usually just one or two clicks—to figure out whether you're searching in the right subject area. If you click on a subject area and none of the topics listed in its subcategories seems to pertain even remotely to your research topic, try a different subject area. As you browse through various subject directories, keep a running list of keywords associated with your topic that you can use in subsequent keyword searches.

EVALUATING YOUR SOURCES

You do not have to spend long in the library to realize that you do not have time to read every print and online source that appears relevant. Given the abundance of print and Internet sources, the key to successful research is identifying those books, articles, Web sites, and other online sources that will help you most. You must evaluate your potential sources to determine which materials you will read, which you will skim, and which you will simply eliminate. The following box offers some evaluation strategies and questions to assist you in identifying your most promising sources.

Strategies for Evaluating Print and Online Sources

Evaluating a Book

- Read the back or inside cover copy for insights into the book's coverage and currency as well as the author's expertise.
- Scan the table of contents and identify any promising chapters.
- Read the author's preface, looking for his or her thesis and purpose.

- Check the index for key words or key phrases related to your research topic.
- Read the opening and concluding paragraphs of any promising chapter; if you are unsure about its usefulness, skim the whole chapter.
- Ask yourself: Does the author have a discernible bias? If so, you must be aware that this bias will color his or her claims and evidence. (See "Analyzing Your Sources," on pages 546–47.)

Evaluating an Article

- Ask yourself what you know about the journal or magazine publishing the article:
  - Is the publication scholarly or popular? Scholarly journals (*American Economic Review, Journal of Marriage and Family*, the *Wilson Quarterly*) publish articles representing original research written by authorities in the field. Such articles always cite their sources in footnotes or bibliographies, which means you can check their accuracy and delve deeper into the topic by locating these sources. Popular news and general interest magazines (*National Geographic*, *Smithsonian*, *Time*, *Ebony*), on the other hand, publish informative, entertaining, and easy-to-read articles written by editorial staff or freelance writers. Popular essays sometimes cite sources but often do not, making them somewhat less authoritative and less helpful in terms of extending your own research.
  - What is the reputation of the journal or magazine? Determine the publisher or sponsor. Is it an academic institution or a commercial enterprise or an individual? Does the publisher or publication have a reputation for accuracy and objectivity?
  - Who are the readers of this journal or magazine?
- Try to determine the author's credentials. Is he or she an expert?
- Consider the title or headline of the article as well as the opening paragraph or two and the conclusion. Does the source appear to be too general or too technical for your needs and audience?
- For articles in journals, read the abstract (a summary of the main points) if there is one. Examine any photographs, charts, graphs, or other illustrations that accompany the article and determine how useful they might be for your research purposes.

Evaluating a Web Site or Document Found on the Open Internet

- Consider the original location of the document or site. Often the URL, especially the top-level domain name, can give you a clue about the kinds of information provided and the type of organization behind the site. Common suffixes include:

  .com — business/commercial/personal

  .edu — educational institution

  .gov — government sponsored

  .net — various types of networks

  .org — nonprofit organization, but also some commercial or personal

(continued on next page)

(Be advised that *.org* is not regulated like *.edu* and *.gov*, for example. Most nonprofits use *.org*, but many commercial and personal sites do as well.)

- Examine the home page of the site:
  - Does the content appear to be related to your research topic?
  - Is the home page well maintained and professional in appearance?
  - Is there an "About" link on the home page that takes you to background information on the site's sponsor? Is there a mission statement, history, or statement of philosophy? Can you verify whether the site is official — actually sanctioned by the organization or company?
- Identify the author of the document or site. What are the author's qualifications for writing on this subject?
- Determine whether a print equivalent is available. If so, is the Web version identical to the print version, or is it altered in some way?
- Determine when the site was last updated. Is the content current enough for your purposes?

ANALYZING YOUR SOURCES

Before you begin to take notes, it is essential that you read critically and carefully analyze your sources for their theses, overall arguments, amount and credibility of evidence, bias, and reliability in helping you explore your research topic. Look for the writers' main ideas, key examples, strongest arguments, and conclusions. While it is easy to become absorbed in sources that support your own beliefs, always seek out several sources with opposing viewpoints, if only to test your own position. Look for information about the authors themselves—information that will help you determine their authority and where they position themselves in the broader conversation on the issue. You should also know the reputation and special interests of book publishers and magazines because you are likely to get different views—conservative, liberal, international, feminist—on the same topic depending on the publication you read. Use the following checklist to assist in analyzing your print and online sources.

Checklist for Analyzing Print and Online Sources

- What is the writer's thesis or claim?
- How does the writer support this thesis? Does the evidence seem fact based, or is it mainly anecdotal?
- Does the writer consider opposing viewpoints?
- Does the writer have any obvious political or religious biases? Is the writer associated with any special-interest groups, such as Planned Parenthood, Greenpeace, Amnesty International, or the National Rifle Association?

- Is the writer an expert on the subject? Do other writers mention this author in their work?
- Is important information documented through footnotes or links so that it can be verified or corroborated in other sources?
- What is the author's purpose — to inform, to argue for a particular position or action, something else?
- Do the writer's thesis and purpose clearly relate to your research topic?
- Does the source reflect current thinking and research in the field?

DEVELOPING A WORKING BIBLIOGRAPHY FOR YOUR SOURCES

As you discover books, journal and magazine articles, newspaper stories, and Web sites that you think might be helpful, you need to start maintaining a record of important information about each source. This record, called a working bibliography, will enable you to know where sources are located as well as what they are when it comes time to consult them or acknowledge them in your list of works cited or final bibliography. In all likelihood, your working bibliography will contain more sources than you actually consult and include in your list of works cited.

Some people make separate bibliography cards, using a 3- by 5-inch index card, for each work that might be helpful to their research. By using a separate card for each book, article, or Web site, you can continually edit your working bibliography, dropping sources that do not prove helpful for one reason or another and adding new ones.

With the digitization of most library resources, you now have the option to copy and paste bibliographic information from the library computer catalog and periodical indexes or from the Internet into a document on your computer that you can edit throughout the research process. You can also track your project online with a citation manager like Zotero, Mendeley, or EndNote. One advantage of the copy/paste option over the index card method is accuracy, especially in punctuation, spelling, and capitalization—details that are essential in accessing Internet sites.

Checklist for a Working Bibliography of Sources

For Books

- Library call number
- Names of all authors, editors, and translators
- Title and subtitle

(continued on next page)

- Publication data:

    Publisher's name

    Date of publication

- Edition (if not the first) and volume number (if applicable)

For Periodical Articles

- Names of all authors
- Name and subtitle of article
- Title of journal, magazine, or newspaper
- Publication data:

    Volume number and issue number

    Date of issue

    Page numbers

For Internet Sources

- Names of all authors and/or editors
- Title and subtitle of the document
- Title of the longer work to which the document belongs (if applicable)
- Title of the site or discussion list
- Name of company or organization that owns the Web site
- Date of release, online posting, or latest revision
- Format of online source (Web page, PDF, podcast, etc.)
- Date you accessed the site
- Electronic address (URL) or digital object identifier (DOI)

For Other Sources

- Name of author, government agency, organization, company, recording artist, personality, etc.
- Title of the work
- Format (pamphlet, unpublished diary, interview, television broadcast, etc.)
- Publication or production data:

    Name of publisher or producer

    Date of publication, production, or release

    Identifying codes or numbers (if applicable)

TAKING NOTES

As you read, take notes. You're looking for ideas, facts, opinions, statistics, examples, and evidence that you think will be useful in writing your paper. As you work through the articles, look for recurring themes and mark the places where the writers are in agreement and where they differ in their views. Try to remember that the effectiveness of your paper is largely determined by the quality—not necessarily the quantity—of your notes. The purpose of a research paper is not to present a collection of quotes that show you've read all the material and can report what others have said about your topic. Your goal is to analyze, evaluate, and synthesize the information you collect—in other words, to enter into the discussion of the issues and so take ownership of your topic. You want to view the results of your research from your own perspective and arrive at an informed opinion of your topic. (For more on writing with sources, see Chapter 14.)

Now for some practical advice on taking notes: First, be systematic. If you use note cards, write one note on a card and use cards of uniform size, preferably 4- by 6-inch cards because they are large enough to accommodate even a long note on a single card and yet small enough to be easily handled and carried. If you keep notes electronically, consider creating a separate file for each topic or source or use a digital research application like those mentioned previously (Zotero, Mendeley, or EndNote). If you keep your notes organized, when you get to the planning and writing stage, you will be able to sequence your notes according to the plan you have envisioned for your paper. Furthermore, if you decide to alter your organizational plan, you can easily reorder your notes to reflect those revisions.

Second, try not to take too many notes. One good way to help decide whether to take a note is to ask yourself, "How exactly does this material help prove or disprove my thesis?" You might even try envisioning where in your paper you could use the information. If it does not seem relevant to your thesis, don't bother to take a note.

Once you decide to take a note, you must decide whether to summarize, paraphrase, or quote directly. The approach that you take is largely determined by the content of the passage and the way you envision using it in your paper. For detailed advice on using your sources, see Chapter 14, "Learning to Summarize, Paraphrase, and Quote from Your Sources," on pages 499–507.

DOCUMENTING SOURCES

When you summarize, paraphrase, or quote a person's thoughts and ideas, and when you use facts or statistics that are not commonly known or believed, you must properly acknowledge the source of your information. You must document the source of your information when you:

- Quote a source word for word
- Refer to information and ideas from another source that you present in your own words as either a paraphrase or a summary
- Cite statistics, tables, charts, or graphs

You do not need to document:

- Your own observations, experiences, and ideas
- Factual information available in a number of reference works (known as "common knowledge")
- Proverbs, sayings, and familiar quotations

A reference to the source of your borrowed information is called a *citation*. There are many systems for making citations, and your citations must consistently follow one of these systems. The documentation style recommended by the Modern Language Association (MLA) is commonly used in English and the humanities and is the style used for student papers throughout this book. Another common system is American Psychological Association (APA) style, which is used in the social sciences. In general, your instructor will tell you which system to use. For more information on documentation styles, consult the appropriate manual or handbook. For MLA style, consult the *MLA Handbook*, 8th ed. (MLA, 2016).

There are two components of documentation in a research paper: the *in-text citation*, placed in the body of your paper, and the *list of works cited*, which provides complete publication data on your sources and is placed at the end of your paper.

IN-TEXT CITATIONS

Most in-text citations, also known as parenthetical citations, consist of only the author's last name and a page reference. Usually, the author's name is given in an introductory or signal phrase at the beginning of the borrowed material, and the page reference is given in parentheses at the end (see Chapter 14, "Integrating Borrowed Material into Your Text," on pages 503–4). If the author's name is not given at the beginning, it belongs in the parentheses along with the page reference. The parenthetical reference signals the end of the borrowed material and directs your readers to the list of works cited should they want to pursue a source.

Consider the following examples of in-text citations from a student paper on the debate over whether to make English America's official language.

In-Text Citations (MLA Style)

Diaz 4

Many people are surprised to discover that English is not the official language of the United States. Today, even as English literacy becomes a necessity for people in many parts of the world, some people in the United States believe its primacy is being threatened right at home. Much of the current controversy focuses on Hispanic communities with large Spanish-speaking populations who may feel little or no pressure to learn English. Columnist and cultural critic Charles Krauthammer believes English should be America's official language. He notes that this country has been "blessed . . . with a linguistic unity that brings a critically needed cohesion to a nation as diverse, multiracial and multiethnic as America" and that communities such as these threaten the bond created by a common language (112). There are others, however, who think that "language does not threaten American unity. Benign neglect is a good policy for any country when it comes to language, and it's a good policy for America" (King 64).

Citation with pronoun in the signal phrase referring to author's name

Citation with author's name in parentheses

Diaz 5

Works Cited

King, Robert D. "Should English Be the Law?" *Atlantic Monthly*, Apr. 1997, pp. 55–64.

Krauthammer, Charles. "In Plain English: Let's Make It Official." *Time*, 12 June 2006, p. 112.

In the preceding example, the student followed MLA guidelines for documentation. The following sections provide MLA guidelines for documenting a variety of common sources. For advice on documenting additional, less frequently cited sources, consult the *MLA Handbook*, 8th ed. (MLA, 2016).

LIST OF WORKS CITED

In this section, you will find general guidelines for creating a list of works cited, followed by sample entries designed to cover the citations you will use most often.

Guidelines for Constructing Your Works-Cited Page

1. Begin the list on a new page following the last page of text.

2. Center the title *Works Cited* at the top of the page (without italics).

3. Double-space both within and between entries on your list.

4. Alphabetize your sources by the authors' last names. If you have two or more authors with the same last name, alphabetize by first names.

5. If you have two or more works by the same author, alphabetize by the first word of the titles, not counting *A*, *An*, or *The*. Use the author's name in the first entry and three unspaced hyphens followed by a period in subsequent entries:

   Twitchell, James B. *Branded Nation: The Marketing of Megachurch, College Inc., and Museumworld*. Simon & Schuster, 2005.

   ---. "The Branding of Higher Ed." *Forbes*, 25 Nov. 2002, p. 50.

   ---. *Look Away, Dixieland: A Carpetbagger's Great-Grandson Travels Highway 84*. Louisiana State UP, 2011.

6. If no author is known, alphabetize by title.

7. Begin each entry at the left margin. If the entry is longer than one line, indent the second and subsequent lines one-half inch (a hanging indent).

8. Italicize the titles of books, journals, magazines, and newspapers. Use quotation marks for titles of periodical articles, chapters and essays within books, short stories, and poems.

▶ Periodical Print Publications: Journals, Magazines, and Newspapers

Scholarly Journal Article

For all scholarly journals—whether paginated continuously throughout a given year or not—provide the volume number (if one is given), the issue number, the year, and the page numbers, separated by commas.

Ercolino, Stefano. "The Maximalist Novel." *Comparative Literature*, vol. 64, no. 3, Summer 2012, p. 56.

Newspaper Article

Bellafante, Ginia. "When the Law Says a Parent Isn't a Parent." *New York Times*, 3 Feb. 2013, natl. ed., p. 27.

Standard Information for Periodical Print Publications

1. Name of the author of the work; for anonymous works, begin entry with the title of the work
2. Title of the work, in quotation marks
3. Name of the periodical, italicized
4. Series number or name, if relevant
5. Volume number (for scholarly journals that use volume numbers)
6. Issue number (if available, for scholarly journals)
7. Date of publication (for scholarly journals, year; for other periodicals, day, month, and year, as available)
8. Page numbers

Magazine Article

When citing a weekly or biweekly magazine, give the complete date (day, month, year).

> Hennigan, W. J. "Nuclear Poker." *Time*, 12 Feb. 2018, pp. 20–25.

When citing a magazine published every month or every two months, provide the month or months and year.

> Kunzig, Robert. "The Will to Change." *National Geographic*, Nov. 2015, pp. 32–63.

If an article in a magazine is not printed on consecutive pages—for example, an article might begin on page 45, then skip to 48—include only the first page followed by a plus sign.

> Mascarelli, Amanda Leigh. "Fall Guys." *Audubon*, Nov.-Dec. 2009, pp. 44+.

Review (Film or Book)

> Lane, Anthony. "Imaginary Kingdoms." Review of *Black Panther*, directed by Ryan Coogler, and *Early Man*, directed by Nick Park. *The New Yorker*, 26 Feb. 2018, pp. 60–62.

> Walton, James. "Noble, Embattled Souls." Review of *The Bone Clocks* and *Slade House*, by David Mitchell. *The New York Review of Books*, 3 Dec. 2015, pp. 55–58.

If the review has no title, simply begin with *Review* after the author's name. If there is neither a title nor an author, begin with *Review* and alphabetize by the title of the book or film being reviewed.

Anonymous Article

When no author's name is given, begin the entry with the title.

> "Pompeii: Will the City Go from Dust to Dust?" *Newsweek*, 1 Sept. 1997, p. 8.

Editorial (Unsigned/Signed)

"Policing Ohio's Online Courses." *Plain Dealer* [Cleveland], 9 Oct. 2012, p. A5. Editorial.

Stengel, Richard. "In Drones We Trust." *Time*, 11 Feb. 2013, p. 2. Editorial.

Letter to the Editor

Lyon, Ruth Henriquez. "A Word to the Editor." *Audubon*, Jan.-Feb. 2013, p. 10. Letter.

▶ Nonperiodical Print Publications: Books, Brochures, and Pamphlets

Standard Information for Nonperiodical Print Publications

1. Name of the author, editor, compiler, or translator of the work; for anonymous works, begin entry with the title

2. Title of the work, italicized

3. Edition

4. Volume number

5. Name of the publisher and year of publication

Book by a Single Author

Desmond, Matthew. *Evicted*. Crown Books, 2016.

When writing the publisher's name, omit business words such as *Co.* or *Company*, but do include shortened versions for university presses (e.g., *Cambridge UP* for Cambridge University Press).

Anthology

Marcus, Ben, editor. *New American Stories*. Vintage Books, 2015.

Book by Two or More Authors

For a book by two authors, list the authors in the order in which they appear on the title page.

O'Reilly, Bill, and Martin Dugard. *Killing England*. Henry Holt, 2017.

For a book by three or more authors, list the first author in the same way as for a single-author book, followed by a comma and the abbreviation *et al.* ("and others").

Cunningham, Stewart, et al. *Media Economics*. Palgrave Macmillan, 2015.

Book by Corporate Author

Human Rights Watch. *World Report of 2015: Events of 2014*. Seven Stories Press, 2015.

Work in Anthology

Include the page numbers of the selection after the anthology's year of publication.

> Sayrafiezadeh, Saïd. "Paranoia." *New American Stories*, edited by Ben Marcus, Vintage Books, 2015, pp. 3–29.

Article in Reference Book

> Anagnost, George T. "Sandra Day O'Connor." *The Oxford Companion to the Supreme Court of the United States*, 2nd ed., 2005.

If an article is unsigned, begin with the title.

> "Ball's in Your Court, The." *The American Heritage Dictionary of Idioms*. 2nd ed., Houghton Mifflin Harcourt, 2013.

Note that widely used reference works do not require a publisher's name. Also note that page numbers are not necessary if entries in a reference work are arranged alphabetically.

Introduction, Preface, Foreword, or Afterword to Book

> Sullivan, John Jeremiah. "The Ill-Defined Plot." Introduction. *The Best American Essays 2014*, edited by John J. Sullivan and Robert Atwan, Houghton Mifflin Harcourt, 2014, pp. xvii–xxvi.

Translation

> Ullmann, Regina. *The Country Road: Stories*. Translated by Kurt Beals, New Directions Publishing, 2015.

Illustrated Book or Graphic Novel

> Moore, Alan. *V for Vendetta*. Illustrated by David Lloyd, DC Comics, 2008.

Book Published in Second or Subsequent Edition

> Eagleton, Terry. *Literary Theory: An Introduction*. 3rd ed., U of Minnesota P, 2008.

Brochure or Pamphlet

> *The Legendary Sleepy Hollow Cemetery*. Friends of Sleepy Hollow Cemetery, 2008.

Government Publication

> Canada, Minister of Aboriginal Affairs and Northern Development. *2015–16 Report on Plans and Priorities*. Minister of Public Works and Government Services Canada, 2015.

Treat the government agency as the author, giving the name of the government followed by the name of the department and agency.

▶ Web Publications

Standard Information for Web Publications
1. Name of the author, editor, or compiler of the work (For works with more than one author, a corporate author, or an unnamed author, apply the guidelines for print sources; for anonymous works, begin entry with the title.)
2. Title of the work, italicized, unless it is part of a larger work, in which case put it in quotation marks
3. Title of the overall Web site, italicized (if distinct from the title)
4. Publisher or sponsor of the site
5. Date of publication (day, month, and year)
6. Location (online database, DOI, URL)
7. Date of access (day, month, and year), only if the date of publication is not listed

Although MLA does not absolutely require URLs in works-cited entries, it does recommend that you include URLs in your works-cited list. Even though URLs can become obsolete in a matter of months and can give a cluttered feel to your works-cited list, they are useful in the short run because they help readers locate your source quickly, especially if your paper is in digital format and the URLs are clickable. Some publishers assign a digital object identifier — a DOI — to each online publication. Because a DOI remains with an article even when a URL changes, you should cite a DOI instead of a URL whenever possible. Insert the DOI or the URL as the last item in an entry, immediately after the date of publication. The DOI or URL is followed by a period. The following example illustrates an entry with the DOI included:

> Young, Michelle D., and Frank Perrone. "How Are Standards Used, by Whom, and to What End?" *Journal of Research on Leadership Education*, vol. 11, no. 1, 2016, doi:10.1177/1942775116647511.

If you're using a URL, do *not* include *http://*. If a DOI or URL extends over more than one line, break the DOI or URL after a slash and before any other punctuation, such as a hyphen or period. Do *not* add spaces, hyphens, or any other punctuation to indicate the break.

Online Scholarly Journals.   To cite an article, a review, an editorial, or a letter to the editor in a scholarly journal existing only in electronic form on the Web, provide the author, the title of the article, the title of the journal, the volume and issue, and the date of issue, followed by the page numbers (if available), and the DOI or URL.

Article in Online Scholarly Journal

Bryson, Devin. "The Rise of a New Senegalese Cultural Philosophy?" *African Studies Quarterly*, vol. 14, no. 3, Mar. 2014, pp. 33–56, asq.africa.ufl.edu/files/ Volume-14-Issue-3-Bryson.pdf.

Periodical Publications in Online Databases

Journal Article from Online Database or Subscription Service

Spychalski, John C. Review of *American Railroads — Decline and Renaissance in the Twentieth Century*, by Robert E. Gallamore and John R. Meyer. *Transportation Journal*, vol. 54, no. 4, Fall 2015, pp. 535–38. *JSTOR*, doi:10.5325/transportationj.54.4.0535.

Magazine Article from Online Database or Subscription Service

Rosenbaum, Ron. "The Last Renaissance Man." *Smithsonian*, Nov. 2012, pp. 39–44. *OmniFile Full Text Select*, web.b.ebscohost.com.ezproxy.bpl.org/.

Newspaper Article from Online Database or Subscription Service

"The Road toward Peace." *The New York Times*, 15 Feb. 1945, p. 18. Editorial. *ProQuest Historical Newspapers: The New York Times*, search.proquest.com/ hnpnewyorktimes.

Nonperiodical Web Publications. This category of Web publication includes all Web-delivered content that does not fit into one of the previous two categories (online scholarly journal publications and periodical publications from an online database).

Online Magazine Article

Swenson, Haley. "Chasing the Loneliness Epidemic Won't Cure What Ails Us." *Slate*, 22 Feb. 2018, slate.com/human-interest/2018/02/chasing-the -loneliness-epidemic-wont-cure-what-ails-us.html.

Online Newspaper Article

Crowell, Maddy. "How Computers Are Getting Better at Detecting Liars." *The Christian Science Monitor*, 12 Dec. 2015, www.csmonitor.com/Science/ Science-Notebook/2015/1212/How-computers-are-getting-better-at -detecting-liars.

Humphrey, Tom. "Politics Outweigh Arguments about School Vouchers." *Knoxville News Sentinel*, 24 Jan. 2016, www.knoxnews.com/opinion/ columnists/tom-humphrey/tom-humphrey-politics-outweigh -arguments-about-school-vouchers-29c77b33-9963-0ef8-e053 -0100007fcba4-366300461.html.

Book or Part of Book Accessed Online

For a book available online, provide the author, the title, the editor (if any), original publication information, the name of the database or Web site, and the URL.

> Piketty, Thomas. *Capital in the Twenty-First Century*. Translated by Arthur
>   Goldhammer, Harvard UP, 2014. *Google Books*, books.google.com/
>   books?isbn=0674369556.

If you are citing only part of an online book, include the title or name of the part directly after the author's name.

> Woolf, Virginia. "Kew Gardens." *Monday or Tuesday*, Harcourt, 1921. *Bartleby.com:*
>   *Great Books Online*, www.bartleby.com/85/7.html.

Online Speech, Essay, Poem, or Short Story

> Milton, John. *Paradise Lost: Book I. Poetry Foundation*, 2014, www.poetryfoundation
>   .org/poem/174987.

Online Encyclopedia or Other Reference Work

> Hall, Mark. "Facebook (American Company)." *The Enyclopaedia Britannica*, 2 Jul.
>   2014, www.britannica.com/topic/Facebook.
> "House Music." *Wikipedia*, 19 Feb. 2018, en.wikipedia.org/wiki/House_music.

Online Artwork, Photograph, Map, Chart, and Other Images

> van Agtmael, Peter. *Ms. Armed Forces*. 2017, Magnum Photos, pro.magnumphotos
>   .com/C.aspx?VP3=SearchResult&ALID=2K1HRGKY5MQG.

Online Government Publication

> United States, Department of Agriculture, Food and Nutrition Service, Child
>   Nutrition Programs. *Eligibility Manual for School Meals: Determining and Veri-*
>   *fying Eligibility. National School Lunch Program*, July 2015, www.fns.usda.gov/
>   sites/default/files/cn/SP40_CACFP18_SFSP20-2015a1.pdf.

Blog Posting

> Kiuchi, Tatsuro. *Tatsuro Kiuchi: News & Blog*, tatsurokiuchi.com. Accessed 3 Mar.
>   2016.

Online Video Recording

> Nayar, Vineet. "Employees First, Customers Second." *YouTube*, 9 Jun. 2015,
>   www.youtube.com/watch?v=cCdu67s_C5E.

▶ Additional Common Sources

Television or Radio Broadcast

> "Federal Role in Support of Autism." *Washington Journal*, narrated by Robb
>   Harleston, C-SPAN, 1 Dec. 2012.

Sound Recording

Bizet, Georges. *Carmen*. Performances by Jennifer Larmore, Thomas Moser, Angela Gheorghiu, and Samuel Ramey, Bavarian State Orchestra and Chorus, conducted by Giuseppe Sinopoli, Warner, 1996.

Film or Video Recording

Scott, Ridley, director. *The Martian*. Performances by Matt Damon, Jessica Chastain, Kristen Wiig, and Kate Mara, Twentieth Century Fox, 2015.

Work of Visual Art

Bradford, Mark. *Let's Walk to the Middle of the Ocean*. 2015, Museum of Modern Art, New York.

If you use a reproduction of a piece of visual art, give the institution and city (if available) as well as the complete publication information for the source.

O'Keeffe, Georgia. *Black and Purple Petunias*. 1925, private collection. *Two Lives: A Conversation in Paintings and Photographs*, edited by Alexandra Arrowsmith and Thomas West, HarperCollins, 1992, p. 67.

Interview

Weddington, Sarah. "Sarah Weddington: Still Arguing for *Roe*." Interview by Michele Kort, *Ms.*, Winter 2013, pp. 32–35.

For interviews that you conduct, provide the name of the person interviewed, the type of interview (personal, telephone, e-mail), and the date.

Proulx, E. Annie. Telephone interview. 27 Jan. 2017.

Cartoon or Comic Strip

Zyglis, Adam. "City of Light." *Buffalo News*, 8 Nov. 2015, adamzyglis.buffalonews .com/2015/11/08/city-of-light/. Cartoon.

Advertisement

Rolex, *Esquire*, Mar. 2018, pp. 10–11. Advertisement.

Lecture, Speech, Address, or Reading

Smith, Anna Deavere. "On the Road: A Search for American Character." National Endowment for the Humanities, John F. Kennedy Center for the Performing Arts, Washington, 6 Apr. 2015. Address.

Letter, Memo, or E-Mail Message

Thornbrugh, Caitlin. "Coates Lecture." Received by Rita Anderson, 20 Oct. 2015.

Matthew Taylor/Alamy

Editing for Grammar, Punctuation, and Sentence Style

ONCE YOU HAVE REVISED YOUR ESSAY AND YOU ARE CONFIDENT THAT you have said what you wanted to say, you are ready to begin editing your essay. During the editing stage of the writing process, you identify and correct errors in grammar, punctuation, and sentence style. You don't want a series of small errors to detract from your paper: Such errors can cause confusion in some cases, and they can also cause readers to have second thoughts about your credibility as an author.

This chapter addresses twelve common writing problems that instructors from around the country told us trouble their students most. For more guidance with these or other editing concerns, be sure to refer to a writer's handbook or ask your instructor for help.

RUN-ONS: FUSED SENTENCES AND COMMA SPLICES

Writers can become so absorbed in getting their ideas down on paper that they sometimes incorrectly combine two independent clauses—word groups that could stand on their own as complete sentences—creating a *run-on sentence.* A run-on sentence fails to show where one thought ends and another begins, and it can confuse readers. There are two types of run-on sentences: the fused sentence and the comma splice.

A *fused sentence* occurs when a writer joins two independent clauses with no punctuation and no coordinating conjunction.

> **fused sentence** The delegates at the state political convention could not decide on a leader they were beginning to show their frustration.

A *comma splice* occurs when a writer uses only a comma to join two or more independent clauses.

> **comma splice** The delegates at the state political convention could not decide on a leader, they were beginning to show their frustration.

There are five ways to fix run-on sentences.

1. **Create two separate sentences with a period.**

> **edited** The delegates at the state political convention could not decide on a leader ~~they~~ `. They` were beginning to show their frustration.

2. **Use a comma and a coordinating conjunction to join the two sentences.**

> **edited** The delegates at the state political convention could not decide on a leader `, and` they were beginning to show their frustration.

3. **Use a semicolon to separate the two clauses.**

> **edited** The delegates at the state political convention could not decide on a leader `;` they were beginning to show their frustration.

4. **Use a semicolon followed by a transitional word or expression and a comma to join the two clauses.**

> **edited** The delegates at the state political convention could not decide on a leader `; consequently,` they were beginning to show their frustration.

5. **Subordinate one clause to the other, using a subordinate conjunction or a relative pronoun.**

> **edited** `When the` ~~The~~ delegates at the state political convention could not decide on a leader, they were beginning to show their frustration.

> **edited** The delegates at the state political convention could not decide on a leader `, who were beginning to show their frustration,` ~~they were beginning to show their frustration.~~

SENTENCE FRAGMENTS

A *sentence fragment* is a part of a sentence presented as if it were a complete sentence. Even if a word group begins with a capital letter and ends with a period, a question mark, or an exclamation point, it is not a sentence unless it has a subject (the person, place, or thing the sentence is about) and a verb (a word that tells what the subject does) and expresses a complete thought.

> **sentence fragment** My music group decided to study the early works of Mozart. *The child prodigy from Austria.*

Word groups that do not express complete thoughts are often freestanding subordinate clauses beginning with a subordinating conjunction such as *although*, *because*, *since*, *so*, *that*, or *unless*.

> **sentence fragment** The company president met with the management team every single week. *So that problems were rarely ignored.*

You can correct sentence fragments in one of two ways.

1. **Integrate the fragment into a nearby sentence.**

   > **edited** My music group decided to study the early works of Mozart, ~~The~~ **, the** child prodigy from Austria.

   > **edited** The company president met with the management team every single week, ~~So~~ **so** that problems were rarely ignored.

2. **Develop the fragment into a complete sentence by adding a subject or a verb.**

   > **edited** My music group decided to study the early works of Mozart. The child prodigy **was** from Austria.

   > **edited** The company president met with the management team every single week. ~~So that problems~~ **Problems** were rarely ignored.

Sentence fragments are not always incorrect. In fact, if used deliberately, a sentence fragment can add useful stylistic emphasis. In narratives, deliberate sentence fragments are most commonly used in dialogue and in descriptive passages that set a mood or tone. In the following passage taken from "Not Close Enough for Comfort," David P. Bardeen uses fragments to convey the awkwardness of the lunch meeting he had with his brother Will:

> I asked him about his recent trip. He asked me about work. Short questions. One-word answers. Then an awkward pause.

COMMA FAULTS

Commas help communicate meaning by eliminating possible misreadings. Consider this sentence:

> After visiting William Alan Lee went to French class.

Depending upon where you put the comma, it could be Lee, Alan Lee, or William Alan Lee who goes to French class.

> **edited**   After visiting William Alan, Lee went to French class.

> **edited**   After visiting William, Alan Lee went to French class.

> **edited**   After visiting, William Alan Lee went to French class.

The comma, of all the marks of punctuation, has the greatest variety of uses, which can make its proper use seem difficult. It might help to think of the comma's role this way: In every case, the comma functions in one of two basic ways—to *separate* or to *enclose* elements in a sentence. By learning a few basic rules based on these two functions, you will be able to identify and correct common comma errors.

1. **Use a comma to separate two independent clauses joined by a coordinating conjunction.**

> **incorrect**   Tolstoy wrote many popular short stories but he is perhaps best known for his novels.

> **edited**   Tolstoy wrote many popular short stories, but he is perhaps best known for his novels.

2. **Use a comma to separate an introductory phrase or clause from the main clause of a sentence.**

> **incorrect**   In his book *Life on the Mississippi* Mark Twain describes his days as a riverboat pilot.

> **edited**   In his book *Life on the Mississippi,* Mark Twain describes his days as a riverboat pilot.

> **incorrect**   When the former Soviet Union collapsed residents of Moscow had to struggle just to survive.

> **edited**   When the former Soviet Union collapsed, residents of Moscow had to struggle just to survive.

3. **Use commas to enclose nonrestrictive elements.**   When an adjective phrase or clause adds information that is essential to the meaning of a sentence, it is said to be *restrictive* and should not be set off with commas.

The woman wearing the beige linen suit works with Homeland Security.

The adjective phrase "wearing the beige linen suit" is essential and thus should not be set off with commas; without this information, we have no way of identifying which woman works with Homeland Security.

When an adjective phrase or clause does not add information that is essential to the meaning of the sentence, it is said to be *nonrestrictive* and should be enclosed with commas.

incorrect   Utopian literature which was popular during the late nineteenth century seems to emerge at times of economic and political unrest.

edited   Utopian literature,which was popular during the late nineteenth century,seems to emerge at times of economic and political unrest.

4. **Use commas to separate items in a series.**

incorrect   The three staples of the diet in Thailand are rice fish and fruit.

edited   The three staples of the diet in Thailand are rice,fish,and fruit.

SUBJECT-VERB AGREEMENT

Subjects and verbs must agree in number—that is, a singular subject (one person, place, or thing) must take a singular verb, and a plural subject (more than one person, place, or thing) must take a plural verb. While most native speakers of English use proper subject-verb agreement in their writing without thinking about it, some sentence constructions can be troublesome to native and nonnative speakers alike.

Intervening Prepositional Phrases

When the relationship between the subject and the verb in a sentence is not clear, the culprit is usually an intervening prepositional phrase (a phrase that begins with a preposition such as *on*, *of*, *in*, *at*, or *between*). To make sure the subject agrees with its verb in a sentence with an intervening prepositional phrase, mentally cross out the phrase (*of the term* in the following example) to isolate the subject and the verb and determine if they agree.

incorrect   The first one hundred days of the term has passed quickly.

                                                    have
edited   The first one hundred days of the term ~~has~~ passed quickly.

Compound Subjects

Writers often have difficulty with subject-verb agreement in sentences with compound subjects (two or more subjects joined together with the word *and*). As a general rule, compound subjects take plural verbs.

incorrect   My iPhone, computer, and television was stolen.

                                            were
edited   My iPhone, computer, and television ~~was~~ stolen.

However, in sentences with subjects joined by *either . . . or, neither . . . nor,* or *not only . . . but also,* the verb must agree with the subject closest to it.

> **incorrect** Neither the students nor the professor are satisfied with the lab equipment.
>
> **edited** Neither the students nor the professor a̶r̶e̶ ^is^ satisfied with the lab equipment.

UNCLEAR PRONOUN REFERENCES

The noun to which a pronoun refers is called its *antecedent* or *referent*. Be sure to place a pronoun as close to its antecedent as possible so that the relationship between them is clear. The more words that intervene between the antecedent and the pronoun, the more chance there is for confusion. When the relationship between a pronoun and its antecedent is unclear, the sentence becomes inaccurate or ambiguous. While editing your writing, look for and correct ambiguous, vague, or implied pronoun references.

Ambiguous References

Make sure all your pronouns clearly refer to specific antecedents. If a pronoun can refer to more than one antecedent, the sentence is ambiguous.

> **ambiguous** Adler sought to convince the reader to mark up *his* book.

In this sentence, the antecedent of the pronoun *his* could be either *Adler* or *reader.* Does Adler want his particular book marked up, or does he want the reader to mark up his or her own book? To make an ambiguous antecedent clear, either repeat the correct antecedent or rewrite the sentence.

> **edited** Adler sought to convince the reader to mark up h̶i̶s̶ ^Adler's^ book.
>
> **edited** Adler sought to convince the reader to mark up h̶i̶s̶ ^his or her^ book.

Vague References

Whenever you use *it, they, you, this, that,* or *which* to refer to a general idea in a preceding clause or sentence, be sure that the connection between the pronoun and the general idea is clear. When these pronouns lack a specific antecedent, you give readers an impression of vagueness and carelessness. To correct the problem, either substitute a noun for the pronoun or provide an antecedent to which the pronoun can clearly refer.

vague   The tornadoes damaged many of the homes in the area, but it has not yet been determined.

                                                          the extent of the damage
edited   The tornadoes damaged many of the homes in the area, but ~~it~~ has not yet been determined.

vague   In the book, they wrote that Samantha had an addictive personality.

edited   In the book, ~~they wrote that~~ Samantha had an addictive personality.

Whenever the connection between the general idea and the pronoun is simple and clear, no confusion results. Consider the following example:

> The stock market rose for a third consecutive week, and this lifted most investors' spirits.

Implied References

Make every pronoun refer to a stated, not an implied, antecedent. Every time you use a pronoun in a sentence, you should be able to identify its noun equivalent. If you cannot, use a noun instead.

implied   After all of the editing and formatting, it was finished.

                                  the research report
edited   After all of the editing and formatting, ~~it~~ was finished.

Sometimes a modifier or possessive that implies a noun is mistaken for an antecedent.

implied   In G. Anthony Gorry's "Steal This MP3 File: What Is Theft?" he shows how technology might be shaping the attitudes of today's youth.

                                                          G. Anthony Gorry
edited   In ~~G. Anthony Gorry's~~ "Steal This MP3 File: What Is Theft?" he shows how technology might be shaping the attitudes of today's youth.

PRONOUN-ANTECEDENT AGREEMENT

Personal pronouns must agree with their antecedents in *person*, *number*, and *gender*.

Agreement in Person

Traditionally, there are three types of personal pronouns: first person (*I* and *we*), second person (*you*), and third person (*he, she, it,* and *they*). To agree in person, first-person pronouns must refer to first-person antecedents, second-person pronouns to second-person antecedents, and third-person pronouns to third-person antecedents.

> **incorrect** A scientist should consider all the data carefully before you draw a conclusion.
>
> **edited** A scientist should consider all the data carefully before ~~you draw~~ a conclusion. *he or she draws*

In today's society, where gender norms are changing, some individuals may identify by different third-person pronouns than *he* or *she*. As a conscientious writer, be sure to understand your audience when determining if and how to incorporate these pronouns.

Agreement in Number

To agree in number, a singular pronoun must refer to a singular antecedent, and a plural pronoun must refer to a plural antecedent. When two or more antecedents are joined by the word *and*, the pronoun must be plural.

> **incorrect** Karen, Rachel, and Sofia took her electives in history.
>
> **edited** Karen, Rachel, and Sofia took ~~her~~ electives in history. *their*

When the subject of a sentence is an indefinite pronoun such as *everyone, each, everybody, anyone, anybody, everything, either, one, neither, someone,* or *something,* use a singular pronoun to refer to it or recast the sentence to eliminate the agreement problem.

> **incorrect** Each of the women submitted their résumé.
>
> **edited** Each of the women submitted ~~their~~ résumé. *her*
>
> **edited** ~~Each~~ of the women submitted their ~~résumé~~. *Both* *résumés*

If a collective noun (*army, community, team, herd, committee, association*) is understood as a unit, it takes a singular pronoun; if it is understood in terms of its individual members, it takes a plural pronoun.

> **as a unit** The class presented its annual spring musical.
>
> **as individual members** The class agreed to pay for their own art supplies.

Agreement in Gender

Traditionally, a masculine, singular pronoun has been used for indefinite antecedents (such as *anyone, someone,* and *everyone*) and to refer to generic antecedents (such as *employee, student, athlete, secretary, doctor,* and *computer specialist*). But *anyone* can be female or male, and women are employees (or students, athletes, secretaries, doctors, and computer specialists), too. The use of masculine pronouns to refer to both females and males is considered sexist; that is, such usage leaves out women as a segment of society or diminishes their presence. Instead, use *he or she, his or her,* or, in an extended piece of writing, alternate in a balanced way the use of *he* and *she* throughout. In some contexts, using *they* for singular antecedents is also considered appropriate because it is less clunky than *he or she* or includes individuals who may identify by different or non-gendered pronouns. Sometimes the best solution is to rewrite the sentence to put it in the plural or to avoid the problem altogether.

sexist   If any student wants to attend the opening performance of *King Lear,* he will have to purchase a ticket by Wednesday.

edited   If any student wants to attend the opening performance of *King Lear,*
he or she
~~he~~ will have to purchase a ticket by Wednesday.

edited   students
If any ~~student~~ wants to attend the opening performance of *King Lear,*
they   tickets
~~he~~ will have to purchase ~~a ticket~~ by Wednesday.

edited   All tickets for
~~If any student wants to attend~~ the opening performance of *King Lear,*
must be purchased
~~he will have to purchase a ticket~~ by Wednesday.

DANGLING AND MISPLACED MODIFIERS

A *modifier* is a word or group of words that describes or gives additional information about other words in a sentence. The words, phrases, and clauses that function as modifiers in a sentence can usually be moved around freely, so place them carefully to avoid unintentionally confusing — or amusing — your reader. As a rule, place modifiers as close as possible to the words you want to modify. Two common problems arise with modifiers: the misplaced modifier and the dangling modifier.

Misplaced Modifiers

A *misplaced modifier* unintentionally modifies the wrong word in a sentence because it is placed incorrectly.

misplaced   The waiter brought a steak to the man covered with onions.

edited   covered with onions
The waiter brought a steak to the man ~~covered with onions~~.

Dangling Modifiers

A *dangling modifier* usually appears at the beginning of a sentence and does not logically relate to the main clause of the sentence. The dangling modifier wants to modify a word—often an unstated subject—that does not appear in the sentence. To eliminate a dangling modifier, give the dangling phrase a subject.

> **dangling** Staring into the distance, large rain clouds form.
>
> **edited** Staring into the distance, ^Jon saw^ large rain clouds form.
>
> **dangling** Walking on the ceiling, he noticed a beautiful luna moth.
>
> **edited** ~~Walking on the ceiling, he~~ ^He^ noticed a beautiful luna moth ^walking on the ceiling^.

FAULTY PARALLELISM

Parallelism is the repetition of word order or grammatical form either within a single sentence or in several sentences that develop the same central idea. As a rhetorical device, parallel structure can aid coherence and add emphasis. Franklin Roosevelt's famous Depression-era statement "I see one-third of a nation *ill-housed*, *ill-clad*, and *ill-nourished*" illustrates effective parallelism. Use parallel grammatical structures to emphasize the similarities and differences between the items being compared. Look for opportunities to use parallel constructions with paired items or items in a series, paired items using correlative conjunctions, and comparisons using *than* or *as*.

Paired Items or Items in a Series

Parallel structures can be used to balance a word with a word, a phrase with a phrase, or a clause with a clause whenever you use paired items or items in a series—as in the Roosevelt example above.

1. **Balance a word with a word.**

   > **faulty** Like the hunter, the photographer has to understand the animal's patterns, characteristics, and where it lives.
   >
   > **edited** Like the hunter, the photographer has to understand the animal's patterns, characteristics, and ^habitat^ ~~where it lives~~.

2. **Balance a phrase with a phrase.**

faulty   The hunter carries a handgun and two rifles, different kinds of ammunition, and a variety of sights and telescopes to increase his chances of success.

several types of guns

edited   The hunter carries ~~a handgun and two rifles~~, different kinds of ammunition, and a variety of sights and telescopes to increase his chances of success.

3. **Balance a clause with a clause.**

faulty   Shooting is highly aggressive, but photography is passive; shooting eliminates forever, but photography preserves.

edited   Shooting is ~~highly~~ aggressive, but photography is passive; shooting eliminates ~~forever~~, but photography preserves.

Paired Items Using Correlative Conjunctions

When linking paired items with a correlative conjunction (*either/or*, *neither/ nor*, *not only/but also*, *both/and*, *whether/or*) in a sentence, make sure that the elements being connected are parallel in form. Delete any unnecessary or repeated words.

incorrect   The lecture was both enjoyable and it was a form of education.

educational

edited   The lecture was both enjoyable and ~~it was a form of education~~.

Comparisons Using *Than* or *As*

Make sure that the elements of the comparison are parallel in form. Delete any unnecessary or repeated words.

incorrect   It would be better to study now than waiting until the night before the exam.

to wait

edited   It would be better to study now than ~~waiting~~ until the night before the exam.

WEAK NOUNS AND VERBS

The essence of a sentence is its subject and its verb. The subject—usually a noun or pronoun—identifies who or what the sentence is about, and the verb captures the subject's action or state of being. Sentences often lose their vitality and liveliness when the subject and the verb are lost in weak language or buried.

Specific Nouns

Always opt for specific nouns when you can; they make your writing more visual. While general words like *people*, *animal*, or *dessert* name groups or classes of objects, qualities, or actions, specific words like *Samantha*, *camel*, and *pecan pie* appeal to readers more because they name individual objects, qualities, or actions within a group. Think about it—don't you prefer reading about specifics rather than generalities?

> **weak noun** The flowers stretched toward the bright light of the sun.
>
>   tulips
> **edited** The ~~flowers~~ stretched toward the bright light of the sun.

Strong Verbs

Strong verbs energize your writing by giving it a sense of action. Verbs like *gallop*, *scramble*, *snicker*, *tweak*, *fling*, *exhaust*, *smash*, *tear*, *smear*, *wrangle*, and *flog* provide readers with a vivid picture of specific actions. As you reread what you have written, be on the lookout for weak verbs like *is*, *are*, *have*, *deal with*, *make*, *give*, *do*, *use*, *get*, *add*, *become*, *go*, *appear*, and *seem*. When you encounter one of these verbs or others like them, seize the opportunity to substitute a strong action verb for a weak one.

> **weak verb** Local Boys and Girls Clubs in America assist in the promotion of self-esteem, individual achievement, and teamwork.
>
>   promote
> **edited** Local Boys and Girls Clubs in America ~~assist in the promotion of~~ self-esteem, individual achievement, and teamwork.

While editing your essay, look for opportunities to replace weak nouns and verbs with strong nouns and action verbs. The more specific and strong you make your nouns and verbs, the more lively, descriptive, and concise your writing will be.

When you have difficulty thinking of strong, specific nouns and verbs, reach for a dictionary or a thesaurus—but only if you are sure you can discern the best word for your purpose. Thesauruses are available free online and in inexpensive paperback editions; most word processing programs include a thesaurus as well.

SHIFTS IN VERB TENSE, MOOD, AND VOICE

Shifts in Tense

A verb's tense indicates when an action takes place—sometime in the past, right now, or in the future. Using verb tense correctly helps your readers understand time changes in your writing. Shifts in tense—using different verb tenses within a sentence without a logical reason—confuse readers. Unnecessary shifts in verb tense are especially noticeable in narration and process analysis writing, which are sequence and time oriented. Generally, you should write in the present or past tense and maintain that tense throughout your sentence.

> **incorrect** The painter studied the scene and pulls a fan brush decisively from her cup.
>
> **edited** The painter studied the scene and ~~pulls~~ pulled a fan brush decisively from her cup.

Shifts in Mood

Verbs in English have three moods: *indicative*, *imperative*, and *subjunctive*. Problems with inconsistency usually occur with the imperative mood.

> **incorrect** In learning a second language, arm yourself with basic vocabulary, and it is also important to practice speaking aloud daily.
>
> **edited** In learning a second language, arm yourself with basic vocabulary and ~~it is also important to~~ practice speaking aloud daily.

Shifts in Voice

Shifts in voice—from active voice to passive voice—usually go hand in hand with inconsistencies in the subject of a sentence.

> **incorrect** The archeologists could see the effects of vandalism as the Mayan tomb was entered.
>
> **edited** The archeologists could see the effects of vandalism as they entered the Mayan tomb ~~was entered~~.

WORDINESS

Wordiness occurs in a sentence that contains words that do not contribute to the sentence's meaning. Wordiness can be eliminated by (1) using the active voice, (2) avoiding "there is" and "it is," (3) eliminating redundancies, (4) deleting empty words and phrases, and (5) simplifying inflated expressions.

1. **Use the active voice rather than the passive voice.** The active voice emphasizes the doer of an action rather than the receiver of an action. Not only is the active voice more concise than the passive voice, it is a much more vigorous form of expression.

   passive   *The inhabitants of Londonderry were overwhelmed* by the burgeoning rodent population.

   active   *The burgeoning rodent population overwhelmed* the inhabitants of Londonderry.

In the active sentence, *The burgeoning rodent population* is made the subject of the sentence and is moved to the beginning of the sentence—a position of importance—while the verb *overwhelmed* is made an active verb.

2. **Avoid "There is" and "It is."** "There is" and "It is" are expletives—words or phrases that do not contribute any meaning but are added only to fill out a sentence. They may be necessary with references to time and weather, but they should be avoided in other circumstances.

   wordy   There were many acts of heroism following the earthquake.

   edited   ~~There were~~ Many acts of heroism ~~following~~ followed the earthquake.

Notice how the edited sentence eliminates the expletive and reveals a specific subject—*acts*—and an action verb—*followed.*

3. **Eliminate redundancies.** Unnecessary repetition often creeps into our writing and should be eliminated. For example, how often have you written expressions such as *large in size, completely filled, academic scholar,* or *I thought in my mind*? Edit such expressions by deleting the unnecessary words or using synonyms.

   Sometimes our intent is to add emphasis, but the net effect is extra words that contribute little or nothing to a sentence's meaning.

   redundant   A big huge cloud was advancing on the crowded stadium.

   edited   A ~~big~~ huge cloud was advancing on the crowded stadium.

   redundant   After studying all night, he knew the basic and fundamental principles of geometry.

> **edited** After studying all night, he knew the basic ~~and fundamental~~ principles of geometry.

4. **Delete empty words and phrases.**   Look for words and phrases we use every day that carry no meaning—words that should be eliminated from your writing during the editing process.

> **empty** One commentator believes that America is for all intents and purposes a materialistic society.

> **edited** One commentator believes that America is ~~for all intents and purposes~~ a materialistic society.

Following are examples of some other words and expressions that most often can be eliminated.

basically	I think/I feel/I believe	really	truly
essentially	it seems to me	severely	very
extremely	kind of/sort of	surely	
generally	quite	tend to	

5. **Simplify inflated expressions.**   Sometimes we use expressions we think sound authoritative in hopes of seeming knowledgeable. We write *at this point in time* (instead of *now*) or *in the event that* (instead of *if*). However, it is best to write directly and forcefully and to use clear language. Edit inflated or pompous language to its core meaning.

> **inflated** The law office hired two people who have a complete knowledge of environmental policy.

> **edited** The law office hired two people who ~~have a complete knowledge of~~ *are experts.* environmental policy.

> **inflated** The president was late on account of the fact that her helicopter would not start.

> **edited** The president was late ~~on account of the fact that~~ *because* her helicopter would not start.

SENTENCE VARIETY

While editing your essays, you can add interest and readability to your writing with more sentence variety. You should, however, seek variety in sentence structure not as an end in itself but as a more accurate means of reflecting your thoughts and giving emphasis where emphasis is needed. Look for opportunities to achieve sentence variety by combining short choppy sentences, varying sentence openings, and reducing the number of compound sentences.

Short Choppy Sentences

To make your writing more interesting, use one of the following four methods to combine short choppy sentences into one longer sentence.

1. **Use subordinating and coordinating conjunctions to relate and connect ideas.** The coordinating conjunctions *and, but, or, nor, for, so,* and *yet* can be used to connect two or more simple sentences. A subordinating conjunction, on the other hand, introduces a subordinate clause and connects it to a main clause. Common subordinating conjunctions include:

after	before	so	when
although	even if	than	where
as	if	that	whereas
as if	in order that	though	wherever
as though	rather than	unless	whether
because	since	until	while

short and choppy   Short words are as good as long ones. Short, old words—like *sun* and *grass* and *home*—are best of all.

combined   Short words are as good as long ones ~~short,~~ old words—like *sun* and grass and *home*—are best of all.
           , and short,

                                                                    —RICHARD LEDERER,
                                                      "The Case for Short Words"

2. **Use modifiers effectively.** Instead of writing a separate descriptive sentence, combine an adjective modifier to convey a more graphic picture in a single sentence.

short and choppy   The people who breed German shepherds in Appleton, Wisconsin, are also farmers. And they are wonderful farmers.

combined   The people who breed German shepherds in Appleton, Wisconsin, are
           wonderful
also farmers. ~~And they are wonderful farmers.~~

3. **Use a semicolon or colon to link closely related ideas.**

short and choppy   Pollution from carbon emissions remains a serious environmental problem. In some respects it is the most serious problem.

combined   Pollution from carbon emissions remains a serious environmental
           ; in
problem. ~~In~~ some respects it is the most serious problem.

4. **Use parallel constructions.** Parallel constructions use repeated word order or repeated grammatical form to highlight and develop a central idea. As a rhetorical device, parallelism can aid coherence and add emphasis.

> **short and choppy**   The school busing issue is not about comfort. It concerns fairness.
>
> **combined**   The school busing issue is not about comfort. ~~It concerns~~ *but about* fairness.

Sentence Openings

More than half of all sentences in English begin with the subject of the sentence followed by the verb and any objects. The following sentences all illustrate this basic pattern:

> Martha plays the saxophone.
>
> The president vetoed the tax bill before leaving Washington for the holidays.
>
> The upcoming lecture series will formally launch the fund-raising campaign for a new civic center.

If all the sentences in a particular passage in your essay begin this way, the effect on your readers is monotony. With a little practice, you will discover just how flexible the English language is. Consider the different ways in which one sentence can be rewritten so as to vary its beginning and add interest.

> **original**   Candidates debated the issue of military service for women in the auditorium and did not know that a demonstration was going on outside.
>
> **varied openings**   *Debating the issue of military service for women,* the candidates in the auditorium did not know that a demonstration was going on outside.
>
> *In the auditorium,* the candidates debated the issue of military service for women, not knowing that a demonstration was going on outside.
>
> As they *debated the issue of military service for women,* the candidates in the auditorium did not know that a demonstration was going on outside.

Another way of changing the usual subject-verb-object order of sentences is to invert—or reverse—the normal order. Do not, however, sacrifice proper emphasis to gain variety.

usual order   The crowd stormed out.

inverted order   Out stormed the crowd.

usual order   The enemy would never accept that.

inverted order   That the enemy would never accept.

Compound Sentences

Like a series of short, simple sentences, too many compound sentences—two or more sentences joined by coordinating conjunctions—give the impression of haste and thoughtlessness. As you edit your paper, watch for the word *and* used as a coordinating conjunction. If you discover that you have overused *and*, try one of the following four methods to remedy the situation, giving important ideas more emphasis and making it easier for your reader to follow your thought.

1. **Change a compound sentence into a simple sentence with a modifier or an appositive.**

   compound   Richard Lederer is a linguist, and he is humorous, and he has a weekly radio program about language.

   appositive   Richard Lederer ~~is a~~ linguist, ~~and he is humorous, and he~~ has a weekly radio program about language. *,a humorous*

2. **Change a compound sentence into a simple sentence with a compound predicate.**

   compound   Martin Luther King Jr. chastises America for not honoring its obligations to people of color, and he dreams of a day when racism will no longer exist.

   compound predicate   Martin Luther King Jr. chastises America for not honoring its obligations to people of color, and ~~he~~ dreams of a day when racism will no longer exist.

3. **Change a compound sentence into a simple sentence with a phrase or phrases.**

compound   Women have a number of options in the military, and the responsibilities are significant.

with a phrase   Women have a number of options in the military, ^with significant responsibilities^ ~~and the responsibilities are significant.~~

4. **Change a compound sentence into a complex sentence.**

compound   Farmers are using new technologies, and agriculture is becoming completely industrialized.

complex   ^Because farmers^ ~~Farmers~~ are using new technologies, ~~and~~ agriculture is becoming completely industrialized.

Thematic Writing Assignments

GREAT WRITING BEGINS WITH THE IDEAS WE FORM AS WE READ.
When we read, we follow the logic of people with different backgrounds and beliefs. We reach conclusions that challenge us to reflect on the world and our experiences in new ways. We spend time wandering through someone else's mind, discovering insights we love and outlooks that strike us as odd — sometimes at the same time. Just as visiting a new place forms lasting memories, reading shapes our perception. When we sit down to write, we discover that we have important things to say. Things that we *must* say.

This appendix helps you practice the leap from reading to writing, using readings and visuals that are already part of the book. Each cross-chapter cluster reveals multiple aspects of engaging topics and shows how different writing strategies and a range of ideas work together to bring a single subject to life. Specific assignments help you articulate your reaction and enter into the conversation. You may find that additional reading selections in *Subject & Strategy* could also relate to the ideas in the essays we have listed here; do not hesitate to use them if they contribute to your writing.

Whether your instructor uses these thematic writing assignments in class discussion, for weekly assignments, or as a reference for your final paper, or whether you decide to use these ideas as inspiration for your own essay topic, this appendix is a concrete guide for practicing reading as a writer.

Note: For a complete, alternative thematic table of contents, see pages xliii–xlviii.

DISCOVERIES AND EPIPHANIES

As this cluster of essays shows, discoveries and epiphanies often happen when we learn something ourselves or about the world around us. Perhaps it's accepting something about ourselves, such as our need for stability and home (as LeeLee Goodson does) or understanding that society treats us differently (as Issa Rae does). Write an essay in which you narrate the process of self-discovery, or use your personal epiphany to illustrate how society works or treats others.

EDUCATION

Write a brief essay identifying and defining three to five principles that you believe are the foundation of a strong education. Consider: What environments were most conducive to your personal learning? What other factors contributed to the success of those experiences? Did you have an instructor or a mentor, or did you teach yourself? Should students always have complete access to information, or are there advantages to limiting content? How important is it for students to enjoy what they learn? How does Adler's discussion of how to mark up a text translate into electronic books or documents? How might it need to be adapted?

FAMILY AND RELATIONSHIPS

In many ways, our connections to others define us. People we have lost (as Mitch Albom notes), relationships we are afraid of changing (as is the case between David Bardeen and his brother), reciprocal friendships of the type Howard Solomon describes, or even elegant neighbors who take an interest in our lives (as with Maya Angelou's Sister Flowers)—our bonds to others can shape our decisions and the path our lives take. Write an essay about a meaningful relationship in your life. Who is the person who has affected you most? Are they a parent, a sibling, a friend? In what way have they influenced your life, and how have you influenced them in return? What challenges has your relationship faced, and are those challenges the cause of internal communication or external forces? Can your relationship be classified as a certain kind of relationship, such as a friendship, romantic partnership, classmate pairing, or something else?

GENDER

Write an essay about your experience with the gendered cultural expectations discussed by the authors above. Do such expectations help people find themselves, or are they too quick to gloss over our human vulnerabilities? Do you feel pressure to conform to gender stereotypes, or have you ever pressured others to do so? How might these stereotypes have contributed to Bardeen's hesitations and Porizkova's experiences?

GROWING UP

Growing up is a process of discovery—both inward facing self-discovery, as you determine who you are and how you see yourself, and outward facing discovery of the world, as you determine how the people and societies around you see themselves and how they see you. Write a reflection about the most important thing you discovered growing up. Was it the value of service, as in Caitlin McCormick's case? The distinction between what you do and who you are that Toni Morrison describes? How to reject fear, like Junot Díaz, or the true impact of gendered messages Deborah Roffman highlights? Was your discovery positive or negative? Does it reflect a reality you wish to change, and if so how might you go about doing so? How does your experience compare with one of these authors' experiences?

THE IMMIGRANT EXPERIENCE

Junot Díaz, *The Terror* 92

Jake Jamieson, *The English-Only Movement: Can America Proscribe Language with a Clear Conscience?* 530

Michael Jonas, *The Downside of Diversity* 357

Bharati Mukherjee, *Two Ways to Belong in America* 242

Amy Tan, *Mother Tongue* 294

Why might an essay on immigration focus on individuals instead of a whole society? What are the pros and cons of the micro and macro perspectives? Are they mutually exclusive? Write a brief reflection detailing the ways in which each author used his or her scope to further their message. Conclude with how they'd likely respond to one another. How might Mukherjee and Tan react to Jonas and Jamieson? What might all four say about the changing American dream?

MORAL VALUES

Barbara Bowman, *Guns and Cameras* (student essay) 234

William Galston, *Telling Americans to Vote, or Else* 406

Nikki Giovanni, *Campus Racism 101* 415

Abraham Lincoln, *Second Inaugural Address* 398

Anahad O'Connor, *Coca-Cola Funds Scientists' Effort to Alter Obesity Battle* 365

Mark Peters, *Virtue Signaling and Other Inane Platitudes* 333

Andrew Vachss, *The Difference between "Sick" and "Evil"* 247

Judith Viorst, *The Truth about Lying* 273

Jeannette Walls, *A Woman on the Street* 125

What moral obligations do we have to one another? Do our obligations increase when they apply to people we are closely connected to, or not? Which value system takes precedence when two moral systems conflict? Write a short essay exploring the nature of morality and individual responsibility to enact change. Do the same moral values and obligations apply to everyone, or does identity differentiate responsibility? Does Jeannette Walls have the responsibility to help her mother, or is she unable to accept the values of her parents? How can the systems of corruption or moral ambiguity detailed by Nikki Giovanni, Anahad O'Connor, or Andrew Vachss be dismantled, and what is your individual obligation to contribute to that effort?

THE NATURAL WORLD

Write a journal entry in which you explore how technology, urbanization, and modern life shape the way that humans experience nature. Compare Connor's idyllic isolation in nature to Barbara Bowman's thoughts on hunting. How might nature — or biological processes — be a threat to humans' health and well-being? What drives scientists to learn more about nature? How does science endanger the natural world, and how might it protect that world? What should be our relationship to nature?

PEER PRESSURE

Peer pressure in this selection of readings is overwhelmingly negative — it pressures us to be overcommitted and busy, to risk our health to look "good," to conform to damaging stereotypes, engage in behaviors and relationships we don't enjoy, and sublimate our own preferences to those of the group. Is this the experience you have had with peer pressure? Must peer pressure always be a bad thing? Brainstorm a list of areas of life that could be positively impacted by peer pressure, and write a journal entry about your own experience with group expectations. Were you a part of the group, or the odd one out? Explore the expectation from both sides — is the group or the individual more justified?

PEOPLE AND PERSONALITIES

What does it mean to be you? Is who you are innate, or are you a result of your environment? Write an essay in which you explore what it means to be an individual. How do your values, beliefs, and behaviors affect the way others see you? Do you fit into a specific personality type? How do these selections prompt you to reevaluate your personality? How has your identity been shaped by where you grew up or by people you've known?

POVERTY, ECONOMICS, AND INEQUALITY

Poverty is part of a chain of consumption, habits, and economic forces often outside an individual's control. Write an essay in which you define poverty and economic inequality. To what extent are your answers influenced by the country in which you were born? Have you ever participated in philanthropy or volunteered to assist the disadvantaged? Do you feel any responsibility to do so? In what ways do these selections prompt you to rethink your purchasing habits?

POWER OF LANGUAGE

What affects how we construct our sentences, our tone, and our message? Are the factors psychological, sociological, biological, or some combination of the three? Write a reflection comparing how Shaun King or Richard Lederer might identify the power and purpose of language. To what extent is precision important in our word choice, even when discussing a simple thing like coffee? How important is such precision when discussing more abstract ideas? How can thoughtless words be harmful? How might Mark Peters respond to Derald Wing Sue?

RACE IN AMERICA

Race is one of the most critical social (and political, and economic) issues of American life. As these selections indicate, there is no one solution to solve racial inequality. How has race affected your life? Identify one system or structure at your college or in your community that unfairly privileges one race over another and then write a short op-ed about the history of this system and possible changes to make it more equitable. Next, journal about the experience of writing the op-ed: What did you learn from your writing about how race affects the way you move through world? What is the best way to make your voice heard and to enact change? Can the solutions you proposed be scaled up from one issue at one college to multiple systems, or even be applied to America as a nation?

SENSE OF PLACE

How does place affect who we are? Write an editorial for your local or college newspaper about how the geography of your community contributes to its identity. Imitate the ways in which Ramírez and Cunningham describe their emotional, nostalgic connections to specific elements of their hometowns. Consider how perception plays a role in your understanding of a community, as an insider or an outsider, particularly keeping in mind the issues Ramírez raises. Address how large-scale trends like increased population, demographic shifts, and urbanization could affect your community in thirty or fifty years.

SENSE OF SELF

As these essays show, authors write about their search—and discovery—of their identities at all stages in life. Write a narrative essay in which you explore the primary ways you define yourself—perhaps by gender, sexuality, race, class, where you're from, hobbies, career goals, appearance, politics, religion, or some other way. (Chances are you identify with several of these intersecting identities.) Compare your experience to the experiences of two or more authors in this group. For example, if you identify as a writer of color, how does your sense of self as a writer compare with Russell Baker's experience? And how does your identity as a person of color compare with Issa Rae's experience? How does the intersection of those identities create your unique sense of self?

TECHNOLOGY IN MODERN LIFE

Technology fosters social connections, but it also disconnects us from real-life surroundings. With so many apps, networks, and social sites, social media and technology are not just reflecting society but reshaping it. Write an essay about what we gain—and perhaps lose—when we focus on our devices instead of what's around us. Brainstorm a list of ways that technology impacts your life on a daily basis. Is there anything you couldn't do without technology? Is there anything that would be better without technology? How has technology affected the ways you interact with family, friends, and acquaintances? Why are we obsessed with our screens? How has your perspective evolved over time? How important is it to form impressions and make decisions without influence from social media? Is that even possible in today's media landscape?

THE WORLD OF WORK

Write an essay in which you identify a problem with society's current approach to work and then propose a solution. You may respond directly to the type of work described by any of the authors in this cluster, or you may decide to introduce an author's solution to work and improve it based on your own ideas. For example, do you think our society should pay more attention and respect to the types of work that Connors, McCormick, and Rebanks describe? What would that accomplish? Do you, like Smith, think we should be wary of robots in the workplace? Why? Should we identify with our careers in the way Goodman or Morrison describes? If not, what should our relationship to our jobs be?

WRITERS ON WRITING

Write an encouraging essay on the importance of writing, aimed at an audience of infrequent writers. Include advice on how to develop writing skills. What are common *writer* mistakes, and what are the best ways to avoid them? What is the importance of *reading* as a writer? What can new writers learn from experienced writers, such as those who appear in this cluster. What can Alison Bechdel's comic teach your audience about the writing process (page 24)?

Glossary of Rhetorical Terms

Abstract See *Concrete/Abstract*.

Allusion An allusion is a passing reference to a familiar person, place, or thing drawn from history, the Bible, mythology, or literature. An allusion is an economical way for a writer to capture the essence of an idea, atmosphere, emotion, or historical era, as in "The scandal was his Watergate," or "He saw himself as a modern Job," or "Everyone there held those truths to be self-evident." An allusion should be familiar to the reader; if it is not, it will add nothing to the meaning.

Analogy Analogy is a special form of comparison in which the writer explains something unfamiliar by comparing it to something familiar: "A transmission line is simply a pipeline for electricity. In the case of a water pipeline, more water will flow through the pipe as water pressure increases. The same is true of a transmission line for electricity." See also the discussion of analogy on pages 228 in Chapter 8.

Analytical Reading Reading analytically means reading actively, paying close attention to both the content and the structure of the text. Analytical reading often involves answering several basic questions about the piece of writing under consideration:

1. What does the author want to say? What is his or her main point?

2. Why does the author want to say it? What is his or her purpose?

3. What strategy or strategies does the author use?

4. Why and how does the author's writing strategy suit both the subject and the purpose?

5. What is special about the way the author uses the strategy?

6. How effective is the essay? Why?

For a detailed example of analytical reading, see Chapter 1.

Appropriateness See *Diction*.

Argument Argument is one of the four basic types of prose. (Narration, description, and exposition are the other three.) To argue is to attempt to convince the reader to agree with a point of view, to make a given decision, or to pursue a particular course of action. Logical argument is based on reasonable explanations and appeals to the reader's intelligence. See Chapter 12 for further discussion of argumentation. See also *Logical Fallacies; Persuasion.*

Assertion An assertion is the thesis or proposition that a writer puts forward in an argument.

Assumption An assumption is a belief or principle, stated or implied, that is taken for granted.

Attitude A writer's attitude reflects his or her opinion on a subject. For example, a writer can think very positively or very negatively about a subject. In most cases, the writer's attitude falls somewhere between these two extremes. See also *Tone.*

Audience An audience is the intended readership for a piece of writing. For example, the readers of a national weekly newsmagazine come from all walks of life and have diverse opinions, attitudes, and educational experiences. In contrast, the readership for an organic chemistry journal is made up of people whose interests and educational backgrounds are quite similar. The essays in this book are intended for general readers — intelligent people who may lack specific information about the subject being discussed.

Beginnings/Endings A *beginning* is the sentence, group of sentences, or section that introduces an essay. Good beginnings usually identify the thesis or controlling idea, attempt to interest the reader, and establish a tone. Some effective ways in which writers begin essays include telling an anecdote that illustrates the thesis, providing a controversial statement or opinion that engages the reader's interest, presenting startling statistics or facts, defining a term that is central to the discussion that follows, asking thought-provoking questions, providing a quotation that illustrates the thesis, referring to a current event that helps establish the thesis, and showing the significance of the subject or stressing its importance to the reader.

An *ending* is the sentence or group of sentences that brings an essay to closure. Good endings are purposeful and well planned. Endings satisfy readers when they are the natural outgrowths of the essays themselves and convey a sense of finality or completion. Good essays do not simply stop; they conclude.

Cause and Effect Analysis Cause and effect analysis is one of the types of exposition. (Process analysis, definition, division and classification, illustration, and comparison and contrast are the others.) Cause and effect analysis answers the question *why?* It explains the reasons for an occurrence or the consequences of an action. See Chapter 11 for a detailed discussion of cause and effect analysis. See also *Exposition.*

Claim A claim is the thesis or proposition put forth in an argument.

Classification Classification, along with division, is one of the types of exposition. (Process analysis, definition, comparison and contrast, illustration, and cause and effect analysis are the others.) When classifying, the writer arranges and sorts people, places, or things into categories according to their differing characteristics, thus making them more manageable for the writer and more understandable for the reader. See Chapter 9 for a detailed discussion of classification. See also *Division; Exposition.*

Cliché A cliché is an expression that has become ineffective through overuse. Expressions such as *quick as a flash*, *dry as dust*, *jump for joy*, and *slow as molasses* are all clichés. Good writers normally avoid such trite expressions and seek instead to express themselves in fresh and forceful language.

Coherence Coherence is a quality of good writing that results when all sentences, paragraphs, and longer divisions of an essay are naturally connected. Coherent writing is achieved through (1) a logical sequence of ideas (arranged in chronological order, spatial order, order of importance, or some other appropriate order), (2) the thoughtful repetition of key words and ideas, (3) a pace suitable for your topic and reader, and (4) the use of transitional words and expressions. Coherence should not be confused with unity. See *Unity*. See also *Transitions*.

Colloquial Expressions A colloquial expression is characteristic of or appropriate to spoken language, or to writing that seeks its effect. Colloquial expressions are informal, as *chem*, *gym*, *come up with*, *be at loose ends*, *won't*, and *photo* illustrate. Thus, colloquial expressions are acceptable in formal writing only if they are used purposefully.

Comparison and Contrast Comparison and contrast is one of the types of exposition. (Process analysis, definition, division and classification, illustration, and cause and effect analysis are the others.) In comparison and contrast, the writer points out the similarities and differences between two or more subjects in the same class or category. The function of any comparison and contrast is to clarify—to reach some conclusion about the items being compared and contrasted. See Chapter 8 for a detailed discussion of comparison and contrast. See also *Exposition*.

Conclusions See *Beginnings/Endings*.

Concrete/Abstract A *concrete* word names a specific object, person, place, or action that can be directly perceived by the senses: *car*, *bread*, *building*, *book*, *Abraham Lincoln*, *Chicago*, or *hiking*. An *abstract* word, in contrast, refers to general qualities, conditions, ideas, actions, or relationships that cannot be directly perceived by the senses: *bravery*, *dedication*, *excellence*, *anxiety*, *stress*, *thinking*, or *hatred*.

Although writers must use both concrete and abstract language, good writers avoid using too many abstract words. Instead, they rely on concrete words to define and illustrate abstractions. Because concrete words affect the senses, they are easily comprehended by the reader.

Connotation/Denotation Both connotation and denotation refer to the meanings of words. *Denotation* is the dictionary meaning of a word, the literal meaning. *Connotation*, on the other hand, is the implied or suggested meaning of a word. For example, the denotation of *lamb* is "a young sheep." The connotations of *lamb* are numerous: *gentle*, *docile*, *weak*, *peaceful*, *blessed*, *sacrificial*, *blood*, *spring*, *frisky*, *pure*, *innocent*, and so on. Good writers are sensitive to both the denotations and the connotations of words, and they use these meanings to their advantage in their writing. See also *Slanting*.

Contrast See *Comparison and Contrast*.

Deduction Deduction is the process of reasoning from a stated premise to a necessary conclusion. This form of reasoning moves from the general to the specific.

See Chapter 12 for a discussion of deductive reasoning and its relation to argumentative writing. See also *Induction*; *Syllogism*.

Definition Definition is one of the types of exposition. (Process analysis, division and classification, comparison and contrast, illustration, and cause and effect analysis are the others.) Definition is a statement of the meaning of a word. A definition may be either brief or extended, part of an essay or an entire essay itself. See Chapter 10 for a detailed discussion of definition. See also *Exposition*.

Denotation See *Connotation/Denotation*.

Description Description is one of the four basic types of prose. (Narration, exposition, and argument are the other three.) Description tells how a person, place, or thing is perceived by the five senses. Objective description reports these sensory qualities factually, whereas subjective description gives the writer's interpretation of them. See Chapter 5 for a detailed discussion of description.

Dialogue Dialogue is conversation that is recorded in a piece of writing. Through dialogue writers reveal important aspects of characters' personalities as well as events in the narrative.

Diction Diction refers to a writer's choice and use of words. Good diction is precise and appropriate—the words mean exactly what the writer intends, and the words are well suited to the writer's subject, intended audience, and purpose in writing. The word-conscious writer knows that there are differences among *aged*, *old*, and *elderly*; *blue*, *navy*, and *azure*; and *disturbed*, *angry*, and *irritated*. Furthermore, this writer knows in which situation to use each word. See also *Connotation/Denotation*.

Division Like comparison and contrast, division and classification are separate yet closely related mental operations. Division involves breaking down a single large unit into smaller subunits or breaking down a large group of items into discrete categories. For example, the student body at your college or university can be divided into categories according to different criteria (by class, by home state or country, by sex, and so on). See also *Classification*.

Dominant Impression A dominant impression is the single mood, atmosphere, or quality a writer emphasizes in a piece of descriptive writing. The dominant impression is created through the careful selection of details and is, of course, influenced by the writer's subject, audience, and purpose. See also the discussion of dominant impressions on pages 114–16 in Chapter 5.

Draft A draft is a version of a piece of writing at a particular stage in the writing process. The first version produced is usually called the *rough draft* or *first draft* and is a writer's beginning attempt to give overall shape to his or her ideas. Subsequent versions are called *revised drafts*. The copy presented for publication is the *final draft*.

Editing During the editing stage of the writing process, the writer makes his or her prose conform to the conventions of the language. This includes making final improvements in sentence structure and diction, and proofreading for wordiness and errors in grammar, usage, spelling, and punctuation. After editing, the writer is ready to prepare a final copy.

Emphasis Emphasis is the placement of important ideas and words within sentences and longer units of writing so that they have the greatest impact. In general, the end has the most impact, and the beginning nearly as much; the middle has the least. See also *Organization*.

Endings See *Beginnings/Endings*.

Essay An essay is a relatively short piece of nonfiction in which the writer attempts to make one or more closely related points. A good essay is purposeful, informative, and well organized.

Ethos *Ethos* is a type of argumentative proof having to do with the ethics of the arguer: honesty, trustworthiness, and even morals.

Evaluation An evaluation of a piece of writing is an assessment of its effectiveness or merit. In evaluating a piece of writing, you should ask the following questions: What is the writer's purpose? Is it a worthwhile purpose? Does the writer achieve the purpose? Is the writer's information sufficient and accurate? What are the strengths of the essay? What are its weaknesses? Depending on the type of writing and the purpose, more specific questions can also be asked. For example, with an argument you could ask: Does the writer follow the principles of logical thinking? Is the writer's evidence convincing?

Evidence Evidence is the data on which a judgment or an argument is based or by which proof or probability is established. Evidence usually takes the form of statistics, facts, names, examples or illustrations, and opinions of authorities.

Examples Examples illustrate a larger idea or represent something of which they are a part. An example is a basic means of developing or clarifying an idea. Furthermore, examples enable writers to show and not simply tell readers what they mean. The terms *example* and *illustration* are sometimes used interchangeably. See also the discussion of illustration on pages 153–59 in Chapter 6.

Exposition Exposition is one of the four basic types of prose. (Narration, description, and argument are the other three.) The purpose of exposition is to clarify, explain, and inform. The methods of exposition presented in this text are process analysis, definition, division and classification, comparison and contrast, illustration, and cause and effect analysis. For a detailed discussion of each of these methods of exposition, see the appropriate chapter.

Fact A fact is a piece of information presented as having a verifiable certainty or reality.

Fallacy See *Logical Fallacies*.

Figures of Speech Figures of speech are brief, imaginative comparisons that highlight the similarities between things that are basically dissimilar. They make writing vivid and interesting and therefore more memorable. The most common figures of speech are these:

Simile—An implicit comparison introduced by *like* or *as*: "The fighter's hands were *like* stone."

Metaphor—An implied comparison that uses one thing as the equivalent of another: "All the world's a stage."

Personification—A special kind of simile or metaphor in which human traits are assigned to an inanimate object: "The engine coughed and then stopped."

Focus Focus is the limitation that a writer gives his or her subject. The writer's task is to select a manageable topic given the constraints of time, space, and purpose. For example, within the general subject of sports, a writer could focus on government support of amateur athletes or narrow the focus further to government support of Olympic athletes.

General See *Specific/General.*

Idiom An idiom is a word or phrase that is used habitually with a particular meaning in a language. The meaning of an idiom is not always readily apparent to nonnative speakers of that language. For example, *catch cold, hold a job, make up your mind*, and *give them a hand* are all idioms in English.

Illustration Illustration is a type of exposition. (Definition, division and classification, comparison and contrast, cause and effect analysis, and process analysis are the others.) With illustration the writer uses examples—specific facts, opinions, samples, and anecdotes or stories—to support a generalization and to make it more vivid, understandable, and persuasive. See Chapter 6 for a detailed discussion of illustration. See also *Examples.*

Induction Induction is the process of reasoning to a conclusion about all members of a class through an examination of only a few members of the class. This form of reasoning moves from the particular to the general. See Chapter 12 for a discussion of inductive reasoning and its relation to argumentative writing. See also *Deduction.*

Introductions See *Beginnings/Endings.*

Irony Irony is the use of words to suggest something different from their literal meaning. For example, when Jonathan Swift proposes in "A Modest Proposal" that Ireland's problems could be solved if the people of Ireland fattened their babies and sold them to the English landlords for food, he meant that almost any other solution would be preferable. A writer can use irony to establish a special relationship with the reader and to add an extra dimension or twist to the meaning of a word or phrase.

Jargon See *Technical Language.*

Logical Fallacies A logical fallacy is an error in reasoning that renders an argument invalid. Some of the more common logical fallacies are these:

Oversimplification—The tendency to provide simple solutions to complex problems: "The reason we have inflation today is that OPEC has unreasonably raised the price of oil."

Non sequitur ("it does not follow")—An inference or conclusion that does not follow from established premises or evidence: "It was the best movie I saw this year, and it should get an Academy Award."

Post hoc, ergo propter hoc ("after this, therefore because of this")—Confusing chance or coincidence with causation. Because one event comes after another one, it does not necessarily mean that the first event caused the second: "I won't say I caught a cold at the hockey game, but I certainly didn't have it before I went there."

Begging the question—Assuming in a premise that which needs to be proven: "If American autoworkers built a better product, foreign auto sales would not be so high."

False analogy—Making a misleading analogy between logically unconnected ideas: "He was a brilliant basketball player; therefore, there's no question in my mind that he will be a fine coach."

Either/or thinking—The tendency to see an issue as having only two sides: "Used car salespeople are either honest or crooked."

See also Chapter 12.

Logical Reasoning See *Deduction; Induction.*

Logos *Logos* is a type of argumentative proof having to do with the logical qualities of an argument: data, evidence, and factual information.

Main Idea See *Thesis.*

Metaphor See *Figures of Speech.*

Narration Narration is one of the four basic types of prose. (Description, exposition, and argument are the other three.) To narrate is to tell a story, to tell what happened. Although narration is most often used in fiction, it is also important in nonfiction, either by itself or in conjunction with other types of prose. See Chapter 4 for a detailed discussion of narration.

Objective/Subjective *Objective* writing is factual and impersonal, whereas *subjective* writing, sometimes called *impressionistic* writing, relies heavily on personal interpretation. For a discussion of objective description and subjective description, see Chapter 5.

Opinion An opinion is a belief or conclusion not substantiated by positive knowledge or proof. An opinion reveals personal feelings or attitudes or states a position. Opinion should not be confused with argument.

Organization In writing, organization is the thoughtful arrangement and presentation of one's points or ideas. Narration is often organized chronologically. Exposition may be organized from simplest to most complex or from most familiar to least familiar. Argument may be organized from least important to most important. There is no single correct pattern of organization for a given piece of writing, but good writers are careful to discover an order of presentation suitable for their audience and their purpose.

Paradox A paradox is a seemingly contradictory statement that may nonetheless be true. For example, "We little know what we have until we lose it" is a paradoxical statement.

Paragraph The paragraph, the single most important unit of thought in an essay, is a series of closely related sentences. These sentences adequately develop the central or controlling idea of the paragraph. This central or controlling idea, usually stated in a topic sentence, is necessarily related to the purpose of the whole composition. A well-written paragraph has several distinguishing characteristics: a clearly stated or implied topic sentence, adequate development, unity, coherence, and an appropriate organizational strategy.

Parallelism Parallel structure is the repetition of word order or form either within a single sentence or in several sentences that develop the same central idea. As a rhetorical device, parallelism can aid coherence and add emphasis. Roosevelt's statement, "I see one third of a nation ill-housed, ill-clad, ill-nourished," illustrates effective parallelism.

Pathos A type of argumentative proof having to do with audience: emotional language, connotative diction, and appeals to certain values.

Personification See *Figures of Speech.*

Persuasion Persuasion, or persuasive argument, is an attempt to convince readers to agree with a point of view, to make a given decision, or to pursue a particular course of action. Persuasion appeals heavily to the emotions, whereas logical argument does not. For the distinction between logical argument and persuasive argument, see Chapter 12.

Point of View Point of view refers to the grammatical person of the speaker in an essay. For example, a first-person point of view uses the pronoun *I* and is commonly found in autobiography and the personal essay; a third-person point of view uses the pronouns *he, she,* or *it* and is commonly found in objective writing. See Chapter 4 for a discussion of point of view in narration.

Prewriting Prewriting encompasses all the activities that take place before a writer actually starts a rough draft. During the prewriting stage of the writing process, the writer selects a subject area, focuses on a particular topic, collects information and makes notes, brainstorms for ideas, discovers connections between pieces of information, determines a thesis and purpose, rehearses portions of the writing in his or her mind or on paper, and makes a scratch outline. For some suggestions about prewriting, see Chapter 2, pages 26–33.

Process Analysis Process analysis is a type of exposition. (Definition, division and classification, comparison and contrast, illustration, and cause and effect analysis are the others.) Process analysis answers the question *how?* and explains how something works or gives step-by-step directions for doing something. See Chapter 7 for a detailed discussion of process analysis. See also *Exposition.*

Publication In the publication stage of the writing process, the writer shares his or her writing with the intended audience. Publication can take the form of a typed or an oral presentation, a photocopy, or a commercially printed rendition. What's important is that the writer's words are read in what amounts to their final form.

Purpose Purpose is what the writer wants to accomplish in a particular piece of writing. Purposeful writing seeks to *relate* (narration), to *describe* (description), to *explain* (process analysis, definition, division and classification, comparison and contrast, illustration, and cause and effect analysis), or to *convince* (argument).

Revision During the revision stage of the writing process, the writer determines what in the draft needs to be developed or clarified so that the essay says what the writer intends it to say. Often the writer needs to revise several times before the essay is "right." Comments from peer evaluators can be invaluable in helping writers determine what sorts of changes need to be made. Such changes can include adding material, deleting material, changing the order of presentation, and substituting new material for old.

Rhetorical Question A rhetorical question is a question that is asked but requires no answer from the reader. "When will nuclear proliferation end?" is such a question. Writers use rhetorical questions to introduce topics they plan to discuss or to emphasize important points.

Rough Draft See *Draft*.

Sequence Sequence refers to the order in which a writer presents information. Writers commonly select chronological order, spatial order, order of importance, or order of complexity to arrange their points. See also *Organization*.

Signal Phrase A signal phrase introduces borrowed material—a summary, paraphrase, or quotation—in a researched paper and usually consists of the author's name and a verb (for example, *Daphna Oyserman contends*). Signal phrases let readers know who is speaking and, in the case of summaries and paraphrases, exactly where the writer's ideas end and the borrowed material begins. For suggestions on using signal phrases, see pages 503–04 in Chapter 14.

Simile See *Figures of Speech*.

Slang Slang is the unconventional, very informal language of particular subgroups of a culture. Slang, such as *bummed*, *split*, *wicked*, *fresh*, *dis*, *blow off*, and *cool*, is acceptable in formal writing only if it is used purposefully.

Slanting Slanting is the use of certain words or information that results in a biased viewpoint.

Specific/General *General* words name groups or classes of objects, qualities, or actions. *Specific* words, in contrast, name individual objects, qualities, or actions within a class or group. To some extent, the terms *general* and *specific* are relative. For example, *dessert* is a class of things. *Pie*, however, is more specific than *dessert* but more general than *pecan pie* or *chocolate cream pie*.

Good writing judiciously balances the general with the specific. Writing with too many general words is likely to be dull and lifeless. General words do not create vivid responses in the reader's mind as concrete, specific words can. However, writing that relies exclusively on specific words may lack focus and direction—the control that more general statements provide.

Strategy A strategy is a means by which a writer achieves his or her purpose. Strategy includes the many rhetorical decisions that the writer makes about organization, paragraph structure, syntax, and diction. In terms of the whole essay, strategy refers to the principal rhetorical mode that the writer uses. If, for example, a writer wishes to show how to make chocolate chip cookies, the most effective strategy would be process analysis. If it is the writer's purpose to show why sales of American cars have declined in recent years, the most effective strategy would be cause and effect analysis.

Style Style is the individual manner in which a writer expresses ideas. Style is created by the author's particular selection of words, construction of sentences, and arrangement of ideas.

Subject The subject of an essay is its content, what the essay is about. Depending on the author's purpose and the constraints of space, a subject may range from one that is broadly conceived to one that is narrowly defined.

Subjective See *Objective/Subjective.*

Supporting Evidence See *Evidence.*

Syllogism A syllogism is an argument that utilizes deductive reasoning and consists of a major premise, a minor premise, and a conclusion. For example:

All trees that lose leaves are deciduous. (*Major premise*)

Maple trees lose their leaves. (*Minor premise*)

Therefore, maple trees are deciduous. (*Conclusion*)

See also *Deduction.*

Symbol A symbol is a person, place, or thing that represents something beyond itself. For example, the eagle is a symbol of the United States, and the bear is a symbol of Russia.

Syntax Syntax refers to the way in which words are arranged to form phrases, clauses, and sentences as well as to the grammatical relationship among the words themselves.

Technical Language Technical language, or jargon, is the special vocabulary of a trade or profession. Writers who use technical language do so with an awareness of their audience. If the audience is a group of peers, technical language may be used freely. If the audience is a more general one, technical language should be used sparingly and carefully so as not to sacrifice clarity. See also *Diction.*

Thesis A thesis is a statement of the main idea of an essay. Also known as the *controlling idea*, a thesis may sometimes be implied rather than stated directly.

Title A title is a word or phrase set off at the beginning of an essay to identify the subject, to capture the main idea of the essay, or to attract the reader's attention. A title may be explicit or suggestive. A subtitle, when used, extends or restricts the meaning of the main title.

Tone Tone is the manner in which a writer relates to an audience—the "tone of voice" used to address readers. Tone may be described as friendly, serious, distant, angry, cheerful, bitter, cynical, enthusiastic, morbid, resentful, warm, playful, and so forth. A particular tone results from a writer's diction, sentence structure, purpose, and attitude toward the subject. See also *Attitude.*

Topic Sentence The topic sentence states the central idea of a paragraph and thus limits and controls the subject of the paragraph. Although the topic sentence most often appears at the beginning of the paragraph, it may appear at any other point, particularly if the writer is trying to create a special effect. See also *Paragraph.*

Transitions Transitions are words or phrases that link sentences, paragraphs, and larger units of a composition to achieve coherence. These devices include parallelism, pronoun references, conjunctions, and the repetition of key ideas, as well as the many conventional transitional expressions, such as *moreover, on the other hand, in addition, in contrast,* and *therefore.* See also *Coherence.*

Unity Unity is achieved in an essay when all the words, sentences, and paragraphs contribute to its thesis. The elements of a unified essay do not distract the reader. Instead, they all harmoniously support a single idea or purpose.

Verb Verbs can be classified as either strong verbs (*scream, pierce, gush, ravage,* and *amble*) or weak verbs (*be, has, get,* and *do*). Writers prefer to use strong verbs to make their writing more specific, more descriptive, and more action filled.

Voice Verbs can be classified as being in either the active or the passive voice. In the active voice, the doer of the action is the grammatical subject. In the passive voice, the receiver of the action is the subject:

Active: Glenda questioned all the children.

Passive: All the children were questioned by Glenda.

Also, voice refers to the way an author "talks" or "sounds" in a particular work as opposed to a style that characterizes an author's total output. Voice is generally considered to be made up of a combination of such elements as pacing or sense of timing, word choice, sentence and paragraph length, or the way characters sound in a written composition.

Writing Process The writing process consists of five major stages: prewriting, writing drafts, revision, editing, and publication. The process is not inflexible, but there is no mistaking the fact that most writers follow some version of it most of the time. Although orderly in its basic components and sequence of activities, the writing process is nonetheless continuous, creative, and unique to each individual writer. See Chapter 2 for a detailed discussion of the writing process. See also *Draft*; *Editing*; *Prewriting*; *Publication*; *Revision.*

Acknowledgments (continued from page iv)

Jennifer Ackerman, "The Genius of Birds" excerpted from *The Genius of Birds,* copyright © 2016 by Jennifer Ackerman. Used by permission of Dutton, an imprint of Penguin Publishing Group, a division of Penguin Random House LLC. All rights reserved.

Mortimer Adler, "How to Mark a Book." Originally published in *Saturday Review of Literature,* July 6, 1940. Reprinted by permission.

Mitch Albom, "If You Had One Day with Someone Who's Gone" originally appeared in the September 17, 2006, issue of *Parade.* Copyright © 2006 ASOP, Inc. Reprinted by permission of the author.

Maya Angelou, "Sister Flowers," "Chapter 15" from I KNOW WHY THE CAGED BIRD SINGS by Maya Angelou, copyright © 1969 and renewed 1997 by Maya Angelou. Used by permission of Random House, an imprint and division of Penguin Random House LLC. All rights reserved.

Nancy Armour, "James Harrison Is Right, You Shouldn't Get a Prize for Showing Up," *USA Today,* August 18, 2015. © 2015 USA Today. All rights reserved. Used by permission and protected by the Copyright Laws of the United States. The printing, copying, redistribution, or retransmission of this Content without express written permission is prohibited.

Alicia Ault, "How Do Spiders Make Their Webs?" *The Smithsonian Magazine.* Copyright 2015 SMITHSONIAN INSTITUTION. Reprinted with permission from Smithsonian Enterprises. All rights reserved. Reproduction in any medium is strictly prohibited without permission from Smithsonian Institution.

Russell Baker, "Discovering the Power of My Words." Copyright © 1982 by Russell Baker. Reprinted by permission of Don Congdon Associates, Inc.

David P. Bardeen, "Not Close Enough for Comfort," *The New York Times,* February 29, 2004. Reprinted by permission of David Bardeen.

Suzanne Britt, "Neat People vs. Sloppy People." Reprinted by permission of the author.

Cody Cassidy and Paul Doherty, "What Would Happen If You Were Attacked by a Great White Shark?" excerpted from *And Then You're Dead: What Really Happens If You Get Swallowed by a Whale, Are Shot from a Cannon, or Go Barreling over Niagara.* Copyright © 2017 by Cody Cassidy and Paul Doherty. Used by permission of Penguin Books, an imprint of Penguin Publishing Group, a division of Penguin Random House LLC. All rights reserved.

Roger Cohen, "The Organic Fable," *The New York Times,* September 7, 2012. Copyright © 2012 The New York Times. All rights reserved. Used by permission and protected by the Copyright Laws of the United States. The printing, copying, redistribution, or retransmission of this Content without express written permission is prohibited.

Philip Connors, "A Talent for Sloth," originally appearing in *Lapham's Quarterly.* Used by permission of Philip Connors.

Junot Díaz, "The Terror," *The New York Times,* June 28, 2015. Copyright © 2015 The New York Times. All rights reserved. Used by permission and protected by the Copyright Laws of the United States. The printing, copying, redistribution, or retransmission of this Content without express written permission is prohibited.

Lars Eighner, "On Dumpster Diving" from *Travels with Lizbeth: Three Years on the Road and on the Streets.* Copyright © 1993 by Lars Eighner. Reprinted by permission of St. Martin's Press. All rights reserved.

Linda S. Flower, "Writing for an Audience" from *Problem-Solving Strategies for Writing,* Fourth Edition. Copyright © 1993 Harcourt College Publishing. Reprinted by permission of the author.

Thomas Friedman, "My Favorite Teacher," *The New York Times,* January 9, 2001. Copyright © 2001 The New York Times. All rights reserved. Used by permission and protected by the Copyright Laws of the United States. The printing, copying, redistribution, or retransmission of this Content without express written permission is prohibited.

William Galston, "Telling Americans to Vote, Or Else," *The New York Times,* November 6, 2011. Copyright © 2011 The New York Times. All rights reserved. Used by permission and protected by the Copyright Laws of the United States. The printing, copying, redistribution, or retransmission of this content without express written permission is prohibited.

Ilana Gershon, "The Quitting Economy," originally appearing in *Aeon,* July 26, 2017. Copyright © 2017 by Aeon Media Group Ltd. aeon.co. Used with permission.

Sara D. Gilbert, "The Different Ways of Being Smart" from *Using Your Head: The Many Ways of Being Smart.* Copyright © 1984 by Sara Gilbert. All rights reserved. Used with permission.

Nikki Giovanni, "Campus Racism 101," *Racism 101.* Copyright © 1994 by Nikki Giovanni. Reprinted by permission of HarperCollins Publishers.

Natalie Goldberg, "Be Specific" from *Writing Down the Bones: Freeing the Writer Within,* by Natalie Goldberg, © 1986 by Natalie Goldberg. Reprinted by arrangement with The Permissions Company, Inc., on behalf of Shambhala Publications Inc., Boulder, Colorado. www.shambhala.com.

Jason G. Goldman, "How a Kids' Cartoon Created a Real-Life Invasive Army," Originally appearing in *Nautilus,* May 30, 2017. Copyright © 2017 Jason Goldman. Used with permission.

Ellen Goodman, "The Company Man." Copyright © 1979 The Washington Post Company. Reprinted with the permission of Simon & Schuster, Inc. All rights reserved.

Linda Holmes, "The Sad, Beautiful Fact That We're All Going to Miss Almost Everything," *NPR.org,* April 18, 2011. © 2011 National Public Radio, Inc. Used with the permission of NPR. Any unauthorized duplication is strictly prohibited.

Michael Jonas, "The Downside of Diversity," *The Boston Globe,* August 5, 2007. Copyright © 2007 by Michael Jonas. Used with permission.

Shaun King, "No, I Won't Be Writing about Black-on-Black Crime," *New York Daily News,* June 29, 2017. Copyright © 2017 Daily News, L.P. (New York). All rights reserved. Used with permission.

Stephen King, "Reading to Write" from *On Writing: A Memoir of the Craft.* Copyright © 2000 by Stephen King. Reprinted with permission of Scribner, a division of Simon & Schuster, Inc. All rights reserved.

Tim Kreider, "The 'Busy' Trap," *The New York Times,* July 1, 2012. Copyright © 2012 The New York Times. All rights reserved. Used by permission and protected by the Copyright Laws of the United States. The printing, copying, redistribution, or retransmission of this Content without express written permission is prohibited.

Anne Lamott, "Shitty First Drafts" from BIRD BY BIRD: SOME INSTRUCTIONS ON WRITING AND LIFE by Anne Lamott, copyright © 1994 by Anne Lamott. Used by permission of Pantheon Books, an imprint of the Knopf Doubleday Publishing Group, a division of Penguin Random House LLC. All rights reserved.

Richard Lederer, "All-American Dialects." Reprinted by permission of the author.

Caitlin McCormick, "4 Standout College Application Essays on Work, Money and Class," *The New York Times*, May 12, 2017. Copyright © 2017 The New York Times. All rights reserved. Used by permission and protected by the Copyright Laws of the United States. The printing, copying, redistribution, or retransmission of this content without express written permission is prohibited.

Cherokee Paul McDonald, "A View from the Bridge," originally published in the *Sun Sentinel, Sunshine Magazine* (Fort Lauderdale, FL). Copyright © 1989 by Cherokee Paul McDonald. Used with permission.

Roger McNamee, "I Invested Early in Google and Facebook. Now They Terrify Me," *USA Today,* August 8, 2017. Copyright © 2017 USA Today. All rights reserved. Used by permission and protected by the Copyright Laws of the United States. The printing, copying, redistribution, or retransmission of this Content without express written permission is prohibited.

John Metta, "I, Racist," *Those People,* April 14, 2017. Copyright © 2017 by John Metta. Used with permission.

Toni Morrison, "The Work You Do, The Person You Are," originally appearing in *The New Yorker,* June 5 & 12, 2017. Copyright © 2017 by Toni Morrison. Reprinted by permission of ICM Partners.

Bharati Mukherjee, "Two Ways to Belong in America" originally published in *The New York Times,* September 22, 1996. Copyright © 1996 by Bharati Mukherjee. Reprinted by permission of the author.

Anahad O'Connor, "Coca-Cola Funds Scientists Who Shift Blame for Obesity Away from Bad Diets," *The New York Times,* as it appeared in *The Dallas Morning News,* August 9, 2015.

Index

Instructor's Manual

Fifteenth Edition

Subject & Strategy

A Writer's Reader

Paul Eschholz • Alfred Rosa

Instructor's Manual

Subject & Strategy
A Writer's Reader

FIFTEENTH EDITION

Paul Eschholz
University of Vermont

Alfred Rosa
University of Vermont

bedford/st.martin's
Macmillan Learning

Boston | New York

Preface

The purpose of this instructor's manual is to suggest responses to the questions and prompts that accompany each selection in *Subject & Strategy*, and to offer support as you plan your course using the textbook. Naturally, there are no substitutes for your own experience with each essay and for common sense about what will challenge and engage your students. Our intent in writing this manual is to save you time, not to dictate answers. On occasion, you may disagree with our interpretation or emphasis, but we trust that the suggested responses will be useful at least as starting points for class discussion.

Planning Your Course

Many instructors who use *Subject & Strategy* begin the course by having their students read the first two chapters of the text: "Reading" and "Writing." There, students will find guidelines for reading analytically and for using reading in the process of writing. Of particular interest in Chapter 1 are Cherokee Paul McDonald's "A View from the Bridge" (pages 5–11), which provides a step-by-step model of active reading, and Thomas L. Friedman's "My Favorite Teacher" (pages 13–15), which invites students to apply what they have learned. This Instructor's Manual includes additional study questions and possible responses for these Chapter 1 readings. In Chapter 2, students are encouraged to develop an effective writing process, in part by examining a case study of a student paper in progress. Many instructors choose then to assign Chapter 3, "Writers on Writing," that features essays in which well-known writers, including Anne Lamott and Stephen King, express both the joy and hard work of writing.

The arrangement of this book suggests one possible sequence for teaching Chapters 4–12: the movement from narration through the subsequent rhetorical strategies, culminating with argumentation, where those strategies are all brought to bear. Each chapter is self-contained, however, so that you may follow any sequence you prefer, omitting or emphasizing a chapter, according to the needs of your course and your students.

Chapter 13, "Combining Strategies," and Chapter 14, "Writing with Sources," are typically introduced in the latter weeks of a course — or in the second semester, if you're using *Subject & Strategy* over the entirety of the student's first year — after students have mastered some of the basic rhetorical strategies and are ready to move on to more advanced work. In Chapter 13, students learn how to use more than one strategy to achieve their purpose; a sample student essay and three professional essays demonstrate the possibilities. Chapter 14 offers sound, detailed advice on effectively integrating sources through quotation, summary, synthesis, and paraphrase and on avoiding plagiarism. This chapter features three essays that integrate outside sources, and it provides questions and prompts that direct students' attention to those integration techniques. Chapter 15, "A Brief Guide to Researching and Documenting Essays," which is especially useful in courses that require students to do independent research, offers advice on finding and evaluating sources and on the mechanics of documentation. This chapter includes up-to-date guidelines for the Modern Language Association's documentation style. You may wish to encourage students to consult Chapter 16, "Editing for Grammar, Punctuation, and Sentence Style," during the final stages of revising and proofreading a piece.

Several sections in the book may be particularly helpful as you plan your course. In addition to the complete **Contents** on page xxvii of *Subject & Strategy*, you may enjoy the alternative **Thematic Contents** on page xliii; you'll find some suggestions for **Thematic**

Writing Assignments in the Appendix on pages 581–89, offering a structured and useful way of connecting the book's readings and visuals through topical questions that resonate with students.

We have also provided **Sample Course Plans** on pages xii–xx of this manual. One of the example syllabi is arranged by rhetorical strategy, much like the main book organization, and the other is arranged by theme, an option we have highlighted with the Thematic Contents. We hope either of these can provide you with a starting point for planning your own course.

Using the Material Accompanying the Readings

This edition includes **chapter-opening images** for every chapter, increasing the opportunities for discussing and studying how visual rhetoric works. The chapter-opening images in each rhetorical modes chapter (Chapters 4–13) are particularly useful for underlining the importance and ubiquity of the strategies. A "Visualizing the Strategy" activity—new to this edition—includes a brief discussion of the visual and prompts students to enact their visual literacy skills to answer questions about the image, considering the creator's rhetorical choices and evaluating its effectiveness.

The introductions to the strategy chapters define and explain the strategy using annotated extracts from published writing. The **Using [the Strategy] across the Disciplines** section in each chapter shows students how rhetorical strategies can be used outside the composition classroom—whether in the humanities, the natural sciences, or the social sciences. **Practical Advice for Writing and Essay Using [the Strategy] sections** offer advice for every stage of the writing process, with special emphasis on revising. The chapter introduction concludes with an **annotated student essay** that uses the strategy, as well as a new student interview in which the student writer reflects on his or her writing process, followed by a prompt for students to consider their own process for writing using the chapter strategy. We have found that model student essays like these can be especially helpful in introducing novice writers to the various rhetorical strategies and establishing realistic expectations for their own work.

The **headnotes**, **prompts**, and **questions** that accompany each professional selection focus on different aspects of the essays:

- *Headnotes* offer biographical and publication information, as well as some insight into the selection's content and how the reading employs the mode under discussion.
- *Preparing to Read* prompts are prereading exercises—often used by instructors as journal prompts—that encourage students to explore what they already know about the topic of the essay. (Suggested discussion points are included in this manual.)
- *Thinking Critically about the Text* prompts are intended to engage students with an issue, a concern, or an idea raised in the selection they have just read. (Suggested responses are included in this manual.)
- *Questions on Subject* are designed to focus students' attention on the author's purpose and on the major points of the essay, as well as to promote class discussions of the selection. In addition, they provide a convenient means of checking comprehension. If you desire, these questions might be used as the basis for content quizzes. (Suggested answers are included in this manual.)
- *Questions on Strategy* focus students' attention on analyzing the various strategies the authors have used in composing their essays. In answering these questions, students are encouraged to put themselves in the author's place and understand how they may use the same strategies in their own writing. Through this analysis, students come to a better understanding of the principles of good writing. There are also questions that ask students to examine passages in each selection where the

writer has used *multiple* strategies in support of the dominant pattern of development. These questions illustrate and reinforce the points made in Chapter 13, "Combining Strategies." (Suggested answers are included in this manual.)

- *Strategy in Action* activities follow each reading and encourage students to explore both the practical and the academic uses of the various rhetorical strategies. Many of these activities are visually based; all of them can be used as icebreakers to launch class discussion of a particular reading.

- *Writing Suggestions* can be found at the end of each selection. To encourage student competency in researching and documenting students' work, several prompts are specifically labeled "Writing with Sources." We've also included some "Writing in the Workplace" prompts to help students envision how to carry the strategies into their professional careers. (Additional writing suggestions for each chapter are included in this manual.)

We are very interested in hearing from anyone who has constructive ideas about either *Subject & Strategy* or this manual. We are always receptive to thoughts on how our book might be made even more useful for teachers and students. We can be reached at the Department of English, 400 Old Mill, The University of Vermont, Burlington, VT 05405-4030.

Paul Eschholz
Alfred Rosa

Contents

Sample Course Plans

Sample Course Plan Organized by Rhetorical Strategy

15 Weeks

Instructor Information:
Instructor:
Email:
Office Location & Hours:

COURSE MATERIALS

- Eschholz, Paul and Alfred Rosa. *Subject and Strategy: A Writer's Reader.* 15th ed., Bedford/St. Martin's. ISBN 978-1-319-13195-1, 2019.

In this course, students will write essays between 500-800 words (roughly two to three pages), each using a different rhetorical mode as a primary writing strategy.

At the end of the semester, students will submit a final portfolio which includes all the notes, drafts, and other materials at the end of the semester.

Students should consider visiting the Writing Center between classes while working on the various papers. They can help with all stages of the writing process: brainstorming, developing ideas, identifying main point, planning organizational structure, revisions, and more.

COURSE SCHEDULE

*Readings should be read *before* coming to class on the day they are listed as "assignments."

Week 1, Class 1: Preliminaries
In class: Review attendance, syllabus, texts, course requirements
Assignments:

- Read Chapter 1: Reading (3)
- Read Stephen King, "Reading to Write" (71)
- **Paper #1:** Something you read which influenced you or had a significant effect on you. Be prepared to explain the subject and topic of your first paper in Week 1, Class 2.

Week 1, Class 2: Introduction to Writing
In class: Students will share the subject and topic of their paper, followed by a discussion of the writing process. Full class examination of one student paper.
Assignments:

- Read Chapter 2: Writing (25)
- **Paper #1:** Be prepared to share the thesis of your paper in class on Week 2, Class 1.

Week 2, Class 1: Narration

In class: Narration as a rhetorical strategy. Discuss reading. Students work with each other's drafts.
Assignments:

- Read introduction to Chapter 4: Narration (79)
- Read David P. Bardeen, "Not Close Enough for Comfort" (97)
- **Paper #1:** First draft due. Bring two copies for conferencing. Class discussion of your thesis statement.

Week 2, Class 2: Narration (cont.)

In class: Discuss readings. Students will consider which approach best suits the subject of their second paper.
Assignments:

- Read Junot Díaz, "The Terror" (92)
- **Paper #2:** Select a live event or moment which you could never forget. This will be the subject of your narration paper.

Week 3, Class 1: Description

In class: Discuss reading. Freewrite: Write for five to ten minutes, describing a moment that occurred today before class. Go into as much detail as possible and share discoveries.
Assignments:

- Read introduction to Chapter 5: Description (113)
- Read Jim Tassé, "Trailcheck" (student essay) (120)
- Read Philip Connors, "A Talent for Sloth" (142)

Week 3, Class 2: Description (cont.)

In class: Discuss readings. Students exchange and review each other's papers. Peer review.
Assignments:

- Read Jeannette Walls, "A Woman on the Street" (125)
- **Paper #2:** Bring two copies of a draft for peer conferencing.

Week 4, Class 1: Illustration

In class: Discuss readings.

- Read introduction to Chapter 6: Illustration (153)
- **Paper #2:** Revised draft due
- **Paper #3:** Write an essay on one of the following statements, using examples to illustrate your ideas. You should be able to draw some of your examples from personal experience and firsthand observation.
  - The latest trend is [ridiculous/worth paying attention to].
  - In advertising, [*group of people*] are portrayed as [*characteristics*].
  - Grades [are/are not] a good indicator of what students have learned.
  - Every college campus has its own unique culture and language.

Week 4, Class 2: Illustration (cont.)

In class: Discuss readings. Peer review.
Assignments:

- Read Natalie Goldberg, "Be Specific" (168)
- Read Jennifer Ackerman, "The Genius of Birds" (172)
- **Paper #3:** Bring two copies of this essay for student conferencing.

Week 5, Class 1: Process Analysis

In class: Discuss process analysis as a writing strategy. Discuss readings.
Assignments:

- Read introduction to Chapter 7: Process Analysis (191)
- Read Alicia Ault, "How Do Spiders Make Their Webs?" (220)
- **Paper #3:** Revised draft due
- **Paper #4:** Write a directional or evaluative process analysis on one of the following topics:
  - How to rent an apartment
  - How to cook in a dorm
  - How to prevent an argument
  - How to make up after a fight
  - How to make a really good meal
  - How to buy the perfect gift
  - How to get into shape
  - How to break a bad habit

Week 5, Class 2: Process Analysis (cont.)

In class: Discuss the reading.
Assignments:

- Read Cody Cassidy and Paul Doherty, "What Would Happen if You Were Attacked by a Great White Shark?" (211)
- Read Ashlie Stevens, "Why We All Scream When We Get Ice Cream Brain Freeze" (217)

Week 6, Class 1: Comparison and Contrast

In class: Review the readings. Exchange and review each other's process papers.
Assignments:

- Read introduction to Chapter 8: Comparison and Contrast (225)
- Read Andrew Vachss, "The Difference between 'Sick' and 'Evil'" (247)
- **Paper #4:** Due

Week 6, Class 2: Comparison and Contrast (cont.)

In class: Discuss readings.
Assignments:

- Read Suzanne Britt, "Neat People vs. Sloppy People" (238)
- Read Paulina Porizkova, "America Made Me a Feminist" (253)
- **Paper #5:** Write an essay in which you compare and contrast two objects, people, or events to show at least one of the following:
  - Their importance differences
  - Their significant similarities
  - Their relative value
  - Their distinctive qualities

Week 7, Class 1: Division and Classification

In class: Consider division and classification as a rhetorical strategy. Discuss readings.
Assignments:

- Read introduction to Chapter 9: Division and Classification (259)
- Read Judith Viorst, "The Truth about Lying" (273)
- Read Sara Gilbert, "The Different Ways of Being Smart" (280)

Week 7, Class 2: Division and Classification (cont.)

In class: In-class editing of final draft.
Assignment:

- **Paper #5:** Due

Week 8, Class 1: Definition

In class: Consider definition as a rhetorical strategy, especially when combined with other strategies.
Assignments:

- Read introduction to Chapter 10: Definition (303)
- Read Deborah M. Roffman, "What Does 'Boys Will Be Boys' Really Mean?" (323)
- **Paper #6:** Select a word or concept you feel has been misunderstood. Write a sentence describing what you consider is the existing definition and another sentence describing your definition.

Week 8, Class 2: Definition (cont.)

In class: Discuss readings and student topics for Paper #6.
Assignments:

- Read Mark Peters, "Virtue Signaling and Other Inane Platitudes" (333)
- **Paper #6:** Draft an essay that includes the two definitions from last class and argues why this distinction matters.

Week 9: Class 1: Cause and Effect Analysis

In class: Consider cause and effect analysis as a rhetorical strategy and the challenges of using the strategy. Peer review.
Assignments:

- Read introduction to Chapter 11: Cause and Effect Analysis (339)
- **Paper #6:** Draft due. Bring in two copies to workshop with peers.

Week 9, Class 2: Cause and Effect Analysis (cont.)

In class: Discuss reading. In class free write: Spend 5-10 minutes writing about how advertising uses cause-and-effect claims to sell products.
Assignments:

- Read Anahad O'Connor, "Coca-Cola Funds Scientists' Effort to Alter Obesity Battle" (365)
- **Paper #6:** Revision due

Week 10, Class 1: Argumentation and Writing with Sources

In class: Discuss argumentation as a writing strategy supported by other strategies.
Assignments:

- Read introduction to Chapter 12: Argumentation (377)
- Read Nancy Armour, "Participation Awards Do Disservice" (402)

Week 10, Class 2: Argumentation and Writing with Sources (cont.)

In class: Discuss readings. In-class journaling: Write a paragraph explaining whether or not you find the articles convincing and why.

- Read John Metta, "I, Racist" (432)
- Read Shaun King, "No, I Won't Be Writing about Black-on-Black Crime" (445)

Week 11, Class 1: Argumentation and Writing with Sources (cont.)

In class: Discuss readings and use of sources.
Assignments:

- Read introduction to Chapter 14: Writing with Sources (497)
- Read Lisa Wade, "American Hookup" (524)
- **Paper #7:** Select one of your previous papers and add 3-5 sources to enrich your essay.

Week 11, Class 2: Revising

In class: Discuss readings in preparation for the production of final portfolios.
Assignment:

- **Paper #7:** Print/copy your sources and bring to class.

Week 12, Classes 1 & 2: Revising

In class: Revise and edit.
Assignments:

- Read and reference Chapter 16: Editing for Grammar, Punctuation, and Sentence Style (561)
- **Paper #7:** While students are meeting one-on-one with instructor, the class will review each other's essays and note suggested revisions.

Week 13, Classes 1 & 2: Conferences with Instructor

While students are meeting one-on-one with instructor, the class will read their weakest pieces aloud to one another and note suggested revisions.
Assignment:

Portfolio: Bring a copy of all papers written for the class. Have several questions ready for the instructor.

Week 14, Classes 1 & 2: Student Presentations

Each student will adapt their strongest paper in a three-minute presentation, in whatever mode, medium, or genre they choose. Each presentation will be followed by a discussion and suggestions for the author.
Assignment:

Continue revising papers based on feedback.

Week 15, Class 1: Final

Portfolio Due

Sample Course Plan Organized by Theme

15 Weeks

Instructor Information:
Instructor:
Email:
Office Location & Hours:

COURSE MATERIALS

- Eschholz, Paul and Alfred Rosa. *Subject and Strategy: A Writer's Reader.* 15th ed., Bedford/St. Martin's. ISBN 978-1-319-13195-1, 2019.

In this course students will write essays between 500-800 words (roughly two to three pages), each emphasizing a different theme.

At the end of the semester, students will submit a final portfolio which includes all the notes, drafts, and other materials at the end of the semester.

Students should consider visiting the Writing Center between classes while working on the various papers. They can help with all stages of the writing process: brainstorming, developing ideas, identifying main point, planning organizational structure, revisions, and more.

COURSE SCHEDULE

*Readings should be read *before* coming to class on the day they are listed as "assignments."

Week 1, Class 1: Preliminaries
In class: Review attendance, syllabus, texts, and course requirements.
Assignments:

- Read Stephen King, "Reading to Write" (71)
- **Paper #1:** Something you read which influenced you or had a significant effect on you. Be prepared to explain the subject and topic of your first paper in Week 1, Class 2.

Week 1, Class 2: Introduction to Writing
In class: Students will share the subject and topic of their paper. Discuss the writing process. Draft thesis statements in class.
Assignments:

- Read Chapter 2: Writing (25)
- **Paper #1:** Be prepared to share the thesis of your paper in class on Week 2, Class 1. Full class examination of one student paper

Week 2, Class 1: Working with Drafts
In class: Discuss reading. Class discussion of thesis statements. Peer review.
Assignments:

- Read Anne Lamott, "Shitty First Drafts" (62)
- **Paper #1:** First draft due. Bring two copies for conferencing.

Week 2, Class 2: Sense of Self

In class: Discuss theme.
Assignments: Read Russell Baker, "Discovering the Power of My Words" (57)

- **Paper #1:** Revision due
- **Paper #2:** Select an incident that contributed to your sense of self and/or gave you a new awareness of yourself.

Week 3, Class 1: Sense of Self (cont.)

In class: Discuss reading and challenges of Paper 2. Outlining workshop.
Assignments:

- Read David P. Bardeen, "Not Close Enough for Comfort" (97)
- Read Amy Tan, "Mother Tongue" (294)

Week 3, Class 2: Family and Relationships

In class: Discuss readings. Peer review.
Assignments:

- Read Mitch Albom, "If You Had One Day with Someone Who's Gone" (178)
- **Paper #2:** Bring in a draft of Paper #2. Bring two copies for conferencing.

Week 4, Class 1: Family and Relationships (cont.)

In class: Discuss reading.
Assignments:

- Read Howard Solomon, Jr., "Best Friends" (student essay) (312)
- **Paper #2:** Submit revision of Paper #2.
- **Paper #3:** Write an essay about a family member or friend who played a significant role in your life.

Week 4, Class 2: Family and Relationships (cont.)

In class: Discuss reading. In pairs, students share who they picked for their essay subject and why, generating notes to contribute to their papers.
Assignments:

- Read Maya Angelou, "Sister Flowers" (135)
- **Paper #3:** List 3-5 qualities of the person who is the subject of your paper.

Week 5, Class 1: Moral Values

In class: Discuss theme and readings.
Assignments:

- Read Judith Viorst, "The Truth about Lying" (273)
- Read William Galston, "Telling Americans to Vote, Or Else" (406)
- **Paper #3:** Due

Week 5, Class 2: Moral Values (cont.)

In class: Discuss readings.
Assignments:

- Read Anahad O'Connor, "Coca-Cola Funds Scientists' Effort to Alter Obesity Battle" (365)
- Read Mark Peters, "Virtue Signaling and Other Inane Platitudes" (333)
- **Paper# 4:** Select a value you wish people shared or a value you observe but believe is harmful and writing an essay in support of or against this value.

Week 6, Class 1: Moral Values (cont.)

In class: Review reading, and consider it as a model for writing.
Assignment:

- Read Barbara Bowman, "Guns and Cameras" (student essay) (234)

Week 6, Class 2: Moral Values (cont.)

In class: Peer review.
Assignment:

- **Paper #4:** Draft due. Bring two copies to class for conferencing.

Week 7, Class 1: Sense of Place

In class: Discuss theme and reading.
Assignments:

- Read James Rebanks, "A Shepherd's Life" (106)
- **Paper #4:** Revision due

Week 7, Class 2: Checkpoint

In class: How is class going so far? What questions, challenges, or strategies have you encountered? Optional consultation with instructor.

Week 8, Class 1: Technology in Modern Life

In class: Discuss theme and readings.
Assignments:

- Read Pamela Paul, "Save Your Sanity, Downgrade Your Life" (371)
- Read Roger McNamee, "I Invested Early in Google and Facebook. Now They Terrify Me." (426)
- **Paper #5:** Choose an aspect of technology in modern life and argue whether that technology is improving or harming life.

Week 8, Class 2: Technology in Modern Life (cont.) & Research

In class: Discuss reading, and how and why to conduct research. Freewrite: Given that it will be impossible to consume everything produced, by the end of your life what will you hope to have read, seen, or heard?
Assignments:

- Read Chapter 15: A Brief Guide to Researching and Documenting Essays (539)
- Read Linda Holmes, "The Sad Beautiful Fact That We're All Going to Miss Almost Everything" (491)

Week 9, Class 1: Research (cont.)
Research Workshop with Librarian

Week 9, Class 2: Technology in Modern Life (cont.)

In class: Discuss readings. Peer review workshop of annotated bibliography.
Assignments:

- Read Noah Smith, "Don't Assume Robots Will Be Our Future Coworkers" (464)
- **Paper #5:** Bring two copies of annotated bibliography (2-4 sources) for peer review.

Week 10, Class 1: Technology in Modern Life (cont.) & Writing with Sources

In class: Discuss effectively incorporating sources and avoiding plagiarism.
Assignment:

- Read introduction to Chapter 14: Writing with Sources (497)

Week 10, Class 2: Working with Sources

In class: Editing of final drafts in-class; turn in.
Assignment:

- **Paper #5:** Due

Week 11, Class 1: The Power of Language

In class: Discuss theme and readings.
Assignments:

- Read Russell Baker, "Discovering the Power of My Words" (57)
- Read Jake Jamieson, "The English-Only Movement: Can America Proscribe Language with a Clear Conscience?" (530)
- **Paper #6:** Write a researched argument about an aspect of language in today's society using one of the following rhetorical strategies in *Subject & Strategy* as an organizing principle: cause and effect, comparison and contrast, process analysis, division and classification.

Week 11, Class 2: The Power of Language (cont.)

In class: Discuss readings and addressing counterarguments. Workshop thesis statements, outlines, and research plans.
Assignments:

- Read Shaun King, "No, I Won't Be Writing about Black-on-Black Crime" (445)
- Read Derald Wing Sue, "Racial Microaggressions in Everyday Life: Is Subtle Bias Harmless?" (439)

Week 12, Classes 1 & 2: Conferences with Instructor

Week 13, Classes 1 & 2: Revising

In class: Revise and edit. Peer review.
Assignments:

- Read and reference Chapter 16: Editing for Grammar, Punctuation, and Sentence Style (561)
- **Paper #6:** Bring two copies of your draft for peer review.

Week 14, Classes 1 & 2: Student Presentations

Each student will adapt their strongest paper in a three-minute presentation, in whatever mode, medium, or genre they choose. Each presentation will be followed by a discussion and suggestions for the author.
Assignment:

Continue revising papers based on feedback.

Week 15, Class 1: Final

Portfolio Due

CHAPTER 1   Reading

A View from the Bridge (p. 5)
CHEROKEE PAUL MCDONALD

ASSIGNMENT QUESTIONS

Preparing to Read

The great American philosopher and naturalist Henry David Thoreau has written: "The question is not what you look at, but what you see." We've all had the experience of becoming numb to sights or experiences that once struck us with wonderment; sometimes, however, with luck, something happens to renew our appreciation. Think of an example from your own experience. What are some ways we can retain or recover our appreciation of the remarkable things we have come to take for granted?

■ Thinking Critically about the Text (Instructor's Manual Only)

The jogger and the kid are very different from each other, but they share an interest in fishing. What role does the tarpon play in this story? What can a shared interest do for a relationship between two people?

■ Questions on Subject (Instructor's Manual Only)

1. Why is the narrator angry with the kid at the beginning of the story?
2. What clues lead up to the revelation that the kid is blind? Why does it take the narrator so long to realize it?
3. "Why don't you get yourself some decent equipment?" the narrator asks the kid (paragraph 19). Why does McDonald include this question? Speculate about the answer.
4. The boy boasts that one day he will catch big sport fish, too. Why does the narrator say he "wished [he] could be there when it happened" (paragraph 48)?

■ Questions on Strategy (Instructor's Manual Only)

1. Notice the way the narrator chooses and actually adjusts some of the words he uses to describe the fish to the kid. Why does he do this? What is McDonald's desired effect?
2. By the end of the essay, we know much more about the kid than the fact that he is blind, but, after the initial description, McDonald characterizes him only indirectly. As the essay unfolds, what do we learn about the kid, and by what techniques does the author convey this knowledge?
3. McDonald is able to move his story along rather quickly by being selective about what he tells the reader. For example, examine paragraphs 9–13, and explain how the author moves the action forward.
4. This essay, descriptive in theme and intent, is structured as a **narrative**. What makes the combination of story and description effective? Suppose McDonald had started his essay with a statement like this: "If you really want to see something clearly, try describing it to a blind child." How would such an opening change the impact of the essay? Which other rhetorical strategies might McDonald have used along with the new opening?

RESPONSES

Preparing to Read

Something happens in this essay: McDonald tells the story of an event that helped revive his narrator's sense of wonder and appreciation. This assignment asks students to remember and describe a similar event in their own lives. It is designed to elicit both narrative and description, the strategies McDonald uses. It also asks students to consider the cause and effect of apathy, a question that is central to McDonald's essay but one with which he deals only indirectly.

Thinking Critically about the Text (Instructor's Manual Only)

The tarpon is something of value to both the narrator and the kid, but because they perceive the fish in profoundly different ways, each can add to the other's ability to appreciate it. Each enriches the other's understanding and enjoyment of something they both like. A shared interest (in this case, the tarpon) allows a connection to occur between two people who otherwise would pass each other by. At the end of their encounter, the narrator is better able to see and appreciate both the fish and the kid.

Questions on Subject (Instructor's Manual Only)

1. There are two aspects to the narrator's frustration. The first aspect is that he is exercising and doesn't want to break stride and interrupt his workout. The second is that the kid's demand at first seemed unreasonably simplistic, and thus selfish.

2. The kid wore wrap-around sunglasses (paragraph 3); he was "fumbling" with his rod and reel (4); he could not see the shrimp by his foot (10); his fingers "felt" for the drag setting (16); he thought he had lost the fish when the line went slack (20); and he asked the narrator to tell him what the fish looked like (29). The narrator does not realize the kid is blind because he is preoccupied with his jogging and because the kid is a competent angler whose behavior does not arouse suspicion.

3. The narrator has developed enough admiration for the kid's skill to notice with regret the inadequacy of his equipment. Because he cannot see it, though, the kid is probably unaware that his gear is not "decent."

4. The narrator and kid have developed a symbiotic relationship that allows them both to see events in a new way: The kid sees the fish for the first time through the narrator's description, and the narrator appreciates the details of things that he once took for granted, like fishing technique and what a tarpon looks like. Catching a sport fish would not only be a huge victory for the kid, and the narrator would love to share in that victory, but being there would also give the narrator another chance to experience the heightened appreciation of detail.

Questions on Strategy (Instructor's Manual Only)

1. The narrator seeks to use words and phrases that are familiar to a child. He also looks for words that appeal to a sense other than sight (e.g., he starts to say that the fish is three feet long, but he then changes to the more concrete and sensory phrase, "as long as one of your arms" [33]). The effect is a description both accessible and vivid.

2. We learn that the kid is courteous; he says "please" (paragraphs 5 and 8) and "thanks" (12 and 42). He is, against all odds, a capable, determined fisherman (15, 24, and 47). Both the act of fishing and the fish itself give him tremendous delight. We see his joy in hooking and playing the fish (15 and 22), his pleasure in the narrator's description, and

his desire to set the fish free (37). McDonald uses dialogue and telling details to convey this knowledge to us.

3. There are several things to notice here. First, McDonald omits any description or flourish and concentrates on describing the events efficiently. Second, in paragraph 10, McDonald leaves out the customary "I said," phrase, instead incorporating it into the next paragraph. Third, McDonald uses two complex sentences (9 and 11) that contain a lot of information and read more quickly and smoothly than several short sentences would.

4. The narrative structure is effective because it adds suspense to the piece. The reader does not realize that the kid is blind until paragraph 31, and this revelation adds great impact to the narrator's description of the fish. Also, the narrative includes dialogue, which McDonald uses to great effect. McDonald's point is made indirectly, by illustration, in the narrative essay; to open the essay with a thesis statement would require a shift of strategy from story to argument. Students will have various ideas about how McDonald might have supported a different opening; some possibilities are illustration, exemplification, description, and cause and effect.

My Favorite Teacher (p. 13)
THOMAS L. FRIEDMAN

ASSIGNMENT QUESTIONS

Preparing to Read

If you had to name your three favorite teachers of all time, who would they be? Why do you consider each one a favorite? Which one, if any, are you likely to remember twenty-five years from now? Why?

▪ Thinking Critically about the Text (Instructor's Manual Only)

What do you think Friedman means when he states, "The Internet can make you smarter, but it can't make you smart" (paragraph 11)? What, according to Friedman, is missing on the Internet? Do you agree?

▪ Questions on Subject (Instructor's Manual Only)

1. Hattie M. Steinberg taught her students the fundamentals of journalism — "not simply how to write a lead or accurately transcribe a quote, but, more important, how to comport yourself in a professional way and to always do quality work" (paragraph 3). According to Friedman, what other fundamentals did she introduce to her students? Why do you think Friedman values these fundamentals so much?

2. Why do you think Friedman tells us three times that Hattie's classroom was Room 313 at St. Louis Park High School?

3. According to Friedman, what went wrong when the "huge dot-com-Internet-globalization bubble" (10) of the late 1990s burst? Do you agree?

4. Why did Steinberg have her students read the *New York Times* first thing every morning?

1. Friedman claims that his high school journalism teacher, Hattie M. Steinberg, was "someone who made the most important difference in my life" (1). What descriptive details does Friedman use to support this **thesis**?
2. Friedman punctuates his description of Steinberg's teaching with short, pithy sentences. For example, he ends paragraph 2 with the sentence "She was that good" and paragraph 3 with "She wanted to teach us about consequences." Identify several other short sentences Friedman uses. What do these sentences have in common? How do short sentences like these affect you as a reader? Explain.
3. What details in Friedman's portrait of his teacher stand out for you? Why do you suppose Friedman chose the details that he did? What **dominant impression** of Hattie M. Steinberg do they collectively create?
4. In paragraph 7, Friedman quotes Steinberg directly. What does he gain by having her speak for herself?

RESPONSES

Preparing to Read

You might want to remind students that these do not have to be schoolteachers. Their favorite teacher could be a person who taught them how to tie their shoes, play piano or soccer, or use their computer. Teachers can be found everywhere.

Thinking Critically about the Text (Instructor's Manual Only)

Students may have varying interpretations of what Friedman means by this statement. Many will probably mention that the Internet provides information, but it does not teach the user how to use or interpret the information, nor does it help the user to develop character when applying or borrowing the information.

Questions on Subject (Instructor's Manual Only)

1. At the end of paragraph 10, Friedman presents characteristics that represent Steinberg's understanding of fundamentals: "reading, writing, arithmetic; church, synagogue, and mosque; the rule of law; and good governance." Friedman uses this series of items to illustrate how the principles and aspects of journalism that Steinberg taught her students also applied to larger concerns of life.
2. Friedman's repeated references to Room 313 reflect the deep impression that the activities within that room made on him and the amount of time he spent there during high school. Now when he thinks of his teacher and the experiences he had with her, he thinks of Room 313.
3. Friedman believes that, in the rush to make a lot of money quickly, the dot-coms "forgot the fundamentals of how to build a profitable company." Students may or may not agree with Friedman's statement. Ask students whether they believe that the same thing happened in the nation's housing, banking, and financial markets in recent years.

4. Steinberg had her students read the *New York Times* every morning because that's how "real journalists start their day" (paragraph 9). Specifically, Anthony Lewis and James Reston start their day reading the paper. Of course, it was also a way to expose students to well-thought-out, well-written models of journalism and analysis. Ask students how reading models of good writing can improve one's own writing, a method they'll use as they encounter the student and professional selections in *Subject & Strategy*.

Questions on Strategy (Instructor's Manual Only)

1. Friedman's examples point out key aspects of his own career in journalism, thereby establishing the important role Hattie Steinberg played in his life. One example, his interview with an advertising executive for his high school newspaper — during which the advertising executive used a four-letter word that Friedman and Steinberg decided to print — taught Friedman about the consequences of one's behavior. He also describes his first published story for the school paper, for which he covered a lecture by and then interviewed Ariel Sharon. This event indicates the direction his career followed, focusing on issues in the Middle East. Friedman says that the *New York Times* was delivered every morning to Room 313, emphasizing how the paper exerted an enormous influence over his approach to journalism, beginning the professional path that led him from being Steinberg's student to a successful columnist for the *Times*. Finally, Friedman's example about the "dot-com-Internet-globalization bubble" (paragraph 10) that burst impresses upon readers the real secret to success that Steinberg passed on to him: fundamentals that transferred across different industries, jobs, and areas of life.

2. Examples of short sentences in Friedman's essay include the following:

   "She wanted to teach us about consequences" (3).

   "Competition was fierce" (4).

   "His name was Ariel Sharon. First story I ever got published" (4).

   "She was a woman of clarity in an age of uncertainty" (5).

   "These fundamentals cannot be downloaded" (11).

   In each case, the short sentence emphasizes the key point developed in the paragraph in which it appears. Students' opinions about how the sentences affect them as readers may vary, but most will probably acknowledge the way in which the sentences dramatically emphasize the main ideas presented throughout the essay or the manner in which they create a sense of rhythm and fluency in the prose by varying sentence length and structure.

3. Students' opinions about which examples stand out for them and why Friedman chose those examples may vary. Whichever details they select, however, the general idea or dominant impression conveyed should reflect Friedman's emphasis on Steinberg's stern but principled and committed behavior toward her students.

4. By letting Steinberg speak for herself, Friedman is able to "show" what his teacher was really like. Her words are direct, deliberate, and stern, which supports his description of her. The quote thus increases Friedman's credibility with readers. Also, the quote varies the writing style, piquing reader interest and keeping their attention through to the end of the piece.

Sample Worksheets for Peer Review

In a typical peer critique session, a student reads her or his paper aloud to one or two students. The students then discuss the paper, and the reviewers take notes that the author can use during revision. A few different worksheets are often helpful, and we've provided the following two models.

The reviewer should record the author's responses to specific questions.

Author Name:
Paper Title:
Reviewer Name:

Peer Critique Worksheet: Answers from the Author
(Reviewer asks questions, author answers verbally, and reviewer records responses.)

1. Have you focused your **topic**?
2. Does your **thesis statement** clearly identify your topic and make an assertion about it?
3. Is the **writing strategy** you have chosen the best one for your purpose?
4. Are your **paragraphs** adequately developed, and does each support your thesis?
5. Is your **beginning** effective in capturing the reader's interest and introducing the topic?
6. Is your **conclusion** effective? Does it grow naturally from what you've said in the rest of your essay?
7. Have you accomplished your **purpose**?

Each peer reviewer should also complete an evaluation reflecting his or her thoughts about the paper, which may differ from those of the author.

Author Name:
Paper Title:
Reviewer Name:

Peer Critique Worksheet: Answers from the Reviewer

1. What is the **purpose** in this essay?
2. What is the **thesis**? Where is it stated?
3. Is the **thesis statement** sufficiently focused?
4. Does each **paragraph** support the thesis? If not, what can the author do to correct the problem?
5. Is the **organization** of the essay the best one for the material?

---

6. What is the **strongest part** of the essay? What can the author do to build on that aspect of the essay?
7. What is the **weakest part** of the essay? What can the author do to correct any problems?
8. What might the author add to the draft?

The first two chapters, the chapter introductions, and the glossary in *Subject & Strategy* may be especially useful to students as they complete these two worksheets.

CHAPTER 3   Writers on Writing

Learning to Write Dumb Things Again (p. 52)
RICARDO RODRÍGUEZ-PADILLA

Preparing to Read
This prompt will encourage students to reflect on their literacy and consider the connections between creativity, work, and school, as well as the way their childhood literacy transferred to their current work in college. Some students may not remember their childhoods as well as others. Be prepared for some students having no recollection of these early years and these early interests.

Thinking Critically about the Text
Montaigne's contemporaries criticized him as being self-indulgent because he often wrote personal anecdotes and went on tangents in his writing. It is just these tangents and individuality which Rodríguez-Padilla advocates for in his essay. Montaigne's genre of personal essay was a challenge to the writing style of his day; however, Montaigne's work has retained relevance because the personal story has a timelessness other forms of writing may lack — which is the irony of this epigraph.

Discussing the Craft of Writing
1. Rodríguez-Padilla uses the second person (*you*) to call the reader into action; he wants readers to return to the "dumb" writing of the childhood. He speaks with the audience directly in order to connect to the child within the reader. His argument is that the reader's authentic voice and personal story matters — and worth the risk of eschewing, at least for a time, the conventions of the traditional educational system. Had he used "I," he may have been able to inspire the reader through his own personal story.
2. "Dumb things" are those things that teachers and academic institutions may disregard as informal or unprofessional writing. These include personal stories, memories, tangents, fantasies, and stories involving a variety of characters and plots. The writer implies that within these so-called "dumb" details we find what matters to us most, and we discover our shared humanity.

3. We first write, he says, when we discover the depth and breadth of self-expression writing allows (paragraph 3). We write to communicate beauty (4) or because we think up "dumb" storylines (5). We write because we make our parents and early teachers proud (4). His motive is to re-inspire people who once loved to write to reclaim their passion for writing.

4. The paradox is the more we are willing to write about "dumb things" and forget about trying to be the next great novelist, the more likely we are to become just that. Student opinions will vary.

5. Student experiences will vary. The majority of formal academic writing likely requires the author to be invisible, but some will have had training, perhaps in an anthropology class where they can discuss their interactions. The increase of blogs and social media has increased the personal narrative as a means for self-expression, as well.

6. Student answers will vary. Hopefully, students will be tempted to try returning to some of this "dumb" writing and write for creativity and pleasure. Perhaps you can encourage experimentation through a free-write after discussing this essay. Ask students, for example to take twenty minutes and write a story using the line Rodríguez-Padilla offers: "The silverware's ready, Mrs. Halifax."

Discovering the Power of My Words (p. 57)
RUSSELL BAKER

Preparing to Read
Since few students will have had specific "writing teachers," most will probably write about an English teacher or a history teacher who gave them assignments. These questions encourage students to think about the kinds of writing instruction they have received, their personal reactions to that instruction, and the long-term benefits. The questions prepare them to relate to Baker's personal experience.

Thinking Critically about the Text
Most students will be able to relate to the expository essay format to which Baker refers; such essays include the five-paragraph essay (introduction, three body paragraphs, and conclusion). Students write these essays about plays or classic literature, usually quoting the text or citing cases to prove a point about a theme — for example, loss, gender, irony, or a character's true nature (good/evil). Unlike "The Art of Eating Spaghetti," these traditional essays do not ask students to bring forth their own personal experiences, write in the first person, or convey a story for its own sake. Traditional expository essays teach structure and how to build a case, use evidence, and find themes.

Most students will expect that Baker would understand just the kind of writing assignments that the cartoon is depicting: assignments that make the mind "numb" (paragraph 6). Baker came to prim Mr. Fleagle's class believing, "Of all forms of writing, none seemed so boring as the essay" (6). Students will probably believe that Baker would find it ironic that writing for the teacher does not produce the kind of piece that instructors find really exemplary, whereas writing about something personally meaningful found in an assignment, as Baker did in "The Art of Eating Spaghetti," produces material more likely to be "the very essence of the essay" (12).

Discussing the Craft of Writing

1. Baker describes Mr. Fleagle as having a "dullness and inability to inspire. He was said to be stuffy, dull, and hopelessly out of date" (paragraph 2). He looked roughly seventy years old and prim, wearing "severe" eyeglasses and sporting primly cut hair. His clothes included vested suits, neckties, and starched shirts. His facial features matched his style; he had a pointed jaw, straight nose, and a way of speaking with grammatical accuracy and acuity. He appeared to be a "comic antique." Baker creates the dominant impression of Mr. Fleagle as someone from an earlier era by juxtaposing him with a younger and free-spirited person.

   You may want to ask students to describe Baker based on the picture of him at the beginning of this essay. He too has a formal appearance and seems about the age of Mr. Fleagle. What insight can they gain from this?

2. Because writing requires the author's intelligence and general life experience, choice enables a writer to find a hook or something inspiring. This inspiration, in turn, gives the writing momentum and infuses the reader with the author's own passion, something that Baker thought Mr. Fleagle seemed unable to do.

3. Baker describes the experience of seeing the topic as "produc[ing] an extraordinary sequence of mental images. Surging up from the depths of memory came a vivid recollection of a night in Belleville . . ." (7). Baker has a visceral response to the title: The night reminds him of the joy of being with his family, of laughter, and of everyone's inability to feel adequate when eating this new food. Like writing, nobody knew how to eat spaghetti primly and properly, so they laughed about their awkwardness. They had to throw "what was proper" out the window and just slop through themselves. This is exactly what Baker does when he writes the essay.

4. Whereas Baker believed that writing what came to him and not writing in a controlled manner would cause him to fail the assignment, his passion and ability to write about something true and meaningful captured the power of the personal essay.

5. Baker felt touched that someone would be moved by his words rather than by his analysis. In expository essays, writers quote from the text and rarely speak in the first person. In his spaghetti essay, Baker felt he used his voice and his true self. In addition, Baker's words infected the class with the kind of passion and inspiration he experienced when he wrote the essay and when he ate the meal. He communicated something important and personally meaningful through words. Others wanted to hear his words, too. Despite his distaste for the prim and proper approach, he found writing has something to offer.

6. Mr. Fleagle does not necessarily need to inspire students; he needs to help his students find inspiration in themselves. The narrative offers several insights into writing. First, a writing teacher should not be judged by his or her mannerisms, but rather by his or her ability to help students find their own words. Writing can be many things: a way to describe a play and to communicate with others. Writing can be a powerful way to communicate a personal experience to others who care about what you have to say. It is important not to give up on writing even if the topics do not appeal. When inspired, even the most reluctant English student has something to say.

Shitty First Drafts (p. 62)
ANNE LAMOTT

Preparing to Read

Students will most likely view writing first drafts as a chore. They may say that they have a pattern of frustration, false starts, and procrastination. Some will even say they have written first drafts and turned them in as final drafts.

Thinking Critically about the Text

Some students may find Lamott's use of the word *shitty* offensive or even unprofessional; however, they should see that the word is in keeping with Lamott's light-hearted tone and the frustration writers often feel. Another word might not have captured her feelings as acutely.

Discussing the Craft of Writing

1. Lamott means that nonwriters have a romantic view of the writer's life and process — that words flow freely from the writer's mind to the page. In reality, writing is difficult, and writers often find themselves blocked or doubtful of their abilities.

2. By "more or less," Lamott means that while in the thick of the process, it's hard to have perspective on how effective the process is or how well one is using it. Her sentiments are personal, but they do reflect a predicament many writers face.

3. Lamott suggests that first drafts are more about psychology than content and that the real hurdle is believing in oneself enough to get ideas down on paper. Content is something that can be refined in subsequent drafts, when the writer has gained confidence from surmounting the most difficult part of the process: the first draft.

4. Lamott's thesis statement is located in paragraph 3: "For me and most of the other writers I know, writing is not rapturous. In fact, the only way I can get anything written at all is to write really, really shitty first drafts."

5. Lamott infuses her essay with black humor: "All right, one of them does, but we do not like her very much" (paragraph 1); "One might hope for bad things to rain down on a person like this" (2); "Some readers took umbrage at my comparing mounds of vegetable puree with various ex-presidents' brains" (5); "I'd obsess about getting creamed by a car before I could write a decent second draft" (7). In paragraph 4, when encouraging writers to let themselves explore, she writes, "If one of the characters wants to say, 'Well, so what, Mr. Poopy Pants?' you let her." The word *poopy* brings the reader back to the title word, *shitty*. The absurd phrase demonstrates how relaxed readers may allow themselves to be during this first draft stage. Her use of humor mirrors some of the negative thoughts writers often have. Many students will likely appreciate and identify with Lamott's candor and sense of humor, though student opinions about the effectiveness of the humor will vary.

6. Lamott discusses her difficulties so that readers can better understand how much work writing truly entails. Students will find this information reassuring because it shows them that even professional writers have difficulties.

Writing for an Audience (p. 67)
LINDA S. FLOWER

Preparing to Read

Student responses will vary. This prompt is designed to get students thinking about audience — how their diction and tone can differ according to the audience. The truthfulness of students' accounts will probably vary as well. If you have an ethnically diverse class, the answers might vary more dramatically. The answers to the questions can tell us so much about our society as it does about each other's family, race, and the type of relationship we have with a best friend.

Thinking Critically about the Text

According to Flower, "the real purpose of a paper may be for you to make connections between two historical periods, to discover for yourself the principle behind a laboratory experiment, or to develop and support your own interpretation of a novel. A good college paper doesn't just rehash the facts; it demonstrates what your reader, as a teacher, needs to know—that you are learning the thinking skills his or her course is trying to teach" (paragraph 9).

Discussing the Craft of Writing

1. A competent writer will look at the distance between him- or herself and the audience, a distance created by differences such as age or background, knowledge about the topic, attitudes toward it, and personal or professional needs. The writer must analyze those needs, clarify what the reader needs to know, and adapt that knowledge to the reader.

2. Flower defines *knowledge* as a "conscious awareness of explicit facts and clearly defined concepts" that "can be easily written down or told to someone else." *Attitude*, on the other hand, is an "image" or "a loose cluster of associations" (paragraph 4). The distinction is important because "a reader's image of a subject is often the source of attitudes and feelings that are unexpected and, at times, impervious to mere facts" (5). Once aware of this, writers can bridge the distance between themselves and the reader through word choice and examples.

3. Students can begin by defining *connotation*: word associations derived from personal experience, reading, and the influence of others, as opposed to *denotation*, the literal meaning of a word. Flower uses the word *lakes* to illustrate the clusters of associations that are connected with a word. Engage students in a discussion of the examples; for example, ask them how *home* differs from *house*.

4. Students' responses may vary, though Flower seems to make conscious attempts to direct her diction and examples at a college audience. The second paragraph asks students to imagine themselves writing to their parents about a wilderness survival expedition they would like to join. The writers must bridge the gap between themselves and their New York City parents by communicating their desire to join this expedition in language their parents can understand. In her discussion of needs, for instance, Flower focuses on writing done on a job and in college courses—both examples of the kinds of writing that concern college students.

5. Using jargon might impress readers, but when the language used is too technical for the reader, he or she tunes out. Writers can use definitions, meaningful examples, description, comparison and contrast, and tone to bridge the gap between themselves and the reader. By asking classmates, friends, or parents to review writing, these readers' different backgrounds can help clarify areas which may be unclear to certain audiences.

Reading to Write (p. 71)
STEPHEN KING

Preparing to Read

Most students will see a connection between reading and writing. At a very basic level, reading can offer something to write about. Students may also say that, when they read, they get more exposure to the written word, providing them with an understanding of how good writing is supposed to look and on a deeper level, even unconsciously, an understanding of the structure and sound (voice) of good writing, all of which can help them when they write. Some students, however, might say that reading and writing are not connected. These students might struggle with reading but like writing. For these individuals, writing can lead back into reading: The more they write, the more they begin to appreciate what others have written. It is possible that a few students may say that they don't want to be influenced by others' writing or that when they read a lot they have trouble getting started with their own writing. In these cases, the reading might either intimidate the students or overwhelm the students' ideas or voice. Ask students what they hope to get from reading. (Pleasure? Knowledge?) Do they prefer some types of writing over others? What might they learn from those preferences? How might their reading lead to writing, and how might their writing also lead to reading?

Thinking Critically about the Text

When King says that "quite often the bad books have more to teach than the good ones" (paragraph 2), he means that one learns what not to do as much as what to do as a writer when reading poor writing. Bad prose may be more instructive because it is easier to avoid the pitfalls of bad writing than it is to achieve the grace of great writing. Some writers might despair when reading remarkable works like *The Grapes of Wrath*, feeling they will never write anything as good. But there is inspiration in exemplary work, too. One can't achieve great heights in writing unless she or he has been "swept away" (6) by such.

Discussing the Craft of Writing

1. King seems to find the word *zestful* artificial (and thus a mark of bad writing). He emphasizes that he doesn't think he's ever used *zestful* because for him it became synonymous with artless writing after he read that "terrible" story where Leinster "had fallen in love with the word" (3). It was like a "vaccination" against using words that don't feel natural (and repeating them dully). King learned what to avoid in his writing by reading terrible fiction.

2. Examples of different styles that King experienced through reading include not only the bad prose of Leinster, *Valley of the Dolls*, *Flowers in the Attic*, and *The Bridges of Madison County*, but also the "green and wondrous" work of Ray Bradbury, the "clipped . . . stripped, and hardboiled" James M. Cain, and the "luxurious and Byzantine" Lovecraft (paragraph 8). King states that developing a writing style doesn't "occur in a vacuum" (8). He learned by imitating a variety of styles he admired. According to King, "[y]ou have to read widely," try on different styles, and thereby develop the tools you need to write well (8).

3. King believes it is impossible to be both a writer and a member of polite society because writers who write "truthfully" (paragraph 10) cannot be concerned with whether or not they are perceived as rude or offensive in their work (and they likely will be).

4. King does not like TV because an aspiring writer does not have enough time both to read widely and to watch TV. "Reading takes time," and writers need time "to do some serious turning inward toward the life of the imagination" (paragraph 11).

5. King points out that not everyone gets joy out of a pursuit like writing, using for an example the dilemma of his son Owen, who "fell in love with Bruce Springsteen's E Street Band, particularly with Clarence Clemons, the band's burly sax player" (paragraph 13). But when Owen practiced on his saxophone, there was "no joy in it" (15). King says playing a musical instrument is the same as reading and writing. You need to find pleasure in it so it will not feel like a "rehearsal." The importance of reading, even for those

who don't love writing, is that "[t]he more you read, the less apt you are to make a fool of yourself with your pen or word processor" (17).

6. Student reactions will vary. A Klout score is a numerical measure between 1 and 100 that rates someone's influence on social media. The cartoon highlights a contemporary obsession with one's popularity on social media. How many "likes" one gets on Facebook, for example, can perhaps be taken as a measure of the value of one's worth or success. King would likely find the cartoon humorous because he would agree that writing must be evaluated based on its quality, not its popularity alone.

CHAPTER 4   Narration

The Terror (p. 92)
JUNOT DÍAZ

Preparing to Read
Not all students are avid readers. If students struggle to find responses, prompt them to share the books (or poems or plays) they read for class while in middle school and ask whether any of the material made an impact on them. Remind students that the impact can be either positive or negative.

Thinking Critically about the Text
Students may share stories about being bullied. If they do not, you can ask them to share a story about someone they know who was bullied or if they remember bullying someone else.

Questions on Subject
1. Díaz attributes the name-calling he experienced to "white middle-class bigotry" (paragraph 2). There must have been stories circulating that people from the Dominican Republic ate dogs. They called him a "sand nigger" likely because he was a darker-skinned man from an island country.

2. Díaz most likely told his brother that he was having a great time because he was ashamed of the bullying and because his brother — who was sick with leukemia — had his own struggles. Díaz may not have wanted to burden his brother and likely believed his sick brother could do little to help him.

3. "Being afraid" suggests a more constant state of being whereas "fear" suggests a momentary emotion. People living in war-torn countries, for example, are *afraid*. They live "in" fear. Fear is a more momentary experience, like when we lose control of our car in a snow storm. We experience fear in that moment, but we do not necessarily say that we are afraid of driving. Díaz's fear became constant — immutable like his brown skin.

4. Díaz attributed his safety to his vigilant efforts to avoid the brothers. If he changed the game, even very slightly, he feared disturbing the universe's delicate balance. It is possible, however, that the brothers lost interest in him immediately after the fight. But Díaz had to gather the courage to test their disinterest in him. He had to challenge his belief that he was safe only if he hid. In doing so, he freed himself.

Questions on Strategy

1. By providing the context first, the reader sees the narrator as even more vulnerable. Many readers appreciate the tenderness of that life stage and may be touched by his brother's sickness. This causes readers to feel sympathy for the narrator even before he takes his beating. By the time he is beaten, readers jump to his defense. If he had described the beating in the first paragraph, readers may not have felt as close to him. Díaz's structure creates the possibility that the reader, along with Díaz, feels personally attacked.

2. Díaz offers these details about his brother, "40 pounds lighter and barely able to piss under his own power, looking as if he were one bad cold away from the grave" (paragraph 3). The details show the brother's proximity to death. The details are fresh and reflect the sensibilities of an adolescent, not an adult. The phrase, "barely able to piss under his own power" may shock some readers. Because it is an uncommon way to describe leukemia, the statement may increase reader alertness. The observation might be something that stands out to an adolescent.

3. By shifting tenses, Díaz brings the readers into the action. Successful writing carries writers through a variety of emotions at varying tempos. Shifting tenses brings readers into the fight, making it hard for the reader to turn away.

4. In paragraph 2, Díaz places himself in the seventh grade. In paragraph 3, Díaz lets us know his father left the year prior. After the family fell into poverty, his brother was diagnosed with leukemia. In paragraph 5, we learn the "beat-down" occurred after his brother was already in the hospital. In paragraph 6, we learn Díaz goes home to an empty house and returns to school the next day with a black eye. Díaz exists in a state of fear from the beat-down until sophomore year in high school (13). As a sophomore, he faces his fears and presumably lives the rest of his days feeling much less afraid. The sequence of events tells readers the age of the author, the context in which he was living, and the duration of the fear.

Not Close Enough for Comfort (p. 97)
DAVID P. BARDEEN

Preparing to Read

Students will have a variety of stories about people keeping secrets from them. This prompt is an opportunity for students to reflect on how secrets have affected their relationships. You may want to ask students if they think keeping secrets from people can be a good thing or a hurtful thing.

Thinking Critically about the Text

Will once questioned David about his sexual orientation, so he probably was not totally surprised by David's revelation. When David came out, Will asked several questions, perhaps suggesting a lack of surprise. However, Will's calmness could be a reflection of the distance that had grown between the twins. Knowing his brother had kept a secret from him may have also made Will feel betrayed and not trusted. For Will, David's sexual orientation could be further proof that they had more differences than similarities, making closeness even more challenging.

Questions on Subject

1. Bardeen probably had many reasons for not telling his brother sooner. As a teenager Bardeen seemed afraid of his sexual orientation and withdrew from most relationships

(paragraph 11). Later, he probably feared being rejected by his brother and losing their close relationship. Maybe he thought Will would push him away, fearing that he too might be gay or be labeled gay.

2. It is often said that twins feel closer to each other than to any other person in the world and that twins share an almost psychic bond. However, twins are individuals who have their own feelings, thoughts, and desires; like many siblings, they keep secrets from each other. The word *romantic* refers to the idealized but impractical belief that the relationship between twins is different from that between other siblings. In fact, an individual can hardly ever truly be known by another, even if a twin.

3. Bardeen apologizes to his brother for keeping such a large secret from him. Will's response to David is, "No I think it's great" (paragraph 17), which can be read as Will thinking that David apologized for being gay.

4. Bardeen probably hoped that coming out would bring him and his brother closer together, or at least explain some of the distance they felt. Students may think this hope was unrealistic because the gulf between the brothers seemed so wide. At the same time, the revelation might offer the brothers some insight into why their relationship waned.

Questions on Strategy

1. Bardeen uses first-person point of view because coming out is telling one's own story in one's own voice. Third-person point of view would create the sense that Bardeen was hiding himself and not being honest to himself or his audience about his secret.

2. Bardeen bookends his coming out to others (paragraphs 3–6) with his conversation with his brother, contrasting how "easy" it was to confide in people who didn't know him with how difficult it was to confide in someone with whom he was once extremely close. Paragraphs 3 through 6 explain how Bardeen built up the courage to talk to Will and the process he went through to come out to other people in his life. Had Bardeen begun his narrative with paragraphs 3 through 6, the gravity of his discussion with Will — the deliberation and thoughts he was having as they talked — would not have been expressed with the same urgency or emotion.

3. The dialogue shows the nature of the brothers' relationship and how hard it has become for them, despite the closeness they once shared, to talk to each other. The clipped dialogue captures the tension of the conversation.

4. Bardeen uses short sentences and sentence fragments to reflect his fear and hesitation about coming out to his brother. The clipped sentences illustrate how difficult it is for the brothers to communicate now that they have grown apart.

The Work You Do, The Person You Are (p. 102)
TONI MORRISON

Preparing to Read

Student experiences will vary based on their work experience (or lack thereof), and a discussion may focus on the difficulty of work, the type of work, or the importance of early jobs to future careers. The question should prepare students to talk about the role of work in their lives, particularly how it does — or will — relate to their personal identities.

Thinking Critically about the Text

Morrison passes the advice she received to the reader in an attempt to convince them to accept it for their own lives. Readers will likely reflect on their own present or past jobs to see how closely they relate to Morrison's experience.

Questions on Subject

1. The most profound pleasure for Morrison was "the pleasure of being necessary to my parents" (paragraph 3). The money she earned helped pay for "real things" like insurance policy payments and food.

2. Morrison says in the 1940s children were "needed"; they cared for siblings, worked the farm, and/or earned money (3). Today, she does not think most families rely on children in the same way; families now do more to serve children than children do to serve the family.

3. Morrison's employer began to offer her used clothes she could buy. Initially Morrison was impressed by the clothes and bought some items. She said that to her, with only two dresses to wear to school, these clothes seemed an improvement.

4. She thought her mother would tell her to quit. This suggests that her mother had a strong influence over her decisions and that children may be more likely to make career choices based on what they believe their parents want than what the child wants for herself.

Questions on Strategy

1. Morrison does not begin with a clear context of her employment situation. She identifies the employer only with the capitalized pronoun *She* or *Her*. Students may find this beginning disorienting but may also appreciate the opening strategy of placing readers directly in the scene, helping them identify with the narrator.

2. Morrison begins paragraph 4 with "in those days" to shift the essay from the personal narration to a reflection on the times more generally. Paragraph 5 begins with "little by little," which alerts readers that the storyline is moving forward and conveys that a length of time has passed. She starts paragraph 6 with "still," indicating she will continue with the same narrative thread.

3. With this technique, Morrison demonstrates that we make meaning out of what people say or do not say. Communication is about more than words exchanged. We interpret and may turn a moment of advice into a set of guidelines to follow, which she renders as a numbered list.

4. By using pronouns, readers have a sense of the employer as being distant and indifferent. She is not someone Morrison can relate to. Additionally, the capital letter shows the power differential.

A Shepherd's Life (p. 106)
JAMES REBANKS

Preparing to Read

Students' varying experiences in or feelings toward their hometown may make for a compelling discussion about their motivations for attending their school or pursuing a career. Reflecting on the relationship between their origins and their career paths will prepare them to consider Rebanks's return to his sheep farming roots.

Thinking Critically about the Text

Student answers will vary, but the prompt is designed to encourage students to consider how Rebanks rejected what was expected of him or what was considered a better path. Students may also have experiences where they have felt put down for their life decisions instead of empowered.

Questions on Subject

1. Displaying their "brightness" would have been dangerous for two reasons: the students tended to be very physically aggressive, so acting different may have made one stand out as a target. And as he mentions in paragraph 6, people could easily become outsiders. When labeled an outsider, one could not easily be accepted back in.
2. Rebanks creates a dominant impression of chaos and destructive behavior by describing what the classrooms looked like after the students tore them apart and recounting a story about a student who climbed up on the roof. Details of teacher-student interactions also create an impression of an authoritarian education.
3. Rebanks realized the teacher was communicating her patronizing view of the Lake District. She saw is as a place to flee, not a place to settle down and live. She thought only unintelligent people stayed and her job was to inspire them to think and move beyond the confines of their upbringing. Rebanks becomes incensed at this insult to his family and to the work they did, as if it were not good enough.
4. Rebanks hates the implication that "staying local and doing physical work doesn't count for much" (paragraph 7). He believes instead that all work matters and that staying in one's hometown does not necessarily mean one is stagnant.

Questions on Strategy

1. In paragraph 2 Rebanks sets up a shift between the main narrative and specific examples: he writes, "There was a chasm between that headmistress and us." The rest of the paragraph describes that chasm. By using "daydreaming" as a strategy, he shares his reflections without losing the setting of the assembly. He starts paragraph 5 with "On another occasion" to alert readers that he will tell another specific story.
2. The single-sentenced paragraph 3 sets up a longer description of daily life in the classroom, and it highlights Rebanks's place in the story as well as his skills and character at the time.
3. The teacher values going out and seeing the world, academic intelligence, and white-collar jobs. Rebanks finds this insulting of not only the students in the school but their parents and grandparents as well.
4. William Wordsworth was a nineteenth-century English Romantic poet who used the Lake District for poetic inspiration. Romantics considered a life well lived as one in which a person has many different experiences, including relationships, emotions, travel, and generalized diversity. The teacher wanted to instill these values in her students, and she also wants to present an idea of education and experience that may clash with the students' rural livelihoods. Rebanks's response reveals that her reference to Wordsworth was not aspirational but offensive to the students.

ADDITIONAL WRITING SUGGESTIONS FOR NARRATION

1. Using Junot Díaz's, David P. Bardeen's, Toni Morrison's or James Rebanks's essay as a model, narrate an experience that gave you a new awareness of

yourself. Use enough telling detail in your narrative to help your reader visualize your experience and understand its significance for you. You may find the following suggestions helpful in choosing an experience to narrate in the first person:

- my greatest success or failure
- my most embarrassing moment
- my happiest moment
- a truly frightening experience
- an experience that, in my eyes, turned a hero or an idol into an ordinary person
- an experience that turned an ordinary person I know into one of my heroes
- the experience that was the most important turning point in my life

2. Each of us can tell of an experience that has been unusually significant in teaching us about our relationship to society or to life's institutions — schools, social or service organizations, religious groups, government. Think about your past, and identify one experience that has been especially important for you in this way. After you have considered this event's significance, write an essay recounting it. To bring your experience into focus and to help you decide what to include in your essay, ask yourself: Why is this experience important to me? What details are necessary for me to re-create the experience in an interesting and engaging way? How can my narrative be most effectively organized? What point of view will work best?

3. While growing up, we have all done something we know we should not have done. Sometimes we have gotten away with our transgressions, sometimes not. Sometimes our actions have no repercussions; sometimes they have very serious ones. Tell the story of one of your escapades, and explain why you have remembered it so well.

4. Many people love to tell stories (that is, they use narration) to illustrate an abstract point, to bring an idea down to a personal level, or to render an idea memorable. Often, the telling of such stories can be entertaining as well as instructive. Think about a belief or position that you hold dear (e.g., every individual deserves respect, recycling matters, voluntarism creates community, people need artistic outlets, nature renews the individual), and try to capture that belief in a sentence or two. Then, narrate a story that illustrates your belief or position.

5. **Writing with Sources.** As a way of gaining experience with third-person narration, write an article intended for your school or community newspaper in which you report on what happened at one of the following:

- the visit of a state or national figure to your campus or community
- a dormitory meeting
- a current event of local, state, or national significance
- an important sports event
- a current research project of one of your professors
- a campus gathering or performance
- an important development at a local business or at your place of employment

In order to provide context for your article, consider interviewing one or more people involved and/or doing some background research on the object of your narrative. For models of and advice on integrating sources in your essay, see Chapters 14 and 15.

6. Take some time to study Grant Snider's "Life in the Woods," reproduced at the beginning of the chapter.
   - Take a few minutes to describe what's going on in this illustration. Who is the character? Where is he or she? What happens? Next, consider how you know this. What aspects of the narrative are conveyed by written elements? What parts are conveyed by visual elements only?
   - Write a short paper in which you discuss what you discovered about the differences between visual and written narratives.

7. **Writing with Sources.** Consider broadening and deepening your exploration of the differences between visual and written narratives by reading what others have to say about using visuals to convey meaning. (One good source for such discussion is Scott McCloud's *Understanding Comics*.) Alternatively, consider writing a paper in which you compare and contrast two genres (graphic novels and films, perhaps) used with a single work or two examples from the same genre (for instance, Gene Luen Yang's *American Born Chinese* and Marjane Satrapi's *Persepolis*, two graphic novels). For models of and advice on integrating sources in your essay, see Chapters 14 and 15.

CHAPTER 5   Description

A Woman on the Street (p. 125)
JEANNETTE WALLS

Preparing to Read
Some students may see the homeless as a kind of "other" people with whom they have little in common and maybe even fear. There is a tendency to think of the homeless as a unified group rather than as individuals that share a single attribute: They have no fixed roof over their head. Students may try to generalize about their hygiene and how they use their time. Students may share stories of homeless people they have met that help characterize them as unique individuals with varying experiences and motivations.

Thinking Critically about the Text
Seeing her mother helps Walls see herself. For most readers, seeing someone who is homeless won't prompt this reflection because someone who is homeless will seem very different from themselves. Walls cannot so easily discount the differences because the homeless person she saw was her mother. When Walls walks back into her own home, she sees it through her mother's eyes. Nice furnishings and a comfortable existence are a stark contrast to her mother's dumpster diving.

Questions on Subject

1. From Walls's presentation of her dialogue with her mother, her mother *seems* happy. She does not complain or bemoan her situation. Yet the state of her body and her lack of self-care might suggest otherwise. We cannot know from the essay how truly happy her mother is, although she seems less perturbed than her daughter regarding their differences in lifestyles.

2. Walls's mother tells Walls that she thinks people are too wasteful, but she has also asked for perfume in the past, so we do not really know whether she is against all material possessions as an absolute principle, or if she feels she just does not need them for herself. It seems she doesn't approve of her daughter's values, but we do not know to what extent this has to do with material possessions.

3. Walls's mother might not like to see her daughter's apartment because, in seeing it, she herself might have to face the painful difference in their life circumstances. It might be easier to judge her daughter's lifestyle in an abstract way rather than face it literally. Just as it was difficult for Walls to see her mother dig through the trash, perhaps it would have been as difficult for her mother to see Walls's apartment.

4. Her mother is trying to make Walls see how uncomfortable Walls is with herself. She wants Walls to see the importance of self-acceptance. She believes her daughter focuses on the wrong things in life. We do not know whether this means her choice of career, her choice of husband, or how she values and uses money. Her mother's criticism is broad. Presumably, readers will share more of Walls's values than her mother's, so students will have to reflect on their own values to answer this question. Does valuing creature comforts mean that one's values are confused? Student answers will vary.

Questions on Strategy

1. Walls describes her mother with "long hair streaked with gray, tangled and matted, and her eyes had sunk deep into their sockets" (paragraph 2). She seems to enjoy her life, "rooting happily through the Dumpster" (5). Her mother was also someone who used to be active (cliff diving) and artistic (painting in the desert) and in fact still values commenting on the arts (a recent Picasso exhibit). She seems articulate and educated. She is also a married woman with a husband who seems to share her values.

2. Walls describes herself as someone living on Park Avenue, well-dressed (wearing heels) with an active social life (she was headed to a party when she saw her mother). She is someone who has invested time in designing a home that feels comfortable and appealing to her. She has spent time framing artwork and creating a cozy atmosphere. She has a husband who works late, presumably with a good and high-paying job. Walls tells the reader and her mother that she is embarrassed by her parents' lifestyle. We know that she has offered to help them multiple times, and they have refused.

3. The single sentence in paragraph 4 encapsulates very clearly Walls's shame (hiding in the seat) and the difference in their lifestyles (she lives on Park Avenue and takes taxis around the city). Its brevity draws attention to these issues, emphasizing their importance to the piece.

4. Words representing Walls's life include *Park Avenue, overdressed, elevator man, polished wood floor, Vivaldi, Persian rugs,* and *overstuffed leather armchair*. Words representing her mother's life include *Dumpster, trash, childish glee, tangled, matted, grime,* and *bulky*. These terms highlight the difference in their lives. Walls is living a stereotypical highbrow lifestyle in New York City, surrounded by the expensive objects in her home, classical

music, and fashionable clothes. Her mother is living with seemingly more glee, but she does not groom and survives on the scraps others leave behind.

The Barrio (p. 130)
ROBERT RAMÍREZ

Preparing to Read
Students always find something to write about when describing a neighborhood in which they've lived. They often focus on their house or apartment, school, places they frequented, family, or friends. We like to ask how many students have lived in a single town or city or at the same address their whole lives, live in an ethnic neighborhood, or live in the same town or city as their grandparents or other relatives. Students who come from older, more established neighborhoods often have different stories to tell about their sense of community than do students from the suburbs. A sense of community can grow out of a shared history and feelings of connection to a place. Students cite ethnicity and extended families as factors contributing to a sense of community.

Thinking Critically about the Text
Most students have mixed feelings about wanting to visit or live in the barrio. Many are curious enough to want to visit, but few are willing to commit to live there. Invariably they start by pointing to the positive qualities of life in the barrio, especially the strong feelings of family. However, they always come back to the negative elements—the severe overcrowding, the feelings of being trapped, and the perpetuation of the past at the expense of a future.

Questions on Subject
1. *Barrio* is a Spanish word that refers to a chiefly Spanish-speaking neighborhood, typically in a city in the southwestern United States. Ramírez generally describes barrios as isolated communities "fenced off by railroads, canals, and expressways" (paragraph 2). The train image transports readers into the barrio in the opening paragraphs and out at the end. The train tracks are a reminder of the boundary between the barrio and the outside world.
2. One way that the barrios of the Southwest are paradoxical is that they are traditional communities hemmed in by signs of progress (railroads and highways). In addition, while the barrio is enclosed, once inside, the boundaries become quite fluid, so that "[m]embers of the barrio describe the entire area as their home" (paragraph 4).
3. For the residents of the barrio, it is "a refuge from the harshness and the coldness of the Anglo world" (4); as a result, most members of the barrio have no desire to leave. Rejected by the outside world, these castoffs have banded together in the barrio where all their needs—material as well as emotional and spiritual—are met.
4. In paragraph 13, Ramírez explains how the bright neon colors of the houses catch viewers' eyes and stimulate their curiosity. The "orange, chartreuse, lime-green, yellow, and mixtures of these and other hues" highlight the individuality of each home (13). The outside world stands in sharp contrast. While the barrio is refreshing, the Anglo suburb is "narcotizing like revolting rows of similar houses, which neither offend nor please" (13).

Questions on Strategy

1. Ramírez compares the fences in the barrio with the walls of the Anglo community to symbolize the easy interaction among the people of his culture compared with the isolation and separation within the Anglo world.

2. Metaphors appear in a number of places throughout Ramírez's essay:

   Paragraph 1: "this pulsing light . . . beats slower, like a weary heartbeat"

   Paragraph 4: "from the angry seeds of rejection grow the flowers of closeness between outcasts, not the thorns of bitterness"

   Paragraph 5: "the warmth of the tortilla factory is a wool *sarape*"

   Paragraph 17: "Their houses, aged and bent, oozing children, are fissures in the horn of plenty."

   These metaphors compare things common to the barrio with other things that are relevant to it. The wool *sarape* is as common as the factory. The horn of plenty, broken and empty, is also a metaphor for the people of the barrio.

3. Had Ramírez begun his description of the barrio with the negative aspects of life there, he would have risked having readers misunderstand the intent of his essay. Ramírez wants us to understand that life in the barrio is satisfying and necessary. He saves the sadder aspects of life there until the end, so that readers do not confuse his desire for our understanding with a desire for pity.

4. The shopkeeper extends credit to those unable to pay (paragraph 7). The young men perform rituals of manhood for the approval or disapproval of the old men who only watch (10). Families—extended, large, inclusive of neighbors—maintain the sense of belonging, order, and tradition that keeps the people of the barrio here. Even the poor of the barrio serve as a visual reminder of the attitudes and isolation of the Anglo community outside its borders (11 and 12).

5. In paragraph 12, Ramírez talks about the barrio as "closeness." He says, "The feeling of family, a rare and treasurable sentiment, pervades and accounts for the inability of the people to leave. The barrio is this attitude manifested on the countenances of the people, on the faces of their homes, and in the gaiety of their gardens" (12). In paragraphs 17 and 18, however, Ramírez presents the darker side of the barrio. This is the barrio of the families who have not achieved a sense of financial security. These "poorer barrio families remain trapped in the nineteenth century and survive as best they can" (18). One gets the impression from Ramírez that change is occurring in the rest of the world and that the outside world is leaving the barrio behind. Change "eludes their reach, in their own backyards, and the people, unable and unwilling to see the future, or even touch the present, perpetuate the past" (2).

Sister Flowers (p. 135)
MAYA ANGELOU

Preparing to Read

Students may talk about someone who came to their aid but may also refer to a song, an author, an instrument, or a sport that gave them comfort during a time of struggle. Encourage them to consider whether music, books, and sports are sometimes enough, or are people needed at these times? What are the downsides of relying on just one thing?

Thinking Critically about the Text

Marguerite had recently been raped and, as such, was sought out as a body, not for her mind or as a person. She needed to be validated as she was — a whole person. Plus, when one is healing, love and acceptance can be very helpful. Being liked by others takes people beyond their immediate surroundings and gives them hope and perspective.

Questions on Subject

1. Angelou's main point is that Sister Flowers carried herself with respect. Sister Flowers was able to show grace in all weather, hot or cold, and gave Marguerite an example of how to carry herself despite the storm in her life. Marguerite says, "[S]he made me proud to be Negro, just by being herself" (paragraph 11).

2. Sister Flowers always seemed to keep a slight distance from others. She wore gloves, remained proper, and was not sloppy in her communications. She did not encourage dropping one's guard and letting others make her vulnerable. She carried herself with grace and strength first and foremost, and then with kindness.

3. For Marguerite, reading became an escape, a wonderful way to develop her mind, but reading alone could not reconnect her with people and teach her how to reach out to others. Too much reading without speaking could make her too internal and could cause her to withdraw from the world.

4. Angelou makes a powerful statement in paragraph 13: "It was fortunate that I never saw her in the company of powhitefolks. For since they tend to think of their whiteness as an evenizer, I'm certain that I would have had to hear her spoken to commonly as Bertha..." For Marguerite, Sister Flowers's image within the black community as a leader and role model would not have necessarily been acknowledged by the white community. Sister Flowers's power extended within and not necessarily beyond the black community.

Questions on Strategy

1. Angelou creates the dominant impression of a woman who respected herself and others. Sister Flowers wore gloves, nice dresses, and hats. She was independent of the church yet did not rebuff others. She spoke well and was educated, but she did not look down on people with less education. Angelou creates this impression by remarking on her dress and describing her interactions with the less educated, such as Marguerite's mother.

2. Angelou incorporates numerous visual descriptions of Mrs. Flowers: "She had the grace of control" (paragraph 2), "thin without the taut look of wiry people" (2), [h]er skin was a rich black that would have peeled like a plum if snagged" (3). Angelou also describes her hats, clothing, and ways of walking, noting that Mrs. Flowers would "drift off the road" (9) or "continue her easy gait up the hill" (8). In contrast, Marguerite's mother is described as "shelling peas" (8). Angelou also uses sound to bring the reader close to Mrs. Flowers, describing her as "soft-voiced" (10). She begins describing the house with reference to its scents, "the sweet scent of vanilla had met us as she opened the door" (29), and continues with visual imagery: "I looked around the room that I had never in my wildest fantasies imagined I would see. Browned photographs leered or threatened from the walls . . . I wanted to gobble up the room entire . . ." (32).

3. Angelou gives clues that the mother might have asked Sister Flowers to give her daughter "a little talking to" in two instances: in paragraph 9, when her mother tells Marguerite to run and play while she talks with Sister Flowers; and in paragraph 15,

when Sister Flowers says, "I've been meaning to talk to her, anyway." Momma knew that Marguerite would respect and respond to Sister Flowers; everyone did. She also knew that she was not able to assist her daughter. She put pride aside and accepted that someone else might be able to help. While Margeurite's mother was not highly educated, she demonstrated her love for her daughter and had the ability to identify someone who could help.

4. By having Marguerite imagine the conversations, Angelou helps readers get insight into her perspective and feelings of shame and helps them better understand Mrs. Flowers's strength and Marguerite's desperate need for reassurance.

A Talent for Sloth (p. 142)
PHILIP CONNORS

Preparing to Read
Students responses will vary. Some may find final exams or paper writing a lonely endeavor, or they may be introverted and prefer activities they can pursue alone. Students can reflect on their social habits and how that may influence the type of education or career they are pursuing.

Thinking Critically about the Text
A reader, writer, and fire lookout all need to be patient, show up every day, and have great attention for detail to notice important changes and shifts. Readers and writers work with a mental landscape, whereas the fire lookout is looking at a physical landscape. Students may draw other connections.

Questions on Subject
1. Connors loves watching the landscape and getting to know it — and himself — intimately.
2. Connors came to dislike his work copyediting when he began to see it as "blind striving." He also described it as, "day after day the guillotine of an evening deadline stretching into the murky distance" (paragraph 10). In both jobs, he is barely noticed or remarked upon when he does his job well, and most of his work is conducted in silence and solitude.
3. The profession might soon be extinct. As proof, he writes, "Ninety percent of American lookout towers have been decommissioned, and only around five hundred of us remain, mostly in the West" (4).
4. Student opinions about Connors's degree of laziness will vary. Fire lookout requires discipline, and even though he is not doing physical labor, he must be alert at his post and perform his job on a regular schedule, even if nothing happens for weeks. Ironically, it is because not much happens that his job is more difficult; it would be easy to slack off or sleep. As Connors shows, nature, and his careful observance of it, is anything but lazy.

Questions on Strategy
1. In paragraph 3, Connors provides a description of the landscape. Some is objective and some is subjective, or poetic. For example, he describes winds of over seventy miles an hour (objective; wind speeds can be measured) and the "sweet smell of burning pine" (subjective; others may not find the smell sweet). Though his language is poetic, "The fires of June, when dry lightning connects with the hills…" is an objective description;

"the thunder makes me flinch as if from the threat of a punch," is subjective. But the paragraph has many descriptions which seem a mix of both; do ladybugs emerge in great clouds? Or, do they just look like great clouds when there are so many awaking from hibernation?

2. Connors describes his experience of his different jobs specifically, with details about copyediting and being a fire lookout, respectively. He carefully selects detail to help readers imagine what he sees all day. Connors uses narration to keep readers connected to this foreign experience.

3. Connors creates a dominant impression of beauty and dramatic natural changes in the environment. In paragraph 7, he uses nouns like *warble, hermit thrush, pine, clouds, meadow,* and *coffee.* These words remind readers that even in a world of seeming quiet, there is much diversity, and there is much to see. Verbs such as *boil, piss, observe, note, rouse, attain, shifts,* and *devote* show us that even in quiet, nature is quite active.

4. The blanket of snow creates a sense of quiet and isolation; many animals hibernate in the cold winter, and many people avoid leaving their houses when they can. The contrast between the fire lookout tower rising into the mist and the cabin capture the stark isolation of the tower as opposed to the more comforting and familiar experience of a house structure. Knowing that Connors was the photographer shows that no one else was present; he is the sole living figure of the photo, and he's not even in it.

ADDITIONAL WRITING SUGGESTIONS FOR DESCRIPTION

1. Most description is predominantly visual; that is, it appeals to our sense of sight. Good description, however, often goes beyond the visual; it appeals as well to one or more of the other senses — hearing, smell, taste, and touch. One way to heighten your awareness of these other senses is to purposefully de-emphasize the visual impressions you receive. For example, while standing on a busy street corner, sitting in a classroom, or shopping in a supermarket, carefully note what you hear, smell, taste, or feel. (It may help if you close your eyes to eliminate visual distractions as you carry out this experiment.) Use these sense impressions to write a brief description of the street corner, the classroom, the supermarket, or another spot of your choosing.

2. Select one of the following places, and write a multiparagraph description that captures your subjective sense impressions of that particular place.
   - a busy doctor's office
   - a bakery
   - a dorm room
   - a factory
   - a gas station
   - a cafeteria
   - a farmers' market
   - a library

3. At college you have the opportunity to meet many new people, students as well as teachers. In a letter to someone back home, describe one of your new acquaintances. Try to capture the essence of the person you chose and to explain why this person stands out from all the other people you have met at school.

4. The readings in this chapter on description focus on people (Jeannette Walls and her mother, Sister Flowers) and places (a barrio, a forest from a fire look-out tower). Write an essay in which you compare and contrast any two of these readings. Here are some questions to get you started:
   - If you choose to write about the selections that describe people, ask yourself what features of those people the authors concentrate on. What features do they leave out or downplay? Which person do you get to know best, and why?
   - If you choose to write about a selection focusing on a place, ask yourself what techniques are employed that contribute to a better understanding or appreciation of the place. What is the dominant impression the author portrays?
   - If you choose to compare or contrast two different subjects (a person with a place, for instance), consider how the descriptions might be reversed. Could the description of a person also apply to a place or a thing? How are the adjectives similar? How is the imagery different?

5. **Writing with Sources.** Writers of description often rely on factual information to make their writing more substantial and interesting. Using facts, statistics, or other information found online or in your college library, write an essay describing one of the people, places, or things in the following list. Be sure that you focus your description, that you have a purpose for your description, and that you present your facts in an interesting manner.
   - the Statue of Liberty
   - the Great Wall of China
   - Donald Trump
   - LeBron James
   - the sun
   - Disney World
   - the Hubble Space Telescope
   - Ruth Bader Ginsburg
   - a local landmark

   For models of and advice on integrating sources in your essay, see Chapters 14 and 15.

6. **Writing with Sources.** As a way of getting to know your campus, select a building, statue, sculpture, or other familiar landmark and research it. What is its significance or meaning to your college or university? Are there any cere-monies or rituals associated with the object? What are its distinctive or unu-sual features? When was it erected? Who sponsored it? Is it currently being used as originally intended? Once you have completed your research, write a description of your subject in which you create a dominant impression of your landmark's importance to the campus community.

   You and your classmates may want to turn this particular assignment into a collaborative class project: the compilation of a booklet of essays that introduces readers to the unique physical and historic features of your campus. To avoid duplication, the class should make a list of campus landmarks, and each student should sign up for the one that he or she would like to write about. For models of and advice on integrating sources in your essay, see Chapters 14 and 15.

7. **Writing with Sources.** Study the photograph by Gordon Parks that appears at the beginning of this chapter (page 112). First, respond to the photograph, answering the questions in the "Visualizing Description" prompt: What does

the image convey to you? How would you characterize the figure of the woman, the presence of the American flag, and the broom and mop? Do you see any significance in how the woman and the inanimate objects are positioned in the photograph?

Next, do some research on Parks's work. (You might start by searching for the Library of Congress's online exhibit entitled "Ella Watson, U.S. Government Charwoman.") Be sure to find out why the photo is commonly called *American Gothic*. What is its connection to American painter Grant Wood's iconic painting of the same name? In what ways is Parks's photograph a parody of or commentary on Wood's painting?

Finally, write an essay describing the photograph and discussing its history and the message you think Parks means to convey. For models of and advice on integrating sources in your essay, see Chapters 14 and 15.

8. **Writing in the Workplace.** You are working for your local weekly newspaper, and your boss has assigned you to do a profile of a local celebrity for a series on getting to know important people in the community. Interview your subject and describe the person both objectively and subjectively, telling of the person's background and achievements so as to make lively reading for the average weekly newspaper reader. What special qualities do you detect in your subject? What contributions has the person made to the community? What weaknesses has the person overcome? What triumphs has your subject achieved? What stands out for you about your subject, and what is it that readers will most want to know about this community figure?

CHAPTER 6   Illustration

Be Specific (p. 168)
NATALIE GOLDBERG

Preparing to Read
This exercise puts into practice the advice Goldberg gives in the first three sentences of her essay: "Be specific. Don't say 'fruit.' Tell what kind of fruit—'It is a pomegranate.'" The term *woods* is general; *redwood forest* is specific. Because nearly all students will at some time have walked in a woods of some sort but very few will have seen an actual redwood forest, it might be interesting to ask whether the second part of their response to the exercise is more detailed and precise than the first—and, if so, why. Explore the possibility that words can sometimes be more evocative than memory.

Thinking Critically about the Text
Students are asked to examine and expand their specific knowledge of aspects of their own environment. Goldberg says that we might gain by this activity because knowing the names of things grounds us, clears the mind, and makes us more awake and "more friendly toward the environment" (paragraph 3). It surprises her that so few people are able to name the plants and trees in their own yards; it is cheating to ask others because they can provide only unreliable, secondhand knowledge. Besides, it is important to know with certainty for oneself.

Questions on Subject

1. According to Goldberg's example (i.e., addressing a girl by her name rather than by "girl"), people—and by extension, things—are dignified when they are recognized by name as specific individuals instead of as members of a general class. The term *integrity* implies uniqueness, wholeness, and self-worth.

2. To know the name of something "connects us to the earth"; it makes us more awake and friendly toward the environment (paragraph 3). It allows us to "[penetrate] more deeply" into what is in front of us and to learn from it (5); it grounds us and makes us more attentive in a group (6).

3. A writer needs to know not only the name of a particular thing but also the month, day, and moment of the context in which it is important (paragraph 4). Precision in *time* is as important as precision in identity in making a subject real and immediate to the reader.

Questions on Strategy

1. The quoted lines of poetry by William Carlos Williams support Goldberg's thesis that it is important to "be specific" in order to learn and know. Williams grounds his poetry in precise, concrete descriptions of familiar objects, starting with their names. It is his belief that intimate knowledge of the things closest to us leads to a broad understanding of the world and our important ideas about it. Goldberg does the same by listing and naming many things to show the value of precision and how naming grants dignity.

2. The lists help define the term *specific* because each is made up of particular members of a general category. They forcefully show that names do, in fact, convey very precise images; each name on the list removes a particular object from its category by bringing to mind a picture of that object in a setting furnished by the reader's imagination.

3. Goldberg is addressing writers. In paragraph 4 she quotes William Carlos Williams: "Write what's in front of your nose." She mentions writing groups (paragraph 6) and gives advice to "a writer" (7).

4. Goldberg's illustrations of naming help define her central concept that knowing the names of things helps both writers and readers achieve an appreciation and understanding of their world. Definitions are abstract; examples of any kind make them more specific and concrete for the reader.

The Genius of Birds (p. 172)
JENNIFER ACKERMAN

Preparing to Read

Students will likely list dolphins, elephants, rats, monkeys, and pigs as intelligent animals. Ravens, like elephants and monkeys, also use tools; though, because their strange call, black color, and scavenger diet have associated them with various superstitions, they are often forgotten for their intelligence. These questions will likely prompt students to consider how they associate animal intelligence with anthropomorphic qualities.

Thinking Critically about the Text

Student answers will vary, but bird behaviors such as flying into glass panes may inspire discussion. Bird traits involving creativity, often associated with human art, or those involving logic, may also lead to skepticism.

Questions on Subject

1. We now see birds as highly intelligent whereas in the past we thought them stupid because of their behavior and the physical properties of their brains.

2. These are the animals people usually associate with intelligence. Chimps and apes, in particular, are notable examples of "human cleverness" because of humans' biological similarities and their social relationships.

3. Crows in New Caledonia make their own tools and transmit methods for making these tools to new generations.

4. "Bird brain" came from the idea that the small size of their brains denoted a capacity for instinct only, no complex thought. It was based on the assumption that a small brain was necessary for flight, but also meant sacrificing intellect.

Questions on Strategy

1. The point of the essay is to challenge common assumptions about birds. To do this, Ackerman needs to effectively set up the notion she plans to challenge; in this case, that birds are stupid. She provides examples of the many associations people have about birds and linguistic phrases that reflect these biases.

2. Student answers will vary.

3. Ackerman devotes so much space to Alex because his accomplishments were a turning point in our understanding of bird intelligence. Furthermore, this extended example helps readers understand the various kinds of intelligence in one kind of bird. In other words, it is not that every bird has one intelligence, but some birds are intelligent in many different ways.

4. Throughout, Ackerman seeks to show similarity between animals whose intelligence used to be thought very different (e.g., apes and birds). In paragraph 12, Ackerman begins with a comparison of brain structure between humans and birds: "Like our brains, the brains of birds are lateralized." In paragraph 13, Ackerman compares songbirds to humans in the way we learn songs and language. This approach supports her main purpose of correcting mistaken assumptions and of showing that birds and humans are *both* intelligent and even have similarities.

If You Had One Day with Someone Who's Gone (p. 178)
MITCH ALBOM

Preparing to Read

This question helps students first identify the person with whom they would like to share one more day, if they had it. When reading the essay, students will already have someone in mind and will have a chance to answer before learning Albom's and his friends' perspectives.

Thinking Critically about the Text

Albom's mother is shocked to the point of disbelief and denial when learning of her father's death. "Dead? How could he be dead? Hadn't she seen him the night before, when she kissed him goodnight?" (paragraph 2). Rabbi Wolpe still thinks about the sudden loss of his father: "[A]t some moment every day, he is an eleven-year-old boy who lost his dad to a sudden heart attack in 1938" (16). Maury De Young just sat under a tree and cried after his son was killed in a car accident. The shock of losing someone suddenly seems to have made these losses harder because they could not say goodbye and cannot change their last interaction with the person. With a death from old age, people have time to say goodbye, talk about the past, heal any wounds, and tell the person they love them. Because they can just slowly start to let go, there may be less denial than in cases of sudden loss.

Questions on Subject

1. Albom's mother cried because she, too, wanted to have several more minutes with her lost loved one.

2. They all responded by saying they would do normal activities together. Most of them wanted just to express their love and appreciate the simple pleasure of the other person's company. The life lesson Albom draws is that the simple day-to-day things are precious and we should cherish them. This is reminiscent of the John Lennon lyrics, "Life is what happens when we're busy making other plans."

3. Rabbi Wolpe meant that his father is trapped in the time and way that he remembers him. Because he can no longer interact with his father, Wolpe's memories are all that exist of him.

4. She did not want to disappoint her father or his high expectations for her learning. We later learn that he encouraged her to become a doctor. She remembers her last assignment and perhaps feels guilty that she did not live up to his hopes. The event represents how, at times when something happens suddenly, time slows and we remember everything in great detail. The essence of her relationship with him was his desire for her to excel and her desire not to disappoint.

Questions on Strategy

1. Answers will vary. By opening with his mother's story, Albom shares with the reader a sense of his family and their experience, setting an intimate tone for the story. Albom also ends the essay with his mother's experience and how it made him appreciate the present moment even more. Her experience of loss taught him what is important in his own life in the present.

2. Albom asks this question of each of the people featured in the essay, and their answers structure the essay. By asking the rhetorical question, he brings readers closer to the subject and makes them part of the discussion he leads. He wants readers to realize that they too desire the simple experiences, not just the wild ones.

3. In paragraph 10, Albom says, "I began to pose this scenario to other people—friends, colleagues, readers. How would they spend a day with a departed loved one?" The answers come from people around the country, two of whom held religious positions, as a pastor and as a rabbi. Despite their titles and different beliefs, facing sudden loss equalized them all. They all support his findings that most people want to relive the simple things together, forgive each other, and let others know how much they were loved.

4. In paragraphs 3 and 4, Albom repeats the concept of a "lie," the initial denying of a sudden loss. "'You're a liar,' my mother said." The next paragraph begins, "But it wasn't a lie." He challenges the reality in his mother's head. He uses a similar technique between paragraphs 14 and 15. He writes, "Some might say, 'That's such an ordinary day.'" Then the next paragraph starts with "Maybe that's the point." This reasserts that, in fact, the ordinary is the extraordinary. It is okay to repeat it, both in an essay and in life.

The "Busy" Trap (p. 184)
TIM KREIDER

Preparing to Read
College students are notoriously busy, skimping on sleep to meet competing academic and social demands. This can be a good opportunity to bring the classroom discussion around to time management and to set realistic expectations regarding the time it takes to research, write, and revise.

Thinking Critically about the Text
Student opinions will vary. Some who define success as career accomplishments may believe that being busy is necessary, that we are here in life to engage in activities and that busyness is a sign that one is living a full life. In the Jewish tradition, for example, life accomplishments are seen as the purpose of life. Some might note the cost on relationships, creativity, and joy. Students may note that people who provide for others (children or aging parents) might need to be busy to bring in enough income.

Questions on Subject
1. Kreider does not say so directly, but readers can imply that people might have to face a feeling of emptiness without all that busyness. They might also question some of their decisions and their relationships. He does suggest that people might have to face that their activities are not ultimately all that important or meaningful.
2. From reading the *World Book Encyclopedia,* Kreider likely acquired knowledge, developed a love of learning, and nurtured his sense of wonder. By creating animated films, he developed his creativity and had a vehicle for self-expression. Playing in the woods with friends, he developed a connection to nature, skills of working with others, and maybe — because the game was a form of combat — a sense of competition.
3. By "real writing," Kreider likely means writing that feels solid, is authentic, and represents his true voice. He was not just producing words but writing in a way that he felt connected to them. Constant interruptions and other obligations have kept him away from "real writing." He is suggesting that we lose quality when we are overcommitted. He would likely consider this essay "real writing" because he is talking about something that matters and that could change behavior and how people live their lives. Real writing has that power.
4. Kreider uses "bad influence" ironically. Those who believe in busyness will advocate for more work and less play. They would consider people like Kreider distractions. In this playful line, he helps readers see the absurdity of all this commitment. His essay asks subtly, "Why are we so afraid of play?"

Questions on Strategy
1. Kreider compares people who are busy to people who are exhausted. Exhausted people, he says, are those committed to back-to-back shifts in the intensive care unit (ICU) or people commuting long distances to multiple minimum-wage jobs. Busy people are those, he says, with self-imposed obligations such as activities and classes. Through the comparison, he makes the distinction that not everyone who has a full schedule is running away from downtime and also speaks to potential critics who will want to argue that some people are legitimately busy. The comparison also helps readers to identify the two types in themselves: Some of our commitments are legitimate, and others are to elevate self-importance or run from the quiet.

2. In paragraph 7, Kreider says, "I feel like a reprobate who does not deserve to live on any day that I do not write." In paragraph 10, he says that idleness is as important to the brain as "vitamin D is to the body and deprived of it we suffer a mental affliction as disfiguring as rickets." Students may identify other examples as well.

3. Kreider's audience seems clearly to be people who are busy (but perhaps *not* people who are exhausted). He is writing to others he believes are caught up in the "busy trap" as a way to encourage them to free themselves from what he believes he himself has escaped.

4. Student response will vary based on their background knowledge, but context clues should tell them that each of these examples represents an important moment that arose out of being *not* busy.

ADDITIONAL WRITING SUGGESTIONS FOR ILLUSTRATION

1. Write an essay on one of the following statements, using examples to illustrate your ideas. You should be able to draw some of your examples from personal experience and first-hand observations.
   - Television has produced a number of "classic" programs.
   - Every college campus has its own unique slang terms or phrases.
   - All good teachers (*or* doctors, secretaries, auto mechanics, sales representatives) have certain traits in common.
   - Reality television is an accurate (*or* inaccurate) reflection of our society.
   - Good literature always teaches us something about our humanity.
   - Recycling starts with the individual.

2. College students are not often given credit for the community volunteer work they do. Write a letter to the editor of your local newspaper in which you demonstrate, with several extended examples, the beneficial impact that you and your fellow students have had on the community.

3. How do advertisers portray older people in their advertisements? Based on your analysis of some real ads, how fair are advertisers to senior citizens? What tactics do advertisers use to sell their products to senior citizens? Write an essay in which you use actual ads to illustrate two or three such tactics.

4. Most students would agree that in order to be happy and "well adjusted," people need to learn how to relieve stress and to relax. What strategies do you and your friends use to relax? What have been the benefits of these relaxation techniques for you? Write an article for the school newspaper in which you give examples of several of these techniques and encourage your fellow students to try them.

5. The Internet has profoundly altered the way people around the world communicate and share information. One area in which significant change is especially evident is education. While having so much information at your fingertips can be exciting, such technology is not without problems. What are the advantages and disadvantages of using technology in the classroom? Write an essay in which you analyze the educational value (or the temptation for distraction) inherent in bringing technology into the classroom. Document your assessment with specific examples.

6. Some people think it's important to look their best and, therefore, give careful attention to the clothing they wear. Others do not seem to care. How much stock do you put in the old saying "Clothes make the person"? Use examples of the people on your own campus or in your community to argue your position.

7. **Writing in the Workplace.** Your boss at your internship asks you to evaluate one aspect of the company's operation (customer service, advertising/promotion, internal communications, employee morale, community service, etc.). After selecting an aspect of the company you want to evaluate and talking with customers and/or other employees, write a memo to your boss in which you use examples to document your findings.

CHAPTER 7 Process Analysis

How to Mark a Book (p. 204)
MORTIMER ADLER

Preparing to Read
Answers will vary according to what works for the individual student. Students may answer with some of the strategies they will read about (taking notes, writing in the margins). You might begin discussion for this prompt by asking what kinds of texts students have problems reading or for what purposes they read.

Thinking Critically about the Text
Answers will vary according to students' answers to the "Preparing to Read" prompt. Have students discuss what they learned and how they might modify their own reading strategies.

Questions on Subject
1. The first kind of book owner "has all the standard sets and best-sellers — unread, untouched" (paragraph 6). The second has many books — some read — "but all of them as clean and shiny as the day they were bought" (paragraph 6). And the third has books that are "dog-eared and dilapidated, shaken and loosened by continual use, marked and scribbled in from front to back" (6). In Adler's eyes, the third type is the only one who "owns" books because these books have been actively devoured by the owner.

2. Adler claims that writing in the book you are reading keeps you awake, helps you think a book through, and helps you remember your thoughts and the author's (paragraph 9). Most students readily agree with Adler's points.

3. In Adler's schema, the conversation should be a series of questions or remarks to a person who is not present (the author). Marking a book carries on the conversation by attempting to engage the reader and author in a dialogue. It is an expression of difference between the reader and the writer, the result of questioning oneself and the "teacher."

4. Answers will vary.

Questions on Strategy

1. Adler assumes throughout the essay that he is talking to nonbelievers, so he addresses the unspoken objections of his readers. However, in addressing his readers as nonbelievers, his argument could alienate those who do believe what he says or make the nonbelievers even more resistant to his ideas.

2. "You shouldn't mark up a book which isn't yours" (paragraph 3). This sentence lets the reader know that marking up books can be done only after they are bought or owned. "There are two ways in which one can own a book" (4). Building on the idea of ownership introduced in paragraph 3, this sentence clarifies the direction of paragraph 4 by distinguishing the two ways in which books can be owned (by payment and by writing in them). The phrase "[c]onfusion about what it means to *own* a book" (5) — suggesting that there is a confusion in the term *ownership* — unifies the rest of paragraph 5 by setting up another explanation for ownership. "There are three kinds of book owners" (6). Moving from the concept of ownership to that of owners, this sentence provides a schema for the types of people who own books.

3. These verbal cues indicate that Adler's process analysis is directional. In the first fourteen paragraphs he is describing not *how* to do something but *why*. He begins with his thesis, and then he supports his argument with several points. It is not until the second half of the essay that he explains how to go about marking books. This method is necessary to Adler's purpose. He assumes that his readers have been told all their lives, under threat of punishment, not to write in books or simply that to write in a book is to deface it.

4. Throughout his process analysis explanation, Adler explicates three main ideas using cause and effect reasoning: that writing in the book you are reading keeps you awake, that writing in the book helps you think a book through, and that writing in the book helps you remember your thoughts and the author's. In this sense, his description of reading has an effect on the reader's interest and understanding. The cause of this effect is Adler's method of reading. In taking the time to explain the benefits (effects) of each step in his process (causes), he persuades his readers that they should try his method.

What Would Happen If You Were Attacked by a Great White Shark? (p. 211)
CODY CASSIDY AND PAUL DOHERTY

Preparing to Read

Student answers will vary. Some people are often preoccupied with especially gruesome or exotic deaths, especially if they are well represented in film or other shared cultural experiences. By asking readers to consider their own levels of fear regarding sharks, these questions prepare them to learn about the actual level of risk. This helps sets up the juxtaposition. You may want to ask students if would answer these questions differently after reading the article.

Thinking Critically about the Text

Students may say that the concession helps readers relax and enjoy the essay without too much fear a shark attack will happen to them. Others may feel it makes the information less relevant and unnecessary; or that though it is an unlikely scenario, it is still a serious one that the authors trivialize with humor.

Questions on Subject

1. Cassidy and Doherty write for a general reader who may have thought about shark attacks but likely will never experience one. We know the article is not for experts because they do not use technical terms and adopt a humorous tone.

2. The authors claim sharks would likely bite you out of curiosity. In paragraph 6, they challenge the theory that sharks bite humans because they confuse them with seals. Sharks approach and attack seals differently, so this challenges the confusion theory. Also, in paragraph 3, they cite the fact that when researchers examine shark attack victims, they find that the sharks have rarely eaten anything.

3. Sharks have "bad table manners" because they do not chew, often eating in one bite. The good news is if they bite you in one way, you'll likely live. The bad news is if they unevenly severe your femoral artery, you will likely bleed to death.

4. Much has to do with how the femoral artery is severed, if the shark bites it. If it is a clean sever, the body can retract the artery and you can stop the bleeding. If the shark severs it at an angle, you will likely bleed to death.

Questions on Strategy

1. Using the second person makes the reader pay attention and gives the sense that they are being given important information; we hear second person when we hear emergency exit instructions and other important information. The second person also establishes the hypothetical nature of their essay, as if they are writing, "Suppose you…"; this also helps readers imagine themselves in the scenario.

2. In paragraph 1, the authors tell readers, "you're like the squirrel in the ocean." This simile draws a parallel between how sharks feel about eating us and how we feel about eating squirrels; it also draws a comparison to our relative inferiority in the food chain. In paragraph 3, the authors talk about sharks biting a human as being like children playing with peas on their plate. The writers are trying to put the shark world in human terms so readers can imagine how sharks behave. Student reactions will vary.

3. Paragraph 16 is set up using an *if…then* construction to explain different outcomes of the "process." In paragraph 17, the authors use the transitional phrase, "four minutes after the attack…" and later in the paragraph, "After that…" to signal the order of the process.

4. The essay is an informational process analysis because it describes an occurrence in detail, without explaining how to replicate the process or judging the effectiveness of the process.

Why We All Scream When We Get Ice Cream Brain Freeze (p. 217)
ASHLIE STEVENS

Preparing to Read
This question helps students think about their own preconceptions about brain freeze. Many will likely discover how little they have thought about it and may be surprised how

much research has been done. The question stimulates curiosity about this and other peculiar things they may rarely stop and notice.

Thinking Critically about the Text

By moving between informal language and scientific language, Stevens achieves her goal of both hooking the general reader *and* educating this reader. The casual language makes the essay accessible and helps orient her reader, who is likely not a scientist. The casual language hooks the reader, then she teaches the readers something scientific and then goes back to a casual tone. This helps the reader hang in through the more complex explanations. Students will say whether they believe she is successful or not.

Questions on Subject

1. The cold from the ice cream causes the blood vessels and capillaries on the roof of our mouth to constrict; the body registers this constriction as pain. The message shoots up to the brain, which has no pain sensing fibers itself but has a covering — located on the top of the head — that receives the pain message.
2. Stevens compares the brain to a computer, a common analogy that helps readers understand the brain as a mechanical system.
3. In both cases, the area we feel the pain is not the area in distress.
4. Ice cream headaches help researchers understand how the brain processes pain signals and how those processes are impacted by genetics, sex, and age.

Questions on Strategy

1. Stevens uses several conjunctions to begin sentences, making them fragments. Beginning with "but" and "and" creates a logical flow from one point to the next and keeps the tone conversational.
2. First, Stevens introduces the topic. Then she explains, via Rau, how the brain processes the ice cream shock. Then she moves into the implications. Students will say whether or not they find this effective.
3. In paragraph 2, Stevens writes "But first, a lesson in terminology" to announce that she will announce terms, including the medical term for brain freeze. Since the brain doesn't actually freeze, the entire essay is in service of defining the actual, medical term as different from the colloquial one. The definitions of medical terms help Stevens explain the process.
4. She uses the verbs *slurp* and *dive* as part of the casual description of how we eat ice cream. The verbs used to describe the physiological processes show the body's struggle to make sense of the input, *trying, knows, interprets, process.*

How Do Spiders Make Their Webs? (p. 220)
ALICIA AULT

Preparing to Read

You might ask students to break into pairs or small groups to discuss their writing processes rather than trying to share these as a class. Expect a wide range of responses, and encourage students to discuss not just the process itself but why it is so intriguing and what they would like to learn about it that they do not already know.

Thinking Critically about the Text

Because spider web fibers are stronger than steel, we could use these fibers to replace the use of steel in bridges, railways, and building materials. Spider web fibers could also be used for safety belts or used to drill or for any number of other purposes.

Questions on Subject

1. In paragraph 5, Ault quotes an expert who says that spiders use webs offensively and defensively. Vibrations in the strands alert spiders to predators. Webs also trap prey.

2. In paragraph 2, Ault describes spider silk by saying that it is "stronger than steel and has impressive tensile strength . . ." Spider silk is known, therefore, for both its strength and elasticity. Scientists find it valuable because no human-made substance has that combination. Because spider silk cannot yet be fully replicated, scientists have only just begun to discover its possible uses.

3. Spiders also use web-building to create defensive systems that can alert them when prey is nearby.

4. The fact that spiders build their webs at night adds a bit of mystique to these already curiously powerful animals. Building at night makes them seem secretive and strategic as well as powerful.

Questions on Strategy

1. Ault's purpose, as stated in the article, is to pique our interest in spiders as powerful engineers and planners. This helps us both appreciate spiders and consider what might be possible for us if we could produce what they do. Paragraph 1 hooks readers and piques their curiosity about these creatures. She speaks of them in such a positive light, describing them as "skillful engineers, gifted with amazing planning skills. . . ." Without saying so directly, she asks readers not to pass them off as useless creatures or be afraid of them.

2. Ault creates the impression that webs are very sophisticated creations made of some of the world's finest materials. She begins the essay by talking about the quality of the material and then describes in paragraphs 10 to 15 how the orb weaver spider makes its web. This description helps readers appreciate the amount of strategy and work that goes into the average web. She describes how the spider pulls the silk from its glands (paragraph 11), then how the web "balloon" soars to make its first connection (12), how the spider selects the best attachment points (12), and then how the spider constructs the interior of the web. The fact that spiders of the same species have the same process demonstrates that the process it not haphazard but is hard wired.

3. Ault quotes only Jonathan Coddington, the director of the Global Genome Initiative and senior scientist at the Smithsonian's National Museum of Natural History. Students might say that an expert on spiders would be a good addition to the essay. Also, they might point out that, since this publication was in the *Smithsonian* magazine, perhaps it would have added more credibility to also include experts *not* part of that institution.

4. The essay begins by introducing the topic and the purpose of the essay — to increase the appreciation for spider web materials as well as spiders' planning skills. Ault begins by talking about the spider web materials (paragraphs 2–7), describes the process of building a web (8–14), then talks about how the web is used to capture prey. The essay concludes with a list of companies investing in spider silk. In paragraph 5, the question

"why build webs?" alerts readers to a shift in topic. Paragraph 12 begins with the word *eventually*, which tells the readers that Ault is lapsing time in order to show them the next part of the process. The use of the word *then* throughout tells us that she is still describing the process.

ADDITIONAL WRITING SUGGESTIONS FOR PROCESS ANALYSIS

1. Write a directional or evaluative process analysis on one of the following topics:
   - how to make a viral video
   - how to adjust bicycle brakes
   - how to save photos you take on your smartphone
   - how to throw a party
   - how to add, drop, or change a course
   - how to play a particular game
   - how to develop confidence
   - how to change the oil in a car

2. Think about your favorite pastime or activity. Write an essay in which you explain one or more of the processes you follow in participating in that activity. For example, if basketball is your hobby, how do you go about making a layup? If you are a photographer, how do you develop and print a picture following traditional methods? If you are an actor, how do you go about learning your lines? If cooking is your passion, how do you get ready to prepare a particular dish? Do you follow standard procedures, or do you personalize the process in some way?

3. Write to a person who is a computer novice, and explain how to do a Web search. Be sure to define key terms and to illustrate the steps in your process with screen shots of search directories and search results.

4. With a partner, in a small group, or as an entire class, brainstorm either an informational or directional process analysis for a familiar process or activity. You might also approach the process from a humorous angle. Here are some suggestions. Choose one:
   - applying to college
   - choosing a major
   - getting a paid internship
   - contacting a professor to request an extension
   - binging on Netflix
   - finding a job

   If you worked on the steps or aspects of the process with a partner or in groups, share them with the rest of the class, or create a presentation. Did you all focus on the same elements? Were the processes organized or presented in the same order? How does sharing the results make the process analysis more accurate and complete?

5. **Writing with Sources.** Do some research and then write an informational or evaluative process analysis on one of the following topics:
   - how your heart functions
   - how a U.S. president is elected
   - how ice cream is made
   - how a volcano erupts
   - how the human circulatory system works
   - how a camera works
   - how an atomic bomb or reactor works
   - how a recession occurs

   For models of and advice on integrating sources in your essay, see Chapters 14 and 15.

6. **Writing with Sources.** If you are scientifically minded or simply want to know more about evolution, research some subprocesses that contribute to the evolutionary process, using books, journals, articles, videos, and online resources. Some of the subprocesses that you may want to pursue include adaptation, selection, divergence, genetic drift, natural selection, mutation, and bipedalism. Consider an educated, general-interest reader to be your audience, so be sure to define technical terms. For models of and advice on integrating sources in your essay, see Chapters 14 and 15.

7. **Writing with Sources.** The opening illustration for this chapter on page 190 is an informational process analysis about how baked goods are recycled into plastics. Do some research in your library or online and write a set of detailed directions for carrying out that process. You will need to explain how to get the ingredients, how much of each ingredient is needed, and the types of required equipment and machinery, as well as explicit directions for carrying out the process. As with any other good set of directions, you need not only to say what to do but also what not to do. Mention where the process can go wrong at every point and what the components and ingredients should look like at each step. For models of and advice on integrating sources in your essay, see Chapters 14 and 15.

8. **Writing in the Workplace.** You have just been hired to be the person in charge of small gift giving for a local nonprofit organization. Among your various responsibilities is the writing of letters of acknowledgment for gifts to the organization. Prepare several letters thanking donors and explaining how their contributions will be used. One should be a general letter suitable for most donors. The second letter should be one in which the donor makes the gift in memory of someone and wants that person's family to be notified of the gift. You will need to make up a name for your organization, a fictitious name for the donor, and one for the person in whose memory the gift is being made. Before starting to draft your letter, think about what needs to be said in each situation. Also be sure to carefully consider the tone of your letter.

CHAPTER 8 Comparison and Contrast

Neat People vs. Sloppy People (p. 238)
SUZANNE BRITT

Preparing to Read
This prompt functions on the assumption that we all fall prey to the trap of stereotyping. You might prepare for this prompt by asking for a list from the class about the kinds of stereotypes they have seen or experienced.

Thinking Critically about the Text
Britt breaks her distinction between neat and sloppy people along moral lines. She claims that neat people are lazy, mean, and immoral; sloppy people are planning, caring, and loving. Chances are students will know about exceptions to Britt's categories. You might begin a discussion by asking why Britt's categories are too reductive.

Questions on Subject
1. Referring to the distinction between neat and sloppy people as a "moral" one is pure irony. With this sarcastic reference, Britt may well be making fun of all other socioeconomic and political debates in which superior morality is claimed by both sides of a decidedly nonmoral debate. The use of a pseudomoralistic tone helps Britt make her point.

2. The "heavenly vision" and "precise plan" held dear by sloppy people is the concept of "someday": someday they will accomplish everything. Of course, because "someday" is always somewhere in the future, it never arrives. As a result, sloppy people remain sloppy.

3. Sloppy people tend to be packrats—people who collect things and never throw anything away—whereas neat people clear everything away, often while still in use. Basic truisms like this one provide the foundation from which Britt takes off in exaggeration. Ask your students to give some well-known characteristics of neat and sloppy people, then discuss whether each one has merit or is just an unwarranted stereotype.

Questions on Strategy
1. Britt starts almost every paragraph repeating the type of person she will discuss further, "neat" or "sloppy." The reader can never get lost and can follow the singsong tone of the essay. Between paragraphs 5 and 6, she makes a smooth transition from her discussion of sloppy to neat people. She begins paragraph 5 with "Sloppy people can't bear to part with anything," and the last sentence in the paragraph smooths the transition to neat people: "A neat person would just bulldoze the desk." She starts paragraph 6 with "Neat people are bums." Most students will find this essay delightfully easy to follow.

2. Because this is an exaggerated, humorous essay, it would be to Britt's disadvantage to point out the similarities between the two types of people she is trying to show at opposite ends of the spectrum. Similarities are inherent; answers will vary depending on each student's particular viewpoint. This will make for a lively class discussion, and the variety of examples given will ensure that students understand the strategy being discussed.

3. In this essay the block system of contrast is actually an extended version of point-by-point contrast; Britt presents an idea, backs it up with outrageous details, and then goes on to contrast it with its counterpart. If simple point-by-point contrast had been used, much of the entertaining hyperbole would have been lost and the essay would have been dull.

4. Britt's use of examples in this essay is effective only because she goes to such absurd lengths to exaggerate her purpose and point. In paragraph 4, Britt writes the following about sloppy people: "the books spill from the shelves onto the floor, the clothes pile up in the hamper and closet, the family mementos accumulate in every drawer." Compare these examples to what she writes in paragraph 6 about neat people: "They have cavalier attitudes toward possessions, including family heirlooms. Everything is just another dust-catcher to them. If anything collects dust, it's got to go and that's that." Britt's statements of comparison and contrast need examples like these to make clear the comparison between the moral sloppy person and the immoral neat person. The comparisons or contrasts remain plain statements without support if Britt does not use examples.

Two Ways to Belong in America (p. 242)
BHARATI MUKHERJEE

Preparing to Read
Views will likely be influenced by whether or not students are themselves immigrants (particularly those who are in the United States to go to college) or whether their parents, grandparents, or close family members were immigrants. It may be useful to ask students to react to the phrase "We are a nation of immigrants." Current American political debates may have galvanized student views as "for" or "against" immigration. Ask students how black-and-white pro/con arguments might oversimplify an issue — regardless of where they themselves fall on the debate. It may be productive to allow a debate on these issues, or it may be more useful to create a neutral climate in the classroom. Issues in the news that are likely to come up: Is Donald Trump's 2016 campaign proposal to build a wall between the United States and Mexico unconstitutional and biased or a necessary step toward a "secure" border? What groups are more likely to feel that immigrants "take our jobs" or are "criminals"? What groups are more likely to believe recent immigrants do work "that no one else will do," like farm labor or housecleaning? Does media coverage inflame or simply inform us about the immigration debate? Mukherjee's essay helps students think about immigration from the perspective of the immigrant. You might ask students why an immigrant would want to be an American citizen and why an immigrant would want to stay a citizen of a parent country.

Thinking Critically about the Text
Mukherjee's sister plans to subvert the intention of the law by working within the letter of it. For students, the sister's plan can be an important reminder that policies that restrict the rights of U.S. immigrants, whether here legally or illegally, feel like personal attacks; immigrants are personally affected by laws that are largely theoretical for most Americans. Student responses will range from sympathy to accusations of hypocrisy. It might be helpful to ask students what they would do if they were wearing the immigrants' shoes.

Questions on Subject

1. There might be disagreement on the thesis of Mukherjee's essay. It could be argued that her thesis is implied and concerns the contributions of immigrants to America or the injustice of American immigration laws. However, the most powerful point on the subject is personal and supports Mukherjee's thesis as: "The price that the immigrant willingly pays, and that the exile avoids, is the trauma of self-transformation" (paragraph 15). She presents this statement directly at the end of the essay, after spending some pages describing that very phenomenon. It might be useful to ask students if they agree or disagree that this is the thesis of the essay.

2. Mukherjee's arguments in favor of citizenship grow out of her personal preferences: "I need to feel like a part of the community I have adopted…I need to put roots down, to vote and make the difference that I can" (paragraph 15). Her sister's arguments for retaining her Indian citizenship are similarly personal; she feels like an Indian, and she wants to retire to India (4).

3. At the end of paragraph 11, Mukherjee asks, "Which of us is the freak?" Student responses will vary. Note, however, that Mukherjee goes on to imply that neither sister is a freak; they simply have different priorities, and their actions can be traced back to those priorities. Mukherjee's sister's decision seems more surprising, yet if you understand her reasoning, it seems entirely rational.

4. Mukherjee means that when a person emigrates from a homeland and becomes a citizen of a new country, her or his identity is deeply changed. Mukherjee rejected "three thousand years" of family tradition when she chose her own husband and decided not to return to India (paragraph 5). She went from being an Indian woman to being an American woman of Indian ancestry; her sister, on the other hand, is "here to maintain an identity, not to transform it" (9).

Questions on Strategy

1. Mukherjee's essay is a combination of block and point-by-point organization: She considers both sides of one issue, she takes a longer space to consider one experience or point of view, and then she returns to the dialogue.

2. This pattern of organization is appropriate because it allows Mukherjee to present the complexities of her subject; a simple point-by-point analysis of the pros and cons of citizenship would minimize the ambiguities inherent in her decision to become a citizen and her sister's decision to remain an alien.

3. Mukherjee chooses to let Mira speak for herself in this essay, allowing her to make arguments with which Mukherjee herself disagrees. If Mukherjee had merely summarized her sister's words, Mira's reasoning wouldn't have been as clear and her persuasive points would have been muted. Allowing Mira to speak for herself shows respect for her views.

The Difference between "Sick" and "Evil" (p. 247)
ANDREW VACHSS

Preparing to Read

Students may define evil in various ways, offering simple or complex descriptions. Some may say evil is simply purposefully harming another. Others may talk about actions and attitudes that lack compassion or caring for others. Some students may associate evil with more extreme cases, such as genocide, school shootings, or even villains such as the Joker from the *Batman* series. A discussion of fictional villains may also be useful because these characters are often less complicated than real figures, making it easier to pinpoint what makes them evil. For example, the question of whether every Nazi was evil is more complicated than determining Lex Luthor's evilness. Much scholarship has been dedicated to understanding, locating, and reflecting on evil. Remind students that the topic is an open one.

Thinking Critically about the Text

Student answers will vary as they speculate about why "our society distrusts the term *evil*." Maybe, in part, it's because *evil* has religious and comic book overtones. It has an inhuman, otherworldly quality to it that we do not often want to see or acknowledge as existing in the world in which we find ourselves. The concept of evil can be difficult to deal with and understand for several reasons. If evil exists, we actually might see ourselves as called on to take action. We have in our culture what Vachss feels is confusion between "sick" and "evil." Vachss believes we have a tendency to excuse behavior for this reason: We allow the topic to be confusing so we do not have to face the truth or the tough decisions.

Questions on Subject

1. In the first paragraph, Vachss asks, "Are those who abuse their positions of trust to prey upon children . . . sick . . . or are they evil?" How we answer this question will determine how we react to the actions of these people. If we see them as sick, we in effect see them as blameless and treat them as victims. This takes the focus away from the children and the evil inflicted upon them. Perpetrators are not held responsible for their behavior in the same way if we label them as sick.

2. Vachss believes psychology's approach and euphemisms result in allowing us "to absolve the predator of responsibility for his behavior" (paragraph 19). We do not hold people accountable if we call them sick.

3. Vachss believes we are so quick to declare predators as sick because "sickness not only offers the possibility of finding a cure but also assures us that the predator didn't really mean it. After all, it is human nature to try to understand inhuman conduct" (paragraph 25). In doing this, we do not hold people accountable, he believes. We cannot fight evil if we do not acknowledge it for what it is.

4. Vachss wants his readers to work toward amending the laws. Students might consider writing their state legislatures and asking that members of the religious community be required to report child abuse when they suspect it. In 2002 (when this article was written), members of religious communities were not required to report abuses, allowing much abuse to occur. Students may or may not find Vachss's argument convincing, though they might respect how he asked for very direct action.

Questions on Strategy

1. Vachss's thesis is in the second paragraph when he says, "we need to answer that fundamental question. Because without the truth, we cannot act. And until we act, nothing will change." In his mind, the distinction between "sick" and "evil" must be made clear so that we can address wrongs and protect our children.

2. In the article, Vachss tells the reader that his life's work has been the protection of children and that he has conducted this work in a wide variety of settings. His commitment and breadth of experience count as his expertise. In the introduction to the essay, readers

learn more about him. He has been the director of a maximum-security prison, worked as a lawyer to protect children, and has written extensively on crime. All these experiences contribute to his expertise and authority as a writer.

3. In paragraphs 6 to 14, Vachss works to make very clear the difference between "sick" and "evil" so that readers will agree that a clear and important distinction exists that is "beyond dispute." He uses a powerful and graphic "sick" example—a woman putting her baby in the oven to eradicate the devil—and an equally powerful "evil" example—the renting of a baby to pornographers. He then, using one-sentence paragraphs, aims to clarify even further how they are different: "sickness is a condition" (9) and "evil is a behavior" (10). In paragraph 14, he provides an example to clarify this distinction. Fantasizing about child abuse is sick, whereas actually acting on the idea is evil. Students will then discuss how they responded to the examples.

4. Student responses will vary. This absurd example highlights Vachss's point that every action could be considered a sickness. We must draw the line somewhere. Some students will find the extreme nature of the example very illustrative of his point. Some might find it too bizarre an example to be convincing.

America Made Me a Feminist (p. 253)
PAULINA PORIZKOVA

Preparing to Read
Student answers will vary based on their experiences or beliefs, but these questions will likely prompt discussions of recent feminist activism such as the Women's Marches and social media activism such as #yesallwomen and #metoo. You might discuss HeForShe and similar initiatives that focus on the importance of men's feminism to create change. This prompt also helps students clarify their own definition of an association with feminism.

Thinking Critically about the Text
Porizkova's multicountry experiences taught her that in comparison to contemporary European women, American women were not as powerful or as valued as in other places. She noted the difference in pay, the shame around talking about sex, the use of the word "slut," and even doctors' unwillingness to talk about the body. She observed that in America, her body seemed to belong to everyone but herself.

Questions on Subject
1. Porizkova inferred that French men found women as "dangerous objects to treasure and fear" (paragraph 12). In response to what she considered patronizing behavior (treating her as too delicate to care for herself), she became sexually assertive. The men either retreated or thought her a prostitute.

2. Student opinions will vary, but the questions may prompt useful discussion of sexual behavior on college campuses.

3. Porizkova seems surprised and disappointed to have discovered that American women were far less free than they had a reputation for being and implies that American culture is the most conservative she had encountered.

4. In France, Sweden, and the Czech Republic, a woman knows her place (paragraph 12), but in the United States, a woman receives conflicting messages. She is told on the one

hand to rise up and then is quickly smacked down when she does. This helps her justify the resurrection of the term "feminist" when in America, because she needed it to make a place for herself.

Questions on Strategy

1. Porizkova primarily uses a block comparison likely to help readers understand each country separately. This organization helps highlight the ways in which each country's culture treated women.

2. Porizkova begins several of her paragraphs by identifying the country she is going to discuss (e.g., "In Czechoslovakia" in paragraph 3 and "In Sweden" in paragraph 4); this orients the reader and announces a shift in focus or a new contrast. Paragraph 12 contains several uses of parallelism to announce quick comparisons of European cultures, then shifts to an entire paragraph on American culture in the next paragraph, highlighting her point about the conservatism of America.

3. Her thesis is at the end of the essay: The word *feminist* needs to be resurrected to help women put an end to the cage of mixed expectations in which they find themselves. She puts it at the end because she wants to carry readers slowly to her point and to use the "journey" through different cultural experiences to explain how she has shifted from her opening statement of once feeling that *feminism* meant insecurity.

4. Porizkova uses definition to describe the role and meaning of "woman" in each country. She uses cause and effect to describe how men's attitudes changed the behavior of women, including how she altered her personal behavior to rebel against cultural norms.

ADDITIONAL WRITING SUGGESTIONS FOR COMPARISON AND CONTRAST

1. Write an essay in which you compare and contrast two objects, people, or events to show at least one of the following:
   - their important differences
   - their significant similarities
   - their relative value
   - their distinctive qualities

2. Select a topic from the list that follows. Write an essay using comparison and contrast as your primary means of development. Be sure that your essay has a definite purpose and a clear direction.
   - two television situation comedies
   - two types of summer employment
   - two people who display different attitudes toward responsibility
   - two restaurants (or other establishments)
   - two courses in the same subject area
   - two friends who exemplify different lifestyles
   - two video streaming services
   - two attitudes toward death

3. Most of us have seen something important in our lives — a person, place, or thing — undergo a significant change, either in the subject itself or in our own perception of it. Write an essay comparing and contrasting the person, place, or thing before and after the change. There are many possibilities to consider.

Perhaps a bucolic vista of open fields has become a shopping mall; perhaps a favorite athletic team has gone from glory to shame; or perhaps a loved one has been altered by decisions, events, or illness.

4. Use one of the following "before and after" situations as the basis for an essay of comparison and contrast:
   - before and after an examination
   - before and after seeing a movie
   - before and after reading an important book
   - before and after a big meal
   - before and after a long trip

5. Interview a professor who has taught for many years at your college or university. Ask the professor to compare and contrast the college as it was when he or she first taught there with the way it is now; encourage reminiscence and evaluation. Combine strategies of description, comparison and contrast, and possibly definition as you write your essay.

6. **Writing with Sources.** Two of the essays in this book deal, more or less directly, with issues related to the definition, achievement, or nature of manhood in America: "What Does 'Boys Will Be Boys' Really Mean?" by Deborah M. Roffman (p. 323) and "How Boys Become Men" by Jon Katz (p. 325). Paulina Porizkova's essay in this chapter, "America Made Me a Feminist" (p. 253) also raises similar issues of gender attitudes and behavior based on her own personal, multinational experience. Read these essays and discuss with classmates the broad issues they raise. Choose one aspect of the topic of particular interest to you and write an essay in which you compare, contrast, and evaluate the assertions in these essays. For models of and advice on integrating sources in your essay, see Chapters 14 and 15.

CHAPTER 9   Division and Classification

The Truth about Lying (p. 273)
JUDITH VIORST

Preparing to Read
The prompt will elicit a subjective response (allow room for a variety of views). You might ask students about the times they have lied — whether it was to conceal or to avoid hurting feelings. Discuss these personal experiences before you have students try to define and then classify types of lies.

Thinking Critically about the Text
Lying has always been understood as a negative social practice, but Viorst offers a number of examples of lies that can protect or keep trust. These sections promote another understanding of lying. Answers will vary on the necessity of these lies. Have students discuss whether telling the truth is the better alternative.

Questions on Subject

1. Viorst is wary of giving advice on lying because "too many people would promptly disagree" (paragraph 1) without taking time to really consider the topic or examine the consequences.

2. There are contradictions inherent in both the "protective" and "peace-keeping" categories of lies. The very fact that these lies are rationalized as being for the "good" of oneself or others is contradictory: If lying is bad, how can some lies be good?

3. In telling a protective lie, one would make the assumption that the truth would be too damaging to the listener. Students will likely disagree with this assumption. Discuss it.

4. A peace-keeping lie is told primarily to prevent the teller from having to experience discord resulting from the truth; protective lies are told to spare the feelings of others from a damaging truth. Thus, the basic difference between the two categories is that peace-keeping lies are told to protect the teller, whereas protective lies are told to protect the listener.

Questions on Strategy

1. Viorst categorizes lies as social lies, peace-keeping lies, protective lies, and trust-keeping lies. This is an adequate division for the writer; other people may have other categorizations. Ask your students if they can think of any additional categories.

2. Viorst accommodates those with steadfast views on lying by first assuring the reader that she "can't present any ultimate conclusions" (paragraph 1) and then by showing within each section circumstances that could justify the lie or not, depending on the individual view of the reader. She challenges her audience by posing direct questions — such as "What about you?" — at the end of each section.

3. Beginning in paragraph 45, Viorst opens her essay to the thoughts of others. In this way, the readers are given a cross-section of people who lie and a variety of reasons they do — a clever way for Viorst to reinforce her point without direct claims. At the end, the reader is unsure if he or she has been lied to throughout this essay — a very effective way to conclude a selection on lying.

4. The examples used by students in this response will depend on each individual. Viorst's use of examples strengthens her classification of lies. She gives the reader categories and then provides examples of her distinctions about lies. In paragraph 3, after classifying social lies, she writes, "Will you say to people, when it simply isn't true, 'I like your new hairdo,' 'You're looking much better,' 'It's so nice to see you,' 'I had a wonderful time'?" Viorst shows and tells at the same time. As a result, the reader gets a complete picture of what she is talking about.

The Different Ways of Being Smart (p. 280)
SARA GILBERT

Preparing to Read

Students may respond by citing IQ tests, exam scores, or grades to determine intelligence, which you may direct into a conversation about the ability to measure smartness. Students will also likely come up with a familiar distinction between "book smart" and "street smart" or "common sense smart," which will prepare them to engage with Gilbert's divisions. The question also encourages readers to define their own kind of intelligence.

Thinking Critically about the Text

Gilbert wants readers to understand that 1) having one type of intelligence does not mean you do not have others, and 2) that each form of intelligence has value and requires similar skills to develop. She writes to show the connections — and perhaps nuanced differences — between common assumptions of the types students may have identified in the "Preparing to Read" prompt and the scientific research on the topic.

Questions on Subject

1. The overlap supports her argument that we have many kinds of intelligence because she explains how each kind draws on similar mental skills. However, just because overlap may occur does not mean it has to, which sustains her purpose for writing and dividing.

2. She wants to make sure readers understand these categories are useful to help us understand certain aspects of intelligence, but they are not designed in order to put us into boxes. We are people, not types.

3. Each type of intelligence draws on the same ingredients. She underscores the idea that even though people have different kinds of intelligence, we draw on the same skills to develop them. This is important for her purpose of breaking down the hierarchy of intelligence to show they are all important and all require skill.

4. Athletic achievement, like other forms of intelligence, also requires practice, intense concentration, self-control, and persistence. These are all qualities that can be put to use in more "intellectual" forms of intelligence. Students will say whether they find these claims convincing.

Questions on Strategy

1. In paragraph 10, Gilbert illustrates how a book-smart versus an art-smart person would take an exam; she uses these examples to compare and contrast this experience for each of them. This supports her argument that there are different kinds of intelligence and they affect how we initially approach problems. In paragraph 12, she illustrates how a body-smart person might best study for a test. This also supports her argument that different intelligences do better with different approaches even if they all require patience and practice to develop.

2. Most people associate intelligence with "book smarts," related to formalized learning and study. She starts there to acknowledge the assumption and then moves to other types of "smarts" to encourage readers to broaden their idea of *intelligence*. Student reactions to this order will vary.

3. Many of her paragraphs begin by identifying which kind of smart she will talk about next. These serve as transitions to help readers follow her explanations through the different types. Paragraph 12 starts with, "The people we're calling *body-smart* ..." and paragraph 14 starts with "Persistence is also an important quality of *street-smart* people." Italicizing the types also helps readers follow. This reinforces the idea that multiple kinds of intelligence overlap, so she needs to keep clarifying terms.

4. The final three paragraphs call on the reader to see if they can recognize people with these different types of intelligence. She reinforces her argument that people have multiple forms of intelligence but will be more dominant in some areas over others. Her last paragraph introduces an important new idea — that people develop a particular intelligence in response to home or larger social environments. This poises her essay (and her readers) to begin further discussions and consider her argument's implications beyond the scope of her writing.

All-American Dialects (p. 286)
RICHARD LEDERER

Preparing to Read
This question helps students begin to classify themselves based on their regional accent. People rarely think of their speech as unique; they usually see the strange words and accents "other" people use. This question develops self-awareness. Use student answers and experiences to celebrate the diversity of your classroom. With students, generate a list of regional terms and expressions students use or may identify with other regions (e.g., "highway" vs. "interstate" vs. "expressway").

Thinking Critically about the Text
Students may list better communication as an advantage to uniform language, or feeling included rather than made fun of for the way one speaks. Lederer does not discuss how certain accents are more privileged than others. Students speaking a more homogenized version might find it easier to feel proud than those speaking a dialect more often associated with lower levels of education and/or income. Ask students if they can think of a better metaphor than a "pie." This could lead to a useful discussion of the complexities of the "melting pot" metaphor.

Questions on Subject
1. Lederer argues one dialect is not better than another or more correct; therefore, Lederer argues for people to have pride in using their dialect.
2. By "American rugged individualism" Lederer means the American value of being beholden to no one and able to put oneself above others. This supports his main idea that people do not have to all conform to the same accent or colloquialisms.
3. There was a time that people's regional accents were so consistent and unique they could be identified by an outsider simply by hearing how they pronounced (or could not pronounce) certain words. Our language used to be able to indicate our region. With television and radio some of these regional differences have flattened.
4. In paragraph 17, Lederer talks about how linguist Donald Lance helped find the residence of a woman with amnesia. Just by the words she used and her pronunciation he deduced she came from West Pennsylvania. In paragraphs 18 and 19, he recounted how linguist Roger Shuy accurately profiled Unabomber Ted Kaczynski. From Kaczynski's manifesto, Shuy deduced his religious background, education, age, and geographical origin.

Questions on Strategy
1. Lederer reinforces how a variety of regionalisms can be used to make the same point, and all are successful forms of communication. What one group considers "incorrect" or unintelligible may be considered correct by others. Language accuracy is determined by usage; if everyone in a region agrees on a certain word for a certain object and a specific pronunciation for that word, then that is correct for that group. This reinforces his claim that different does not mean wrong.
2. In paragraph 6, he *defines* the different meaning of milk shake, depending upon the region. Some use ice cream, and some just milk. This shows that not just the pronunciation can change but also the meaning. In paragraph 13, in his description of Southernisms, the reader can *compare and contrast* how they say various basic words with how Deep

Southerners might do so. This enables readers to experience the difference. The entire essay *divides* American English into regionalisms but also *classifies* them as part of the national language "pie."

3. At the end of paragraph 1 he writes, "we talk in melodies." This helps the reader orient toward language as something beautiful and charming, not simply functional. His last sentence, "May our bodacious language remain tasty and nourishing" (25), likens language to food.

4. Lederer includes references to songs, novels, poems, and plays to help readers pay attention to the fact that language is everywhere. Note, he does leave out television and movie references, likely because he sees these as more often flattening our speech rather than delivering to us more local varieties to appreciate.

Mother Tongue (p. 294)
AMY TAN

Preparing to Read
After students have discussed how their speaking might change in different contexts, move the conversation into a discussion of how different writing situations also affect language. You might point out that a text or a social media post invites a very different style of writing than an academic essay or a professional cover letter.

Thinking Critically about the Text
Students may respond differently to the idea that someone would find their writing "easy to read." Some may consider it a compliment, whereas others may consider it an indicator that the piece was not academic or professional enough. It might depend on the audience for whom it was intended. If a piece is not able to communicate its ideas to an intended audience, however, then it has failed its task. Why would we ever want to write a piece that is purposefully hard to read? To prove our own intelligence?

Questions on Subject
1. In paragraph 3, Tan introduces the main idea of the essay: "Recently, I was made keenly aware of the different Englishes I do use." We know she will talk about the use of different kinds of English in her experience.

2. In paragraph 3, Tan introduces the standard English she learned in school. She offers the following phrase as an example of this English, "the intersection of memory upon imagination." She describes this kind of English as having "carefully wrought grammatical phrases . . . normalized forms, past perfect tenses, conditional phrases . . ." In paragraph 4, she talks about the kind of English she uses with her mother. She calls this "the language of intimacy" and "family talk." In paragraph 6, she provides an example. Tan experiences this family English as "vivid, direct, full of observation and imagery" (7). To those not familiar with this type of English, the communication would be seen as filled with errors (according to Standard American English). The verbs are incorrectly conjugated and sometimes missing altogether. Articles and direct objects are also often missing.

3. Tan felt ashamed as a child because she considered her mother's English "broken," "fractured," and "limited" (8). Now she considers her mother's English "simple" (21) but still full of imagery and containing the passion, intent, and unique manner of the speaker. It is full and complete even if it is neither wholly English nor wholly Chinese.

4. Students will respond differently to this question. Some may argue there are correct answers on many English tests. There are rules of grammar, and there are relations between words that can be identified. Many may agree that, while these rules exist, English and the humanities — because they are often about interpretation — have more possible answers than math and science.

Questions on Strategy

1. Tan's purpose in this essay is to show how she came to see English not as one static language that could be spoken correctly or incorrectly but rather as a form of communication that can have many iterations. In paragraphs 2 and 3, she tells readers that she sees the forms of English she uses as variations. Then she tells how she came to see them that way rather than one as broken and the other as correct.

2. She organizes them based on where she uses them; at home, at work, in the hospital, and so on.

3. Some students may struggle with the example and appreciate Tan's explanation. In paragraph 6, Tan chooses to show versus tell. Something would have been lost had she just tried to describe the language. Readers would have had an incomplete picture. Actually quoting her mother helps readers see the differences between the two Englishes introduced in the essay.

4. The limitations of her mother's English are only limitations when compared to standard English taught in school. Tan realized over time that the simple English her mother used still communicated a great deal. Her mother's English may have been wrong grammatically, but it did not lack in meaning and effectiveness. This shows us that language does not have to be correct to be powerful and understood. This seeming contradiction works to encourage readers to be less judgmental about what they perceive to be "broken English."

ADDITIONAL WRITING SUGGESTIONS FOR DIVISION AND CLASSIFICATION

1. To write a meaningful classification essay, you must analyze a body of unorganized material and arrange it for a particular purpose. For example, to identify for a buyer the most economical cars currently on the market, you might initially determine which cars can be purchased for under $3,000 and which cost between $25,000 and $35,000. Then, using a second basis of selection — fuel economy — you could determine which cars have the best mileage within each price range.

   Select one of the following subjects and write a classification essay. Be sure that your purpose is clearly explained and that your bases of selection are chosen and ordered in accordance with your purpose.

   - attitudes toward physical fitness
   - reasons for going to college
   - attitudes toward the religious or spiritual side of life
   - choosing a hobby or recreation
   - college professors
   - college courses
   - ways of financing a college education
   - parties or other social events

2. We sometimes resist classifying other people because doing so can seem like "pigeonholing" or stereotyping individuals unfairly. In an essay, compare and contrast two or more ways of classifying people, including at least one that

you would call legitimate and one that you would call misleading. What conclusions can you draw about the difference between useful classifications and damaging stereotypes?

3. Use division and classification to explain your school or town. What categories might you use? Would you divide your subject into different types of people? Would you classify people by their spending habits? What are the other ways in which you might explain your school or town? What other rhetorical strategies might you incorporate to strengthen your presentation? You might want to look at the Web site of your school or town to find out what categories it uses to present itself.

4. **Writing with Sources.** Do some research on the most recent presidential election or another political campaign that interests you. Reread or watch online major news coverage of the last days of the election and identify at least three qualities that were mentioned most often for the final contenders. What categories or classes do these qualities belong to? Write an essay in which you discuss how this division and classification of the candidates' qualities might have contributed to the winner's victory. Also consider who did the dividing: Was it the media? The public? For models of and advice on integrating sources in your essay, see Chapters 14 and 15.

5. **Writing with Sources.** Using the terms "museum floor plan," search online for formatted layouts of museum floor plans, perhaps for the Smithsonian Institution museums such as the National Museum of Natural History. Consider museums that you've visited in the past or museums you hope to visit in the future. Look at a few different plans and then select one with exhibit categories that interest you. Brainstorm a list of things that might appear in each category and write a paragraph about why those items would be a good fit for the museum's overall purpose, focus, and audience. Be sure to reference specific parts of your floor plan in your explanation. For models of and advice on integrating sources in your essay, see Chapters 14 and 15.

6. **Writing with Sources**. Writers use division and classification to generate new ways of understanding topics, and some use it to revisit subjects of lasting interest on which they wish to offer fresh insights. Select a topic for your essay and then decide which approach you want to take. If you think you're devising an original classification, do some research first to see whether others have, in fact, already written on the same topic. Note, for example, that much has already been written about types of love, types of war, types of lies, types of students, types of humor, types of bosses, types of poetry, and types of cars. If you are writing a classification that has been treated before, you will want to learn all you can about the way other writers have already treated this subject. Naturally, you will want to offer fresh ideas rather than simply offering examples of what others have already found to be true.

7. **Writing in the Workplace.** You are starting a new business, either a nonprofit charitable organization in which you are looking for donors or a for-profit business for which you need customers. Develop a fund-raising plan or a marketing plan in which you divide and classify your potential donors and customers. Be sure that your plan identifies the classes and subclasses of donors and customers that would maximize your desired outcome. When classifying, consider such demographics as age, sex, income, race, ethnicity, location, and likely proficiency with social media.

CHAPTER 10   Definition

What Is Poverty? (p. 317)
JO GOODWIN PARKER

Preparing to Read
Students will have various responses to the prompt because *poor* is an ambiguous term that will lead to many interpretations. You might prepare for this prompt by asking about the multiple meanings of the word *poor*. Keep in mind that Parker's poverty encompasses more than economics.

Thinking Critically about the Text
Much of Parker's essay works by attempting to create empathy in the reader. She tries to place the reader in her conditions and times. Students' responses to the prompt will vary; take time to discuss a few of the responses. Discuss how personal experience affects one's opinion on a subject.

Questions on Subject
1. Parker could not have the operation that was recommended for her because she could not afford it, she was afraid of it, and she did not have the time or resources to take care of her children during the time it would take her to recover (paragraph 3). She quit her job because she was spending more on day care than she possibly could afford and still be able to feed her family (3).
2. Parker claims that asking for help is humiliating and shameful and results in getting the runaround. The only reason that she is compelled to seek help in spite of all of this is for the sake of her children (paragraph 6).
3. Readers are not given a precise reason for the husband's departure; they are merely told by Parker that she purposely "destroyed" her marriage (8). She claims that she hopes her husband has been able to better himself because "[h]e never could hope with us to drag him down" (8).
4. Parker is implying that those without money are taken advantage of in insidious, humiliating ways. The neighbor obviously expects sexual favors as payment for a ride.

Questions on Strategy
1. Parker wants to make people aware of the plight of the poor. She drives home—very forcefully—the misery and squalor of poverty by using extended definition. The reader is placed in Parker's scene.
2. Parker uses narrative, description, some negative and some synonymous definitions in this essay. There are no statistics or quotations from other sources. Parker leaves such information out because she does not want her definition of poverty to become impersonal.
3. The most striking details Parker uses are those that were obviously meant to be the most disturbing, such as an infant's skin peeling off with an old diaper, insects everywhere, and the stench of poverty: "watching gnats and flies devour your baby's tears when he cries" (paragraph 5); "insects in your food, in your nose, in your eyes, and

crawling over you when you sleep" (5). The emotional impact comes from the realization of the terrible toll that poverty exacts on children, especially babies. Most readers can identify with the basic needs of food and shelter; when they are faced with the images of children deprived of even these basic needs they respond emotionally. By using description and examples, Parker's definition of poverty is not read about but felt (almost experienced).

4. "Poverty is an acid that drips on pride until all pride is worn away" (paragraph 13) and "Poverty is a chisel that chips on honor until honor is worn away" (13) describe the corrosive destruction of poverty and mirror—through repetition—the drudgery that must be endured by those being systematically eaten away and destroyed by poverty. The metaphoric imprisonment reflected in the phrase "the bars of my poverty" (10) reinforces the feelings of being trapped, helpless, and desperate. The reader responds to the raw force and emotion of these phrases as much as to the plain, simple words and phrases used elsewhere.

What Does "Boys Will Be Boys" Really Mean? (p. 323)
DEBORAH M. ROFFMAN

Preparing to Read
The expression "boys will be boys" will likely bring to mind stereotypes of crude, sexual (especially if thought of in the context of "locker room talk"), and possibly violent behavior. This expression implies that it is natural for boys to, for example, enjoy rough physical play, be quick to anger, bully or worse, be interested in sports, have an aversion to domestic labor, pursue casual sex, and behave irresponsibly in a relationship. The expression also implies that there is an inherent and socially acceptable quality to these characteristics and behaviors.

Thinking Critically about the Text
Roffman wants her readers to understand how "astonishingly negative" (paragraph 9) and insulting the expression is about boys. Instead of finding the "messy . . . selfish . . . insensitive" (9) depiction of boys accurate, Roffman finds it an implicit condemnation of boys as "animals" (10). Roffman believes that "[w]e need to explain why the notion that 'boys will be boys' embodies a bogus and ultimately corrupting set of expectations that are unacceptable" (22) because accepting such a pervasive cultural stereotype allows boys to take advantage of their relationships with adults and girls (19), while at the same time it hurts their self-respect and confidence (20, 24).

Questions on Subject
1. Roffman's students suggested that she did not want to view the episode of *Family Guy* in class because of: "The language? The women dressed like 'bimbos'? The implied sexual acts? The mistreatment of the mother?" (paragraph 4). She responds to these questions by informing the students that it is "the less obvious images and messages that got [her] attention" (5). Instead, she objected to the "underlying assumption in the show, and often in our society, that boys, by nature, are bad" (5).

2. When Roffman revealed her reason for not viewing the show in class, some of the boys reacted to the show with indignation and anger. According to Roffman, "It was a good

moment: Recognizing for the first time the irony that maybe it was they who were really being demeaned . . ." (paragraph 6).

3. Roffman objects to the advertising and entertainment industry practice of glorifying and sexualizing women's bodies because it inherently assumes that the man looking at the ad is "just another low-life guy who lives and breathes to ogle and grab every large-breasted woman he sees" (paragraph 18). Roffman finds the adult responses to these images and messages to be disturbing because they "aren't nearly as clued in about how destructive these ubiquitous images and messages can be for boys" (14).

4. Roffman sees the source of the "boys will be bad" stereotype in the "time when men were the exclusively entitled gender," as "[m]any did behave badly, simply because they could" (paragraph 15). She suggests that such gender myths have staying power because "as stereotypes go, they can be remarkably invisible" (16).

Questions on Strategy

1. Roffman's purpose in writing this essay is to show that "no matter how demeaning today's culture may seem toward girls and women," it may be "fundamentally more disrespectful of boys and men" (paragraph 8).

2. Roffman's intended audience is adults who might see nothing wrong with the "boys will be boys" stereotype. In paragraph 7, the pronoun *you* refers to the reader, and in paragraph 8 the pronouns *us* and *we* refer to society as a whole. Boys and children are referred to but not addressed, as if they are not the intended audience, and adults are referred to as part of the discussion.

3. The series of questions Roffman asks in paragraph 10 functions to solidify her argument that the "boys will be boys" stereotype is disrespectful to men and harmful to society. The questions imply that when we think about boys more seriously, we will not accept a superficial and one-dimensional view of them as "animals." "Is it possible . . . we really think . . ." is a rhetorical construction that does not need an answer. Therefore, these questions allow her to build her case for what is problematic about the stereotype.

4. Roffman's analogy is intended to explain how a boy in today's society is unable to tell how he is being manipulated by these stereotypes. By presenting the boy as a fish in water, Roffman clearly explains how pervasive these stereotypes are.

The Company Man (p. 329)
ELLEN GOODMAN

Preparing to Read
Students will have a variety of career paths in mind. Encourage students to discuss the expectations of those diverging paths. Are there any expectations or sacrifices that are similar for the majority of the paths? Are there expectations that students consider unfair but will submit to anyway?

Thinking Critically about the Text
Goodman adds these details because many readers may make similarly false assumptions. They assume they are healthy because they do not engage in the riskiest behaviors. The details help her correct this false assumption. Phil's employer supported and

encouraged his long hours. The end of the essay shows us that the employer is looking for someone like Phil who will sacrifice health for work. The entire work environment and the demands of the job supported or encouraged his lifestyle choices, leading to his untimely death.

Questions on Subject

1. Goodman mentions the concept of Type A personality in paragraph 2. She defines it as a "workaholic."

2. Phil invested all of his emotional, mental, and physical energy in his work. There was nothing left for his wife, his children, or himself. The stress of the job and his singular focus on his work, she claims, killed him. He died of exhaustion and ill health from too much stress. She does not mean that the job killed him in the sense that the ceiling collapsed on him. His body collapsed under the weight of the job itself.

3. Goodman suggests that Phil worked as hard as he did in order to become president one day (paragraph 3). He may have also worked this hard to hide from his life, himself, and his family. He may have had fears of intimacy that made work feel more comfortable than home. Also, as time went on, he had developed no other interests and therefore had no reason not to work. He was not a very fully developed person. Students may offer other explanations.

4. Not including the specific profession in the essay has several advantages. First, more readers can identify with Phil. They might be an executive or know executives. In addition, not mentioning the exact profession stresses the point that it did not matter what Phil was doing. He was not, Goodman suggests, committed to the mission of his career or company. He was driven by stress and ambition.

Questions on Strategy

1. Goodman's purpose in this essay is to help readers check themselves and their loved ones to see if they are working themselves to death. Or, if not to death, to consider how obsession with work might rob people of rich, happy, and healthy lives. In paragraph 2, she emphasizes the short reflection period of those attending the funeral. They knew why Phil died and thought briefly about their own choices. Her essay expands and develops this period of reflection. She presents him as a man who did not live, who emotionally abandoned his wife and died young. She paints a tragic picture of Phil and encourages readers not to make the same mistake.

2. Waiting until paragraph 3 helps readers project their own experiences first. They can imagine themselves or someone they love dying that way. This pulls readers in and helps them connect emotionally with the content.

3. A company man is someone who works long hours, sacrifices his body for the company (4). She uses as evidence his long hours (working six days a week, several of them late) and health habits (being overweight and eating at his desk). The people he knew and the activities he did all related to work; he had no outside activities or interests (4). The impression was that he was not his own person, but actually *belonged* to the company.

4. The numbers referring to the company give the impression of nameless employees all competing against and then replacing one another. Phil's age shows us how young he was when he died and the youth of his wife. Forty-eight is young to be a widow. Fifty-one is young to die, especially when one is affluent and has access to health care. The numbers help paint the picture of Phil's life without having to say literally that he died young or that the company had many employees to replace one another.

Virtue Signaling and Other Inane Platitudes (p. 333)
MARK PETERS

Preparing to Read
This question enables students to examine their own behavior before reading how Peters makes sense of this new online realm of awareness raising, idea sharing, and cause engagement. By admitting their own behavior first, readers will likely pay greater attention to Peters's critiques. Use the discussion to generate examples of recent social media activism or ways people share their causes.

Thinking Critically about the Text
Students may argue that promoting causes online *can* help raise awareness and financial contributions to organizations. They may also say that just because someone promotes a cause on social media does not mean they are not also doing something actively for that cause. Peters does not offer any statistics about the offline activism of those who promote causes online.

Questions on Subject
1. Virtue signaling is a form of communication that occurs mostly online, in which people express sentiments or support without actually taking any actions. Peters argues this online behavior gives people the illusion that they have made a contribution when in fact they haven't changed anything.
2. Peters explains how the term emerged in political context in which the right critiqued the left. In regards to social media, Peters's argument shows how words can be useful beyond the contexts which spawned them.
3. Humblebrag is "self-aggrandizement cloaked in humility" (9). Like virtue signaling it refers to behaviors commonly seen on social media.
4. This question allows students to critique Peters's argument or express their agreement with the inutility of promoting causes online.

Questions on Strategy
1. If readers answer "yes" to any of these rhetorical questions at the beginning of the essay, they have participated in virtue signaling. The questions hook readers, helping them see how they might be participating in the behavior the article critiques. Some readers might feel attacked and, as a result, be turned off. He could have begun the essay listing these behaviors versus listing them as questions. This likely would not have been as compelling for readers.
2. In paragraph 7, he cites lexicographer Orin Hargraves who studies self-glorifying online behavior. By referring to academics and experts, the article becomes more of a study of the term than just a critique of the behavior, and it gains authority as an important issue instead of just one writer's musings.
3. In paragraphs 3 and 4, Peters compares and contrasts different ways in which conservatives use the term, both to critique liberals and one another. In paragraph 7, he compares virtue signaling to prayer shaming. Later in the paragraph, he compares and contrasts these terms to humblebragging, which helps him identify different behaviors and the socio-political work each technique aims to achieve.
4. Peters's article offers readers vocabulary for the new discourses emerging online. He helps readers understand where these terms came from and will reflect before engaging

in causes online if they are not planning to take any action. Peters wants readers who say they care about causes to stop typing and actually help.

ADDITIONAL WRITING SUGGESTIONS FOR DEFINITION

1. Write an essay in which you define one of the following words by telling not only what it is but also what it is *not*. (For example, one could say that "poetry is that which cannot be expressed in any other way.") Remember, however, that defining by negation does not relieve you of the responsibility of defining the term in other ways as well.
   - leadership
   - patriotism
   - wealth
   - failure
   - family
   - loyalty
   - creativity
   - humor

2. Think about your school, town, or country's identity. How would you define its essential character? Choose a place that is important in your life and write an essay defining its character and significance to you.

3. **Writing with Sources.** Karl Marx defined *capitalism* as an economic system in which the bourgeois owners of the means of production exploit the proletariat for their own selfish gain. How would you define *capitalism*? Write an essay defining *capitalism* that includes all six types of definition: formal, synonymous, negative, etymological, stipulative, and extended. Do some research in the library or online to help with your definitions. For models of and advice on integrating sources in your essay, see Chapters 14 and 15.

4. The opening visual for this chapter, on page 302, defines various types of coffee drinks using a highly graphic style. Visual definitions can be an excellent complement to text-only definitions because our brains are often able to process them more quickly. Using the coffee-drinks image as a model, create a coherent set of visual definitions for types of pasta. Search online or in your library or supermarket to find the names of six to twelve different pasta shapes or doughs. You may want to combine a few select words with your images to clearly distinguish what your illustration represents, as was done in the coffee-drinks image. To create your visual, either sketch by hand or use photo and graphics applications, keeping in mind that simple visuals often have greater resonance with viewers. Once your visual definitions are complete, write a paragraph explaining what your visual would uniquely add to a set of more traditional, text-only definitions. In what ways might the images affect your choice of pasta to purchase, prepare, or eat?

5. **Writing with Sources.** In discussing the power of labels that define identity, psychiatrist Thomas Szasz once wrote:

> The struggle for definition is veritably the struggle for life itself. In the typical western two men fight desperately for the possession of a gun that has been thrown to the ground: Whoever reaches the weapon first, shoots and lives; his adversary is shot and dies. In ordinary life, the struggle is not for guns but for words: Whoever first defines the situation is the victor; his adversary, the victim. . . . In short, he who first seizes the word imposes reality on the other; he who defines thus dominates and lives; and he who is defined is subjugated and may be killed.
>
> — From *The Second Sin*

Take some time to think about words like *gay*, *retarded*, or *jock*, whose meanings in our culture have become contested — that is, challenged by some who are offended by the way(s) in which those words are used. What other defining labels have you encountered or observed? After doing some research in your library as well as on the Internet, write an essay in which you explore the power of labels to define. For models of and advice on integrating sources in your essay, see Chapters 14 and 15.

6. **Writing in the Workplace.** One pressing social issue facing all-women's colleges today is the question of how to define the term *female* when considering student applications. Some colleges, such as Smith, have changed their acceptance criteria to include transgender students who currently (or used to) identify as female, whereas other women's colleges are still sorting out what definitions they will accept. Suppose for a minute that you are a dean in the admissions office at one of these schools, preparing for a meeting to set the guidelines for your applicant pool. In preparation for your meeting, write a definition essay to explain your understanding of female and what it means with regard to acceptance at your school. To make your definition clearer to your reader, you might consider employing one or more of the other methods, which will almost certainly include classification and might benefit from the inclusion of a relevant narrative.

CHAPTER 11   Cause and Effect Analysis

How Boys Become Men (p. 352)
JON KATZ

Preparing to Read
Katz's essay closely explores some of the more painful rituals through which boys in mainstream American culture establish gender identity. This prompt asks students to recall and evaluate related childhood experiences of their own. It might be interesting for students to

discuss the differences between the experiences cited by girls and those recalled by boys. Discussion might also reveal interesting differences and similarities between Katz and students of varied cultural backgrounds.

Thinking Critically about the Text

Students' responses will vary. Their answers will reveal significant assumptions that stem from their personal backgrounds. Note that Katz does not attempt to tell where "Boy Justice" comes from; therefore, students will have to support their answers with illustrations from their own experience and reading.

Questions on Subject

1. According to Katz, women see men as a "giant problem" because they do not understand the boyhood "Code of Conduct," which is often carried into adulthood. The perceptive student might detect the circular logic in this argument — that women don't understand men because they don't understand male culture. Follow-up questions might include "What is the origin of this Code of Conduct?" and "Do boys learn it from men or culture, or is it somehow innate?"

2. Answers will vary.

3. "More than anything else, boys are supposed to learn how to handle themselves" (paragraph 7). Students' answers about what girls are supposed to learn will vary; some believe they need to learn how to handle themselves as well, how to act modestly or in a "lady-like" way.

4. Men gain sensitivity "when they lose their jobs, their wives, or their lovers. Others learn it through a strong marriage, or through their own children" (paragraph 19). Students will identify various other factors that might promote male sensitivity. It might be interesting to discuss their reasons for considering those other factors.

Questions on Strategy

1. Katz's audience is young women, whom he addresses specifically as "you" in paragraphs 4 and 18.

2. Katz begins his essay by referring to men as "we" and follows with a long example in which the chief male character is "I." Men do not appear as the abstract "them" until paragraph 15. The change shifts the emphasis away from a narrative account of boyhood experience to a generalization of how men behave in American culture.

3. The location of the quotes in paragraphs 16 and 17 makes the transition from an emphasis on the personal and anecdotal experiences of boys to a general and objective analysis of the behavior of men.

4. Katz's first anecdote, which tells about the boy who refuses to be chicken, opens the essay (paragraphs 1 and 2) and illustrates his argument that boys are acculturated to accept pain rather than show fear. His second anecdote (7 through 14) centers the essay. It recounts his personal memory of telling on a tormentor and suffering for it. Katz's final narrative (20 through 23) ends the essay with an account of a bullying episode he witnesses as an adult, showing that the youthful male behavior he deplores (both the bullying and its acceptance by the victim) is still prevalent in our society. In the paragraphs between narratives (3 through 6 and 15 through 19), Katz analyzes how the characteristics of men in our society are rooted in their behavior as boys.

The Downside of Diversity (p. 357)
MICHAEL JONAS

Preparing to Read
Students may believe that people who live in ethnically diverse communities demonstrate stronger civic engagement and interconnectedness than people who live in homogeneous communities because they are exposed to wider and more diverse ideas. Students may believe that lack of exposure to diversity breeds passivity in homogeneous communities.

Thinking Critically about the Text
Despite Putnam's findings that ethnic diversity might be a liability, he argues that it can be "ultimately valuable and enriching" (paragraph 37). This seeming contradiction is explained when he writes, "Experience shows that social divisions can eventually give way to 'more encompassing identities' that create a 'new, more capacious sense of "we"'" (34).

Questions on Subject
1. The effects of greater social diversity include "tension and discord" and a loss of civic engagement (paragraph 20). However, "the creative tensions unleashed by those differences in the workplace may vault those same places to the cutting edge of the economy and of creative culture" (31). Putnam believes the losses are significant enough that efforts should be made to mitigate them, and he has done work to promote "efforts . . . to increase civic connections in communities" (39).
2. Putnam worried that his findings would subject him to "liberal attacks" (paragraph 15), but his "worst fears" were "about how his results could be used" by conservatives and even racists (33) at a time of "intense political debate, from immigration to race-based admissions to schools" (4).
3. Evidence that runs counter to Putnam's research on ethnic diversity yielding a "civic malaise" (paragraph 21) is found in "the vigor often associated with urban centers, where ethnic diversity is greatest" (29). "[A] parallel line of emerging research suggests [diversity] can be a big asset when it comes to driving productivity and innovation" (29). "'[B]y hanging out with people different than you, you're likely to get more insights. Diverse teams tend to be more productive'" (30). Political scientist Scott Page calls it "the diversity paradox" (32).
4. For increasing social capital within diverse ethnic communities, Putnam suggests expanding "support for English-language instruction and investing in community centers and other places that allow for 'meaningful interaction across ethnic lines'" (paragraph 37).

Questions on Strategy
1. Jonas's essay reports the research findings that indicate ethnic diversity causes diminishment of social capital. Other causes were considered, such as "greater income ranges, higher crime rates, and more mobility among their residents" (paragraph 16), but "the connection remained strong" (18). The effects of diversity on members of a community were "distrust," withdrawal, disaffection, and isolation (18).
2. Conservative think-tank fellow John Leo criticizes Putnam's presentation of his findings because Leo says social scientists are supposed to be objective and neutral. Leo says, "You're just supposed to tell your peers what you found" (paragraph 38). Instead Putnam frets about his findings and suggests that, despite the ill effects of diversity in the short term, in the long term diversity could create new ties that expand the definition of "we"

(34) and suggests programs for creating more community ties in diverse neighborhoods (37). Leo's criticisms are answered by John Wolfe when he says, "Social scientists are both scientists and citizens" and that he "sees nothing wrong in Putnam's efforts to affect some of the phenomena he studies" (40). Student opinions will vary.

3. In his essay, Jonas quotes from numerous expert sources but none so much as John Putnam. He depicts the controversy over Putnam's findings through the reactions of other experts, such as Scott Page, John Leo, and John Wolfe. This technique separates the findings from the controversy and gives Putnam's research more credibility as evidence in the essay.

4. Jonas appears objective in his treatment of Putnam's work. He explores the implications for immigration and other issues, goes into detail about contradictory evidence in relation to big cities, and brings in views that oppose Putnam's. This builds credibility for the information in the essay. Jonas may possibly be tipping his hand that he supports diversity by his sympathetic portrayal of Putnam's advocacy and fears about how his research might be used by conservatives.

Coca-Cola Funds Scientists' Effort to Alter Obesity Battle (p. 365)
ANAHAD O'CONNOR

Preparing to Read
Weight and health can be very sensitive topics. If you have concerns over discussing these issues in class, consider asking students to journal on the topic, or steer the conversation to depictions of weight (and weight gain/loss) in the media.

Thinking Critically about the Text
Students will likely have a different feeling about how the medical advice is being used *after* reading the article. You might want to ask if they can imagine how they thought of this advice *before* reading.

Questions on Subject
1. Coke has been promoting the medical advice that, in order to stay fit, people need to balance calories taken in with calories burned. Their message is suggesting to people that, if they find themselves overweight, it is because they are not moving enough, not because soda is unhealthy. The title prepares the readers for an argument about the true cause of obesity and the potential effects of Coca-Cola's marketing.

2. O'Connor believes that a combination of lack of exercise and ingesting too many calories causes obesity.

3. The Global Energy Balance Network is a group that "promotes the argument that weight-conscious Americans are overly fixated on how much they eat and drink while not paying enough attention to exercise" (paragraph 2). Coca-Cola's support of this network includes a great deal of funding for this calorie balance approach to health. The network, with Coca-Cola's support, may promote the idea that if you work out more, you can eat more. The soda company loves this idea because it can continue to promote sports and its soda together. It makes it look like a health-conscious company when, in fact, it is not.

4. Coke supports the idea that health involves balancing the calories eaten with the calories burned. By creating opportunities for exercise, Coke would seem to be removing barriers from people buying more of their product.

Questions on Strategy

1. The entire article hinges on two important questions of cause-and-effect. The first is whether or not poor eating is a major contributor to obesity (paragraphs 17, 20, 21, 23). The second is whether or not the funding from Coke is likely to influence the findings of the Global Energy Balance Network (4, 6, 12, 16).

2. O'Connor would likely say that it does not make them corrupt, but it does make them suspect. You can tell that O'Connor is skeptical of Blair's defense because his bracketed note includes the phrase "allegedly by accident" and he follows the quote with a paragraph noting that studies suggest that corporate funding often biases scientific findings. Stylistically, we feel that Blair and O'Connor are in conversation with each other, with Blair offering a statement that O'Connor then refutes.

3. If people believe that sugary drinks like Coca-Cola have a serious impact on their health, they may stop buying them and sales will drop off, making Coke lose money. Also, proposed tax increases on sugary drinks (meant to encourage people to buy healthier alternatives) will impact how often consumers purchase soda. Paragraphs 4 to 6 provide evidence for these views.

4. Quotations will vary. The reasoning behind the sources may include presenting an opposing argument in order to refute it and presenting evidence in support of the central claim.

Save Your Sanity, Downgrade Your Life (p. 371)
PAMELA PAUL

Preparing to Read
Many people may take technology for granted and may not stop to think about the effects of technology on their lives. Feeling anxious, having headaches, and even an inability to focus can all be caused by frenetic time on devices. This article and its associated questions might be the first time students have stopped to think about technology as something optional or something they can mitigate. If leading a class discussion or activity with this prompt, try finding ways for students to recognize their dependence on technology.

Thinking Critically about the Text
Paul describes how mitigating technology's influence on her life has been beneficial. Because she focuses on the benefits of reducing the use of technology, readers could critique her for not addressing the life-saving and time-saving advantages of technology. Students may also find her argument weakened by its reliance on the author's personal experience and may not be representative.

Questions on Subject
1. Paul considers technology a cause of the mind-boggling speed at which we live — its omnipresence can be annoying and disruptive in people's personal lives. Ironically, the

increasing reliance on technology has resulted in a desire to simplify and return to nostalgic technologies such as typewriters.

2. Technology can be "intrusive and annoying" (paragraph 4). "Techno-stress" is the physical and psychological effect of staring at screens for countless hours (9). Many experience online harassment (10). Kids stop playing with each other and are starting to play with their devices instead, losing touch with what it means to be a socially adept human (11).

3. Paul contrasts work life with home life. The divide between work and home has dissolved or at least shrunken for many; email, portable phones, and chat-systems like Slack keep us connected all the time. Reducing dependence on technology would help re-establish a healthier work-life balance. At work, we often operate in teams, making on-going communication essential and collaborative technology useful.

4. Paul writes that Americans yearn for simplicity and nostalgia. She points to best-selling self-help books that aim to keep readers from feeling overwhelmed (8) and an A.P.A. study that reports how worried people are about the impacts of social media, including the threat of online harassment (9).

Questions on Strategy

1. Paul's purpose is to have readers pause and think about the effect of technology on their own lives and think about ways they might mitigate its influence. She shows readers that they do have some choice in the role it plays.

2. This one sentence paragraph emphasizes Paul's strategy in the face of technology's ubiquitous presence: downgrading.

3. In paragraph 5, Paul illustrates ways in which even tweens are scaling back. In paragraph 6 she defines "digital detoxes." In paragraph 8, she demonstrates Americans' interest in nostalgia by listing books about simplification. Citing Pixar's film *WALL-E*, she illustrates a possible future if we continue using our devices at an increasing rate. Students may find others.

4. Paul's tone is one of concern and sometimes frustration about technology's influence; she is adamant about taking steps to reduce its influence on her life, especially at home. She refers to her work life as accelerating at a "boggling speed" (3). By calling technology "intrusive and annoying" (4) we know she is not an unequivocal fan of its presence in her life. Her one paragraph statement, "I deliberately downgraded," shows her adamancy. Students may find similar words to describe her tone.

ADDITIONAL WRITING SUGGESTIONS FOR CAUSE AND EFFECT ANALYSIS

1. Write an essay in which you analyze the most significant reasons for your decision to attend college. You may want to discuss your family background, your high school experience, people and events that influenced your decision, and your goals in college as well as in later life.

2. It is interesting to think of ourselves in terms of the influences that have caused us to be who we are. Write an essay in which you discuss two or three of what you consider the most important influences on your life. Following are some areas you may want to consider when planning and writing your paper:
   - a parent
   - a book or movie
   - a religious leader

- a teacher or coach
- a friend
- a hero
- your neighborhood
- your ethnic or cultural background

3. Write an essay about a recent achievement of yours or about an important achievement in your community. Explain the causes of this success. Look at all of the underlying elements involved in the accomplishment, and explain how you selected the one main cause or the causal chain that led to the achievement. To do this, you will probably want to use the rhetorical strategy of comparison and contrast. You might also use exemplification and process analysis to explain the connection between your cause and its effect.

4. **Writing with Sources.** Decisions often involve cause and effect relationships; that is, a person usually weighs the possible results of an action before deciding to act. Write an essay in which you consider the possible effects that would result from one decision or another in one of the following controversies. You will need to do some research in the library or online to support your conclusions.
   - taxing cars on the basis of fuel consumption
   - requiring an ethics course in college
   - mandatory licensing of handguns
   - cloning humans
   - abolishing grades for college courses
   - raising the minimum wage

   For models of and advice on integrating sources in your essay, see Chapters 14 and 15.

5. **Writing in the Workplace.** A position paper gives advice on an issue and may incorporate any combination of the different development methods you're studying in this book. Most likely, however, it will place the greatest emphasis on cause and effect analysis and argumentation. The purpose of a position paper is to make a case for a way of regarding a topic and for taking action on it. Rather than a review of research that explores all that's been said about a topic or issue, or an essay that allows you to show your own thinking about it, the position paper presents a question, considers the pros and cons of various courses of action, and makes a recommendation.

   Say that you are an executive at the Javro Coffee Roasters Company, and the board of directors is interested in moving toward a fair-trade business model. Fair trade means selling coffee from beans that are raised on environmentally sustainable plantations, where workers are paid according to a fair and equitable wage scale, and where all business transactions are transparent and ethical. At the board's request, write a position paper on the feasibility of pursuing the fair-trade model, the pros and cons of the approach, and your recommendation about whether Javro should adopt it.

CHAPTER 12   Argumentation

Ain't I a Woman? (p. 395)
SOJOURNER TRUTH

Preparing to Read
Many students might respond that they have never attended a rally but have heard speeches on television. Others will recall a speaker who spoke at their high school or gave the graduation address. Ask students how they might react to a speech by Donald Trump, Barack Obama, Stephen Colbert, Steph Curry, Beyoncé, Nelson Mandela, Hillary Rodham Clinton, Sonia Sotomayor, or Kanye West. Which speakers would they be likely to trust or view skeptically?

Thinking Critically about the Text
We've had success having a student read Truth's speech aloud to the class before starting the discussion. In this way, Truth's down-home idiomatic images come to life. While students find different things memorable about the speech, most agree that her claims for the importance of women and her positioning of Christ's mother in Christianity are memorable. Most students can't believe that a black woman was speaking this way in the 1800s prior to the Civil War.

Questions on Subject
1. When Truth says, "Where there is so much racket there must be something out of kilter" (paragraph 1), she means that if women of the North and the African Americans of the South are making a lot of noise about their rights, something must be unequal. She believes that white men are going to find themselves in a "fix" (1) because they will cease to dominate the rights of each group.
2. Truth's credentials as a woman are that she is as strong as a man, she has plowed and planted, she has borne the lash, she has eaten as much as a man, and she has had thirteen children.
3. Truth uses the cup metaphor to show that women's rights and African Americans' rights have nothing to do with intellect. The cup is a metaphor for human rights and deservedness, and people are "mean" who will not allow others the rights that they deserve, especially when those recipients are given less to begin with.
4. Truth counters the argument that "women can't have as much rights as men, 'cause Christ wasn't a woman" (paragraph 4) by saying that Christ came from God and a woman, and that "Man had nothing to do with Him" (4).

Questions on Strategy
1. Truth's purpose is to point out how strong women are and that they don't need to be "helped into carriages, and lifted over ditches, and to have the best place everywhere" (paragraph 2). She sets herself up as a strong example and role model for her white audience. It's important for her to define a woman in the terms that she does because the men in the audience don't see women in the same way.

2. Truth's comments regarding "[t]hat man over there" (paragraph 2) and "that little man in black" (4) let her audience know that she isn't defined by what men say. She thinks for herself.

3. By repeating "And ain't I a woman?" four times in paragraph 2, Truth tries to convince the audience that she's for real. She believes what she says and she has the authority (being a woman) to make her argument. She also asks the audience to speculate on what the fuss is all about (paragraph 1), what "this thing in the head" (intellect) is (3), and why this has anything to do with women's or Negroes' rights. Her rhetorical questions let the audience stop and consider her questions and draw their own conclusions. She then asks, "Where did your Christ come from?" (4). Here she makes it very clear that Christ came from God and a woman, that "[m]an had nothing to do with Him" (4). Truth presents this answer as a fact. Because she does not expect the "little man in black" (4) to answer her question, she answers for him.

4. Truth's tone is forceful, defiant, passionate, and convincing. Answers will vary, but most students point to phrases and clauses like "Ain't I a woman?" (paragraph 2), "Look at me!" (2), "Look at my arm!" (2), "no man could head me" (2), "little man in black" (4), "Where did your Christ come from?" (4), and "the men better let them" (5).

Second Inaugural Address (p. 398)
ABRAHAM LINCOLN

Preparing to Read
Even amidst all the social media feeds and news sources, the State of the Union address still attracts attention and sets the tone for the national political climate. For students who are not from the United States, you may want to ask if the leader of their country offers similar addresses and, if so, what role these speeches play in that society.

Thinking Critically about the Text
When a piece is written to be read aloud, readers have to imagine where the pauses might have been and which words may have been emphasized or downplayed. In his speech, Lincoln uses shorter phrasing than a written piece might include; this allows for pauses and emphasis. His tone is galvanizing and unifying. He wants the war to end and the result to be a unified country. So even in his desire to conquer the Confederacy in the Civil War, he is careful to plant the seeds for reconstruction.

Questions on Subject
1. The context of Lincoln's speech is his second inaugural address, which took place during the Civil War. The main idea of Lincoln's first paragraph is that this short speech will not include an update on the war or a prediction regarding its outcome.

2. Lincoln's is against the "unrequited toil" (paragraph 4) of slavery and recognizes that the right to own slaves was the cause of the Civil War (3).

3. In paragraph 3, Lincoln points to slavery as a cause of the war. The meaning of the war, for Lincoln, is to ensure the United States remains one country. He puts the timing of the war's ends in God's hands, but calls on listeners to assist and help finish it.

4. Lincoln chastises the South for choosing war over national survival (3). Though he does not admonish outright the South for its use of slaves, he does warn the South against the

consequences of the offence by quoting from the Bible: "Woe unto the world because of offenses; for it must needs be that offenses come, but woe to that man by whom the offense cometh" (4).

Questions on Strategy

1. Lincoln appeals to *ethos* in his delivery of the speech; it is his second inaugural address, so he has the authority of being a newly re-elected president. He also appeals to the Christian God and quotes the Bible to demonstrate his knowledge. He appeals to *logos* when he uses the "one-eighth" statistic to show how many people were bonded in slavery and when he uses cause and effect analysis to identify slavery as the cause of the war (paragraph 4). The last paragraph uses *pathos* to galvanize support to finish the war; he uses words like *strive, wounds, care, widow, orphan, cherish,* and *peace* (5), all of which evoke emotion.

2. Lincoln uses parallelism in paragraphs 3 and 4: "all dreaded," "all sought," "all knew." He emphasizes the similarities of both the North and the South, though they were on different sides, using parallel sentence structures that draw comparisons in paragraph 4: "Neither party," "Neither anticipated," "Each looked," "Both read."

3. He uses deductive reasoning when he says that if both sides pray to the same God for opposite outcomes, logically, "the prayers of both could not be answered" (3); therefore neither side can believe God works solely for them.

4. Lincoln wants his audience to continue fighting to the end of the war. His last paragraph is all about action: "let us strive on to finish the work we are in, to bind up the nation's wounds…" (5). He wants citizens to do so in the spirit of long-term peace, not as a form of punishment to the South.

Participation Awards Do Disservice (p. 402)
NANCY ARMOUR

Preparing to Read
Consider taking an informal poll of your students and asking them if they remember participation awards as being particularly meaningful or meaningless. Compare your results to Armour's statement that most children do not find such awards to be of value.

Thinking Critically about the Text
Armour says that Harrison's behavior ought not distract from the strength of his message about participation trophies. This inclusion has the added benefit of reminding readers not to reject all of someone's comments because they have made mistakes in some areas of life. Student opinions will vary.

Questions on Subject
1. Participation trophies give young people a distorted view of life. Later, they may be shocked at "the harsh realities of life . . ." (paragraph 5). Also, not having to work for anything seems to be contributing to a larger sense of depression and even increased stress (5). Armour's thesis is in paragraph 3: "someone had the misguided notion that kids should live in la-la land where everything is perfect, there are no hardships or heartbreaks, and you get a shiny trophy or a pretty blue ribbon just for being you."

2. In paragraph 9, Armour explains the rationality of "everybody-gets-a-trophy" proponents. They say that these trophies encourage children always to try their best and persevere. She also says in paragraph 11 that the participation trophies are designed to protect children.

3. Students will have varying opinions. Some may say that Armour does not cite enough statistics or proof to convince all readers that they are really more depressed *because* of participation trophies. They might be stressed out because of the pressure of technology or because of unavailable parents, or because they are in a culture of emotionally unavailable people, and so on. In other words, she does not sufficiently prove that participation trophies are the *cause* of this depression or show us how widespread this depression and stress actually are.

4. Armour believes that adults give these trophies as an "affirmation that our kids are as wonderful as we think they are. It's also a way to fool ourselves into thinking that we are sheltering them, at least temporarily, from the cold, cruel world" (paragraph 14). Adults can think they are being good protectors of ideal children.

Questions on Strategy

1. Armour wants to startle readers and provide a bit of a wake-up call for them. This is a similar lesson she wants children to learn; she thinks that losing may teach children that life is not always fair. Students may note that not winning is not necessarily teaching children that life is not fair but that it actually *is* fair. The old adage "life isn't fair" applies to this argument only if children are losing because the judges are biased. This may occasionally be the case, but in most instances children lose because someone else is stronger. In any event, the opening phrase creates the emotional jolt in the reader, which is similar to the one she wants to create for children.

2. Armour means that children are told a lie when they receive these participation trophies. She says that they are taught incorrect lessons about the world and that the trophies decrease the value of their true wins. Awards mean more when earned. Children will be taught lessons of real value when they are allowed to win *and* lose.

3. Merryman's quote shows there might be a real long-term benefit to holding back on these participation trophies. Her comment suggests that we might better serve children's overall success if we delay their rewards. Let them be disappointed and learn how the game of life really works. If we can allow ourselves to do this, they might have real wins later on, wins that are far bigger than we could have imagined. The quote suggests that being a great parent might mean letting children struggle a bit.

4. Saying that children do not value the trophies suggests that we are not really giving them anything by giving them these false prizes. They do not have the meaning suggested by many people that "everybody gets a trophy." This claim also supports the idea that the trophies are for the parents, not the children.

Telling Americans to Vote, or Else (p. 406)
WILLIAM GALSTON

Preparing to Read

If students do not seem engaged in the topic, you might ask whether they have encountered any politicians whom they do not approve of or any they particularly like. Once they are engaged in having opinions about the results, it will be easier for students to see why voting matters.

Thinking Critically about the Text

Galston does not believe that democracy can function properly when a majority of the population does not vote. Students might consider Galston's argument *focused* and/or *logical*. It is a focused argument because it has only one objective: to convince readers to make voting mandatory. It is a logical argument because he substantiates his claims about the importance of voting.

You could add a class discussion that points to a significant and dangerous hole in Galston's argument. Many people *not* voting face barriers to doing so. For example, they may not have child care or transportation. They may be on drugs or have an undiagnosed mental illness because they do not have health care. Or they may have trouble with the language. The fine imposed on people who can barely pay their electricity or other basic bills could be devastating and demoralizing. What, if anything, does Galston offer about helping people overcome the barriers that make it hard to vote? He suggests that people do not vote because of laziness, but people in lower socioeconomic groups face real challenges. Enforcing this practice without exploring and addressing why people do not vote can further subjugate them financially and morally.

Questions on Subject

1. Galston means that U.S. citizens talk about and the U.S. government grants people lots of rights (freedom, clean water, education, representation), but the government does not ask for much action in return.

2. Argument one: "[A] democracy cannot be strong if its citizenship is weak" (paragraph 5). Argument two: Democracy is not democratic if large groups of people are underrepresented. Viewpoints will be missing (6). Argument three: Low voter turnout polarizes the country. Elections end up being dominated by "hard-core partisans" (9).

3. In paragraph 8, Galston acknowledges that enforcing voting would "impose greater burdens on those with fewer resources." He says that this will make it *more* likely that these people will vote. They have more to lose by paying the fine. In paragraph 13, he acknowledges there is no guarantee that the mandatory voting policy in Australia would work in the United States. He also acknowledges that the idea of mandatory voting contradicts the freedoms stated in the U.S. Constitution. He suggests that a handful of states with varying civil traditions try mandatory voting to see how well it works. He encourages a variety of people to monitor and consider the consequences. Students will offer additional rebuttals to the counterarguments Galston advances.

4. Those with fewer resources often do not vote. As a result, their needs are less well articulated. Participation in voting would help them feel a "sense of participation in national politics" (paragraph 7).

Questions on Strategy

1. The title uses a more shocking tone than the article itself. The title grabs readers' attention with drama, but the article aims to win them over with logical argument. The title helps Galston attract a wide audience; the logical argument style within the article helps him retain that audience.

2. The jury duty comparison at the start of the article helps diffuse dissent immediately. All readers can recognize the argument that 'Hey, you're right, we do have to go to jury duty.

How is this different?' By drawing a comparison to a requirement that already exists, Galston can show that his idea is not anti-American but rather an extension of an existing tradition.

3. The Australian comparison is strong because the country has many similarities to the United States and because it had great success with mandatory voting laws. Students may note that Australia may not have the same level of diversity as the United States (economically or ethnically) and this might have a big impact on the program's success anywhere else.

4. The clear argumentation style helps Galston maintain close contact with readers. They cannot drift off or get lost. To make the structure even more clear, he could have added headings with the name of each argument.

The Organic Fable (p. 411)
ROGER COHEN

Preparing to Read
Do most students eat on campus or off? Students on meal plans have very different concerns than those who prepare their own food, but all should be able to offer opinions about what matters to them and why.

Thinking Critically about the Text
Students will say whether they are convinced by Cohen's argument. Many have likely read materials in support of organics, and Cohen's singular essay might not be enough to change their opinions. If he could prove that there really was no difference for *all* foods, then maybe people would stop buying them. There's a list called the "dirty dozen" that talks about the twelve foods where it matters most to buy organics. Cohen does not talk about these twelve foods. Perhaps in these foods it really does make a difference. He says that the long-term impact could be that we will not be able to feed the planet if we use only organic farming processes. Cohen does not address the argument that part of the reason we cannot feed the planet is actually the large consumption of beef. You may want to ask students to research how much land and water cattle require and the pressure this places on the planet. Population increase is another important factor. Then, with the whole class, discuss whether the consumption of bovine products (especially in the United States and China) has a greater or smaller impact than organic farming on our future ability to feed the planet.

Questions on Subject
1. Cohen is making a logical argument. We know because he cites sources to back his claims. He wants to persuade readers but through logic rather than through manipulative language.

2. Cohen means that "organic" is more a designation used to sell products at a higher price than to provide meaningful value and nutrition. He cites the Stanford University study as an example; this study found that organic fruits and vegetables provided no additional benefits.

3. Cohen says that the organic movement will not support genetically modified foods because "that would go against the ideology and romance of a movement which says: We

are for nature, everyone else is against nature" (paragraph 12). He believes that, in order to feed a growing planet and reduce our dependency on pesticides, we will need to rely on genetic modification.

4. Cohen means that he values people above the planet. For him there is an either/or choice to be made. Likely, one does not have to choose, but he makes this shocking statement to push back on the cultural proclivity toward organics. He is trying to show people that buying organics might not necessarily be more loving than advocating for processes that will feed more people. This statement could possibly offend readers who think of themselves as caring *because* they buy organics.

Questions on Strategy

1. Cohen's thesis is the entire second paragraph. Using a long sentence as a full paragraph, he can both challenge the obsession with organics as a concept and demonstrate what he believes is the potential impact of moving to a solely organic way of farming on the growing population on earth.

2. In paragraph 3, Cohen cites the Organic Trade Association to highlight the amount of money spent on organic foods. He uses this statistic to support his point that many people are becoming increasingly obsessed with organics. In paragraph 5, he cites the Stanford University study to support his claim that organics are not actually better. In paragraph 9, he cites the requirements of the Department of Agriculture for foods labeled organic to support his point that organic labeling at least has some restrictions—unlike terms such as *natural*.

3. By saying three positive details about organics, Cohen shows that he is educated on the subject and tries to bring back readers he may have offended with his earlier claims and who may be shocked by the Stanford University study. These positive details could help proponents to feel less betrayed by the results of the study.

4. Cohen focuses more on the fact that organics are not as healthy—likely because he wants to pull people away from buying the products. Most people buy organics for their own health, not the planet's health. If he wants to change their minds, he must speak to their primary concerns. This was an important strategic decision. He connects the ideas by suggesting that, if you think you are saving the world by eating organic, think again. He makes the claim that nonorganic might actually be the more humanitarian choice.

Campus Racism 101 (p. 415)
NIKKI GIOVANNI

Preparing to Read

You may want students to consider whether race relations on their campus are typical. Does it matter whether the campus is in an urban or a rural environment, on the East or West Coast, in the North or South, or religious or secular? Encourage students to cite specific examples in support of their views.

Students may notice that Giovanni teaches at Virginia Tech University. Although this article was published before the April 2007 shooting incident at Virginia Tech, you may want students to consider how a massacre like that equalizes all races. The killer did not care about the race of his victims; his pathological behavior was the result of numerous factors, including a general hatred toward people and an untreated mental illness. How did his race play into people's conception of the shootings?

Thinking Critically about the Text

Students may have fiscal responsibilities to pay for college or food. Students want college to be a social environment as well: They may participate in theater, the newspaper, or sports, all of which can take substantial amounts of time and energy. In addition, students have friends, go to parties, and fall in and out of love. All of this goes on while they are living together in dorms or off-campus housing. Students have many new experiences in a new environment that demand their attention. Each student will have different priorities, and his or her academic interest and capabilities will have a great effect on classroom successes. Students may argue that much of their education comes from their out-of-class activities. Their education goals may include participating in all of the wonderful activities college has to offer.

Questions on Subject

1. Giovanni's audience is predominantly black college students. The first paragraph does not identify the race of the young people in the postcards. By the third paragraph, where Giovanni writes, "You're going to interact," we know for sure that her intended readers are black students.

2. Giovanni dismisses the notion that it is hard to be a black student in a predominantly white college in paragraph 3. She then goes on to illustrate that many experiences are far worse than being in a white college: such as being in jail, not being educated, or joining the military because of limited opportunities. In addition, she dismisses the notion by pointing out that black students will have to interact with a white world anyway. She wants to instill the idea that being in college is an opportunity.

3. Giovanni wants black students to see themselves as typical students because the keys to success are the same for everyone. They should not alienate themselves from the white world; there is only one world, and they can handle it.

4. Giovanni uses the questions and answers starting in paragraph 13 to show black students how to respond to ignorant and "stupid questions" from white students. She encourages her readers to choose self-control and empowerment over victimization.

Questions on Strategy

1. Giovanni argues for black students to take control of their own futures and to find ways to achieve academic success. Her thesis is stated in paragraph 4: "There are discomforts attached to attending predominantly white colleges, though no more so than living in a racist world."

2. At the start of her essay, Giovanni wants to give readers a sampling of the attitudes young people have about education. The short sentences reflect the quick or rash decisions that some students make about their education.

3. Her personal narrative offers an example of how she handled living in a white world, which in turn gives her authority to write about the subject. Because Giovanni has succeeded in a white world, she has the authority to advise others.

4. These Q&A examples, in line with her title, "Campus Racism 101," provide a manual for dealing with racism. The article gives black students both keys to success and concrete ways to deal with the kinds of racism she knows they will face.

On the Subject of Trigger Warnings (p. 422)
SIOBHAN CROWLEY

Preparing to Read
You might ask students if they have had courses where their instructors use trigger warnings. Or, if you use them, you could discuss why. There are certain courses that lend themselves more to these possibly triggering events: courses on conflict resolution, genocide studies, wars, gender and violence, and so on. Instructors in these and related courses could say at the beginning that material might be intense at times and create ways of talking about that triggering material together in class.

Thinking Critically about the Text
The author's teaching experience is relevant in that she has spent a great deal of time in the classroom. However, students might also argue that she has some bias because she may not want to alter her curriculum to incorporate trigger warnings. Ask students to find textual support for their position.

Questions on Subject
1. Crowley argues that trigger warnings might end up robbing students of the opportunity to face their fears through the lens of critical analysis. Students will say whether or not they agree.
2. Crowley agrees with the college president that students should not be coddled by being protected from every troubling detail. But her reason is more precise; she thinks potentially triggering materials could be left out of courses where they are not essential, rather than major courses which go in to greater details.
3. The first concern is that students will not be professionally qualified (paragraph 3). The second is that student will be unprepared to face triggering content after graduation (5).
4. Students may have a variety of interpretations, but it is likely that Crowley means that facing difficult issues can give someone a firmer foundation for encountering potential future life challenges.

Questions on Strategy
1. Crowley makes her argument on the basis of her authority as both an instructor and as a student. Students will share whether they find her position convincing.
2. In paragraph 4, Crowley notes that it would not hurt someone majoring outside of the humanities to miss out on the content of *Othello*. This is a concession to her argument in paragraph 3 that a student or instructor would have "glaring blind spots" if they skipped over certain triggering topics each time they appeared in the canon.
3. Crowley primarily uses a deductive approach in that she states her thesis first, then proves it through a series of claims supported by evidence.
4. Student opinions on the effectiveness of the conclusion will vary. The conclusion challenges students to face difficult material, rather than run from it.

I Invested Early in Google and Facebook. Now They Terrify Me. (p. 426)
ROGER MCNAMEE

Preparing to Read
For students who have grown up with these technologies, alternatives to constant use might not seem obvious. Because peers likely use them constantly, students may fear being left behind socially. Is an individual expected to choose isolation? To get students thinking about whether the companies have any responsibility to mitigate some of the addicting effects of the technology, ask them to consider or investigate how algorithms and data collection practices work among big players like Facebook, Google, and Twitter.

Thinking Critically about the Text
Some students might think McNamee's participation makes him part of the problem or hypocritical. He is not necessarily using any of his financial gains in these companies to help mitigate the issue. If he suggests the companies bear some responsibility, does not he — as an early investor — also bear some? You may want to ask students how else he might contribute.

Questions on Subject
1. "Brain hacking" (7) is a social media platform's ability to influence the emotional state of the user simply by sending them different content.
2. People are willing to sacrifice their health and well-being to use these technologies constantly.
3. McNamee blames the "advertising business models that drive companies to maximize attention at all costs, leading to ever more aggressive brain hacking" (8). In other words, the fault is with these companies' reliance on advertising income, which makes data mining imperative.
4. The financial incentive for these companies to sell advertising as effectively as possible is enormous; therefore, McNamee believes change would come only if consumers force changes at Facebook and Google. He is not specific about what those changes should be.

Questions on Strategy
1. *Ethos* is the primary rhetorical appeal in the first paragraph. McNamee states his credentials as an investor and as someone who has benefitted from these companies financially and who, therefore, has a large stake in their success. This authority makes his claim that he is "terrified" more shocking (*pathos*).
2. By highlighting the causes (advertising models which promote addiction) and the effects (sleep deprivation, addiction, and emotional swings curated by platforms), McNamee identifies a problem's cause and helps readers become aware of the effects of these technologies on their lives. He raises readers' awareness and then inspires them to take action to both curtail these behaviors in themselves and the policies within these corporate giants.
3. McNamee uses the analogy of Google and Facebook being like nicotine, heroin, gambling, and alcohol, which are all highly addictive. Students will comment regarding whether they find this analogy effective — some may consider it an extreme comparison. Does technology ruin lives the way heroin can? Is getting off technology really harder than giving up smoking?

4. McNamee's audience is the average technology user. His readers likely all have smart phones and spend a significant amount of their time looking at computer screens each day. Yet, they are not technology professionals — we know this because he does not use jargon or refer to obscure Web sites. The piece is not for an academic audience because he references studies without giving the full details. This audience is likely addicted in ways they cannot recognize and unaware about how these internet monopolies manipulate them and use their data. He shapes his writing to make average technology users aware of their own behaviors and how they are being influenced.

ARGUMENT CLUSTER
Race and Privilege: How Do We Address a System of Bias?

I, Racist (p. 432)
JOHN METTA

Thinking Critically about the Text
Student responses will vary. You may want to ask them if there were certain experiences that they themselves faced or certain people or environments that helped them better understand the race issues around them.

Examining the Issue
1. The topic is race. Metta does not want to discuss it because he thinks people around him, even those who love him, will say he is overreacting or being too sensitive. He also says that people will point out how much better things are today than they were forty years ago. He keeps his mouth shut because it is part of an unspoken agreement in the culture that nice liberal friends ought to be kept comfortable.

2. Student answers will vary. It might be beneficial to discuss the following question in class: If someone is a member of a minority group, does that mean that person cannot be racist? There may be the assumption that only white privileged people can be racist.

3. Students' answers will vary. Metta's claim that the discourse works to protect white feelings does ring true. You may want to ask whether they think the Black Lives Matter campaign works to protect white feelings.

4. "Tone policed" refers to the ways in which people angry about racism are shushed back into silence. Those operating in the institutions that perpetuate racism often try to control the angry expressions of those pointing out instances of racism.

5. Student answers will vary based on experience.

6. Metta quotes his sister, who defines how people in the North and South deal with race: "down here, at least people are honest about being racist" (paragraph 6). Throughout the essay, he is alluding to and pointing to what could be considered "racist" — that even white, liberal people can be racists. He also indirectly defines what racism is, such as moving out of a black neighborhood for "better schools" (6). He says that racism is not slavery and avoids using certain racial slurs or the term *segregated public spaces*. He says

that racism is really about cops attacking and killing an innocent man, the death of a twelve-year-old from playing with a toy gun, or making movies with only white people. He also defines a racist system as one that allows upward mobility only for some.

7. Metta means that prosperity and opportunity are correlated with being white not black. Moving away from black people for a "better life" is a way of further separating people on racial lines and perpetuating the systemic oppression of black people.

8. Metta believes racism exists to keep white people in power.

Racial Microaggressions in Everyday Life: Is Subtle Bias Harmless? (p. 439)
DERALD WING SUE

Thinking Critically about the Text
Students may think awareness is enough to interrupt the pattern of these microaggressions. Others may advocate for more robust changes such as policy changes or consequences for such aggressions. You may want to ask how interrupting microaggressions could violate free speech rights. When is bias allowed? When is it not?

Examining the Issue
1. In paragraph 6, Sue says that microaggressions are comments that, "on the surface, appear like a compliment or seem quite innocent and harmless, but nevertheless, they contain what we call demeaning meta-communications or hidden messages." He finds these messages concerning because those receiving such communications can experience "an erosion of their mental health, job performance, classroom learning, the quality of social experience and ultimately their standard of living" (paragraph 10).

2. Reiterating that the aggressions are unconscious has at least two purposes. First, it tells the reader that Sue is not blaming people for being purposefully hurtful. This keeps readers from being defensive. Labeling the behavior unconscious also encourages readers not to absolve themselves just because they may not be consciously aware of their actions. He encourages everyone to look a little deeper. This strengthens Sue's argument because it supports his claim that there is a subcategory of aggression that is not overt. Students may say that it weakens his argument because they believe aggression requires consciousness.

3. Sue introduces the term *microassaults*, which are uttered consciously and intentionally either with words or with the use of symbols. *Microinsults* are verbal and nonverbal but more subtly convey a diminishing attitude toward another culture or heritage. Microinsults can be unconscious. Symbols, like flags, would be less likely to be part of this category, but you can discuss with the class the Confederate flag debate and whether the use of the Confederate flag would be considered a microassault or microinsult. The third category is *microinvalidations*. This category dismisses the thoughts or feelings of another race. It creates an exclusionary atmosphere. The major differences have to do with the consciousness level of the speaker and the subtlety of the message.

4. In paragraph 12, Sue says that "our research suggests that microinsults and microinvalidations are potentially more harmful because of their invisibility, which puts people of color in a psychological bind: although people of color might be insulted, they are often

uncertain why, and perpetrators are unaware that anything has happened and are not aware they have been offensive." People of color are punished for speaking up or psychologically hurt by not speaking up, Sue claims.

5. The personal story tells the reader that Sue is a person of color. The narration quickly draws the reader into the dynamic that the article will examine. Most readers can easily visualize the situation. The narration acts to hook readers and even cause them to consider if they have ever been victims or perpetrators of a similar act.

6. Sue includes the history of the term *microaggression* to introduce the term in context before defining it.

7. Sue calls them "brief" and "everyday" to highlight the subtle nature of such dynamics. They are not big demonstrations of racism. This encourages readers to be on the lookout for the ways these microaggressions are evident around them. The reference to the terms also suggests how such insults build up over time, adding a little more pain every day. Over time this can contribute to the erosion of a person's self-esteem.

No, I Won't Be Writing about Black-on-Black Crime (p. 445)
SHAUN KING

Thinking Critically about the Text
By including the actual message, readers can see not only the critiques King receives, but the hateful manner in which the critiques are delivered. This shows readers that King continues to write despite many critics and much pushback. Student opinions will vary about whether King is ignoring one social problem in favor of another. Some may say focusing on one issue actually amplifies his voice; even the criticism gives him notoriety.

Examining the Issue
1. King claims that his life mission "is to call out injustice" (paragraph 5). The injustice he focuses on in this selection is black people being held fully accountable for any crimes they commit while white criminals, such as cops who kill black people, often escape punishment.

2. King describes the cases involving the white cops not held accountable for their crimes involving the deaths of Eric Garner, John Crawford, Tamir Rice, Sandra Bland, and others.

3. King asks, "Right now, without Googling it, can you name even one white officer in jail for killing somebody on the job?" (paragraph 6). The question challenges readers to disprove his point; the fact that answering his question is difficult proves his point.

4. King sets up his use of parallelism when he uses the phrases, "I don't write about…" and "I write about." He uses this structure to justify focusing on cops who escape accountability. The rhythmic style of the phrasing helps emphasize his point.

5. King points to prisons overflowing with African Americans who have been convicted without fair trial and who serve sentences more extreme than their crimes may have deserved.

6. King means that many people see African Americans as perpetrators or potential perpetrators, whereas white people are often given the benefit of the doubt. Students will share opinions.

7. King's critics cited in the article use name-calling (*ad hominem* attack), either/or thinking (either he writes about all crime or he does not care about justice), and hasty generalizations (he does not write about a particular incident, so he does not care about justice).

8. King appeals to *ethos* in the beginning of his essay when he relays how many messages he gets from people trolling him. To have so many messages implies that he is a well-known writer on these issues.

ARGUMENT CLUSTER
The Changing Nature of Work: What Is the Value of a Career – Now and in the Future?

The Gingham Apron (p. 454)
CAITLIN MCCORMICK

Thinking Critically about the Text
When writing a college admissions essay, applicants ideally represent their worldview as well as their other interests and accomplishments. McCormick may not have emphasized, for example, all the NGO work she had done in a non-admissions essay. Admissions officers likely enjoyed this essay because it showed both a very astute and adult understanding and appreciation of her upbringing while also distinguishing her as a self-directed individual who could present herself articulately. The *New York Times* likely appreciated her textured representation of the service industry, showing an understanding of class issues and privilege. Have students tell what questions they were asked for their college admissions essays, if they had them, or what their strategies were when writing.

Examining the Issue
1. Growing up, McCormick hated the hospitality business because she felt "conditioned in excessive politeness" (paragraph 3). She also found her own life interrupted by the business, almost missing her own birthday party (5), and she disliked seeing how guests treated her parents and the housekeeping staff.

2. McCormick's experiences taught her that people often take service people for granted, taking out their personal aggressions and expecting a great deal without offering much kindness or financial remuneration in return.

3. By "raw grit," McCormick means helping people in a way that requires handling the multiple moods and various needs/requests of people in a direct way. This kind of service requires being emotionally and physically available to serve people no matter their state or their request. This takes endurance and determination.

4. By "microaggression," McCormick means that people could express their feelings about the service received through the amount of their tip, if they tipped at all. Housekeeping, for example, often received fewer tips. She sees this as dismissing their contribution. She interprets people's expression of dissatisfaction through withholding or reducing tips as a kind of aggression.

5. McCormick uses logical reasoning when critiquing the behavior of some guests. For example, if someone has some unusual request — such as having one's room cleaned two times a day — a tip is a logical expectation. By outlining the abuse, she has seen her parents and their staff suffer, and she attempts to persuade readers to treat service people kindly and with respect. By taking the time to build a logical case, she can persuade readers without preaching. This offers a more subtle form of persuasion.

6. McCormick uses narration in the opening of the essay to talk about her early life at the bed and breakfast. She used cause and effect to show, for example, how a guest's uncommunicativeness (cause) resulted in McCormick almost missing her own birthday party (effect). She shows the irrationality of people's behavior, for example, by describing that the cause of one client yelling at her parents was a delayed taxi, which was not their fault. She uses illustration when she describes the various demanding behaviors of clients and the various efforts her parents made to meet client needs.

7. Student opinions will vary. McCormick shows how much can be learned by careful observation in any context, especially a work context. Many students may have been taught that learning only occurs in books and in a classroom.

8. Student answers will vary regarding the connection between physical work and the mind. You may want to refer them to Sara Gilbert's article in Chapter 9, "The Different Ways of Being Smart."

The Quitting Economy (p. 457)
ILANA GERSHON

Thinking Critically about the Text
Students will write whether they feel the article has shifted their ideas about how economic models affect the workplace. Many students, having grown up in a world in which people change jobs frequently, may not identify with the sense of change that Gershon writes about. Students might be excited by the idea that whatever job they take after college will not be their only job. This sense of options and freedom might appeal to, rather than scare, them. Others might find the notion of constant change overwhelming and unappealing.

Examining the Issue
1. Gershon's key metaphor equates each person with a business. The rest of the essay discusses the effect of living in a world where everyone sees themselves in this way. She considers how this view affects our relationships, sense of community, and work culture.

2. Gershon's thesis is that neoliberalism has created a quitting economy, where it is desirable for employees to move from job to job and company to company rather than remaining loyal and climbing the ladder.

3. Hayek's core conviction was that "markets provided the best means to order the world" (2). He opposed having the government provide services to citizens because he believed "private interests most efficiently handle these services" (3).

4. Gershon means that taking a neoliberal stance on the economy trickles down into all levels of society. It affects our relationships (how we mentor) and how we think about our careers and our attitudes about the institutions within which we work.

5. The American Airlines example (which showed the company being forced to pay shareholders rather than employees) supports her claim that market demands end up serving

shareholders, rather than companies and their employees. Market forces are not an effective way to care for people's needs or the organizations for which they work.

6. A good job used to be defined by being in a good location, with a good salary, with good benefits and a good office culture; now, however, a good job is defined by how mobile it makes an individual employee. Are the skills transferable? Will the company's name be respected by others so that one will be an appealing candidate elsewhere? This new model has also made it easier for young people to start their own businesses — many have been very successful, and it allows workers freedom to change careers.

7. Passion has replaced company loyalty. Companies seek passionate people willing to work long hours on projects without either party having to commit long-term.

8. The effect of a neoliberal approach to life, Gershon claims, is that we have developed a quitting economy. She shows how the effect of shareholder pressure at American Airlines took money from worthy employees. She shows how the desire for work mobility has diminished company loyalty.

Don't Assume Robots Will Be Our Future Coworkers (p. 464)
NOAH SMITH

Thinking Critically about the Text
Students will share any personal concerns about the economy and about robots replacing humans. Some might say it depends on the job: Plumbers will likely not be replaced, nor will teachers, but taxi drivers and waiters might be. Students' level of concern might relate to their own personal career aspirations. You might want to ask them how this might affect various groups within our society rather than just considering how robots may affect their own career choices and opportunities. What about cashiers and others, for example, who can more easily be replaced by robots?

Examining the Issue
1. "Skill-biased technological change" (paragraph 1) means that "people who are technically savvy, mentally flexible and educated will reap greater and greater rewards while everyone else sees their wages decline" (1).

2. He says the robot based revolution has not occurred yet because if it had, we would see far more productivity and higher unemployment (2).

3. Luddites were originally British textile workers in the nineteenth century known for protesting technologies which they feared would soon replace them. Because they found themselves actually benefitting from the changes, the term has become one of derision, referring to those who fear technology but will ultimately benefit from technological advancement.

4. Economists assume that the relationship between technology and humans is fixed; technology will complement humanity, not replace it (5).

5. Smith uses the Industrial Revolution as an example when new technologies "resulted in an abrupt acceleration of wealth generation" (9). Until the Industrial Revolution, advances (steel, plumbing, etc.) had done little to change per capita wealth. It defied all prior lessons of history. Students will say whether they find this example effective.

6. The chart illustrates the abrupt acceleration of wealth after about 1800, when the Industrial Revolution was taking place. Although the United States and Western Europe experienced the changes earliest, other nations eventually followed, all breaking previous growth records. The chart helps readers *see* the size of the change, rather than just imagining it. This underscores his point. If such a shift has happened before, it could happen again.

7. The "nature of technology is that it changes the world in ways that are totally new and unanticipated" (12).

ADDITIONAL WRITING SUGGESTIONS FOR ARGUMENTATION

1. Think of a product that you like and want to use even though it has an annoying feature. Write a letter of complaint, in which you attempt to persuade the manufacturer to improve the product. Your letter should include the following points:
   - a statement concerning the nature of the problem
   - evidence supporting or explaining your complaint
   - suggestions for improving the product

2. Select one of the position statements that follow and write an argumentative essay in which you defend that statement.
   - Living in a dormitory is (or is not) as desirable as living off campus.
   - America should (or should not) be a refuge for the oppressed.
   - Interest in religion is (or is not) increasing in the United States.
   - We have (or have not) brought pollution under control in the United States.
   - The need to develop alternative energy sources is (or is not) serious.
   - Fraternities and sororities do (or do not) build character.
   - Fair play is (or is not) a thing of the past.
   - Human life is (or is not) valued in a technological society.
   - The consumer does (or does not) need to be protected.
   - America should (or should not) feel a commitment to the starving peoples of the world.
   - Money is (or is not) the path to happiness.
   - Animals do (or do not) have rights.

3. Think of something on your campus or in your community that you would like to see changed. Write a persuasive argument that explains what is wrong and how you think it ought to be changed. Make sure you incorporate other writing strategies into your essay — for example, description, narration, or illustration — to increase the effectiveness of your persuasive argument.

4. Read some articles in the editorial section of today's paper (in print or online), and pick one with which you agree or disagree. Write a letter to the editor that presents your point of view. Use a logical argument to support or refute the editorial's assertions. Depending on the editorial, you might choose to use different rhetorical strategies to reach your audience. You might use cause and effect, for example, to show the correct (or incorrect) connections made by the editorial.

5. **Writing with Sources.** Working with a partner, choose a controversial topic like the legalization of medical marijuana. Each partner should argue one side of the issue. Decide who is going to write on which side of the issue and keep in mind that there are often more than two sides to an issue. Then each of you should write an essay, trying to convince your partner that your position is the most logical and correct.

   You'll both need to do research online or in the library to find support for your position. For models of and advice on integrating sources in your essay, see Chapters 14 and 15.

6. **Writing in the Workplace.** You're a summer intern at a midsized news Web site. A freelance journalist sends you the final draft of his commissioned article so that you can correct any grammar mistakes before it's read by your boss. As you read it, you realize that a few sentences stand out for their distinct, different style. You run those sentences through a search engine and, sure enough, the freelancer plagiarized them from an independent, personally run blog. Write a thorough, professional e-mail to your boss, explaining the situation and why the plagiarism is a concern. Can you run the piece? How would doing so affect the credibility and reputation of the journalist? To what extent must freelancers produce original content? How might the freelancer defend his actions? Would that defense matter? Since you're on a deadline, propose a solution to your boss. What next steps can your organization take to accurately and ethically report on the story?

CHAPTER 13   Combining Strategies

On Dumpster Diving (p. 481)
LARS EIGHNER

Preparing to Read
In this age of conservation and recycling, many students may have thought very hard about how they use things and how they choose to discard them. This question asks them to analyze not only what they do with waste but how and why they do it. The class may also want to discuss how the thought of ultimately disposing of goods influences their decisions when they are buying them, which will lead into the "Thinking Critically about the Text" question.

Thinking Critically about the Text
Eighner's essay underscores how wasteful we are and emphasizes that everything we buy ultimately ends up somewhere. Yet, as a society, we are often urged to buy more and acquire more. In the "Preparing to Read" prompt, students were asked to discuss personal experience. Here they must ponder the question in the context of Eighner's essay and the potential effect personal beliefs may have on society and the environment as a whole.

Questions on Subject

1. There is the stage of shame and self-loathing; the stage of discovery, where the scavenger discovers the wealth to be found in Dumpsters; and the stage of professionalism, when the diver is willing and able to eat from Dumpsters. Eighner provides vivid examples of the goods to be found in the Dumpsters that move scavengers through their period of shame. Items such as a working calculator and still-frozen ice cream indicate the thoughtlessness with which people throw things away (paragraph 6). The discussion of food to be found and consumed in Dumpsters is more prosaic, but Eighner again provides specific examples.

2. Eating from Dumpsters requires scavengers to use their senses and common sense to evaluate the food, to know Dumpsters in an area and check them regularly, and to always question why something may have been discarded (paragraph 9). Canned food, dry food, raw fruits and vegetables, peanut butter, and yogurt are good things to eat from Dumpsters (10 and 11). Dysentery is a hazard that Eighner mentions, but it can be inferred that there must be others (12).

3. Eighner has learned to take what he can use and let the rest go (paragraph 13) and that material being is transient (14). He has learned not to grab for objects just for the sake of having them, and he has found a peace that he believes eludes the "rat-race millions," confounded as they are by their consumer society (16).

4. Because a novice diver is often tempted to take whatever he or she can carry, the ability to find something of true value is indeed an art. One must know where to find it and how to identify a worthy find. Eighner shows the reader, one item at a time, how much thought goes into selecting each find.

Questions on Strategy

1. Eighner discusses the concrete aspects of Dumpster diving to teach readers what it is like—what can be found in Dumpsters, how scavenging affects its practitioners, what makes it a potential hazard, and so on. It is only from this base of knowledge that he can then discuss the abstract, particularly the transience of material objects. For those who have never found things such as new running shoes or working calculators in Dumpsters, a discussion of transience may have little meaning. Eighner's concrete experiences give his abstract lessons credence.

2. Eighner's discussion of just how much good material can be found in Dumpsters does make scavenging sound almost attractive, but most readers will still be repelled by the idea of it—particularly when it comes to eating. By mentioning the grim reality of how regularly one struggles with disease when eating out of Dumpsters, Eighner maintains credibility in the eyes of the average reader and acknowledges the opinion most readers will have that "Dumpster diving has serious drawbacks as a way of life" (paragraph 12). The mention is brief, though, because the drawbacks to scavenging do not contribute to Eighner's purpose for writing the essay, which is to communicate what he has learned from all the good stuff he has found in Dumpsters.

3. Students should be able to provide a brief process analysis. Eighner's choice of title reflects his desire to communicate what he has learned from the process of Dumpster diving, not to present how to do it.

4. Students should identify many of the examples previously discussed. They will probably give various answers to the second part of the question, but students should touch on one of the following three characteristics: The examples are surprising, in terms of what can be found in Dumpsters; they are presented with candor and frankness, especially when

Eighner discusses food; and they are presented quickly but effectively, so that it is very easy to picture the objects and to understand their implications.

The Struggle (p. 486)
ISSA RAE

Preparing to Read
Students who have culturally dominant identities may not be as aware of their identities as students in the minority. Identities become prominent for people often when they feel these identities as increasing their vulnerability or when these identities are under attack. For example, a black student in school with mostly white students will likely be more aware of his or her blackness than the white students. When an identity makes someone feel different or feel more vulnerable, she is often more aware of it. Being gay, a teenage mom, handicapped, etc. all can become prominent identities when they are not the norm. Discuss these issues with students and ask them to contribute personal experiences. You may also decide to focus on other subcultures that students may not regularly think of, such as band members, skateboarders, or fandom.

Thinking Critically about the Text
While Rae begins the essay referring to talking about blackness as "tiring," in paragraphs 6 and 7 she talks about how she slips between heightened awareness and anger and apathy. By the end of the article, she considers it more of a choice whether or not to think about it or chooses to think about it in empowering ways.

Questions on Subject
1. By "militant," Rae means being someone who is consistently, entirely, and uncompromising dedicated to a cause. To "demilitarize" herself means no longer requiring herself to talk about blackness all the time. She does not need to wear the identity like a military uniform, constantly and unequivocally serving its cause.
2. In paragraph 9, Rae describes moving to Los Angeles to a middle school where her blackness was constantly questioned, as opposed to her experience in Potomac, Maryland, where she and her peers never put much thought to their races.
3. Judgement 1: That Rae was not really black because she lacked certain knowledge or characteristics. Judgement 2: That Rae's behavior was uncharacteristic of a black person, meaning she broke various stereotypes.
4. At the end of the essay, rather than dividing the world into black and not-black, she challenges the definition that there is one blackness. Black people have just as much variety as white people, even though mass media promotes limited definitions. Rae decides. to only focus on the benefits of being black and being a black woman, eschewing the notions of racism and marginalization to see herself as free and empowered.

Questions on Strategy
1. Her attitude is positive, but not naïve. Rae talks about her struggle (as the title suggests) with a tone of frustration but emerges passionate, adamant, and proud of herself.

2. Rae primarily uses illustration with two major examples of times when she was made to feel like she wasn't "black" enough. Supporting strategies are description, narration, and process analysis in the journey she takes to self-discovery.

3. Rae challenges the idea that blackness means one thing and that existing racism and marginalization need to limit people. She also wants people to know they do not have to have their lives dominated by cultural attitudes about their identity.

4. Rae uses the examples of Al Sharpton, Cornel West, Jesse Jackson, and Tavis Smiley to illustrate how some people make blackness the subject of their whole lives. She also uses examples when she describes the two most common situations she found herself in while living in Los Angeles. She shares examples of exactly what people said to her and the intention of those comments. This illustrates the preconceived notions of blackness people tried to impose on her.

The Sad, Beautiful Fact That We're All Going to Miss Almost Everything (p. 491)
LINDA HOLMES

Preparing to Read
Students will experience different levels of pressure to keep up with various media. The fear of missing out has become such a phenomena there is now even a common acronym for it: FOMO. Usually, people feel pressure to keep up if their social and/or professional status could be affected by not being perceived as up-to-date. Ask students to explore why they feel anxiety about missing some type of entertainment but not others. Are there social ramifications?

Thinking Critically about the Text
The audience for this essay is likely those who attempt to keep up. Those who do not care about keeping up will not be interested in this article; they have already surrendered to apathy. Holmes wants to advise and support those still striving and interested in engaging in the world but find themselves overwhelmed with the abundance of resources and the impossibility of consuming them all.

Questions on Subject
1. There is so much more being produced to replace older entertainment. Beyond more books, mediums like Netflix, Amazon, and iTunes also compete for attention, and the Internet makes entertainment from around the globe more available.

2. We can either *surrender,* or we can *cull*, meaning we can either stop trying to keep up or just be more discerning about what we consume. But we could also work in teams and present our chosen entertainment to others. Students may come up with additional responses.

3. Because being "well-read" has become nearly impossible, it can no longer be the destination for which one strives. Holmes argues that it is unachievable. Because of this, she says, we must *cull*.

4. Holmes says the fact that we will miss out on so much means humanity produces much worth consuming. This speaks well of humanity's productivity and talent, that more good work is produced than we can consume. Students will say whether they agree.

Questions on Strategy

1. Holmes uses a hypothetical scenario as her process analysis in paragraphs 2 and 3. This scenario proves her point that consuming even a fraction of the world's books is impossible. This enables her to set up her main argument that we must *cull*.

2. Holmes redefines what it means to be "well-read." The old definition might have been moderately achievable, but the notion must be redefined in the modern era to mean "making a genuine effort to explore thoughtfully" (paragraph 21). This redefinition is part of the essay's purpose; we must cull in order to be well-read. She also defines culling versus surrender, as a means of advocating for culling.

3. Holmes compares and contrasts surrendering versus culling. Culling takes mastery and surrender means giving up (19).

4. The amount of media (books, music, film, etc.) is like an ocean. All we have is a small cup representing our time on the planet. We can pretend all the materials are not there, or we can accept we just have one small cup and make the best use of it we can. Students will say whether they find this conclusion effective. Her conclusion puts the challenge back in the hands of the reader.

ADDITIONAL WRITING SUGGESTIONS FOR COMBINING STRATEGIES

1. Select a piece you have written for this class in which you used one primary writing strategy and rewrite it using another strategy. For example, choose a description you wrote and redraft it as a process analysis. Remember that the choice of a writing strategy influences the writer's "voice"; a descriptive piece might be lyrical, while a process analysis might be straightforward. How does your voice change along with the strategy? Does your assumed audience change as well?

2. **Writing Across the Disciplines.** Select an essay you have written this semester, either for this class or for another class. What was the primary writing strategy you used? Build on this essay by integrating another strategy. For example, if you wrote an argument paper for a political science class, you might try using narrative to give some historical background to the paper. For a paper in the natural sciences, you could use subjective description to open the paper up to nonscientists. When you're finished, ask yourself: How did use of the new strategy affect your paper?

3. The choice of a writing strategy reflects an author's voice — the persona he or she assumes in relation to the reader. Read back through any personal writing you've done this semester — a journal, letters to friends, e-mail. Can you identify the strategies you use outside formal academic writing, as part of your natural writing voice? Write a few pages analyzing these strategies and your writing voice, using one of the rhetorical strategies studied this term. For example, you could do a cause and effect analysis of how being at college has changed the tone or style of your journal writing or social media posting.

4. Find a local newspaper editorial dealing with a controversial social or educational problem. Outline the issues involved and the strategies that the editorial writer used to present his or her argument. Then assume that you — a concerned citizen — are given equal space in the newspaper to present an opposing viewpoint. Make notes for a rebuttal argument and for the development strategies you might use to support your argument, considering, for

example, narration, process analysis, comparison and contrast, and/or illustration. Finally, write your response to the editorial and submit a copy to the newspaper that published the original piece. (This writing suggestions expands on the "Combining Strategies in Action" activity in the essay by Issa Rae, "The Struggle.")

CHAPTER 14   Writing with Sources

How a Kids' Cartoon Created a Real-Life Invasive Army (p. 518)
JASON G. GOLDMAN

Preparing to Read
Unless a student grew up on a farm or lived in a very rural area, they likely did not have ongoing direct contact with wild animals. Within this vacuum, films, books, and television shows have been able to shape how generations of young children see animals. You may want to also ask how YouTube videos of funny animal moments or experiences at the zoo might also affect perceptions of animals.

Thinking Critically about the Text
Beyond Japan, there are many ecosystems which have been interrupted by the introduction of foreign species. In Florida, for example, people have released pythons into the wild and these pythons have flourished at the expense of native species. Plant species have also proven invasive and harmful to ecosystems, such as the Asian plant family kudzu overtaking the southeastern United States. The essay serves as a warning not to turn wild animals into pets and not to release foreign fauna into regions where they are not native.

Questions on Subject
1. Sterling North's memoir, which became a popular Disney film called *Rascal* as well as the Japanese anime series *Araiguma Rasukaru*, captured the fascination of Japanese children who demanded to have raccoons as pets.
2. Raccoons are not suitable as pets because they are "friendly when young, but as they age they become more aggressive, harder to control, and post a potential threat to humans" (paragraph 5).
3. In Japan, wild raccoons now cause roughly US $300,000 worth of agricultural damage a year. They have moved into homes, temples, and shrines. In cities they hunt the carp and goldfish in decorative ponds (6). They prey on native mammals (the vole, snakes, dragonflies, butterflies, and others) and are pushing out the red fox, native owls, and grey herons (7-8).
4. Goldman says there is no good solution to the current problem (12). The best thing that can be done, he believes, is to increase wildlife education helping people understand the differences between what can become a pet and what — if introduced to the region — could affect ecosystems.

1. The summary is necessary because without understanding this charming story about a boy and his raccoon (or being familiar with the resulting film), readers might struggle to understand how the notion of raccoons as pets became so appealing. The original story is also important because in it, Sterling has the realization that raccoons do *not* make good pets.

2. In paragraph 2 Goldman narrates the true story of Sterling North who befriended a raccoon. This helps readers become enchanted with the idea of a raccoon friend and also shows why they do not make good long-term companions. In paragraph 4, he narrates how the raccoons came to the island of Japan to explain the influence of television on the Japanese ecosystem (also cause and effect analysis). Goldman uses cause and effect analysis in paragraph 6 to show the effect raccoons have had on the agricultural industry. In paragraph 7, he shows the effect of the raccoons on the indigenous mammals of Japan.

3. The research supports the point that raccoons spread infectious diseases (paragraph 9), which supports Goldman's larger point that raccoons do not make good pets and have harmed Japanese ecosystems and culture.

4. This long quote is integrated well. Goldman uses clear attribution tags and correct punctuation to identify the quote, which flows well with the language of the paragraph to support his claim that the Japanese are not eager to kill the wild raccoons. He uses the transition "indeed" to incorporate a summary of more research in the following sentence.

American Hookup (p. 524)
LISA WADE

Preparing to Read
A standing joke in pop culture (particularly in high school or college film and TV) is people's differing definitions of what "hooking up" means, so students may have fun discussing the term. But students may demonstrate various comfort levels writing about the sexual behavior and the hookup culture around them. They may also vary regarding their awareness of what others are doing. As Wade points out, students tend to perceive more hooking up than actually exists. You might consider having students submit a percentage of the college student body they think is "hooking up" and discuss the ranges in perception that students reveal.

Thinking Critically about the Text
Students will reflect on the levels of depression and anxiety they observe in themselves and their peers. Students' answers will also reflect how they perceive college life for prior generations. You may also point out that support for victims of rape, counseling services, and anti-harassment services, and so on, have actually increased in past decades. Many college students may have suffered in silence or stigma in the past, whereas now college students are more vocal about their unhappiness.

Questions on Subject
1. In paragraph 4, Wade cites journalists who say the hookup culture allows women to put their careers and educational aspirations ahead of their marriage aspirations. She also cites two social scientists who argue that ambitious women from economically stable

families handle hookup culture quite well. So, in fact, secure, driven women thrive in these contexts, suggesting women are not victims (but maybe even promoters) of this culture.

2. In Bogle's landmark study, students overestimated the amount of hooking up by their peers by at least 25 percent. The premise of the debate is wrong because people are not hooking up nearly as much as students think they are. The focus should be more on perception of hooking up than on actual encounters.

3. "Hooking up" means having a sexual encounter outside the context of a committed relationship. In paragraph 16, Wade defines "hookup culture" as being a climate in which students expect to be able to have these encounters whenever they want. In this culture, they perceive their peers as hooking up all the time. The distinction is important for her argument because the perception that everyone hooks up regularly increases the levels of anxiety and depression of students more than the sexual behavior itself.

4. "Moral panic" refers to a concern (individual or collective) that all or part of the community has lost track of its values. Communities control one another as much through social norms as through laws, arguably more so. When groups push the boundaries of accepted norms, others may be concerned that their community is on the verge of crisis and collapse. The term connotes fear of an irreversible degradation and loss of control over sexual behavior.

Questions on Strategy

1. Surveying other writers is crucial to establish her authority (*ethos*) and to ensure that her argument reflects more than the personal opinions of the author. Additionally, proving the disparity between the amount of student hook-ups vis à vis the *perception* of hooking up requires data.

2. Wade's argument is a cause-and-effect argument. She considers the increase of college students' self-reported depression, anxiety, and feelings of being overwhelmed as an effect of hookup culture. She also is careful to distinguish the "hookup culture" as the cause of this emotional distress rather than the actual sexual behavior. This distinction could assuage some of the moral panic she anticipates in some of her audience.

3. In paragraph 16, Wade refers to the hookup culture as being a climate. As a climate, it can be no more easily removed than fog. Students will speak to the efficacy and resonance of this simile.

4. By surveying students from various parts of the United States (as well as schools of various levels of prestige), Wade proves that hookup culture transcends status or geography; it flourishes on college campuses throughout the country.

The English-Only Movement: Can America Proscribe Language with a Clear Conscience? (p. 530)
JAKE JAMIESON

Preparing to Read
For some students, English will not be their first language, and they will have experiences to share about learning English in the United States. Although most students are likely to say that they would work hard to learn the predominant language of a chosen country, it

might be useful to talk about how difficult that might be for some people. You might ask students if they've tried to learn another language before, and if so, how easy or hard it was for them. Or, ask students whether they have visited a country where English was not the predominant language and what their experience was like. Were they grateful to find people who could speak English? If they moved to that country, would they feel similarly grateful to have the opportunity to speak English? Responses will vary on how students would feel if laws forced them to learn and use the predominant language as quickly as possible. Would they feel welcome?

Thinking Critically about the Text

Responses will vary regarding whether students agree with Jamieson's claim that "[t]here are so many sets of variables that it would be hard to defend the argument that there is only one culture in the United States" (paragraph 3). The mainstream cultural idea of a two-parent house-in-the-suburbs family does have many variations, but traditionally the white middle class (Anglo-Saxon descent) has been considered the dominant American culture. Students might be asked how they fit into that "mainstream" and whether the prevalence of that idea of mainstream has the cultural power to still be considered "the norm."

Questions on Subject

1. Jamieson wants to answer this question: "Should immigrants be required to learn English or should accommodations be made so they can continue to use their native languages?" (paragraph 1). Jamieson notes that the melting-pot idea of assimilation is in reality "a giant cauldron" where differences "are boiled away in the scalding waters of discrimination" (1) and quotes language diversity advocate James Crawford that discrimination is behind the English-only laws (8). He goes on to point out that English-only laws have been linked to anti-immigration laws (12) and that the English-only sentiment is concentrated in areas with large Spanish-speaking populations (12). Jamieson sees the official-English requirement as a form of discrimination that violates the constitutional right of citizens not only to freedom of speech (7, 14) but also to "life, liberty, and the pursuit of happiness" (14). In his last paragraph, he quotes columnist Myriam Marquez's assertion that whatever language is spoken, a more multiethnic American cultural landscape is inevitable.

2. Jamieson counters the people who argue that the melting-pot analogy is valid by indicating that the kind of harmonious assimilation the analogy alludes to is a myth, that in fact the melting pot is "a giant cauldron" where differences "are boiled away in the scalding waters of discrimination" (1). Jamieson counters the melting-pot myth of "harmony and the only way to dissipate the tensions that inevitably arise when cultures clash" by asserting that immigrants have not always come to this country because they wanted to "embrace American values" (2) and, further, that there's no consensus on what the "'American way' of doing things" is (3). His evidence: "Not everyone in America is of the same religious persuasion or has the same set of values, and different people affect vastly different styles of dress" (3). Student responses to whether this is a persuasive counterargument will vary. Some may add to the counterargument from their own experience of "variables" (3); others may indicate that Jamieson's evidence of cultural variation is weak.

3. In paragraph 6, former senator Bob Dole is quoted as saying that English "is the ticket to the 'American Dream,'" and Greg Lewis's quotation shows what he means: To "succeed in America," a person needs to be fluent in the dominant language of the country. While few would disagree with this statement, some—like language diversity advocate James Crawford—might argue that success could occur in occupations that service a group that

doesn't have English as the dominant language. Some might say that when political commentator Greg Lewis supports Dole's position by saying, "it's just the way it is," Dole's position is revealed to allow for, accept, and in this way, promote discrimination.

4. In his concluding paragraph, Jamieson leaves his readers with three important questions:

   - "Do we plan to allow everyone in this country the freedom of speech that we profess to cherish, or will we decide to reserve it only for those who speak English?"
   - "Will we hold firm to our belief that everyone is deserving of life, liberty, and the pursuit of happiness in this country?"
   - "Or will we show the world that we believe in these things only when they pertain to us and people like us?"

Jamieson aligns himself with those who find English-only legislation in violation of the constitutional rights invoked in the first two questions. The third question is a rhetorical chastisement directed at those who would use English-only rules to violate the Constitution. Student responses are likely to vary as to whether they agree or not with Jamieson.

Questions on Strategy

1. Jamieson's thesis is found in the question in the first paragraph: "At the center of the discussion about immigrants and assimilation is language: Should immigrants be required to learn English or should accommodations be made so they can continue to use their native languages?" While not a statement, the essay is organized as an answer to this question. The implied thesis is that English-only legislation constitutes discrimination.

2. Jamieson's focused argument is organized in a linear fashion, from an implied assertion to evidence to conclusion, including proof and counterproof and a classical appeal to ethical behavior. Opposing viewpoints are included to show their inadequacies and thereby strengthen Jamieson's own position. His goal is to change the reader's mind about a controversial issue. He presents his thesis, then explains his points: First he defines the issue in the form of a question. Then he presents his evidence through his own reason supported by the expert testimony from Clarkson and Marquez that English-only laws are a form of discrimination. He includes quotations from Dole and Krauthammer to represent the opposite point of view so that he can argue against it, moving back and forth between these authorities to compare and contrast views. He concludes with an ethical appeal not to discriminate but to uphold the constitutional rights of those who are not fluent English speakers.

3. Signal phrases that introduce quotations in Jamieson's essay include the following: "According to former senator and presidential candidate Bob Dole . . ." (paragraph 6), "Many of them, like Myriam Marquez, readily acknowledge . . . but fear that . . ." (7), and "According to language diversity advocate James Crawford . . ." (8). He brings in point and counterpoint with these quotes, which allows him to argue against Dole's position with the support of Marquez and Crawford.

4. Jamieson supports Crawford's assertion that English-only advocates are "bigoted, anti-immigrant, mean-spirited, and steeped in nativism" (8) with an example in paragraph 9 of a Texas judge who ruled that a mother's speaking only Spanish to her child constituted abuse: "'relegating her to the position of housemaid.'" He stood firm on this ruling, even though he later apologized to housekeepers. With this example, Jamieson shows how English-only beliefs rely on the notion that languages other than English are not only associated with lower socioeconomic groups but are also deemed inferior, with second-class discriminatory status.